# Manage
# Software
# Testing

# Other Auerbach Publications in
## Software Development, Software Engineering, and Project Management

**Accelerating Process Improvement Using Agile Techniques**
Deb Jacobs
ISBN: 0-8493-3796-8

**Advanced Server Virtualization: VMware and Microsoft Platforms in the Virtual Data Center**
David Marshall, Wade A. Reynolds and Dave McCrory
ISBN: 0-8493-3931-6

**Antipatterns: Identification, Refactoring, and Management**
Phillip A. Laplante and Colin J. Neill
ISBN: 0-8493-2994-9

**Applied Software Risk Management: A Guide for Software Project Managers**
C. Ravindranath Pandian
ISBN: 0849305241

**The Art of Software Modeling**
Benjamin A. Lieberman
ISBN: 1-4200-4462-1

**Building Software: A Practitioner's Guide**
Nikhilesh Krishnamurthy and Amitabh Saran
ISBN: 0-8493-7303-4

**Business Process Management Systems**
James F. Chang
ISBN: 0-8493-2310-X

**The Debugger's Handbook**
J.F. DiMarzio
ISBN: 0-8493-8034-0

**Effective Software Maintenance and Evolution: A Reuse-Based Approach**
Stanislaw Jarzabek
ISBN: 0-8493-3592-2

**Embedded Linux System Design and Development**
P. Raghavan, Amol Lad and Sriram Neelakandan
ISBN: 0-8493-4058-6

**Flexible Software Design: Systems Development for Changing Requirements**
Bruce Johnson, Walter W. Woolfolk, Robert Miller and Cindy Johnson
ISBN: 0-8493-2650-8

**Global Software Development Handbook**
Raghvinder Sangwan, Matthew Bass, Neel Mullick, Daniel J. Paulish and Juergen Kazmeier
ISBN: 0-8493-9384-1

**The Handbook of Mobile Middleware**
Paolo Bellavista and Antonio Corradi
ISBN: 0-8493-3833-6

**Implementing Electronic Document and Record Management Systems**
Azad Adam
ISBN: 0-8493-8059-6

**Process-Based Software Project Management**
F. Alan Goodman
ISBN: 0-8493-7304-2

**Service Oriented Enterprises**
Setrag Khoshafian
ISBN: 0-8493-5360-2

**Software Engineering Foundations: A Software Science Perspective**
Yingxu Wang
ISBN: 0-8493-1931-5

**Software Engineering Quality Practices**
Ronald Kirk Kandt
ISBN: 0-8493-4633-9

**Software Sizing, Estimation, and Risk Management**
Daniel D. Galorath and Michael W. Evans
ISBN: 0-8493-3593-0

**Software Specification and Design: An Engineering Approach**
John C. Munson
ISBN: 0-8493-1992-7

**Testing Code Security**
Maura A. van der Linden
ISBN: 0-8493-9251-9

**Six Sigma Software Development, Second Edition**
Christine B. Tayntor
ISBN: 1-4200-4426-5

**Successful Packaged Software Implementation**
Christine B. Tayntor
ISBN: 0-8493-3410-1

**UML for Developing Knowledge Management Systems**
Anthony J. Rhem
ISBN: 0-8493-2723-7

**X Internet: The Executable and Extendable Internet**
Jessica Keyes
ISBN: 0-8493-0418-0

## AUERBACH PUBLICATIONS
www.auerbach-publications.com
To Order Call:1-800-272-7737 • Fax: 1-800-374-3401
E-mail: orders@crcpress.com

# Manage Software Testing

**Peter Farrell-Vinay**

## CRC Press
Taylor & Francis Group
Boca Raton London New York

CRC Press is an imprint of the
Taylor & Francis Group, an **informa** business
AN AUERBACH BOOK

CRC Press
Taylor & Francis Group
6000 Broken Sound Parkway NW, Suite 300
Boca Raton, FL 33487-2742

First issued in paperback 2019

© 2008 by Taylor & Francis Group, LLC
CRC Press is an imprint of Taylor & Francis Group, an Informa business

No claim to original U.S. Government works

ISBN-13: 978-0-8493-9383-9 (hbk)
ISBN-13: 978-0-367-38770-9 (pbk)

| Library of Congress Cataloging-in-Publication Data |
| --- |

Farrell-Vinay, Peter.
   Manage software testing / Peter Farrell-Vinay.
      p. cm.
   ISBN-13: 978-0-8493-9383-9 (alk. paper)
   ISBN-10: 0-8493-9383-3 (alk. paper)
   1. Computer software--Testing. 2. Computer software--Evaluation. I. Title.

QA76.76.T48F37 2008
005.3028'7--dc22
                                              2007008293

**Visit the Taylor & Francis Web site at**
**http://www.taylorandfrancis.com**

**and the CRC Press Web site at**
**http://www.crcpress.com**

# Contents

# List of Figures

# List of Tables

# Preface

This book is written for:

- Testers who want to become test managers and need to get a new perspective on all the things they already know.
- Test managers who want answers to some very pressing questions all in one place.
- Project managers who want to know what they should expect from their test team, what they can do with it, and what it will mean.
- Quality assurance staff who want to know what to look for in a testing environment and how to measure it when they find it.
- Lecturers who realize that test management is another critical role which can mean the difference between success and failure on a project, and which might form the basis of a new course.
- Investment analysts who want to know what might go wrong with their investments, why, and how to stop it.
- Project office staff who want to know how to integrate the information they get from the test team.
- Auditors fed up with being pilloried by the Public Company Accounting Oversight Board and worried that something about Sarbanes–Oxley might have escaped them.

It is intended to pull together a lot of issues to give a strategic, risk-based management view of testing and how it relates to every stakeholder involved. In particular it is focused on lifting readers above the testing battlefield, concerned with the *what* and *how* of bug finding but also looking at the *why*.

The book's structure is as follows:

- The Introduction and Chapter 2 set out the **issues**. The issues are simple and so are the questions underlying them. The answers to those questions must be equally simple to be useful. Getting the answers *isn't* simple and that's why a lot of this book is devoted to how the test manager gets answers and interprets them.
- Chapter 3 begins the discussion of **risk**, which carries on throughout the book.
- Chapter 4 tells you how to **plan and manage tests**, and discusses possible starting points.
- Chapter 5 looks at **web** testing.
- Chapter 6 puts testing into the context of several **life-cycle models**.
- Chapter 7 and Chapter 8 look at the things you must do and have ready for use, your **tools, processes, and support systems**, your eyes and ears, the kinds of testing you may need to do, and the documents you need to work with.
- Chapter 9 examines the **test team** in its context, who they interact with, how, and why.
- Chapter 10 looks at the problems of **outsourcing**, third-party service provisions, and how to accept a release.
- Chapter 11 through Chapter 13 look at **test techniques** in as much detail as you will need to know, and show how they get you the answers you need.

- Chapter 14 covers **unit testing** and why it will save you time and money by reducing risk during system testing.
- Chapter 15 through Chapter 17 go into **system, performance, and usability** testing.
- Chapter 18 deals with the issues needing to be backed by **metrics**. Metrics are only useful if they answer a question. I have tried to put all the basic questions in and give you worked examples to show how to get the answers. I've put in the equations to show the basis, but where things have got complex I have put some of the equations in Excel spreadsheet format.
- Appendix A contains **examples** of reports and plans as well as case studies.
- Appendix B contains **checklists** with questions you need answers to in more detail. Although this book is not concerned with reviews, inspections, or audits, these may prove useful in either.
- Appendix C contains approaches to **categorizing bugs**.
- Appendix D lists **tools**.
- **References**, a **glossary**, and the **index** are located at the back of the book.

Managing testing is like managing a battle. Part of the time you need to fight the battle and part of the time you need to be above the battle, thinking. Thinking above the battle requires that you ask questions. If you don't ask the right questions, you will never get the answers. The answers must help you and the test team *do* something. At the back of my head I hear the voice of an awkward Highland-Scottish project manager asking, "*Aye, but what does it buy me?*"

It's a good question and this is an answer.

## Assumptions

This book has been written with a number of assumptions:

- That software is best developed according to a plan which respects a life-cycle. The life-cycle used here is compatible with that shown in the IEEE *Glossary of Terms.*
- That for planning and management purposes, all activities in a project are broken into work packages of approximately two person-weeks duration, each with some definable work-product to be checked and signed off as complete. (This may seem like administrivia. On a well-run project it is one of the things which makes it a well-run project. In a not-entirely-well-run-project it isn't done, because it would highlight the project's deficiencies too clearly.) It's worth doing because it makes you think more clearly about what you're trying to do, and if you can't plan it, what makes you think you can do it?
- That code is developed in units.
- That the integration of large-scale software is planned as a series of separate steps, each with its own set of tests. There are development environments which greatly simplify this.
- That you want a book on test planning and management, not quality assurance, reviews, or auditing.
- That you are testing systems of up to 200 KLOC. For such systems the usual method of unit and system testing applies. Beyond such a size it may be preferable to include a preliminary series of subsystem integration tests and subsystem tests before the full integration and system tests. This is because, with very large systems, perhaps some feature may prove extremely problematic when finally system tested, and it's better to find such bugs early. Other than that, the book is applicable to managing the testing of systems of any size.

## Book's Website

http://web.mac.com/petersv1/Web/Manage_Software_Testing/Welcome.html

# Acknowledgments

My first thanks go to my wife Janna, who encouraged me to finish this book. Sanjeev Richariya and Zahid Chaudhary were kind enough to review it, make many good points, and save me from many gaffes. Mariena Somasundaram, Samantha Glenn, and Matt Dreisin provoked many of the questions.

# About the Author

Peter Farrell-Vinay has been a test manager and consultant to major corporations, institutes, and governments. He has managed teams of up to 30 in billion-dollar safety- and mission-critical projects. He has written *Software Quality Assurance — What it Buys You and What It Will Cost You* (Technical Communications Ltd., 1992).

# 1
# Introduction

We all know what testing is. We've been doing it for years, in and out of school. We took tests, and teachers gave us marks and told us we were good, bad, or indifferent. People had got the idea that tests might be used to predict things about other people.

In 1904 a Frenchman called Alfred Binet was given the task of deciding whether or not children were subnormal. Monsieur Binet was a member of a committee of Eminent Frenchmen, each eager to propose his own Theory of Child Intelligence and How It can be Determined. M. Binet listened, extracted from each Eminent Frenchman a set of tests, added many of his own invention, and tried them out on sets of children. From the behavior of the children he decided which tests were useful. He then threw out those tests which failed to predict successfully, and tried again.

What did these tests prove? Nothing. They *indicated* the level of a child's intelligence at the time the test was administered. They did not *prove* that the child has great ability or potential. They have been given to an enormous number of children. They are still in use today.

Mr. Cyril Burt was a psychologist interested in predicting the ability of children. The British government wanted to reduce the cost of education. They reached a position whereby Mr. Cyril Burt provided (much) questioned figures that "proved" that it was possible to predict a child's ability, and the British government imposed a test on all British children at the age of 11 (called the 11-plus), which determined whether a child would go to a Grammar school (for the brighter) or a Secondary-Modern school (for the less-bright). Many studies have shown that the tests were very bad predictors of a child's ability and have blighted the lives of a generation of children. Britain still has a terrible shortage of graduates and technicians, but Mr. Cyril Burt was knighted.

## 1.1 Conclusions

1. Theories can be disproved.
2. Theories can be very useful and good predictors within a limited range of environments.
3. Tests only work in a limited range of environments.
4. Conclusive tests are very difficult to write.
5. There is always someone who believes despite the evidence.
6. Test the tests before you use them.
7. Faking test results can be a way to social advancement — but destroys your reputation.

## 1.2 What Has This Got to Do With Software?

We build software. Software incorporates a lot of intelligence. So do children. We want to know if software or children have absorbed knowledge and are likely to succeed in some future world. Our software flies aircraft, helps us drive cars, and administers medicine. Since we would rather not be flown, driven, or cured by an incompetent, we want to feel confident that our software is capable of behaving properly under all circumstances. So we test it. Unfortunately, we occasionally make the mistake of believing that the tests we devise will always predict something useful. Sometimes they don't.

## 1.3   If It Isn't Planned, It Won't Happen

Testing can only be managed successfully if management understands the processes of testing, the reasoning behind those processes, the intermediate products,[1] their limits, how to estimate them, and how to recognize trouble early. For this reason this is not a book about how to write tests. If you need to know about testing, buy several of the books in Appendix D. If you need a definition of test manager's terms of reference, then see Appendix B. If you want to know how to manage testing, read on.

## 1.4   Let's Not Test

Testing is very expensive and its results are often embarrassing. So there are many politically-adept people ready with plausible arguments explaining why testing can be reduced, curtailed, or its implications glossed-over. Here are some of their favorites, followed by a possible rebuttal or work-around. If you think such politically-adept people are really too dim to bother with, then either you've just left university, have led a very cloistered life, or have only worked for really great companies.

1. *We don't need that level of testing.* Whatever that level of testing is, they don't want it. Perhaps because it'll show that the product, or system is bug-ridden, and their job is on the line, alternatively that it'll delay release, and they'd rather (very temporarily) satisfy a customer (and their boss) with a timely release than a usable one.

   But there are limits to testing, and perhaps your boss knows what they are better than you. Ask yourself: is the thing I want to test essential? Will a failure matter? Is a failure probable? Is the risk low-probability/high-consequence? It is better to be boring and explicit than to assume. Remember the level of testing should always relate to the risk the product or system poses to all the stakeholders.

   Put together the case as shown in section 1.5.

2. *It costs too much.* The issue is simply how much they will pay to manage a risk. The risk might be somewhere between *"will we have any (more) customers if this release fails?"* and *"is it worth spending one more week to find bugs when the few we have found in the last 3 weeks were trivial?"* See Chapter 3.

   Estimate what it will cost if the software is late or fails. Then counter the question with "*It costs too much for what? The risk the system represents to the company? The budget you agreed to last week without me, or any relation to the cost to the company if the system fails?*"

   Put the question another way: "*Why not just build the software and release it? To hell with the customers. They won't know. Think of the money and time you can save by sacking all the testers.*" (Be prepared to make this argument because if ever anyone thinks you're too scared to argue for your job — you're out. Persist.)

   "*You don't want to test; fine, don't test.*" (Then they'll accuse you of "being silly.")

   "*Fine, so we agree you do want to test.*" (Pause here. Let someone deny the obvious.)

   "But you don't want to test a lot. At least not with as much rigor as I do. So how much do you want? How much is enough?"

   This should trigger a counter-attack along the lines of "*testing is very costly in itself,*" "*testing is costing us time to market,*" or "*there are still too many bugs being found in the field.*"

   To each of these, show your figures. When they fail to come up with their own figures, make this bitingly clear. "*You're worried about the bottom line. Funny. So am I. But I'm prepared to back my arguments with figures and proof. You just hand-wave.*" (Yes, the gloves are off). For the sorts of figures and 'proof' you need, look at section 4.6.

---

[1] *Specifications, manuals, and prototypes*: anything created to help build the deliverable.

3. *It'll take too long.* This might be just "*it costs too much*" in another guise. The argument may be couched in terms of "*getting the developers the information they need fast.*" In reality it doesn't matter how fast you get the information to the programmers if most of it's missing because test coverage was terrible. The question remains the same: *what is the risk?* Look at Chapter 3.

   If, though, the complaint is that developers are told about bugs too late for them to be able to fix in an agile manner, then it needs investigating. How long does it take you to run a full system test (as a proportion of the time they spend building the software), and how good is your coverage?

4. "*Testing*" *is never ready.* Often true. The test team which is ready for system test is one which has had a stable and unchanging requirements specification 4 months before system testing was due to start, and a stable test environment for 3 months beforehand (assuming it uses automated tests). It is rare that requirements are so stable that every one is already covered by a test when testing begins: often some tests are being written and reviewed while other tests are being run. Yes, it's the customer's fault. What does that buy the test team? They just have to get ready as best they can. See section 4.6.5 and section 6.6 for more on this.

5. *We never know how long testing will take* (Aka *we don't know how many bugs are in the release*). There are ways of finding out. See Chapter 18. Did you warn them how many there'd be or how long it would take? Did they want to know? Did the testers find bugs? Were they testing every day, or was there extensive downtime as development tried to get a release to work? Were there enough testers? Did you make your schedules unrealistically short? Did the testers agree to it? See section 4.6.5 in Chapter 4.

   This is your problem. Deal with it by getting an estimate both of the number of bugs to be found and the length of time it will take to find them. Look at section 18.10.

6. *It's too academic* (alternatively, *we're not NASA*). It's true that some academic ideas don't scale to industrial use, but the real reason is *they* don't (want to) understand either what you're proposing to do or what will happen if you don't. (This argument is also the managerial equivalent of the "*real men don't eat quiche*" argument in that such a manager believes himself/herself to be practical and thus non-academic.) Don't expect senior management to repeat that line of defense to customers or investors.

   Bankruptcy is quite academic while it happens to someone else. Answer this by saying that everything you are doing is industry-standard (privately ensure that any academic approaches you might use are proven first). Ask them what they would do. Don't wince or laugh. Write a brief paper of not more than two sides outlining your proposals. You have a major re-education job on your hands.

7. *It isn't in the plan* (they mean "*budget,*" but don't want to say so). Nor was the sinking of the *Titanic*. Are they suggesting that very little testing be carried out or are they opposing that extra bit of testing you feel is needed? Were you one of the planners? If you weren't, then write a paper as shown in section 1.5; if you were, explain how the situation has changed, as it does in any project. Explain the risks to be run if they don't add it to the plan (and the budget).

8. *Testing stops us getting the product out.* Whoever uses this argument is quite unconcerned for the ill effects the product's state may have on customers. They have probably miscalculated the release date too, and now face the prospect of explaining why the release is late. Testing is there to stop the company and customers from being damaged by buggy systems.[2]

---

[2] A nice example: A computer system to cut crime and give Brits the chance to check the status of resold cars is running millions of pounds over budget, three years late, and won't be complete for another year. Disclosures obtained by Tom Brake, the Liberal Democrat spokesman for transport, *reveals the contract to computerise the ... system, (suffered) delays ... caused by staff at the Vehicle and Operator Services Agency (VOSA), implementers of the scheme, and the IT contractor. His evidence ... indicates both the Agency and contractor underestimated the migration stage of the project, with progress further **hindered by extensive software testing*** (author's italics). Note the unchallenged allegation that it's the **testing** which **hinders**, not the fact that the system doesn't work properly. (Source *Contractor UK* Website).

9. *Customers are crying out for this release and you testers are holding everything up.* Oh gosh, that's terrible. Well, we'd better stop testing and release It Immediately. They'll never cry out for another one.

10. *Testing makes us look bad.* This sounds so much like the waffle of the brain-dead; you might be surprised anyone would propose it. It was said by someone (probably) under great pressure and with little experience (let's be nice). If testing makes that person look bad, then what does a bug-rich release do? Thought: is that person about to resign anyway?

11. *Testing doesn't add value.* It's not there to add value. It's there to preserve value, the value that the development team has put into it.

12. *By the time the testers have found all the bugs, the market will have gone away.* See the story "If at First You Don't Succeed, Then Bungee Jumping's Not for You" in Chapter 7. If you're competing in a market, this implies you have competitors. Are you relying on them making the same really crass mistake this argument implies? Markets have this horrid habit of rejecting bad products. If this release is a feature too big, then remove that feature. Else keep testing.

13. *Nobody cares about these bugs.* Everyone cares about the bug that's stopping them from doing something. This sort of reaction means either you haven't got them to agree on a way of classifying bugs or they're arguing about the lesser bugs. What do these bugs mean? That some feature is missing, or absent, and users don't care? If the latter, then remember that a system infected with a thousand tiny bugs is possibly as unusable as one with a couple of big ones, and user dissatisfaction may soon come to the boil. See section 17.2 for a little story.

14. *Testing isn't the answer.* This was said of a finance system which should have been tested and never was, didn't work, and whose remaining users fled. The person who said that was later found running another failing project. He had never quite worked out what the question was either.

15. *The developers do all the testing* and other sources of belly laughs. Developers develop. Ask them to seriously system-test what they build and you'll be looking at a fascinating expanse of empty chairs. This is probably what this person told the board or anyone else too dim to consider the implications. The person who said that lost his job as CEO seven months later.

16. *Please don't damage the system.* OK, this was said 20 years ago and the person concerned will never make the same mistake again. But it illustrates perfectly what happens when someone who should know better gets a faulty paradigm into his[3] head. If you can get people to explain how they view the system, you can probably clear away a lot of misconceptions.

17. *By the time the users have found that bug, we'll have released a patch.* Sorry, why does the release need to be made anyway if you are going to release the patch so soon? Is it to fix a very embarrassing bug? If so, can you imagine how happy users will be to find the patch contains another bug? Because with that sort of inattention it will, and they'll find it as well. Probably immediately. This too is the sort of excuse someone might dishonestly put to a (not very bright) board, not to testers.

18. *We don't have time to write the requirements specification.* If they say this to you at the interview, and the project is allegedly "close" to making a critical release, then you have options:
    * Take the job (and enjoy being a scapegoat).
    * Fight your corner.
    * Don't take the job.
    The requirements specification is of critical importance to the following stakeholders:
    * Testers who need a specification to test against.
    * Developers who need a specification to know what to develop.
    * Technical writers who need a specification to know what they have to write about.
    * Marketing which needs a specification to sell the product.
    * Project and test management need a requirements specification to get some idea of system sizing.

---

[3] Sexism. If there's one thing that enrages my wife more than sexism, it's the habit of writing *s/he*, or *his, or hers* repeatedly. She finds it tedious to read and understands that the use of *his, him,* or *he* are nothing other than a linguistic oddity confined to the English language. Italians, French, and Germans manage perfectly well by relating the pronoun's gender to the object rather than the subject: viz. *il suo computer, la plume de mon oncle* etc. Therefore for *his* read *hers,* etc.

There are variants:
- We don't write specifications.
- The product is too advanced/complex for a specification to be written.
- That's too process for this year.[4]

Before we all go down with a bad attack of structured sneering let us recall that:
- To have a complete requirements specification is impossible (never mind what the IEEE says), because to be complete the specification would have to say everything the system must be able to do, and to do that you would have to have the system itself. So most sensible people settle for a requirements specification sufficient to meet the stakeholders' needs.
- Needs change, therefore requirements specifications must change. Requirements specifications can't change if they don't exist.
- In the past there was a race of absolutists who wanted cast-iron definitions of everything before they would release a development cent. They leave a long shadow in the collective memory.
- Read [Hooks] for an excellent and simple explanation of what happens if you don't write good requirements specifications. Note the NASA diagram showing how failure to get the requirements right leads to big cost overruns.

If people simply want to insist that requirements change and they must be free to change them as the market evolves, then:
- Remember that there has to be a cut-off date after which no changes can be made to a release (if you are ever to test it sufficiently).
- Ensure that there is someone tasked with both keeping the requirements up-to-date and distributing copies to all stakeholders in a timely fashion (possibly someone with an interest in keeping things up-to-date, like the testers).

Otherwise, do you really want to work for people so badly in need of taking Software Engineering 101?

19. *The testers never find the important bugs.* This is a serious criticism: if, despite having adequate specifications, your team is failing to find serious bugs which users later discover, and you were able to complete all your tests, either you or your team or both are no good. But take heart: at least someone is worrying about bugs.

20. *The testers never find all the bugs anyway.* Probably true. To test such that every possible bug is found would probably bankrupt the company. To test until every severity 1 or 2 bug is found and fixed is essential. See Appendix C for a classification scheme.

## 1.5  Something to Do When You Really Hit Opposition

Here are some of the things they don't want to look at (and you do). Use these as the basis of a report to provide an outline for discussing

1. How much newer projects have slipped as a result of having to pull people off them in order to try to fix the mess created during older ones.
2. The cost of fixing post-release bugs, possibly because that doesn't come out of their budget or they don't care how frustrated the developers get in having to build patches rather than design new bits of the system. Get the data from time sheets. Look at:
   - The equation in section 18.13
   - Table 3.4
   - Section 7.4.6
   - Section 14.8.2

---

[4] I'm sorry. We had this tacit agreement that we were going to use the English language, and here I go breaking it. What I *think* the person who said this meant, was that writing requirements specifications was something he associated with high-ceremony, process-oriented companies. And that he wanted his company to become just like that really fast. Er, next year.

3. The relationship between stopping testing "too early" and delaying getting the next release out (because the developers are spending all their time bug-fixing). Measure this by looking at the bug detection curve, the test runs, the time sheets, the overtime, and the 3rd-line support calls (problems per user month). If it looks like the one in Figure 1.1, then it seems highly probable that the release was snatched away from testers at the moment they were finding the most bugs. Note that only a third had been fixed. Were they the most critical? Find the number of 3rd-line support calls (problems per user month) made against that release and compare them with those made for a "well-tested" release whose bug detection curve looks like the one in Figure 1.2. (Notice, though, that this release had far too many unfixed low-level bugs in it.)

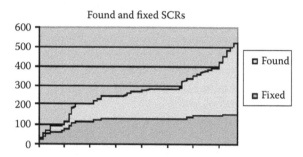

**FIGURE 1.1**  Found and fixed bug detection chart

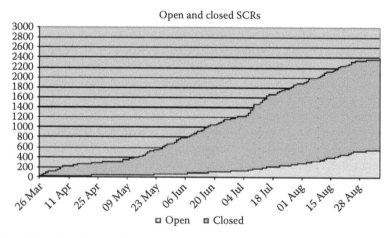

**FIGURE 1.2**  Overall bug detection profile

4. The number of lines of code per bug in each release over the last two years, and show it on a chart. Are things getting better or worse? (See Figure 18.19 for a nasty example.)
5. Number of bugs found in the field compared with those found during system testing (try to see how easy is it for some user to raise a bug report, and how easy is it for you to read it). Go and talk to real users. If there are very few bugs reported from the field it is probably because that's difficult for users to do.
6. The number of click-outs or click-throughs on a web page. If you're testing a web application, create some user action logs and look at them. At what point do people click out?
7. The number of 3rd-line support calls (measured as problems per user month in some companies) and which bits of the system provoked the most. (Why wasn't the buggiest bit tested better? Review the tests and find out.) The support desk is either:
   • Overwhelmed with calls
   • Already abandoned by customers because it doesn't work
   • Regularly hand-holding important users

8. The amount they are spending on training (because the system is unusable out of the box or the user interface is terrible). Beware: some companies like it like this — users spend a lot on training consultants and the company earns even more revenue.

9. The extraordinary number of releases made to the field. (How many major releases do they make a year? How many minor releases, how many patches?) Rule of thumb: you should have one major release per annum, one minor, and a maximum of two roll-up patches. Why? Because otherwise:
   - Your development and testing staff will be falling over themselves trying to get releases out, they will be unfocused, disorganized, and chaotic, and people will leave.
   - The market will correctly perceive that your testing process, and probably much else, is inadequate.

10. The number of developers and testers who left in the last year.

11. The overtime amount. (To cope with the chaos. Relate them to the release dates. If you can't observe a pattern, then it's because you haven't been given the real release dates. Check in the configuration management database. There's always a bit of overtime worked around the time of a major release. How big is that bit?)

12. The number of abandoned test runs. There are two good reasons and one bad one for abandoning test runs:
   - The number of bugs is so high that the testers spend more time filling in bug reports than in testing.
   - Important parts of the system simply do not work.
   - The developers arbitrarily change the test environment (thus halting the use of the present release) or impose a new release by simply installing it over the existing one.

    The first two are unfortunate; the last is unforgivable and indicates that the development function is out of control. If the last happens, then it can mean that some part of the system never gets tested until too late and that developers don't hear of bugs in time because test coverage is poor. You can get this data from the test management tool or direct from the testers.

13. The risk the project runs. Is there a risk log? Review it.

14. The number of bugs is being introduced with each fix. This will really make people scream. The truth is, all fixes induce some bugs. Hopefully the ratio is less than 1:1 fixes to new bugs. See section 2.7.2 for more on this.

15. How many extraordinary delays occurred before the first release, because key parts of the product had neither been prototyped nor modeled and were found not to work far too late for corrective measures to be taken?

Structure your report like this:

1. The project environment.
2. What the project is supposed to be doing.
3. What's happening, and the evidence.
4. What we need to do.
5. How we'll know if we're succeeding.
6. What will happen if we don't do what's needed.

Keep it short (no more than 4 pages, and preferably two), keep it conclusive. Say nothing you cannot support with evidence.

## 1.6 Conventions

- [Names] refer to a reference in the list at the back of the book.
- |a| is the absolute value of a, e.g., (|-5|=5).
- min(a, b) is the minimum of a or b, e.g., (min(10, 11) = 10).
- $\hat{N}$ is an estimate of N.
- { sets | of | things } are held in curly brackets and separated with vertical strokes.

## 1.7    Apologies

If this book seems so far to be a little diatribe against management, then please accept that:

1. I know and have worked for many intelligent managers who have been very tough over dates and resources, but didn't want their name sullied by bug-filled releases. They are very good people to work for.
2. There are the unhappy few for whom avoidance of responsibility has become a way of life.

More cautions:

1. **We have seen the enemy and it's us**. When we've seen past the technology, we realize that most of the problems we face are the ones we create for ourselves.
2. **Definitions of quality are a bit like quality of life**. If the subject is raised, then you know there isn't much. If a product does what it says on the tin and someone will pay for it, that's quality.
3. **Why words get in the way**: software engineering is a lexicographer's delight. It's nice to know someone is happy with the plethora of terms, acronyms, and subtle distinctions that the subject has spawned. The definitions used in this book are contained in the Glossary at the end. As far as possible, this glossary is consistent with the IEEE glossary. To make this book as short as possible, polite phrases such as "*it is highly advisable to*" have been avoided in favor of a simple if direct command: "do this" or "do that." If the reason for the command isn't obvious, it has been added.
4. **Errors, faults, bugs, problems, and defects**. Much time is spent on defining them. A simple distinction may help: in this book an error or problem is humanly visible; a fault, bug, or defect is the underlying cause. I have mostly used the word "*bug*."

Many of the things in this book are so obvious everyone knows about them. Perhaps you know them. I'd rather bore you than mystify you.

## 1.8    Some Basics

### 1.8.1    Experts and Novices

Of course you're not a novice. Whoever suggested that? But, er, just check:

1. The novice has no idea of what to attend to in the mass of data he sees every day. So he attends to everything, gets overloaded, and misses the vital signs.
2. The expert has anticipated most problems, concentrates on the essentials, and thus has time to look for the unexpected.
3. There is also the hapless person for whom unwelcome news is simply ignored because it conflicts with his pre-existing views. You've never met one? Lucky you.

See [Dixon 1] and [Dixon 2] for more on experts, novices, and, er, the others. There is no quick way to become an expert. But there is a way of preparing for surprises, somewhere between expert and novice. It's called strategy and planning. Writing all those Very Wonderful documents is a way of simulating the project, getting it all down on paper, and thus externalizing it, like a script or a set of stage directions or a program.

There are few things more embarrassing than reading something you wrote at a moment's notice under great pressure. Revising what you jammed down last night is a great way of giving yourself time to rethink, focus on essentials, and think through your plan so you know you are happy with it. This way you give yourself space in which to ask "*...and what could go wrong here?*" and work out a solution beforehand.

# Story

S ir Peter Hall was once an unknown, aspiring theatre director: a novice. He finally got his Big Break directing a play, and bought a copy of the play, some paints, and cardboard, an enormous blank bound book, and hastened off to a rented cottage for a month.

In the cottage he made a model of the theatre with all the actors, lights, scenery, etc. He cut up the copy of the play into individual sheets and pasted them into the blank bound book, leaving a blank page between each page of dialogue. Then, looking at the model theatre, he annotated the dialogue scene-by-scene until he knew exactly where everyone should be, what their cues were, roughly what the lighting should do, and what noises-off were needed.

The day came when he entered the theatre and placed his enormous book (which impressed everyone) on a table in the middle of the auditorium.

"Act one, scene one, darlings," he called. The cast dutifully took their places, and he started to direct them exactly as his notes showed.

After an hour he realized that something was wrong. Nothing gelled. The cast just weren't behaving like the bits of cardboard. They were scruffy, misbehaved, and awkward. He'd just have to get up there on stage and show them. So he did, and the play gelled and was a great success, because he knew that play backwards. Indeed, he was well on his way to becoming an expert.

Moral: with the script in your head you can play it any way you want.

## 1.8.2   Let's Hear It for Strategy

Testing is a way of answering questions. Questions such as *"Does it work? Is it any good? Can we use it?"* are big, but they can be split into smaller questions such as *"Have we used it like the users will? Have we tested it all? Did we build it the 'right' way? Is it fast enough?"*

These are all strategic questions but because testing as an activity is accepted as Something We Ought To Do (more in principle than in practice), managers and testers tend to lose sight of them. This book is intended, among other things, to remind everyone that testing occurs for good reasons, and these need to be made explicit if they are to be understood. The place for this is not the test plan but the test strategy document. See section 8.3. See also [Minto] for good ways of thinking and writing strategically.

The test strategy document is a way of exposing your thoughts on what you are testing and why. It provides the rationale for the test plan and the overall approach to testing, and thus helps you to keep such thoughts in a place where they are more likely to be read. To some extent it subsumes some of the contents of the quality plan (see section 8.21), while leaving (say) the activities and the schedule to change as progress dictates. As a manager you must be able to work part of your time at a strategic level so that you can align your work with the company's needs. You will be expected to share your strategic thoughts with other managers and of course the board. Use the test strategy document for this.

## 1.8.3   Planning and Specifying

Testing takes time. So you need a test plan to manage that time. Tests get planned in test plans. These may be self standing or part of quality plans (see section 8.21 in Chapter 8). Generally speaking, quality plans define a project's overall approach to quality, and thus shouldn't change throughout the project's life unless something most important happens. Test plans may change as the risk the product is perceived to pose changes. Test plans say who does what, when, and what they produce. See section 8.5 for an example; also see Chapter 6 and section 4.4 for an overview of the processes you'll need to plan for.

# Story

"**D**on't be ridiculous," said my boss, when I told him that we were spending at least 33% of the project's money on testing. "Go and look at the time sheets."[5]
So I did. I was wrong. We weren't spending 33% of our resources on testing: it was 35%.

All tests exist to answer some question. **Unit, integration, and system tests** answer the questions "*Do the units do what they're supposed to? Do the components integrate properly? Does the system do what is required of it?*" To minimize risk, these questions are answered in phases: unit, integration, and system testing. Since testing will certainly cost a third and perhaps more than half the total cost of the project, planning and managing it is a major problem.

Tests get specified in test specifications (yes, some people call them test plans, but this is wrong). The test specifications may in fact be inputs directly to some test tool. If not, they should contain at least the essence of the test as shown in section 8.8.

## 1.8.4   Reviews

Testing is one of the main methods of demonstrating that the requirements of a project are met. Another method is reviewing. This book is not concerned with how to review or how to manage a review, other than test-readiness reviews. Look at [Freedman], [Wiegers], [Gilb], [Hollocker], and [Yourdon] in the list of references at the back of the book for books on reviewing. As a test manager you'll want to review all critical documents as part of an overall validation and verification (quality control) strategy for the project. This is shown in the test plan.

## 1.8.5   Baselines

All tests derive from some baseline, usually a specification. Even a piece of code or some manual may be a part of a suitable baseline; anything will do, providing the following rules are adhered to. The baseline must:

1. Be changeable (because the world changes) and any changes to it must be controlled.
2. Only be interpretable in one way.
3. Contain enough information to be *useful*. It need not be *complete* (things seldom are). For a "complete" baseline for a system you would need to have the system itself. By useful I mean that it can be transformed into something else. Thus a requirements specification can be transformed into a design specification, and a system test specification, and even a user manual.
4. Be humanly-visible. If the baseline involves (say) astrophysical movement then this must be defined in some terms (possibly involving telescopes, satellites, or Foucault's pendulum) that involve some humanly-observable event.
5. Be stable. "*I think it should do this*" isn't a baseline. "*User X believed the system should do this*" **is** a baseline if it's written and agreed by stakeholders.

If the relationship between a test and its baseline cannot be determined, the test is meaningless.

---

[5] The company sensibly had all staff fill out time sheets showing how much time was spent on various project phases. I included unit and system testing.

Remember however, that testing does not, and cannot prove that some software conforms to specification. By the nature of proof itself, all that a test can show is that:
- (rather negatively) An attempt to make the software fail with respect to some specification has itself failed
- (rather positively) That the software worked

This can be taken only as an implication that the software has passed that test, and therefore conforms to that specification on which the test was based. By passing some test, all that can reasonably be deduced is that the test failed to find any bugs in that software.

*Example*: a very expensive motor-car is being road-tested. The baselines of the test are the specifications for that car plus all the last-minute tweaks made to its software, suspension, fuel injection system etc. It is a bright summer's day. The test consists of the following procedure:
1. Start up the car.
2. Drive for 100 miles at speeds of up to 70 mph.
3. Stop the car.

Assuming that the car passes such a test, what can we conclude from it? We can assume that under the circumstances of a bright summer's day the car can be persuaded to start, be driven, and stop. This is unlikely to convince us that we should buy it. We may remember that snow, and rain sometimes fall, that the roads may be covered with ice, that a hundred-and-one mishaps may befall us. We might write some more-rigorous test procedures involving icy roads, the Sahara desert, flood water, and hurricane-force winds. Eventually it will occur to us that what we are really trying to do is to prove that under some circumstance the car will **not** work.

This is the essence of testing. This is why testing is difficult. To be able to think of every circumstance in which some system, be it a car, a database, or a can of beans, will not fulfill its intended function, is an art that requires talent, numeracy, and imagination. That is why good testers are intelligent pessimists.

## 1.9   The Players

In a large (30+ developers) company lots of people are involved in testing. In smaller companies the roles may overlap (see Figure 1.3). Here's a brief guide:

1. **Assessment and certification bodies** who certify that your processes (and sometimes products) meet one or more standards and that the system is safe. They need to see test results to be sure the process is working.
2. **Business analysts and tech writers** write the specifications and know the system from the users' viewpoint. Make sure you give them feedback on the specifications and their testability in a timely manner.
3. **Configuration manager** is in charge of managing the configurations and releases of all software and hardware. He may be the same as the project librarian. His moment of glory comes at integration test time when close cooperation with the test manager ensures a quick turn-round of intermediate releases and patches. This is utterly essential for the smooth running of any project.
4. **Customer staff** are the people who will end up using the system. They will often be kept away from the developers by the combined efforts of customer management and developer management. This is because contact with customer staff might reveal to the developers how little customer management understands about what customer staff really do, and even call into question the rationale behind the system. Developer management don't want developer staff upsetting customer management with ill-judged questions that begin with phrases like "*what's the point of…?*" or "*why don't you simply…?*" Customer staff are however essential both for writing the requirements specifications and for checking that those parts of the system test concerned with the human–computer interface are realistic, and workable.

5. **Customer** is the person who pays for the product. Note that the customer may never actually use the product, or may not use it until too late. For this reason developers and testers need access to customer staff.

6. **Design authority** tries to keep the design of the system consistent, elegant, and architecturally coherent. He remembers the justification for the design decisions and is usually some sort of oracle on the system's behavior. The test manager will thus consult him frequently. He will usually have defined the system's interfaces.

7. **Developers** are the staff who write real code and sometimes low-level designs. As such they may also be responsible for writing and executing the unit tests for that code. If so, have all the unit tests checked by someone else, preferably a tester. Make sure they know as soon as you've found each bug you can reproduce. Monitor their relations with testers to ensure that they are neither too close (which could subvert testing rigor, particularly if bugs aren't accorded the right classification) nor too distant (such that antagonism occurs). They may also have to handle third-line *Support* if no one else can.

8. **Human resources** recruit staff and get them trained. They are also good at being a third party when discussing staff career prospects. If you want good staff you need to talk to them very seriously.

9. **Independent safety advisor** is usually appointed to oversee and approve the safety case which will be constructed by the safety manager, and staff with test input to show that the safety claims have been met. Testing will have a major input to the safety case, and the relationship between you and the independent safety advisor is critical. The independent safety advisor will as his title suggests be independent of the company. He is only concerned that the system be safe to use and operate.

10. **Line manager** has overall financial responsibility for the project. The project manager reports to him, the quality assurance manager should not. The line manager will undoubtedly pressurize the project manager to minimize spending.

11. **Project director:** very big projects have several managers reporting to a director who will operationally run the test, quality assurance and safety managers. In that case there may usually be separate quality and safety directors as well for exception-reporting purposes.

12. **Project librarian** is in charge of all the project documentation. May also be the configuration manager and if not, will often report to him. A good role for an aspiring and meticulous junior. Ensure he has a deputy.

13. **Project manager** is in charge of all aspects of the project except (hopefully) design. He writes the project plan and the quality plan. He is ultimately in charge of the project's quality and safety. He may be in charge of the test manager. He will have some financial authority and report to the line manager. He will issue and sign-off the workpackages. He may be aware of the dangers of cutting corners but will be under pressure to do so from the line manager. If he fulfills the role of Design Authority, and the development team has more than 5 staff, then beware of conflicts over design. He will authorize a release.

14. **Quality assurance manager** is in charge of the quality system. He assures the process whereby the system is required, designed, built, tested, installed, and handed over. He has nothing to do with either reviewing, or testing but acts as the channel whereby any serious quality concerns can be revealed to senior management as required by ISO 9000. He or his staff audit the project and its facilities.

15. **Quality assurance representative** reports to the quality assurance manager and is responsible for assuring the quality of the processes by signing off the quality plan — and thus implicitly any separate test plans — and auditing the project against the quality system. He has no responsibility for testing, or reviewing. He must be satisfied that all the quality controls on the project are satisfactory and will thus be particularly concerned with such issues as reviews, testing, and configuration management.

16. **Requirements manager** manages the acquisition, maintenance, modeling, integration, documentation, and review of requirements. The project manager or design authority often holds this role. On occasion it has been the test manager's job.

17. **Safety assurance manager** is in charge of safety. He will assure the safety management system as required by whatever safety standard the project follows. He will often report both to the project's line management, and to an Independent Safety Advisor who is independent of the project, and probably of the company.

18. **Safety staff manage** all safety-related aspects of the system and need to be sure that safety-critical bits are tested with sufficient rigor. They too have to interact with assessment bodies in preparing the safety case. They will typically review test specifications and recommend tests. They report to the safety assurance manager.

19. **Security manager** is in charge of all the security aspects of the organization, its products (if any), and operations. He will call on the services of the test team on occasions. He will normally be in charge of planning and executing security-related matters including penetration testing.

20. **Suppliers** interface with most of the other parties. Their relations with the test manager and test group can become fraught since test staff are the persons most likely to identify embarrassing flaws in the suppliers' work. Their relations with the quality assurance manager and staff may also become problematic should audits identify problems. The suppliers' reaction may be to cast doubt on the test group's ability.

21. **Support desk staff** are the heroes and heroines who have to deal with the customers with the problems which the test group should have found. They will typically deal with most of them themselves ( *"Well, have you tried switching it on?"*) but the real bugs will come your way. The ratio of bugs which are referred for patches by the Support desk to the number of bugs found while testing is a measure of your success. They are a mine of knowledge about the history of the product, the horrors of the last release, and configuration testing.

22. **Test manager** is in charge of writing the test strategy, and test plan, or the test parts of the quality plan. He may report to the project manager or to the line manager. As such he may come under pressure to cut corners. This would be very serious if no quality assurance manager or quality assurance representative exists to whom he could turn to limit that pressure. He must run the testing group and be the principal conduit through which test result are made known to the project. He reviews tests. He must have a separate exception reporting line to someone with a major and financial stake in the success of the project, such as the managing director, the project director, or the line manager.[6] He may be in a position to refuse to make a release. He must always be able to refuse to sign-off a release.

23. **Testers** are responsible for controlling the quality of deliverables by specifying, writing, executing, and analyzing tests; may also be programmers though they will not be the same staff responsible for writing the system/components to be tested. They need testable specifications, releases, and your support. They should also be reviewing the specifications. They report to the test manager but may indirectly report to the project manager should they be split among feature teams.

There is inevitably an adversarial relationship between testers and developers. This is no bad thing: developers are trying to get something working and the testers are trying to show it doesn't. The keys to success are patience, a sense of humor, clear definitions of responsibilities, a plan, and good staff. So what else is new?

These roles are shown in simplified form in Figure 1.3. They depend on two distinctions being drawn:

1. Between the quality assurance and quality control roles of the QA department, and the testers
2. Between the testing and development roles

---

[6] I'm sure you can guess why.

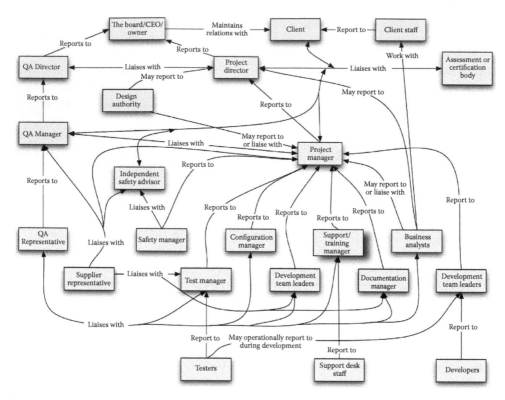

**FIGURE 1.3** Project roles and relations

If the roles in your project differ greatly from those shown above ask yourself what the political and technical effects of those differences will be, and plan accordingly. The next section explains why.

# 1.10 Quality Assurance and Quality Control

Many problems arise in software development because these two activities are confused. The confusion arises for historical and practical reasons:

- Quality control is concerned with controlling the quality of some products of some processes, be they documents, software, or motor cars. It is concerned to find bugs, and in so doing assure[7] management and the customer that the product (specifications, code, plans, manuals) is correct.
- Quality assurance is concerned with looking at the process by which the products are produced. Quality assurance staff may not be technical experts in the area of the project they are monitoring, in fact it's probably better that they aren't; otherwise they might be tempted to get involved in the technical details and lose the big picture. This is why it is wrong (for example) to expect QA staff to sit through the whole of a review. They should be invited of course, but only to confirm that the review is being properly run. Similarly they should only expect to attend test runs as witnesses, not as proof that code is bug-free.

Managers have found it convenient to confuse the two in an attempt to save money while still obtaining ISO 9000 certification. Since one of the roles of QA staff is to check that the testing process is running well, it follows that if QA staff test, then they must check themselves...

---

[7] Here's where the confusion arises.

## 1.11  Processes, Tools, Products, and Standards

# Story

T here was a man with a nail to whom everything looked like a hammer, and a little boy with a hammer to whom everything looked like a nail.

If you have no processes defined, and no standards to match your product, or processes against, almost anything will look pretty good.

There is a tribe called Software Quality Methodists (who have various gods including ISO 9000, CMM, and Six Sigma) who by contrast see any company without a wall full of paper defining processes, and practices, as a fertile space in which they can impose their own Very Wonderful Solutions.

You can have some great products built by a very few good people who know how to work around each other like cooks in a busy kitchen, but things get more difficult when such groups grow, and are replenished. If you want to be a big, dedicated organization you'd better get your own structure in place. But structure and process are relatively easy to determine, impose, and support. Product quality requires:

- A really clever product vision
- Clever people to build
- Clever people to test
- A stable and helpful environment in which to build
- A management which understands the vision, and the process, its weak points, and how to apply pressure most productively to achieve that vision
- Great salespeople (the others may get you a great product but they won't be around for long if it doesn't sell)

If you want a supportive structure, then it's best that the people who have to do the work define it, live with it, and modify it as they see fit. The only time management should need to take a lead in the matter is if the staff cannot decide in a timely manner, or there is insufficient money for the tools.

# 2

# The Big Questions You Need Answers To

---

## Story: Hadrian's Wail

Once upon a time there was a British software house. It had a won a Command, Control, and Communication project with a police force which lived in the shadow of Hadrian's Wall. It was a big contract, bigger than anything the software house had ever done before. But they had done lots of other C3 contracts before (well, three), and so this one wasn't going to be any more difficult. So they wrote specifications, on paper, with pencils (makes them easier to correct). The planners of the project had not envisaged the number of terminals required (this was in an age before PCs, but after the invention of the word processor). As the project "progressed," the numbers of developers dwindled from 365 at the rate of about 1 per day. There was a large number of tests written by a dedicated test team. Fairly early on they started testing, and found, unsurprisingly, a large number of bugs.

Deadlines loomed. There was no chance of simply declaring a delay and fixing the bugs. In desperation the managers decided to throw out all the tests which found bugs, but not to substitute them with any others. So when the police chiefs came to the demonstration nothing untoward was visible and it was proposed to install the system forthwith.

Imagine how happy the policemen were with a system which both lacked key features and whose response time was best measured with a calendar. The British software house went swiftly bankrupt. The new chairman, who had taken over on the day the trials started, never had a chance to resolve anything.

---

If you're thinking strategically you will start with Where You Are Now. Then you'll look at the Big Questions. This section is structured to get you going with a set of Big Questions and the answers you need to continue with. Each answer is further decomposed into pointers to other parts of the book.

## 2.1 Why Do We Test?

Testing enables us to answer questions about the software or the system as a whole, at least with some level of confidence. One of the objectives of this book is to help you think in terms of the questions you need to ask, which testing can answer. These questions concern the product, the users, the user's commercial and operating environment, and the product's operating environment. There are two questions in particular:

1. Is the product ready for release? See section 4.6.5.
2. Have we sufficient test coverage? See section 2.8.

Managing testing requires that you ask these kinds of questions so that if the answer is "no," it will be very clear to all concerned **why** it is "no."

## 2.2 How Do We Test?

There are many techniques for testing. Some can be applied to more than one test phase. None ensures bug-free software: each has its own strengths, limitations, and costs.

- **Functional** (black-box) methods can be applied to any unit, build, or system, since they assume no knowledge of how either was constructed or what it contains. Such methods require a sufficient and unambiguous specification if they are to be effective. (Devising black-box tests for some code from its specification at the time the specification is written is a useful verification of the specification; if it can't be done, the specification isn't good enough.) This is what you will normally do for a system test.
- **Structural** (white-box) methods can also be used on any unit or build, but are cheapest to devise when used on structured programs, e.g., well-written programs in a structured language. These are usually applied to unit tests.
- **Dynamic analysis** techniques are derivative methods which assume that a particular technique such as condition tables, finite state machines, object-orientation, or functional programming, has been used to develop the software; we use knowledge of that technique to determine the *test cases,* so these have very special areas of application. These can be applied at both system test and unit test times. These are usually applied to unit tests.
- **Static analysis** techniques can best be used before integration, and can also point to the need for more-rigorous unit testing. These require using tools to analyze the source code (see section D.11). These are usually applied to unit tests.
- **Symbolic evaluation** carried out by an automated symbolic evaluation tool places no special requirement on the unit, except of course that it be in the language evaluated by the tool. This involves "dry-running" the code, and recording the output values of variables algebraically rather than using specific values for input variables (see section 7.9). This is usually applied to unit tests.

Table 2.1 lists the techniques and summarizes their strengths and weaknesses. The techniques are described later. For lists of tools and sources, see Appendix D.

## 2.3 When Do We Start Testing?

Before we can release software for use we must be able to demonstrate both to the customer as well as to ourselves that the software works. This is demonstrated by attempting to prove it does not work. These attempts take place at four critical moments in the development of software:

1. The end of the coding phase, when each unit or separately compilable unit is tested in isolation.
2. At the end of the integration phase, when the entire system is tested to demonstrate that every feature works as required. Integration testing per se is rare today, given the improvements in compilers.
3. As soon as a reasonably stable system is available, when we test to see if its performance is sufficient (when code turmoil has fallen enough, see Chapter 18).

**TABLE 2.1**   The use of testing methods

| Technique | Can reveal | Cannot reveal | No. of test cases |
|---|---|---|---|
| Algorithm complexity | Complexity, validity, optimality, and computational limits of an algorithm, and its effects | Algorithm unsuitability | As required |
| Boundary-value analysis | Bugs on boundaries and bugs related to output domain | Bugs from combinations of inputs | No. of input and output equivalence classes + no. of equivalence class bounds |
| Feature testing | Anything tested for | Doesn't test all the code equally, doesn't always reflect use in the field | As required |
| Cause–effect graphing | Specification ambiguities and inconsistencies, combinations of inputs | Some boundary bugs | No. of input equivalence classes + no. of output equivalence classes |
| Decision (branch) coverage | Outcomes of simple decisions | Units without decisions, multiple entry points, incorrect conditions in decisions | No. of decision outcomes, McCabe metric |
| Decision tables | Which conditions should not affect the decision (but might)? | Logic bugs in the original decision table | No. of columns in the decision table |
| DU paths | Incorrect operations or no operations on variables | Wrong specification | At least one per path |
| Dynamic dataflow | Data behavior in a running program | Total path coverage | Code instrumentation as required plus tools |
| Equivalence class partitioning | One representative of each input class | Bugs from combinations of inputs, bugs related to output domain structure, and bugs on equivalence class boundaries | Number of input equivalence classes |
| Executable assertion | Correctness of code at assertion point | Anything unrelated to the assertion | As many assertions as required |
| Execution-time and resource use analysis | Execution-time, order, control-flow, wait-time, and resource use of each module | Faulty execution or resource use | Not applicable |
| Fault injection | Control-flow errors, inability to manage illegal data, illegal data states, and code bugs | It may show bugs in compiled code, but identifying which source instructions they refer to may be too expensive an exercise to be undertaken | As required |
| Linear code sequence and jump | As statement coverage plus $n$ paths | As expensive as the number of jumps covered, requires a tool to be done inexpensively | As required |
| Multiple decision coverage | All outcomes of all conditions in all decisions in all combinations | Units without decisions | No. of decision/condition/outcome combinations |
| Mutant analysis | Finds bugs similar to the mutation | Depends on mutant strategy approximating reality | See section 13.6 |
| Path analysis | Computational, path, and missing path bugs | Wrong paths | At least one per path |
| Random data selection | The probability of failure given some random input | Any case not tested for | As required |
| Statement coverage | Incorrect processing | Some decision, or decision/condition outcomes, e.g., incorrect logic flow | No. of paths |
| Symbolic evaluation | Equivalence classes of inputs | Feasible paths excluded by manual intervention (e.g., in path pruning) | As the symbols evaluated |

4. At various times (as soon as possible) when we test the human–computer interfaces to see if the system is usable.

Additionally we exercise some form of validation on a specification which needs some form of validation by creating an executable model. Other informal tests may occur at any time throughout software projects, but are outside the scope of this book.

---

# Story

---

*Note:* You will be punished for "not starting system testing on time."

"Yes, but we didn't have any specifications, and we only had two extra features added yesterday. We've had no time to write the tests."

"*So? You should have said so earlier.*" (I'm not exaggerating much. Even if you only heard the news 10 minutes ago there are those who will say anything, no matter how silly, to deflect blame from themselves.)

---

This is called *getting stitched-up*. Avoid it early by sending all relevant parties a memo identifying the entry criteria you will adopt for deciding when you are ready to start system testing (see section 8.5.9). Stand to one side and admire the smoke, flames, and bangs with equanimity. Remember that this way you will focus much-needed attention on the exit criteria.

## 2.4   When Do We Stop Testing?

We stop testing when we realize that the system is so buggy that testing it anymore is pointless, or when all the following are true:

1. The number of bugs found is close enough to the number you expect to find. See section 18.10.
2. All the tests have been run.
3. All the code has been exercised.
4. Every feature has been shown to work (with every other).
5. Every use case scenario has been exercised.
6. Code turmoil has fallen enough. See section 18.9.8.
7. Feature stability is sufficient. See Figure 8.25.
8. The system can be shown to be within some Reliability, Availability, and Maintainability Profiles defined in the test plan.
9. The number and severity of outstanding bugs has fallen to a satisfactory level.
10. When all regression, smoke, and confidence tests pass.

See section 8.5.9 for more on this.

Some projects are 'sticky'; that is, no matter how much work you do there always seems to be more. Having an exit criterion at least gives you a measure of how sticky the project is.

1. **An example:** management desperately wants to release v.1.0. It still has 8 priority-1 bugs unfixed, to say nothing of the 50 priority-2s. Releasing it would probably cause severe problems for a large number of customers, and perhaps bring down the company. But management is getting hysterical. The Directors don't hear what management tells you and (unless you tell them) never will. The Directors would be horrified if they ever understood the risks which management is proposing to run.

2.  **Yet another example:** it doesn't matter how many bugs they fix, the developers always seem to leave new ones in the code. Management has realized that the situation is getting terminal. Try to resolve this by:
    - Demonstrating it's true (see section 2.7.2 and section 18.10.2.2)
    - Proposing setting up an ad-hoc group to assess the code and unit-test the most-changed parts in an effort to stem the tide

Avoid the hysteria, risk, and disruption of personal relations by having a release exit criteria defined, understood, and accepted well in advance. See section 8.5.9. Make sure the Directors know this and are happy with it. This way they have a simple question for you, and you can say "*Yes, we met the criteria*" or "*No.*"

## 2.5   What Do We Test It Against?

---

# Story: What the Bleep Was That?

---

Once upon a time a man invented an automatic garage door opener. It used a low-power, short-wave transmitter operating on a little-used frequency, which the user kept in the car. It sold very well, and the man made a lot of money.

Then Sputnik was launched. Guess what little-used frequency the Sputnik designers used.

And as Sputnik bleeped its way over America, garage doors opened and closed.

Moral: There are things you can specify and things you can test for and there are things you'd never ever *think* of guarding against.

---

Here's a selection:

1.  Our **belief in real-world events.** You can have all the specifications you want and they still won't define every possible event in the real world, like the last example.
2.  **Specifications.** What kind of specifications?
    a.  Specifications which match the level of testing we need to perform. Normally these are *Requirements specifications,* which are the basis (or "*baseline*") of system tests; *Design specifications,* which are the basis of subsystem tests; and *Module specifications,* which are the basis of module tests (Aka unit tests). As things get more complex you may use *HW/SW Interface specifications,* which are the basis of HW/SW interface tests; *KPIs (Key Performance Indicators),* which are the basis of performance tests; and *User Interface specifications,* which are the basis of usability tests. When web testing you may need to use user action logs and transaction flow maps. In principle every kind of test has some baseline.[1]
    b.  *What if the specifications don't exist, e.g., when testing games software?* There are times when specifications that existed at the start are no longer useful. To expect programmers to define what they're doing while they are in creative full flow would be like asking a centipede to think

---

[1] There are tests whose baselines cannot be written. When early models of a production car first roll off the line they are subjected to special usability tests. These are conducted by drivers expert in the specifications of the car and the expectations of users. Armed with enough monitoring gadgetry to sink a boat, they drive the car along lanes and motorways, through mud, rain, and snow. Their objective is to fractionally improve the overall handling of the car. Their results are fed back to the powertrain, steering, suspension, and braking specialists of the production line. Their baseline is essentially their experience of cars and their expectations.

about how to walk: you could ask, but the centipede would fall over. In practice centipedes walk and (games) programmers program. While games programmers may appear to work in an unstructured manner, in reality they create and tear down structures as they need them. Thus if there's a need for a video insert, be sure that one will be scripted and built in. The tester must create what baselines are required if only by writing them himself. Such baselines can be minimal and make sense to the testers alone. If you don't have baselines you can use a notation like the ones discussed in section A.4 and section 8.2.1, and Do It Yourself.

3. **Baselines.** Have we identified the baseline documents (or whatever)?
   a. Who owns them?
   b. Are they going to change?
   c. How much warning will we get before they change?
   d. Are they sufficient for use as a baseline?
   e. Have we reviewed them?
   f. Have we fed our review comments back to the owner?

   A faulty or missing baseline is the first sign that things will go wrong. Another is that the document (or whatever) is insufficient for testing against. "*Bang the table*" by reviewing whatever is there and commenting clearly and succinctly on its shortcomings. This is not simply self-protection, but a wake-up call to management that there are going to be problems.

   Testers need to be in the requirements loop. Having the test team review all the requirements is one of the smartest things management can do. The test team need those specifications, are going to use those specifications, and will be more likely than developers to find fault with them. They need to review all the changes, too. The person who says, "*I can't see any reference to X*" is on the way to earning a year's salary by seeing a problem now rather than just before the system testing started.

4. **Existing systems.** Sometimes a system is built to replace another. The old system may be all you get to use as a baseline. If so, write a requirements specification as discussed in Chapter 8.

5. **Real-world data.** There's no user interface. There's a system A, which processes something from system B and generates something to be used by system C. Only the data is real. You have to test it. Naturally there's no specification for the thing in between. Write an interface specification as discussed in Chapter 8. Look at server log entries to find what real traffic has occurred.

6. **Gossip and hearsay.** Don't ignore it. Developers can be very touchy about being refused permission by a pressuring project manager to fix unstable and otherwise risky bits of code. If this happens they'll often love to tell you where the really risky bits are. Similarly a hard-to-repeat bug can be discussed with a sympathetic developer who can offer insights on why it might have appeared.

## 2.6   What Do We Test it With?

1. Tools which simulate inputs.
2. Real-world sample and faked data.
3. Tool harnesses which simulate an environment.
4. Tools which manage tests.
5. Test scripts which simulate users.

See Chapter 7 for more on tools and data.

## 2.7   Are We Getting Better or Worse at Finding Bugs?

The only absolute answer to this question is to identify the bugs reported from the field as a proportion of those found in-house for any release. This measure, however:

1. Ignores those bugs users cannot be bothered to report, perhaps because they are so bad that they are about to abandon use of the system or product.
2. Is only available when it is no longer useful, some months after the release.

An alternative is to:

1. Identify a series of indicators (number of bugs found by testers as a proportion of the whole, average number of bugs found per day, total number of bugs found as a proportion of estimated bugs found, priority-1s and priority-2s as a proportion of all bugs found).
2. Compare them with previous releases and observe the fluctuations.
3. Use a bug-seeding tool to estimate how many bugs remain in the system (when enough of the system has automated tests written).

See also section 2.7.2 and section 18.10.2.2.

## 2.7.1 Why Didn't We Find That Bug Earlier?

This is a cry frequently heard as deadlines approach. There could be a number of answers:

1. The testers were not able to complete testing due to a new release being loaded.
2. The bug was not in an earlier release (reload that earlier release and see).
3. The bug could not be tested for earlier because some part of the release did not work and inhibited the test's ability to "see" the bug.
4. The bug was in some part of the system not originally planned for the release for which a test has only just been written.
5. The bug was found while running some other test.
6. The bug was in a part of a system which was not the focus of testing.
7. The bug would have been found eventually, but the tester hadn't run the test (which would have found it) yet.
8. And yes, maybe if we'd been more thorough we'd have found that bug earlier.

Circulate a spreadsheet like the one shown in Table 2.2.

**TABLE 2.2**  Late-found bug list

| SCR No. | Headline | Tester | Date raised | Severity | Outcome | Why not found earlier |
|---|---|---|---|---|---|---|
| 7690 | Text Editor: Intermittent error and unable to shutdown NewSystem | Feroza | 03.11.04 | High | May be Critical. Being monitored. If not will be moved to Callisto | Ad hoc test |
| 7738 | Notes Editor—TAB button does nothing | Mat | 04.11.04 | Medium | | Intermittent problem. Test has been produced after the Minor Transactions UI spec (which required all Notes Editor UI tests to need rewriting). |
| 7708 | Schedules—Pasting of bulleting lists has XML appear in the TextEditor Schedules—Pasting of numbered lists has XML appear in the TextEditor | Mat | 04.11.04 | High | TextEditor Shortcuts | Passed in Drop 21. Found while executing this test but not as a result of it. Passed in Drop 21. Found while executing this test but not as a result of it. |

Just having the list and having already got the answers from the testers will help you both bat back some criticisms and give you better insights into how tests should be managed.

### 2.7.2   How Many Bugs Are Being Introduced with Each Fix?

Microsoft suffered from this problem in the 1980s. It is called the *infinite defect loop*. It caused major delays to their development of Windows 3.0. The WinWord project took five years, starting in 1983, and was delayed for the same reason.

Infinite defect loops have many causes, beginning with an inadequate architecture, but persist because of subtle, frequent changes. Software that exhibits this tendency is probably entropic. A less-polite phrase to describe it is "*spaghetti code.*"

To eliminate or minimize this, Microsoft uses an approach called synch and stabilize (see Chapter 4). To find this out, you will need to look at two sources:

1. The test history. Look at the execution of tests over the last three to four test runs. How many problems have repeatedly recurred? How many tests have found a bug, had it fixed, and had it recur? See Figure 8.25.
2. The configuration management database. Use this to get the data you need to assess requirements and code turmoil. See section 18.9.8.

See also section 18.10.2.2.

### 2.7.3   What Are the Primary Root Causes of Our Bugs?

The obvious answer to this is to look in the mirror. Of course, the root cause of all bugs is human failing. More usefully, a number of other causes can be determined:

1. The process or phase. Is there evidence that an undue number of bugs are deriving in or from some phase? Would they have been found by better unit tests or system tests? Could the bug have been found by a more rigorous review? This is data that can be got from the bug reports. Most root cause analyses of bugs stop here and shouldn't. (See section 18.10.2.2 for an example of an out-of-control process that generates out-of-control code.)
2. The tool used: yes, a bad workman blames his tools but maybe the compiler gives misleading messages, maybe the development environment is poor, maybe the allegedly reusable code is, er, terrible, maybe the unit testing tool doesn't cover all the input ranges it promised to. Ask the developers.
3. The people involved: if each developer has a particular area of responsibility, then it shouldn't be difficult to work out that Fred or Freda is in need of, er, further development.
4. The feature involved: some features are buggier than others (surprise). This too is data which can be got from the bug reports.

See section 7.6.1 and section 18.9.8. Also read [Reason] for a fascinating account of human error.

### 2.7.4   Which Features Are the Most Buggy?

Providing bugs are feature-related this is simple and can result in pie-charts like the one shown in Figure 2.1. Using such charts it is easy to prioritize the development effort in bug fixing as well as reviewing where testing effort is best applied (the buggiest features have the greatest number of changes, which often implies the greatest number of newly-introduced bugs).

Beware though that feature A may exhibit more bugs than feature B, because you have more tests for feature A.

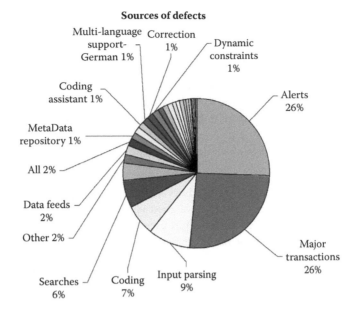

**Sources of defects**

FIGURE 2.1 Which is the buggiest feature?

## 2.7.5 Are We Creating More or Fewer Bugs?

This can be determined by:

1. Relating the number of bugs found per build to the number of changes (creates, updates, and deletes) of each build. Assume 4 builds: A, B, C, and D. If the total number of bugs found in each build is proportional to the number of changes to that build (a large number of changes equates to a large number of bugs, and a small number equates to a small number of bugs), then the release is probably stable. If (measured over a number of builds) the relationship of changes to bugs found is inversely proportional (that is, more bugs are found as the number of changes falls), then you possibly have a problem.

2. Measuring the number of bugs found in each iteration of each test. Assuming you can run all the tests to completion on each build, *how many bugs do the tests find on each build? Is the number growing, fluctuating, or reducing? If it is not reducing overall, then is the number of priority-1 bugs reducing?*

However, there are other possibilities. Table 2.3 shows 6 cases. The prerequisites are above the thick, black line and the conclusions below it.

TABLE 2.3  Identifying whether testing or development is affecting quality

| Case | 1 | 2 | 3 | 4 | 5 | 6 |
|---|---|---|---|---|---|---|
| Have the tests been revised or the test regime changed? | Y | N | N | N | Y | Y |
| Are the numbers of bugs found by unit tests increasing? | N | N | Y | Y | N | N |
| Is the defect rate/KLOC much greater than in the last release? | Y | Y | Y | N | N | Y |
| Is code turmoil high? | N | N | N | — | — | Y |
| Is there evidence of increased code complexity? | N | Y | — | — | — | — |
| Testers are getting better at system testing | Y | | | | N | Y |
| Developers are creating more bugs | | Y | Y | | | |
| Developers are reducing the number of bugs | | | | Y | | |

## 2.8   How Do We Measure Our Test Coverage?

Test coverage is a measure of the degree to which a test exercises some feature(s) or code. Test coverage relates the tests produced to the software or features under test such that we can estimate:

1. The degree to which a test exercises the software or features.
2. The software or features which are insufficiently exercised.
3. Given the number of bugs found and the test coverage, the confidence we have in the system's attributes at any moment.
4. The minimum number of tests which need to be run to provide some level of confidence in the quality of the system.

*Caveat:* test coverage is another example of small boys with hammers to whom everything appears to be a nail. Thus there are many papers published, full of good advice on code coverage in unit testing. There is very little on feature coverage; [Memon] is the rare exception.

Is your test coverage getting better, or worse? There are several ways of measuring it:

1. Test coverage by feature. The specification says the system has the following *n* features plus start-up and shut-down. Do we have a test (set) for every feature plus start-up and shut-down? See section 15.2.
2. Test coverage by GUI icon. The user interface has a number of screens, buttons, pull-downs, tabs, menus, etc. Do we have them all listed (see section 8.2 for an example), and do we have tests which execute every one? See section 15.4 for more on this.
3. Test coverage by instrumentation. Use a code instrumentation tool to instrument a build, and then test that build using the system tests already prepared. The tool output should be able to indicate how much coverage in code terms the system had. Note that this need not occur for every build once sufficient code coverage is assured. See section 12.9 for more on this.
4. Test coverage by structure. When unit testing you need to be sure you have exercised some minimum part of the code. Testing should include Statement coverage, Decision (branch) coverage, Condition coverage, All-DU-paths coverage, and Linear Code Sequence and Jump (LCSAJ) (see Chapter 12). Beware of anyone claiming "code coverage" when all they are doing is running Ncover when building: they may have filtered out unexercised lines and will only have exercised at best all the statements in the unit. Decision, branch, DU-paths, etc., will probably **not** have been covered.
5. Test coverage by scenario. Users have a number of goals which they want to achieve. They achieve them using a number of (parts of) features. In doing so they set up subtle feature interactions, which no other coverage approach will mimic. Use user action logs (if necessary) to validate your proposed scenarios, and user profiles to identify scenario sets. Naturally use cases form the baseline of such an approach. See section A.1 in Appendix A.
6. Test coverage by transition. Typically on web applications, but also in more conventional applications, there is a number of "paths" a user may take to achieve a goal. These paths need to be identified possibly in the form of a state transition diagram (typically from URL to URL in the case of a web test) such that a minimum number of paths can be identified and traversed. This is something of a hybrid of test coverage by structure and test coverage by scenario, and is invaluable when testing web applications.
7. Test coverage by web script, web page, application, and component. Having identified the risk level of the website (see section 5.2), you can then decide the level of coverage necessary to mitigate that risk by selecting the test types from section 5.5.

Why does this matter? Because you want to minimize the risk of not having covered all the possibilities of having a fatal bug in the released system. Test coverage cannot be complete, any more than requirements specifications can be (see section 1.4 for a discussion of this). But you can make a good engineering decision on what sort of test coverage you need based on the risk the system poses.

The coverage type(s) you choose (should) relate to the probability of finding bugs, and thus to the degree to which you are minimizing the risk the product poses.

## 2.8.1 Code Level Test Coverage Estimation

At the code level, test coverage is intimately related to test type, and there is no independent criterion against which the various types of test (and therefore the various types of coverage) can be measured. In the test plan you need to establish the types of test and the coverage to be obtained therefrom. Criteria range from the banal (but essential) all-statements-executed to the near-impossible all-paths-executed.

Before determining the amount of code level test coverage, it is useful to decide:

1. Whether any parts of the system have a high criticality (note that this excludes safety-critical parts, all of which must have the highest-possible level).
2. Which features and code areas are likely to be the most-highly used.
3. Which units are the most complex.
4. Which units have been changed the most often since being submitted to configuration management.
5. Which units have generated the most bugs so far (this will clearly change; if the test plan is being written at the high-level design stage, then, presumably, no units will have been coded so far; however, as the test plan is revised later in the project cycle, experience will suggest that some units are bug-prone).
6. What sort of inputs the system should withstand.
7. What the history of similar systems has suggested (this can be derived from bug reports; if they can be related either to features or particular parts of the code, it will be possible to build a code profile of the more problematic and use this as a guide to the type and quantity of tests to be run).

Having defined these issues it will be easier to relate the test types as shown in section 2.2 to the particular software bugs. See [Wei-Tek] for details of a minimal approach to test coverage of embedded medical devices complete with examples and toolkit.

## 2.8.2 System Test Coverage Strategies

Here are three approaches:

1. Major features first. Create tests which will exercise all the principal features first, to give maximum coverage. This will probably be the same as the regression test. Then exercise each feature in some depth.
2. Major use cases first. As major features. Requires that you know both the user profile and the use profile. The test must be end-to-end such that some real-world user objective is reached.
3. Major inputs and outputs. If the application is I/O dominated, then identify the most common kinds of inputs and outputs and create tests to exercise them.

These can be followed by:

1. All GUI features
2. All functions with variations
3. All input/output combinations

Note that various test management tools will give you coverage metrics showing the proportion of *requirements "covered" by a test, test cases run*, etc. These are of course purely arbitrary; just because a tester has associated a test case to a requirement doesn't mean that the requirement has been adequately covered. That's one of the things you as test manager must check.

## 2.9   Are There Any More Embarrassing Questions?

At some point management may start to look seriously at their costs. Here are some questions to get them going:

1. How much does product development, maintenance, and support cost the company? How does quality relate to cost, and stability to milestones?
2. Why does a particular product's schedule keep slipping while other product schedules stay on track? Is resource allocation adequate, and management stable?
3. How many worker-hours have gone into a particular product? How are they apportioned among requirements management, planning, design, implementation, testing, and support? Do staff record them on their time sheets? How long does it take to resolve customer complaints?
4. How stable is each software component? What is the appropriate level of quality?
5. What can be done to minimize the rate of field failures and the cost of fixing bugs, improving milestone accuracy, quality, and optimizing resource allocation?
6. Do any of those very low-severity bugs, which no one can be bothered fixing, mask a much more serious bug? (Answer: *If the level of code turmoil* (see section 18.9.8) *is high, then "yes."*)

$3$

# Risk Management

---

## Terminal Litigation

T here was once an Italian computer manufacturer whose British subsidiary sold an expensive system to a large solicitors' practice. It was a client-server system and buried in the contract was a phrase to the effect that the system would support up to 160 clients. The contract was signed and much spumante[1] flowed. No one at the manufacturer's end had read the details of the contract, much less understood it. No one had ever tested such a system with more than 5 clients and no one had informed the Head of Quality Control of the contract's existence, much less of its provisions.

This was an interesting experience for the Italian computer manufacturer whose litigation experience had hitherto been confined mostly to the Italian legal system. The solicitors won their case (the contract was according to the laws of England and surprise, surprise, they wrote it). Many other problems became known over the years. The Italian computer manufacturer later sold mobile (cell) phones, and has not fielded a computer system since its entire stock of (unsaleable) PCs was destroyed in a mysterious fire.

---

Risk is the probability of something happening, multiplied by the cost if it does.

The mere mention of the word *risk* scares many project managers. It has become taboo like death or taxes. Testing is a major defense against risk, and the wise test manager knows how to use risk as a lever to get more resources and time, and allocate these according to the perceived risk. There are four major sources of risk:

1. The **product;** in that it may not work properly with the result that some loss occurs to the developers (see section 3.1.3 for more on this).
2. The **project;** in that it may be late with the developers incurring some penalty clause, or reduced probability of gaining some later contract, exposed to some danger due to an external dependency on a supplier, greatly exceeding its cost envelope, lack of skills, or other resources.
3. The **users;** in that they may use the product *"wrongly,"* in a way that was not allowed for and which, while no blame need be associated with the developers, might prejudice the probability of the developers winning similar contracts in future.
4. The **environment;** which includes competitors, the government, the banks, the weather, etc.

---

[1] Italian sparkling wine.

## 3.1 How to Manage Risk

Here is a process for managing risk (see Figure 3.1). Risk should be tracked through the project plan, but in the event that this has not been done, perform your own risk assessment. From such an analysis, write a prioritized set of risks together with the risk reduction plan and a maximum which can reasonably be spent to meet each risk. This can be fed into an equation of the type shown in section 7.9.2. From this you can define some cost limits for the amount of testing you can afford to do, and these can be fed back into the plan and used to justify the test team's work.

- **Plan how to manage the project's risks.** The Risk Management Plan documents how risks will be managed. It is a subset of the project plan and is written before the project begins. See [IEEE 1540-2001] for a standard to follow. See also [Boehm 91].
- **Identify risks.** One simple approach is to get representatives of all the affected groups in a room and have a workshop. Circulate a provisional list to excite attention. Get their ideas down onto large sheets of paper you can blu-tack to the walls. Circulate a revised list after the meeting. Repeat the process half-way through the project, and identify how many have not occurred, and how many unforeseen ones *had* occurred. Use [Carr M], the kinds of risk mentioned earlier, and look at each workpackage in the plan to identify how each could be compromised by being unfinished, late, or simply giving a wrong output. Identify what the knock-on effect of such an event might be. Look at the users, and identify how each stakeholder class might be negatively affected by a system failure (look at section 7.7.3). Look at the development, test, training, and support environments, and identify weak points (for example, see section 8.5.17). See [Wallace] for a list of fifty-three major risks and their relationships.

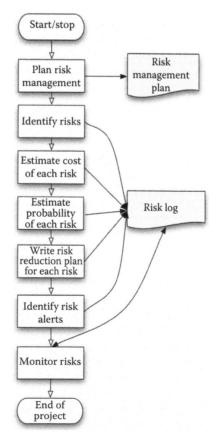

**FIGURE 3.1** A risk management process.

- **Estimate risk costs, probabilities, and exposures** (see Table 3.1).
- **Write the reduction/mitigation plan for each risk.**
- **Identify the risk alerts.** Taking the list of risks, identify what are the first signs you might get that the risk will eventuate. What can you do to get those signs earlier? How can you get such a sign to trigger an alert?
- **Monitor the risks** using the risk log in section 8.17 and the alerts.

## 3.1.1   Risk Alerts

These are the triggers used to identify when a risk is imminent. Typical test-related triggers are:

- Reduction in the number of lines of code per bug found.
- Finding an unacceptably-high number of priority-1 and -2 bugs in a build.
- Finding an unacceptably-high number of bugs in a component.
- Late arrival of signed-off specifications for use as a baseline.
- Failure of performance tests to achieve targets.
- Growing code complexity.
- Growing code turmoil.

Monitoring such risks is easier when an alerting system is in place.

The existence of a risk log allows the test team to identify priorities and provides a good basis for deciding the mix of tests to be planned.

## 3.1.2   Risks as Drivers

Risks can be grouped by *sources* (as shown above) and by *kinds*. A risk *kind* is for example that something doesn't work, that it works too late, too slowly, at the wrong time, or that it has unintended side-effects. These groups are sensitive to risk drivers in that a driver can change a whole group of risks. Thus the product risk *kind* may be composed of the following subrisks:

- That features A, B, and D don't work correctly.
- That features C, and D are too slow.
- That features B, and E are highly susceptible to environmental change, and that the proposed move from database X to Y will cause many problems.

These risks might be related to (say) the failure of the project to use an appropriate *development method* (the project is mostly staffed by new graduates with some experience in Visual Basic, and none in design. No high-level designs are being developed, nor is any prototyping). When in week 26 a new project manager is appointed he speedily junks all the existing code, changes the development approach, sacks the team leaders, reorganizes the development process, and puts a workable plan in place. The failure of the project to use an appropriate development method was having a knock-on effect throughout the whole of the project. It was a source of risks and a major driver. Here are some more:

- Use of an inappropriate (unrelated to the risk) method or process.
- Lack of customer involvement. Apart from the obvious need for a sufficient set of requirements there is the need for feedback to users of (fragments of) the proposed solution.
- Dissimilarity to previous projects. If "we've never done anything as (big/complex/different) as this before" is an issue, then beware.
- Project complexity. This is relative to the experience of an organization. What might exhaust some organizations will be run-of-the-mill to others.
- Requirements volatility. If such changes aren't allowed for, the project will soon deteriorate.

This list appears to be merely a set of big risks, however each point shown will affect a range of related risks. When the existence of the big risk is recognized, the subsidiary risks can be tackled together rather than in isolation.

### 3.1.3   Product Risk

Among the various risks the project may pose, the product risk in particular needs to be decomposed since some features are more risk-bearing than others. Recognize and track them from the moment requirements are written. While it may not be possible to assign a cost to the risk from the outset, it should be possible to assign a hazard potential (*High, Medium,* or *Low*) to each requirement such that it can be eventually transformed into a risk. In this way you can:

- Identify the features most in need of early prototyping, or formal specification.
- Determine the level and rigor of tests needing to be written.
- Assign the bug fixing priorities.
- Assign effort.
- Monitor the feature status.
- Identify when the features are likely to be used, from the operational profile (this will give you the risk exposure factor).

Table 3.1 lists some frequently-mentioned risks and things you can do to mitigate them.

### 3.1.4   Risk Exposure

Every component or feature represents a risk however small. However it may not represent a risk *all* the time. It may be very rarely used. So it's useful to understand how often it will be used in order to gauge whether to devote a lot of resources to testing it. Risk is only exposed when a threat is present.

Why is this important? You need to be able to:

- Identify costs in order to assess the value of taking some mitigating action.
- Factor in the exposure to the hazard of a project, user, or product, however brief.
- Ensure both that the exposure period is valid and that your testing represents it.
- Distinguish between a low-risk, constant-exposure threat and a high-risk, low-exposure one.

Note that a number of authors confuse *risk* with *risk exposure.*

We can express exposure (in this case of a feature) as an equation [Sherer]:

$$X^F(T) = \sum_i p(U_i^F) \sum_j p\left(\frac{H_j}{U_i^F}\right) C_j(T)$$

where

$X^F(T)$ = exposure of feature $F$ during time $T$

$p(U_i^F)$ = probability of use $i$ of feature $F$

$p\left(\dfrac{H_j}{U_i^F}\right)$ = probability that hazard $j$ occurs when feature $F$ is being used by i

$C_j(T)$ = consequence (cost) of hazard $j$ occurring during time $T$

**Example 1.** A system's feature might be the daily printing of a report. User profile analysis shows this to be utterly critical on 2.25 days every week and not important otherwise. An analyst uses the report. The Chairman also wants the report but will do nothing with it. The non-availability of the report will at non-critical times still have a cost of wasted time of US$5. If the report is wrong the cost incurred by the analyst will be US$5m. If the analyst doesn't get the report on time the cost is US$3m.

**TABLE 3.1**  Project risks and how the test team can help mitigate them

| Risk | Test activity |
|---|---|
| Unclear, or misunderstood scope, or objectives<br>Misunderstood requirements | Review the specifications for testability (all part of your job) and then complain loudly when anything is unclear.<br>Note that testers will be writing a version of the requirements in the form of their test objectives. If the requirements are unclear to them, they will be unclear to the developers, the technical writers, the support team, and the users. |
| Conflicting system requirements | The test group is one of the best placed to identify these early. See the story in section 4.43. |
| Undefined project success criteria | Insofar as a test group is there to answer questions, defining the project success criteria is a primary task for them. See section 4.18. |
| Unrealistic schedules and budgets | Complaining that a 500 man-day project has allowed 5 man-days for system-test preparation and execution will not make you loved, but at least this way no one can complain you didn't warn them, and you'll have time to prepare your exit. A closely-reasoned memo to the project manager may be just what he needs to subtly deflect the blame from himself (*"and then of course the testers always say they need more time"*), and still render the schedule a little less suicidal. |
| Failure to gain user involvement | This calls for award-winning levels of tact. Talking directly to users can upset the marketing people (*"We talk to clients"*), the project manager (*"No one talks to clients without my approval"*), and the client (*"I'm not having my staff being upset by a lot of silly questions…"*). If in doubt back off. But if there's resistance at the client end this is an indicator that something's wrong with the relationship, and if you are to be sure to test the system exactly as the client's staff use it… |
| Continuous requirement changes | As with the unrealistic schedules and budgets this is an area where some project managers need the moral support of an unhappy test manager. You need to determine the amount of extra work some requirement change will cost because you have to write extra tests for it. Even if the developers cannot imagine the effect of a change, you can. Managing requirements changes simply requires that you declare that there are times when changes can be made economically, and times when they can't. Create time windows wherein changes can be accepted, and deadlines by when they must be agreed. Assess every change against a schedule, and keep the price of change firmly in front of the project manager. |
| Conflicts between users/users with negative attitudes towards the project | The underlying causes of these are usually political, with group A believing that the system will somehow cause them some slippage downwards with respect to group B. The ostensible basis of such a conflict may be objectively determinable such as *"(the proposed system) doesn't give us what we need."* In this case the test group can either take details, or show group A their fears are met by some set of tests. |
| Users not committed to the project | If project management suspects some user group of being less than committed, the test group can become a litmus test by requesting help from that user group in determining the everyday use of the system. |
| High level of technical complexity | The wise project manager will choose a strategy involving prototypes and single-thread integration. The wise test manager will encourage this and make test staff available to create informal test fragments to test prototypes. |
| Dependency on outside suppliers | See section 10 for a discussion. |

- Dividing the critical day by the number of days it might be run gives us a probability figure of 2.25/5 days in which the feature is used.
- The report might be at risk for several reasons (see Table 3.2).

**TABLE 3.2**  Hazard/consequence

| ID | P | Consequence |
|---|---|---|
| a. | 50% | Report unavailable for analyst |
| b. | 20% | Report unavailable for chairman |
| c. | 30% | Report wrong |

We can express this set of hazards and probabilities as a diagram as shown in Figure 3.2 and as another equation:

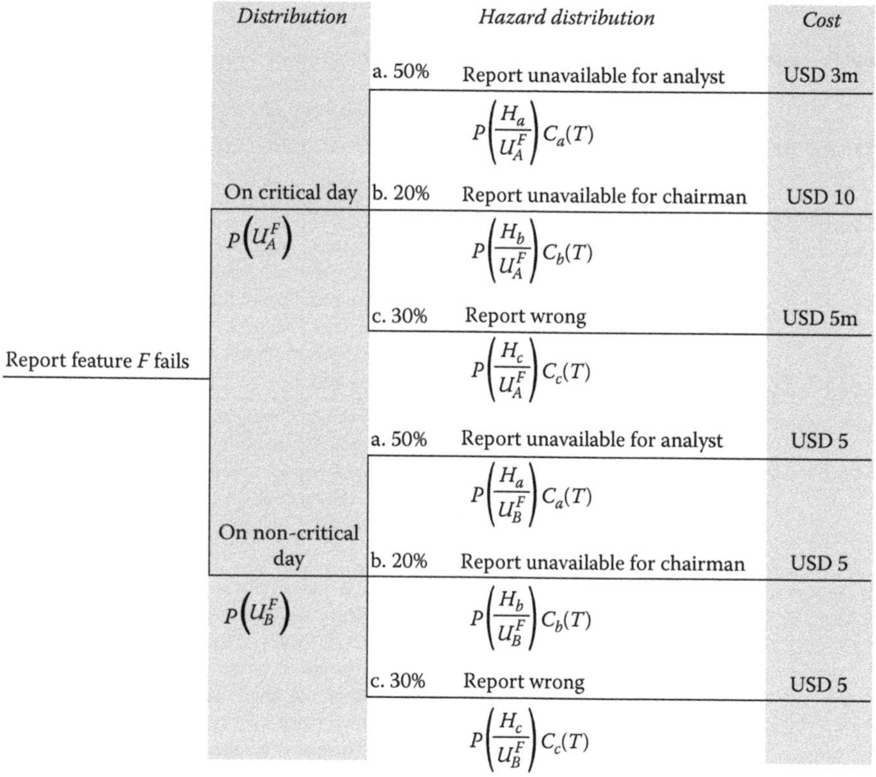

| Distribution | | Hazard distribution | Cost |
|---|---|---|---|
| | a. 50% | Report unavailable for analyst | USD 3m |
| | | $P\left(\dfrac{H_a}{U_A^F}\right)C_a(T)$ | |
| On critical day | b. 20% | Report unavailable for chairman | USD 10 |
| $P\left(U_A^F\right)$ | | $P\left(\dfrac{H_b}{U_A^F}\right)C_b(T)$ | |
| | c. 30% | Report wrong | USD 5m |
| | | $P\left(\dfrac{H_c}{U_A^F}\right)C_c(T)$ | |
| | a. 50% | Report unavailable for analyst | USD 5 |
| | | $P\left(\dfrac{H_a}{U_B^F}\right)C_a(T)$ | |
| On non-critical day | b. 20% | Report unavailable for chairman | USD 5 |
| $P\left(U_B^F\right)$ | | $P\left(\dfrac{H_b}{U_B^F}\right)C_b(T)$ | |
| | c. 30% | Report wrong | USD 5 |
| | | $P\left(\dfrac{H_c}{U_B^F}\right)C_c(T)$ | |

*Report feature F fails*

**FIGURE 3.2**  Hazard/consequence decision tree

$$X^F(T) = p\left(U_A^F\right)\left[p\left(\frac{H_a}{U_A^F}\right)C_a(T) + p\left(\frac{H_b}{U_A^F}\right)C_b(T) + p\left(\frac{H_c}{U_A^F}\right)C_c(T)\right] +$$

$$p\left(U_B^F\right)\left[p\left(\frac{H_a}{U_B^F}\right)C_a(T) + p\left(\frac{H_b}{U_B^F}\right)C_b(T) + p\left(\frac{H_c}{U_B^F}\right)C_c(T)\right]$$

which when evaluated looks like this:

$$1,350,003 = (2.25/5) * ((0.5 * 3000000) + (0.2 * 10) + (0.3 * 5000000)) + (2.75/5) * (((0.5 * 5) + (0.2 * 5) + (0.3 * 5)))$$

This represents the total risk exposure of this feature. To assess the reliability of the software see section 18.6.

**Example 2**: A lightning strike can only hit a space vehicle during the exit and entry phases — in other words when it is in some atmosphere. For the rest of the mission the vehicle's lightning risk exposure is nil. During launch and re-entry periods the probability is kept low by ensuring that no launches, or re-entries occur in discharge-potential weather (risk mitigation 1). If a strike occurs, the vehicle is built to minimize any upset for example by keeping its computers well shielded (risk mitigation 2). The risk of a lightning strike remains the probability of a strike (when exposed) times the cost.

**Example 3.** A project has all its testing off-shored in another continent. There is a threat that the test results are not provided in a timely manner, and are of insufficient quality due to cultural and time-zone differences. There is a plan to collocate the testers with the developers in three months time. The risk exposure thus lasts until the developers and testers are on the same site, and have minimal cultural, and time-zone differences.

(Counter) **Example 4.** An ejector seat will only be used once. The probability of its being used per 1000 flight hours in peacetime is low. In wartime it is quite high. The threat against which it is designed (an uncontrollable aircraft) is thus exposed very rarely. The probability of it being needed when such a threat is present is 1. There are some risks whose exposure can be considered constant.

## 3.2 A Worked Example

Assume a project to build a release 7.0 of the QuanGO product. The product has four major features:

1. An Alerts Management System (AMS) (to tell staff when some stock is low)
2. An ODBC interface (to interface to the databases)
3. A Stock Management System (to manage the warehouse)
4. A web interface (so salesmen and major customers can see stock levels and order)

It is proposed to rewrite the Alerts Management System and add a voice input ordering system.

1. *What are the risks?*
   - It doesn't work.
   - It contains serious bugs.
   - The release will not be made on time.
   - The project will suck in resources from the rest of the company which had been allocated to other projects.
2. *What are the probabilities and costs?* From Table 3.3, it is a simple matter to calculate the total risk the project faces (probability * cost). Note that *exposure* in this case is considered to be 100%.
3. *What are the sources?* Following is a list of possible sources. You will need this if you are to attack the problem. Each of these can contribute to a single risk such as *it doesn't work.*
   - Developer expertise: the old AMS was, frankly, clunky. It was written in VB4, made no use of .NET, and was a major source of bugs. It is proposed to rewrite it in C#. All the developers are experienced in Java. None has any major C# experience. None has any experience of .NET though management believes their expensive knowledge of J2EE will "carry across."
   - Complexity: although the AMS worked, it did so inconsistently. A look at the code reveals why. There is a risk that the new version will be as badly designed.
   - Lack of requirements: the old AMS was itself a kludge of a bought-in source from a now-defunct Alerts company. There are consequently no requirements for the new AMS other than "it should do what the old one did."
   - Voice input is much touted and terribly fashionable, but not yet proof against good folks from Aberdeen and the Adirondacks and their challenging speech. Thus either user HR has to be kept in the loop to ensure that staff pronunciation is of an acceptable level (not a core skill of HR departments), or there could be problems.
   - No definition of throughput: The existing system handles twenty simultaneous users. The proposed system must handle 2000. No work has been done to show that the database could handle this level of throughput let alone the rest of the system.
   - Age: The current development hardware is 5 years old and must be replaced.
   Note that these are *threats* not *risks*. The lack of developer expertise (for example) is not in itself a risk but a threat. No one will refuse to buy your software because none of your programmers has a PhD. They might if your programmers are a bunch of cowboys. The risk is simply that they

**TABLE 3.3**  Simple risk

| Risk name | Prob. | Cost (US$) | Comments | Risk (US$) | Alerts | Mitigation |
|---|---|---|---|---|---|---|
| It doesn't work. | 0.5 | 1,125,000 (cost of lost sales) | It gets released without major features or with major features not functioning. The last three releases did. | 562,500 | High levels of code complexity, turmoil, unit test failures. | Create demonstrator versions for all major features and have them performance-tested early. |
| It contains serious bugs. | 0.7 | 350,000 (the cost of the next bug-fixing release) | The last three releases did. | 245,000 | When actual bug level exceeds expected. | Ensure all critical units are unit-tested. Have all unit tests reviewed, and some code quality tools. |
| The release will not be made on time. | 0.99 | 75,000 (average cost of the last three overruns) | None of the last eight releases did. | 74,250 | When any workpackage is late in delivery by more than one day. | Review the schedule in the presence of test and developer staff. Identify weak areas. Allow for contingency of 25%. |
| The project will suck in resources from the rest of the company. | 0.7 | 65,000 (cost of resources) + 75,000 (cost of delays to other projects) | Every one of the last four releases did. | 98,000 | Any request for more staff by any manager. | None. No other project is more important. Get staff lists from the other project and cherry-pick their best people. |
| | | | (probability * cost) | 979,750 | | |

don't buy *because* the product doesn't work, because your developers are a bunch of cowboys. The risk "*it doesn't work*" can for example be broken down into a series of other risks:

- The old features fail.
- The new features fail.

Each of these can then be decomposed into a list of features and tested for. Some of these features represent greater risks than others. Thus you can:

- Identify an hierarchy of risks and thus test objectives.
- Monitor the degree of the risk, with reference to the bugs found and the amount of coverage obtained so far such that you can determine the amount of risk involved in releasing at any point.

If you then relate the features by criticality, you can order your tests and testing such that the biggest risks are prioritized and monitored.

4. *What are the solutions?* Table 3.4 shows that the cost of reducing the risks are lower than the total risks. No estimate is given for the cost to later releases of having kludgy, unmaintainable code in the system. This is left as an exercise. From this table it is a simple matter to calculate the total risk the project faces (probability * cost). Note that exposure in this case is considered to be 100%.

**Conclusion.** This is a very primitive and partial attempt at demonstrating how to think about and estimate project risk. It's something a project manager should do. It's something test managers often end up having to do in order to fight their corner, and ensure they have the company focusing realistically on the state of the project and what needs to be done to preserve its quality. For more on risks see section 8.16, 8.17, and B5 in Appendix B.

**TABLE 3.4**   Cost of risk mitigation

| Solutions to (causes of) risks | Cost (US$) | Delay (elapsed) |
|---|---|---|
| Hire a C# guru for six months | 60,000 | 0 |
| Send all development staff on a C# course | 20,000 | 1 |
| Rewrite entire system[a] | 250,000 | 8.5 |
| Write and review proper requirements specifications including throughput | 30,000 | 1 |
| Limit voice input (optionally research a different voice input engine) | 0 | 0 |
| Plan to spend six tester-months for every developer-year spent on the project (figure represents increase over original budget)[b] | 70,000 | −4 |
| Buy code quality tools | 100,000 | −1 |
| Have critical features prototyped and performance-tested, so that any potential shortcoming is known well-enough in advance | 122,000 | 3 |
| Total | 652,000 | 8.5 |

[a]  If the system is so clunky that rewriting it is the better option, then the alleged elapsed delay of 8.5 months is far *less* than the time taken to demonstrate that the old system is unfixable. However this plan is being made well before that unhappy point will be reached and the delay against the original (highly-unrealistic) plan becomes evident.

[b]  This will speed up the project by getting bugs found earlier.

## 3.3   Hazard Analyses and Testing

Hazard analyses were once used mostly by the "safety" industry as one part of preparing a "safety case" in order to have a system accepted and used. Any system which can cause or fail to prevent death, or injury must have a "safety case" prepared in most countries whose governments are concerned for the well-being of their people.

Today hazard analyses are also recognized as invaluable means of identifying financial, or indeed any kind of critical loss. The process is briefly shown in Figure 3.3. Alternatively put, the process is like this:

- Identify all the hazards (and write a hazard list).[1]
- Model the hazards using an FTA to identify what might — if it fails — provoke the hazard (based on the fact that we have only the haziest notion of what the system will resemble).
- Put the hazard list and the constraints we want to put on all the undesigned bits of an unbuilt system into the requirements specification.
- Design a system against the requirements specification. (Review the system to ensure it meets all these constraints.)
- Undertake an FMECA to see what would happen if some combination of components fails and the probability of this happening.
- Test the components of the system and the system as a whole to see if we can get some evidence that neither the failure of any individual component nor some (rather small) group thereof will cause a failure, with sufficient probability to satisfy the people who approve the safety case.

This is a very simplified view of what can happen with a safety- or otherwise mission-critical system analysis. It isn't cheap. It requires a lot of thought on the part of engineers and it requires that every bit be tested to prove that nothing bad will happen in the time frame of interest. It is a lot less expensive than an accident, or losing several million dollars in a faulty trade.

[1]  Aka *Hazard Log*: same dog, different collar.

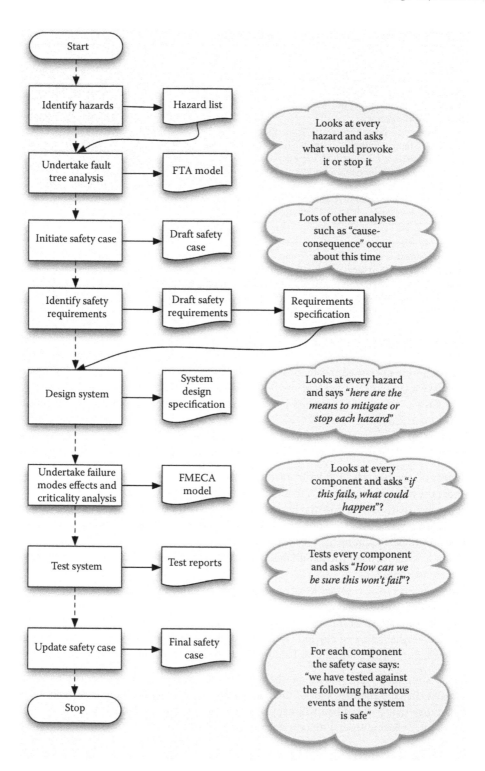

**FIGURE 3.3**  Hazard analysis process

# 4

# Test Planning and Management

---

## Story

There was once a project manager from an agency. He ran a small project in a Big Corporation. He believed in spreadsheets. The Big Corporation had an ethos of planning badly, optimistically, without tools, and then lying when they were found out. All the senior staff saw the project manager coming, and he saw them.

So when at these immensely-jolly meetings they loved holding, they tried to get him to commit to some date, he always told them that he would check his spreadsheet first, and just occasionally he agreed.

This made all the Big Executives inwardly wrathful, and they made Terribly Amusing Jokes about how he planned to make love to his wife with the aid of his spreadsheet. To his face. And he made no sign of having heard them.

His project finished a week late, and theirs finished 24 weeks late. He had several children.

---

This section discusses the principles of testing, relates testing to the project life-cycle, and examines the problems of planning, estimating, and managing the testing process.

## 4.1 Testing Principles

*...and this is where the story really starts.*

**Neddy Seagoon**

Testing is described in this book as a series of processes, each of which uses a number of inputs and generates a number of outputs. These processes and outputs are the result of the application of a number of (sometimes painfully-acquired) principles:

- The purpose of all quality activities is to minimize risk. Risk involves the probability of something happening, the results (including the cost) if it does, and the actions to be performed to either remove or minimize the risk or cope with the results. All project activities need to be judged against this criterion, and the related quality activity begun. A bug represents a kind of risk.

- The purpose of testing is to find bugs. Any test that merely shows that, under some conditions software functions as expected, is only useful as a regression test, that is, to demonstrate that the system is minimally capable of functioning.
- A successful test is one which finds a bug. There are 5 kinds of bugs:[1]
  a. The bug which exists in terms of some specification. (The specification says that *having pressed F1 a Help menu will always be displayed*. On pressing F1 a help menu is not displayed. Therefore there is a bug.)
  b. The bug which can be imagined. (The early DOS message that said *keyboard not present press F1*.)
  c. The bug which can't be imagined. (*The specification says that* having pressed F1 a Help menu will always be displayed. *I have just pressed F1 and while a menu was displayed, it is now obscured by the smoke billowing out of the machine.*) These bugs depend on some interaction between the system and the "real" world. The latter cannot be completely specified.[2]
  d. The bug which has been foreseen but not sufficiently allowed for. (*The possibility of an aircraft destroying a building because a turbine compressor disk broke off and caused the aircraft to crash, because a turbine blade melted, because the turbine blade heat sensor didn't sound the alarm in time, because there was a delay in the software.*)
  e. The non-functional bug. By non-functional I mean some part of the system where the failure criterion can only be specified by a (set of) range(s) of values, such as (say) performance or usability. See Chapters 16 and 17 for more on this.
  The sorts of bugs which *can* occur suggest the sorts of tests to be written to find them. By definition no tests can be written for the type "c" bug, but because they exist, every effort should be made to imagine them. Writing good tests means imagining the unimaginable.
- Testing cannot prove the absence of bugs, only their presence.
- If a program produces a correct output from many test inputs then it may produce correct output from any input. Sometimes it doesn't. Even flawless software can generate drivel if the inputs are corrupt enough.
- A test can find a bug only in terms of some baseline; some specification which determines what a bug is. This baseline can exist on paper or in someone's head ("It shouldn't have done *that!*"), but to be useful it must be objective and evident. There are (almost) no oracles to determine the correctness of every output in every circumstance. A good tester may have an instinctive knowledge of what is "incorrect" behavior — he will then spend the time required to show why it is "incorrect."
- Testing costs at least half of all the other project activities. Even if this hasn't been planned it's what will happen anyway. Therefore it's better to plan. This requires that we set priorities and make choices.
- Testing cannot be complete. Any non-trivial system will use too many combinations of inputs to allow for every one to be tested. Testing can only cover a small fraction of these in the time-scale required.
- Testing must stop at some point. Because testing costs a lot, some ratio of time spent testing to the number of bugs discovered needs to be established at the outset. This ratio should increase proportionally to the risks inherent in the system.
- Testing requires independence; for an unbiased measurement of software quality, you need an unbiased person to measure it. Thus testing needs to be independent of designing and coding, for example:

---

[1] There is another way of classifying errors shown in Appendix C.

[2] Much learned ink has been spilt in an effort to make this clear. If you don't have a maths PhD but disagree, then read Douglas R. Hofstader *Gödel, Escher, Bach, an eternal golden braid*. Basic Books, 1979.

- At the lowest risk level this may simply mean that a second programmer checks the unit tests written by the developer.
- At the highest risk level there may be a separate group completely independent of the software developers, charged with integration and system testing. While this may appear expensive it is always cost-efficient for large projects.

- Tests must be repeatable. It is not enough that a bug be seen. Each test should find the bug as many times as is required for the developers to be able to find the cause of the bug.
  - Developers can really help here: they may be able to advise on probable scenarios.
  - Developers would probably appreciate a QuickTime movie of your tester's screen travels too.
- The probability of the existence of more bugs in a section of a program is proportional to the number of bugs already found in that section [Myers G].
- Bugs remain in software after testing because both the testers and the developers have the same view of the way the software will be used.
- The use of randomly-generated test data reduces the likelihood of shared oversights remaining.
- Testing carried out by selected *test cases*, no matter how carefully and well-planned can provide nothing but anecdotes [Mills 87].
- Mathematical modeling will not reveal discrepancies between the model being used and the real world. Only testing will do that [Parnas].
- 20% of the units contain 80% of the bugs [Endres, Boehm 75].
- In testing nothing succeeds like failure. If you're trying to convince people of the need to test longer, harder, or with more tool support, the evidence of failure in terms of enraged, fee-paying users is the best support you can get. But you'll get it too late.
- Software exhibits weak-link behavior: failures in even unimportant parts of the code can have important repercussions elsewhere.
- You never know the environment in which software will have to work throughout its life [Voas].
- The existence of a tool changes the nature of the problem.[3] Therefore systems as yet unbuilt will be used in ways we cannot imagine.

Like other project activities, test planning and test design are themselves subject to errors and omissions. Therefore the major test documents should be independently reviewed before testing. The formality of such a review will vary as the risk; in any event it is essential that someone, other than the author of a test specification, examine it for adequacy, feasibility, and traceability.

## 4.2  Laws

There is no such thing as a scientific law. All scientific "laws" are in fact useful rules of thumb which have (mostly) not yet been disproved. Boyle's law for example has been shown to be false (at certain temperature extremes). Boyle's law is however very useful as a way of understanding the relationship between temperature and pressure. Murphy's law states that *if it can be done wrongly someone will do it wrongly* (there are lots of variations on this but Capt. Murphy, U.S. Army, had seen too many recruits throwing a hand grenade pin really well to have any doubt about his definition). The following "law" is offered in the hope it'll be useful, if not 100% accurate:

Farrell-Vinay's law: *if it can go wrong it will not go wrong until the last opportunity to fix it has passed.* Thus only when it's released will the major news agency discover that its Word processor "eats" text in a "Pacman"-like manner.

The importance of this law lies primarily in the way it saps your confidence that you have tested thoroughly, and spurs you to greater efforts.

---

[3] Manny Lehman (private communication).

## 4.3   Test Management Principles

*I keep six honest serving men*
*(They taught me all I knew);*
*Their names are What and Why and When and How and Where and Who.*

**Rudyard Kipling**

Here are some principles acquired, like most painful experiences, when I was trying to do something else.

- If you can't plan or process model it, what makes you think you can do it?[4]
- Never put into a plan what you can put into a strategy document. Only put the unchanging essentials into the strategy document. Any part of the plan which doesn't somehow depend on the strategy document is probably not thought through properly. Any part of the strategy document which isn't reflected somehow in the plan is a risk.
- As soon as you have finished the plan, go through it and see what you can cut out.
- Limit the things you monitor to the phase you are in, the start of the next phase, and the top priority alerts.
- If you lose several of the arguments listed in section 4.6, leave. Unless it changes, the organization won't last long anyway.
- Anyone should be free to raise a bug. If bugs are duplicated the test manager can weed out duplicates daily at the bug clearing meeting.
- You must have access to all bugs reported from the field.
- You are paying test staff primarily for their ability to think. If they cannot or will not do this, then sack them.
- Testers need to work with the best. It's part of your job to keep the idiots out.
- Pay your staff the compliment of reviewing at least a sample of their tests. If you can't be bothered why should they?
- Testers can concentrate on details: you must be able to both take an overview, *and* to concentrate on details.
- Testers know the value of everything and the cost of nothing: you must know both.
- If your processes are wrong you'll be forever fighting them.
- The more your processes are tool-based the fewer documents you'll need: you only write a document because there's no tool capable of holding the information.
- If no one really needs a document it won't be read. A document is there to remind you, to tell you how to do something, to tell someone else something or to help you think. If it doesn't, don't write it.
- Do not accept the unacceptable. Even if your customers do. Because someday they won't. Try and be somewhere else when that happens.
- We all hate bureaucracy. We all *need* bureaucracy, if only to get paid. This book is full of bits of it. Exclude them if the risk is low enough. It's your job to keep bureaucracy off tester's backs as much as possible.
- You're a manager, you can't see everything, you need to keep tabs on what's happening, and you need to be able to refer to things: you can't always do this with a quick chat.
- If in doubt ask: what's it for, what happens if I don't, what does it buy me, and what does it cost me?

---

[4] Based on an aphorism of Fred Brooks, author of *The Mythical Man-Month*.

## 4.4 Life-Cycles and Four-Wheel-Drive Karmas

There is a large number of life-cycles around. You need to be aware of their strengths and weaknesses, and the subtle ways they can (be used to) louse up projects. A fervent belief on a particular life-cycle untrammeled by any concern for its weakness is an early danger sign in a project manager.

Remember that life-cycles only exist as models; they're simply attempts at describing what we do.

### 4.4.1 Who Cares about Process Models?

Life-cycle or process models are only useful in that they help us think about how we develop systems. If we fail to have any process we get chaotic. If we have the wrong process we can at least rethink it.

In the end process models subtly influence thinking. What matters in any project is that the artefacts: specifications, code, manuals, and tests get written, tested, and used.

### 4.4.2 The Waterfall Model

The waterfall [Royce] is the best known. It consists of 5 phases:

1. Requirements (in which the customer requirements are written).
2. Design (in which the high and low-level design documents are written).
3. Code (in which the code is written and (hopefully) unit tested).
4. System test (which is where we come in).
5. Installation and cutover: (in which the finished (!) system is installed, the users are trained, and the system is put to use).

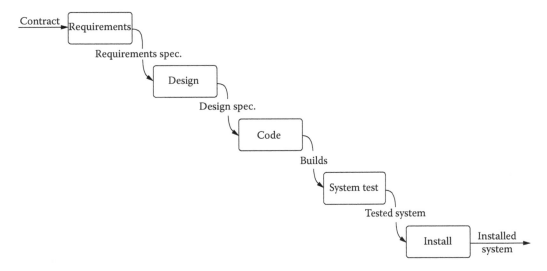

**FIGURE 4.1** The waterfall model

This is an approach which everyone says is out-of-date and which everyone uses more or less. It suffers from the dangers that:

- Bureaucrats believe such phases are finite and cannot be iterated upon.
- It doesn't allow for parallel activities such as prototyping or the development of user interface specifications (which in themselves require their own life-cycle) or for safety-critical system issues such as the development of a safety case.
- It makes no mention of contract preparation, project management, reviews, or audits.
- It implies that system testing starts only when coding is finished.
- It says nothing about software reuse.

It has the merit that:

- Each phase generates some baseline deliverable.
- It is well-known.
- It has been used for many years.
- It is very adaptable.
- Each process can be decomposed into others.
- You can add any process you want.

If people can simply accept that:

- Each phase may have to be repeated (as requirements change, as prototypes evolve).
- It needs to be seen in parallel with a number of other life-cycles with which it must stay synchronized.
- It can be modified for prototypes and software reuse.
- Testing input begins at least as early as requirements definition (and arguably it is as well to have the test team review the request for proposal and contract for test implications).
- Any change to requirements, design, or code must be (manually) reflected through all levels of documentation to ensure all documents are consistent (which rarely happens).

then it is perfectly usable.

### 4.4.3   Cooper's Stage-Gate Process Model (Figure 4.2)

Cooper's *stage gate* model is a variant of the waterfall. It splits the life-cycle into six stages separated by "gates." Each gate is a decision point. It differs from the waterfall in that the activities in each stage may be simultaneous [Cooper].

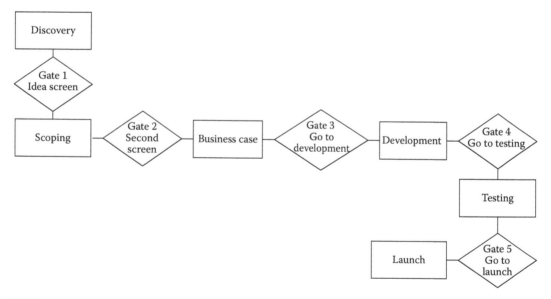

**FIGURE 4.2**   Cooper's stage-gate process model

- **Discovery stage:** a product manager thinks of a new idea for a product.
  - **Idea screen:** the idea is presented to potential stakeholders for their buy-in.
- **Scoping stage:** the market for the product is assessed and key features are identified.
  - **Second screen:** the idea is re-presented to potential stakeholders for their buy-in, but with more-rigorous requirements and other information.

- **The business case stage:** in which the product, market, organization, project management and environment, competitors, budget, RoI, and legal issues are defined.
  - **Go to development** is the moment at which the organization can commit to the large budget required for development.
- **The development stage** includes requirements refining, design, code, and build. Its output is a product ready for beta testing.
  - **Go to testing** is the moment when the testing budget and the marketing and operational plans must be committed to. It is based on the continued existence of a market opportunity.
- **Testing** is system and acceptance testing at internal and friendly customer sites. It generates a product fit for launch.
  - **Go to launch:** is the moment when marketing and training plans become operative.
- **Launch** the product.

It is easy to see a number of critical dangers in this approach:

- Half the activities are oriented to the development of a business case. Since this is likely to occupy between 5–10% of the total manpower, more detail on the other 90–95% of the manpower's activities would be useful.
- No allowance has been made for the (inevitable) requirements changes.
- Testing is relegated to the penultimate activity. The possibility that the requirements are deeply flawed will thus tend to be hidden. Similarly the testers will not learn how to use the product until too late causing considerable delay. The tests they prepare may thus need much rewriting.
- That a decision can be taken on the marketability of a product which has yet to enter beta testing requires enormous faith in the ability of developers. The amount of iteration between the development and testing groups is not shown, and the delays (which will also affect the go-to-market decision) can be considerable.

To make such a process work it is imperative that testers:

- Focus on the earliest access to the requirements as they are assembled.
- Get early access to prototype versions so they can prepare tests.
- Provide review and possibly modeling feedback to management such that inconsistent or missing requirements be identified asap.

# Story

One test team identified by modeling that a check reader had to guess when the "last" check was in the tray.
This led to a small but crucial requirements change and avoided some major downstream embarrassments.

## 4.4.4 Spiral Model (Figure 4.3)

The spiral model [Boehm 88] is based on the need to iterate. It contains as many iterations as are necessary to bring a product to fruition. Each iteration requires that the participants plan, define their life-cycle, prototype, analyze risks, write requirements, build models, detailed designs, code, unit, and system tests, and install.

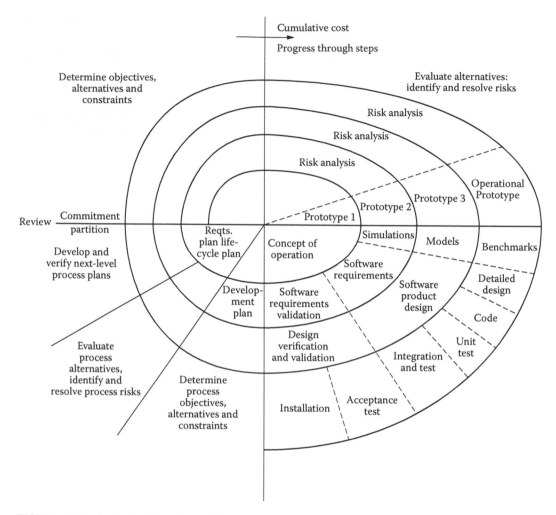

**FIGURE 4.3** Boehm's spiral life-cycle model

The spiral model has a number of advantages:

- It is flexible and allows for multiple iterations.
- It employs prototyping extensively.
- It allows for the coexistence of other models (indeed it expects candidate models to be proposed and adopted if useful).
- It makes risk evaluation explicit.
- It acknowledges the need to validate requirements and design.
- It was originally designed with a particular need to accommodate COTS, and is therefore more amenable to software reuse.

Its dangers are:

- It is less easy to allocate phases to groups and responsibilities than other models.
- It requires that staff are well-versed in software engineering.
- It requires much team self-discipline in the capture of emerging requirements.
- It does not acknowledge the need to have test input from the start of the project.
- It allocates particular phases to requirements definition and high- and low-level design.
- It doesn't make the baselines explicit.

- It doesn't allow for process decomposition.
- Much prototype code may eventually be used in the final version.
- It must be very tool-supported to work or it will either decay or become enmeshed in the bureaucracy it was intended to minimize.

The implications of this for the system testing team are that:

- The status of emerging requirements must be constantly reviewed.
- The team is committed to validating both the requirements and the design.
- Any use of prototype code in the production version will require much more rigorous unit testing than is normal.

## 4.4.5   Prince II

Prince II is a stage-oriented project management approach which is promoted by the British government. The words *test manager, test team, requirements, functional,* or *specification* do not appear in the glossary or indeed anywhere else in the manual [Prince II]. Its approach to testing is naive and based entirely on the requirements of ISO 9000. It is easy to see why the British government has suffered from so many project failures. The British government, aware of the problem, has reviewed a number of IT projects and issued a report [McCartney] which makes a number of useful recommendations concerning requirements management and testing while stopping short of mentioning a test manager or team. None of these has resulted in any change to Prince II. As a test manager you will need to ensure:

- That you have a role at all to play despite Prince II and McCartney
- That the requirements specification exists, is properly managed (if not under your control), and all changes to it are controlled
- That the project manager understands the need to institute reviews early
- That the project manager understands the implications of [McCartney] and the need to change the use the project makes of Prince II as a result

Prince II is intended to be used with SSADM. SSADM is a relatively little-used approach sponsored by the British government. It is based on Shlaer-Mellor notation with some extensions to cover Entity-Relationship modeling, and state machines. It supported by a toolset. See www.webpoedia.com/TERM/S/SSADM.html for more.

## 4.4.6   Synch and Stabilize

This is an approach favored by Microsoft. It consists of three phases: planning (specification and review), development (several — usually 3 — subphases developing feature sets of decreasing priority plus a period of optimization), and stabilization (beta test and finalization). The process is characterized by feature teams consisting of 3–8 programmers, (an equal number of) testers, and technical writers who work jointly on a feature. Microsoft planning allows for a buffer time of between 20–50% of the total project time to allow for unplanned events.

The coherence of each feature is underpinned by a nightly build in which much social opprobrium attaches to the programmer whose code "breaks the build." Each build (however incomplete) is regression-tested. Testers are thus kept very close to evolving features. Internal testing is then augmented by external testing by off-shore suppliers and friendly customers. See section 18.9.6 for some statistical justification of this approach.

Managing this test process requires that:

- Staffing levels are comparable to Microsoft's. Thus in addition to the 1: 1 developer-tester ratio you will need a further backup of off-shore testers.
- Testers not only manually test the features but create/write unit tests and script automated tests as well.

- The company not only creates a daily build for each platform but tests it thoroughly such that at any time after the first of the three development phases, it has a shippable product. See section 18.13 in Chapter 18 for some metrics concerning this.
- The functional specifications (in Microsoft's case typically written by product managers) are reviewed and untestable requirements identified.
- The monitoring of the state of each feature enables testers to determine what levels of features are in a release. In Microsoft up to 30% of the feature set can change, many low priority features are deleted as deadlines loom.
- The interactions between features be identified and tested for as subtle interactions can prove disastrous. (Example: version 6 of MS Word for Windows would crash were a table, inserted in a *footer*, to have its cell widths adjusted. Windows 2004 has subtle timing interactions between the toolbar and the text which scripting exposes. The predecessor of Access was simply thrown away.) The test manager must thus find a way of identifying potential interactions, and testing for them. Solution: write a feature–feature interaction matrix showing which features cannot interact with which, and the names of the tests which cover the feature–feature interaction of those which do (see Figure 15.12).
- The test manager:
  - Identifies the known weaknesses and feeds details back to all testers.
  - Monitors the degree of coverage, robustness, and execution history of all automated tests (if testers ever get much "behind the curve" it will severely delay release since system testing will uncover even more bugs).
  - Ensures that testers (mostly) have the tools and training they need.
  - Ensures that automated feature-interaction tests are prepared.
  - Reviews automated tests.
  - Monitors the degree of coverage of test suppliers.

  If the management attempt to emulate the Microsoft approach to develop products of comparable size to Microsoft's (c. 170 KLOC) *without* the right staffing ratios, approach, or time, chaos will ensue. Note that:
  - The best view of the system's functions lies in the system tests.
  - Netscape attempted a similar approach but used three developers per tester, and had no buffer time or daily tests. It lost the browser war by being too slow delivering and too slow in performance.

See [Cusumano 1] and [Cusumano 2] for more on this. Note that the Microsoft Solutions Framework (a near clone of SSADM) does not appear to be used by Microsoft Product Groups. Mention of it provoked wry grins when mentioned to some senior staff working on Word.

## 4.4.7 (Rational) Unified Process

This consists of four phases:

1. Inception in which the business case is established
2. Elaboration in which the scope of the system is defined, risks are identified and resolved, and the architecture designed
3. Construction in which the low-level elements of the system are coded or designed, and minor releases each containing an increment of the system's features
4. Transition in which a beta release is made and system-tested.

The phases correspond to a number of models, several of which can be baselines for system and unit testing (Figure 4.4). These models are supported by a number of diagramming techniques. The solid lines in Figure 4.5 indicate required diagrams and the dotted lines indicate optional ones. The test phase exploits primarily the Class diagrams but may also use Component and Deployment diagrams. Sequence diagrams have had timing constructs attached as shown in [*UML* TP].

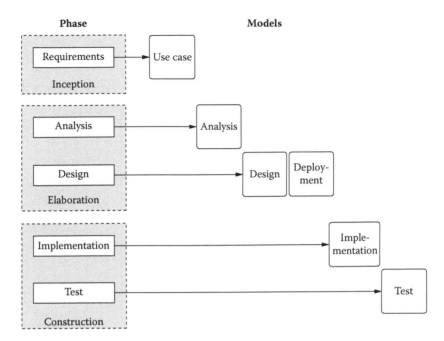

**FIGURE 4.4** UP phases and models

It is quite possible to get the data required from *UML* diagrams for the purpose of system testing (see section 8.2.1). However unit *test cases* cannot be so simply designed from an *UML* model, and are probably best derived using a tool such as xUnit or its equivalent.

The UP approach has the following dangers:

- Baseline maintenance: because you are not allowed to *decompose* in *UML* the possibility of inconsistency is considerable.
- Baseline definition: you need to look at several models to check what is your baseline.
- Sloppiness: the approach is as rigorous as users make it. If used well you will have a lot of support, and test development will be greatly simplified. Otherwise…

## 4.4.8 Executable Models

Executable models are built using graphic tools using such notations as finite-state machines, *UML* or XML. There is a number of reasons for spending the time and money required to build such models:

- Much of the system to be built will be constructed from existing components or using known technologies. Some may be unknown and these need to be prototyped. The results will be small demonstration fragments.
- Some specifications are so large that they contain critical inconsistencies which are best exposed by using a graphic notation such as *UML*. *UML* can now be used to generate executable code.
- The feasibility of some models cannot be determined from simply reading the specification, particularly where timing is concerned. An executable model can give early warning.

The models exist at three levels:

- **Prose**: the informal specification of the use case such as A.2.10 in Appendix A.
- **Diagram**: which can be any *UML*, state case, or other diagram supported by the modeling system.
- **Code**: which generates a pseudo user-interface. In the case of the *Informal specification* example, the interface can be made to resemble an ATM as shown in Figure 4.6. Yes folks, you can get a relatively realistic picture to play with.

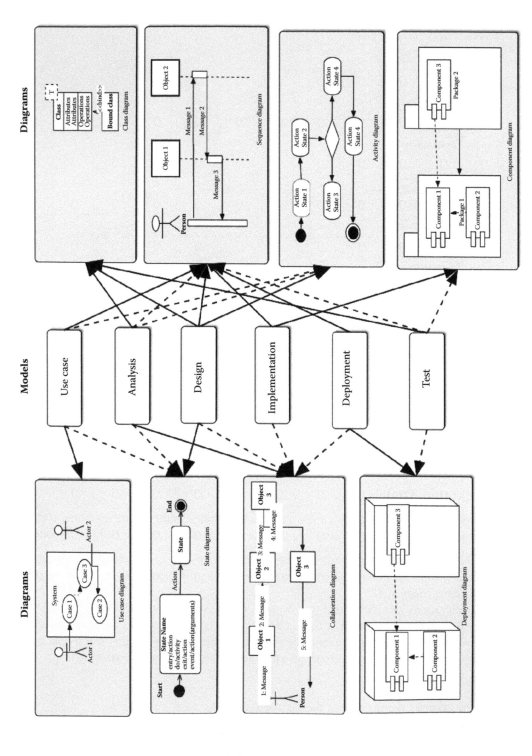

**FIGURE 4.5** Standard *UML* models and supporting diagrams

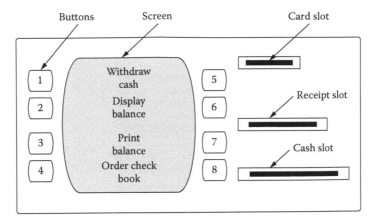

**FIGURE 4.6** The "Display Options" point of the "Withdraw Cash" use case

By using such a model with a customer it becomes far easier to define requirements at levels satisfactory to all stakeholders. Such a model can provide a baseline for system test objectives (Figure 4.7).

These solutions imply the following approach:

1. Specify new and reusable domains. This can include both server and client domains as well as legacy code.
2. Create Use cases using use case diagrams supported by sequence diagrams, providing a *Platform-Independent Model* (PIM) for each domain.
3. Create static models using class diagrams for all the objects in each PIM and determine the relations between the classes. By this point it should be possible to identify most of the risks the project faces.
4. Create dynamic models using state charts, state tables, and interactions by:
   - Identifying all the class life-cycles.
   - Identifying the timing constraints.
   - Summarizing complex interactions using class collaboration diagrams.
   The ability to submit a fragment of a PIM for validation at this stage is a key factor in using this approach. By identifying problems at this point a test team can obtain great leverage on the system's eventual quality. It will have the effect of:
   - Greatly speeding system testing.
   - Validating requirements early.
   - Identifying performance requirements and constraints.
5. Define action behavior using an *Action Specification Language* (ASL).
6. Identify domain–domain interfaces (domain contract). There is a need to check the interfaces between domains: since a bridge provides a mapping between two (or more) domains, the scope of the ASL used to describe it is no longer that of a single domain, and may thus be ambiguous.
7. Create *Processor-Independent Module/Platform-Specific Implementation* (PIM/PSI) tests using the use cases and sequence diagrams and the ASL (to define external stimuli). This involves:
   - Identifying use cases specific to a domain to act as baselines.
   - Identifying bridges to act as the baselines for multiple domain testing so as to be able to answer the question *"have we tested each domain interface?"*
   - Creating test scripts capable of exercising each domain and each domain–domain interface.
   - Creating target system test scripts (which will be collections of those above).
   - Creating stubs and test methods to exercise those stubs, through the simulator during preliminary integration attempts, using unfinished domains. This will normally be the responsibility of programmers.

   Code-level bugs and initial conditions for model execution can be injected using the ASL code.

   Note that the test method creation facility, while mostly designed for developer use, can also be used to create domain-level test environments.

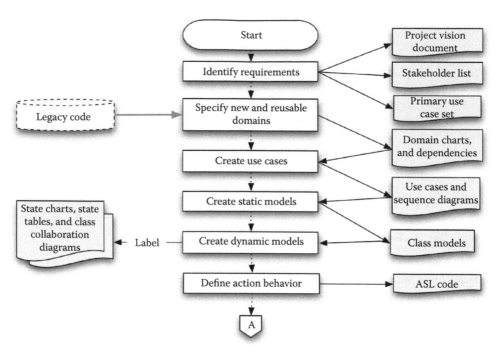

**FIGURE 4.7**  Executable *UML* (x*UML*) process model A

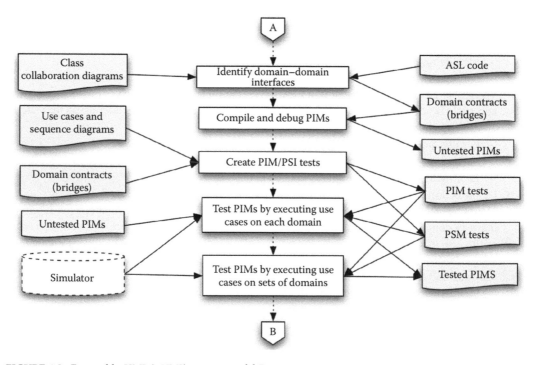

**FIGURE 4.8**  Executable *UML* (x*UML*) process model B

Look for "cannot-happen" effects in the code. These indicate illegal events which should be thrown up by a simulation.

8. Compile and debug a PIM using a *Virtual Execution Environment* (VEE). (This may also involve preliminary timing tests which will be performed by programmers.)

9. Test each PIM by executing use cases on each domain using a simulator and a special-purpose code generator.
10. Test a set of PIMs by executing use cases on sets of domains and thus test the domain–domain bridges. Note that this may reveal further requirements which may affect system test readiness.

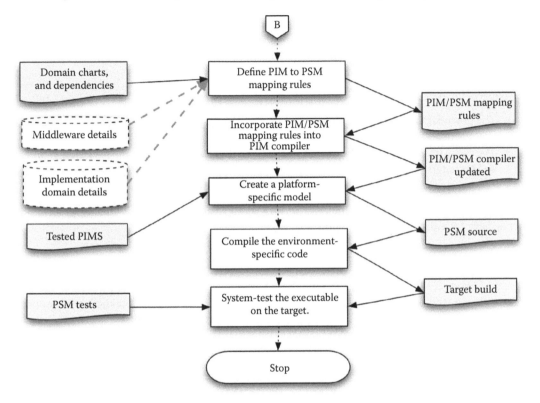

**FIGURE 4.9** Executable *UML* (x*UML*) process model C

11. Define PIM to PSI mapping rules.
12. Incorporate PIM/PSI mapping rules into the PIM compiler.
13. Create a *Platform-Specific Model* (PSM) compliant with a component model such as CORBA, using a supplied or purpose-built VEE plus optional manual modifications. It may interface with existing systems using such protocols as IIOP, RMI, or SOAP, and also with such middleware as CCM, J2EE, or MQSeries. This generates environment-specific code.
14. Compile the environment-specific code to produce an executable.
15. System-test the executable on the target. Note that any defects found will lie in either the original models or the mapping rules. At this point the key functionality should not, theoretically require testing. Testing can thus concentrate on non-functional requirements such as performance and usability.

The advantages of the x*UML* approach are that:

1. Developers can build precise models.
2. The models can be executed and tested early.
3. The process is well-defined.
4. The system allows for the reuse of components.

Note that:

1. The model shown above has eliminated much of the iterative interaction which surrounds the creation and validation of PIMS.

2. The approach excludes all GUI design issues.
3. Algorithm-proving is assumed to occur separately.

See [Atkinson] and [Raistrick] for an overview.

At least 3 toolsets (Virtual Engineering Environments or VEEs) for executable *UML* were available as at October 2005:

1. Kabira Technologies (www.kabira.com) — ObjectSwitch.
2. Project Technologies (www.projtech.com) — BridgePoint.
3. Kennedy-Carter (www.kc.com) — *UML/xUML*.

The dangers for system testing are:

1. The potential for losing sight of the user requirements (as opposed to the design) since these are neatly embedded in the models.
2. The ease with which the model can be changed such that a system test baseline can change without system testers realizing it.
3. Few existing automated test tools will interface to the system.

The modeling approach, with its emphasis on early testing, means that many quality problems will already have been dealt with beforehand.

### 4.4.9  Formal Methods

Formal Methods (FM) are the use of techniques of formal logic and discrete mathematics in the specification, design, and construction of computer systems and software. These allow the logical properties of a computer system to be predicted from a model of the system using logic to calculate if a system description:

- Is internally consistent
- Has certain properties
- Has a correctly-interpreted requirements specification

Systematic checking of these calculations may be automated using such languages as Z and VDM.

Formal modeling of a system usually entails translating a system description from a non-mathematical model (dataflow diagrams, object diagrams, scenarios, *UML*, English text, etc.) into a formal specification, using one of several formal languages. FM tools can then be employed to evaluate this specification to check its *completeness* and consistency.

FM techniques and tools can be applied to the specification and verification of products from each development life-cycle: requirement, high- and low-level design, and implementation.

Formal methods force users and developers to use a common language in requiring and designing systems. The baselines against which system tests are defined remain as essential as before but by using a formal language essential relationships can be defined and proven. See Figure 4.9.

See section A.11 to get a sense of how a system test can be developed from a formal specification.

The dangers of using a formal specification are:

- Staff and users may claim they cannot understand it.
- The use of the formal specification may be subverted by inconsistencies with the natural language specification.
- The formal specification takes time and some mathematical ability to create and prove.

### 4.4.10  Extreme, Agile, and Rapid Development

These represent essentially a reworking of various approaches to minimize the administrivia of software development and leave coders freer to code. Such approaches do not necessarily hinder system testing (and

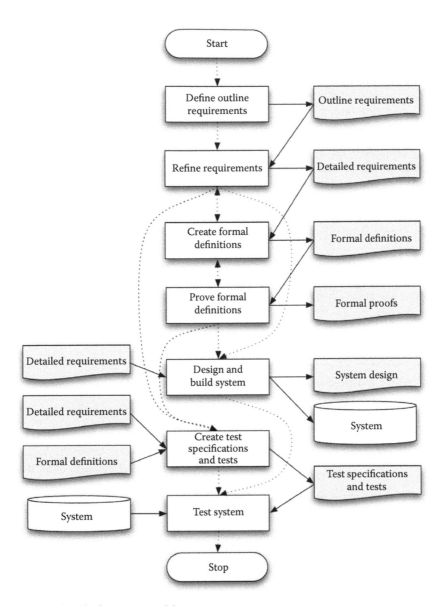

**FIGURE 4.10** Formal methods process model

the "Extreme" approach, if correctly followed will at least result in a lot of unit tests being prepared), providing that we can identify the requirements the coders satisfy. This is supposed to happen with the aid of "*user stories.*" If it doesn't, testers must write their own baselines, possibly as described in section 8.2. Additionally developers need to take long hard looks about how the architecture evolves, if it is not to become entropic.

The dangers of Extreme, Agile, and Rapid development are that:

- The requirements will evolve and need to be captured.
- Developers remain unaware of subtle feature interaction until the end.
- The approach needs to be feature-driven (which it mostly is) with frequent builds of features matched by frequent system tests of those features as they evolve.
- Integration remains a hazardous time because of the subtle feature interactions.
- The concern for (unit) test-driven development, will tend to produce good code but isn't enough to ensure successful product release.

- Developers need to be highly-motivated, responsible, and competent, taking the requisite time to document what they are doing. Typically they are supposed to document requirements as soon as these are stable. Check for airborne pigs.
- Since it relies on the customer's ability to write "*user stories*" and if customers narrate their stories with their usual level of precision (and no one checks), then the integration phase will be problematic, and acceptance testing will be distinguished by the number of snapped pencils, gritted teeth, and people crying in corners.

System testing (sometimes mis-referred to as *acceptance testing* by agile methods promoters) remains as agile as the persons doing it. For system testing to match the agility of other phases of development, it is essential that the requirements are captured as they evolve, and that the testers write tests as features are built rather than at the end. One way of capturing evolving requirements is to write them down as notes in the *test cases*. Thus the persons who have most need of the information are those who capture it. If testers are distributed among development teams they are in a good position to capture and maintain these requirements.

The purpose of agility is to be able to react fast to market changes and emerging requirements. If the price of agility is too high in terms of poor quality code or delayed time-to-market (because of the confusion agility can generate) then either an "agile" approach isn't or you haven't managed the consequences well enough.

# 4.5   Starting from Where You Are

This is always where you are urged to start. Here are 4 scenarios:

## 4.5.1   You're Not Really Testing

> *It's not our job to find bugs.*
>
> **Test manager of an Italian bank**

People lose the plot and so do organizations. There are those who want appearances above all else. The Italian bank was one. A major energy utility was another. They had test coordinators who waved their hands about and steadfastly refused to find problems. The bank test manager was eventually sacked and the utility was sold, handing over all its testing to a big-5 consultancy as soon as they realized that not one of the 25+ systems being developed, worked.

How could this occur? Big organizations can themselves become entropic and lose the plot (see [Farrell-Vinay] for more on incompetence). In this case political power, and position maintenance, override any concern for the well-being of the organization. Big organizations have big programs of work. They have big program managers on big salaries who report to an even bigger Program Director. The prospect of delay terrifies them. They believe that the testers are the people primarily responsible for the delay (after all they, the program managers, never actually *use* the wretched systems). Therefore they ensure that the testers are hobbled. This hobbling occurs as follows. They:

- Don't have test managers, but have test "coordinators."
- Let the suppliers do the testing (so the test coordinators can "coordinate" their testing).
- Stick rigidly to Prince II and avoid thinking of the consequences.
- Prevent the test manager from refusing to accept inadequate systems by accepting them behind his back.
- Where, by some oversight, they have any testers who test seriously, they isolate them — by threatening the tester with the sack or suggesting he's "not a team player" very firmly so he knows it will appear in his year-end assessment.

So sniff the job specification to see if it smells of anything like this. Do you *really* want this job?

Remember: few high-flyers stay in a role more than 24 months. Some big projects last more than 24 months. All the program managers and program directors consider themselves to be high flyers. So they will have left before the project is seen to be a disaster. If (some) investment analysts have only got 6-month horizons why should senior managers think any farther?[5]

## 4.5.2   Starting Up a New Test Function

You are faced with absolutely nothing. No lead testers, no testers, no tools. You have to recruit everyone. There may be a very good reason why they are only now starting a test function, which, if you are wise, you will discover. (When is the release date? *How* long?) The best possible reasons are (in descending order of attractiveness):

- That everything is new, and a far-sighted project director wants to have a *Testing* function as fast as possible, even before requirements are written.
- That testing was hitherto informal but it happened, and now it's getting too big and needs to be managed.
- That testing was done by some other group which is now to be (or has just been) sacked.

Write a report on the status of the project. Look particularly at any results obtained so far. See section A.10 in Appendix A. Then write your test strategy document. You are probably very lucky in that you have a green-field to work on.

## 4.5.3   Taking Over an Old Test Function

Your predecessor left for some very good reasons. Make sure they were only salary- or competence-related. Spend some time assessing where you are now with the aid of the checklists in Appendix B. Remember:

- There is no advantage in change for change's sake.
- To ask testers, developers, and management how much value the test team has added so far.
- To listen for the sound of people being tactful. An old test function might also be a failing test function (see below).
- That you can be faced with a number of test leaders each of whom has their own view of what testing is about. They may tell you something new. You may have to tell them something they need to know. Establish yourself. Nicely. Out there are people who need you and are prepared to like what you do. Be prepared to explain. Be prepared to insist on essentials.
- To look at the tests and the testers. Review both, and trace some tests back to their baseline(s). Trace some other baselines back to the tests.
- To look at the user group message boards. Are there signs of people giving up with the company?

Write a report on the status of the function. Look particularly at the results. See section A.10 in Appendix A. Look at:

- Proportion of developer hours versus tester hours
- Proportion of bugs found before release compared with those found after release
- Number of pages of requirements/functional specifications, for each release compared to the number of tests for the last 3 releases. How much has that proportion varied?
- Proportion of requirements covered by tests

For indications of what is going wrong as well as the checklist in section B.7 in Appendix B.

---

[5] "Investment analysts only hold a stock for 6 months." Clarence H. Brooks, private communication.

## 4.5.4  Reforming a Failing Test Team

How did management know the function was failing? (Table 4.1)

**TABLE 4.1**  Complaints made about a failing test function

| Complaints | Questions |
| --- | --- |
| Testing could never repeat their bugs. Testing gave poor feedback or were no help in debugging. | Did you change the test environment? Do the testers have scripts which enabled them to repeat the tests? Are the scripts detailed enough to permit this? (*Some managers attempt to destroy testers' reputation by driving one build after another onto the test environment regardless of whether the previous build was completely tested.*) Testers are not supposed to help debug even when they write unit tests. Their responsibility stops when they can demonstrate a bug at will, given a limited number of attempts.[a] |
| Testing's view of a bug was arbitrary. | Do you have a bug classification scheme? Can you demonstrate this arbitrariness on 6 bugs? (*This is really a sign of poor management. No tester should raise a bug unless they can repeat it given a number of attempts.*) Do you have a sufficient baseline against which they can test? |
| More bugs were found by the users than the testers. | Assuming that the testers were allowed the time, specifications and tools they needed to test with this is a very serious accusation. |
| Testing doesn't read or understand the functional specifications. | Assuming that the specifications were available to the testers in a timely manner and in readable format this is a very serious accusation. |

[a] OK this is a gray area. Here's a rule. If a tester can always demonstrate the existence of a bug given (say) 10 attempts, then it exists. It is asking too much to say "you must be able to demonstrate it at will at every attempt."

Test functions fail for several reasons:

- The decision to release was taken with out reference to the test team. (*Check if there was a memo authorizing the release: was the former test manager's signature on it? Ask the testers.*)
- The specifications were poor and very late. (*Check the release dates and the dates on the specifications. Read the specifications.*)
- The test manager failed to:
  - Ensure testers had adequate baselines: ask the testers for copies of the baselines. (*Check with the project manager.*)
  - Support testers in their complaints about inadequate baselines. (*Baselines have always got some bugs. If the test manager hasn't complained about something…*)
  - Conduct a test readiness review (*or if he did, he never left any record of it*).
  - Report on the status of the tests to the management and the testers.
  - Define test start/stop criteria.
  - Provide any metrics such that some sense of the success or failure of the testers or the project could be unequivocally defined.
  - Plan.
  - Sack incompetent testers. (*Look for big difference between the persons raising the greatest and smallest number of bugs. Look for near-duplicate bugs which are not marked as such.*)
  - Check whether a bug had already been raised. (*Look for a large number of bugs marked as "duplicate."*)
  - Clarify that testers and developers were on opposite sides of the fence. (*Look for references to "partnership" in memoranda.*)
  - Protect testers from any unjustified criticism of them by the project manager. (*"Testing only raised x bugs, I could have raised more on my own."*[6])
  - Provide leadership, training, or advice.
  - Stop the project manager from:
    - Deciding arbitrarily that a bug wasn't

- • Dictating what parts of the system should be tested, and when
  - – Stop the developers from imposing new releases on the test team before existing ones were fully tested
  - – Stop testing when it was evident that the release was useless
- • The testers:
  - – Were poor quality (*check their tests, and the descriptions of the bugs they found — that'll tell you how poor; see who raised the same bug 20 times with slightly-different wording*)
  - – Had too little time or too few tools. *Check:*
    - • *How much time was wasted by repetition*
    - • *If the tests are held electronically*
    - • *How long it takes to raise a bug*
  - – Had no smoke or regression tests so it was some time before it realized that some features were missing (*ask the testers to show them to you*)
  - – Had no smoke tests so it could not immediately reject a release because it lacked essential features (*ask the testers to show them*)
  - – Were in a different time-zone to the developers or the users
  - – Were not reviewing their work (*review it yourself, and ask the testers to explain the errors you've found, and why they didn't find them themselves*). *Check the dates the faulty tests were written, and see if perhaps the testers were simply unmotivated rather than that they had too little time.*
  - – Were expected to both find the bugs, and identify them in the code so the developers merely had to make the change. (*If true, immediately refuse to continue such a policy. Its purpose is simply to inhibit testers from finding problems. Developers are far better placed to know which pieces of code are likely to contribute to a problem or even which features were, er, left unfinished.*)
  - – Were unable or unwilling to examine scripts in an effort to determine likely sources of bugs
- • The tests:
  - – Did not cover all the features of the product
  - – Were not configuration-managed
  - – Were unrelated to the release they were used on
  - – Were not prioritized or related to the risks the project ran
- • The users are in revolt.

See also the checklist in section B.7 in Appendix B.

# 4.6  Arguments You Need to Win

These are so obvious you may feel they're not worth raising. Surely no company would be so silly...

## 4.6.1  General

- • Assess the risk to the company of the system failing and get a test budget which reflects this risk.
- • Get an agreement between testers, developers, and management:
  - – On the classification of bugs, their priorities, and severities
  - – On test priorities (limits the occurrence of the question *"why didn't we find this bug earlier?"*)
  - – On the maximum number of each kind of bug which can remain in a released system (and yes, this means it can't be released if this is exceeded)
  - – On the baseline against which testers test
  - – On the amount of unit testing to be done and who will do it

---

[6] Best said privately to a stressed test manager struggling with a complete lack of specifications and a thoroughly-buggy release in which anyone can find bugs. Wait until the end of the test and then gently ask the project manager if he could have found a quarter of what the test team found. In front of the test team.

>   – That testers will review the baseline for the tests and be able to have it changed
>   – On the risk and responsibility for premature releasing

## 4.6.2   Test Inputs

You must have access to the following:

- A baseline against which to test. (Needn't be a specification. Could be just an earlier version of the system. Must be unambiguous.) If you don't have this (because the developers are just throwing the software over the wall), then you must be free to create one as you go. Start with the user manual. If you can't get a baseline then it will be impossible for you to determine if:
    - The developers have included that feature in the release
    - You've found a bug or a feature
    - The bug's been fixed
    - You've tested that feature already
    - Whether a bug is serious or trivial[7]
- A way of managing that baseline. The baseline will change. If that change is unclear or if you're not aware of the change, you may not know until enraged customers call.
- A basis for determining the severity of a bug. Sounds obvious but it isn't. The seriousness of a bug can be measured in terms of what it will cost you (the test manager), the test team, the developers, the company, and of course the customer, and the customer's customers. The obvious classifications are: *Critical, High, Medium,* and *Trivial.* OK, what do they mean? Does *Critical* mean that the customer loses data or that an operator loses their life? Does *High* just mean *Critical* (but there's a workaround)? It would be good to ensure the developers have some basis for determining the fix priority too. See Appendix C for a classification scheme but remember that what matters in the end is how a bug will be perceived by the end user.
- Authority over the testing staff. This isn't obvious either. Those organizations which operate by feature teams may pride themselves on their intellectual agility because each team is equipped with a business analyst, some programmers, a lead, and a tester. It can be a good way to work. But when a release is made it is imperative that the distributed testers work as a team to test that release, exchange ideas between themselves, and are not distracted by pleas from the developers to test some newly-fixed bug. See section 9.3.
- Access to statistics: people will ask you questions such as those in section 1.4 and you need to be able to get answers based on statistics gleaned from the code (the configuration management tool), the bug tracking tool, and the test management tool.

## 4.6.3   Test Environment

You must have a stable test environment with the following tools:

- Bug-management tool (otherwise it will be impossible to discuss bugs let alone fix them).
- Test specification and management tool. (Otherwise you will not be able to specify tests unambiguously nor show that some bug has been fixed. It will be impossible to specify regression tests, and lots of clever test ideas will be lost because there will be no way to trap them.)
- Separation from the development environment so that your test environment is as much like the end users' as possible. (Otherwise you'll have — for example — the same clutter of unused .dlls etc. that the developers have, which masks from them the bugs suffered by the users who don't have the same .dlls. When you are system testing it must be impossible for anyone other than

---

[7] Dear reader, you think this is obvious? True. No one would be so silly? False.

yourselves to affect the test environment. Thus it must be impossible for developers to terminate testing of a client/server release by simply changing the server software.)

- Reasonable time to test in. If you are having releases of software for system testing in less than every two weeks, then something is seriously wrong with your test-and-build cycle. The usual excuse is "we need to know if the fixes we have applied work." The answer to that is either *"test them yourself, and don't hand them over to us until you are sure that they do"* (this makes people very cross because they thought that was your job) or if they want you to test fixes (as opposed to systems) then you will either need an extra member of staff to work with a developer team or you will need to reorganize how you work.

- All bugs of a given priority are fixed before a release is made. Assuming that it be agreed that all severity-1 and -2 bugs, plus some proportion of severity-3 and -4 bugs are fixed before the next release be made, it is pointless making a release with only some of the severity-1 and -2 bugs fixed, since the failure to fix other bugs may leave big problems in the code. Alternatively, when the developers finally fix them, the fixes may themselves provoke further bugs. A really silly variant of this argument is *"we plan to make another release to customers soon. The outstanding bugs are so deep in the system that the customers won't have had time to find them before we make the next release."* Result: when they fix the outstanding bugs they uncover/create further bugs which delay the fix so long the customers have plenty of time to discover the original problem.

It would be nice to have the following tools:

- Code coverage analyzer (see section D.10 in Appendix D) to allow you to see which lines of code had been executed after some set of tests have been run.
- Dynamic analysis tool (see section 7.9) to see what the code is doing, and allow you to advise developers on which bits to optimize, and the testers on which features may contain the most bugs.

### 4.6.4 Management

- **Independence**: The test manager must be functionally independent of development. Safety-critical development standards emphasis this. Non-safety-critical projects need to ensure it happens because:
  - Developers (and their project manager) may want to get releases out fast, don't want to hear how many bugs there are, and don't face the users or the shareholders.
  - By the time that senior management realizes there's a problem it will be too late to save the project, the product or the company.
- **Release management**: The test manager or his boss should be able to prevent a release to the field. If they can't, then they can bear no responsibility for any bugs found later. Essentially testing is a way of answering the question *"is the system ready to be released."* If the answer is "no," then ignoring that answer is another way of saying *"we don't need to test."* At this point the wise test manager polishes his CV and sends it off. Since the project manager is ultimately in charge of quality, a release must ultimately be his responsibility.
- **Why might the answer be "no"?**
  - Because you still have some severity-1 or -2 bugs in the system
  - Because the testers tell you it's not ready.
  - Because you haven't exercised enough of the code.
  - Because there should be x bugs, and you haven't found them yet. See Chapter 18.
  - Because code turmoil is still too high (see section 18.9.6).
  - Because the bug-detection rate is still too high. Look at the curve in the Figure 4.11.

The curve shown in Figure 4.11 is of a test cycle which is finding a growing number of bugs. Clearly there is a large number of bugs still to be found.

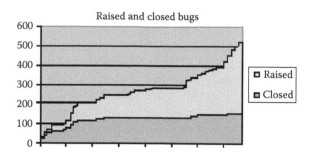

**FIGURE 4.11**  A bug detection curve of a project which is a long way from release

## 4.6.5   Release Readiness

Releases should not be made without your agreement. If a release isn't ready, you, the test manager must be able to say "*no, that's not going out.*" Getting everyone to accept both this principle and the basis on which it's established is one of the earliest battles you must win. If you are overridden by the project manager (and you are after all acting *for* the project manager) then make sure it is clear that it's his responsibility.

A release is ready when:

- All the tests have been run.
- Test coverage is sufficient (see section 2.8 for more on this).
- It has all the features required in it and they are stable (see Figure 8.25).
- All the bugs needing to be fixed have been.
- *Code turmoil* is low (see Chapter 18).
- The reliability (see section 18.6.2) is satisfactory.
- Testing has not revealed any more bugs of above some level of severity for some time.
- The bug detection profile has flattened (see section 7.6.2 *Bug tracking graphs* in Chapter 7 for more on this).
- The expected number of bugs have been found (see section 18.10).

If this last bullet point sounds vague then remember that what matters is the risk the release poses. As test manager you need to define what release risk means.

The chart in Figure 4.12 shows a project in which many bugs have been found in the past but which is now quite stable and with few bugs being found in the last few days. Assuming that the bugs not closed are trivial, a release could be made shortly.

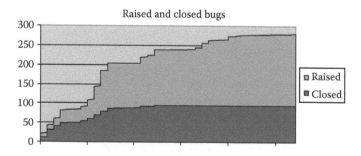

**FIGURE 4.12**  Release readiness shown in terms of a bug curve

You may hear occasionally this argument: *"What matters is not the total number of bugs found but the number of bugs remaining to be fixed."* This is mostly daft because:

- Until you find them you won't know what bugs need fixing.
- Developers may inject bugs *as* they fix them.

There are two ways of showing these problems:

- If *Code turmoil* is high it is probable that bugs are being introduced. See Chapter 18.
- If previously bug-free units (and the tests which go with them) show new bugs it is probable that they weren't there before. See Figure 8.25.

So you need to monitor the *Fix backlog metric* (see section 18.9.1). The total number of bugs matters because by counting the total number of bugs found we can answer the following questions:

- Have we found the total we expected to find?
- Are we finding fewer and fewer bugs per day, consistently?

Only then will you know whether the total number of bugs needing to be fixed is realistic. Remember also that if the developers whose work you test tend to create bugs as they fix them, then you could be greatly underestimating the number of bugs needing fixing anyway.

But if the answer to these questions is "yes," and we've exercised all the code, and we've tested all the features, then the software is ready for release.

See [Johnson] for details of the LEAP open toolkit and experience in estimating project size and bug numbers.

## 4.6.6   Test Outputs

You should write:

- A test plan (see Chapter 8). Even if no one wants to see it, and it isn't contractually-required, write it anyway. It'll help you think. You need this to get an overview of where you and your team are going. It's just a plan with activities, schedules, and responsibilities. It isn't a test specification (see below).
- A test (case) specification (see Chapter 8) because what the developers build to, and what you test, aren't the same thing. They are simply two views. You need your own. Thus the requirements specification may say good things about the information appearing on a screen. The test case specification goes into detail about how you are to test that screen and what happens when you press button "B." If you are wise and minimally-funded you will have written this using test management software. The test case specification may (if it's embedded in the test management tool) also be the tests you will run.
- Test reports (see section 8.18).
- Release notes.

You will find it useful to write a test strategy document (see Chapter 8).
Internal test standards are useful to convince assessment bodies and train new testers with. In practice however much of their function can be subsumed into:

- A test process model showing the inputs and outputs of the test process, the tools supporting it, the inputs to metrics, and the subprocesses
- Test tools (in practice much paper otherwise used to write test specifications on can be saved by using a good test management tool preferably with a built-in bug management tool)
- Templates for creating documents with checklists for reviewing documents against

# 5
# Testing and the Web

## Hallo, Hallo Statue?

There was a voice-recognition company with a really good product. It was the premier product in its field. It had a managing director who is an expert in the field. He was really concerned for quality: he said so. One day he (at last) realized that there were problems with the product. Buyers just weren't buying. He invited all his senior people round to a hotel, including the QA manager. The QA manager had nothing to do with testing. He was a true QA manager and audited the company processes. He had noted that there was:

- No test manager
- No testing worthy of the name being undertaken before the release
- Interference by senior staff (Aka the managing director) in the release process (which guaranteed frequent and non-functioning releases)
- Considerable problems with customers
- Very faulty configuration management

So, when asked, he stood up and said so. He was sacked the next day. The managing director was sacked by the board after 6 months and the company was wound up after three years, and a refinancing operation had still failed to institute a sufficient test process.

The web is another example of a disrupting technology (like RAD and XP) requiring that a lot of old lessons get relearned. These lessons are:

- All approaches to non-trivial software development require disciplined and trained practitioners.
- Any information which isn't written down gets forgotten.
- Users can't read code, don't very much like diagrams, and need some specification to sign off before they'll part with their money.
- Changes have ripple effects throughout systems.
- Developers, testers, and test managers need to have some objective way of deciding if a bug exists.
- If developers want to take a risk, and try and integrate a system in a big bang they are simply ignoring 60 years of experience, and will eventually realize that unit and integration testing reduce risk, and save time.

Early web development was characterized by many programmers quickly hacking simple static websites with minimal features and quite terrible graphics, using simple tools. The sites were image threats only. As the commercial web developed, the ghastly possibility that such sites represented a commercial threat too was realized, and some degree of formality and accountability began to reassert itself, to counterbalance the supremacy of developmental speed. In short People Who Mattered realized it didn't matter how fast a site was developed if it was "wrong."

# 5.1   How Websites Work

Web development is dominated by architectural concerns. Figure 5.1 is a typical web architecture corresponding to level 4 in Table 5.1.

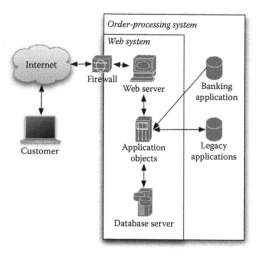

**FIGURE 5.1**   A typical web architecture

There are many web system types, all of which have similar architectures to the one shown above. The elements of the architecture can interact as shown in Figure 5.2.

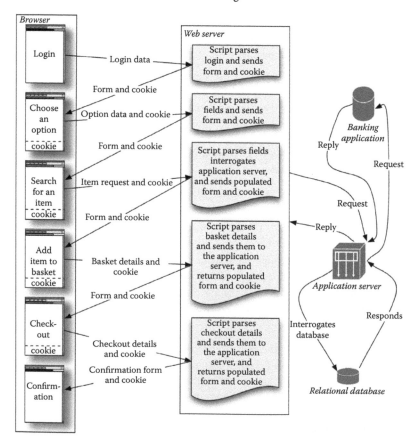

**FIGURE 5.2**   Web interactions

The browser pages communicate with the web server using details (form fields filled, check-boxes ticked, etc.) sent to the web server along with a cookie which identifies the particular browser. A series of scripts held by the web server interprets the details and calls an application (legacy, COTS, or new). The application in turn interrogates a database or a banking application (for payment and credit card details), and then returns data to the web server. The web server creates a page and returns it with a cookie to the browser.

Variations of this approach will include closed internets for suppliers to (say) car companies or clients of private trading systems.

## 5.2   Website Risks and Problems

Not all websites carry the same level of risk. Table 5.1 attempts to identify a hierarchy of risks. Level 5 seems improbable but see [Birman].

Who cares? Well, getting the risk level wrong can be fatal. [Carr N] (*IT doesn't matter*) writes that what makes a resource unique is not ubiquity but scarcity: the core functions of IT are available to all companies. Thus when a resource is central to competitiveness but inessential to strategy, the risks it creates are greater than the advantages it confers. If your site fails, you're dead. If your competitors' sites fail you have an advantage. Take electricity: no one today builds a plant so as to be near an electricity source, but if the electricity fails...

Where Carr is wrong is in assuming that all computer systems are broadly similar and thus commoditize-able and replicable. Bricks, lumber, tiles, cement, and plans are all commodities but some houses are still better than others, and on the web we can live where we choose. There are lots of personal music players, so how does Apple get 80% of the market in 2006? Why is Wal-Mart so phenomenally successful year on year?

What distinguishes the winners from the losers in the web game is the ability to provide a unique and satisfying web experience. Since there are no barriers to market entry, everyone and their dog can, and does have a website. Unfortunately most of these are at best "coach" class. The failures believe industrial-strength websites can be created both painlessly and fast.

"Good enough" is alleged to be the enemy of perfection. "*I don't want perfection,*" screams a project manager, "*I just want a site that works.*" The issue of course remains *risk*: do you want to risk your site selling diamond rings at US$2.99? Can you be sure you have enough control over the development and testing processes to be sure that that doesn't happen? Someone once thought they had.

---

# It's Hard to Make It Easy, and Easy to Make It Hard

Apple's seamless combination of music player and download service has yet to be challenged by devices from Samsung, Sony, or Creative, or from services such as Napster or RealNetworks' Rhapsody.

"Apple set the bar ... it just worked,"[1] said a spokesman for a competing and so-far-unsuccessful music service. "That's one of the things — it's hard to make it easy, and easy to make it hard."

---

[1] No, you don't seriously believe that Apple just set up iTunes with a couple of hackers and a copy of DreamWeaver, do you? Nothing that good "just worked."

**TABLE 5.1**    Web test approaches

| Level | Characteristics | Test approach and order |
|-------|-----------------|-------------------------|
| 1 | The website is purely informative and no user input is possible. May include company email. Less than 10 pages. | Simple manual check for browser and graphics display, content accuracy, and email link every time the website is changed. Check for link-rot, accuracy, emailing ability and spelling. |
| 2 | As 1 but also downloading of company literature. | As 1 but also check download. |
| 3 | As 2 but contains major marketing details. Supports sales outlets. | As 2 but:<br>• unit tests of the web-application's components<br>• a series of integration tests wherein each application's relationship with the client page is tested first for functionality, then performance: application/web page (set)<br>    • smoke tests<br>    • feature/scenario tests<br>    • usability tests<br>    • non-functional feature tests.<br>These may need to use stubs and drivers.<br>• full system tests of all applications working together |
| 4 | As 3 but commercially-critical website. Has security implications since it involves credit cards and thus legal implications should user details be revealed. Implies goods will be delivered either physically or via the net, and thus connects to logistic and other delivery applications. Involves major legal liabilities in the event of failure.<br>May have legacy applications | As 3 but:<br>• treat each legacy application as a component and perform a separate component test on it<br>• integration test all legacy applications with the web applications.<br>• performance test major feature set(s) to show maximum latency<br>• security-test all the website to conform to the company security policy<br>• perform an FMECA on the website<br>• integrate the banking application and integration-test this with the bank's test environment.<br>• security-test all websites to ISO/IEC17799 |
| 5 | Safety-critical website containing information whose inaccuracy may lead to loss of life or an interface whose failure may lead to loss of life. | As 4 but also FTA on the problem domain as part of a safety case. |

The main problems with web testing are:

1. The heterogeneous nature of both the component origins (new, legacy, COTS) and the running environments, with components executed on different servers, browsers, WAP phones, PDAs, and kiosks.
2. The number of concurrent users of widely varying skill levels.
3. The possibility of massive load fluctuations as a website gains popularity.
4. The apparent ease with which the look and feel of a website can be changed which tempts those ignorant of the problems of web development and testing to insist on widespread changes at short notice, sometimes by staff with little experience of coding let alone software design.
5. The consequent difficulty in establishing and maintaining baselines for web applications.
6. The degree to which companies depend exclusively or greatly on the web for their sales.
7. The need for frequent site maintenance which has an increasingly entropic effect.

Web testing presents some unique challenges. See [Nguyen], [Gerrard], [Splaine], and [Andrews] for discussions of how to meet them.

## 5.3 Web Test Planning

In addition to the normal test plan contents consider the following issues:

- **Information gathering**. Assuming that the site is underspecified:
  - Undertake a scoping exercise to identify every document, script, manual, or specification which may be useful. Send a memorandum from both yourself and the project manager asking for information.
  - Identify from the results:
    - A list of all components of the website (html, scripts, servlets, applets, web, and legacy applications)
    - A list of all the website features
  - Create a cross-reference between feature and component
    - Against this list identify:
      - Any item which may form a baseline against which to test, who owns the item, and where it is held
      - The development group responsible
      - The tester(s) responsible
      - The manager concerned for the item or feature
      - The baseline documents, code, etc.
      - The components which are under-documented
      - The priority of each component
      - The tests to be written
  - Give this list to a tester to keep updated.

  This list is a major weapon in your battle to impose order on website testing. As testers explore the site the discrepancy between what is supposed to be there and what isn't, can provoke some major battles and you will need back-up and proof that information is missing.

- **Client configuration identification** (OS, browser, language, plug-ins, cookies, screen resolution, color depth). You may find it advisable to identify a limited number of sets, only one of which will be tested exhaustively. Once this is shown to be working the others can be tested. See www.codehouse.com/browser_watch/ for some statistics on OS, Browser, plug-ins, cookies, screen resolution, and color depth. Remember to start with something small which can unequivocally be shown to work (or not) and which can then be scaled up.
- **Test coverage determination**. Identify some basis on which you can report test coverage. See section 5.5.11 below.
- **Test ordering**. This is strategy-dependent (see Table 5.1) and depends on the degree your website is dominated by web applications. Ensure that (for example) you answer one performance question conclusively and unquestionably before attempting to answer another.
- **Test environment determination**. Ensure that your environment doesn't either affect other users or can be affected by them. You need to be completely separate from developers and the real world to be sure that it hasn't been polluted.
- **Data source determination**. Ensure the data is as real or valid as possible. In the worst case (the site is totally new, the user profile ranges from nuns to terrorists, the numbers as vague as a politician's promise) look for the worst case (the entire population of Brazil attempts to download the HD version of "The Sound of Music," in Chinese at 0500 GMT on Sunday (say)), and

extrapolate from that. Check that the data obeys the business rules of the system and that referential integrity isn't compromised when the data is loaded. Two approaches can be taken:

- Use the web server log to extract user data.
  - Modify scripts to capture data and archive it.
  - The data can then be rendered anonymous as required. This kind of data suffers however from the problems that it is true for a particular website structure and popularity level. As the website is modified, the URLs used by a user may no longer exist; should the site become heavily used (and thus slow), users may use it differently.
- **Data auditing**. Apart from the commercial considerations of accountability consider how you will test the auditability of data. Which logs hold it and how securely are they kept?
- **Tool acquisition and use**. Ensure your staff has had time to accustom themselves to the tools and that the tools work. Highly conscientious staff may refuse to accept that a tool is failing and blame themselves. Insist on demonstrations. Use outside agencies for one-off events but develop staff for repeat events: consultants and agencies take their ability with them. Compromise: hire a consultant to mentor your staff. Buy load-testing tools only if their repeated use is foreseen, otherwise use open source tools (and give staff time to learn them) or (for one-off events) hire specialists with their own tools.
- **Early execution**. You will always be squeezed, so consider using a comparable pseudo-website to the one you intend to performance test against. If your company develops many websites there may be one with comparable size and architecture against which you could at least test the loads. As soon as the thread of some complete action is available test that. If nothing else it will help accustom the tester to the tool.
- **Early alerting**. Design your environment such that you can get feedback to developers and management asap. You will be time-boxed. Here are alerts of disaster:
  - We can't get a separate environment.
  - We can't get the tools.
  - The tools don't work.
  - We can't code the tools.
  - The tools cause the system to crash.
  - The tools give faulty readings.
  - The data is unrealistic/unobtainable/unusable
  - The tools slow the system unacceptably.
- **Capacity**: scaling the system is not a question of merely adding a server (changing the structure will simply change the stress levels within the system) but rather of identifying:
  - When the system will run out of capacity such as to affect latency, (try rehosting a copy of your current system on a minimal hardware set and seeing where the bottlenecks are — never use the backup system for testing unless you want the primary system to fail)
  - How much warning you will get and how you will be warned?
  - How many parts of the system from internet connection through web server cluster to legacy system must be changed?
  - How system elements (such as video) will require dedicated servers, and how this will affect server pages and load balancing.
  - How you will test mirror sites, particularly if one crashes and traffic is re-routed
  - How pages and scripts need to be restructured to minimize latency (see section A.7)
  - How you will manage to upgrade servers and server farms while keeping a 24/7 site. Will the system reconfigure itself and load-balance correctly?
  - How you will test to show that these issues have been identified and resolved.
- **Disaster recovery**: how will you test the transfer to an emergency site?
- **Division of responsibilities**. You must ensure that there is a clear division of responsibilities between testers and developers. It is in principle uneconomic to have testers do anything other than look for bugs. It should not therefore be testers' primary responsibility either to locate the

source of bugs or to review code in an effort to imagine where bugs might be found. This is work which is far better left to developers.

- **Quality of Service constraints**. The user of a service stipulates a SLA with the provider and the latter agrees to ensure proper levels of QoS. QoS testing of a website attempts to break SLA constraints, by provoking the system to take different paths through the service workflow, which (may) produce different QoS values.
- **Size**. See [Reifer] for an adaptation of the CoCoMo model to the web. This yields an effort/ duration estimate 1/3 of which should be allocated to testing.
- **Checklists**. Use those in *Web issues checklist*.

## 5.4 Web Performance

Web performance is dominated by the following issues:

- **Website structure**: a good structure is one which allows the majority of users to do what they want most efficiently. If this is difficult to determine, think what a bad structure would be, and how you would recognize it (slow, boring, hard to navigate). Then don't do that.
- **System architecture**: there's always a bottleneck. If there isn't you must have a lot of resources standing idle. Whom do you want to please, your customers or your accountant?[2] Have your system as fully tuned as possible before starting testing, otherwise your first set of results will spur everyone to do what they should have done already and time will be wasted.
- **Logistics interface**: unless you sell downloadable software (and the downloads are fast), there's always the need to move the goods. This means the relationship between the site and the fulfillment medium (a man and a truck), has to be tightly integrated. And tightly-integrated systems can collapse when something small happens, if they have poor feedback loops and no buffer space. End-to-end testing means you need to test the relationship between a "*buy*" button being pressed and the happy recipient signing for the goods. Performance testing of those systems means finding ways of stressing them out, with (logically) big loads.
- **Internet connection**: At present the fastest available connection to the internet for private use is 11 MB. An internet T3 connection is 44.736 MB; an Optical Carrier 12 (OC12) is 622.08 MB. By the time you read this there will be other standards, thus the Abilene network (abilene.internet2.edu) is 10 GB. Ensure you have enough bandwidth in your connection that your figures are not skewed by interference from the company's commercial connection. Note that a few European countries have private 100+ MB connections, due partly to a lack of legacy technologies to hobble them. Remember: Ms. Jones is still using a 56k modem and she buys a lot.
- **Medium**: customers access the web using PDAs, WAP phones, 3G phones, browsers, RSS feeds, and kiosks. The service(s) available to each medium (as well as the download speed) differs. Here the issues are screen size, definition, and channel width.
- **Obligations**: Apart from the contractual obligations to fulfilling customer requests, there is also the need to satisfy contractual obligations expressed in an SLA, commercial obligations to banks and legal obligations to governments.
- **Targets and measures**: You need to have measures which are common across stakeholders. In particular you need to measure how:
  - The users behave: how fast, and when, do users arrive, how many pages do they access, how long do they stay on each page, and on the site as a whole, how fast do they abandon the site, how many give up trying, what are their browser settings.
  - The site behaves: does the site load many client-side scripts, how fast do pages load, is the database a bottleneck, does the site require a lot of ftp downloads?

---

[2] No, no, let me guess.

You need to see the relationship between targets and measures: Marketing will want as many hits as possible to convert into sales. However as response times (latency) grows users will abandon the site. The cost of abandonment has to be balanced against the cost of response times.

See Chapter 16.

## 5.5 Web Tests

The diagram in Figure 5.3 (based on Figure 5.1) shows the various areas of web functionality and how they can be tested. This is a suboptimal approach. One might well ask, *"why not begin with a requirements specification as in any other mission-critical system?"* One answer is simply that they are sometimes missing or incomplete, and that one has to deal with the world as it is. Another is that websites are frequently assembled from legacy and other systems and, since they evolve a lot, keeping track of baselines is a major, if necessary, task. The baselines of each of the bits of the systems are shown below.

- The website system test (sometimes referred to as *large scale integration test)* covers all the site features, its performance, usability, and security. It will usually involve one or more tester's machine(s) containing a number of test tools (see Appendix D). The baseline of the test will be the overall website requirements specification (however expressed). See section 5.5.1.
- The browser test covers all the .html code, the spelling, graphics, plug-ins, client-side scripts, applets, components, and compatibility issues which browsers throw up. The baseline of this test will be the .html, any client-side scripts, and the sets of browsers and operating systems which the site supports. Wise companies will also have a series of card mockups used by graphic designers both to satisfy clients and interact with human factors' experts. See section 5.5.2.

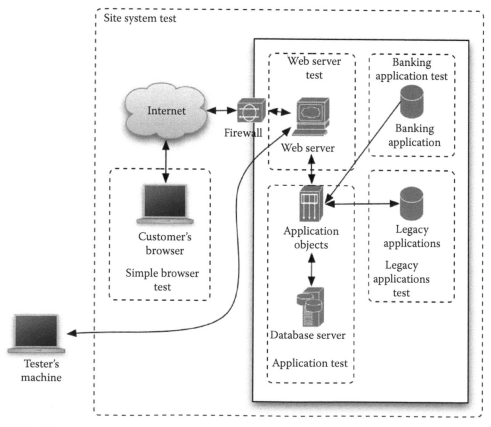

**FIGURE 5.3** Web test architecture

- The web server test tests the ability of the web server scripts to respond sufficiently to the browser and pass on requests to application objects. The baseline of the test is the set of server side scripts which pass requests to the rest of the system. See section 5.5.3.
- The application tests covers the application objects and their relations with the database(s) and the legacy applications. The baseline of the test is the set of application specifications and interface definitions. See Chapter 8.
- The banking application will usually be tested in relation to a special banking application test suite maintained by the bank providing the application. The baseline of the test is the interface and features specification provided by the bank. See section 5.5.3.
- The legacy application tests will (hopefully) be those originally created for the legacy applications which have been thereafter maintained The baseline of the test is the set of requirements specifications from which the applications were developed. See section 5.5.6.

From this the value of identifying all the interfaces employed is evident. Fortunately many of these are identified in the CGI, and various APIs, but interfaces with the legacy applications need to be identified, and specified. All the elements in this architecture have interfaces. These need to be recorded to simplify integration and system testing. See section 8.4.

Those experienced in web development will know that many of the specifications mentioned above as baselines will not exist. The degree to which they *do* exist is evidence of the recognition of the risk the company runs in developing the site. Note that insofar as the information can be obtained unambiguously and easily from code, that is a sufficient baseline.

## 5.5.1   Website System Test Approaches

Since web pages can be put together fast using specialized tools, the temptation to make on-the-fly changes has meant that there is no clear distinction between unit (or developer) tests and system tests. Understanding what might go wrong depends to a large extent on testers having an intimate knowledge of the code. This in turn tempts:

- Developers to shed their unit testing responsibilities onto testers.
- Testers and developers to duplicate each others' work.
- Testers to become distracted from the task of system-testing a site.

These issues need to be clarified in the test plan and the web test process beginning with a search (repeated regularly) for baseline-relevant data. Here are some approaches to the tests:

- **Transaction link tests.** These are baselined on single end-to-end transactions. Having identified these from some requirements specification, determine all the browser elements, components, applications, and scripts needed to get it to work, and build a pseudo-site capable of undertaking it. This way you will answer the following questions:
  - Can we undertake this transaction?
  - How fast can we get it to run?
  - What are the interfaces?
  - How many of these transactions can the system support at once?
  - Does the system successfully add, delete, and update records?
  - How much of the system did we have to stub to get this to work?
  - Did this leave the database as it should be?
  - Do our automated tests work?
  This is nothing more than the "threaded" integration strategy. This approach may be opposed on the grounds that "*it's too early for this sort of thing*": which means "*I think you're about to show that my code doesn't work.*" As indeed you probably will.

- **All links test**. This simply checks that all links work and reach the *right* page. Curiously, this cannot always be automated. While a tool will indicate which links fail, only a human will know if a clicked link arrives at the right page. Use this as an exercise to draw a spreadsheet of website pages. This will give you an idea of the amount of work involved and the degree of test coverage achieved. Dynamically-created links (such as on a news website) can be tested generically. When compared with the html, such a spreadsheet can also reveal unhittable pages.

- **Bash the browser.** This is *not* recommended but without any specifications it is what you may end up doing, at least until the test team understand how the system is supposed to work. It consists simply of exploring what features the browser offers and activating every control possible therein. This may at least give you the information you need to write a requirements specification.

Overall website requirements specifications may have to be assembled and maintained by the test team (if no one else will). Websites cost: no one pays out that sort of money and stays in business without a pretty good idea of what they want. If nothing else, you will get ideas for scenario or transaction tests from the memoranda, and position papers generated while the business tried to identify what it wanted. If nothing else the graphic design people will have a brief: get a copy of that.

## 5.5.2   Browser Tests

Web test specifications sometimes derive from attention to the code and the bugs it may exhibit. Testers being in the position of men with only a large nail of a web to test, and no hammer of a requirements specification or other baseline, will look for whatever hammers are to hand, and will read the raw code if nothing else.

The danger with such an approach is that:

- It may deteriorate into a browser-bashing session in which testers unsystematically attack every screen element presented.
- It doesn't allow for potential state changes or subtle feature interactions which "real" transactions may cause.

There is a large number of tools available to check the html. Servlets and applets will need to be unit tested. In this respect, as in many others, there is little difference between web, and any other kind of testing.

## 5.5.3   Web Server Tests

The server-based components do things such as:

- Security checks
- Order processing
- Credit checking and payment processing
- Business logic (possibly using a separate set of business rules) to interact with a database
- Creation of *live* pages possibly using ASP or JSP

These require a system test but without a UI. Consider using a unit-test tool to interface with the components. Once you have a way of bypassing the lack of the UI you can execute what are in effect system tests of the features of each of these subsystems and end-to-end tests of the various scenarios. These may involve passing transactions to a separate (possibly legacy) application or fulfilling them directly. Servers need to be upgraded so ensure you have a means of testing a server upgrade before it is returned to use. These too need to be unit tested.

## 5.5.4   Bank Application Tests

A key part of any site is the integration of the site with one or more credit or debit cards or other payment service. The steps vary as the service but are generically:

1. Create a **project plan** to define the major activities, tasks, dependencies, dates, and resources required to produce the deliverables to implement the service within the merchant's environment. This will include:
   a. A schedule for interim checkpoint reviews of the project plan
   b. Selection of a *Merchant Server plug-In* (MPI) software supplier
   c. Identification of an MPI implementation location, at the merchant, payment service provider, or acquirer locations
   d. Installation, integration and testing of the MPI
   e. Development and agreement of dispute resolution procedures
   f. Obtaining merchant password, URL of the production card issuer server and card issuer root certificate
   g. Changes to server configurations, DNS, routing tables, firewalls, procedures, and operational issues
   h. Production rollout details
2. **Identify an MPI software supplier** by assessing the MPI software's compatibility and integration requirements, with the merchant's existing software. This will include:
   a. Preparation of all authentication data relevant to the location of the final "*Buy*" page or "*Check Out*" button
   b. Presentation of authentication data to the MPI
   c. Assessing the answer returned by the MPI after it receives the authentication response.
3. Prepare a **diagram** of the merchant's existing or proposed **commerce platform** for the supplier's review.
4. **Review the MPI proposal** with the supplier and identify any other steps required to install the MPI. Modify the plan.
5. **Unit- and stress-test** the MPI interfacing software.
6. **Unit-test** the MPI interfacing software.
7. **Conduct:**
   a. System testing
   b. Compliance testing
   c. Product integration testing on a remote web-testing environment that:
      i. Provides the equivalent of all components of the card issuer's secure infrastructure
      ii. Provides a facility for production readiness testing of *Access Control Server* (ACS) and MPI component implementations
      iii. Verifies that compliant, secure ACS components are integrated at issuer or issuer processor sites
      iv. Verifies that MPI components integrated at a merchant or merchant aggregator sites, comply with all subject processing requirements, and are production-ready.
8. **Populate** the card issuer database with the merchant data.
9. **Obtain from the acquirer:**
   a. The URL of the production directory server
   b. The card-issuer root certificate
   c. The acquirer-assigned merchant password.
10. **Install the card-issuer root certificate** in the MPI.
11. **Install the merchant ID and the merchant password** (obtained from the acquirer) in the MPI.
12. **Change the code** to enable the MPI software to point to the production card-issuer directory server.

## 5.5.5 Credit Card Use Process

Figure 5.4 illustrates the essentials of the payment process.

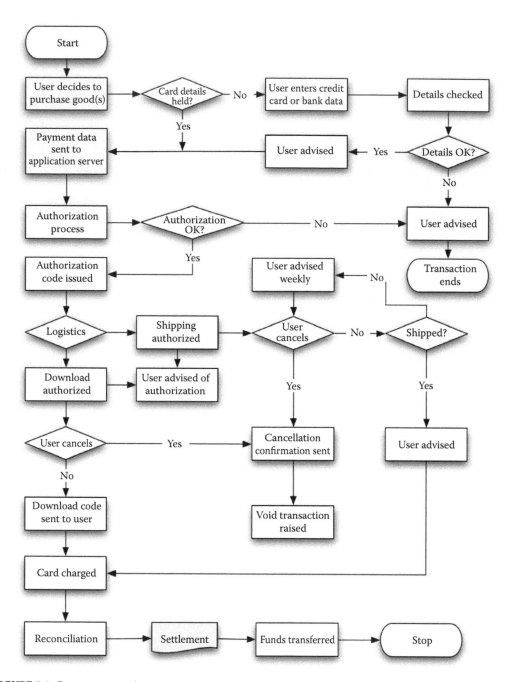

**FIGURE 5.4** Payment processing

There is a bottleneck problem when transactions are to be authorized which can be resolved by simply advising the user that the authorization details will be advised along with any download codes, batching the transactions, and forwarding them to the credit card issuer at a low-traffic moment. Downloaded (soft) transactions cannot use this approach since the whole point of such a transaction is to allow the user download access fast. In practice an email advising the user that the download code will be sent within 30 minutes is usually satisfactory.

Note that other methods are used:

- PayPal (www.paypal.com) used both escrow accounts, and credit card authorizations to speed web transactions
- 1-Click™ allows a user to simply click a button to authorize payment. This requires that the browser has cookies on.

Both these approaches require similar flows to the one above for the purposes of getting the user authorized. All approaches involve a lot of security issues most of which are hidden from the merchant's website.

## 5.5.6   Legacy Application Tests

Some issues to be considered when testing legacy applications in the web:

1. There will (almost certainly) be no requirements or any other specifications. What you will be offered is (possibly) a peek at the code. If the legacy application was bought from a supplier you may not even get that.
2. The interface to the web may ignore little-used but essential features known only to the staff who (rarely) used them. The people may already have left. Their absence of both the features and staff will not be noticed until too late (Year-end accounts, leap-years, month-end reconciliations, journaling).

In both these cases be prepared to fight for the use of a technical writer or literate tester, and the time to get a requirements specification written. (You will be accused of empire-building, colonization of the development process and worse.) The time you (and, ultimately everyone else) will save will outweigh such considerations. Have the technical writer excavate all the memoranda, manuals etc. relating to all the applications to be cared for, from wherever the organization hid them and then spend the time assembling what can be found. Let him use a notation like the one in section A.4 in Appendix A and section 8.2.1. Ask the operators of the legacy system, talk to the trainers, find out if anyone recently-retired could be recalled to help. If the system is important enough to be front-ended by the web it must have had some real users recently. Be prepared to have him model the interface as well since this may considerably clear his thinking (and everyone else's). One upshot of this rigor is that you may well discover problems which have been known of and ignored for years.

Do not accept any suggestions that testers can discover what they need from the source code. The developers who will be subjecting the source to unit tests etc. (won't they?) will doubtless find the source code valuable. You need to test what it does for users. When hidden behind a browser this may be most unclear.

## 5.5.7   Scripting Language Risks

Scripting languages such as Perl, PHP, TcL, ASP, Jscript, VBScript, and Cold Fusion are the duct tape of the internet. They are powerful, agile, and essential. It is unwise to expect testers to have to examine any but the least-complex of scripts to determine the logic of some event (the least-complex scripts will possibly be bug-free). It is essential that such scripts be designed and unit-tested. Undisciplined scripting is the enemy of good architectural design. The complexity which such scripting induces make debugging and bug isolation a developer's curse. One argument in favor of having testers read scripts is that they will become more aware of the kinds of errors which may occur. Writing (other than unit) tests to find such errors will not be successfully informed by deep code knowledge so much as by a definition of the website's requirements and the possible user scenarios.

## 5.5.8   Web Unit Testing

High-criticality websites need to be unit tested. The scope of a web unit is the server/client page. Server pages are static only in the sense that they contain the logic by which a page is built for transmission to a client. Client pages are static only in that they are built by the server. They are often as varied in content as the logic of the server page allows.

Each client page can be considered as being built from:

- Business logic
- Database results
- Scripts and applets
- Frames containing screen icons, fields, graphics, pull-downs, etc.
- Links

There remains thus a problem of granularity. If a page is very complex it might be less risky to test individual elements. The baseline of a browser page web unit test can be expressed as a decision table wherein some combination of page state (before test), input variables, and user input actions will lead to a page state (after test), expected outputs, and expected results. Similarly the baseline of a server page web unit test can be expressed as a decision table wherein some combination of page state (before test), and input variables will lead to a page state (after test), expected outputs and expected results.

Drivers and stubs can be developed from such a baseline. A driver is built (probably using a scripted test tool) to populate a client page's input forms and generate the test events. The driver page will include some script functions and the Document Object Model (DOM) allows its interaction with the page under test. Stubs can be developed either as client pages, server pages, or web objects. Their complexity will depend both on the type of interaction between the page under test, the component to be substituted, and on the internal complexity of the component(s).

Server pages are usually more complex than client pages due to scripting languages and such technologies as ASP and JSP. Thus a server page can receive data from a client page through predefined objects, manage a user session, redirect a session to other web pages, interact with other objects on the web server, interface to a database or a file, and send or receive an e-mail.

## 5.5.9   Dynamic Server Page Creation

Dynamic Server Pages (DSP) can create a large number of page types thus complicating testing.

One solution is to use the rules contained in the DSP scripts to generate a number of tests each of which is self-checking in that a user or a script can check the page contents against the page specifications both of which are evident from the page. The number of page *types*, however large, is finite. The contents however (take, for example, eBay) is infinite.

Another solution is to identify the primary (or most-used) pages and test those most.

If a dynamic server page scripting engine is used, and it fails, it will stop the entire site until restarted. A failed individual CGI script will simply affect an individual browser session.

## 5.5.10   Web Reliability Testing

There are two main sources of *un*reliability in a website:

1. The browser–web server connection (discussed below)
2. Everything else (see section 16.8)

Web performance is a bit like the quality of life. You know if it's ever mentioned that it's either bad or non-existent. You need to be able to calculate it. Here's the process:

1. Draw a *reliability block diagram* of your system. It could look something like the diagram in Figure 5.5.

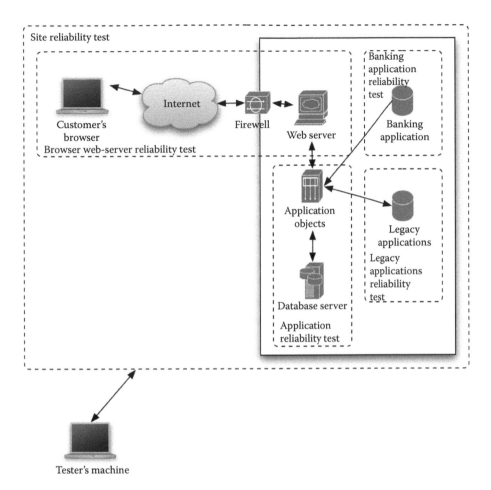

**FIGURE 5.5** Simple reliability block diagram

2. Identify the possible paths. Each element of the diagram (Browser (Br), Internet (In), firewall (Fi), web server (We), application objects (Ap), banking application (Ba), legacy application (Le), and database server (Da)) has some level of reliability. That is: there is a probability of failure once every so many years, days, minutes, or seconds. A request goes from browser to:
   - Web server
   - Legacy application
   - Database server, or
   - Banking application.

   Thus to calculate the probability of a request going to the legacy application and back, failing over (say) 1 hour we can (with reference to section 18.6.4) write an equation thus:

$$R_{sys}(transaction) = (R_{Br})^2 \bullet (R_{In})^2 \bullet (R_{Fi})^2 \bullet (R_{We})^2 \bullet (R_{Ap})^2 \bullet (R_{Le})$$

   Note that reliability of each item except the legacy system has been squared since they will be encountered both on the outward and return journeys of the transaction.

3. Get the reliability of the components. We can draw a table of the reliabilities over one hour as shown in Figure 5.6.

| Item | Reliability |
|---|---|
| Customer's browser R(Br) | 0.998 |
| Internet R(In) | 0.99997 |
| Firewall R(Fi) | 0.999996 |
| Web server R(We) | 0.995 |
| Application objects R(Ap) | 0.996 |
| Banking application R(Ba) | 0.9999998 |
| Legacy application R(Le) | 0.92 |
| Database server R(Da) | 0.99991 |

**FIGURE 5.6** Probabilities of failure

4. Calculate. We can evaluate these figures thus:

$$0.998^2 * 0.99997^{\,2} * 0.999996^2 * 0.995^2 * 0996^2 * 0.92$$

which in Excel notation looks like:

$$=POWER(B13, 2)*POWER(B14, 2)*POWER(B15, 2)*POWER(B16, 2)*$$
$$POWER(B17, 2)*B19 = 0.8998792047$$

which is pretty bad. Assuming that some 500,000 people hit that site every hour some 50,060 (500,000 * (1 − 0.8998792047)) will have a failed transaction. This is entirely due to the lousy reliability of the web server, the application objects, and the legacy application. If these were all improved to 0.999999 the reliability would increase to 0.999890005 and only 55 transactions per hour would fail.

5. Mitigate
   a. If we double the web server in parallel, the calculation (with reference to section 18.6.5 in Chapter 18) is

$$0.999975 = [1 - ((1 - 0.995) * (1 - 0.995))]$$

   which when plugged back into the original equation gives us 45,550 transactions failing.
   b. If the legacy application is only failing due to stress then double and load-balance it. This will drop the number of failures per 500,000 to 9,194.
   c. Alternatively treble and load-balance it (with reference to section 18.6.6). This will drop the number of failures per 500,000 to 6032.

From this, three questions remain:

1. How do we calculate the reliability of each element of the transaction?
   a. Create a test harness for each element of the transaction and subject it to an increasingly-heavy transactional load. Find out the point at which it fails (and make sure the system isn't simply shedding load), and then subject it to a load just below that point for a long period of (say) a month. Ensure that the harness is capable of restarting immediately after the system fails. Count

how many times it fails during that period (say it is 6). Then over a period of 30 days * 24 hours (=720 hours) it fails 6/720 times per hour or 0.00833333 times. Rounded up this gives us 0.01.

   b. Look in the logs of the various servers to see which transactions failed. Create a load on the browser, and see how many http requests arrive at the web server.

2. How do we help improve the reliability of the legacy application?

   a. Create a test harness which will:

      i. Annotate the code so you know what module is being called when

      ii. Punish the code

      iii Tell you:

         A. Where the bottlenecks are

         B. Which units were being used when the failure occurred.

3. How do we calculate the reliability of code outside our control?

Give it a $10^{-9}$ probability[3] of failure and ignore it unless you have any reason to doubt that probability, in which case get the log data. If you are paying the bank a fee for the privilege of using their system, they should be able to give you some reliability figures.

## 5.5.11   Web Test Coverage

We can use:

1. All URLs and transitions between them within the website
2. All transaction types ({ navigation | data | order creation and submission })
3. A set of scenarios which users are expected to take possibly (preferably) culled from user action logs
4. All servlets
5. All applets
6. All scripts
7. All applications (legacy, COTS, and new)
8. All components

There remains the problem of state. Apart from the possibility that browser variables may affect browser behavior, the ostensibly stateless behavior of the browser (it just submits requests and displays whatever it's sent) masks the reality that the website taken as a whole has a state which may affect the browser's behavior in that (for example) having established that some item is in stock user A orders it. Before the request can be satisfied user B has already ordered it. User A is blocked and on checking again discovers the item is "on back order." Similarly travel websites may differ in the order in which airlines are displayed following a request for a given flight depending on the availability and price of seats for that flight.

## 5.5.12   Web Test Tools

Static elements of websites can be tested automatically by such spider-like programs (see section D.13 in Appendix D), which follow recursively all possible static links from a Web page in search of errors such as broken links, misspellings, and HTML-conformance violations. For automatic testing of dynamic components, including executing client-side scripts, and form interactions, use either:

---

[3] A generally-accepted limit for ultra-reliable code.

- Scriptable "capture-replay" tools that record user-defined testing scenarios and then generate scripts (sequences of browsers' actions) that can be run on browsers or
- Non-scripting "wizard" -based test generators

Generating server workloads. There are two approaches:

1. **Trace-based**: which exactly mimics a known workload but is a "black box" approach and it's difficult to change parameters of interest.
2. **Analytic:** which creates a workload synthetically allowing models to be inspected and parameters varied.

## 5.6   Monitoring Issues

Once functioning, you need to ensure a website stays that way. This can be done either through a paid service or using shareware tools. You need to check:

- Availability: is the website visible? (Can it be pinged?)
- Linkrot: ensure that all the links in your site are always current and that any hosted links are themselves current.
- Link speed checks: to ensure that the page can be speedily reached.
- Download: that downloads are fast and correct.
- Back-end connections: do calls to legacy and web applications succeed? Are databases unduly slow? (Because they are very big?)
- Memory leaks: is there any evidence? Which database drivers are you using?
- Traffic volume: is this increasing unduly?
- Click-out rates: are users abandoning your website as soon as they find it?
- Security alerts: are all your systems upgraded to counter the latest threats?

# 6

# The Overall Test
# Life-Cycle

We need a test process that is closely integrated with whatever software life-cycle the project believes it is using and that brings discipline to the manner in which the what-to-test, when-to-stop, and who-does-what questions are answered. Testing requirements at each phase of the project have to be defined. The cycle shown in Figure 6.1 is very simple, obvious, and true for (almost) any kind of test.[1] If it doesn't happen, you have a problem.

A typical software life-cycle contains the following activities, not necessarily in the order shown here:

- Initiate, plan, and set up infrastructure
- Write the requirements
- Design the architecture
- Code and unit test
- System test
- Document and train,
- Install, cutover, support, and evolve[2]

As test manager you need to relate these activities to the life-cycle being used as discussed in section 4.4 in Chapter 4. The following sections identify the test-related activities that should occur irrespective of the life-cycle adopted. As with all processes it is necessary that they are clear to the staff engaged in them. The following description is simplified in that the phases described will normally overlap one another and may be simultaneous.

## 6.1   Initiation Phase

This is the period, before the project starts, when the system is first identified, perhaps as part of some future component or as a stand-alone.

- If possible, **review the tender or the contract** to see what testing commitments have been made.
- Undertake a **sizing exercise** to get some sense of how many tests you must write. Note section 18.12 in Chapter 18.
- **Identify the configuration management** and change control processes to be applied to all documents. Note that if your requirements specifications derive from such other documents as business process models or system specifications, then you need to track changes to these documents as well if you are going to modify your tests in a timely manner.

---

[1] The exception is, of course, the test automation process.
[2] Start again generating the next version (and fixing this version's bugs which were found in the field).

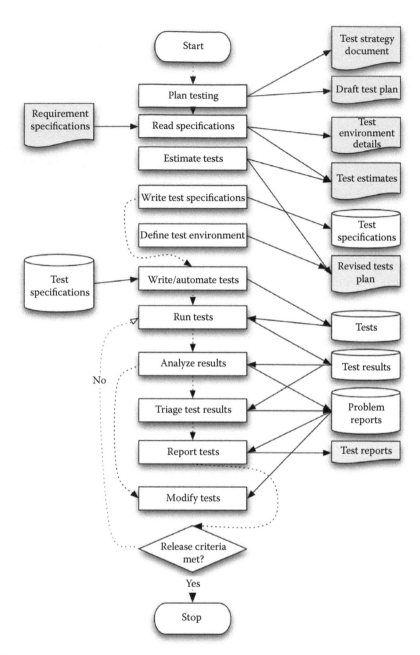

**FIGURE 6.1**  A test process

- Draft a **test strategy document** as described in section 8.3 in Chapter 8. Use this to identify what is exceptional about this project before getting into the detail of test planning. When you are in the throes of test planning, use this as a way of abstracting out strategic issues.
- Then draft a skeleton **test plan** showing all the testing activities of the project, preferably as a separate document or as part of a draft quality plan (see section 8.21). This should indicate the objectives, management, and processes of all the testing activities of the project as well as any risks and commitments which justify them. Orient the test plan to the testing deliverables and establish who is responsible for each deliverable and its testing. Get some sense of timing in place with a Gantt or PERT chart (Figure 6.2). Check the test plan against the project plan and ensure that the dates match and the stakeholders agree.

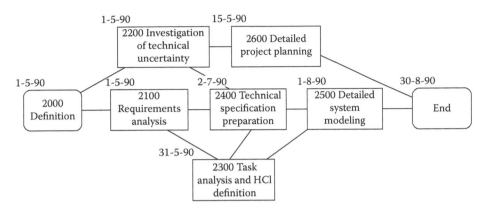

**FIGURE 6.2** A PERT chart of the system definition phase

The test plan can follow the IEEE model [IEEE 1012] mentioned in section E.2 in Appendix E. However this could usefully be augmented with two extra sections covering reliability profiling and risk. These are discussed in Chapter 18. Review the test plan with the project manager.

- Write a **process model** of how you are going to test the software and what items (documents, code, tests, reports, etc.) will pass between the stakeholders and you. Show in particular how you will interface with developers, configuration management, project management, external suppliers, and the customer. Show all the support systems you will need such as:
    - A bug management tool (at its simplest this can be an Access database) to record the bug reports and display the quantity and type found to date (see section 7.6)
    - A configuration management tool to manage the test specifications and software (if your organization doesn't have a suitable one already)
    - Test harnesses and test management software
    - Test automation software
- Identify, evaluate, and obtain what you need. Put it under configuration management.

## 6.2 Requirements Analysis Phase

The software requirements specification forms the baseline of the system tests. Writing it will permit much of the detail of the system-test phase of the software test plan to be completed and allow those responsible for the system testing to begin specifying the system tests. During this phase:

1. **Review the requirements specifications.** They may be all you will ever be given to define the features you must test. If you are using automated test tools you will need to be sure that the requirements specifications contain enough detail to allow testers to manually-test the system before they start preparing them. See section B.5 in Appendix B. If the specification is purely textual consider modeling it using some requirements specification tool. You will be unhappily surprised how many bugs the specification contains.

   If you realize that the specifications are grossly inadequate and that nothing will be done in time to improve them, have a senior member of your team write a better version. See [Gervasi] and section 8.2.1 for examples. See [Kwan] for some interesting horror stories of what happens if you don't.

2. **Identify the usability-testing requirements** (see section B.12 in Appendix B) in terms of:
   a. The usability requirements in the requirements specification, with particular attention paid to user-critical moments (*"... press this button at the wrong moment, Sunshine, and ..."*)
   b. The user population and some definition of their talents (*"... he can't walk and chew gum at the same time ..."*)

    c. The possible environments or circumstances in which the users might be trying to use the system (*"…if the prime minister would kindly remove her handbag from my keyboard…"*)

    d. The user's objectives (*"…I'm trying to write a news story…"*)

3. **Identify the safety-testing requirements** (see section B.10 in Appendix B) in terms of:
    a. The user population
    b. The safe and unsafe states, changes between them, and ability to recover from a failure
    c. Hazards
    d. Safety-related functions
    e. Safety performance
    f. Human interface
    g. Testing requirements

4. **Identify the security-testing requirements** (see section B.11 in Appendix B) in terms of:
    a. The user population
    b. The secure and insecure states and interfaces
    c. The 3rd-party security subsystems to be used
    d. The threats and defenses

5. **Identify the performance-testing requirements** in terms of section B.14 in Appendix B. Also see Chapter 16 for more on this.

6. **Identify the operational profile** as discussed in section 7.7.

7. **Identify feature interactions.** As the system is used (particularly operationally) subtle interactions may emerge (for example, the use of tables in footers in Word 6.1, the instability in Word v.x when inserting cross-references, etc.). To identify all the feature interactions you will need to:
    a. Identify the features in each operational profile
    b. Identify all the scenarios the users will adopt
    c. Identify which feature interactions are *not* covered by a scenario (see section 15.10.10)
    d. Identify test objectives to cover the missing interactions
    e. Create a matrix of them (see Figure 15.12 for details of how to prepare one)
    f. Enter any bugs you find in the bug management tool (see section C.2 in Appendix C for advice on documentation bugs). Don't be persuaded that these aren't real bugs by the developers or management.[3] Knowing how many bugs you found in each phase (and indeed each document) is critical for predicting bug totals. And if the bugs aren't recorded how can you be sure they'll be fixed?

8. **Plan and specify** (in outline) **the system tests:**
    a. Identify a subset of the system tests for smoke test purposes
    b. Identify a subset of the system tests for regression test purposes[4]
    c. Identify another subset of the system tests for system test dry-run purposes
    d. Identify and add any tests required for customer acceptance if not yet included

9. **Review the tests.** See section B.7 in Appendix B.

10. **Design, code, or acquire the test tools.** It may seem better to wait to do this until unit design has begun but there won't be enough time then.

Probably a few of these details will not exist at the time you are planning, and their absence will come as a warning to both you and the project manager.

---

[3] *"I don't feel these issues are best placed in the defect management database"* was one attempt, swiftly demolished by asking where else they would go and how they should be tracked.

[4] Regression and smoke testing answer different questions. Smoke tests simply say *"It's worth testing this build"* (or not) and need to be short. Regression tests answer the question *"Has any feature broken since (the last build/moving the build onto a different OS/language etc.?"* This takes longer.

If the software is highly-critical it may be preferable to have the system modeled by a part of the test team using a formal methods tool in order both to check the feasibility and correctness of the assumptions and to generate tests automatically. See section 4.4 for a discussion of such tools.

Preparing the system test specifications acts as a major control of the testability of the software requirements specification itself. Each system test should be clearly related to the requirement from which it was derived. Three major problems may appear:

1. **Requirements are incomplete.** Every menu and window has perhaps been specified within the definition of each feature. But not every interaction perhaps. Alternatively, users (and everyone else) may expect some feature to be present but because they were quite obviously essential they were forgotten. Requirements may simply emerge as a result of users (in this case, testers) interacting with the system ("...*Well, of course you need to be able to save files...*").

2. **Requirements confusion.** The specification was ambiguous. The testers read it one way and the developers another: see the little story in *Terms Used* in the Glossary.

3. A specification may be written in such a way as to render it **untestable.** Consider Figure 6.3.

> The system will contain an FX1700 processor with an FQ1400 unit, and a ZZ2100 unit.

**FIGURE 6.3**   An untestable requirement (just what contains what?)

For this reason it can be essential that requirements specifications are written but changeable. The potential for requirements change can be a root cause of problems. See [Lutz] for more on this.

# 6.3   Architectural Definition Phase

In this phase the overall design of the system is completed. Integration testing has often been obviated by the use of better software development environments wherein all interfaces are already checked before units are compiled. If such checking cannot take place or if (for example) preliminary partial integrations can take place with only stubs and drivers available, as in web system development, then this phase still needs planning. This phase will show:

- The subsystems into which the system features have been allocated.
- The interfaces between the subsystems which are the basis for the integration test specifications. Find out where these are defined and, if any aren't but you still have a responsibility for testing them, write them yourself using section 8.4. From this, whoever is in charge of building the releases can derive the *Integration tree* (see section 8.5.16) which will define the order in which the software will be integrated and built.

During this phase:

- Update the test plan with any integration test details. Alternatively if the system is large, write a separate integration test plan.
- Review the software/software integration using section B.16 in Appendix B.
- Define the software scaffolding for the integration tests.
- Specify the integration tests.
- Identify any regression tests.

Note that this will require that the subset of the system tests identified in the last phase be included as regression tests, so that the overall features of some integrated system at the end of some integration step can be demonstrated. This will guard against a successful integration delivering software for system testing which doesn't in fact work.

Apply the following controls:

- Each integration step should be identifiable in the integration tree (see section 8.5.16 in Chapter 8).
- Each set of integration tests should be related to an identifiable integration step. The definition of the interfaces can often be checked by those responsible for preparing the integration tests.

## 6.4   Coding and Unit Testing

In this phase the detailed design of the system is completed and the units coded, tested, and debugged. You will probably need some modifications both to the unit tests and the test plan itself. During this phase:

- Complete the test plan.
- Create the unit test specifications, software, and procedures.
- Review (a sample of) the unit tests prepared by the developers for coverage, consistency, and other attributes (see section B.15).
  - Review the test inputs for these and all the other tests.
  - Assess the structural coverage of the unit tests.
- Estimate the remaining number of bugs to be found and the time to be spent testing.

Apply the following controls:

- Relate each unit test to a unit specification (which can simply be the unit header).
- Test the unit tests by bug seeding (see section 18.10.5).
- Peer-review each unit before unit-testing.
- Relate unit test severity to code complexity (see section 18.8.4) and expected unit use.
- Relate unit test execution time to the expected use of the unit.
- Review unit tests. Re-review those which found no bugs if bugs are found later during integration and system testing time.
- Review the unit test environment (tools, etc.).
- Modify any unit test which has found a bug (otherwise there will be a tendency for the tests to train the code to pass them).
- Get the code size and details to help in determining bug numbers (see section 18.10).

When a unit passes a unit test, put the code under configuration control. Access to and control of the unit-tested code should be with the project librarian.

Unit testing is not a clearly-delimited phase and so apply these controls whenever a unit is ready for submission (as soon as a program declares some unit to be ready for a build). See section 4.4.6 for the Microsoft approach and Chapter 14 for more details generally.

## 6.5   Software/Hardware Integration

Sometimes new software needs to be integrated with new hardware. Do not attempt this with untested software and untested hardware if you value your schedule.

Wherever possible, software should first be tested with hardware emulation software such as an In-Circuit Emulator (ICE) and hardware should be tested with hardware test programs. Any such support software and hardware should be suitably validated before use and maintained under configuration control.

Any software embedded in a piece of hardware should be tested as a separate system first with a full system test. Then their interfaces should be tested by placing each subsystem in an emulator. Once system tests have been conducted on all such subsystems they can be amalgamated, and an overall end-to-end system test conducted.

## 6.6 Test Readiness Review

The purpose of a test readiness review is to determine:

- How ready the test team is to undertake system (and later) testing (*Have tests been written to cover every requirement? Is the system sufficiently-documented?*)
- To what extent the tests already executed demonstrate the system's readiness for release
- To what extent the system's unit and other tests already undertaken indicate the system's readiness for system testing
- How representative the data proposed to be used during system testing is

Inputs to the review are:

- The baseline documents, test plans, test objectives, and tests (which may include automated tests)
- Results of pre-system test activities such as early test runs which demonstrate that the tests are capable of finding problems
- Results of installation and smoke tests

The review will (minimally) use section B.7.4 in Appendix B. The output of the review should be a report identifying:

- What still needs to be done to improve baselines and tests
- The degree of coverage expected to be achieved
- The weaknesses so far discovered
- The risks remaining

## 6.7 System-Testing Phase

System testing is the moment when the project's success or failure becomes evident. It is the first time that the system is being used in anything like the way and the environment it was intended for, and is often the moment at which the customer can observe the system in action.

During this phase the system is tested against its requirements. Since some parts of the system may be expensive to test or the contract requires you to invite customer representatives to observe them, dry-run the system tests beforehand. System tests tend to be long, drawn-out affairs for the following reasons:

- Many features aren't ready.
- Those features which *are* built have so many bugs in them that they can only be partly used.
- Fixing the bugs exposes more bugs.
- Many tests aren't ready.
- The process of fixing bugs induces more of them.
- The testers discover new ways of testing features not evident from the specifications.
- Subtle and unwanted feature-feature interactions occur.

During this phase:

- Execute the full system tests. If they derive from business process models, then at some point execute them in the context defined by those process models.
- Evaluate the results.
- Write the bug reports.
- Correct any bugs discovered.
- Write the system test summary report.
- Update the system test specifications, procedures, and software.
- Modify the tests.

- Review the number of bugs expected to be found.
- Get the system to a sufficiently stable state to allow customer representatives to attend the acceptance test.

See Chapter 15 for more on this.

---

# Story: Bankruptcy Alert

T he test manager wasn't prepared to authorize the release. Testers were still finding a lot of bugs each day. Some were serious. The CEO believed that only by regular releases could the product's market profile be maintained. So he tried to pressure the test manager, who resisted and was sacked.

The company never employed another test manager, and failed 27 months later, despite a further three rounds of funding.

---

## 6.8   Beta Testing

Beta testing is the moment your wonderfully-crafted product finally arrives before "real" users. You need to balance the amount of effort you need to do it, with the minimal response they mostly give you.

Beta testers:

- Are the nearest you will get to real-world users.
- Are sometimes from companies whose senior staff are old friends of the marketing people. The other staff will know this and may resent it since they never get taken out to lunch.
- Have many other things to do besides play with your software. So you need to look at why they would do it anyway:
  - Because they already use the software and they want to know:
    - If it's worth continuing with it,
    - If the features they've been screaming at you for the last 18 months are finally there.
  - Because they might, just possibly, recommend it for purchase, and taking part in the beta test process is the cheapest way of accessing a copy.
- Aren't testers. They've (mostly) no idea of how to report a bug, and will happily tell you everything is wonderful, even when they've given up on the software upon seeing how big the manual is.
- Have some very odd software on their machines which makes installation hell and teaches you some useful configuration lessons early on. In the unlikely event that a beta tester runs your stuff thoroughly and finds it good, then you have a friend for a long time.
- Can find bugs you have never thought of.

See section 15.12.

## 6.9   Certification- or Acceptance-Testing Phase

During this phase the system is tested against the customer's acceptance requirements. Since (hopefully) these have been included in the system tests, all that is usually required is for the customer acceptance/certification subset to be re-run. This phase can usually be obviated by having customer representatives attend the system testing phase. The exception to this is when the client insists on *challenge testing* (see section 15.13.2).

Note that there is an environment problem inherent in certification. A system certified for use in one environment needs recertification either if a part of that system changes or the environment changes. Any change may thus become most expensive. See also [Kelly 2].

Certification testing will include but not be limited to performance testing. See Chapter 16 for more details.

Microsoft (and other companies) has Gold certification schemes against which your software can be assessed.

## 6.10 Documentation, Help, and Training Phase

During this phase the documentation and training materials are prepared and reviewed. Test staff are invaluable as course guinea-pigs and document reviewers. The business process models can be tested before cutover. See section 15.10.7 in Chapter 15 for more details.

## 6.11 Install, Coexist, Cutover, Support, and Evolution Phase

During this phase the software is installed and a series of tests are run to answer the big questions of this phase:

1. *Does the software install properly? Does it interfere with anything else? How will we know if it doesn't?*
2. *Does it coexist with the other systems? How will we know if it doesn't?*
3. *How would we know that cutover has failed?*
4. *Having cutover, if anything goes seriously wrong, can we revert to a previous state with minimal cost?*
   a. Identify the cost of a system failure.
   b. Test the cutover, see if any part of the old database and any network-coexisting system is affected.
   c. Run the new system simulating loads at critical performance periods for a period indicating a sufficient reliability. See section 16.8 in Chapter 16, the discussion in section 18.4 in Chapter 18, and the *Resilience Checklist* (section B.14.4) in Appendix B. Ensure that every transaction type has been run. Simulate clock changes for new year, leap year, etc.
   d. Identify whether it is necessary and cost-effective to have some way of capturing all transactions made on the new system such that they can be applied to the old one.
   e. Write a procedure to roll back to the old system and perform it.
   f. Test if the old system can handle an update of all the transactions previously made on the new system before roll-back.
5. *Will any systems coexisting on our company network affect or be affected by this release?*
   a. Identify a means of providing syntactically-correct but semantically irrelevant and harmless outputs to any dependent systems.
   b. Create a version of the system to use the harmless outputs to operational systems and run it.
   c. Monitor all related systems.
6. *Do the Support staff have sufficient knowledge of the system to handhold users through their installation?*
   a. Identify all the new or changed features of the system.
   b. Check the Support staff's training program.
   c. If necessary rotate all members of the Support staff through the installation testing and general system testing, working as part of the test team.
   d. Prepare a list of the most-often-occurring bugs from the buggiest features and make it available to Support staff.
7. *Are we going to be overwhelmed with bugs?* This could happen if:
   a. Your estimates were hopelessly wrong. Check them, then have a colleague check them.

b. Your beta tests didn't show the bugs they were supposed to. Read the bugs they did find; are these bugs found by people playing with the system or using it in earnest?

c. You have a history of being overwhelmed by bugs. Check with Human Resources to find out how many Support staff left after the last big release. Look at the test logs. Read the mails on the user sites. If no big increase in 3rd-line Support calls (real bugs which have to be checked by the test group) occurred after the last big release but a lot of Support staff left, they were probably badly-prepared. If there were a lot of bugs and a lot of Support resignations/dismissals, then maybe Support took the blame for poor testing.

8. *Do we have a sufficient contractual relationship with our suppliers of subsystems to be sure they will respond in a manner which will not leave us exposed?*

a. Check the contract: are there time limits and penalties? What happens if a customer finds a severity-1 bug in their software tonight? In how much time must they get a patch to you? How big is the risk to your company if they don't?

b. Check the history of your company's relations with that supplier. Have they ever provided a severity-1 fix on time? Do they regularly provide fixes on time? What happened when they failed the last time?

9. *Which of our tests was insufficient?*

a. Review all the 3rd-line support calls and fixes against the tests which should have found them.

b. Identify any trends such as a particularly-buggy or particularly undocumented feature or insufficient time spent performance testing or bugs occurring at a particular time or in a particular configuration.

c. Review the test process model, test plan, and test specifications to identify what changes should have been made to detect the bug. Write a report if only as an *aide-memoire* for the next time.

d. Have the test suite changed and rerun the tests to exhibit the bug(s) in the old release. Run the tests against the new fix.

See also section 9.7.7.

Consider creating a model office environment with copies of both old and new systems completely separate from the operational systems but including copies of all other network-coexisting systems. Once the model office environment has been created and the tests have been run once, switch off the network-coexisting systems not known to be codependent, and re-run the tests. This should allow you to identify if network-coexisting systems are really independent of the existing system:

- The system is installed either in your own or customer organizations.
- A low-traffic time is identified and the cutover made.
- The old system is retained for as long as is considered safe and then decommissioned, and the software archived.
- Bug reports are received from Support. As each bug is received it should be analyzed, and the test which should have found it should be analyzed to see why it didn't and then modified or replaced.
- Tests are analyzed and modified.
- A new release is planned.

# 7

# Testing Processes and Infrastructure

## If at First You Don't Succeed, Then Bungee Jumping's Not for You

There is a company in Seattle. It makes, among other things, operating systems. One of them is called DOS. It wanted to make a better one. It tried. It was quite proud of its second attempt, and asked an Internationally Big Manufacturer to test it. For technical reasons (in which the phrase "*not with a bargepole*" appeared) the testing was subcontracted to a British software house. The results were predictable and unwelcome. Much blood was washed out of Seattle carpets, and attempts numbers 3.0 and 3.11 were made.

Moral: whenever any manager tells you that what matters is time-to-market and not quality (*"because that's how Microsoft does it"*), remember that that's what some people *say* Microsoft does. And maybe it's in Microsoft's best interests to have competitors throwing badly-tested software onto the market certain in the belief that this way they are "competing head-on with Microsoft." The reality is rather different: in key areas Microsoft tries to get it right before they get it to market. Don't compete head-on with a brick wall.

This section covers the tools and documents you will need to manage and run your tests.

## 7.1 Initiation

### 7.1.1 Test Strategy

Use the test strategy document to hold and refine your overall views of the job, keep a sense of your direction and priorities, and all the rarely-changing stuff. Review it every six months or when something major happens to the project's objectives or environment. See section 8.3 and of course section 1.8.2 for more details.

## 7.1.2　Test Plan

See section 8.5 for more details of a test plan document. Create one for each release (put any rarely-changing stuff in the test strategy document).

Use the test plan to stay focused on the problems of this particular release. Completely rewrite this document for each release or every six months (whichever is sooner). For faster-changing projects consider using a test monitoring document (later in this chapter) instead.

# 7.2　Keeping the Configuration Management System in Order

There are three principal causes of software change:

1. To correct some bug
2. To add some new feature
3. To adapt to a changing environment

It is well known [Hetzel] that corrections are a prime source of bugs. These occur for two reasons:

1. Changes are made to code without such changes being reflected in higher-level specifications. Consequently:
   - The specifications are increasingly inconsistent with the code.
   - It is not possible to analyze the effects of the change.
   - The changes have unforeseen side effects.
   - The change is itself faultily-applied.
2. Changes are made without sufficient reviews or tests.

Keeping your configuration management system in order is critical to defending the development environment against uncontrolled changes. Do this by using:

- Item acceptance reviews
- Testing code changes

## 7.2.1　Item Acceptance Review

Item acceptance reviews are "gates" through which a release, document, or indeed anything about to go under configuration management must pass. On any non-trivial development they are essential. An *item*

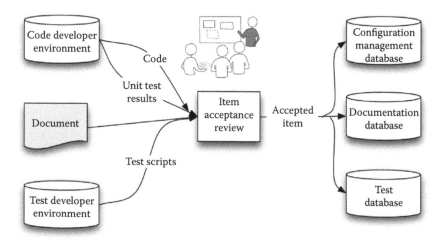

**FIGURE 7.1**　Item acceptance review process

in this context refers to any software including documentation and test scripts, which is maintained under configuration control. This is mostly a configuration management issue but it has been included because such reviews require that the item has been tested and found to be bug-free before the review. The input to the review will normally consist of:

- The written agreement of the design authority that the item be changed.
- The item documentation which may be a cover note describing the item, the changes made, the old and new version numbers, and the person(s) responsible for the authorization and execution of the changes. This documentation is normally in the form of a *Release note* (see Chapter 8).
- The item itself, possibly held on disk in a special secure area and identified by a special filename.
- Any item test results which demonstrate that the item has been tested to some level.
- In the case of large items such as entire subsystems, the reports of configuration or function reviews may be necessary.
- The item tests should it have been necessary to change those as well.
- A checklist which all parties can use to ensure and demonstrate their agreement, that all the required actions have been executed.

The keys to success of item acceptance reviews are preparation and formality. The item acceptance process as indicated by the checklist must have been previously agreed by all parties. If any part of the checklist cannot be signed, it is the responsibility of the moderator either to reconvene the review (if the discrepancies are too large) or to ensure that any minor changes are made and the necessary signatures obtained. A pedantic participant can be worth their weight in gold during such reviews and when well prepared, they can require seven minutes per item or a day per major subsystem.

## 7.2.2 Testing and Reviewing Changes

As a test manager you may have suffered from having changes made arbitrarily and without reference to you. When the project realizes that untested changes are counter-productive, you will be involved in their review and approval. As with all specifications and code, a review is the simplest and most economic way of identifying bugs. This can precede the *Item acceptance review* or (if the change is well understood) can be that review itself. Such a review can be done by one person though it may be even more effective to collect a number of proposed changes together and have them reviewed by several people. These people may have a collective title such as *Change Control Board*. The points to remember are:

- The design authority for the software to be changed must be an approver.
- Include all the specifications which reflect the change, in the review. The simplest approach is to have someone propose the change(s) to the relevant code and documents all together, and then have the reviewers review them from the requirements specifications onwards.
- Ensure that all aspects of the new feature or bug, and all the side effects are considered.
- Formally note the change under the following headings:
  - Change description
  - List of specifications, and units affected, including their version numbers
  - Test documentation, changes required in the test plan, test specifications, procedures, etc.

This approach might appear to be very inflexible and unagile. It doesn't have to be provided:

- The change control board is kept small.
- The process is understood by everyone involved.
- Change meetings are prepared for by the members, so decisions can be taken quickly.
- All changes have been reviewed.

*Agility* rather is *promoted* by *not* leaving hostages to fortune in the form of unforeseen change implications and inconsistent documents. Real agility means changing direction faultlessly.

### 7.2.3  Making and Testing Code Changes

The procedure for making and testing code changes involves the use of two libraries:

1. The personal library of the programmer making the change[1]
2. The system-build library which holds unit-tested code ready for system testing and eventually system-tested code for release and evolution

The procedure is as follows:

- The programmer authorized to make the change obtains a copy of the unit(s), and unit test(s) from the system library, and moves them to the programmer's personal library.
- The changes are made to the code and unit tests as required, and are then unit tested in the programmer's personal library.
- The changed code and unit test results are reviewed by the Change Control Board and are either rejected (in which case the programmer reworks the code to the Change Control Board's satisfaction) or approved, in which case the code is incorporated in the build.
- Any integration tests for the build incorporating the changes are updated and once the build is successfully integration tested, the units are moved into the integration library. Bias the regression-testing parts of the integration tests particularly to exercise the changed units.
- The system tests for the build incorporating the changes are updated and once the build is successfully system-tested, the units are moved into the system build library. To speed the release try using the two charts prepared (see Figure 7.8 and Figure 7.9 for details) to show the system test coverage, such that those tests affecting the changed units can be run immediately after the smoke, confidence and any regression tests. In this way a new release can be made:
  - Unofficially as soon as the changed units have been exercised
  - Officially as soon as the tests have all been run to some level of satisfaction

Complete a system test after an unofficial release since there is always the risk of unexpected side effects.

The test environment should be stable, with all development of the test configuration suspended during testing.

Daily builds *alla Microsoft* are an invaluable means of testing that the automated build scripts work.

## 7.3  Test Environment

Test development, execution, and management are simpler with a test environment. Here's a list of desirable features:

1. **Scheduler.** A place to create, review, display, and send alerts concerning meetings, project deadlines, and tasks to team member's calendars.
2. **To Do** list(s).
3. **Project tasks**, showing:
   a. Deliverables to and from the project
   b. Milestones
   c. Workpackages
   which can be stored, edited, and viewed by all team members.
4. **Requirements management**. This should both interface to existing requirements tools and yet allow testers to enter requirements baseline data for test-group use alone (there may be contractual reasons why the original requirements specification or tool data cannot be changed). Users should have user-definable fields in which to enter requirement data. Requirements can then be assigned to team members. Requirements should be maintained in a central repository along with the history of each requirement's evolution.

---

[1] Assumes no integration testing of compiled units need occur which today is usually the case.

5. **Test case management**. The tool should *support* test case identification and development. Each test case should:
   a. Be traceable to one or more requirements.
   b. Be assignable to a team member.
   c. Relate to at least one test script. If the script detects a bug this should automatically provoke the raising of a bug report.
   d. Have several statuses: { under development I completed I run I passed I failed }. "Failed" will automatically generate a bug record.
   e. Have a change history.
   f. Relate to a feature.
6. **Bug management**. Bug reports are typically raised when a test case fails. The bug report should include details of the case, the script, the baseline, and the test run. The tool should also provide a place to track *support* issues and enhancement requests.
7. **Logging**. The tool should simplify the logging of test run events other than bugs such as the non-availability of an environment, the beginning and end times of test runs, and environment changes.
8. **Reporting**. The tool must provide a number of standard reports and allow users to generate their own. See section 8.18 in Chapter 8.
9. **Document storage**. The tool should function as a central repository for all test documents.
10. **Interface** to test creation toolset.
11. **Import, and export facilities** to enable requirements, test scripts, and documents to be imported, exported, and attached in XML.

Several such environments exist both commercially and as shareware.

# 7.4   Test Automation

Test automation is the development of tests, usually using scripts or special script-generating tools, to simulate user actions on a GUI. This simulation can either test all the features of a GUI using a simulated single user or simulate the behavior of thousands of users executing similar actions in a short time frame in order to test the performance not of the GUI but of the rest of the system when under a load.

## 7.4.1   Why We Should Automate Our Tests

Here are some reasons:

- Some manual tests take a long time to run: if they concern stable features they can be automated.
- End-to end load and performance tests cannot be run without some automation.
- Smoke and confidence tests need to be run fast, possibly overnight, so as to be able to reject a release speedily if it is no good: developers need to know fast if there are problems in a release. With big (> 100 KLOC) systems only automated testing can do this.
- Tests on a large number of configurations need to have a repeatable component to give an early warning of incompatibility.
- Some parts of manual tests can be repetitive, and small automated tests can speed them up greatly.
- Tests involving subtle interactions between user inputs (for example user-entered codes) cannot cover all possible combinations in a timely manner without automation.
- If you can implement several use cases end-to-end, and they will need repeating: automated tests guarantee repeatability.
- Merely writing the automated tests exposes some bugs.
- Test automation can help database population and file generation.
- Some developers write individual automated tests for their own benefit and these can be grouped and reused by testers. Persuading developers and testers to use the same unit, system, and performance test toolset can reap big rewards.

- If the system will have > 3 releases in its life or you need to build a regression suite.
- If some of the features need exhaustive testing. Compilers are good examples.
- If the cost of maintaining the test is high then only automate the bare minimum of features.[2]
- The more tests are automated, the more time is available to keep scripts up-to-date and look for subtle bugs manually. The reverse is also true. Test automation is a constant battle to stay ahead of changes and still find the bugs.

## 7.4.2  Why We Shouldn't Automate Our Tests

Don't automate tests if

- Automating a test can bias test design and construction in favor of automation rather than bug-finding.
- Automated tests don't "see" some quirks a human can see (and only humans can investigate).
- Some testers have little programming expertise.
- Some of the features will be rarely-used and could be left for later.
- Much of the user interface will change.
- There will be few releases and little repetition of manual tests.
- The system uses a lot of special-purpose objects which the tool cannot "see" or which require special programming.
- You cannot (yet) implement any complete end-to-end use of the system by some user (corresponding to a use case perhaps).

## 7.4.3  How Do We Maximize Automated Test RoI?

- Identify the core test actions and automate them first with later variants added as the system evolves.
- Make changes to the tests with spreadsheets full of different data.
- Reduce the tests to a set of individually-callable functions which can be recombined as test sets.

## 7.4.4  When Do We Automate Tests

This is tool-dependent. Plan and design test automation as soon as requirements specifications are available. The outline of a test or a function can often be prepared before the feature is available. Completing the test (which may involve considerable, some or no scripting, depending on the tool) however requires that the system be available.

In the case of system test tools the key issues are:

- Whether the tool can "see" the objects on the screen which it has to manipulate.
- How much effort is required to maintain the test once written. This is tool-dependent. Get your suppliers to demonstrate the tools first.
- How much effort is required to run the test.
- How can the tester can be sure that some action (pressing a screen "button," pulling down a "pull-down") has actually occurred.
- How well does the tool interface with other tools such as Word and Excel.

In the case of performance test tools there are three moments when you should automate:

- As soon as you have some idea of the system's structure you should consider building a demonstration model to show if there are any bottlenecks. This may need the developers to build it for

---

[2] Much effort has been expended by test software companies on ensuring that such a cost remains minimal. The jury remains out on whether they have succeeded in the long term.

you and for you to create the tests. But note that the cost of this work can be balanced against the cost of finding out, rather late, that the system is simply too slow.

- As soon as you have an end-to-end thread available which you can test with. Developer resistance to this may indicate exactly why you need to do it. An end-to-end thread may be unrealistically slow since it contains much unoptimized code but at least it will warn developers how much optimizing remains to be done. And they can remember Michael Jackson's two rules for optimizing:
  - – Don't optimize.
  - – Don't optimize yet.

  This is another good reason for having threaded integration.
- When system testing is almost finished and the code is reasonably stable.

### 7.4.5   What We Would Have to Do to Automate Our Tests

1. **Identify a suitable tool**.
2. **Design the tests.** Some things never change: tests need to be planned and specified as like anything else. Most automated testing tools however provide facilities to let you specify tests long before the test is scripted.
3. **Review the test designs.** You should still be able to use such designs for manual testing at a pinch. Identify one test which is the highest possible priority because it represents the most probably-exercised path through the system. List the other cases in order of priority. Check your priorities with the developers, marketing, and any user representatives. The top-priority tests should be part of the smoke, confidence, and regression test sets.
4. **Automate and run that test** such that it can be copied and modified to provide different use scenarios.
5. **Automate and run the other tests** according to the (revised) priorities.
6. **Consider using a code profiling tool** to assess how much of the code is really exercised by the automated test tool. This will have a delaying effect on the code which may give rise to spurious timing problems.
7. **Document the tests** (minimally) such that:
   a. Each function (*"open a file," "close a file"*) has a simple and obvious name.
   b. A set of tests can be related to a particular build and archived off.
   c. Someone else can run that suite other than the person who wrote it.
   d. A regression suite and set of smoke and confidence tests are identified and maintained.

### 7.4.6   What It'll Cost Us to Automate Our Tests

The cost of test automation can be broken down thus:

- The cost of assessing the tools on the market
- The cost of the tool
- The cost of training staff to use the tool
- The cost of creating the automated tests
- The cost of maintaining the automated tests
- The (possible) cost of a code profiling tool
- The cost of having a special build for use with the code profiling tool
- The cost of assessing the results
- The cost of integrating that tool into whatever dashboard you want to run your tests with

### 7.4.7   How We'll Know if We've Automated Our Tests Successfully?

- When we can show that our test suite exercises all the code (apart from those error messages best tested by hand)

- When we can show that our test suite exercises 100% of the features
- When the test suite finds serious bugs
- When the test suite can be run overnight
- When the test suite can be reused for other scenarios than the ones you thought of at the start
- When we have time at the end of the test cycle to investigate oddities better

## 7.4.8   Open Source GUI Test Tools

Freeware GUI test tools are primarily functional test harnesses except that they automate a graphical user interface. Some rely on other harnesses like xUnit and provide mechanisms for faking mouse and keyboard input, similar to the way the commercial WinRunner™ tool interfaces with TestDirector™ (now Quality Center). Only choose an open source GUI tool which supports object-based automation. Then check how many of your objects it *can't* "see."

## 7.4.9   About GUI Testing

Early GUI test tools were "analog" in that that they recorded mouse movements using X-Y screen coordinates alone. Analog capture and replay of test scripts requires much maintenance to the extent of rewriting all the test scripts whenever there is a change to the GUI. Analog scripts may also be sensitive to changes in screen resolution, color depth, and where the window is placed on the screen.

Later GUI test tools were object-based and recognized many of the objects in a graphical application, like buttons, menus, and text input widgets, and referred to them symbolically rather than by screen coordinates. This technique was more resilient to changes in the GUI design, screen resolution, etc., though the tests still needed to be changed if a GUI control changes; additionally some controls were often not recognized if the developers used custom-developed controls or a toolkit that the tool cannot understand. Object-based tools can also use style-style screen coordinates if necessary.

A newer idea is "keyword-driven" testing in which test data is specified as with data-driven testing, but which also uses pre-defined keywords to define actions for a test case to take. The keywords represent a very simple specification language that non-programmers may be able to use directly to develop automated tests. You still need automation engineers to implement the things that the keywords do and with that comes all the usual issues of GUI automation.

Keyword-driven tests tend to employ "Wizards" to create functions. These "Wizards" generate code. If you want to maintain your functions or do anything clever with them you may still need to write code.

## 7.4.10   Libraries

Test-script maintenance can be reduced by creating a library of GUI object functions such as *"open a file", "Close a file", and "Write to a field(x)"*; thus, when the application changes, only the changed object's function needs to be changed.

## 7.4.11   Data-Driven Tests

Most commercial tools allow you to create scripts and then populate them from a spreadsheet or database with run-specific data such as "employee name", "employee address", etc. Each test run can thus simulate the entry of different data. This is where test automation shows big RoI.

## 7.4.12   Multiple-Function Test Tools

A new generation of test tools can be used for unit, system, and performance tests. They can also be used for HTML and link checking. This can save considerable time at the price of requiring some organization.

## 7.5  Monitoring Test Progress

You have to deal with 6 issues when monitoring test progress:

1. How much test coverage do we need? See section 2.8.
2. How many tests do we need to write to achieve that level of coverage? See section 18.12.
3. How many tests have been written?
4. How many tests have been run? See section A.6 in Appendix A.
5. How many bugs have been found?
6. Have we found as many as we expected? See section 18.10.

### 7.5.1  Test Monitoring Document

Create a spreadsheet such as the *Test monitoring document* in section 8.6 for daily use. Keep it on your lap-top and use it at meetings. It should tell you:

- The expected and actual number of tests to be developed
- The expected and actual number of tests run
- The proportion of units of a release that have been tested
- The number of system features tested
- The priority of each feature
- The test coverage of each feature
- Bugs found per feature
- Bugs found to date (*expected* against *actual*)

### 7.5.2  Test Objectives

The details of tests can confuse. Ensure each test has a simple title by which you can recognize it. This will enable you to connect the test to the strategic question you are trying to answer and act as a placeholder for the test architect.

As tests are planned, relate them using the test objectives in your spreadsheet and group them by feature. See section 8.8.3, sections 14.4 and 14.5.1, section A.1, section A.3, and section A.11.7 in Appendix A for examples of the sources and types of test objectives.

### 7.5.3  Test Scripts

Manual test scripts are best kept in a test management tool. Alternatively they can be prepared in a spreadsheet for later importation into a test management tool. Automated test scripts need to be reviewed and configuration-managed. Both manual and automated scripts can be reused by being assembled into "runs" or batches, covering a set of objectives, a use case, or a scenario.

Keep test scripts configuration-managed: you may find that you may need more than one version of each in order to create different test packs for different releases.

## 7.6  Bug Management Process and Tool

The bug-management process (Figure 7.2) will typically have 7 stages. All should be tool-supported:

1. **Execute tests or reviews.** Testers run system and/or unit tests and gather results. Note that it is usually pointless bureaucracy to record unit test failures of the unit tests executed by developers. Only when a unit test fails on submission to configuration management is it worth recording. The unit tests should occur before the unit is submitted for configuration management and the unit should never be admitted if the unit fails.

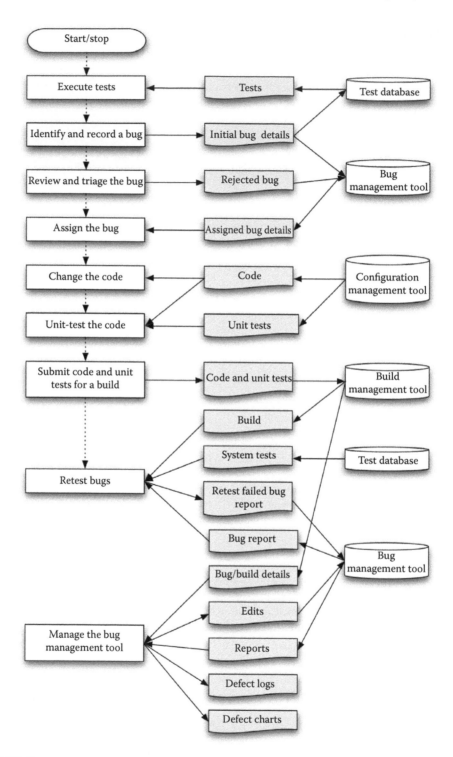

**FIGURE 7.2** Bug management process

2. **Identify and record bugs.** Testers analyze the results, identify bugs, and submit a *bug report* (see Chapter 8 for an example). Note that everyone in a project should be free to submit bug reports. This has several advantages:
   a. All whinges can be dealt with in the project manager's time.
   b. Verbal whinges can be quickly repressed: *write it up in a bug report!*
   c. Everyone knows how to get a whinge answered.
   d. The project manager can direct all bugs to a deputy.
   e. Field or customer-discovered bugs are included along with developer- and tester-discovered bugs. It is more likely in this way that patterns of bugs will emerge.
3. **Review and triage bugs.** Bug reports are reviewed by the test manager, the project manager, the design authority, the configuration manager, a user representative, and possibly senior developers. There are various outcomes:
   a. The bug is confirmed.
   b. The bug severity is changed because it has been mis-classified. See Appendix C.
   c. The bug is assigned a priority. This simply determines the speed with which it will be fixed and is usually related to the degree to which the bug delays testing. It is not necessarily related to bug severity.
   d. The bug is confirmed but cannot be resolved by the developers — it may be in the compiler or in some COT software which will not be changed in time. The user representative and management agree that the bug exists and must remain unfixed.
   e. The bug is confirmed but is being addressed in a bug-management plan which will become operative at a later date.
   f. The bug report is rejected for the following reasons:
      i. The bug is already raised. (If bugs are raised by more than one test group then note this: it will help you estimate the number of bugs in the system. See section 18.10.4 in Chapter 18 for more on this.)
      ii. The bug report has been wrongly-raised — the system is working as specified (note that on occasions the specification may be wrong and the rejected bug report can become the basis of a specification change request).
4. **Assign bugs.** The bug is assigned to a developer to fix.
5. **Fix and unit-test bugs.** The developer makes the fix, unit-tests it, updates the headers in the various code files which have been changed, and marks the bug as ready for inclusion in the next "build." The configuration manager will then incorporate the changed code in the next "build." The change may also require changes to user documents and these should be reviewed too.
6. **Retest bugs.** After finishing the smoke and confidence tests, the system test team retests the unit-tested bug fixes, and marks them as either "closed" (if the bug no longer appears) or "open" otherwise. For bug-fix-only releases this will then be followed by a regression test.
7. **Manage bug database.** The bug management tool manager:
   a. Identifies all the unit-tested bug fixes to be included in the next *build*
   b. Monitors the state of unit-tested bug fixes in the present *build* to ensure they are tested as early as possible
   c. Generates bug logs and bug charts
   d. Lists the rarely-occurring, irreproducible, but potentially-dangerous problems
   e. Looks for patterns of, and in bugs
   f. Issues an updated bug metrics log

This is a simple bug cycle and the one you evolve will probably differ. One probable cause of such a difference is the use of the change request, whereby all bug reports authorized to be fixed have that authorization embodied in a change request form, thus uniting the flow of information from bugs, with that deriving from customer- or other-inspired changes. Other changes may derive from differing terms used by the tool supplier.

### 7.6.1 Tracking Bug Reports

Testing is the prime means of providing objective information both about the quality of the software as well as the process that produced it. To save time it is essential that all bugs and accompanying fixes, as well as any enhancements, are tracked on a database. See Appendix D for details of some commercially-available ones.

### 7.6.2 Bug-Tracking Graphs

The bug reporting database should also be able to produce graphs showing:

- The expected number of bugs found and their type
- The actual number of bugs found and their type
- The number of bugs fixed
- The length of time some bug has been in the software
- The number of outstanding bugs discovered over one month ago but not yet fixed
- The cause of each bug. See Appendix C for a classification scheme
- Which units have the most bugs

Quite apart from the reassurance such graphs can give to senior management, they can also provide considerable reassurance to project management and staff. The sorts of graphs which can be obtained are shown in Figure 7.3, which is a chart of the bugs accumulated during a typical system testing phase over a period of twenty-five days. The curve forms an S-shape of which the beginning and the end show: first the difficulty normally experienced in running tests for the first time and secondly; that by the end of the cycle very few bugs are being found.

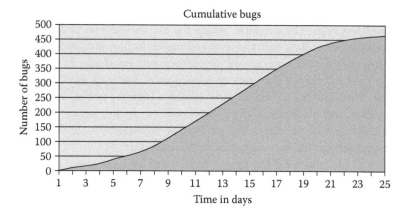

**FIGURE 7.3** Cumulative bugs chart

Figure 7.4 shows the bugs and fixes occurring on a project during the system testing period. The discrepancy between the two curves shows that insufficient effort is being applied to bug fixing. This will delay the next system-test phase unless corrected.

Figure 7.5 shows the bugs and fixes occurring on a project during the system testing period. The discrepancy between the two curves up to day 18 shows that insufficient effort had been applied to bug fixing and that this had then been rectified.

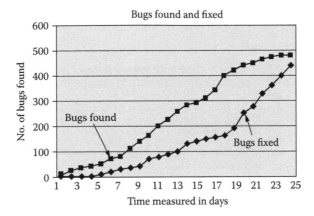

**FIGURE 7.4** Chart showing cumulative bugs and fixes

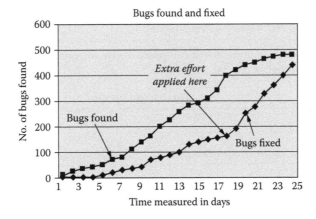

**FIGURE 7.5** Chart showing cumulative bugs and fixes with the addition of extra effort from day 18

Figure 7.6 shows the bugs found during the system testing period ordered by priority; eleven priority-1 bugs have been found.

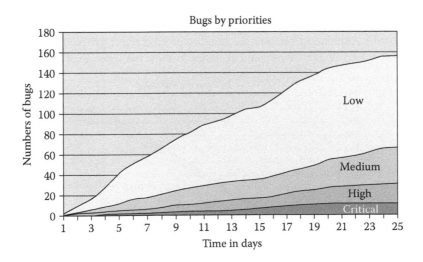

**FIGURE 7.6** Chart showing cumulative bugs found, split out by priorities

Figure 7.7 shows the bugs found and predicted during the system testing period. The slight discrepancy is normal, and can indicate either that the tests are more successful than expected or that the estimates were a little optimistic.

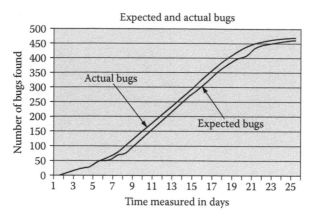

**FIGURE 7.7**  Chart showing bugs found and bugs predicted

Figure 7.8 shows that the system under test is composed of five features and that all the system tests are expected to be run by the end of day 24.

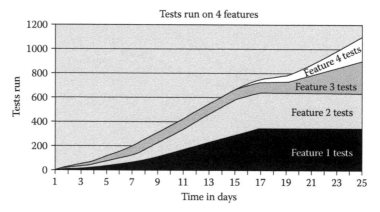

**FIGURE 7.8**  Proportions of system tests run on 5 features

Figure 7.9 shows the relationship between the number of units executed successfully and otherwise, throughout a system test. Similar charts could be drawn to show the coverage of statements or features.

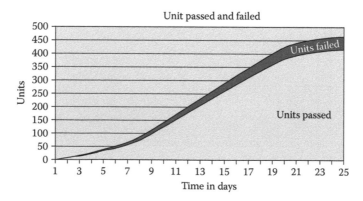

**FIGURE 7.9**  Proportion of units executed with and without bugs

From this relationship it can be seen that only some seventy-one units are buggy (13%). These units can then be analyzed as discussed below to see whether the bug lay in the coding or the design, if for example the buggy units are more complex than those without a detected bug, what kind of unit they were, what sort of bugs predominated, whether a particular sort of test tended to find a particular kind of bug. This in turn will lead to some replanning and divergence of effort to ensure that the unit tests are changed to find those bugs.

## 7.6.3 Bug Analysis

As tests are run, a quality profile of the software can be developed. Quality profiles using analyzers may be run on the software before testing but it is as the software is being tested that the software's behavior and the importance of the tool-derived profiles become evident.

It is useful to distinguish between bugs, and failure. A *failure* is only the expression of the existence of one or more bugs. A failure is what we see: for example when a radio starts to smoke. The bug which causes the smoke lay in plugging the aerial into the power point.

Bugs can be analyzed using the following headings:

1. What kind of bug? Use [Beizer 3] or Appendix C to classify the bugs.
2. Where was the bug made? In a specification? In a manual? In the code? The answer to this question helps answer several others:
   a. Which units have the greatest number of bugs?
   b. Is there any correspondence between the most bug-laden units, and any other unit characteristics such as complexity (see section 18.8.4), size, or number-of-changes?
   c. Which units/interfaces/features should be most heavily tested?
   d. Is any (part of any) specification particularly bug-related?
   e. Which variables have provoked the bug to throw a failure?
3. When was the bug made? In which phase of the project was the bug committed? (See Table 7.1 for an illustration.) This can show:
   a. How many bugs have persisted through two or more phases,
   b. Which reviews or tests failed to find the bug.
4. Who made the bug (and using what tools)? Which groups, individuals, and environments were involved? Note that a degree of collective responsibility is required: it is pointless blaming some programmer for a bug in some unit if that unit has been reviewed. Similarly if bugs can be traced to the use or non-use of some tool, such a relationship can provide management with new insights.
5. What was done wrong? This can be partly answered by using the classification shown in Appendix C. A fuller answer can be derived from the following questions:
   a. Why was the bug made? Answers to this question are central to improving the software project process. See section 15.7.1 as a means of analyzing the operations most likely to expose bugs. Those bugs remaining in the system for more than one phase provoke the further question: why wasn't the bug found earlier?
   b. In which phase was the bug made?
   c. How often should the bug have been caught by a test?
   d. Which test(s) should have caught it?
   e. Which review should have caught it?
   f. Which bugs were related to it?
   g. Which test group found it (if there is more than one)?
6. Which program constructs have to be changed most frequently? (See section 13.6 for more on this).
7. What is the relationship between the bugs? (An analysis of the circumstances likely to cause the bug. See section 15.7.1 for an example.)
8. What could have been done to prevent this bug? This is an antidote to the pious hand-wringing that frequently succeeds a major problem.

9. Which test approach (could have) found this bug? The answers to this question help us decide:
   a. Which testing methods are most effective at finding what kind of bug
   b. (When the system is in use) Which kinds of bugs we failed to find and which kinds of extra tests are needed

By setting up a system to answer such questions well before testing begins, management has the information required:

- To make tactical decisions during the testing and support phases
- To make strategic decisions during the planning phase of the next project
- To justify such choices to senior and customer management

## 7.6.4 Bug Source Table Example

From the bug details to the bug management database you can create a pivot table in Excel as shown in Table 7.1. This partial table shows that 45% of critical bugs are being introduced by design and 50% are being introduced by coding.

Trap the data as it is created, typically at bug triage sessions where those most-knowledgeable are together.

**TABLE 7.1**  Where the bugs spring from

| Count of features affected | | Severity | | | |
|---|---|---|---|---|---|
| Feature affected | Created in activity | Critical | High | Medium | Low |
| AE: Coding | Coding | 12 | 11 | | 2 |
| | Design | 1 | 7 | 2 | 1 |
| | Requirements definition | 1 | 4 | | |
| AE: Create/Save/ Delete | Coding | 5 | 5 | | 3 |
| | Design | 7 | 16 | 1 | 4 |
| | Requirements definition | 2 | 1 | | 1 |
| AE: Display | Coding | 2 | | | 2 |
| | Design | 2 | 4 | 1 | 3 |
| AE: Menu | Coding | 1 | 4 | | |
| | Design | | 1 | 1 | 4 |
| | Requirements definition | | 1 | 1 | |

## 7.6.5 Bug Detection Effectiveness

A more-detailed analysis shown in Table 7.2 demonstrates that although the requirements review was fairly effective (thirty-nine bugs found out of sixty-four), the architecture design review ($43/(64 + 106 - 39)$) was not. On deployment sixty-six bugs were found out of a total of 374 so the bug elimination level (or overall bug removal effectiveness) *so far* is 82%. Note that:

- You will be unable to complete this table until the release to which it refers is removed from service. Only then can any deployment (field) bugs be totaled.
- The table assumes that at each stage the bugs discovered at a previous stage have been removed.

Calculate the bug detection effectiveness as shown in Figure 7.10.

$$\textit{Quality gate effectiveness} = \frac{\textit{Phase total}}{\displaystyle\sum_{\textit{Quality gates reached}} \textit{quality gate total} - \textit{previous phase totals}} \times 100\%$$

**FIGURE 7.10**  Quality gate effectiveness

**TABLE 7.2**    Where the bugs were caught

| Phase/quality gate | Requirements | Design | Coding | Documentation | Phase total | Detection effectiveness (%) |
|---|---|---|---|---|---|---|
| Requirements review | 39 | | | | 39 | 60 |
| Architecture design review | 10 | 33 | | | 43 | 32 |
| Code review | 5 | 55 | 70 | | 130 | 50 |
| System test | 8 | 12 | 66 | 10 | 96 | 59 |
| Deployment | 2 | 6 | 33 | 25 | 66 | |
| Quality gate total | 64 | 106 | 169 | 35 | 374 | |

## 7.6.6   Bug Detection and Injection Analysis

At some point the question will be asked: *"how good are we at finding bugs in the same phase in which we fix them?"* Table 7.3 shows an answer for one project. Each cell in the *Bug Detection (%)* column is calculated using the data from the *Phase Total* column of Table 7.2. Every cell in the *Bug Injection (%)* column is calculated using the data from the *Quality gate total* of Table 7.2. From this table it is evident that the review process is weakest at the coding stage with no review of the documentation occurring at all. System testing only finds 25% of the bugs and many management initiatives are urgently required.

**TABLE 7.3**    Where the bugs were created and caught

| Phase | Bug detection (%) | Bug injection (%) |
|---|---|---|
| Requirements | 10 | 17 |
| Design | 11 | 28 |
| Coding | 34 | 45 |
| Documentation | | 9 |
| System test | 25 | |
| Total | 80 | 100 |

$$Bug\ detection\ \% = \frac{100 \times Phase\ total}{Total\ bugs}$$

**FIGURE 7.11**   Bug detection effectiveness

$$Bug\ injection\% = \frac{100 \times Quality\ gate\ total}{Total\ bugs}$$

**FIGURE 7.12**   Bug injection

## 7.7   Operational Profiles

An operational profile is a quantified characterization of how a system will be used. It helps to ensure that the most-used features of the system are tested and is of great value when testing high-traffic systems. It is also valuable for determining:

- Which functions are the least-likely to be used. If any of these are safety or mission-critical (for example a nuclear shut-down routine) then we can identify these as high-risk/low-use components for special testing.
- Which features to build first (because it is easy to see which will be the most-heavily-used).
- Early that the system has too many operations to be testable (because the combination of operations will be very high and it is in the combinations that the worst bugs hide), and thus influence design decisions.

A profile consists of a set of disjoint alternatives (only one can occur at a time) with the probability that each will occur. If A occurs 60% of the time and B 40%, for example, the operational profile is A = 0.6 and B = 0.4.

It requires some currency such as transactions-per-hour in order that the alternatives can be usefully expressed. See section D.7 in Appendix D for details of some measures and the organizations defining them.

It requires about one person-month to prepare for an "average" project of about 10 developers, 100,000 source lines, and a development interval of 18 months [*Musa 4*].

The process has 6 steps:

1. Find the customer profile.
2. Establish the user profile.
3. Establish risk levels.
4. Define the system-mode profile.
5. Determine the functional profile.
6. Determine the operational profile.

Not all these steps are essential. Any feature change should be reflected as a change to the operational profile.

## 7.7.1 Find the Customer Profile

The customer is the type of institution or business using the system. This may be (for example): schools, hospitals, military, church, retail, manufacturing, and others with proportions of 10%, 21%, 5%, 5%, 25%, 33%, and 1%. This is also known as the customer base.

## 7.7.2 Establish the User Profile

Each customer contains users who will use the system in some form or some way. Each group of users has an occurrence probability of ever being involved with the system. This may vary as the system develops and more customer types are drawn into the system's use. Those people who will never use the system and are unconcerned with it, have an occurrence probability of zero. Some users however may be the customer's customers. Some user types (such as system administrators and operators) may be common across customer types.

At this point it should be possible to generate a table like the one shown in Table 7.4.

TABLE 7.4  Sample user profile

| User group | Customer group 1 probability = 0.6 | | Customer group 2 probability = 0.4 | | Total user group probability |
| | User group probability within customer group | Overall user group probability of customer group | User group probability within customer group | Overall user group probability of customer group | |
|---|---|---|---|---|---|
| Public users | 0.900 | 0.540 | 0.900 | 0.360 | 0.900 |
| Operators | 0.070 | 0.042 | 0.050 | 0.020 | 0.062 |
| System administrator | 0.010 | 0.006 | 0.035 | 0.014 | 0.020 |
| Support desk staff | 0.020 | 0.012 | 0.015 | 0.006 | 0.018 |

### 7.7.3 Establish Risk Levels

Risk is simply the probability of something happening multiplied by the cost if it does. Each outcome of the system will have a risk associated with it. In the case of Word the failure to print a document correctly could be catastrophic if airline pilots depend on that document for their wing de-icing profile or if that document is used by railway signalers to determine which parts of a railway system are "possessed" by a railway company to run trains on and which are "possessed" by railway maintenance staff carrying out permanent-way repairs.

Each feature and mode in a system will thus have a risk level. The operational mode levels will usually dominate. Thus training mode is less risky than the operational.

### 7.7.4 Define the System-Mode Profile

Systems operate in various modes: start-up, "normal" use, shut-down, training. A system-mode profile is the set of system modes and their associated occurrence probabilities. In each mode a system will allow users to use some set of functions. Many of these will be common to more than one mode. Each system mode will therefore have an operational (and possibly a functional) profile. Systems may change mode according to environment such as traffic levels. The basis on which systems can change mode needs to be established.

System modes aren't necessarily disjoint: thus one user may be in training mode, while another uses the system, and a third acts as an administrator performing non-exclusive operations. For each user group you then define the system-mode profile (see Table 7.5).

**TABLE 7.5**   Sample system-mode profile

| System mode | Occurrence probability |
|---|---|
| Business use | 0.756 |
| Personal use | 0.144 |
| Operators | 0.062 |
| System administrator | 0.020 |
| Support desk staff | 0.018 |

### 7.7.5 Determine the Functional Profile

Each mode will consist of a number of features or functions to which some user group will have access. Hopefully, these are defined in the requirements specification but could (at a pinch) be redefined (as shown in section 8.2) from a manual. These can be related to a process model of the system such that the functions being accessed can be shown along with their probability (Figure 7.13).

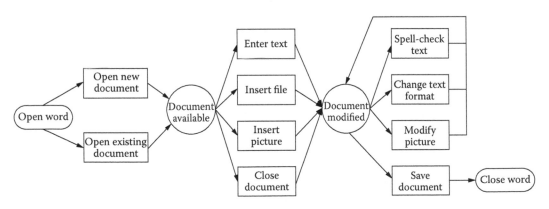

**FIGURE 7.13**   Product use process model

Some functions should be duplicated: mission- or safety-critical functions might exist in training and operational modes. Each will thus need quite different approaches to testing.

Each function will have a number of parameters, each with a range of values. Some will dominate processing more. Thus for example in Word, the "Ctrl+n" feature is used where $n$ = { P(rint) | A(ll) | S(ave) | F(ind) | ... }. This will have a big effect on document structure. Conversely changing the typeface of the "Normal" style involves little processing other than a lot of inheritance but has as many values as Word has typeface files.

Testing (in Word) thus requires at least that you use:

- Ctrl+$n$, where $n$ = { O(pen) | P(rint) | A(ll) | S(ave) | F(ind) | N(ew document) ... }
- Normal style (typeface = { Ariel | Times New Roman | OpenSymbol | Bodoni Ornamental }).

Input variables such as "Ctrl+$n$" are key input variables. These differentiate one function or operation from another. Additionally each interacts with another. The probability of a user hitting "Ctrl+S(ave)" is heavily dependent on their having hit "Ctrl+O" first. Conversely there is no reason (other than aesthetic) why a user should choose "Helvetica" rather than "Ariel." Each must be tested for and thus each will form an explicit operational profile (with every variable). Conversely changing the Normal style typeface requires an implicit operational profile (with sample variables).

The distinction between implicit and explicit operational profiles is important because implicit profiles are usually much smaller and manageable.

**TABLE 7.6**  Sample explicit functional profile

| Input state | Occurrence probability |
|---|---|
| Ctrl+S | 0.42 |
| Ctrl+O | 0.21 |
| Ctrl+N | 0.12 |
| Ctrl+F | 0.07 |
| Ctrl+A | 0.06 |
| ... | ... |

Implicit profiles require far fewer variables: the sum of all examples from all sets of interest. Explicit profiles by contrast require the product of all possible key input variables. This can get big (Table 7.6). Create a key input variable matrix (Figure 7.14) to see which interact and how. Include the environmental and configuration variables in this. In this matrix key inputs (in this case MS Word commands) are shown in column and row. The figure should be read like this:

Ctrl+S (First) can be followed by Ctrl+O (Second)

because there is a "1" in cell D3. Thus it is normal to be able to open a document after having saved another.

Ctrl+V (First) cannot be followed by Ctrl+C (Second)

because there is an "−" in cell H9 and because it is impossible to copy something without choosing it first (ignore the possible use of the mouse in this example).

Note that in Word v.x we can close a document with the *Find* window open. It is then impossible to open another document. This is a bug.

Note that this table could have been written in the form of a state machine. In addition the variables shown here are very few. If there were many more variables affecting the change of state, some other means of defining them would be required.

If some sets of key input variables interact, those sets can be used to define explicit operational subprofiles. Then each subprofile can be used as a key input variable with an associated occurrence probability together with those key input variables that are independent of it, to determine an implicit operational profile.

| ◇ | A | B | C | D | E | F | G | H | I | J | K |
|---|---|---|---|---|---|---|---|---|---|---|---|
| 1 | | | | | | Second | | | | | |
| 2 | | In the context of MS "Word" | *Ctrl + S* | *Ctrl + O* | *Ctrl + N* | *Ctrl + F* | *Ctrl + A* | *Ctrl + C* | *Ctrl + V* | *Ctrl + F* | |
| 3 | First | *Ctrl + S* | | 1 | 1 | 1 | 1 | – | 1 | 1 | |
| 4 | | *Ctrl + O* | 1 | | 1 | 1 | 1 | – | 1 | 1 | |
| 5 | | *Ctrl + N* | 1 | 1 | | 1 | 1 | – | 1 | 1 | |
| 6 | | *Ctrl + F* | 1 | 1 | 1 | | 1 | – | 1 | 1 | |
| 7 | | *Ctrl + A* | 1 | 1 | 1 | 1 | | 1 | 1 | 1 | |
| 8 | | *Ctrl + C* | 1 | 1 | 1 | 1 | 1 | | 1 | 1 | |
| 9 | | *Ctrl + V* | 1 | 1 | 1 | 1 | 1 | – | | 1 | |
| 10 | | *Ctrl + F* | – | – | – | – | – | – | 1 | | |

**FIGURE 7.14** Key input variable matrix

## 7.7.6 Environmental Variables

Identify all environmental variables, identify those which have the largest effects, and add them. In the Word example a major environmental variable might be the operating system { Mac OS | Windows | UNIX }. Another might be the loads under which the system will normally and exceptionally operate.

## 7.7.7 Occurrence Probabilities

There are several sources of usage probabilities:

- System logs
- Special-to-type user profiles created by recording user keystrokes
- Error reports
- Process models
- Surveys
- System logs (particularly if the system involves file transfer)
- Estimation

This will be less than useful for systems which have yet to be fielded. In such cases look for analogous systems (possibly the one to be replaced) and, by identifying the critical use cases, identify functions of interest. Each use case can be thought of as a set of functions. Table 7.7 is an example from a temporary services agency about install a new system. From these scenarios (two of which are themselves functions — log-in and log-off) we can identify the probability of calling each function.

**TABLE 7.7** Scenario probability of occurrence for an employment agency

| | Annual Total | Percent | User mode (80%) | Admin mode (20%) | Mac OS (15%) | Windows (85%) |
|---|---|---|---|---|---|---|
| Create candidate | 1, 800,000 | 10.81 | 8.65 | 2.16 | 1.62 | 9.19 |
| Create vacancy | 188,000 | 1.13 | 0.90 | 0.23 | 0.17 | 0.96 |
| Assignment | 180,000 | 1.08 | 0.87 | 0.22 | 0.16 | 0.92 |
| Short list | 188,000 | 1.13 | 0.90 | 0.23 | 0.17 | 0.96 |
| Application | 658,000 | 3.95 | 3.16 | 0.79 | 0.59 | 3.36 |
| Check candidate has started | 180,000 | 1.08 | 0.87 | 0.22 | 0.16 | 0.92 |
| Vary match criteria | 18, 800 | 0.11 | 0.09 | 0.02 | 0.02 | 0.10 |
| Temp to perm | 18,000 | 0.11 | 0.09 | 0.02 | 0.02 | 0.09 |
| Change details | 630,000 | 3.78 | 3.03 | 0.76 | 0.57 | 3.22 |
| Logon | 6, 302,000 | 37.86 | 30.29 | 7.57 | 5.68 | 32.18 |
| Logoff | 6, 302,000 | 37.86 | 30.29 | 7.57 | 5.68 | 32.18 |
| Request P45 | 180,000 | 1.08 | 0.87 | 0.22 | 0.16 | 0.92 |
| | | 100 | 80 | 20 | 15 | 85 |

### 7.7.8   Determine the Operational Profile

The three steps in creating the operational profile are:

- Dividing the test set into runs.
- Identifying the input space.
- Partitioning the input space into operations.

### 7.7.9   Divide the Test Set into Runs

A *run* (in this case) approximates to a scenario in some environment in some system mode. It will normally achieve some user goal (such as printing a document). It is advantageous to define *runs* such that they begin and end at the same logical point (typically with "no document open" if the purpose of the system is document processing) or with minimal interaction between *runs* and can thus be linked if required.

Each *run* will have an associated set of variables and test data. These should determine a unique path through the system's code. The importance of the *runs* (and therefore the time to be spent testing them) depends on the importance of the outcomes of that *run* (or the scenario on which it is based). Look in the error reports of comparable systems for outcomes You Really Don't Want.

### 7.7.10   Identify the Input Space

The program's input space consists of all the inputs it can receive. This should also include illegitimate inputs. This can become extremely large even if limited by section 2.2 in Chapter 2. Once you have identified the input space you will use, look at the inputs you won't use, and try and see if any are critical. Note that the input space is critical to defining parameters for Fault injection as discussed in Chapter 13.

The criteria for deciding on the number of inputs are ultimately the risk that a failure could represent. This risk can be broken down into such issues as section 16.8 in Chapter 16 and the possibility that features interact. This is a matter of engineering judgment.

### 7.7.11   Partition the Input Space into Operations

You can further limit the input space in 4 ways:

- **By relating it to the operations of interest.** The run types you have defined should share the input space, to speed testing. Essentially there is a trade-off between a big operational profile and an efficient test run. "Efficient" in this context means maximizing the possibility of finding bugs by exercising more features rather than a greater range of variables.
- **By input variable ranges.** We can, with some study, identify that some variables dominate within a range or that they are non-uniformly distributed. Where we find such distributions we can divide the runs by input space range.
- **By failure homogeneity.** This means that within that range one failure (as determined by failure behavior) is similar to another. Such failures will usually exercise the same code. The smaller the run, the greater the homogeneity and the cost.
- **By risk.** Irrespective of the probability that they be used, high-risk features must be thoroughly tested. Lower risk levels can however be used to determine testing priorities.

### 7.7.12   Random Acts of Politically-Motivated Testing

The following should be randomized:

- Data (within the required range), to avoid bias.
- Test ordering, to minimize any possibility of order-effect bias. Thus in the case of testing Word, there is value in trying "Ctrl+S"(ave) before "Ctrl+O"(pen) or "Ctrl+N"(ew) to ensure that the system displays the right error message.

See [Musa 4] for more on this.

## 7.8 Static Analyzers

Static analyzers operate on source code and enhance the testing process by analysis of the code and diagnosis of possible bugs before any testing actually takes place. Typical functions are cross-referencing, the detection of undeclared or unused variables, adherence to the generally-accepted or locally-declared coding standards, and code complexity analysis (usually McCabe's [see section 18.8.4] or knot analysis). A common example of a static analyzer is lint, which analyzes C code and is provided with every UNIX system.

### 7.8.1 Lexical and Syntactic Analysis

Static analysis begins by undertaking lexical and syntactic analysis of the source code. A useful test tool will produce a reference listing as shown in Figure 7.15, which is an output of an ADA program showing the source code reformatted to the test tool reformatting standards with a line number for each statement line. This file is the reference for all other outputs of the test tool, which refer to the generated line numbers and associated reformatted statements.

```
1          With TEXT IO
2          use TEXT IO
3
4          procedure TRIANGLE is
5          type MY INT is new INTEGER range 0. . 1000;
6
7          package INOUT INT is new TEXT IO. INTEGER IO(MY INT);
8          use INOUT INT;
9          I, J, K, MATCH: MY INT;
10
11         begin
12             loop
13             PUT("input: THREE NUMBERS (O TO FINISH)");
14             GET(I);
15             if
16                 I = O
                   ...
```

**FIGURE 7.15** Example of a test tool reference listing

### 7.8.2 Programming Standards Violations

Some test tools will search source code for possible programming standards' violations using the relevant language standards. The reporting of any particular violations is optional; and you can define violation penalty marks. Thus static analysis will typically produce a total penalty award for the analyzed source code. This information is listed in the management summary (see Figure 7.16) which also contains the results from complexity analysis (see section 18.8.4), and dynamic analysis in a summary form. Figure 7.16 is a typical management summary report from static analysis: note the reported standards violations and the associated penalty.

### 7.8.3 Test Path Analysis

*Static analysis* also produces an analysis of the test paths (sub paths) contained in the source code. Test paths can be defined as LCSAJs (Linear Code Sequence & Jumps) and each is a sequence of code (a linear code sequence) followed by a control-flow jump (see Figure 7.17).

   LCSAJ coverage is used in dynamic analysis as a rigorous measure of program execution. The concept is language-independent, requiring only that the program reformatting allows them to be expressed in terms of unambiguous statement line numbers. This is undertaken by a static analysis reformatter. See section 12.4 for more on this.

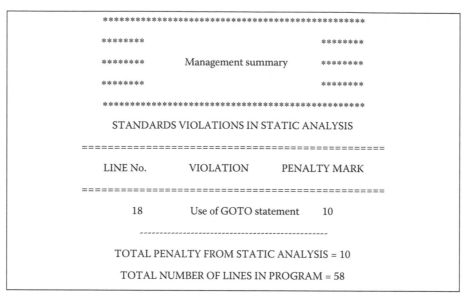

**FIGURE 7.16** Example of a tool management summary

| START | FINISH | LINE No. | STATEMENT | LCSAJ DENSITY |
|---|---|---|---|---|
| | | | ... | |
| START | | 12 | loop | 4 |
| | | 13 | PUT("INPUT THREE NUMBERS (O TO FINISH)"); | 4 |
| | | 14 | GET(I); | 4 |
| | | 15 | if | 4 |
| | | 16 | I = O | 4 |
| | FINISH | 17 | then | 4 |
| | | | ... | |
| | | NUMBER OF LCSAJs IN PROGRAM = 26 | | |

**FIGURE 7.17** Extract from a test path analysis listing showing an LCSAJ

## 7.8.4 Test Coverage Problems

Example: we have a system composed of 5 units and 3 primary features. We can insist that the developers achieve 100% statement coverage of the units. But the tests don't evaluate all the conditions, don't check if the loop conditions terminate, and don't evaluate all logical operators. So we want to exercise all decisions. The IF statement in Figure 7.18 can be satisfied if A and B are true. C is not *necessarily* ever evaluated.

```
IF A & (B, or C)
THEN  D
ELSE E
```

**FIGURE 7.18** Faulty decision coverage evaluation

We can continue this example showing increasingly-complex kinds of measures until we realize:

- The unfeasibility of some paths (see section 12.4)
- A level of unit test complexity such as that shown in Figure 18.29 and the number of executable paths calculated in the equation Figure 18.28

At some point we see that some limit must be set on unit testing and we turn to feature testing. We know that simply testing every GUI element will not show the interactions between the elements and be unrealistic in that no user spends their time simply exercising GUI elements. So we look at scenarios or "paths through the software." And we quickly discover that these are as infinite as the data combinations we might use.

Conclusion: at some point there are no algorithms to guide you and you must use judgment based on risk. If you have read the specifications and/or contract you must have a fairly good idea of the risk involved and the kinds of coverage you will need to be as sure as possible of finding bugs.

## 7.8.5 Structured Programming Verification

This requires a user-defined template to match permitted language constructs against those contained in the subject program (example: IF THEN ELSE ENDIF). A standard template is often supplied with structured programming verification tools which describes the constructs defined by or appropriate to the language, and you can alter it to recognize those used by your group. Templates may contain simple and optional graphs. Figure 7.19 shows some ADA constructs.

```
PROGRAMMING VERIFICATION WILL USE THE FOLLOWING STRUCTURES
-------------------------------------
SIMPLE COLLAPSE
REPEAT
CASE
WHILEDO
IF THEN
IF THEN ELSE
FORLOOP
```

**FIGURE 7.19**  Structured program verification definition (ADA)

Using the templates, all acceptable types of language constructs contained in the program are recognized. The program is said to be properly structured if its graph reduces to a single node after these acceptable constructs have been removed.

Some test tools will also report McCabe's *Essential Complexity* metric, which will exceed unity if the subject program is not properly structured. *McCabe's Essential Complexity* metric is obtained by applying the formula (see section 18.8.4) to the residual graph.

The number of *Essential knots* is also given as a measure of unstructuredness. A structured program will have no essential knots.

Figure 7.20 is an example of a complexity analysis summary.

| \multicolumn{11}{COMPLEXITY ANALYSIS PRODUCES THE FOLLOWING TABLE OF RESULTS} |
|---|
| PROCEDURE | LINES ANLSD | BASIC BLOCKS | AVGE LENGTH | ORD1 INTRVLS | MAX ORD INTRVLS | REDUCE | MCCABE | KNOTS | ESSNL MCCABE | ESSNL KNOTS |
| TRIANGLE | 56 | 19 | 2.95 | 2 | 2 | YES | 8 | 5 | 1 | 0 |
| TOTAL | 56 | 19 | 2.95 | 2 | 2 | YES | 8 | 5 | 1 | 0 |

THE PROGRAM CONTAINS 1 PROCEDURE
THE ESSENTIAL MCCABE MEASURE OF 1 INDICATES THAT THE PROGRAM IS
PROPERLY STRUCTURED

**FIGURE 7.20**  Example of complexity analysis output

## 7.8.6  Dataflow and Procedure Call Analyzers

Procedure Call Information consists of information about which procedures call each other in a program. Each procedure in the program is analyzed in turn and a list of calls to other procedures (including recursive calls), is produced. If the procedure does not call any procedures, then a message is printed. Figure 7.21 shows an example of some procedure call information.

- Dataflow error messages are produced by the dataflow analyzer, and report the three types of dataflow bugs found grouped by error type: UR, DU, and DD errors. In the example shown in Figure 7.22 each message consists of the variable name, the line number, and type of both parts of the error. If either part occurs as the result of a procedure call, this is indicated, as well as any variables declared, but never used.

```
====================================
PROCEDURE CALL INFORMATION
====================================
--------------------------
THE MAIN PROGRAM
main
CALLS THE FOLLOWING PARAMETERS
getname
bearright
----------------------------
PROCEDURE
getname
BETWEEN LINES 371, and 401
CALLS THE FOLLOWING PROCEDURES
error
IS CALLED BY THE FOLLOWING PROCEDURES
main
-----------------------
PROCEDURE
bearright
BETWEEN LINES 406 and 418
DOES NOT CALL ANY INTERNAL PROCEDURES
IS CALLED BY THE FOLLOWING PROCEDURES
main
-----------------------
```

FIGURE 7.21  Example of a procedure call summary

| THE FOLLOWING VARIABLES WERE DECLARED BUT NEVER USED | | |
|---|---|---|
| VARIABLE | DECLARED ON LINE | |
| T      2 | | |
| VARIABLE | UNDEFINE | REFERENCE |
| Y      2 | 5 | |
| TYPE DU ERRORS | | |
| VARIABLE | UNDEFINE | REFERENCE |
| Z      8 | 9 | |
| TYPE DD ERRORS | | |
| VARIABLE | UNDEFINE | REFERENCE |
| X      4 | 6 | |

FIGURE 7.22  Example of dataflow analysis error messages

For example if the program shown in Figure 13.3 was analyzed by a dataflow analyzer the following messages would be produced.

- Procedure parameter analysis (Figure 7.23) consists of information about the types of use for each parameter of a procedure. Each procedure is analyzed in turn and the types of use of its parameters are determined to detect whether the parameter is
  - Referenced only: its value is used but never changed within the procedure.
  - Defined only: it has a value assigned, but this value is never used.
  - Both referenced and defined.
  - Not used in the procedure.

The analysis is carried across procedure boundaries. Thus a variable, which is passed to one procedure and within this procedure is passed as a parameter to another, will be correctly classified depending on its use in both procedures.

```
====================================
PROCEDURE PARAMETER ANALYSIS
====================================
PROCEDURE ONE
PARAMETER X IS REFERENCED INSIDE THE PROCEDURE
PARAMETER Y IS DEFINED INSIDE THE PROCEDURE
PARAMETER Z IS REFERENCED and DEFINED INSIDE THE PROCEDURE
PROCEDURE TWO DOES NOT HAVE ANY PARAMETERS
```

**FIGURE 7.23** Example of parameter analysis output

### 7.8.7 Cross-Referencer

#### 7.8.7.1 General

Cross-referencers refer to all data items used in a program, identifying the type of use of each data item (global, local, or a parameter), and giving a textual representation of the complete call tree of the program under analysis.

#### 7.8.7.2 Output

The output provided by a cross-referencer includes:

- A call tree of the program under analysis produced on a procedure-by-procedure basis in form of a listing of all the procedures, calling and called
- A cross-reference of all data items used in a program organized on a procedure-by-procedure basis listed as follows:

<item name> <attribute code> <list of line numbers>

The <attribute code> field can be any one shown in Figure 7.24.

## 7.9 Dynamic Analyzers

Dynamic analyzers have two uses. First, they collect data to provide quantitative information concerning test coverage. Second, they can identify those portions of code that are used frequently or rarely during normal execution, thus exposing any potential performance bottlenecks.

```
ATTRIBUTE CODES
L       LOCAL VARIABLE

G       GLOBAL VARIABLE

P       PARAMETER

LG      LOCAL VARIABLE USED AS A GLOBAL IN OTHER PROCEDURES
PROCEDURE MAIN   START LINE 160 END LINE 284
CALLS THE FOLLOWING PROCEDURES
NAME CALLED ON LINE
FDPRES 280
...
RDVARS         276
IS CALLED BY NO OTHER PROCEDURE
VARIABLE USE INFORMATION
NAME   ATTRIBUTE   OCCURS ON LINE
RDVARS LG      1309 1316 1615 15304 1908 1948 2054 2077 2672 2751
PROCEDURE GETNAME
START LINE 292 END LINE 375
CALLS THE FOLLOWING PROCEDURES
NAME CALLED ON LINE
ERRMES        359
...
TRACE 357
IS CALLED BY THE FOLLOWING PROCEDURES
NAME   CALLED ON LINE
APPNAME       423
...
RDVARS     LG 1411 1650 1715 1752 1761 1972 2020 2146 2183 2488 2713
VARIABLE USE INFORMATION
NAME ATTRIB OCCURS ON LINE
BUFF   P              292 341 365
...
START P                292
```

**FIGURE 7.24**  Example of the output of a cross-referencer

Test coverage quantification serves two purposes. First, quality control requirements may include a need to demonstrate that each code path, branch, or statement has been executed in the testing process. Second, dynamic analysis tells the programmer how he is progressing in his testing, and helps him to identify those areas of the code that still need to be addressed.

## 7.9.1  Dynamic Analysis Outputs

*Dynamic analysis* can clearly indicate a program's resilience and therefore its reliability. Some *Dynamic analysis* tools report on the effectiveness of test data using Test Effectiveness Ratios (TERs) as shown in Figure 7.25 through Figure 7.29.

The coverage, i.e., the values of the TERs, can be increased by rerunning the instrumented code with extra, different test data sets.

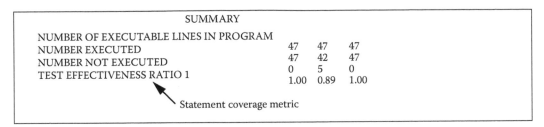

| SUMMARY | | | |
|---|---|---|---|
| NUMBER OF EXECUTABLE LINES IN PROGRAM | 47 | 47 | 47 |
| NUMBER EXECUTED | 47 | 42 | 47 |
| NUMBER NOT EXECUTED | 0 | 5 | 0 |
| TEST EFFECTIVENESS RATIO 1 | 1.00 | 0.89 | 1.00 |

Statement coverage metric

**FIGURE 7.25** Example of statement coverage summary (TER 1)

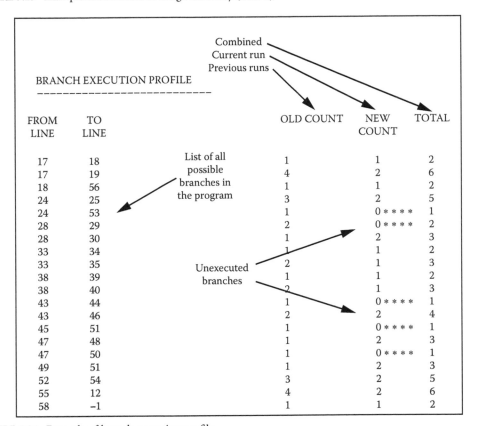

**FIGURE 7.26** Example of branch execution profile

| SUMMARY | OLD COUNT | NEW COUNT | TOTAL |
|---|---|---|---|
| NUMBER OF EXECUTABLE LINES IN PROGRAM | 20 | 20 | 20 |
| NUMBER EXECUTED | 20 | 15 | 20 |
| NUMBER NOT EXECUTED | 0 | 5 | 0 |
| TEST EFFECTIVENESS RATIO 2 | 1.00 | 0.75 | 1.00 |

Branch coverage metric

**FIGURE 7.27** Example of branch execution summary

LINEAR CODE SEQUENCE AND JUMP EXECUTION PROFILE

| FROM LINE | TO LINE | JUMP TO LINE | OLD COUNT | NEW COUNT | TOTAL |
|---|---|---|---|---|---|
| 4 | 17 | 19 | 1 | 1 | 2 |
| 12 | 17 | 19 | 3 | 1 | 4 |
| 4 | 18 | 56 | 0 * * * * | 0 * * * * | 0 * * * * |
| 12 | 18 | 56 | 1 | 1 | 2 |
| 19 | 24 | 53 | 1 | 0 * * * * | 1 |
| 19 | 28 | 30 | 1 | 2 | 3 |
| 19 | 33 | 35 | 1 | 0 * * * * | 1 |
| 30 | 33 | 35 | 1 | 1 | 2 |
| 19 | 38 | 40 | 0 * * * * | 0 * * * * | 0 * * * * |
| 30 | 38 | 40 | 0 * * * * | 1 | 1 |
| 35 | 38 | 40 | 2 | 0 * * * * | 2 |
| 19 | 43 | 46 | 1 | 0 * * * * | 1 |
| 30 | 43 | 46 | 0 * * * * | 0 * * * * | 0 * * * * |
| 35 | 43 | 46 | 0 * * * * | 1 | 1 |
| 40 | 43 | 46 | 1 | 1 | 2 |
| 19 | 45 | 51 | 0 * * * * | 0 * * * * | 0 * * * * |
| 30 | 45 | 51 | 0 * * * * | 0 * * * * | 0 * * * * |
| 35 | 45 | 51 | 0 * * * * | 0 * * * * | 0 * * * * |
| 40 | 45 | 51 | 1 | 0 * * * * | 1 |
| 46 | 47 | 50 | 1 | 0 * * * * | 1 |
| 46 | 49 | 51 | 1 | 2 | 3 |
| 50 | 52 | 54 | 1 | 0 * * * * | 1 |
| 51 | 52 | 54 | 2 | 2 | 4 |
| 53 | 55 | 12 | 1 | 0 * * * * | 1 |
| 54 | 55 | 12 | 3 | 2 | 5 |
| 56 | 58 | −1 | 1 | 1 | 2 |

Unexecuted LCSAJs

List of all the test paths (LXSAJs) in the program)

FIGURE 7.28 Example of test path execution profile

| SUMMARY | OLD COUNT | NEW COUNT | TOTAL |
|---|---|---|---|
| NUMBER OF LCSAJs IN PROGRAM | 26 | 26 | 26 |
| NUMBER EXECUTED | 18 | 12 | 20 |
| NUMBER NOT EXECUTED | 8 | 14 | 6 |
| TEST EFFECTIVENESS RATIO 3 | 0.69 | 0.46 | 0.77 |

Test path coverage metric

FIGURE 7.29 Example of test path execution summary

## 7.9.2 Test Effectiveness

Test Effectiveness Ratios (TERs) 1, 2, and 3 have been defined, where:

$$TER1 = \frac{number\ of\ statements\ exercised\ at\ least\ once}{total\ number\ of\ executable\ statements}$$

$$TER2 = \frac{number\ of\ branches\ exercised\ at\ least\ once}{total\ number\ of\ branches}$$

$$TER3 = \frac{number\ of\ LCSAJs\ exercised\ at\ least\ once}{total\ number\ of\ LCSAJs}$$

The three denominators in the above formulae can be identified during *static analysis* and used as constants in the equations. The numerators are calculated by an inspection of an *execution history* file, generated at run time by the instrumented code. *Coverage* is maximized by running a number of subject program executions with suites of stimulating data. TER 1 and 2 normally reach unity without great effort (although infeasible branches may be discovered), but TER 3 often lags TERs 1 and 2 by some margin, because TER 3 requires a demanding testing strategy to achieve unity. If however, unity can be achieved for TER 3, then the number of undetected bugs remaining in the subject program are substantially reduced.

# 8

# Test Documents

## Call Logged

W hen the test consultant arrived he asked to see a requirements specification. He was met with a blank stare. "You'll have to see the project director about that. You're here to test."

The company made telephone call logging software and was owned by a Big European Corporation.

The test consultant promptly crashed the system twice in two ways creating the blue screen of death each time. People were not pleased.

Then he got some output and wrote a script to analyze it. It showed that telephones were being put down before being picked up and traffic being transmitted to a telephone without it being picked up. He logged each bug.

Then he found several features did not work. By then he had asked several times for a requirements specification and had given up so he wrote up the bug as best he could. By now the staff had stopped talking to each other in his presence.

One morning someone from management came in. "We've got auditors in from Head Office," he said. "Tell them nothing. We're keeping them upstairs at present, but if they ask you anything refer them to the CEO. Fortunately they only speak German."

And no auditor ever appeared.

And a year later the company was sold to an American Corporation for 1.5 million dollars. And (when it realized that it was about to suffer major, indefensible litigation) the Big European Corporation "forgave the debt."

## 8.1 General

The documents outlined in this book are generated by the four essential processes of software testing: test planning, specification, execution, and reporting. In this book however, the documents are generalized to cover the three principal kinds of software tests: System, Integration, and Unit tests.

## 8.2 Requirements Specification

Let us assume that your company has a lot of "sort of" specifications, software, and user manuals but nothing explicit against which you can test. You will need to set your own baseline. Here's how: get a competent technical writer or a literate tester. Grab every document you can and write Testing's own requirements specification. An example *Requirements Specification Table of Contents* is listed in section 8.2.2. And here's how you write it:

1. Take the software out of the box in whatever form it comes and document how you install it. Then starting with the screen you see first, describe everything on it like the example shown in Figure 8.1 (assume that you have found a part of some user guide and are working from that).

---

**Personalized menus**

As an additional feature, Z-System menus now learn from the users about the items they use most often and automatically adapt to provide the user with a personalized menu. You can customize your menus by selecting View > Customize (or by placing the cursor anywhere in the Menu/Toolbar area and right-clicking to display the Customize option). X-System will display the following dialogue:

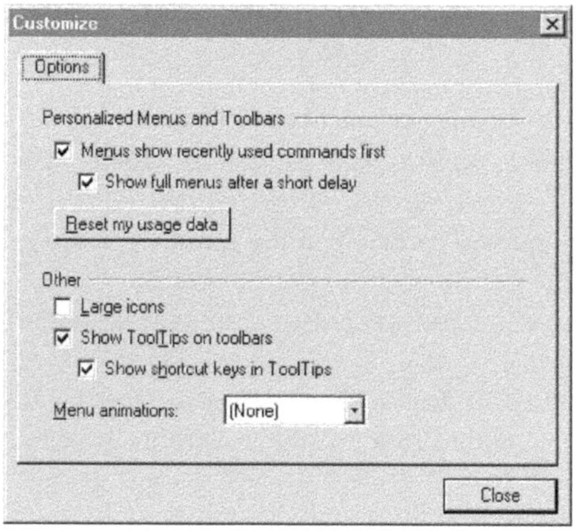

**Figure 1-3 - Customize dialogue**

Make your selections from this dialogue. You may change your customization choices at any time.

---

FIGURE 8.1   Example of a user manual

2. Remember that every single control on every screen has a value (*On/Off, 100 < x > 100*) and a status (*Usable/Greyed out*). See the next section for a way of describing this.
3. In your requirements specification, rewrite the screen and description shown in Figure 8.1 to look like Figure 8.2.
4. Use the notation shown in the next section if it helps or invent your own. If you include screenshots, show the software version number, since interfaces change.
5. Where pressing some button causes some screen to appear (as it usually will), create a separate subsection for that screen, and call it "Dialog Window (<screen name>)," ensuring that <screen name> is what you read on the title bar of the screen. Cross-refer to this section from the button such that you have a line saying something like:

Pressing button (open parasol) brings up screen *3.14.8 Dialog Window (Open parasol)*

6. In Word use the heading levels 7 through 9 for the text so that you have automatic line renumbering. Once the baseline has been released ensure the numbering remains consistent by only adding new sections, sections, subsections etc. immediately before the next highest section. See Figure 8.3.

| 1.1. | Dialog window (Personalized Menus) > Customize (tab(Options) |
|---|---|
| 1.1.1.1 - 1 | X-System menus automatically adapt to provide the user with a personalized menu. You can customize your menus by selecting View > Customize (OR by placing the cursor anywhere in the Menu/Toolbar area and right-clicking to display the Customize option). X-System will display the following dialog: |
| 1.1.1.1 - 2 | Checkbox (Menus show recently-used commands first): the most-recently used commands are displayed at the top of the menu. |
| 1.1.1.1 - 3 | Checkbox (Show full menus after a short delay) Menus are initially displayed with a small double-chevron below and a minimal number of items thereon. After 2 seconds the remaining items are shown and the chevron disappears. |
| 1.1.1.1 - 4 | Checkbox (large icons): keyboard icons are displayed larger. |
| 1.1.1.1 - 5 | Checkbox (Show ToolTips on toolbars): shows a hint message on a yellow field when the cursor is left over the icon for > 2 seconds. |
| 1.1.1.1 - 6 | Checkbox (Show shortcut keys in ToolTips) (only visible if 2.3.4.1 - 5 is checked) |
| 1.1.1.1 - 7 | Dropdown (Menu animations) { None \| Random (menus unfold, or slide open randomly) \| Unfold (menus "unfold" when clicked on) \| Slide (a menu opens whenever one other, or the same menu has been clicked on and the cursor is above it) } |
| 1.1.1.1 - 8 | Button (Reset my usage data): deletes the file concerning the most-recently used menus which is used by 2.3.4.1 - 3. |
| 1.1.1.1 - 9 | The menu items described below are presented in their default arrangement. If you customize your menus to show recently used commands first, the menu options described will not necessarily appear in the same order in your copy of X-System. |

**FIGURE 8.2** Example of a requirements specification

| 1.1.1 | Sub-section | |
|---|---|---|
| 1.1.1.1 | Sub-sub-section | |
| 1.1.1.2 | Sub-sub-section | |
| 1.1.1.3 | Sub-sub-section | |
| 1.1.1.4 | New sub-sub-section | (Goes in here) |
| 1.1.2 | Sub-section | |
| 1.2 | Section | |
| 1.3 | New section | (Goes in here) |
| 2 | Chapter | |

**FIGURE 8.3** Example of where to insert new requirements

## 8.2.1 A Requirements Notation

If no requirements specification or other baseline can be obtained, an emergency solution, mentioned in the last section, is simply to Write Your Own. Do this by starting at whatever entry point you find to access the system (usually *log-in* or even *install*), and then note every possible action using the following notation (for brevity). If nothing else, such an approach will limit the possibility of you testing the same feature twice.

1. Special meanings are often attached to words or symbols such as *shall, will, must,* and [ ].
2. Include references to the source for traceability.

Underlined letters in names refer to the key which is implicitly hit (Table 8.1).

**TABLE 8.1**  A requirements notation of GUI objects

| Symbol/name | Meaning |
|---|---|
| (role chosen + right-click >)Button (Add) | (Example) <u>A</u>dd, <u>D</u>elete, or <u>E</u>dit a role by either choosing the role in the window, and right-clicking on it, and then on the button which is displayed or by simply clicking on the already-displayed button to the right. |
| <keyName1>, <keyName> | Hitting one key after another. |
| <keyName1> + <keyName> | Hitting two (or more) keys simultaneously. |
| … | The preceding item may be repeated. |
| Button (<buttonName>) | A button named <buttonName> such as  OK |
| Button (<buttonName>) with <fieldContents1> + <fieldContents2> + … | When <fieldContents1>, <fieldContents2> are complete <buttonName> can be pressed. |
| Checkbox (<CheckboxName>) | A checkbox like this:  ☑ Check1 |
| child folder | A folder generated by a subprocedure of a procedure. |
| Column (<ColumnName>) | A column in a grid called <ColumnName> and looking like this:<br><br>Column 1 |
| Constraint | Some limitation on the use of the system. |
| Dropdown ({ <pulldownName1> \| <pulldownName2> }) | A dropdown containing a set of items { <pulldownName1> \| <pulldownName2> \| … } of which <pulldownName1 is the visible default> |
| Field (<fieldName>) | A field called <fieldName> looking like this: |
| Flag data | The information that a flag passes. |
| Key (<name>) | Press key <name>: any key such as: A |
| KeyUp | Remove your finger or thumb off the key. |
| Memo (<MemoName>) | A scroll box called <MemoName> like this: |
| menuName1 > menuName2 | Pulling down of one menu after another. |
| MouseUp | Remove your finger or thumb off the mouse key. |
| Tab (<tabName>) | A tab of a window named <tabName> which looks like this:<br><br>\| Notes \| |
| Menu(<menuName1>) | The name of a menu such as "File," "Edit," "View," etc.<br><br>**Word**  File  Edit  View  Ins |
| MenuItem(itemName) | The name of an element in a menu. Thus MenuItem(Open) is:<br><br>File  Edit  View  Insert<br>Project Gallery…<br><br>New Blank Document<br>Open…<br>Open Web Page…<br>Close |

## 8.2.2 Requirements Specification Table of Contents (Figure 8.4)

| | | | |
|---|---|---|---|
| 1 | **Introduction** | 5.2.2 | Understandability |
| 1.1 | Purpose | 5.3 | Performance |
| 1.2 | Scope | 5.4 | Security |
| 1.3 | Background | 5.5 | Timescales |
| 1.4 | Structure of this document | 5.6 | Delivery constraints |
| 1.5 | Definitions, acronyms, and abbreviations | 6 | **System interfaces** |
| 1.6 | References | 6.1 | External interface Requirements |
| 1.6.1 | Government documents | 6.2 | User Interfaces |
| 1.6.2 | Non-Government documents | 6.2.1 | User goals and tasks |
| 1.7 | Standards | 6.2.2 | User characteristics |
| 2 | **System objectives** | 6.3 | Software interfaces |
| 2.1 | General description | 6.3.1 | Subsystem interfaces |
| 2.2 | System features | 6.3.1.1-n | Interface name |
| 2.3 | System modes | 6.3.1.1-n.1 | Requirements applicable to both interfaces |
| 2.4 | System control | 6.3.1.1-n.2 | Interface-specific Requirements |
| 2.5 | Dependencies | 6.3.2 | Interface relationships |
| 2.6 | Assumptions | 6.3.3 | Other system interfaces |
| 2.7 | Constraint explanations | 6.4 | Software packages |
| 2.8 | Expected changes | 6.5 | Communications interfaces |
| 3 | **System-specific requirements** | 6.6 | Database |
| 3.1-n | Use cases 1-n | 6.7 | Operating system |
| 3.2-n | Feature Requirement 1-n | 7 | **Data** |
| 3.2-n.1 | Introduction | 7.1 | Overview of system data |
| 3.2-n.2 | Inputs | 7.1.1 | Data inputs |
| 3.2-n.3 | Processing | 7.1.2 | Data outputs |
| 3.2-n.3.1 | Parameters | 7.2 | Global data model |
| 3.2-n.3.2 | Event sequence | 7.2.1 | Real-world entities |
| 3.2-n.3.3 | Algorithms | 7.2.2 | Relationships between entities |
| 3.2-n.4 | Outputs | 8 | **Support** |
| 3.2-n.5 | Performance | 8.1 | Training |
| 3.2-n.6 | Availability | 8.1.1 | Delivery systems |
| 3.2-n.7 | Bugs | 8.1.2 | Trainee profiles |
| 3.2-n.7.1 | Detection | 8.1.3 | Curricula |
| 3.2-n.7.1.1 | Diagnostic methods | 8.1.4 | Training documentation |
| 3.2-n.7.1.2 | Built-In test | 8.2 | Documentation |
| 3.2-n.7.2 | Reporting | 8.2.1 | Format, style presentation |
| 3.2-n.7.3 | Function during failure | 8.2.2 | System documentation |
| 3.2-n.7.4 | Help and diagnostic facilities | 8.2.3 | User documentation |
| 3.2-n.7.5 | Recovery | 8.2.4 | Operator documentation |
| 4 | **Overall operational requirements** | 8.2.5 | Support documentation |
| 4.1 | Operational parameters | 8.2.6 | Interface documentation |
| 4.1.1 | Start-up | 8.2.7 | Requirements traceability |
| 4.1.2 | Normal operation | 9 | **Acceptance requirements** |
| 4.1.3 | Performance | 9.1 | Introduction |
| 4.1.3.1 | Minimum performance | 9.2 | Standards compliance |
| 4.1.3.2 | Resource capacity | 9.3 | Unit test requirements |
| 4.1.4 | Shut-down | 9.4 | Integration test Requirements |
| 4.2 | Security | 9.5 | System test requirements |
| 4.3 | Safety | 9.6 | Acceptance test requirements |
| 4.4 | Health Requirements | 9.6.1 | Demonstration |
| 4.5 | Integrity | 9.6.2 | Execution |
| 4.6 | Evolution | 9.6.3 | Analysis |

**FIGURE 8.4** Requirements specification table of contents

| 5 | **Constraints** | 9.6.4 | Support |
|---|---|---|---|
| 5.1 | Software design constraints | 9.7 | Inspection |
| 5.1.1 | Reliability | 9.8 | Configuration management |
| 5.1.1.1 | Accuracy | 10 | **Delivery** |
| 5.1.1.2 | Resilience | 10.1 | Deliverables |
| 5.1.1.3 | Consistency | 10.1.1 | Preparation for delivery |
| 5.1.2 | Reusability | 10.1.2 | Delivery schedule |
| 5.1.3 | Testability | 10.2 | Installation aspects |
| 5.1.3.1 | Communicativeness | 10.2.1 | Software installation |
| 5.1.3.2 | Self-descriptiveness | 10.2.2 | Installation-dependent data |
| 5.1.3.3 | Structuredness | 11 | Miscellaneous |
| 5.1.4 | Portability | 11.1 | Development management including |
| 5.1.4.1 | Device-independence | | quality assurance |
| 5.1.4.2 | Self-containedness | 11.2 | Other requirements |
| 5.1.4.3 | Interoperability | 11.3 | Resources |
| 5.1.5 | Efficiency | 11.4 | Available tools and components |
| 5.1.5.1 | Accountability | 11.5 | Other contractual points |
| 5.1.5.2 | Device efficiency | 12 | **Appendices** |
| 5.2 | Ergonomics and HCI | | Index |
| 5.2.1 | Usability | | |

**FIGURE 8.4**   Requirements specification table of contents (continued)

# 8.3   Test Strategy Document

See section 1.8.2 in Chapter 1 for an explanation of why you want to write this. In essence you want to define:

- The situation today
- The top ten problems
- The possible solutions

If this sounds difficult, then you already realize how much thinking is involved. If it sounds easy …

## 8.3.1   Introduction

- **Purpose of this document.** This document is intended as a strategy document for the … project. [*The strategy document identifies the current situation, the problem(s) posed, and one or more solutions together with any criteria for choosing a particular solution and possible measures. From a strategy document <Company name> may write a plan to do something or a specification of a product.*] The Glossary section (at the end of this document) contains all words or phrases having a special meaning in this document.
- **Intended audience.** This document is intended for use by the Test and/or the development team and other project stakeholders.
- **Background.** [*Describe the events which led up to writing this document.*]
- **Scope.** [*The issues central to the strategy and the limits of interest of the strategy document.*]
- **Related documents.** [*Cite any documents referred to by the strategy document or which might be of ancillary interest.*]
- **Conventions.** [*Text in italics is meant for guidance only.*]
- **Assumptions.** [List the assumptions on which the strategy is based (Return On Investment, Market Value Added, value to customers, value to <Company name>). As the document evolves, hopefully this list will grow and become a major focus of concern as the basis of change to the strategy.]

### 8.3.2 The Current Situation

[Describes:

- How the current situation occurred (*what were we trying to do, what happened to stop us*)
- The elements of the current situation (commercial entities, persons, hardware, software)
- The relationship between the elements (the structure of the situation)
- The constraints of the current situation (temporal, financial, managerial)
- The drivers of the current situation (what do the elements want and need)
- The risks
- How it (will) affect(s) <Company name>.]

### 8.3.3 Problem *n* (Repeat as Required)

[Describes:

- The problem
- The causes of the problem
- The effect(s) of the problem
- The costs and frequency of the problem
- Any interrelations with other problems
- The problem's environment.]

### 8.3.4 Possible Solution *n* (Repeat as Required)

[Describes:

- The elements of the solution *(who and what)*
- The relationship between the elements (the structure of the solution, why these elements are there, and why they have this/these relation(s))
- The interfaces with existing solutions
- The constraints of the solution (commercial, financial, temporal, managerial, key boundary condition, operational environments)
- The management of the solution (roles, responsibilities, reporting relations)
- The technical prerequisites of the solution
- The resources required for the solution (software, hardware, human, financial)
- The changes required (to management, system, process, products, features, maintenance, support, training)
- Risks (probability * cost)
- Contingencies (how we allow for the unexpected)
- Process for implementing the solution
- How it will affect <Company name> (in terms of <Company name>'s objectives and targets, in terms of customer relations)
- What will happen if it is not chosen
- Arguments in favor of the approach and against it (with supporting evidence)
- Comparable solutions
- Possible competitive response.]

### 8.3.5 Solution Criteria

[Describes:

- How we will know that the solution resolves the problem (*what degree of leverage would it afford us*)
- Characteristics

- Priorities
- Minimal acceptability criteria (*to <Company name>, customers, and users),*
- What happens if we do nothing.]

### 8.3.6  Recommendations

[Describes:

- The preferred choices
- The justification
- The costs
- The implications
- The alternatives considered
- The reasons why they were rejected.]

### 8.3.7  Metrics

[Describes:

- Solution process metrics
- Solution outcome metrics.]

### 8.3.8  Strategy Document Checklist

1. What are the problems, deficiencies, and opportunities being addressed? Are these symptoms of more basic concerns?
2. Is the context (i.e., problem, scenario, environment) consistent with <Company name>'s overall strategy?
3. Have assumptions and constraints been identified? Are they reasonable? How would changes in them affect the results?
4. Have all reasonable alternatives been considered?
5. Were multiple measures of effectiveness used? Do they relate to the performance thresholds and objectives established for the solution? To overall improvements in features?
6. Have all relevant costs been shown?
7. Are the models clearly identified? Are they appropriate to the system being evaluated? Are the input parameters identified? Can the results be replicated?
8. Has the cost and operational effectiveness been validated through engineering analyses or tests?
9. Does the analysis present all costs and measures of effectiveness for all alternatives? Have equal-cost or equal-effectiveness alternatives been examined?
10. Are the criteria used for assessing alternatives identified? Are they meaningful? Are they consistent with higher order objectives? Are they intuitively acceptable or, if not, adequately explained?
11. Do the results look reasonable? Is it clear from the analysis why the effectiveness measures came out as they did?
12. Were sensitivity analyses conducted showing how changes in technical performance affect utility, cost, and/or schedule? Do the results suggest reasonable ranges or thresholds for performance and cost?]

## 8.4  Interface Specification

Here is a very primitive interface specification template:

- **Glossary:** Includes conventions, abbreviations, explanations of symbols, and glossary.
- **Interface name**.
- **Definition:** Syntax definition for each form.

- **Parameters:** Name of the calling parameters and their type { string I variable I character I real I integer I floating point I none I scalar } and any defaults.
- **Return:** Name of the returned parameters, their type { void I string I variable I character I real I integer I floating point I none I scalar } and meaning.
- **Exception:** Describes the behavior if a problem occurs and known triggers.
- **Usage:** Example describing each operation showing:
  - Informal description
  - Pre/post condition template
  - Typical calling usage (optional)
  - Purpose
- **Constraints/protocol:** Timing, CPU, or memory restrictions, availability, MTBF, MTTR, throughput, latency, data safety for persistent state, capacity, or ordering limitations.
- **Service level:** Non-functional requirements to be met by the services provided by the interface (operations) and covers guarantees regarding any quality or non-functional requirement or constraint to be met by the interface and its operations.
- **Notes:** Limitations on use, pre-requisites, references, standards, and diagrams.
- **Layers:** In the event that the interface is layered, the above-listed sections will be repeated for each layer. Describe the relations between the layers.

## 8.5 Test Plan

The test activities foreseen throughout a project for each particular type of testing are described and coordinated in a test plan. A test plan defines the purpose, scope, approach, resources, and responsibilities of the testing activities. It will also identify each item to be tested, the testing tasks to be performed and the risks associated with each item and activity.

Typical objectives for a test plan are:

- To detail the activities required to ensure the testing is effective,
- To define the test tools and test environment needed to conduct the test,
- To determine the schedule of activities.

The contents of a test plan are:

- **Introduction:** Summarize items and features to be tested.
- **Items to be tested:** List them with version numbers and transmission media.
- **Features/features to be tested/not to be tested:** List them with reasons, and references to the relevant specification, together with a feature/test matrix. See section 15.2 for an example.
- **Interfaces with other systems:** Identify all other systems with which this system must coexist or share data, and the specifications.
- **Business processes supported:** Identify the major business processes, their criticality, and where they are defined.
- **Approach:** For each major group of features, specify the overall approach to testing.
- Test suspension/resumption criteria: list which tests should be repeated.
- **Test deliverables:** Reference the documents in the test document set, test input/output data, and test tools.
- **Environmental needs:** List the hardware, software, supplies, test tools.
- **Responsibilities** for managing, designing, preparing, executing, witnessing, checking, and resolving.
- Staffing and training needs.
- **Schedule** with any additional tasks/milestones not defined in the project plan, their dates, and resources.
- Risks and contingencies.

## 8.5.1   Test Plan Header

A test plan should have a header containing the following fields:

- Project name and identifying number
- Plan date
- Plan manager's name and signature
- Any other signatures required for approval
- Table of contents
- Release number

Summarize the software items and software features to be tested. The need for each item and history may be included. In multi-level test plans, each lower-level plan should reference the next higher-level plan.

## 8.5.2   Introduction (Table 8.2)

TABLE 8.2    Boilerplate test plan introduction
___

**Purpose of system testing**

The purpose of the system test is to provide immediate feedback to the developers about:
- Feature status
- Release status
- Possibility of release failure or delay
- System performance
- Any discrepancies between business and functional requirements and user interfaces

**Scope of system testing**

System testing:
- Covers all issues of installation and use of all parts of the product
- Includes the review of all business and functional requirements, and user interface specifications
- Does not cover training, documentation, performance, or infrastructure testing

**Criteria for seeking developer help in system testing**

Given the difficulty experienced in getting features to work, it is essential that testers can call on help when necessary. Equally developers need to be disturbed as little as possible. The criteria for seeking such help is:
- The feature is under-specified with respect to the delivered system
- The feature is specified in the business or functional requirements
- The feature is included in the release
- The feature can be demonstrated by the developer
- A problem with the feature can be demonstrated by the tester
___

## 8.5.3   Test Items

Specify the:

1. Test items including their version/revision level.
2. The characteristics of their transmittal media which affect hardware requirements or indicate the need for logical or physical transformations before testing can begin (for example, that programs should be transferred from tape to disk).
3. References to the following documents, if relevant:
   a. Requirements specification
   b. Design specification
   c. User guide
   d. Operations guide
   e. Installation guide
4. References to any bug reports (from previous tests) relating to the test items.
5. Any items which are to be specifically excluded from testing.

### 8.5.4 Interfaces with Other Systems

Identify all other systems with which this system must coexist or share data, and where the specifications of the interfaces and data can be found. Show the order (if any) in which this integration should occur. Identify backup facilities to be used in the event of failure of this integration.

### 8.5.5 Business Processes Supported

Identify the major business processes, their criticality, and where they are defined. Relate (or refer to a document relating) each major business objective to the flows involved and the system feature to be used. Identify all flows which will originate or end in other, coexisting systems. Identify how the changeover between the current and the future system will be handled.

### 8.5.6 Features to Be Tested

Identify the software features and combinations of software features to be tested and the corresponding test design specifications.

### 8.5.7 Features Not to Be Tested

Identify any features and major combinations of features which will not be tested and the reasons, if this is not self-evident from the previous section.

### 8.5.8 Approach

Describe the overall strategy and approach to testing. For each major group features or feature combinations, specify:

- The approach which will ensure that these feature groups are adequately tested, in sufficient detail to identify the major testing tasks.
- The major activities, techniques, and tools to be used to test the designated groups of features.
- The minimum degree of comprehensiveness desired, identifying the techniques to be used to judge the comprehensiveness of the testing effort (for example, determining which statements have been executed at least once).
- Any additional completion criteria (for example, bug frequency).
- Any overall criteria to be used to determine whether the test unit has passed or failed testing.
- The techniques to be used to trace requirements.

Identify major constraints on testing such as test-time availability, testing resource availability, and deadlines.

### 8.5.9 Suspension Criteria and Resumption Requirements

Table 8.3 contains boilerplate text for a test approach. Specify the criteria used to suspend all or a portion of the testing activity on the test items associated with this plan. Specify by name or by role the persons with the authority to halt the system tests. Specify the testing activities which should be repeated, when testing is resumed. This will usually be specified in terms of:

1. A number of bugs of a certain severity being encountered (see Figure 8.5).
2. A number of bugs of a certain category being found (see Figure 8.6 through 8.8).

A list of priorities and categories can be found in Appendix C. This section is proposed only for formal system test plans. See Chapter 18.

**TABLE 8.3**    Boilerplate test plan specification of suspension criteria

**Criteria for system test start**

For system testing to begin the following criteria must be met:
• A signed-off system test review report of the baseline specifications (business and functional requirements) for that release exists
• A test plan for that set of tests has been approved by the test and project managers
• All server-side configuration issues are resolved
• All tests have been specified, and manual or automated test scripts are prepared
• Every requirement is matched by at least one test
• Any extra tools needed for test execution are defined, procured, installed, and working
• A smoke test covering the key features of that release has been run on a machine outside the system test environment, without any unacceptable failures occurring
• A confidence test has been run with 70% of the tests passing
• A release note explaining known weak points or unfixed bugs exists

**Criteria for system test interruption**

• Releases collapse. Some releases may appear good, but a day or so of testing reveals major flaws.
• Changes happen. Some need to be accounted for. No addition to a functional requirement is assumed to occur without a corresponding business requirement. Additions to User Interface requirements are excluded from consideration on the grounds that they only concern usability. Any additional feature is expected to be introduced only through a business requirement. System testing will therefore halt when:
    • Any change or addition to any business requirement (for the period required to redefine the functional requirements, add those requirements to the tests, and examine any knock-on effects such (an) addition(s) may have), is made
    • Any changes (as opposed to additions) to four or more functional requirements (for the period required to examine and make the changes to the tests those changes imply) are made
    • More than 50 percent of the proposed functionality as defined in the business requirements cannot be executed

---

**Example:**

Testing will be discontinued on any build if one of the following conditions is encountered:
• 2 severity 1 bugs found,
• 3 severity 2 bugs found,
• 8 priority 3 bugs found.
Testing will not be halted if any lower-severity bug is found. Testing will resume when a new release is available. The test execution order will then be:
• Smoke and confidence tests.
• The tests which found the bugs which have just been fixed.
• The regression tests.
• The rest of the tests.

**FIGURE 8.5**    Alternative boilerplate test plan specification of suspension criteria (severity)

---

**Example:**
Testing will be discontinued on any build if one of the following conditions is encountered:
For all the following categories
- Performance bug (PF);
- Data bug (DA)
- Logic bug (LO)
- Feature bug (CA)

The following aggregate number of bugs is found:
- 2 severity 1 bugs
- 3 severity 2 bugs
- 8 priority 3 bugs

Testing will not be halted for any lower-severity bug. Testing will resume when a new release is available. The test execution order will then be:
- Smoke and confidence tests.
- The tests which found the bugs which have just been fixed
- The regression tests
- The rest of the tests

---

**FIGURE 8.6**   Alternative boilerplate test plan specification of suspension criteria (type)

---

**Criteria for system test resumption**
- The requisite tests have been modified and/or the missing functionality is believed to have been added.
- A new build and release note have been provided.

---

**FIGURE 8.7**   Boilerplate test plan specification of resumption criteria

---

**Criteria for system test end**
System testing implies a handover (to some other group, or a customer). The following criteria must thus have been met for this to happen:
- The release has been provided on CD with a release note explaining known weak points, or unfixed bugs.
- A smoke test covering the key features of that release has been run without any failures occurring.
- A confidence test has been run on that release with 90% of the tests passing.
- No *Critical* bugs, unacceptable to the other group, or a customer, are known to exist in that release.
- 60% of all *High* bugs found in that release have been fixed.
- An installation test using the CD has been completed for that release without any bug being found.
- The last test cycle run on that release has had a 100% coverage of *Must* and *Should* features.

---

**FIGURE 8.8**   Boilerplate test plan specification of system test ending criteria

If the system tests are to be used for acceptance or certification purposes, this section should also define:

- The procedures for agreeing the success of individual tests.
- The procedures for adjudication of tests and the resolution of disagreements.
- The criteria for acceptance and certification if not all the tests have been passed by the release.

### 8.5.10   Test Deliverables

Identify the deliverable documents and to whom (e.g., customer, technical manager, team leader) they are deliverable. The following documents should be included, if they are produced and if they are formal:

- Test plan
- Test design specification
- Test case specifications
- Test procedure specifications
- Test item transmittal reports
- Test logs
- Bug reports
- Test summary reports
- Test input and output data
- Test tools (for example, unit drivers and stubs) may also be included

### 8.5.11   Testing Tasks

Identify:

- The set of tasks necessary to prepare for and perform unit, integration, and system testing
- All inter-task dependencies and any special skills required

### 8.5.12   Environmental Needs

Specify:

- Both the necessary and desired properties of the test environment
- Definitions of the physical characteristics of the facilities including the hardware, the communications, and the system software, the mode of use (for example, stand-alone), and any other software or supplies needed to *support* the test
- The level of security which should be provided for the test facilities, system software, and proprietary components such as software, data, and hardware

Identify:

- Special test tools needed
- Any other testing needs (for example, publications or office space)
- The source for all needs which are not currently available to the test group

### 8.5.13   Responsibilities

Identify the groups responsible for:

- Managing, designing, developing/fixing, preparing, executing, witnessing, and checking
- Providing the test items and the environmental needs: the group may include the developers, testers, operations staff, user representatives, technical *Support* staff, data administration staff, and quality support staff

These may alternatively, be specified in the project plan (see Figure 8.9).

### 8.5.14   Staffing and Training Needs

Specify test needs by skill level. Identify training options for providing necessary skills. Alternatively, this may be specified in the project plan.

**Handover meeting**
Handover from Developers to system testing, or from system test to some other group will take the following form:
- Review the (UAT/system test/Desktop/Server) environment requirements (if unusual)
- Review the release note
- Install the software
- Demonstrate that 90% of all new features are present.

**Release note contents**
The Release note will show:
- Release name, pre-requisites, and release environment.
- bugs fixed and outstanding
- Features allegedly present (as defined by a functional specification, or sub-set thereof).
- Pathnames of ancillary documentation.

**FIGURE 8.9**  Boilerplate test plan specification of handover meeting and release note contents

## 8.5.15  Schedule

Identify the overall test schedule and major test milestones as well as any major item transmittal events.

Define any additional test schedule and milestones needed. Estimate the time required to do each testing task. Specify the schedule for each testing task and test milestone. For each testing resource (that is, facilities, tools, and staff) specify its periods of use.

Use a scheduling method such as a PERT or a Gannt chart. Keep it updated. Use a project planning tool.

## 8.5.16  Integration Tree

This is a definition of the order in which the software will be integrated. It usually applies only to safety-critical or mission-critical systems. The integration will normally be specified in steps. Each step will conform to some identifiable feature such as all operator inputs accepted or all scheduler functions. The set of steps is called an integration tree. An example is shown below.

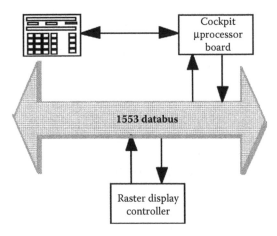

**FIGURE 8.10**  The raster display controller block diagram

In the first place let us imagine that some software to handle a raster display controller is being developed to work as shown in Figure 8.10.

An HOOD (top-level design) diagram is later produced as shown in Figure 8.11.

The software items which constitute the raster display controller can be read off the high-level design and onto an Integration tree as shown in Figure 8.12.

The key to Figure 8.12 is shown in Figure 8.13.

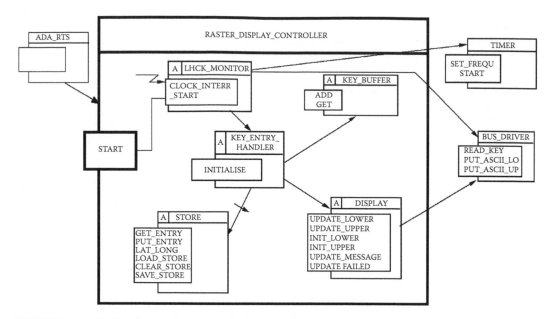

**FIGURE 8.11**  A HOOD diagram for a raster display controller

Figure 8.12 shows an extremely cautious integration strategy, split into 5 steps. In step 1, (on the extreme left) the following units are linked together to form the DISPLAY STEP:

- The driver (a piece of software which will be substituted by whichever units eventually call the system) CALLING DRIVER
- Three other stubs: STORE stub, LHCK MONITOR stub, and KEY ENTRY HANDLER stub
- The ADA run-time-system (ADA RTS)
- The 6 units which together comprise the DISPLAY: UPDATE_LOWER, UPDATE_UPPER INT_LOWER, INT_UPPER, UPDATE_MESSAGE, and UPDATE_FAILED

The features represented by the Display can now be integration tested. In step 2, the following units are linked together to form the STORE and KEY ENTRY HANDLER STEP:

- The driver CALLING DRIVER
- Integrated DISPLAY
- Two other stubs; LHCK MONITOR STUB and KEY ENTRY HANDLER STUB, and the ADA run-time-system (ADA RTS)
- The 6 units which represent the STORE
- INITIALIZE unit which is the only unit of the KEY ENTRY HANDLER
- The ADA run-time-system (ADA RTS)

The logic behind the strategy has to do with the need to get the display working first so that users can get some feedback on their actions. In practice not all of the features can be properly tested since they require the KEY ENTRY HANDLER as well. However this is added in the next step along with the STORE feature. The key parts of the raster display are thus integrated and the LHCK MONITOR and KEY BUFFER are then added before the entire raster display controller is ready to be integrated as a component.

### 8.5.17  Risks and Contingencies

Identify the high-risk assumptions of the test plan. Specify contingency plans for each (for example, delayed delivery of test items might require increased night shift scheduling to meet the delivery date).

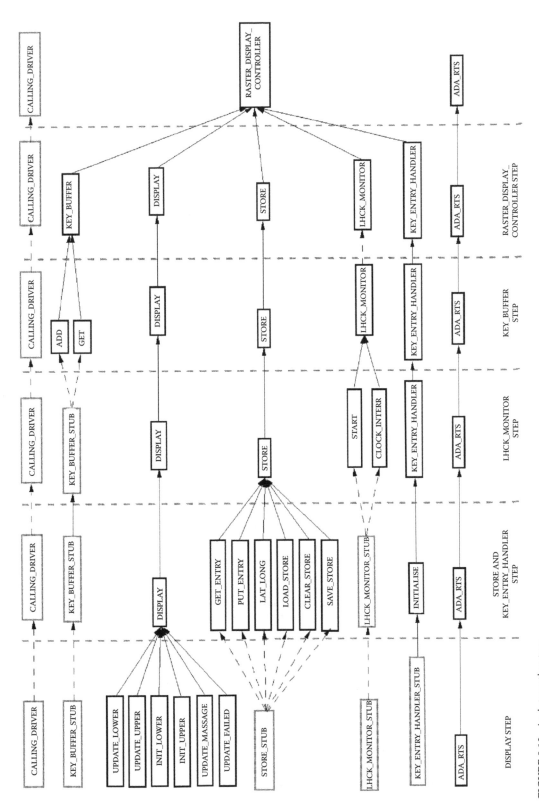

**FIGURE 8.12** An integration tree

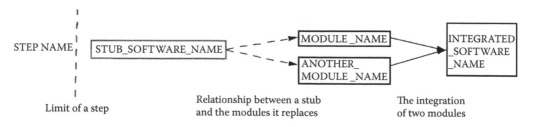

FIGURE 8.13   Key to the preceding figure

## 8.6   Test Monitoring Document

For daily use consider a spreadsheet with the following tabs:

- Document status
- RFC (Request For Change) status
- Test status
- Log
- Crash log
- Raw bug reports
- Weekly bug report count
- Chart: test: execution status
- Chart: overall bug detection profile
- Chart: open and closed critical bug reports
- Chart: release quality profile

### 8.6.1   Document Status

| Wave | Capability | Spec | Tech Author | Developer Team Leader | System Tester | Reqts. spec | Design spec. | Reviewed by System testing | Comments | Doc Lib Location | Sign off progress |
|---|---|---|---|---|---|---|---|---|---|---|---|
| 1 | Minor transactions | NewSystem Level 1 Minor transactions Business Workflow Scenarios | George | Paul 1 | Nat | | 2.00 | Yes | | | |
| | | preparation (Minor transaction Requirements Catalogue)PRS | Fred | | | 1.00 | | Yes | | | Signed off |
| | | NewSystem Minor transactions UI Spec v0.3 | Joan | | | 0.30 | | Yes | | | |
| 2 | Backwards compatibility | Not Found In DocLib - NewSystem Backwards compatibility PFS | Tim | Laxman | Lucy | - | - | | Design spec. draft available | | |
| 2 | Full Classification code functionality | NewSystem Coding PRS | Alistair | Vaso | Lucy | 1.00 | | Yes | | | |
| | | UI spec | Henry | | | | | | | http://www.i me.reuters.c om/doclib/?d | Under review by Usability |
| 2 | Password Security | NewSystem Password Security PFS | Alistair | Ken | Shahir | | 1.10 | Yes | | http://www.i | Signed off |
| | | UI spec | Tim | | | | | Yes | | | |

◄ ► ►| ⬚ Test status   Document status   RFC list   Crash log   Log   Raw SCRS   SCRs per day   SCR analysis   Drop analysis   Drop 6   Charts

FIGURE 8.14   Document status tab

This lists the features and the specifications describing them, the authors of the specifications (aka business analysts), the team leader in charge of developing that feature, the system tester in charge of the feature, the document latest issue number, whether it had been reviewed by the system tester, comments, its URL within the corporate intra-Web and whether it was signed-off. In this it is clear that a number of documents should have been signed-off before testing started and may indicate last-minute changes. Areas of concern can be colored.

### 8.6.2   RFC (Request for Change) Status

As testing progresses it may become evident that minor discrepancies between what the customer wants, and what was specified and built have occurred. Reissuing the entire requirements specification may be very

| RFC Number | Short Description: | Originator: | Owner: | Date Raised: | Priority: | Status: | Describe the Change: | System tester responsible | Time required (In | Status |
|---|---|---|---|---|---|---|---|---|---|---|
| 22 | Unspecified Code handling | Henry | Samantha | 04.07.04 | High | Approved | Markup of Emergency codes No easy way to quickly mark up all Emergency codes in content. This is contrary to the PFS. Emergency codes that quote a Primary Code are being marked up as if they were companies. This is contrary to requirements Emergency codes that quote a single DLC Code are being marked up to reference both Codes for the DLC. If this | Lucy | | Done and tested |
| 31 | BC must not be added for non-English transactions | Rowena | Chris | 4/23/2004 | High | Approved | Currently the string 'BC' is prefixed to all slughines. This must be changed so that it only happens if the language of the item is English (or a variant of English). The issue arose at the National Language Services workshop on April | Andrew ? | | Done |
| 32 | NewSystem Knowledge links via the NewSystem desktop | Vangelis Paul 1 and Chris | | 4/23/2004 | Medium | Approved | Add links for 'NewSystem Knowledge' to the NewSystem desktop via: 1. Start Menu, i.e. Start programmes, NewSystem, NewSystem Knowledge 2. A Launchpad icon 3. Add to the NewSystem drop down menu 4. Add to the | Mat | | Done |

Test status | Document status | RFC list | Crash log | Log | Raw SCRS | SCRs per day | SCR analysis | Drop

**FIGURE 8.15**  RFC list tab

long and involved. To simplify matters some organizations identify each of these changes as a Request For Change, review it with all the stakeholders, and agree it with the customer and senior or contract management. Note that the review must ensure that the requirements specification itself be not compromised. These RFCs are then added to the specifications as the baselines against which all stakeholders must work.

This tab enables a test manager to check the status of all RFCs.

## 8.6.3   Test Status

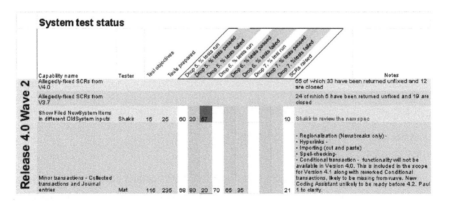

**FIGURE 8.16**  Test status tab

This shows the critical information for each build concerning the feature, the tester in charge, the number of test objectives, and tests prepared, and the percentage run, passed, and failed for each build. By using Conditional formatting on the *tests failed* column those exceeding some limit can be highlighted in red. In this case not only was the feature buggy, but management had decided in mid-release to change the specification.

## 8.6.4   Test Events Log

As testing proceeds and tensions rise, it is invaluable to have a log of events such as *test environment down, build available at 10 am* such that causes of delays, etc. can be simply determined. This log is quite distinct from the *Crash* log.

| Date | Event |
|------|-------|
| 14.May.04 | Paul 1 announces that the latest build is of sufficient quality to meet System entry criteria. A release has been planned for the afternoon. |
| 14.May.04 | Ken announces that X*** codes are not part of 3.8 codes. Peter issues Func Spec 3.8.12. |
| 14.May.04 | 1530 Hours Smoke testing of Drop 5 begins |
| 15.May.04 | 1330 Hours Smoke testing of Drop 5 ends. |
| 15.May.04 | 1331 Hours. Confidence testing of Drop 5 begins |
| 16.May.04 | 1730 Hours Confidence testing ends |
| 17.May.04 | 1340 Hours. System testing of Drop 5 begins. |
| 17.May.04 | 1500 Hours. Richard (Director) announces that more than 3 drops may be made if the System exit criteria be not met. |
|  | 1500 hours. John observed that the Feature Xs exclusion of the Release Note |

◄ ► ►l   Test status / Document status / RFC list / **Log** / Crash log / Raw St

**FIGURE 8.17**   Test events log tab

## 8.6.5   Crash Log

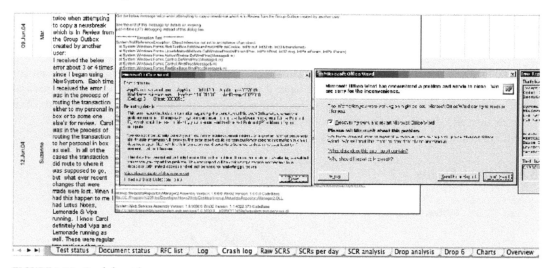

◄ ► ►l   Test status / Document status / RFC list / Log / **Crash log** / Raw SCRS / SCRs per day / SCR analysis / Drop analysis / Drop 6 / Charts / Overview

**FIGURE 8.18**   Crash log tab

Particularly at the start of testing a number of critical events may occur:

- The system may crash, possibly explicably.
- Unrepeatable bugs may be seen.

In those cases testers should be encouraged to submit full crash details plus screenshots not only to the bug-management tool but also to the test manager. Since it is unwise to submit undemonstrable bugs to developers it is essential they be recorded somewhere. This spreadsheet is a good place. After a while patterns can emerge.

## 8.6.6   Weekly/Daily Bug Report Count

| Total SCRs raised by system testing last week = 12 | | Total SCRs closed by system testing last week = 22 | |
|---|---|---|---|
| Tue: 31.Aug.2004 | 5 | Tue: 31.Aug.2004 | 9 |
| Wed: 01.Sep.2004 | 8 | Wed: 01.Sep.2004 | 6 |
| Mon: 06.Sep.2004 | 0 | Mon: 06.Sep.2004 | 4 |
| Tue: 07.Sep.2004 | 4 | Tue: 07.Sep.2004 | 16 |
| Wed: 08.Sep.2004 | 8 | Wed: 08.Sep.2004 | 2 |
| Grand Total | 1358 | Total | 1097 |

◄ ► ►l   Document status / RFC list / Log / Crash log / Raw SCRS / **SCRs per day** / SCR analysi ►

**FIGURE 8.19**   Weekly bug report count tab

Either using an ODBC link to your bug-management tool or a daily dump of raw bug reports into your spreadsheet you can get the weekly running totals of found and cleared bug (SCR reports).

Closing SCRs becomes a major pressure point on testing. Developers need to know their fixes were valid. Closing each bug takes time which testers prefer to spend testing. Bugs are best closed by the tester who found them. But if the bug is evident, a good manager might simply do it himself.

## 8.6.7 Charts

The charts tab draws on a number of pieces of data obtained from the bug-management tool and the test management tool.

1. **Test execution status** (Figure 8.20) is best measured by test execution steps. Why? Because if some tests have only 3 steps and some have 15 it will be very difficult for you to know just how far through test execution you really are. This chart shows that much testing remains to be done, but that very few tests are failing. One confidence test failed[1] and one could not be run for environmental reasons.

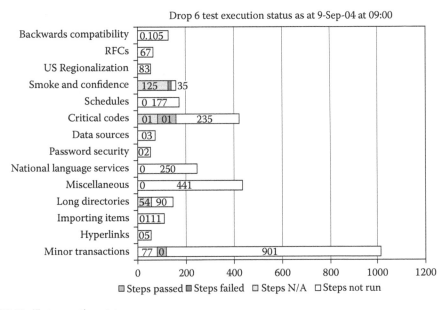

**FIGURE 8.20** Test execution status

2. **Overall bug detection profile** (Figure 8.21). This shows the overall number of bug reports raised against a release. The shape roughly corresponds to the expected "S" curve. The profile looks as if the number of bugs is at last beginning to drop and the release can soon be made.

3. **Open and closed critical bug reports**. The project had four bug report severity levels: *Critical, High, Medium,* and *Low. Critical* implied some feature was missing or didn't work, and there was no workaround. *High* implied there *was* a workaround. The software was not fit for release if any of these bug reports remained. Therefore monitoring them was most important. As in Figure 8.22, the profile has assumed an "S" shape. All "allegedly-fixed" bug reports have been retested and have either been closed or rejected. A worryingly-high number (174) of open bug reports remains.

4. **Build quality profile.** Figure 8.23 shows the number of bug reports raised against each build. Release 6 had only one bug report but it was so critical the release was abandoned. Thereafter the bug profile has fluctuated.

---

[1] Strictly speaking tests only "fail" if they fail to expose a bug they should expose. Software fails or passes. References to tests "failing" means only that they exposed a bug. Tests never pass: only software passes, references to tests "passing" means only that they failed to expose a bug.

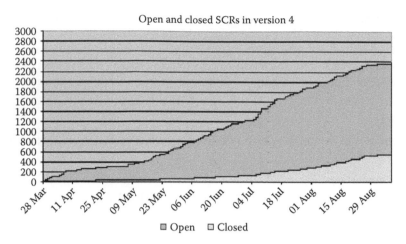

**FIGURE 8.21**  Overall bug detection profile

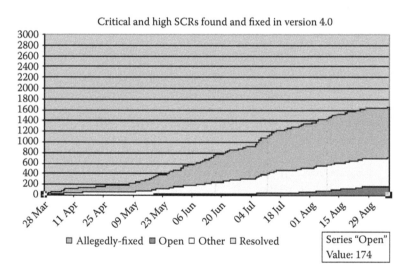

**FIGURE 8.22**  Open and closed critical bug reports

Figure 8.24 shows the same data as in the last chart but as a proportion. Release 13 is still being tested. Note that the right-most (*Medium* and *Low*) bars remain largely static as the releases progress (bad). A large number of critical and high bug reports is still being raised.

5. **Feature stability profile.** Some features are more stable than others. The less-stable are particular candidates for regression-testing. Monitor them by ensuring that the bug-reporting tool can report *by feature* and maintaining a chart like the one shown in Figure 8.25.

This shows the tendency of some features to instability. If the code for those features is also unstable there is a very high probability that bugs are being created as fast as they are being fixed. Look in the source code management system for the degree of *code turmoil* (see Chapter 18) as a check.

## 8.6.8  The Overall Tale

The charts tell a tale of a project which appeared stable until one looked closer. The tell-tale sign was the large number of *Open Critical* and *High* bug reports in Figure 8.23. This told of a persistent inability

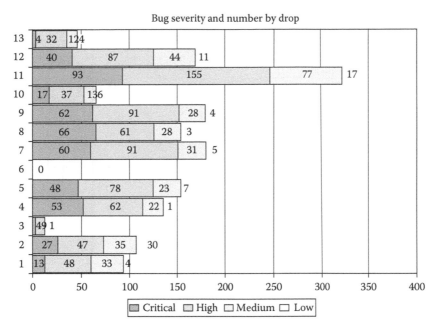

**FIGURE 8.23** Build quality profile expressed as an absolute

to fix bugs without raising more. This habit was even more evident in Figure 8.24 where the number of bug reports raised fluctuated greatly but the proportions remained steady. An improving system would show an increasing proportion of lower-severity bug reports being raised. This didn't.

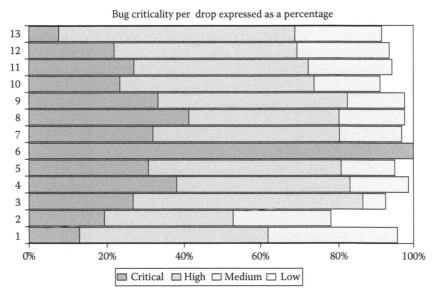

**FIGURE 8.24** Build quality profile expressed as a proportion

| Feature | Function | Test | Drop 18 test status | Drop 19 test status | Drop 20 test status | Drop 21 test status | 27 | 59 | 48 | 23 | 47 | 67 | |
|---|---|---|---|---|---|---|---|---|---|---|---|---|---|
| Alerts 2 | Alert editing functions | (1)Function 3068-A copying an alert or alert series in the AE | No run | Passed | Passed | Failed | | | 1 | | | | In drop 19, 27 failures followed a pass in drop 18, whereas 23 passes followed a preceding failure |
| Alerts 2 | Alert editing functions | (1)Function 3068-B copying an alert or alert series in the AE | Passed | Failed | Failed | Passed | 1 | 1 | | | | 1 | |
| Alerts 2 | Alert editing functions | (1)Function 3068-C copying an alert or alert series in the AE | Passed | Failed | Passed | Passed | 1 | | | | 1 | 1 | |
| Alerts 2 | Alert editing functions | (1)Function 3068-D copying an alert or alert series in the AE | Passed | Failed | Passed | Passed | 1 | | | | 1 | 1 | |
| Alerts 2 | Alert editing functions | (1)Function 3071 delete a new alert | Not compl | Passed | Failed | Passed | | | 1 | | | 1 | In drop 20, 53 failures followed a pass in drop 18 or 19 whereas 47 passes followed a preceding failure |
| Alerts 2 | Correction functions | (1)Function 3050-A (LOW PRIORITY) opening an alert news item correction from inbox | No run | No run | Failed | Passed | | | 1 | | | 1 | |
| Alerts 2 | Correction functions | (1)Function 3051-D spike an alert series correction that has been sent for review | No run | Failed | Passed | Failed | 1 | | | 1 | 1 | | |
| Alerts 2 | Correction functions | (1)Function 3051-E spike an alert series correction that has been sent for review | Not compl | Failed | Passed | Failed | | | | 1 | 1 | | In drop 21, 23 failures followed a pass in drops 18, 19 or 20 whereas 67 passes followed a preceding failure |
| Alerts 2 | Correction functions | (1)Function 3051-F spike an alert series correction that has been sent for review | No run | Failed | Passed | Failed | 1 | | | 1 | 1 | | |
| Alerts 2 | Correction functions | (1)Function 3081-C cancel correcting an alert series | No run | Failed | Passed | Failed | 1 | | | 1 | 1 | | |
| Alerts 2 | Correction functions | (1)Function 3085-B receive and process S77 delete messages for alerts of an existing USN | No run | Passed | Passed | Failed | | | | 1 | | | |
| Alerts 2 | Creation functions | (PRIORITY) create the first alert in a series | No run | No run | Failed | Passed | | 1 | | | 1 | | |

**FIGURE 8.25** Feature stability profile

# 8.7   Test Design Specification

This purpose of this document[2] is to specify refinements of the test approach and to identify the features to be tested by the test design, and its associated tests.

Refer to the associated test plan, if it exists. A test-design specification should address the following:

- Software to be tested
- Testing approach
- Test identification
- Test environment
- Overall pass/fail criteria

## 8.7.1   Software to Be Tested

Define:

- The test items by name and release number
- The features and combinations of features which are the object of this design specification
- All references to baselines in the requirement or design specification
- Any hardware requirements individual pieces of software require

---

[2] This is being shown here as a document to avoid discussing it in relation to a tool. In practice individual tests would almost always be designed, written, and managed using a test tool. Large systems might use such a document to give guidance.

## 8.7.2  Testing Approach

Specify:

- Any refinements to the approach described in the test plan including code instrumentation
- The test techniques to be used
- The method of analyzing test results (for example, comparator programs or visual inspection)
- The results of any analysis which provide a rationale for test-case selection. (for example, one might specify conditions which permit a determination of bug tolerance such as those conditions which distinguish valid input from invalid output)
- The common attributes of the *test cases*. This may include input constraints that should be true for every input in the set of associated *test cases*, any shared environmental needs, special procedural requirements, and case dependencies
- Any overall criteria to be used to determine whether the feature or feature combination has passed or failed
- The test tools to be used including all scaffolding
- The integration order

## 8.7.3  Test Identification

List the identifiers and briefly describe each:

- Test case associated with this design (a particular test case may be identified in more than one test design specification)
- Procedure associated with this test-design specification

## 8.7.4  Test Environment

Specify:

- The hardware requirements
- Dependencies on other software items
- Testing tools, etc.

## 8.7.5  Pass/Fail Criteria

Specify the pass/fail criteria for the overall result of each test set. The detailed pass/fail criteria are specified in the test case specifications.

# 8.8  Test Case Specification

The test-case specification[3] defines a test case identified by a test-design specification. *Test cases* will normally be handled by a test tool and this section can be used as a checklist for deciding on the test case management tool to be used.

Since a test case may be referenced by several test-design specifications used by different groups over a long time period, enough information should be included in the test-case specification to permit reuse.

A test-case specification should address the following:

- Test identifier
- Test items

---

[3] As with a test design document most test case specifications are held in test management tools. This example is shown as a way of identifying the issues any worthwhile test tool must be able to handle.

- Test objective
- Baseline definition
- Input specification
- Output specification
- Pass/fail criteria
- Software environment
- Other environmental needs
- Special procedural requirements
- Inter-case dependencies
- Notes showing how expected bugs may appear

### 8.8.1  Test Identifier

A unique identifier is assigned to each test case.

### 8.8.2  Test Items

Identify and, if necessary, briefly describe the items and features to be exercised by this test case. For each item, refer to the item documents to be used as a baseline for the test.

### 8.8.3  Test Objective

Specify the purpose of the test, perhaps expressed in terms of an attempt to disprove some assertions in some specification.

### 8.8.4  Baseline Definition

Define the baseline from which the objective was derived. This will usually be:

- The requirements specification (for system tests)
- The design specification (for integration tests)
- The unit specification (for unit tests)
- The user guide (for user interface tests)
- The operations guide (for background advice)
- The installation guide (for background advice)

This will enable you to relate the tests to the baselines and check that no baseline remains uncovered. This should also relate the test to a feature so that the number of tests per feature can be determined.

### 8.8.5  Input Specifications

Specify:

- Each input type required to execute the test case; some will be specified by value (with tolerances) while others, such as constant tables or transaction files, will be specified by name.
- Any special relations between the inputs for example with respect to order or timing, expressed in the form of a grammar, state table, or Finite State Machine.
- All data bases, files, terminal messages, memory-resident areas, and values passed by the operating system.
- All required relationships between inputs (for example, timing).
- Where the input should be supplied by the operator and is not described in the test procedures specification, specify:
  - The mode or state the system should be in before the test, including the screen display.
  - The exact operator actions (such as *Press F1, then press ESC-D*) to be carried out.

### 8.8.6 Output Specification

Specify all the outputs and features (for example, response time) required of the test items. Provide the exact value (with tolerances) for each required output or feature. Specify the mode or state the system should be in after the test.

### 8.8.7 Pass/Fail Criteria

Identify acceptable or unacceptable ranges of data or the output of some test tool — typically the results of a comparison between a test-expected-result file, and a test-actual-result file, and is best expressed in terms of some humanly-observable event.

### 8.8.8 Software

Specify the system and application software required to execute this test case. This may include system software such as operating systems, compilers, simulators, and test tools. Allow for the fact that the test item may interact with application software.

### 8.8.9 Other Environmental Needs

Specify any hardware and other environmental needs not covered in higher level test documents, such as:

- Special test rigs
- Specially trained personnel
- Client–server set-up
- Data feeds

### 8.8.10 Special Procedural Requirements

Describe:

- Any special constraints on the test procedures which execute this test case. These constraints may involve special set-up, operator intervention, output determination procedures, and special wrap-up procedures.
- What the expected bugs may look like and leave as many helpful notes as possible for the operator.

### 8.8.11 Inter-Case Dependencies

List the identifiers of *test cases* which should be executed before this test case. Summarize the nature of the dependencies.

## 8.9 Test Procedure Specification

This document specifies[4] any steps for executing a set of *test cases* or, more generally, the steps used to analyze a software item in order to evaluate a set of features. This document should be written for example when:

- A third-party supplier sends a test pack with a release
- When a set of system tests is to be archived, such that staff unfamiliar with the tests can use them
- When a test pack is created from a set of test fragments to cover a particular release or a particular configuration

---

[4] Again, this example is used as a template so you can use it as a requirements specification for the tool you will choose (hopefully).

Refer to the associated test-design specification. A test-procedure specification should address the following:

- The configuration or release for which it is intended
- How to set up the tests
- How to start executing the tests
- How to proceed
- How to perform measurements
- How, why, and when to suspend, restart, or stop testing

### 8.9.1  Purpose

Describe the purpose of this procedure. If this procedure executes any *test cases*, refer to each of them.

In addition, provide references to relevant sections of the test item documents (for example, references to procedures for use).

### 8.9.2  Special Requirements

Identify any special requirements that are necessary for the execution of this procedure. These may include prerequisite procedures, special skills, requirements, and special environmental requirements.

### 8.9.3  Procedure Steps

Include the following steps as applicable:

- **Log:** Describe any special methods or formats for logging the results of test execution, the incidents observed, and any other events pertinent to the test (see section 8.11 and 8.12).
- **Set up:** Describe how to prepare for execution of the procedure.
- **Start:** Describe how to begin execution of the procedures.
- **Proceed:** Describe any actions necessary during execution of the procedures.
- **Measure:** Describe how the test measurements will be made (for example, describe how remote terminal response time is to be measured using a network simulator).
- **Shut down:** Describe how to suspend testing, when unscheduled events dictate.
- **Restart:** Identify any procedure restart points and describe how to restart the procedure at each of these points.
- **Stop:** Describe how to bring execution to an orderly halt.
- **Wrap up:** Describe how to restore the environment so the test may be begun again.
- **Contingencies:** Describe how to deal with anomalous events which may occur during execution.[5]

## 8.10  Release Note

This report identifies an item being transmitted for integration or system testing or release to the field. It includes the person responsible for each item, its physical location, and its status. Note any variations from the current item requirements and designs. A variant of this note may be put on installation CDs.

Specify the names and titles of all persons who should approve this transmittal. Provide space for the signatures and dates.

---

[5] An anomalous event is not necessarily a bug. It might be caused by some test environmental issue. Some are foreseeable and can thus be specified in advance such as power failures.

### 8.10.1 Transmitted Items

Identify:

- The item(s) being transmitted, including their version/revision level
- The item documents and the test plan relating to the transmitted item(s)
- The people responsible for the transmitted item(s)
- The purpose of the release (new feature content, bug fixes, emergency release to the field, for internal use only, etc.)

### 8.10.2 Feature Content

List the features of the software. This may be difficult if the item is a single unit (copy the header), but will be simple when the item represents some release. Identify the features that differ from the last version of the release. Define any restrictions on its use associated with the release.

### 8.10.3 Location

Identify the media and location of the item(s) being transmitted. Indicate how media are labeled or identified. List each file, ordered by media.

### 8.10.4 Status

Identify:

- The status of the item(s) being transmitted (draft I reviewed I reviewed and approved I unit-tested I system-tested I released)
- Any deviations from the item documents, from previous transmittals of these item(s), and from the test plan
- The bug reports which are expected to be resolved by the transmitted item(s)
- Any pending modifications to item documents which may affect the item(s) listed in the transmittal report

### 8.10.5 Release Requirements

List the hardware, firmware, and software required to run the release, complete with version numbers and memory size. List any build instructions.

## 8.11 Test Log

This provides a chronological record of the execution of tests.

### 8.11.1 Description

Include information which applies to all entries in the log:

- The identity of the item(s) being tested including their version/revision levels
- The attributes of the environments in which the testing is conducted (the facility identification, hardware being used — for example, amount of memory being used, CPU mode number, and number and model of tape drives and/or mass storage devices, system software used, and resources available such as the amount of memory available)

### 8.11.2 Activity and Event Entries

For each event, including the beginning and end of activities, record the occurrence date and time along with the author's name and details. Include the following:

- **Execution description:** The test (procedure) identifier being executed, and refer to its specification. Record all personnel present during the execution including testers, operators, and witnesses, and the function of each individual.
- **Procedure results:** For each execution, record the:
  - Visually-observable results (for example, error messages generated, aborts, and requests for operator action)
  - Location of any output (for example, print-outs, and test-actual-result files)
  - Successful or unsuccessful execution of the test
- **Environmental information:** Record any environmental conditions specific to this entry (for example, hardware substitutions, service packs).
- **Anomalous events:** Record the circumstances surrounding the inability to begin execution of a test procedure or failure to complete a test procedure (for example, a power failure or system software problem).
- **Bug report identifiers:** Record the identifier of each bug report generated.

## 8.12 Bug Report

This section shows how a bug report is used to document any event that occurs during the testing process which requires investigation and to lay out the minimum requirements for a bug management system. Bug reports should be raised on any software or document which is configuration-managed. Any software or document which is shared between programmer groups should be configuration-managed.[6]

Tests also exist in order to find bugs. Bugs must be reported (see Table 8.4). The reports must have the following characteristics:

- They should describe the bug such that they can be repeated (this may not always be the case — some bugs are intermittent but need to be reported anyway).
- They should be raised by anyone who finds them. (This can lead to duplication but this is preferable to not reporting them.) See Chapter 6 for more on this.

The person who sees the bug fills in the following fields:

- **project name:** the name and number of the project
- **bug report #:** the number of the bug report; this must be unique
- **controlled item/feature:** the name of the item or feature in which the bug is believed to have manifested itself
- **version/variant:** the version or variant of the controlled item
- **workpackage:** the name of the workpackage responsible for producing the item (if known: this can be added later)
- **name of observer** (appointed by the customer or other body to oversee the testing)
- **bug name:** some very brief, distinct description of the bug which can be used as its title in reports and discussions
- **test identifier:** the name of any test which was being run at the time the bug was observed

---

[6] Keep bureaucracy at bay: stuff which programmers (or testers) exchange informally can be left informal. Documents or code which are exchanged, for example, between program feature groups A and B, and on which group B relies as some description of what group A does, must be configuration-managed.

- **bug details:** add details under the following headings if the formality of the project or the complexity of the bug merits it
    - **summary:** summarize the bug. Identify the item(s) involved indicating their version/revision level (supply references to the test-procedure specification, test-case specification, and test log)
    - **description:** describe the incident in which the bug was evident, avoiding redundancy with other test documents; include the following: *inputs, steps taken* (describe step-by-step) *expected results, actual results, anomalies* (showing the moment the bug is first evident), *date* and *time, procedure step,* (if any) *environment* (if not obvious), *attempts to repeat, testers, the names of any observers*
    - **related activities and observations** that may help to isolate and correct the cause of the bug, for example describe any test-case executions that might have a bearing on this particular bug and any variations from the published test procedure
    - **effect:** indicate what effect this bug will have on the user, the user's business, test plans, test-design specifications, test-procedure specifications, or test-case specifications, such that the severity of the bug is evident
- **signature** of the observer
- **function** of the observer — the group within which the observer works or the responsibility held at the time the problem was observed
- **date** on which the observation was made (optionally the time, too)

**TABLE 8.4** A bug report

| Bug report | | | |
|---|---|---|---|
| project name | | bug report no. | |
| controlled item/feature | | version/variant | |
| workpackage | | name of observer | |
| bug name | | related bug report numbers | |
| test identifier | category | | priority |
| bug details | | | |
| summary | | | |
| description | | | |
| related activities | | | |
| effect | | | |
| signature | function | | date |
| results of investigation | | | |
| effect | | | |
| root cause | | | |
| severity | priority | justification | |
| signature | function | | date |
| action | | | |
| signature | function | | date |

Pass the observation to the project manager to decide what action is to be taken. This may be one of three kinds:

- Investigate the bug
- Resolve the bug
- Do nothing — either because the bug is already known or because its priority is too low

In any case the project manager should ensure that category and (fix) priority are completed as defined in Appendix C.

In the first case complete the following fields:

- **results of investigation:** a definition of the cause of the bug
- **effect:** a definition of all the changes required to resolve the problem; this may consist of a simple reference to a change plan which itself refers to all the documents, code, and tests requiring changes
- **severity** of the bug (see section Appendix C)
- **priority:** there may be lots of high-severity bugs needing fixing; this lets the project manager decide the order
- **justification** if not obvious from the bug description
- **signature** of the person investigating the cause of the problem
- **function** of the investigator — the group within which the investigator works or the responsibility held at the time of the investigation
- **date** the investigation was made
- **related bug numbers:** if the bug has already been reported or if it is believed that the bug is related to others, then add the numbers of the relevant observation reports

In all cases complete the following fields:

- **action** decided by the project manager; this will be either to do nothing, raise a change request or authorize that the bug be fixed
- **root cause** (see section 2.7.3 in Chapter 2 for more on this)
- **signature** of the project manager
- **function** of the project manager with respect to this bug report (useful when the bugs are being assessed by some deputy of the project manager)
- **date** the action was decided

For analysis you could extend the form to include the contents of section 7.7.3.

## 8.13   Test Summary

This document summarizes and evaluates the results of the testing activities.

Specify the names and the titles of all persons who should approve this report. Provide space for the signatures and dates. Address the following:

- **Summary** of the item(s). Identify the item(s) tested, indicating their version/revision level. Indicate the environment in which the testing activities took place.
- For each test item, **refer** to the following documents if they exist or tools: test plan, test-design specifications, test-procedure specification, test-item transmittal reports, test logs, and bug reports.
- **Variances.** Report any variances of the item(s) from their design specifications. Indicate any variances from the test plan, test designs, or test procedures. Specify the reason for each variance.
- **Comprehensiveness assessment.** Evaluate the comprehensiveness of the testing process against the comprehensiveness criteria specified in the test plan (see section 8.5). Identify features or feature combinations which were not sufficiently tested and explain why.
- **Summary of results** including all resolved incidents and their resolutions. Identify any unresolved incidents.
- **Evaluate** each test item including its limitations based on the test results and the item level pass/fail criteria. Add an estimate of failure risk.
- **Summary of activities and methods.** Summarize:

- The test approaches taken including usability and the tools used
- The major testing activities and events
- The resource consumption data, for example, total staffing level, total machine time, and total elapsed time used for each of the major testing activities (see section A.7 in Appendix A)

## 8.14 Usability Test Summary

As section 8.13, but add:

• **Metrics overview** based on the usability metrication occurring so far. Structure this in terms of the questions the metrics are attempting to answer. If you are comparing products or versions you can add a comparison overview here too. Kiviat (Aka "*radar*") diagrams can be useful here (Figure 8.26).

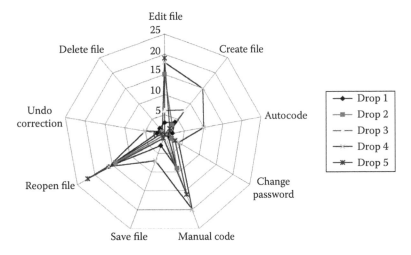

**FIGURE 8.26** Kiviat diagram of task/bug status per release

• **Bug** (or root) **cause analysis** is one in which the causes of each bug are listed in order of severity. Note that the severity can be determined from the table in Appendix C. In particular if a human factors (HF) bug can be shown to have occurred regularly (for example if more than 30% of the users experience it), the column entitled "Fails regularly" can be employed. The causes are of three kinds:
- Functional (X doesn't work)
- Non-functional (the system is too slow and the user times-out with boredom)
- Human: The way information is presented, perhaps the feedback pattern employed is "wrong," inhumane, or otherwise psychologically unwise. This is discussed further in section 17.6.3. This will lead you into some reasoning about Very Wonderful Psychological theories by your HF advisor. Good. Luck.

  Providing this kind of feedback gives management a unique view of the user experience which mere anecdotes lack. Write it so that they can take decisions on it. Don't include recommendations (that's the HF advisor's job), but make them implicit.
• **Weaknesses.** There are probably areas you feel you should have tested differently or more rigorously or you perhaps would have proceeded differently with a Usability Test Candidate (UTC). Here is the place to own up, if only to yourself.

## 8.15    Acceptance Certificate (Figure 8.27)

---

**Acceptance Certificate**

---

Project name

---

Acceptance test

---

| specification reference No | Issue: | Date: |

---

| Accepted item identity | Accepted item description | Version/issue |

---

Concessions

---

| Originator's name | Acceptance test dates |

---

Originator's Signature

---

This certifies that the items defined above meet the Acceptance test specification

---

Authorized on behalf of the customer

---

**FIGURE 8.27**   Acceptance test certificate

Use this when formal customer acceptance or certification tests are required. Have it completed and checked by the project manager (or nominee), and offered to the Customer for signature. Keep the original in the project records.

All references indicated should be provided or marked *Not Applicable*.

## 8.16    Security Risk Analysis Report

Here is a typical table of contents of a security risk analysis report. This report would be used as the basis for implementing and thereafter testing a set of security measures.

### 8.16.1    Introduction

1. Objectives
2. Methods
3. Conclusions

4. Scope and limitations
5. Assumptions
6. Historical factors
7. Difficulties encountered
8. Constraints
9. Information for those conducting future risk analyses
10. Documentation used

## 8.16.2   The Environment

1. Building details
2. Room details
3. Physical access control methods
   a. Fingerprints
   b. Eyeprints
   c. Cards
   d. Keys
   e. Codes
4. External cabling security
5. Network topology
6. Machine specifications
7. Firewall details
8. Router details
9. Security software on all hardware
10. Operating systems used
11. Policies
    a. Security applied
    b. Password control
    c  User and group profiles
    d. Authorization control
    e. Configuration management
    f. Archiving
    g. Production software security
    h. Telephone, cell phone, and fax
    i. Video
    j. Wifi
    k. Internet
    l. Audit access

## 8.16.3   The Risks Section

1. The information assets at risk
2. The threats and vulnerabilities considered
3. The risks, the probabilities of occurrence, and the value loss
4. Business harm
5. Likelihood
6. Third party risk analysis
7. Assessments
   a. Statutory requirements
   b. Contractual requirements

    c.  Business practices
    d.  System deployment
    e.  Business system development
    f.  Business planning
    g.  Business procedure
    h.  Security controls
    i.  Security methods
    j.  Plan
    k.  Personnel security
    l.  Authority
    m. Security management
    n.  Documentation security management
    o.  Data security management
    p.  Security incident management
    q.  System development security
    r.  User access management
    s.  Media security management
    t.  Network security management
    u.  PC, terminal, and mainframe security management
    v.  Other hardware security

### 8.16.4   The Existing Countermeasures Section

1. The major security measures currently in use or in the process of being installed.
2. The threat(s) and risk(s) each countermeasure is intended to address.

### 8.16.5   The Proposed Countermeasures Section

1. A prioritized list of recommended protective measures or safeguards and their costs.
2. A cost–benefit analysis of each countermeasure.
3. The degree of risk acceptance or the remaining exposure after implementation of the recommended protective measure.
4. The effect of implementing technical and procedural protective measures in terms of their effect on the security of information assets.
5. The relationship of recommended safeguards to existing threats, information assets, and risks.
6. The resources necessary to develop, implement, and maintain the protective measures, with particular emphasis on technical security solutions.
7. The security procedures and controls that exist or that must be implemented to maintain the required standards of information integrity and access.

## 8.17   Risk Log

A risk log is a simple means of managing risk. For a more detailed approach see [Levinson] and [IEEE Std 1540-2001]. Table 8.5 is used as an example of major risks to a project.

## 8.18   Daily Test Report

Some organizations prefer a daily test report. It is a good discipline. It could contain:

- **Period covered.** "*This is the test report for release a.b.c. build d of system X for the period 0900 30th–0900 31st June.*" Add a management summary identifying any big bugs found. The number of P1, P2, P3, and P4 bugs found. The number expected to be found.

**TABLE 8.5** Risk log example

| Risk description | Effects and how to assess | Probability | Mitigation |
|---|---|---|---|
| **Requirements tracking —** there is no means in place to relate features in general and requirements in particular to bugs, or parts of code. It is difficult to identify what features are in what state at any time. | Difficulty in:<br>• associating a bug with a feature and therefore deciding whether to declare that feature present in a release,<br>• deciding which features to concentrate on when regression-testing,<br>• identifying which features most need rewriting<br>• identifying common bug patterns.<br>• (Related to *Requirements completeness* below) | 100% | Ensure that as soon as a requirements baseline document be established that all related bugs are raised with a reference to it. |
| **Requirements completeness** — there are no definitions available of the product as a whole. | Insufficient test coverage of the system as a whole showing up in high levels of Support and casually-found bugs | 50% | Extend the product documentation to become useable as requirements specifications. Ensure that release specification is integrated with that documentation. Match all product parts against one or more documents |
| **Testing — system**. It is not possible to system-test any part of a new feature quickly: bugs may only be evident after some feature has been usable for some time. | It is rare that > 10 bugs are found per day. | 25% | Can only be resolved slowly by ensuring that test coverage is greater with each release. |
| **Planning — beta testing**. No beta test has so far been undertaken which has yielded any useful feedback. | Bugs found in the field are quite different to those found in-house. | 40% | Plan for greater involvement by users, who are selected and supported with more care than hitherto. |
| Support interferes with development schedules | Decreasing productivity as developers have to context-switch continually. | 60% | Ensure that the only Support requests accepted are those which are replicated by Support, or which are priority 1 category and require a hotfix. |

• **Features being tested.** List them.
• **Bug profile:** A chart showing the number of bugs found so far, as shown below.

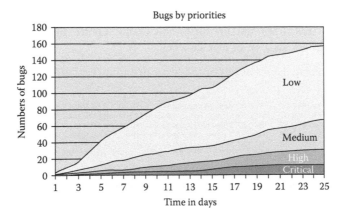

**FIGURE 8.28** Bug detection chart

- (Perhaps weekly) A chart showing which features were the **primary sources of bugs**.

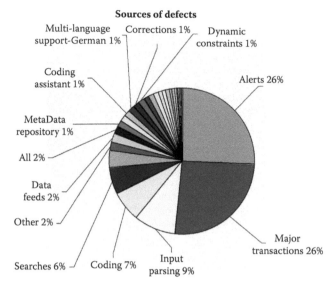

**FIGURE 8.29**  Bug sources

- A list of the **headlines of the bugs** found along with their priority and then name of the person who found them (including a description of the impact on software and system performance, the impact a correction would have on software and system design, and recommendations for correcting the deficiency, limitation, or constraint).
- An **assessment** of the software as demonstrated by the test results.
- The **percentage of tests completed** (i.e., planned versus actual) taken from section 8.6.3.
- The **requirements coverage** status (possibly using the test/feature matrix; see section 15.2 for an example).
- The **documentation** status: which specifications are available, reviewed, changes requested or signed-off, and when.[7]
- The **RFC** (Request For Change) status.
- Any problems of the **test environment** for example taken from the *Test log*.

# 8.19  Reporting Using TestDirector™ (now Quality Center)

We need to report daily on the status of test development and execution. One way is by using TestDirector™ (or its equivalent) and a primary spreadsheet. To populate this primary spreadsheet you need to export a lot of test results from TestDirector™ (now Quality Center) in Excel format.

The primary spreadsheet has a set of tabs showing:

- *<feature>* containing details of sets of tests extracted from TestDirector™

| ◇ | A | B | C | D | E |
|---|---|---|---|---|---|
| 10 | RFC 87 | RFC 87 Support National Service [1]P40 Ret | MANUAL | Passed | |
| 11 | RFC 87 | RFC 87 Support National Service [1]P42 Ret | MANUAL | Passed | |
| 12 | RFC 87 | RFC 87 Support National Service [1]P60 Tra | MANUAL | Passed | |
| 13 | RFC 87 | RFC 87 Support National Service [1]P62 Tra | MANUAL | Passed | |
| 14 | RFC 87 | RFC 87 Support National Service [1]P80 Tra | MANUAL | Passed | |

Ι◀ ◀ ▶ ▶Ι   Data streams ⟍ RFC 87 ⟍ Critical codes ⟍ Schedules ⟍ Smoke &

---

[7] This is a way of negotiating any changes to specifications. Long before you begin system testing you can thus ensure management is aware of the status of your inputs so they have the opportunity to get you better documents earlier. You can also defend yourself against charges of failing to complete testing "on time" by showing how you warned them of document volatility.

- *Overview* containing an amalgamated view of the *feature* tabs

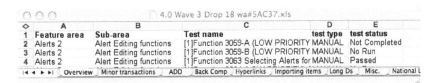

- *Charts* displaying data extracted from the *overview* tab

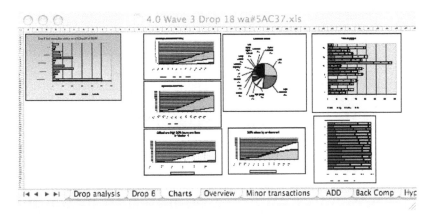

The process works as discussed in the following section.

## 8.19.1   Setting Up the Spreadsheets

1. Open TestDirector™.

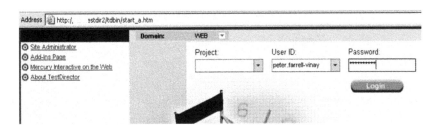

2. Select a test results sheet in the *Test Lab* tab, right-click anywhere on it and "*Select All.*"

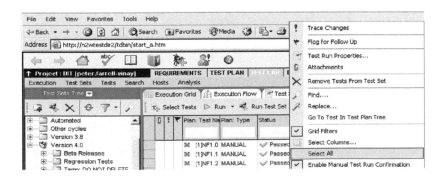

3. The sheet will then be entirely chosen and you can save it as an Excel spreadsheet. Give it a name such as "test x" (this example uses "*RFC 87 test set 1*").

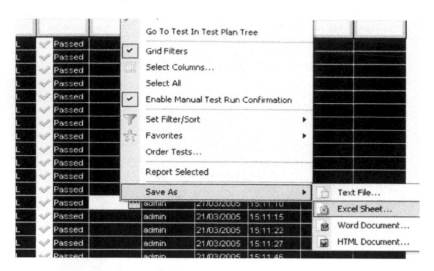

4. Save the Excel sheet to a folder in the "test *files*" directory (in this case "*RFC 87*") overwriting any current one and using its name.

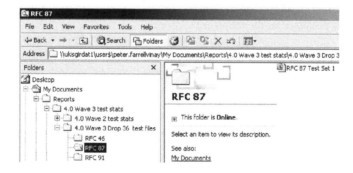

5. If the file is newly-created, open and copy the three critical columns "*Test name, Type*" and "*Status.*"

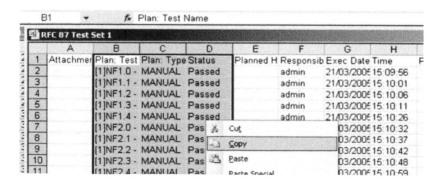

6. Use "*Paste special*" to paste the columns into the related *Feature* tab of your primary spreadsheet, in this case called "*RFC 87.*"

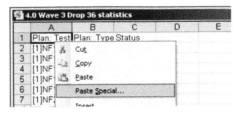

7. And then *"Paste Link."*

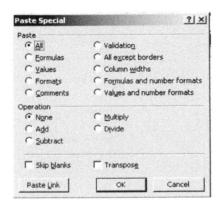

8. When all new test data have been pasted into the *Features* tabs they can be echoed through to the *Overview* tab.

## 8.19.2   Updating the Spreadsheets Thereafter

1. As tests are run the changed test sheets in Test lab can overwrite the existing ones. When all of them are updated with the preceding day's results, use Edit > Links on the main spreadsheet to open all the test results sheets and update the main spreadsheet.

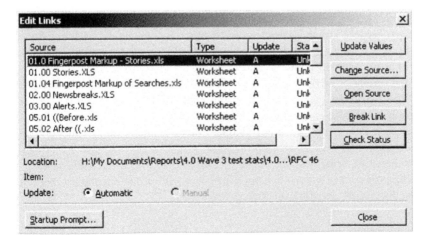

2. Select all the linked documents and press the *Open source* button.
3. If any of the links are rusty use the *Change source* button to change them.
4. Go to the *<release name>* tab and update the data by right-clicking on the pivot table and using the *Refresh Data* command.

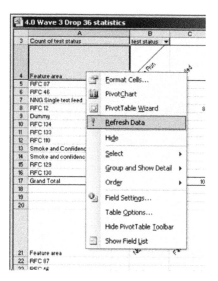

5. At this point all the charts will be updated and a brief overview prepared.

# 8.20   Choosing a Set of Test Documents

The choice of amount and types of software documentation depends on:

- The size and riskiness of the project
- The required visibility of the test process

Suggestions:

- Don't duplicate information between the documents in the test documentation set. Define the common attributes of any group of specifications at the highest possible level. Thus if the environmental needs of all test cases are the same, then define the environment in the master test plan.
- If some or all the content of a section is in another document, then refer to that material in place of the corresponding content. Attach the referenced material to the test plan or make them available to users of the plan.
- Distinguish between *formal* and *working* test documents. *Formal* documents are those which are exchanged between groups or referred to by other documents. For *working* documents, legible notes in a personal log-book are normally sufficient. *Formal* documents should conform to the project's documentation standards and be held within the project file.
- Leave the format of working documents to the discretion of the project manager. Ensure they reflect the scope and purpose of the corresponding formal documents and are available for inspection as evidence of testing.
- Identify each formal test document uniquely with a name, a document number, and an issue number.
- Specify the set of formal test documents in the test plan under *Test deliverables*.
- On a big project have a documentation manager with a documentation plan and a means of holding documents electronically such as *Sharepoint*.

# 8.21 Quality Plan

Use the quality plan to identify how the project manages the overall quality issues. One of these is the need to test.

## 8.21.1 Introduction

Briefly describe the project including its purpose and whether it continues any previous work.

## 8.21.2 Reference Documents

List all documents referenced elsewhere in the text of the plan including national, international and client standards. State the version of each document adopted for use on the project, unless it never gets revised.

## 8.21.3 Quality System

Refer to a document describing the quality system which includes a process model.

## 8.21.4 Organization

List those personnel performing key quality control functions, by function and by name, together with their reporting relationships, responsibilities, and degree of independence from those responsible for system development and use. Say how any change to these staff names or relationships will be made. List any interfaces with independent validation and verification agencies.

## 8.21.5 Associated Plans

List all associated project and plans produced, such as the:

- Project plan
- Configuration management plan
- Documentation plan
- Test and integration plan
- Subcontractor's and client's quality plans

Where specified plans are not yet available, give target milestones for their production. Refer to all mandatory standards to be used on the project. State that all cited optional or project-specific standards are mandatory on the project.

## 8.21.6 Deliverable Items

List each project deliverable, unless it has already been listed in the project plan, when a reference will suffice.

## 8.21.7 Design and Development Standards and Practices

### 8.21.7.1 Project and Product Management

Declare the management methods by specifying standards from the following:

- Project planning procedure
- Project reporting procedure
- Requirements specification procedure

### 8.21.7.2  Process Model

Include a model showing the principal project processes complete with all baselines, responsible groups, and the project environment.

### 8.21.7.3  Techniques and Methods

Specify all project techniques and methods by reference to any standards (e.g., codes of design practice), to define their use in the project. Consider writing project-specific standards for those project areas where none is yet available (e.g., coding in a new language).

## 8.21.8  Quality Control Standards

Specify all standards used for the control of quality on the project.

### 8.21.8.1  Corrective Action

Define a corrective-action process to manage all problems detected in any item under configuration control or in the project activities required by the contract. This must ensure that:

- All problems detected from whatever source are promptly identified, reported, entered, and resolved.
- All problems are related to items under configuration management.
- The circumstances and nature of the problem, together with any other available information are identified and recorded.
- The result of any investigation is recorded.
- The action taken to correct the problem is recorded.
- The status of each problem is tracked and reported.
- Records of the problems are maintained in a database and are available during the project to client.
- Inputs to the corrective action process consist of problem/change reports and other anomaly reports.
- Each problem is classified by category, severity, and priority.
- Trends in the problems reported are analyzed.
- Corrective actions are evaluated to:
  - Verify that problems have been resolved, adverse trends have been reversed, and changes implemented in the processes and items.
  - Help determine whether additional problems have been introduced.

### 8.21.8.2  Reviews

Describe the technical and managerial reviews to be conducted with respect to the system development, either directly or by reference to a standard.

### 8.21.8.3  Testing

Include a statement of the testing strategy to be adopted. Refer to the method of test planning and documentation. Define the level of testing rigor in the *Testing* section.

### 8.21.8.4  Quality Control Records

Specify quality control records selected to match the development method.

### 8.21.8.5  Other Quality Controls

All the elements of the plan apply to all deliverables: hardware, software, documentation, or training.

### 8.21.9  Client-Supplied Material

If there be deliverables or items furnished by the client or other third party used on the project, the quality plan must stipulate their care and control.

### 8.21.10  Quality Milestones

All projects must identify the quality milestones or key events related to the quality control of the deliverables.

Quality milestones shall include:

- Principal reviews
- Completion of key documents (such as the requirements specification)
- Key acceptance/certification events

The timely application of quality control functions tracking these milestones are identified.

### 8.21.11  Unusual Features

Declare any unusual features of the project in this section and identify the standards produced to address them.

### 8.21.12  Risk Areas

Identify all aspects of the project (such as the use of new techniques) which may present a particular risk to project quality and the controls specified to address such risks. Identify each risk by:

- Name
- Probability (%)
- Risk implications
- Dependencies on other events for the risk to occur
- Other events which would be affected were the risk to occur
- Priority
- Risk minimization/avoidance plan

### 8.21.13  Documentation

Identify a structure for the documentation produced during the project and referenced in the quality plan. Indicate the types of document to be generated using as a minimum the following:

- Requirements specification
- Design description
- Test documentation
- User documentation
- Hardware engineering documentation

### 8.21.14  Configuration Management

Refer to:

- The items subject to configuration management, either directly or by reference to a documentation or configuration management plan

- The control mechanisms for identifying, approving, implementing, and recording changes
- The means of controlling changes affecting client or subcontractor contracts
- All quality controls to be exercised on all changes

## 8.21.15  Procurement

Specify the standards required for control of all purchased or subcontracted goods or services. These standards must include provisions for:

- Purchasing
- Goods inwards
- Subcontractor control

Identify all subcontractors involved in the project, along with any special control provisions (such as a subcontract quality plan).

## 8.21.16  Tools

List the items used to support the project. Proprietary tools must be subject to procurement controls.

### 8.21.16.1  Archive Control

Define the methods and facilities used to maintain and store controlled versions of items. State the methods and facilities to be used to protect computer program media from unauthorized access, inadvertent damage, or degradation.

### 8.21.16.2  Records Collection, Maintenance, and Retention

Identify the documentation to be retained, together with the methods and facilities to be used to assemble, safeguard, and enhance this documentation, and shall specify the retention period.

## 8.21.17  Installation

Control the installation, commissioning or any other work on a client's site by standards or other means listed here. Refer to any external standards dictating working practices on client premises.

## 8.21.18  Acceptance

Specify the arrangements for client acceptance of the project deliverables. Describe all quality control activities directly supporting customer handover and any client requirements for certification or delivery paperwork.

# 9

# The Test Team and Its Context

## 9.1 Recruiting the Test Team

# The Gold Team

There was once a team of testers. They were a mix of programmers and operators. The operators knew similar systems backwards, and the programmers knew how to build systems and write scripts. They all knew that testing meant finding bugs early. So they wrote lots of test scripts to test a bank system. In doing this they found lots of bugs in the specifications themselves. (*"Which we know about anyway, and were just going to tell you about,"* said the management. Every time.) They liaised very closely with the developers — so closely that some of them later *became* developers. And the management saw the scripts and were very pleased.

Then they started testing the first build, and the second, and the third. Then they stopped and said, *"Aren't three untestable builds in a week overdoing it a bit?"* and management twitched a little, and they agreed that an experienced tester would check out each build before the team loaded it onto all their machines. And another 10 builds were made before the team started testing again.

And they found bugs galore. And developers fixed, and management sweated, and time passed. And every deadline under the sun was missed, and customers got really edgy. And it got so bad that the project manager slammed the test manager up against a wall and screamed, *"You're doing it on purpose!" "Doing what?" "Finding these errors!"*

But senior management were under no illusions — releasing a poor build could provoke a rich crop of very senior redundancies, because they had built badly in the past and the customers wanted no more of it. Also, they had learned to look at the bug detection chart, and not release until it was nearly flat. So eventually a preliminary demonstration release was made and many agéd fingers were crossed, as just a few customer staff used it in earnest. And three weeks later some interesting bugs were exposed and analyzed, and the testers revised their tests.

Finally the first release was made, and it went up. And it stayed up. And the four key programmers who were warned to be on hand to create emergency fixes found that they had nothing to do and could get on with version 2. And version 2 was built and tested in record time, and was as solid as version 1, so even the accountants started to smile.

## 9.1.1   The Test Manager

The test manager needs a number of qualities. He:

- **Is able to judge people** to distinguish the:
  - Determined from the hangers-on
  - Beginners from the finishers
  - Intellectually-curious from the merely technology-obsessed
- Is able to **distinguish between the true and the useful**.
- Is **methodical**: this is so obvious a prerequisite that it's often overlooked.
- **Listens well** to what is being said. Why? What is *not* being said? Who is telling you? What is their advantage in ensuring you know? He notices what *isn't* being said (and ought to be).
- Is largely **unconcerned for popularity**: he won't be popular at many moments in his career, and he needs to be able to withstand that pressure. He will meet accusations that he is not a *team player* with equanimity. It's not his job to be a nice guy and he knows it. A test manager must have grown out of the need to be loved by his colleagues. His relationship with development and other teams needs to be purely professional because there will be times when that professionalism will come under strain.
- Can **withstand management pressure**: he must have a very tough idea of what must be done and be prepared to fight for it. He will not compromise on essentials. He will know in advance what he can afford to sacrifice. Eventually people will learn not to pressure him.
- Will **back the judgment of his staff**: if staff believe they are liable to be massacred because they're trying to do their job as they see fit, they will either fail or leave.
- Can **curb enthusiasm in staff**, tactfully: good staff may get carried away by the Very Interesting Bug they have just found or the Very Wonderful Tool they have just downloaded. It's the test manager's job to retain the enthusiasm while pointing out that the feature containing the bug is about to be removed for other reasons. (Like: it doesn't work.) And maybe he agrees that the tester can experiment with that tool, later, when the heat's off.
- **Sees what is in front of his eyes**: when a mass of small human interface errors are being regularly found, the implication that the entire system may be simply unusable can be hidden from a test manager locked into day-to-day concerns.
- **Praises staff justly**: this non-trivial ability is highly related to having chosen good staff in the first place, but even then, the difference well-timed praise can exert is considerable, lasting, and can be measured by staff preparedness to work late and weekends. Praise is a currency which can be devalued, particularly by being fulsome. A grimace and an earnest *"nice"* is often all that's needed.
- Is **ruthless**: bad staff must be sacked; it is a gross discourtesy to other staff (however popular the errant person may be) to retain them when they are evidently failing. Bad management also needs to be identified and their effects prepared for.
- Is **instinctive**: irrespective of the reassurances of team leaders or senior management when he feels something is wrong he finds out what it is — it may be himself. There is always someone who prefers emollient phrases to objectivity, and it's not the test manager.
- Is **concerned for process** and support: a good test manager will have several back-of-the-envelope process models, and have looked at:
  - The tools needed to support the various processes
  - The outputs of those processes
- Is **objective**: he will have a limited (and possibly varying) set of objectives which he will attempt to prove he has met with a judicious use of metrics. Everything he does can be related to one or more of those objectives.
- **Motivates**: he will keep testers motivated partly by assessing the risk posed by particularly-critical bugs, and ensuring that the developers, management and testers understand this risk, partly by encouragement, recognition of achievement and feedback, and partly by being a reference point.

- Has a **low paranoia liability**: he will get paranoid anyway, but as Ronald Reagan famously observed: "*I get so worried I'm beginning to have sleepless afternoons.*"
- Is **prepared to admit defeat**: At some point he must (be prepared to) concede that the system isn't too bad and can be released.
- Is **able to philosophize**: a good test manager must always be a philosopher king *manqué*. He will be unhappy if he cannot relate events and phenomena somehow.
- Is **able to stand back** from the fray: there are always bugs, triumphs, and catastrophes. So what? What does this mean for the customers, the company, the share price, the project, and the test team? A test manager must have a sufficient sense of balance that he can evaluate events without undue pessimism (which is a natural tendency of all successful test managers).
- Is **able to get to the thick of the fray**: all test managers must have a slight hankering to test something. It's what gives them an edge. The good test managers can mostly resist this until crises strike.
- **Has been a tester**: You cannot understand a tester's motivations and values if you don't bear the scars.

---

# How to (Not) Choose a Subordinate

E arly in 1944 there was a British Prisoner of War camp near Chester, full of Germans. The camp commandant badly wanted to be part of the invasion of Europe. He pulled strings. Lieut.-General Brian Horrocks heard of him, and decided to pay a visit.

On the appointed day, the camp commandant and all his staff paraded at the front gate, and waited. And waited. And a sergeant came and told the commandant that, er, Horrocks had been and gone. Sir.

"Gone?"

"Yes, sir, came in through the back gate, went straight to the prisoners' mess, sir. Then he left." Horrocks had opened a salt cellar and found no salt.

See en.wikipedia.org/wiki/Brian_Horrocks for other stories of Horrocks. But not *this* story.

---

## 9.1.2   The Testers

Testers are:

- **Literate**: they have no difficulty reading or writing. They'll have to do both. They can spot a split infinitive two paragraphs away and they do.
- **Numerate**: they don't have to know calculus but it would be nice.
- **Programmate**[1]: they must be able to read and write code if they are going to automate tests. So they must either be programmers too or are capable of becoming one.[2]
- **Logical** (which you'd expect if they're literate, numerate, etc., but which means they anticipate trouble in interfaces, specifications, etc., which nicer, more trusting people would miss).

---

[1] \<sigh>Yeah, OK. Sorry.\</sigh> Shakespeare and Chaucer both turned in their graves then. But you read it here first.

[2] This directly conflicts with the claims made by a number of automated testing tools coming onto the market. It is true that they don't necessarily involve scripting in the manner of (say) WinRunner, but (for example) Quick Test Pro includes the facility for writing functions. For non-trivial tests you will need to program.

- **Team players:** they must both be able to work with, and trust each other. There will be occasions when another's judgment is needed. Being a team player no more is part of what makes the transfer to being a test manager painful. Testers must also talk to developers such that the developers don't feel threatened.
- **Tactful, diplomatic, persistent, and firm:** this involves never entering arguments they cannot win.
- **Destructive:** there is no greater challenge than to be told that some system is "rock-solid." Their attitude is similar to General Orde Wingate's: "*No jungle is impenetrable until you have penetrated it.*" Testers refuse to accept "yes" for an answer. They are born skeptics.
- Concerned for **attention to detail**: a phrase can make an enormous difference in a specification; a comma can change the meaning of a sentence. This is how they win their arguments ("*ah, but it says in the spec*"). Their salt-cellars are always full.
- Able to become **domain experts**: it's nice if they are already, but people must start somewhere. Thinking clearly is more important.
- Highly sensitive to **cognitive dissonance**: they can spot a naked emperor at 50 paces, and can decipher 10 kinds of corporate bullshit.
- **Natural pessimists:** irrespective of the enthusiasm of developers and management, they can retain a childlike faith in the system's eventual failure.
- **Technically-competent** rather than geeky: technology is simply something which helps them do a job. They are neither in awe of it nor do they see it as some extension of any personal attribute.
- **Precise** to the point of tedium: people's lives may depend on the number of zeroes to the right of the decimal point.
- Able to **see the implications** of unconnected trivia: the fact that <back-tab><back-tab><back-tab> <text><text><text> was sometimes followed by text vanishing may not occur to the average person.
- Able to **multi-task**: while sometimes they can concentrate on testing a single feature, there will be times in which issues arise concerning several.
- **Methodical:** their sense of order may be more real than apparent, but it's there. They tend to keep notes obsessively, not always in the same place.
- Able to **manage their time**: a good tester knows when to give up and look for some other bug.
- **Creative:** they will think of new ways of testing and new questions to ask.

Testers tend to gross egalitarianism probably because a bug is a bug whoever finds it. Introducing all but the subtlest hierarchies is thus counter-productive. However here is a way of grading them. (Note that simply because someone *can* lead a team it doesn't mean they *must* in order to be considered or paid as a *senior*[3]):

- Basic:
  - Understands the software life-cycle.
  - Executes/maintains *test cases*.
  - Submits/verifies bug reports.
- Experienced
  - As *basic* level.
  - Write *test cases*.
  - Can code.
  - Write/run/maintain automated test scripts, and write test specifications.
  - Provide time estimates.
  - Participate in design/requirement reviews.
  - Mentor new testers during projects.
  - Contribute to maintaining and improving test technology and process.

---

[3] Some people loathe being responsible for others. It is wise to allow them to remain as technical experts alone.

- Can use test tools.
- Can write unit tests.
- Senior level:
  - As experienced level.
  - Write master test plan/report.
  - Mentor mid level testers.
  - Plan/execute system level tests.
  - Manage test automation.
  - Identify and manage metric programs.
  - Drive test process and technology improvements.
  - Able to lead a team.
  - Able to mentor and train all staff levels.
  - Can function as a test consultant
  - Can present to board level.

## 9.2  Test Qualifications

### 9.2.1  International Institute for Software Testing

The International Institute for Software Testing (www.testing.org) offers certification as a:

- Certified software test professional
- Certified test manager

Each requires 10 days training.

### 9.2.2  Information Systems Examinations Board (ISEB)

The British Computer Society runs a 2-level software testing qualification (www.bcs.org/BCS/Products/Qualifications/ISEB/Areas/SoftTest):

- The Foundation Certificate is for software developers, testers, managers, and anyone with an interest in testing. This certificate provides visible evidence that the individual understands the basics of software testing.
- The Practitioner Certificate is for experienced testing practitioners. This certificate demonstrates a depth of knowledge of testing topics and the ability to perform testing activities in practice.

Both syllabi focus mostly on testing with some reference to reviewing configuration management and other quality concerns.

### 9.2.3  American Society for Quality (ASQ)

This has a Software Quality Engineer (CSQE) qualification by examination. The syllabus covers many aspects of quality but little of it is directly concerned with testing. See www.asq.org/training-and-certification.html

### 9.2.4  Quality Assurance Institute

Has a Certified Software Tester (CSTE) grade entirely devoted to testing. See www.softwarecertifications.com

## 9.3  Test Team Structures

### 9.3.1  Stage-Related

There are still some organizations which have special-to-phase validation and verification staff. The justification given is that the systems being developed are so highly-specialized that there is more value in having a specification reviewed (say) by a technical specialist, not responsible for its creation, than by the tester who will use it.

The justification is wholly spurious. Systems needing to be specified by PhDs may need to be tested by PhDs, but they need to be testers (with PhDs), not PhDs who have to be goaded into testing. Compartmenting stages inhibits the development of a development-process-related overview such that the risks inherent in transforming a requirement into a design, test or manual, and a design into code will only be appreciated by the design authority (if then). The persons with a stake in exposing the risks (the users and testers) will be excluded.

None of this however relieves developers of the responsibility for writing and executing their own unit tests.

### 9.3.2  Specialization-Related

Some organizations employ specialists who alone are able to take requirements and design decisions on some feature. In this case it is widely-recognized that validation and verification needs the reinforcement of comparable expertise. This is the basis of the appointment of the Independent Safety Advisor to many safety-critical projects.

Many organizations have a test group. The better ones involve that group at all stages of a system's development from contract negotiation to retirement.

### 9.3.3  Feature-Related

To minimize compartmentization, some organizations have split their development teams into feature teams each of which consists of up to 4 programmers, two testers (a senior and a junior), and a technical author.

(One or two of) the developers write the specifications and feed them back to marketing, the technical author, and the testers.

The teams then develop and the technical author writes up the feature for the manuals.

The testers review the specifications and the manuals, and offer feedback. They also learn how the feature works, and write test objectives, and test scripts. One tester is thus always available for feedback both to the developers and other testers, as well as attending meetings.

There is thus a curious relationship between testers and developers. Developers have to report to the project manager (typically via the team leader). Testers must ultimately report to the test manager. The test manager is thus a safety-net in the event that testers become pressured by developers. There is also a point at which testers *"return to the fold"* and execute system tests as part of the test team. That period is characterized by some strain and sense of betrayal on the part of the developers unhappy that their tester colleagues have shown that the developers' Very Wonderful creations occasionally don't work.

## 9.4  Assessing the Test Team

Despite all the "good" things written of them there are several critical attributes testers must have:

- The ability to find a lot of bugs
- The ability to find them in odd places
- The patience to prepare good tests

To assess any team member solely on the number of bugs they find will lead to bug inflation as multiple manifestations of the same bug are sought rather than different bugs. When assessing team members, bear in mind both the difficulty involved in finding the bug and the apparent bugginess of the feature concerned.

## 9.5   Motivating the Test Team

Don't even try. Test teams smell corporate bullshit at 30 paces and are motivated by:

- The **lust for power**: in finding a bug they are forcing a lot of people who were trying to do something else, to pay attention to that tester, stop what they were doing, and fix it. Running their test team the way (they think) it ought to be run, is a delight known only unto test managers.
- **Attention seeking**: they find a bug, and everyone pays attention to them. They are recognized! Recognizing ability is better value than a company "jolly."
- **Determination to get a good product out**: there is a delight in the silent 'phone, the absence of helpdesk calls, and the flat bug detection graphs. All is well. Unlike developers who (allegedly) crave excitement, testers are only too delighted to have none of it. *"It went out, it went up, and it stayed up"* is a proud boast. *"You should have found that"* is a condemnation.
- **Community buzz**: the water-fountain chat, the recognition not simply of their peers but of the developers. One development team leader said, *"We've never had bugs of this seriousness or complexity raised so early before."* When reported to the test team they almost purred.
- **Self-aggrandizement**: the tester who modestly disclaims all responsibility for finding that difficult intermittent bug has yet to be born. We are modest but not *that* modest.
- **Greed**: they want more money. How unusual.

Testers like the odd company "jolly" as much as anyone else: it's sociable and improves relations. It is not a substitute for the late nights required by poor planning or a recompense for being treated like pariahs because of the embarrassment they provoke. To send testers on courses, to buy them the tools they need, to review their work (and find fault in it), to encourage them to write papers and attend learned conferences are far more effective ways of motivating than feeding and watering them.

## 9.6   Career Progression

Testers:

- Think.
- Write documents.
- Review documents.
- Design tests.
- Write and execute code.
- Manage people.

There is thus nothing in what they do which inhibits a move to other careers within IT. Many have so moved. Testing is in fact an excellent basis for a career in programming since the habit of testing (and thereby getting feedback) is already instilled. Companies can reinforce this by assigning:

- New graduates to act as unit testers, possibly paired with a more-senior programmer, for a *limited* number of months (because otherwise testing will be seen as a career black hole).
- New business analysts (and anyone involved in writing requirements specifications) to system testing such that they learn not to make mistakes in writing requirements specifications.
- Testers with enough programming experience to work as junior programmers (if they really want to program they'll accept).
- Senior testers to work as business analysts or technical writers.
- Test managers to work as project managers.
- Testers to work as second-line help-desk *Support* staff and vice versa.

In practice good testers have so much fun testing that they are often reluctant to move. If testing is ever seen as a repository for poor programmers then you have a big problem.

# Story

A lasdair was not God's gift to programming. Black Jack told him so with his usual sense of tact and camaraderie. "Alasdair, yer effing program disnae[4] effing work!" he screamed. A year later Alasdair was wished onto the test team. He was given a compiler to write test objectives for and a severe dressing down when his specs were reviewed. The test manager had enquired:

"What does this test do?"

"Mmm."

We will draw a veil. Alasdair went away chastened. He wrote. He returned. His test objectives were reviewed and approved. He wrote some tests. He ran them.

There was silence from Alasdair for several days. He arrived early; he left late. And he started finding bugs. Big ones. Ones the Corporation had been plagued with for years Alasdair had found himself.

So he worked as he had never worked before, and then resigned to become a test manager.

## 9.7  Relations

Relations with other staff are conditioned by a company's culture. Here are some indicators of cultures best avoided but, if you have no choice, treated with caution:

- In organizations with few rules inherent in the job, few established routines, where a project manager can approve non-routine decisions, and ride roughshod over developer's calls for clear specifications, and design tools, and time without fear of being criticized, a test manager will soon find that only a disaster will curb such behavior, and will ensure he cannot be seen to have been responsible for that disaster.

- In organizations with few rewards for reliability and predictability, and many rewards for unusual performance/innovation, crises are encouraged as a way of seeking both attention and extra rewards. Project managers will exploit this by working late hours, and expecting development and test staff to do likewise. Get the time sheets and work out the cost of all that overtime first if you want to change such things.

- In organizations which focus on short-term fluctuations and lose sight of long-term objectives, such short-sightedness becomes self-reinforcing. The more the long-term goals go unattended, the more a project manager feels powerless, and the greater the need to prove that he or she is in control of daily events at least. Expect great hostility at triage and bug meetings, and constant questioning of your role, as the failing project manager attempts to distract attention. There will also be many spurious attempts to waste your time with requests for print-outs of test scripts and obscure data. Always provide them and log each request. This will tell you when the bad times occurred for the project manager, and what sort of requests to expect.

- In organizations with conflicting goals, particularly those which fail to appreciate the central importance of IT to its health, a project manager may have to spend half his time re-educating senior management. You can help by explaining what would have happened to the business were the 10 biggest bugs *not* found by your team.

- Some organizations are dominated by a plan-free culture to avoid any possibility of blame for having failed to meet the requirements of that plan. The lack of plans is frequently matched by a

---

[4]  Yes, they are both Scots.

passivity which reinforces the failure to plan by claiming that planning is useless, the situation changes too fast. Procrastination thus becomes institutionalized.

Project and test managers must survive in these dysfunctional states. You need to see the project manager and yourself in relationship to them.

## 9.7.1  Relations with Project Management

Project management is trying to do something very much against the odds. They tend to see testers as the people who stop them. Like everyone else they suffer from a number of shortcomings with very serious effects:

- **Time-discounting**: time is discounted by perceiving events as being farther away in time than they are. Events such as angry customers cancelling, are rarely imagined, much less prepared for. You may notice that, being one of the last activities before a release, testing consequently occupies a diminished space in project management's universe. Counter this by establishing that system testing won't end until a number of criteria are satisfied (see section 4.6.5 in Chapter 4), and ensure that the time provisionally planned for this is likely to be sufficient.
- **Deferred gratification**: we all want to see instant results. Managers (you included) want to see code written, tests running etc., ASAP, and releases hitting the market like clockwork. Counter any tendency to cut corners by writing a process model of how you will develop and run tests, and then identify the outputs, and monitor their development. Write a plan with dates, buffer time, and deliverables, and watch how much you slip. Then you can both:
  - Empathize with the project manager when he panics.
  - Be able to answer the question *"how far behind are you"* when the project manager asks.
  - Know how much buffer time you have left.

  All those intermediate steps will ease the pain of deferring your gratification.
- **Comfort zoning**: project managers have comfort zones like anyone else, and their comfort zone sometimes consists of well-ordered events proceeding to a successful release with a few interruptions most of which the project manager has already foreseen, and allowed for. A test manager's comfort zone consists of large numbers of product-fatal bugs which he, and his trusty team have found, through sheer-hard-work-and-ability, thus saving the company from bankruptcy, chapter-11 restructuring, and unfortunate references in the media. The slight discontinuity between these zones can be minimized by:
  - Checking the project plan and identifying missing actions.
  - Identifying risks early and observing discreetly how many have been avoided or managed well, at discrete intervals, to the project manager.
  - Thinking like a project manager and having the answers to questions ready. In particular showing how project expectations (bugs expected versus found) are being met (or not) as soon as possible.
  - Not making positive announcements until you can be sure they are realistic. Up to that point the most any project manager should be able to get from you by way of a prediction is: *"so far so good."*[5]
- **Cognitive dissonance** is that state where what one wants to see isn't what one sees, and one denies that what one sees is there. People who cannot cope with these signs will avoid sources of such information. Project managers can become so concerned for project success that they refuse to see the warning signs of impending failure. Test managers are prime sources of this information. Expect to be avoided. Counter this (as best you can) by *"developing warm personal relations with the project manager"* (as the psychologist suggests) or by ensuring everyone in the room where

---

[5] In *The Magnificent Seven*, Vin tells the Village Elder of the man who jumped off a 20-storey building *"...and at each floor people kept hearing him say 'so far so good.'"*

you make your reports is well aware of the idea of cognitive dissonance and its implications. Slipping projects and failing systems are strong triggers of cognitive dissonance. The cognitive dissonance inherent in self-deception can, under pressure, result in totemism or optimism raised to the level of ideology. When the difference between emotional and intellectual acceptance becomes too great or if it concerns information no one in the manager's (aspirant) peer group ever bothers with or is socially inhibited from considering, culpable ignorance or denial can occur.

- **Ignorance of process knowledge**: an expert has a mental model of the process order, rationale, and outcomes of his work. He will know which part can be easily automated. Thus he may write several plans, and have a repertoire of scripts[6] or models, each changing as the work evolves but owing something to its predecessor. The incompetent project manager will not use project planning tools or write the project plan until forced to do so. He will see the plan as a threat in that it contains commitments which must be met. The expert project manager has already fought battles to get enough time for margins, and knows that the plan will change, and that schedules will slip. The incompetent project manager refuses to think of such an eventuality. The expert understands how to stabilize projects, will have a wide repertoire of models on which to draw, and can invent new models as the occasion arises. The incompetent relies on repeating previously-used procedures. The competent test manager will have a plan for his test team, and will have published it to everyone who needs to see it well in advance. He will update it as required.
- **Totemism or fixation** occurs when some artefact becomes imbued with particular meaning, its form and use becomes so fixed in a manager's mind that its original purpose is forgotten. It becomes a totem of the manager's existence. Thus a document or tool becomes divorced from its function of conveying information. Examples:
  - Unusable quality systems: a software subsidiary of one multinational has a quality system certified to ISO 9000 only for the packaging of its product: the quality management system says nothing about software.
  - Unrealistic plans or dates (*"that date is cast in concrete!"*)
  - The bottom line: like any good lie, this totem has a grain of truth in it. If some objectionable course of action does less damage to the bottom line than inaction then a totem has been created.
  - Particular machines; the obsessions exhibited by managers and staff for or against Windows, Linux or MacOS are examples.
- **An inability to estimate** is as common a human failing as forgetfulness. It remains a key link in understanding the start of project failure because if exposed, it is difficult to defend. Thus the incompetent's inability to estimate is only matched by their refusal to do so. And let's face it: none of us is good at estimating.
- **Abreaction to information overload**: an expert project manager knows how much attention to devote to every channel of communication and not to attempt to attend to all of them equally. A novice project manager suffers overload and failure. Project and test managers must absorb a large amount of information much of it saturated with *noise*. Some of the information is unexpected, unwelcome, and difficult to process and react to (bug reports for example). Those project managers who have devised filters such as plans and bug triage meetings to reduce or interpret the noise will cope better. Managers dysfunction when the load induced by the need to interpret, exceeds their threshold. This threshold can be determined by one of three reactions to information, characterized by ability, and preparedness to learn:
  - Acceptance as part of an expected event: the information was expected or easily accepted, and few changes are required. If the solution to the problem the information posed is valid, and is in the project manager's repertoire, there is little to perturb the project management process.

---

[6] A way of behaving. A list of steps for approaching a problem. Experts write their own scripts on the hoof. Novices have very few scripts and cannot easily invent them.

- Reorganization as part of an unexpected development: the reorganization is not part of the project manager's repertoire, and must be quickly devised. The project manager learns much, the reorganization may be suboptimal, but it occurs.
- Denial, because the implications of the information require unreasonable change: the greater the impact of information the more strenuously will it be resisted. Denial is a key driver in the:
  - Decision to shoot messengers.
  - Refusal to accept implications. A device for maintaining a position is to accept the facts (*"yes, of course we need to test the product — it says so in the contract"*) but refuse to accept the implications of those facts (*"but that doesn't mean we have to go to all the expense of buying a test tool and writing down all those details"*).
  - Refusal to assess the risks. Insecure managers may be so terrified of these risks that they refuse to examine them.
  - Refusal to analyze: weak managers will refuse to examine why they must repeatedly fire-fight avoidable crises.
  - Refusal to decide: this is particularly evident where the writing of plans is concerned. The existence of a useable plan implies commitments. Such commitment can later be used to demonstrate failure. Writing a plan implicitly criticizes those managers who have not.

Counter information overload by:
- Minimizing the information (but not its importance) you give the project manager.
- Accustoming the project manager to dealing with unpleasant information (such as bug levels) by triage meetings and graphs.
- Prioritizing your reports (*"There is only one big issue today ..."*).
- Ensuring that all your reports have at least one encouraging message. *"We're finding the bugs faster than we expected,"* *"the critical units are mostly freer of bugs than we expected"* (well some of them).

- **Playing games**: some project managers:
  - **Promise:** things will get better (*"we'll do it properly, next time"*).
  - **Pseudochange:** there is an apparent commitment to change, possibly related to some external reference but not to subsequent events. (*The board has adopted a new management strategy.., ... the organization will be certified to ISO 9000...*) This leads to what [Argyris] refers to as *skilled incompetence* whereby much effort is devoted by dominant incompetent groups to appearance management.
  - **Invalidation** (Aka Not Invented Here): some useful alternative or viewpoint is acknowledged as existing but denied validity (*"... an object-oriented approach wouldn't work in our organization..."*).
  - **Messenger-shooting:** the bearer of ill-tidings is labeled as having a personality problem and disposed of *"...we always had problems with that person."* This is why experienced staff become experts at avoiding confrontation with members of dominant and incompetent groups. Having a weak ego helps.
  - **Dualism:** the available choices are limited to two, irrespective of the potential for finding others. Unsurprisingly one is quite unacceptable. Such an approach is invaluable when scapegoats are needed.
  - **Raising questions about things you cannot be expected to know off-hand:** tell him you don't know, log the questions with a date, get the answers, and email them to the manager, copy to every other attendee at the meeting. Keep the log in your notebook and observe:
    - how and if the questions change.
    - If any use was ever made of the answer.
  When you have had enough of this (and the answers were not used) ask the project manager why he needs to know. Then ask him very kindly not to play games with you.

  The best counter to games is being aware that they are being played, ensuring everyone else is aware, seeing if the organization as a whole is capable of reacting intelligently, and for everyone to draw their own conclusions.

## 9.7.2   Relations with Developers

Developers can even be persuaded to see testers and their manager as allies. Since the developers are the people who must fix whatever bugs you find, you are likely to talk to them a lot: Here's how to treat them:

- Never create a bug report of anything that's not repeatable.
- Stick rigidly to the severity levels you have agreed except when you encounter a difficulty, when you can ask their advice.
- Don't talk to them, send them emails, let them talk to you. They need to be disturbed even less than testers.
- Agree a limited number of channels of communication with their team leaders such that only a limited number of developers are ever liable to be disturbed and then only by a tester directly involved in their domain.
- Document everything, not to catch them out but for future reference.

## 9.7.3   Relations with the Independent Safety Authority

The independent safety authority is appointed under a separate contract, usually by the body which will own and operate the installed system, and is commercially and managerially independent of the design and build team. He is there to assess the quality of the work being done on the safety case. Everything in a safety-critical project contributes to the safety case. The role of testing is to provide evidence that the safety targets have been met and the safety arguments (central to the safety case) are therefore valid. The independent safety authority will therefore look for evidence of thorough testing to prove that the system's reliability is as high as reasonably possible and every means has been employed to test with a level of coverage as extensive as is reasonably possible. The question of engineering judgement is thus paramount.

Do not expect guidance from the independent safety authority as to what is reasonable because that would be exceeding his role. Look rather at:

- The independence of the test team from the development team.
- Relationship between the safety plan and the test plan.
- The ability of the test team to access the safety log,[7] the FMECA and the FTA, and see how the testing of the various elements of a system critical to achieving a reliability target of the various *top event* outcomes can be achieved.
- The degree to which
  - Specifications are shown to be testable and tested.
  - The safety of the system as a whole can be tested.
  - The tests show the system can detect failure.
  - Software is reused and the testing of that software in a new environment.
- How the safety analysis has contributed to the test definition (ensure you have a process model) and how this justifies the test objectives, and the extent to which they can be shown to be adequate.
- The integrity level of the test tools being used.
- How the test process
  - Has contributed to the safety case throughout the phases of the project. See [Kelly 2] for an interesting discussion of the generic arguments which will need to be satisfied by testing.
  - Demonstrates correctness of the arguments proposed by the design team.
  - Demonstrates the system's safety in the face of a threat of catastrophic events.
  - Covers hardware/software interfaces.
  - Covers the commissioning and training processes.

---

[7] The safety records log includes the results of hazard analyses, modeling reports, and the results of checking the formal arguments.

The Independent Safety Advisor will conduct audits and reviews looking for evidence both of compliance and non-compliance with the standards your project is following.

## 9.7.4 Relations with QA

The internal quality assurance function of a company is concerned to:

- Maintain and monitor the company quality management system.
- Obtain or maintain certifications to various standards (typically ISO 9000).

In doing this it will:

- Monitor the processes and metrics the company uses.
- Help refine and standardize them.
- Conduct audits, issue audit reports and "close" audit issues.

As far as the internal quality assurance function is concerned, the test processes are just another set to be monitored. They will want to know:

- How you are organized.
- How you relate to other stakeholders in the processes.
- What you plan to do.
- How you model or otherwise describe your activities.
- What evidence you generate.
- How you report your results.
- How you support elements of (say) ISO 9000.

They may repeat a (set of) test(s) you ran, in an effort to see how thorough it was and if their results were any different to yours. They will usually follow some issue (chosen at random) through from start to finish to see that a process *works*. To prepare for them, look at the things you mostly do and ensure:

- You have all your principal processes modeled or otherwise described.
- You can provide evidence of all those processes working.
- You can explain how the tools support them.
- You can relate the processes both to the company standards and the standards used by the certification bodies through which the company is certified.

They may catch you out and create an "observation" that some process is not working as it should. Never resist this. Inquire diligently to know what it was you were *supposed* to have done. Get them to make this very clear. Have them also explain how your failure to do what was wanted detracts from the project's outcome. Then see if their requirement could be said to have been already met in some other way. If you can't, give up. No one will think any the worse of you. Attempting to undermine them is highly counter-productive.

The quality management system which they control (and which is certified under ISO 9000) is there for your use. If it's more trouble than it's worth, negotiate an alternative with the QA department. You'll have to write a standard to keep them happy but it will be worth it and won't invalidate their certification if it's well-written. Note that a standard can be quite minimal and consist of templates, tools, and checklists, providing it can be shown to act as a standard. Ignoring the quality management system is *unwise*.

## 9.7.5 Relations with Sales and Customers

You may be wheeled out to meet customers for two reasons:

- Everything is going well and management want to:
  - Thank you and show how much they trust you by letting you present yourself.
  - Use you as a means of getting orders.
  - Cement relations with a long-standing client.

- Everything is *not* going well and management want to use you as a way of convincing the client that issues are under control.

Treat the occasion as a lightweight audit. When you have finished your presentation you will be questioned. Keep the answers simple. I have managed (as a customer) to cause grave embarrassment to a number of test managers with the question *"how d'you know when you have found a bug?"* We didn't buy.

### 9.7.6 Relations with Certification Bodies

Certification bodies are the nice guys who give you the exciting plaques you see in the entrance hall. They come round and audit you, like your internal quality assurance people. Unlike your internal quality assurance people they have no idea how you work and will thus be a Royal pain, in that you have to explain much that is (for you) obvious. They may well be playing dumb on purpose just to see how well you manage.

If they find that you have somehow infringed the company quality management system, the head on the block is that of the internal quality assurance manager, not you. So when the internal quality assurance manager asks you, nicely, to fix things, that is one of the reasons.

### 9.7.7 Relations with Support

# Story

Support is expensive. There was a Big Corporation which made Big Machines for banks at a plant some distance from head office. The Big Machines didn't exactly work. The cost of supporting them was more than the Big Corporation was getting in income.

The Big Corporation already had a *Product Assurance and Support* group. It did very little of the former and far too much of the latter. It was controlled by *Sales*, which understood little of *Engineering* and cared even less.

*Engineering* therefore set up its own test group called *System Proving*. It found a lot of bugs very early. Suddenly it occurred to the *Product Assurance and Support* that if they didn't test a little more they might find Awkward Questions being asked. So they started testing seriously and found lots of bugs too. The cost of *Support* fell dramatically.

Your organization may have a special *Support* group with its own metric (problems per user month) which will include function failure, training, and usability bugs. You need to find a way accessing all three of these metrics.

This organization will normally consist of two levels of operation: first and second-line (concerned with simple and complex user problems). It should only contact the test team if they are unable to resolve some customer problem and need to escalate it to a third level to determine if it is really a bug. See "Support desk staff" in section 1.9.

The cost of *Support* is a major driver to getting money spent on testing. Unfortunately the advantage of front-loading your costs shows up after the release and the time lag may push the advantage beyond some decision-maker's horizon. See "Time-discounting" under section 9.7.1.

Support know a lot about how real users make mistakes. They can be a great source of help, advice, and training. Some testers may enjoy a *Support* role and vice versa.

### 9.7.8  Relations with Other Test Teams and Third-Party Suppliers

There are four possible sets of relations:

- Your company is buying a product they are testing.
- Their company is buying a product you are testing.
- You have outsourced all or part of your testing to them.
- They have outsourced all or part of the testing to you.

In all cases there are a few fundamental activities to be undertaken:

- Understand each other's companies.
- Identify contact points.
- Identify reporting methods.
- Share CVs (builds confidence), plans, process models (know what they're doing, where the weaknesses are likely to be), standards (are they likely to keep to them?), tool details (to get some idea of the rigor), and results.
- Read the contract (preferably ensure it doesn't get signed without your approval).
- Define the deliverables and the dates.

There is a big advantage in having their staff work alongside your staff for some months. It puts a brain to a face and greatly increases confidence:

See Chapter 10 for more.

### 9.7.9  Relations with the Configuration Manager

The configuration manager doesn't want to have to:

- Create builds every hour
- Be constantly reviewing bugs and proposed changes.

So he has every interest in the best quality product. You are unlikely to be testing his work so he will not be threatened by you. The configuration manager can be a useful source of metrics and will be the person in charge of configuration-managing your test packs. He can sometimes give you advance warning that an alleged change to some specification has not yet been committed and that therefore you might do well to wait before rewriting your tests. Conversely he can warn you of website changes.

## 9.8  The Politics of Testing

*"We don't have internal politics here."* (Smile. Lie.) You don't really believe that either.
*"Conflict between software testers and developers is inevitable"* [Cohen].
*"Who (is doing what to) whom?"* Vladimir Illych Lenin.

You have a bunch of developers trying to build something which works. You have a bunch of testers dedicated to proving it doesn't. Conflict's inevitable, yes? No. In 25 years I have never seen any more conflict between testers and developers than can been expressed by a slight hardening of the voice, a certain resignation, and an upward flip of the eyes.

But that isn't the whole story. Developers are many. The project manager is one. He is the person who is blamed by senior management when a project is late, over budget or fails. The test manager is the person who leads the team which *"delays the project, runs it straight over budget, and demonstrates that it fails."* Note the inverted commas. No project would be delayed if there were no bugs. I'm just proposing the common misperception. Some project managers are terrified of failure. You're not. You're a test manager, and for some project managers you represent failure, and every bug your team, and you find is one more step on a path that leads there.

Organizations have a choice: they can internalize the user-developer conflict within the organization by having a strong test group or leave it externalized with real users becoming increasingly frantic, and eventually refusing to buy. Internalizing this conflict is a sign of organizational maturity.

Where such conflict remains externalized, the role of the test group will be a mere formality. Attempts made at rigorous testing will provoke a number of tactics to be invoked. See section 9.7.1.

Project managers within organizations which have internalized the user-developer conflict feel a need to pressure all aspects of the development process and know the danger of applying too much pressure.

# 10

# Outsourcing

*Doesn't matter how big the engine is — if it ain't got wings, it won't fly.*

**—Decrepit aphorism**

Outsourcing consists essentially of four activities:

1. Find the supplier.
2. Prepare for outsourcing.
3. Tell them what you want.
4. (Don't) Accept what they offer.

Unlike most commercial relations however, the outsource relationship usually involves the handing over of a part of an organization's intellectual DNA which represents a major risk. This DNA consists of extant systems to be maintained as well as new requirements. The distance and occasionally the language barrier involved render issues like testing very prominent.

## 10.1  Dangers of Outsourcing

A number of threats accompany outsourcing. These cannot be shown as risks until their cost and probability of occurrence are determined. The list in Table 10.1 has been adapted from [Aubert].

All competencies can be outsourced. If you have a statutory duty to approve (say) railway signaling or aeronautic systems this is probably too close to your company's core competence to be an outsourcing candidate.

## 10.2  Process of Outsourcing

Figure 10.1 is a view of the outsourcing process limited to the issues most likely to affect a test manager.

### 10.2.1  Identify Outsource Project

1. Identify the reasons why: there are several reasons why people off-shore and some of them are bad:
   - Because it's become fashionable. Be very afraid. A lousy motive brings lousy execution in its train: the result may simply Not Work or the project may collapse.
   - Because the project is failing, and the board wants to defer the moment when they have to reveal this to shareholders.
   - Because the project manager cannot manage.
   Should any of these reasons predominate, treat such projects with caution. The rest of this chapter assumes **none** of these motives apply.
2. Review all outsourcing proposals and plans, relate them to section 10.2.8, and write a report.
3. Assess the threats: use the list in Table 10.1 and write a threat/mitigation list.

**TABLE 10.1** Outsourcing threats and mitigations

| Undesirable outcomes | Contributory threats | How the customer test facility can mitigate the threat |
|---|---|---|
| Unexpected transition and management costs | • Customer inexperience of the activity<br>• Customer inexperience of outsourcing<br>• Opaque legal environment<br>• Development and communication environment discontinuities<br>• Monitoring costs | • Review all outsourcing proposals and plans<br>• Draw up a process model for the outsourcing activity showing quality gates<br>• Review all process aspects of the outsourcing with a view to anticipating problems<br>• Create supplier audit checklists<br>• Analyze supplier development, test, and communication environments<br>• Review the supplier's process model<br>• Identify backsourcing prerequisites |
| Lock-in | • Asset specificity<br>• Limited number of competent suppliers leading to small-number bargaining<br>• Interdependence of contracts<br>• Insufficient incentive to attract a wide pool of suppliers | • Identify reusability and testedness of supplied software<br>• Assess supplier test competence<br>• Model the contract deliverables' interdependence using an influence diagram |
| Costly contractual amendments | • Uncertainty<br>• Technological discontinuity<br>• Task complexity<br>• Customer inexperience in contract definition and negotiation<br>• Indeterminable milestone definitions linked to stage payments | • Contribute test-related elements to overall relationship contract<br>• Review contract to find weak points particularly milestone and quality gate definitions<br>• Review requirements specifications for testability, consistency, and sufficiency<br>• Contribute to and review an SLA |
| Disputes and litigation | • Measurement problems<br>• Customer/supplier inexperience of outsourcing contracts<br>• Cultural discontinuities[a]<br>• Opaque legal environment<br>• Multiple suppliers with overlapping and codependent projects<br>• Security risks | • Contribute to metrics definition and plan<br>• Monitor metrics implementation by supplier<br>• Implement metrics program for incoming deliverables<br>• Create a common glossary, quality plan, and bug severity definition<br>• Ensure the vendor understands not simply what the requirements are, but *why* they are[b] |
| Service debasement | • Interdependence of activities<br>• Performance ambiguity<br>• Supplier inexperience of the activity<br>• Supplier inexperience in providing ancillary support<br>• Supplier size<br>• Supplier financial stability<br>• Task complexity<br>• Mixing two unrelated contract types<br>• Customer failure to set and monitor benchmarks<br>• Customer failure to award related contracts (typically development and support) | • Review supplier's quality management system and map it against the process model<br>• Get supplier to estimate code size and number of bugs[c]<br>• Confirm supplier's adherence to any claimed certification to any international standards<br>• Review, or test deliverables<br>• Liaise with supplier test group<br>• Review supplier benchmark, metrics plan, and implementation<br>• Review contract(s)<br>• Coordinate with supplier in arranging HCI tests on-shore |
| Cost escalation | • Supplier inexperience<br>• Customer inexperience in contract management<br>• Customer failure to monitor and measure the supplier | • Monitor deliverable quality by reviewing, or testing them<br>• Monitor supplier time sheets |
| Loss of organizational competencies | • Closeness of the outsourced work to the core competence of the organization<br>• Customer loss of:<br>– specification and/or SLA competence<br>– installation and support competence<br>– test and approval competence<br>– of innovative capacity | • Install partial releases in simulated operating environment and check for system interface bugs<br>• Review supplier test plans, specifications, and tests<br>• Establish a user stakeholder sounding board to monitor requirements and tests |

**TABLE 10.1** Outsourcing threats and mitigations (continued)

| Undesirable outcomes | Contributory threats | How the customer test facility can mitigate the threat |
|---|---|---|
| Product failure | • Customer failure to:<br> – define requirements and/or SLA with sufficient clarity<br> – define operating environment interfaces with sufficient clarity<br> – clarify the *purpose* of the requirements with sufficient clarity (and the supplier's failure to enquire)<br> – test with sufficient rigor<br>• Supplier failure to test with sufficient rigor<br>• Supplier inexperience in providing ancillary support<br>• Supplier malevolence in injecting Trojan horses and leaving trapdoors | • Review SLA<br>• Check that all metrics used in SLA can be verified independently by the customer<br>• Review the interface and installation specifications<br>• Review the requirements specification and ensure that the purpose of each requirement is known or discoverable<br>• Unit test all units<br>• System-test all system-level deliverables[d]<br>• Compare system-test results from multiple suppliers<br>• Prepare evidence of product failure for liquidated damages litigation |

[a] Both an Admiral and a fisherman know what wet feet mean. Software engineers the world over understand the meaning of "there's a bug." For "*cultural discontinuity*" read "*the customer couldn't write the requirements right and the vendor couldn't read them.*"

[b] "*If that signal goes low the brakes fail.*"

[c] Not for contractual reasons but to see how scared he gets at having to estimate.

[d] You need to be very sure that some bought-in system works **before** deploying it. Apologies if this seems obvious but it wasn't to some big companies. Like AT&T wireless.

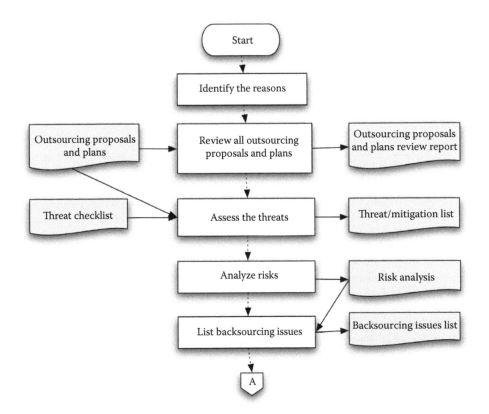

**FIGURE 10.1** Identify outsource project process model A

4. Analyze and quantify the risks.
5. List backsourcing issues.
6. Create an outsourcing process model showing the quality gates.

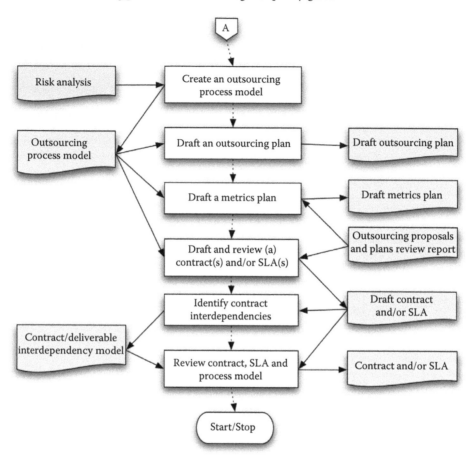

**FIGURE 10.2**  Identify outsource project process model B

7. Draft an outsourcing plan with reference to section 10.2.8.
8. Draft a metrics plan to support the contract(s) and SLA(s). Identify:
   a. The questions you need answering (see Chapter 18)
   b. The tools to be used to collect and analyze the metrics
9. Draft and review (a) contract(s) and/or SLA(s).
10. Identify (possibly with a model) the degree to which one contract depends on the deliverables of another. From this determine a critical path and review which contracts are to be co-awarded, which need coordination, and which can be duplicated either for supplier assessment purposes or to prevent lock-in.
11. Review the process model, SLA(s), and contract(s) by having the customer staff *act out* various supplier roles (it shouldn't be difficult to get people to pretend to misbehave), and thus identify the possible areas of failure and the means by which they can be detected and reviewed. Review the quality gate and milestone definitions.

The critical questions are:

- Are we outsourcing for a Very Good Reason?
- Have we identified every threat?
- Have we identified all the threat mitigations we need?

- How much of the requirements specification do we want to do in-house?
- Do we have a team in place with time to handle this?
- Do we have management commitment?
- If it fails, do we have a plan B?
- On what basis will we choose a supplier?
- Will we choose more than one supplier?
- Will we judge a small (say 4) group of shortlisted suppliers based on a prototype or pilot project which they build for us?[1]
- If we are conscious of *cultural discontinuities,* do such discontinuities really hide supplier or customer incompetence?

## 10.2.2 Find the Supplier

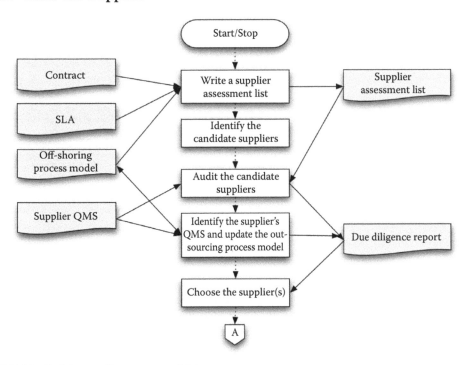

**FIGURE 10.3** Find the supplier process model A

1. Write a supplier assessment list. (Use the lists in Appendix B.) Create supplier audit checklists.
2. Identify the candidate suppliers.
3. Audit the candidates and score them against the criteria.
   a. Assess supplier test competence.
   b. Review the supplier's process model.
   c. Read the proposed staff CVs.
4. Identify:
   a. The supplier's quality management system (QMS) and map it against the process model.
   b. Any claimed certification to any international standards. If you notice any gross shortcomings inform the classification society and seek another candidate supplier.
   c. Any evidence the supplier has ever estimated the code size and bug numbers of other projects.

---

[1]There is an argument in favor of letting (say) three contracts to build a small pilot on terms slightly unfavorable to the supplier on the grounds that only very competent and confident suppliers will bid. This assumes a large group of competent suppliers.

5. Choose the supplier(s). There may be an advantage in minimizing lock-in by having more than one supplier or by having different suppliers developing and testing.

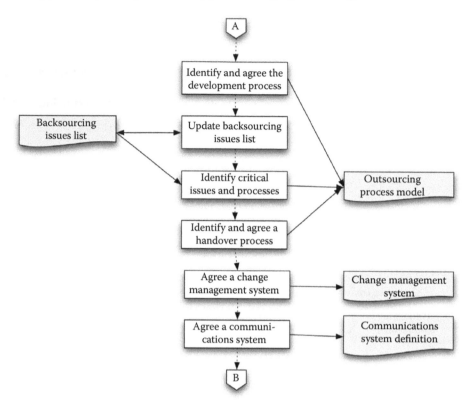

**FIGURE 10.4**  Find the supplier process model B

6. Identify and agree the development process (Figure 10.4) to be used by the supplier using a process model. In particular note where the processes use the common systems mentioned in point 11 below.
7. Update backsourcing issues list.
8. Identify critical issues and processes which must be monitored to warn of relationship failure.
9. Identify and agree a handover process with the supplier.
10. Agree a change management system with the supplier.
11. Agree a communications system with the supplier. This will include the primary contacts, the meetings, the reports and their formats, and the visibility of the supplier development environment by the customer. It will require that you and the supplier use or have access to a set of common systems:
    a.  Email and videoconferencing
    b.  Document management
    c.  Bug management
    d.  Code management
    e.  Test management
    f.  Time sheet management
    Agree email response types and times, and note this in the SLA. This approach uses a common set of unit-testing tools. By having these common systems the supplier-customer relationship can be greatly enhanced from the mutual trust each has or alternatively the failure of either party to use the common systems will act as an early warning.
12. Modify the metrics plan to account for the contract and SLA requirements (Figure 10.5).
13. Negotiate an overall relationship contract. This will cover the major issues including the principles on which testing will occur.

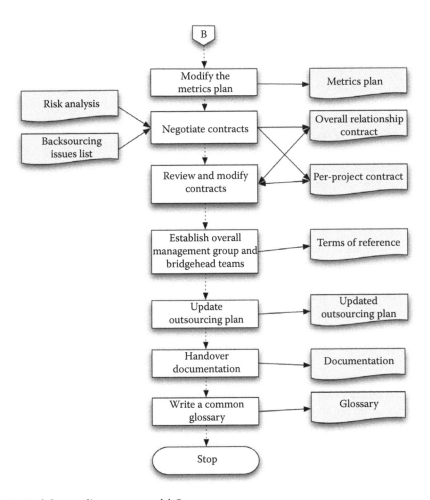

**FIGURE 10.5** Find the supplier process model C

14. Negotiate a per-project contract. This need only be signed much later when requirements have been identified.
15. Review contract(s) to find weak points particularly milestone and quality gate definitions.
16. Establish overall management group and bridgehead teams. There will be usually a management group drawn from both organizations charged with relating the two halves of the project. These will be concerned with the strategic direction. The bridgehead teams will be concerned with day-to-day liaison between the groups and will report to the management group.
17. Handover existing documentation (specifications, code, manuals training materials, and tests) using the common document management system. Off-shore staff should mine all the project documentation and generate:
    a. Indices of all available documents plus "read-mes" describing the contents of each one. (This will help them get some idea of the extent of the project and will add to the customer's trust that the supplier staff comprehend.)
    b. Architecture and network topology diagrams.
    c. Feature descriptions identifying for each feature:
        i. Introduction and background
        ii. References to any plans
        iii. Glossary of feature-related terms
        iv. The requirements and design specifications

    v.   The code fragments

    vi.  The system and unit test designs and tests

    vii.  Any test scripts

    viii. Details of how to set up tests

  d. A matrix relating features and tests to illustrate the degree of coverage so far accomplished (see section 15.2 in Chapter 15 for an example).

  e. Metrics defined and used.

  f. Dependencies (of the feature and its implementation).

  g. Details of bugs found against each feature.

  h. References.

18. Write and agree a common glossary of terms.

The critical questions are:

- Do you have persons on the bridgehead teams who are in control of the respective sides? How do you know they are in control?
- Is there an overall relationship contract in place?
  - Does it include provisions for liquidated damages?
  - Is it enforceable in the supplier's country?
  - Has it been reviewed by the customer test function (if any)?
  - Does it identify:
    - Who writes the requirements specification and the approach to be taken?
    - The deliverables?
    - The stage payments and the criteria for their payment?
    - What sanctions are available if the supplier fails to deliver to time and of acceptable quality?
    - Who writes the acceptance tests?
    - The process of acceptance?
    - How the supplier reports progress to the customer, how often, and against what?
    - What the supplier team reporting structure is?
    - How specification changes and contract extensions are to be accommodated?
    - Performance standards each party must maintain?
    - Termination triggers, consequences, and process?
    - The Quality Management System to be adhered to throughout the relationship and how this QMS will evolve, and be certified?
    - Third-party or other COT software to be incorporated in the final product?
    - Who will be in charge of the acceptance testing of delivered systems?
    - Security issues?
    - Intellectual property rights?
- Are any milestones likely to be cited in liquidated damages litigation?
- Is the customer or the supplier responsible for writing the acceptance tests? If the supplier is responsible, who is in charge of reviewing and accepting them?
- What are the fall-back (backsourcing) positions at each stage of the contract, for the customer, and the supplier organizations in the event that the whole process fails?
- How will the customer monitor the supplier such that the customer gets early warning of problems? Will there be a prototype available for demonstration? Will there be a set of proof-of-concept fragments?
- How will the supplier access updated copies of the customer's operating environment and be notified of the changes?
- Is there an agreed audit process and standard whereby the customer will audit the supplier?
- What redress will the customer have if any third party or COT software fails?
- (How) can the supplier fake the metrics?
- Will the communication links become overloaded?

### 10.2.3   Tell Them What You Want (Figure 10.6)

1. Agree the structure and contents of requirements specifications. Identify and agree the modeling approach to be taken. Incorporate this in a standard possibly with a template.
2. Agree the requirements gathering, identification, definition, and sign-off process. This must include a guarantee of availability of key customer, and supplier staff for requirements gathering purposes. Incorporate this in a development process model.
3. Agree the structure and contents of design specifications. Incorporate this in a standard. This is part of the insurance in the event of backsourcing.
4. Write, review, and agree the requirements specifications and SLA for testability, consistency, and sufficiency. Check the SLA against the metrics plan.
5. Agree the supplier test approach. This will include the standards, tools, and environments to be used. This will be added to the development process model.

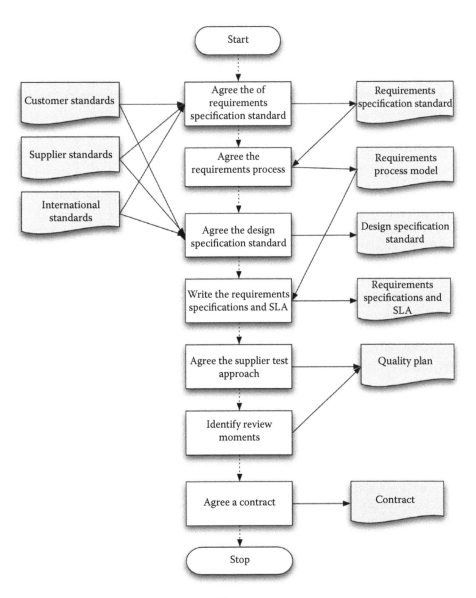

**FIGURE 10.6**  *Tell them what you want* process model

6. Identify review moments for each package of work and update the supplier quality plan (see section 8.21).
7. Agree a contract for the work.

The critical questions are:

- Who writes the system and acceptance tests: the system supplier, another supplier, or the customer?
- How are non-functional requirements to be defined, managed, and tested?
- How are reviews to be coordinated between supplier and customer?
- How can the customer agree that the supplier's non-functional test-bed is comparable to the customer's working environment? (It can't be exact: but at least you should be able to get a populated database and the sets of transactions for several days to be fed in.)
- How does the supplier get access to the information he needs? Does he have access to a person with sufficient clout to get that information?
- What are the quality gates (quality milestones)? Here are some suggestions:
  - The requirements specifications are reviewed and signed-off by the customer.
  - The draft design documents are received and reviewed internally by the customer, and signed-off.
  - The code is unit-tested and the test results sent and signed-off by the customer.
- The supplier's system test has been completed, the customer has assessed the results, and determined if the remaining outstanding bugs represent sufficient grounds for accepting the release.

## 10.2.4  Monitor the Supplier

### 10.2.4.1  Process

1. Review the supplier test, benchmark, and metrics plans, specifications, and tools.
2. Implement and monitor a metrics program for incoming deliverables.
3. Liaise with the supplier test group. Coordinate with the supplier in arranging HCI tests on-shore.
4. Monitor the supplier against the metrics, the process model, the SLA, and the contract.

The primary channels through which the supplier can be monitored are:

- Bug management database
- Test results
- Specification reviews
- Project plan and schedule
- Project status reports
- Time sheets
- Audit reports
- Code quality analyses
- Time sheets
- Metrics drawn from the various management databases and the SLA

Depending on the size you may want to channel all communication through 2–3 people on each side. Some companies have found that it is preferable to treat off-shore staff as merely dislocated, and keep a full network of communications. There will thus be the usual flow of memoranda, change requests, bugs, specs, and other documents.

### 10.2.4.2  Warning Signs to Look for

1. Staff being unavailable or moved to another project without warning. Ensure you have the names of all staff working on your project, and whether they are full- or part-time. Some off-shore suppliers have an average staff turnover of 18 weeks.

2. Simultaneous inaccessibility of bug and configuration management databases. *Possibly means the supplier has experienced major and embarrassing problems or that he is surreptitiously modifying the metrics data acquisition program.*

3. Issues not being dealt with promptly. Email response speed is outside the SLA envelope (*but monitor the email load to ensure that neither side gets overloaded*).

4. Bugs, tests, documents, or code not being added to or changing in the respective management systems.

5. Weekly reports either not arriving or failing to deal with known issues.

6. Senior management being unavailable.

7. Schedules not changing. (*Schedules always change a bit. An unchanging schedule could mean that your supplier has found another, more lucrative contract, and doesn't yet want you to know it.*)

8. Intermediate deliveries are seriously late or of very poor quality.

9. Lack of time sheet data.

10. High overtime being worked by supplier staff.

11. Rising code turmoil just before the release to the customer.

12. Change of project manager, design authority or test manager. *This could be for the good reason that they were no good or for the bad reason that they left because they couldn't stand the project anymore or that they were moved onto another project, and had only been assigned to your project because they were excellent and were likely to persuade you to sign up.*

Considerations: remember that the outsource team may be first rate but at the mercy of management who are not. Therefore be cautious before blaming them and (when on conference calls) listen carefully for the sense of other, unofficially-present people listening to your conversations: a curious formality in the official attendee's speech and undue, and uncharacteristic reticence on their part.

## 10.2.5  Accept What They Offer

This section shows a process for accepting releases from a supplier who has prepared requirements and design specifications, code, manuals, training material, and system and unit tests.

### 10.2.5.1  Assumptions

- The customer has no experience of working with the supplier and therefore needs to ensure that supplier releases are of acceptable quality.
- The customer needs to ensure that should it need to terminate its relationship with the supplier that it has access to sufficient code, tests, and design documentation to enable it either to re-let the contract with another supplier or recommence in-house development.
- The customer has access to various common databases as previously mentioned.
- The solution proposed involves the use of a set of unit test metrics and tools, and the exposure by the supplier of its system tests and practices to the customer. This is shown in terms of a model of the entire build, test, and install process.
- The customer provides an interface specification to the client to ensure the successful coexistence of the new application on the customer network with the other applications.
- The deliverables are usually:
  - Source code
  - Compiled system
  - User documents
  - Test scripts
  - Utilities
  - Training material
- The customer has established a number of quality gates in its relationship with the supplier which consists of processes, documents, metrics, and events.

The customer has five primary quality lead indicators:

1. The requirements specifications
2. The design specifications
3. Access to the source code
4. Access to the source code metrics and unit test results
5. Use of the supplier-generated system tests

The requirements specifications give the first warning of problems by failing to satisfy the business. The design specifications may contain warnings (for example that there is no way of relating them to the requirements) but will need expert interpretation. The metrics and unit test results can warn either that unit tests aren't being run or that the results show the code is poor. The supplier-generated system tests show the degree of system test coverage and the rigor of the supplier's approach. In the long run neither test sets can be falsified since both can be run by the customer. The wise customer will supplement the supplier system tests with his own scenario-based acceptance tests.

### 10.2.5.2 Make a Release (Figure 10.7)

This process assumes a single supplier (there may be several), and a joint requirements-writing activity. In practice the customer may become involved in the design as well, since the delivered system may have to coexist with many others. The supplier's activities are not shown but will include an internal system

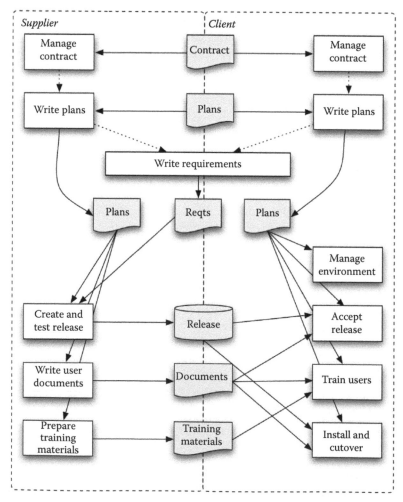

**FIGURE 10.7** Make a release

test before release. The supplier test group will deliver a set of automated system tests along with the release. The key processes are:

- The customer and supplier manage the contract.
- The customer and supplier write plans.
- The customer and supplier write requirements.
- **The supplier creates and tests a release.**
- **The customer accepts a release.**
- The customer manages the customer environment.
- The supplier writes user documents.
- The supplier trains users.
- The customer and supplier install the system and cutover.

The key gates occur in the processes: *the supplier creates and tests a release*, and *the customer accepts a release*.[2] This section focuses on these processes.

### 10.2.5.3   Supplier Creates and Tests a Release (Figure 10.8)

The supplier will create each release using the following process:

- It will design the system based on the requirements.
- It may build demonstration prototypes (which may provoke requirements changes).
- It will code the system, based on the design documents and the prototypes.
- It will create releases of the unit-tested code. It will also send both the unit-test results and the results of the use of an agreed code-quality tool to the customer.
- It will system-test each build internally.
- It will report on the status of each release weekly.
- It will write the user documents and training materials.

## 10.2.6   Customer Accepts a Release (Figure 10.9)

To accept a release the customer will:

- Create and execute acceptance tests using the test tool results, the existing system tests provided by the supplier, and its own acceptance tests.
- Create and execute integration tests either with copies of coexisting systems or with special-to-type hardware.
- Create and execute performance tests.
- Report on the test results daily.

The supplier will train the customer staff.
The supplier and customer will install the new system and cutover.

### 10.2.6.1   Customer-Acceptance Quality Gates

Quality gates will occur when:

- The code analysis tool is used.
- Acceptance tests are executed.
- Installation tests are executed.
- Performance tests are executed.
- The code analyses tool(s) is(are) used.

---

[2] Isn't cutover a key gate then? No. If the customer has already accepted the release the cutover should be a formality, already tested and proven. Leaving cutover as a gate implies exerting quality controls far too late in the process to be effective.

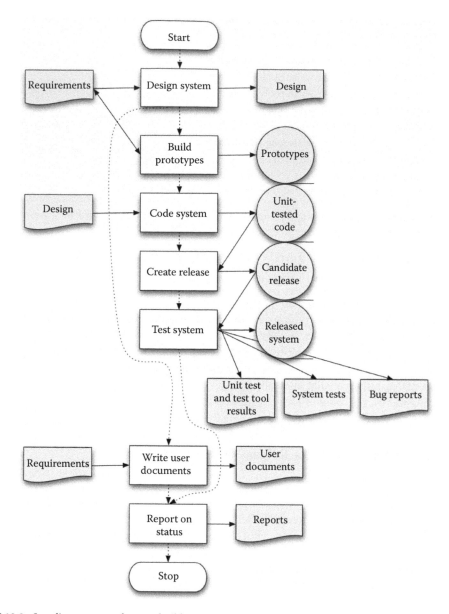

**FIGURE 10.8** Supplier creates and tests a build

The release will be rejected:

- If the results differ greatly from those given by the supplier.
- If the Performance tests reveal that more than *n* Key Performance Quality Measures (KPQMs) have not been met.
- If the functional tests executed by the User Acceptance Test group generate more than 3 *Critical* bugs.
- If the functional installation/integration tests generate more than (say) 0 *Critical* or 3 *High* bugs.

Note that while performance test technology means that the supplier can have already executed performance tests, and have tuned the system to run successfully, it is unlikely that the installation tests will run well at first. This is because execution environments tend to change very subtly, and although the supplier may have a copy of that environment, reality will be slightly different.

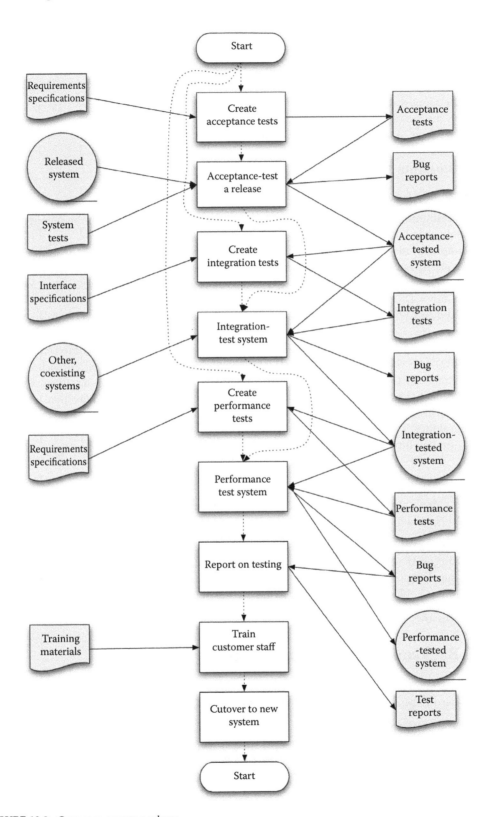

**FIGURE 10.9** Customer accepts a release

The critical questions are:

1. Is the code reusable in the event that the supplier fails?
2. Does the code comply with the acceptance profile? (See section 10.2.7.)
3. Are the unit tests accompanying the code repeatable with identical results?
4. Is the supplier test team competent?
5. Does the installed system coexist successfully with the others in the network?
6. Do we want to let another contract to this supplier?

## 10.2.7  Possible Code Analyses

A number of tests can be specified:

- **Programming standards verification.** These can be defined jointly between the supplier and the customer in a Programming Standard.
- **Complexity metrics.** This will include a limit on the number of control-flow knots and cyclomatic complexity (see section 18.8.4), reachability (see section 7.9.1), LCSAJ density (see section 12.8), and *structuredness* (see section 7.8.5) (Essential Knots = 0 and Essential Cyclomatic Complexity measure = 1)
- **Procedure Call Information including data flow bugs** (see *Dataflow bugs*), procedure parameter analysis (see Figure 7.23 and section 13.4).
- **Dynamic coverage analysis** to show statement coverage (TER1), branch/decision coverage (TER2), LCSAJ coverage (TER3), Procedure/Function Call coverage (P/FCall), Branch Condition Coverage (BCC) Branch Condition and Combination Coverage (BCCC), Modified Condition Decision Coverage (MC/DC). See below for explanations. This will require that all code be instrumented before being run. The supplier will supply the data used for all test runs.
- **Reusability.**
- **Maintainability.** See section 18.8.

## 10.2.8  Plan Structure

To minimize duplication, plans are better arranged in a hierarchy such that each inherits attributes of its superior. Note that:

- No safety plans or cases are shown.
- That a common quality plan is assumed (see section 8.21 for an example).
- All supplier plans shown should be contractual deliverables and adherence to them should be considered obligatory in contractual terms.

Figure 10.10 shows a possible structure.

# 10.3  Backsourcing Considerations

Backsourcing occurs when some client believes that outsourcing involves unbearable costs. Various questions need to be asked at this point by the customer:

- Was outsourcing ever a Good Idea?
- Were we the major cause of the problem? (Are we shipping this project back home only to face identical problems without the time gap?) Did the business change? Did we realize the project was too close to the company's core competence? Did we fail to manage the implication of the list in Table 10.1?
- Did we choose a poor supplier?
- What will it cost us to backsource?
- What do we need to do to backsource?

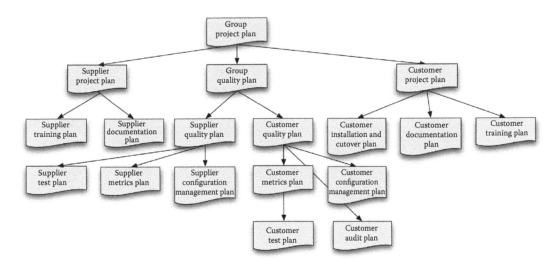

**FIGURE 10.10**  Plan structure

- Identify what evidence we need to collect to demonstrate contract failure and sue.
- Identify what code and documentation we can reuse.

By remaining aware of the need to be able to backsource the customer maintains the potential to do so and keeps his confidence. The supplier will note this.

## 10.4   Testing Proprietary Software

Many systems are constructed from a mixture of new, legacy, and/or bought-in code. It is important that this last category be of at least the same quality as the others, which implies that it should be tested if its failure represents a big-enough risk.

Since full testing of bought-in proprietary software is rarely possible, get evidence of its suitability in the form of:

- A requirements specification or user manual
- Evaluations prepared by others using the software in a similar environment
- Reviews of the software and documentation
- Evidence of testing by the suppliers or a third party

If you can't get the evidence: test it. Perhaps use an outside agency. Note that while your system may be mission-critical, and used by hundreds of users over several networks, the proprietary software supplier may not have tested the software to anything like the same degree of rigor. Thus while [Cusumano 2] declares *"applications such as Word ... are not mission-critical,"* at least one railway company prepares safety-critical documentation using it, and major news organizations use it for their story-writing. Some have abandoned it as being too unstable.

# 11

# Test Techniques: Functional (Black-Box)

## 11.1  Equivalence Partitioning

This technique relies on looking at the set of valid inputs specified for the unit and dividing it up into classes of data that, according to the specification, should be treated identically.

One set of test data is then devised to represent each equivalence class. The premise is that any representative will be as good as any other in the same class at finding bugs in the handling of that class.

Thus if the input data ranges for some system can be identified as (say):

- $100 > x < 100$
- $0 < x > 300$
- $20 > x < 250$

these can be represented as shown below.

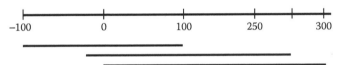

**FIGURE 11.1**  Data ranges

From this it can be seen that the data can be partitioned into the following sub-ranges:

- $[100 \geq x \leq 20]$
- $[20 < x \geq 0]$
- $[0 > x < 100]$
- $[100 \geq x < 250]$
- $[250 \geq x < 300]$

Implicitly, any set of figures, each one drawn from a single sub-range, is as good as any other.

## 11.2  Boundary-Value Analysis

This complements equivalence partitioning by looking at a fruitful source of bugs — the boundaries of the input equivalence classes. *Test cases* are devised that exercise the unit or system with data chosen from these boundaries, and also with data chosen to exercise it on the boundaries of output data as well. For instance, if an input is specified from 0 to 255, the equivalence class partitioning leads to values less than 0, between 0 and 255, and greater than 255 as test input and boundary value analysis would suggest adding the following values:

1, 0, 1, 254, 255, 256

Boundary value analysis is one of the most useful methods of test case design, but not all boundaries (especially on output) are immediately obvious.

# 11.3 Cause–Effect Graphing

Equivalence partitioning and boundary value analysis exercise the unit or system by looking at each equivalence class in isolation, but they do not exercise the unit with different combinations of inputs from the equivalence classes. Cause–effect graphing is a way of doing this while avoiding the major combinatorial problems that can arise.

The technique relates the inputs and input conditions as defined by the specification (requirements, high-level design, or unit) such that for each input or set of inputs some output(s) are defined using either Boolean logic or a graph.

The process is as follows:

1. Partition the assertions of the specification to be tested, either by feature (in the case of system testing), by interface (in the case of integration testing), or by structure (in the case of unit testing). Choose other criteria for partitioning at will.
2. Identify all causes and effects in the specification.
3. Identify each cause and effect by an unique number for each.
4. Draw the cause–effect graph by:
   - Listing each cause as a node on the left-hand side of the paper and each effect as a node on the right-hand side of the paper.
   - Relating the nodes with a line such that each cause and effect be either true or false, given some set of conditions represented by Boolean logic.
   - Annotating the graph with constraints describing combinations of causes and/or effects that are impossible for environmental or syntactical reasons.
5. Convert the graph into a decision table by tracing all the causes for each effect. Each column in the table represents a test objective.
6. Write the tests.

## 11.3.1 Cause–Effect Graph Constructs

Figure 11.2 and Figure 11.3 show constructs that can be used in cause–effect graphing. The causes and effects are identified as shown in Figure 11.4. Construct the graph shown in Figure 11.5.

| Construct name | Meaning | Symbol |
|---|---|---|
| Identity | a causes b |  |
| Not | a inhibits b | 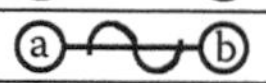 |
| Or | a, or b, or c cause d | 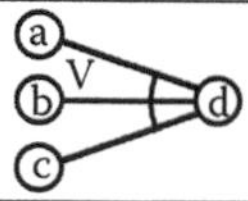 |
| And | a and b cause d | 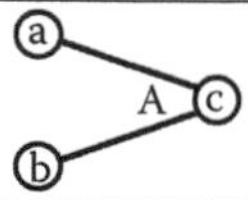 |
| Xor | One of a, or b can be causes, not both(Exclusive OR) | 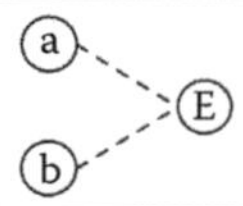 |

FIGURE 11.2  Cause–effect graph constructs

> **Example**
> A database should have each file listed in a 10-section master index by name and location. To display, or list a section in the inquiry mode, the operator must enter a D(isplay), or a P(rint), followed by a numeric character (0-9) to represent the section number, followed by the "return" key.
> Error handling
> If the first character is other than D, or P the system displays:
> INVALID COMMAND
> If the first character is not in the range 0-9 the system displays:
> INVALID INDEX NUMBER

**FIGURE 11.3**  Cause–effect graph example

**Causes**

1. character 1 is a D
2. character 1 is a P
3. character 2 is a digit in the range 0-9

**Effects**

1. Index section is displayed
2. Index section is printed
3. INVALID COMMAND is displayed
4. INVALID INDEX NUMBER is displayed

**FIGURE 11.4**  Cause–effect identification

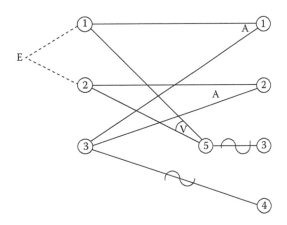

**FIGURE 11.5**  A cause-and-effect graph

Node 5 is an intermediate node to allow us to apply a NOT to the D or the P causes. These are also annotated with an XOR to show they cannot occur simultaneously.

From this graph you can build a decision table as shown in Figure 11.6 with the *test cases* contained in each of the columns and a T(rue) and F(alse) in most cells. Cells with no entries are irrelevant to that test objective. The test objectives uncovered are, on their own, a useful demonstration that the system works as specified. The empty cells are also good starting points for developing further tests to prove that the system doesn't work.

For further details, see [Rich 81].

## 11.4   Random Data Selection

The purpose of random data selection is to exercise software with data chosen to simulate the kind and quantity that is likely to be encountered in practice. The purpose is not to look for bugs of a particular kind, but rather to see what happens according to some theory of practice. Simply choosing random data according to some random number generator may require too much time or else produce illicit data that the unit isn't designed to handle. So the random data should be generated according to some grammar of how the unit will be used. The advantage of random data testing is that it can exercise the

| | Test objectives | | | |
|---|---|---|---|---|
| causes | 1 | 2 | 3 | 4 |
| 1 (character 1 is a D) | T | F | F | |
| 2 (character 1 is a P) | F | T | F | |
| 3 (character 2 is a digit between 0-9) | T | T | | F |
| effects | | | | |
| 1 (Index section is displayed) | T | | | |
| 2 (Index section is printed) | | T | | |
| 3 (INVALID COMMAND is displayed) | | | T | |
| 4 (INVALID INDEX NUMBER is displayed) | | | | T |

**FIGURE 11.6**  Example of a cause–effect decision chart

unit in ways the designers (and the testers) never foresaw. The problem with random data selection is that the theory of how the unit will be used in practice had better be right for the data to be of any use. For state-of-the-art systems this isn't always possible.

Random data testing requires the use of some execution monitoring tool to monitor the execution such that the decision, condition, or other coverage criterion satisfied by the random data can be known. [Munoz] speaks highly of random testing. The 250 cases he generated and used found forty-four bugs at a cost of $1 per test case.

## 11.5   Feature Test Process

The objective of these tests is to demonstrate that the system does/does not possess the features defined in the requirements specification. It is the central technique of system testing, but it can be used in integration testing and occasionally in unit testing.

See section 15.3 for a description of a method to achieve this.

# 12

# Test Techniques: Structural (White-Box)

[Myers G] has suggested that even good black-box testing may only exercise 50% to 70% of the code. We therefore need to supplement black-box testing by choosing further *test cases* that make sure that the unit is fully exercised to some level. This is the purpose of the following white-box techniques. (Note that we cannot use white-box testing alone because we could not be certain of having tested whether the unit had the right feature.) The ideal situation would be to exercise every entry-to-exit path in the unit but often this would involve so many combinations that we may have to settle for a lesser goal.

## 12.1 Statement Coverage

Statement coverage testing requires that you devise a set of *test cases* that together cause every statement in the program to be executed. This is the least you can do.

Some of the *test cases* can of course come from black-box techniques. The aim is to supplement these with others to ensure every statement is executed rather than just 50% or so.

## 12.2 Decision (Branch) Coverage

This requires us to devise enough *test cases* so that each decision has a true and false outcome at least once. The statement coverage criterion will ensure that we exercise every statement and, in particular, every decision. But it will not necessarily exercise every decision outcome. For instance, while one test case (x=0) is sufficient to cover the statement

> if X = 0 then S: = 0 else T: = 0

we cannot be sure that the right action (T: = 0) is taken if X < > 0. The decision coverage criterion makes us devise *test cases* that do this. Multiple decisions (e.g., CASE statements) can be covered such that every possible condition-outcome pair is covered.

This technique requires the use of a pre-processor to insert a branch-reached print message just before each line. When the code is executed the print-out can be visually examined. This process can be speeded up by:

- Writing an expected-branch-reached file
- Dumping the print into an actual-branch-reached print file
- Comparing the expected-branch-reached with the actual-branch-reached print file

This technique will not work if there are timing considerations in the software or if the input is unpredictable. See also section 12.9 for similar approaches.

## 12.3   Condition Coverage

When decisions are made on the basis of complex conditions, the decision coverage criteria can still miss important exceptions. For example consider:

$$if \ X \le \left(\frac{Y}{4}\right) and \left(X \ge 0 \ or \ X \ge Z\right) then$$

To test this adequately we should consider all possible combinations of $X \le (Y/4)$, $X \ge 0$, and $X \ge Z$, related by AND and OR. If we substitute A, B, and C into the conditions we have:

If A or (B or C) then

To define test objectives we need to invert this relationship and find all the possible permutations of the conditions. First we change the ANDs and ORs:

If A or (B or C) then

If A and (B and C) then

If A or (B and C) then

If A and (B or C) then

Then we change the brackets so that the order of processing is reversed:

If A or B or C then

If A and B and C then

If A or B and C then

If A and B or C then

If (A or B) or C then

If (A and B) and C then

If (A or B) and C then

If (A and B) or C then

...

Lastly we look at the individual constructs $X < (Y/4)$, $X \ge 0$, and $X \ge Z$ to see what possible permutations can occur there:

$$X \le \left(\frac{Y}{4}\right)$$

can be permuted as follows:

$$X \ge \left(\frac{Y}{4}\right), \ X > \left(\frac{Y}{3}\right), \ X \ge \left(\frac{Y}{5}\right), \ X < \left(\frac{Y}{3}\right), \ X < \left(\frac{Y}{5}\right)$$

and these permutations can then be substituted back into the equations. Note that the Y/3 and Y/5 are intended to provide boundary coverage. This also provides the *NOT* construct. If the system uses a lot of *reals*, and for example has a maths co-processor, it might be better to exercise the boundaries by:

$$Y/4.00000001 \text{ and } Y/3.99999999$$

This results in a lot of test objectives and is the principal reason why people build test generators. Note that most of the permutations can be made to generate tests which, if the system gives the answer expected by the permutation, show that a bug has occurred.

## 12.4 Path Analysis

Path analysis generates test data to:

- Show computational, path, and missing path bugs
- Cause selected paths to be executed in a program

The analysis begins by defining the possible paths through a program so that each can be at least partly tested.

Given a program like the one shown in Figure 12.1 to generate factorials:

```
1                      READ N
2                      IF N < 0 THEN PRINT "N IS NEGATIVE"
5                      M = 1
6                      IF N = 0 THEN PRINT M
9                      WHILE N > 0
10                         M = M*N
11                         N = N-1
12                         PRINT M
13                     WEND
100 DATA 5, 6, 7, 8, -3, -5, 5,0, 6
```

**FIGURE 12.1** A simple program

We can construct the program tree (also known as a *boundary-interior description tree*) as shown in Figure 12.2.

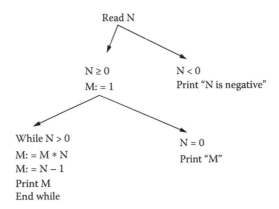

**FIGURE 12.2** A program tree

From this we can define the input data to execute the various paths to be followed using the conditions by substituting symbols for the inputs. This technique is time-consuming but can produce a very precise definition of the test data providing the paths do not contain branches to subroutines, functions, or non-linear expressions involving several variables. In this case there are three objectives to test:

$$N = 0, N < 0, \text{ and } N > 0$$

Having identified tests for each path you need other tests for the algorithms of each path. In this case possible techniques would be to select very large and non-integer values of M.

There are several problems with path testing:

- It is impossible to test all paths. A program with 20 iterations and 5 decision points will require $5^{20}+5^{18}+\ldots+5^1 = 10^{14}$ paths.
- The program may still not match its specification.
- Some specified paths may be missing (for example undefined ELSEs). Data sensitivity bugs will not necessarily be uncovered. Thus if ABS(A-B) has been written rather than A-B the bug may not be detected.
- Some paths may be unfeasible. Consider Figure 12.3.

```
IF X ≤ 4 THEN PRINT "X ≤: 4"        [1]
ELSE PRINT " X >: 4 "               [2]
IF X ≤ 2 THEN PRINT "X ≤: 2"        [3]
ELSE PRINT " X ≤: 2 "              [4]
```

**FIGURE 12.3**  Logically infeasible paths

It is logically unfeasible for the path [2, 3] to be executed. To minimize this problem, construct a control-flow diagram of the unit to be tested, and define the tests required to exercise each node or decision point one-by-one.

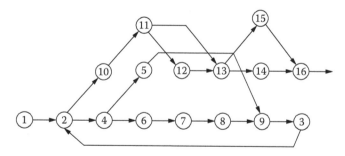

**FIGURE 12.4**  A control-flow diagram

Using Figure 12.4 as an example a first path might be [1, 2, 4, 6, 7, 8, 9, 3], a second might be [1, 2, 4, 5, 9, 3], a third might be [1, 2, 10, 11, 12, 13, 14, 16], etc.

For further details see [Howden 1] and [Rich 89].

In addition code analysis tools are available which can analyze the degree to which some test exercises the possible paths through some software and produce charts like the one shown in Table 12.1.

**TABLE 12.1** Output of a path analysis tool

| | Summary path flow report for diagmodule | | | |
|---|---|---|---|---|
| Procedure name | Times invoked (#) | Existing paths | Paths hit (#) | Paths hit (%) |
| File: print. d | | | | |
| collect | 391905 | 9 | 9 | 100.0 |
| yrstrncmp | 72 | 6 | 6 | 100.0 |
| print BA table | 0 | 21 | 0 | 0.0 |
| print literals | 3476 | 3 | 3 | 100.0 |
| print msg | 712 | 13 | 8 | 61.5 |
| print prompt | 30 | 15 | 14 | 93.3 |
| print range status | 3 | 44 | 24 | 54.5 |
| print test pages | 408304 | 12 | 12 | 100.0 |
| user range | 16384 | 11 | 10 | 90.9 |
| valid response | 194 | 5 | 5 | 100.0 |
| | 821080 | 139 | 91 | 80.02 |

# 12.5  All-DU-Paths Coverage

All-DU-paths testing is a more powerful (because more precise) variant of path testing. A DU-path is that program path that connects the *definition* of a variable with its *use*. By *definition* we mean the modification of the value associated with that variable via an assignment, input statement, or procedure call. A *use* is a reference to the value, usually within some expression. An all-DU-path test should cover all DU paths for all variables in a procedure. The technique also includes means for minimizing the path number. See [Rapps] and [Bieman] for further details.

# 12.6  Execution-Time and Resource-Use Analysis

The purpose of execution time and resource use analysis is to trace performance bugs through monitoring the execution and resource use of a program. This may be done either through instrumented code or special-purpose analyzers.

The results of the analysis show:

- The number of times chosen statements are executed
- The amount of time required to execute a chosen unit
- The most expensive (in terms of resource use) of all the units in the program
- The flow of control over time
- The amount of time the program spent waiting for data entry or some other process to complete
- The amount of CPU and other resource time used

This method is invaluable for optimizing programs. It is incorporated into several software tools. See [Heidler] for more details.

# 12.7  Algorithm Analysis

Algorithm analysis occurs in two stages; *a priori* analysis and *a posteriori* testing.

In *a priori* analysis a function is defined using some theoretic machine such as a Finite State Machine that bounds the (class of) algorithm's use of machine time and memory space to compute an acceptable solution. The logical consistency of the algorithm may be analyzed by rewriting it in a language such as Z (see section A.11 in Appendix A). This analysis will provide evidence of the algorithm's validity, upper and lower computational bound estimates, memory use estimates, and optimality assessment.

In *a posteriori* testing, evidence of the algorithm's use of resources, correctness, and optimality is collected and compared with the *a priori* analysis estimates using a rigorous correctness argument.

Algorithm analysis requires considerable mathematical ability.

# 12.8   Linear Code Sequence and Jump (LCSAJ)

Linear Code Sequence and Jump (LCSAJ) is a linear sequence of executable code which begins at the start of the program or some branch and ends either at the end of the program or some other branch. LCSAJ coverage consists of testing this sequence including one of the paths following the jump and is thus equivalent to statement coverage. There are various kinds of LCSAJs however:

- $LCSAJ_1$ coverage is the equivalent of statement coverage plus one of the paths.
- $LCSAJ_2$ coverage is the equivalent of statement coverage plus both the paths.
- $LCSAJ_n$ coverage (n > 2) is the equivalent of statement coverage plus *n* paths of a case statement or when *n* becomes very large, the equivalent of full path testing; a prohibitively expensive approach.

For low numbers of *n* $LCSAJ_n$ coverage is both feasible and thorough, providing the paths themselves are feasible. For further details of LCSAJ tool support for LCSAJ analysis see section 7.8.3 in Chapter 7.

1. 100% Statement Coverage (TER1)
   - Every statement contained in the code has been exercised by the test data used.
   - Every procedure call has been invoked in combination with preceding constructs.
2. 100% Branch/Decision Coverage (TER2)
   - Every statement contained in the code has been exercised by the test data used.
   - Every procedure call has been invoked in combination with preceding constructs.
   - Every decision branch linking those statements has been exercised.
3. 100% LCSAJ Coverage (TER3)
   - Every statement contained in the code has been exercised by the test data used.
   - Every procedure call has been invoked in combination with preceding constructs.
   - Every decision branch linking those statements has been exercised.
   - Every procedure return has been invoked in combination with preceding constructs.
   - Every zero trip, single, double, triple, or more loop execution has been forced in multi-loop combinations.
   - Every combination of both nested and sequential loops has been forced.
   - All procedure exits have been invoked with all possible exit paths.
   - All branch conditions have been exercised in all combinations.
4. 100% Procedure/Function Call Coverage (P/FCALL)
   - Every Procedure/Function call has been exercised.
   - Every Procedure/Function call return has been exercised.
5. 100% Branch Condition Coverage (BCC)
   - Each Boolean operand within decision conditions has been executed with both a TRUE and a FALSE value.
6. 100% Branch Condition Combination Coverage (BCCC)
   - Each unique combination of the set of Boolean operand values within each decision condition has been executed.
7. 100% Multiple Condition/Decision Coverage (MC/DC)
   - Each Boolean operand value within decision conditions has been executed.

The above-mentioned measures are calculated using the following equations:

$$TER1 = \frac{number\ of\ statements\ exercised\ at\ least\ once}{total\ number\ of\ statements}$$

$$TER2 = \frac{number\ of\ branches\ exercised\ at\ least\ once}{total\ number\ of\ branches}$$

$$TER3 = \frac{number\ of\ LCSAJs\ exercised\ at\ least\ once}{total\ number\ of\ LCSAJs}$$

$$P/FCall = \frac{number\ of\ Procedure\ /\ Function\ Calls\ exercised\ at\ least\ once}{total\ number\ of\ Procedure\ /\ Function\ Calls}$$

$$BCC = \frac{number\ of\ Boolean\ operand\ values\ exercised\ at\ least\ once}{total\ number\ of\ Boolean\ operand\ values}$$

$$BCCC = \frac{number\ of\ Boolean\ operand\ value\ combinations\ exercised\ at\ least\ once}{total\ number\ of\ Boolean\ operand\ value\ combinations}$$

$$MC/DC = \frac{number\ of\ Boolean\ operand\ values\ independently\ affecting\ decision\ outcomes}{total\ number\ of\ Boolean\ operands}$$

## 12.9   Dynamic Analysis Techniques

These are means of analyzing the behavior of a running program, usually in terms of data item use, data operation frequency, and speed, using some instrumentation and one of the following methods:

- **Analyze the existing code** with an interpretive system with access to the symbol table.
- **Add code statements** to print out or write to some log file details of every time some data item is accessed. The instrumentation process is similar to a programmer inserting additional print statements in a program to flag whenever a particular item is executed. The technique improves understanding of the program's execution. Such instrumentation is a prerequisite of dynamic analysis, and requires that code be inserted at strategic points in the program so that the control-flow path can be traced using the dynamic analyzer. Such insertion points are typically at control node jumps, program labels, and the start and finish of the program. These procedure calls write information to an execution history file which is later interrogated by the dynamic analyzer.
- **Read a history of the execution** from a dynamic control-flow analyzer and combine this with output from a static dataflow analyzer. This will indicate the executed parts of the program without the overhead of excessive history but with the disadvantage that no information of the actual data values can be obtained.

See [Fairfield] and Chapter 7 for details of tools to accomplish this.

### 12.9.1   Executable Assertion Testing

Executable assertion testing requires you put assertions into the code which check that the code is correct at the point the assertion is executed and, if not, generate an error message. Derive the assertions from specifications or by reading the code, and put them either at the entry and exit points of units (typically to check that the data used by the units is within bounds) or within units (to check that some function has executed correctly). Typical assertions use set-theoretic constructs such as:

For all I in set S A[I] > A [I+1]
There exists an x such that f(x) = 0

They are added using constructs such as:

```
                         ASSERT <condition>
                         FAIL <bug-handling code>
```

Such assertions will however slow the code and, since they depend on the programmer's knowledge of the code's behavior, may be wrong.

You can write them in comment form and then activate them using a pre-processor in the style of many formal specification notations. Analyze them using an executable assertion analyzer tool which scans the source file for particular strings. The exact string and some of the matching rules are described in a parameter file. Every line of an assertion (including the start and finish special strings) should be part of a normal comment in the source language. Thus were the original source submitted to a compiler it would compile as normal with the assertions treated as comments. Instrumentation is added before and after the expression to sense its truth value. The instrumentation is such that an untrue assertion will cause a "failure" routine to be called which passes a reference number indicating this particular assertion. When the start of an assertion string is read, the subsequent expression is parsed to check that its validity.

In this example, the code shown in Figure 12.5 becomes the code shown in Figure 12.6. For further details see [Presson] and [Rosenblum].

```
with INTE_IO;
with TEXT_IO;

procedure test is
     k : integer;
begin
     k: = 0;
     for i in 0 .. 40 loop
--assert
--
-- (i<40) and (k<300)  ◀──────── Assertion
--
--end assert
     k := k+1;
```

**FIGURE 12.5**  Example of instrumented code

...becomes...

```
with TEXT_IO;
with INTE_IO;
procedure assert fail(n:integer) is
     fail : exception;
begin TEXT_IO.new line;
     TEXT_IO.put("Assertion failure: ");
     INTE_IO.put(n,l);
     TEXT_IO.new line;
     raise fail;
end;
with assert fail;
with INTE IO;
with TEXT_IO;
procedure test is
     k : integer;
begin
     k: =O;                        Expanded
     for i in 0 .. 40 loop          assertion
-- assertion 1
     if not (( i < 40 ) and ( k < 300 ) ) then assert_fail(1)
     end if;
-- end assertion
     k:=k+i;
 ...
```

**FIGURE 12.6**  Example of expanded, instrumented code

## 12.10  Derivative Techniques

The techniques discussed so far have helped to generate test data by looking at what the unit or feature is supposed to do and how it actually goes about it. Some design methods offer us powerful test techniques and if we don't know how the unit was constructed, we lose the benefit of them. This section describes some frequently-used design methods that also offer test techniques.

### 12.10.1  Decision Tables

The functional requirements of some programs can be specified by a decision table. If program is specified in this way, we can carry out checks of specification consistency and *completeness*. Once the tables have been checked for *completeness* and consistency, simple Boolean algebra techniques can be applied to derive a covering set of *test cases* without going through the full $2n$ combinations (where $n$ = the number of possible decisions to be taken). See Figure 11.5 for an example.

### 12.10.2  Finite State Machines

Finite State Machines (FSMs) are frequently used as a means of designing whole systems or simply single units. The FSM modeling and design technique is useful for any system that can be treated as a black-box and that receives sequential inputs, responds by generating outputs depending on the input and the current state and finally changes to a new state.

Review the state-machine model to ensure it is *minimal* (no state is duplicated or redundant), *complete* (every state is shown, every state can be reached from some other state, and can reach some other state), and *deterministic* (the triggers for any transition force a single transition only). If the state-charts describing the state machine are hierarchic, then flatten them by including every transition at the top level.

Test them by testing that:

- Every state can exist
- Every legal transition between states can be made
- No illegal transitions can be made

Test state charts of concurrent systems either by multiplying the existing states (can get big) or by testing each separately and then testing the communication between them (can result in missed transitions). See [Liuying] and Figure A.64 for more.

# 13

# Test Techniques: Static Analysis

## It Isn't Lovely, But It Works

There was a railway company with a computer-based system to allocate the control of parts of its network to contractors. It had no requirements specification but it had a manual which was only about three releases old.

The test consultant said, "I must have a requirements specification if I'm to test this. Otherwise I'll be spending all my time asking questions."

"OK," they said, "write it."

So he did and he found many bugs. And they all got fixed.

This chapter outlines techniques for finding bugs by analyzing some code without necessarily running it. These techniques generally point out both actual and potential bugs by highlighting anomalous behavior — data items that are never read for example.

Very often these investigative techniques can be successfully applied to groups of units forming a larger (but still deterministic) program; many of the analysis code analysis tools that are available are intended to be used in this fashion.

Given the source code of a program we can carry out some analyses without executing the software. For instance:

- Non-standard, anomalous, or dubious programming practices can be identified. These will suggest logical faults: uninitialized variables, unreachable code, incorrectly calculated array bounds, variables set but not read, etc.
- Compliance with interface specifications can be checked.
- Data and control cross-references can be drawn up, perhaps revealing over-coupling, unintended coupling, misuse of global variables or potential synchronization bugs.

Some of these types of analysis can be carried out manually (in reviews for instance) where necessary, but automated static analyzers are clearly preferable. ADA compilers include interface assertion checkers. See Chapter 8 for details of tools and some static analyzers that are available.

# 13.1   Static Dataflow Analysis

Static dataflow analysis determines the presence or absence of those bugs which can be represented as particular sequences of events in a program's execution. It uses two kinds of graphs as input, representing the program structures, and the order in which they can occur.

- The first is a *flowgraph* consisting of a number of nodes representing the program statements and edges representing the order in which they may be executed. Each node is annotated with indications of which program events occur as a consequence of its execution (Figure 13.1).

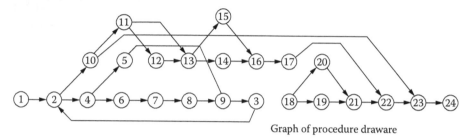

Graph of procedure draware

**FIGURE 13.1**   Static control-flowgraph

- The second is a call graph whose nodes represent procedures and its edges representing which procedures can call which others.

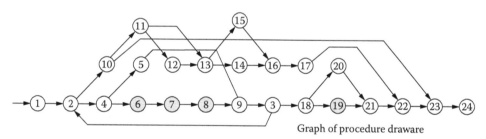

Graph of procedure draware

**FIGURE 13.2**   Dynamic control-flowgraph

Figure 13.2 shows some of the coverage results of dynamic analysis in a graphical form. The control-*flowgraph* of the program is drawn, and those nodes which have been executed are left blank, while those unexecuted by the tests are shaded in grey. Similarly, branches which have been executed are shown as solid lines, while those unexecuted are drawn as dotted lines.

The analysis produces a report showing any (pre-defined) illegal sequences and sample paths which can trigger those sequences. However it can be difficult to annotate all call nodes before the analysis. A bottom-up approach is therefore used with all lower level procedures annotated first showing the possible first and last events which can call the procedure, and then add this information to the call graph of the higher nodes.

Dataflow analysis can typically show uninitialized program variables, and such illegal sequences as attempting to read a file before opening it. It cannot however distinguish between executable and unexecutable paths, and treats arrays as simple variables thereby overlooking illegal array operations. See [Heidler] and section 7.8.6 for more details.

There is a large number of tool suppliers, and a large number of tools is also available in Opensource format. Many Internet sites are devoted to analyzing them. Many are listed in Appendix D.

## 13.2   Dataflow Bugs

Dataflow bugs are sequences of actions on a variable in a program which are suspected to be erroneous. Here's the theory. Any variable in a program can be:

- D(efined), i.e., assigned a value
- R(eferenced), i.e., its value used
- U(ndefined), i.e., its value (if any) is destroyed (e.g., when a variable is first declared it is assumed to be undefined or when a variable goes out of scope it becomes undefined)

Three kinds of dataflow bug can be defined in terms of these states:

1. A variable whose value is undefined may be referenced (UR bug).
2. A variable which has been defined may be redefined without referencing the variable after the first definition (DD bug).
3. A variable which has been defined may become undefined without referencing the variable after the definition (DU bug).

```
1. procedure PROC is
2.                    t, w, x, y, z: integer;
3. begin
4.                    X: = 1
5.                    if y > 0 then
6.                    x: = 2;
7. end if;
8. z: = x+1;
9. end PROC;
```

**FIGURE 13.3**   ADA program listing

In the program segment shown in Figure 13.3:

- The variable x is defined on line 4 and again on line 6; an example of a DD bug.
- The variable y is referenced on line 5, but is not given a value before the reference; an example of a UR bug.
- The variable z is defined on line 8, but becomes undefined (by going out of scope at the end of the procedure) without being referenced; example of a DU bug.

There is also an anomalous use or rather non-use of the variable *t* which is declared on line 2, but is never used.

## 13.3   Control-Flow Analysis

Control-flow analysis, also known as structure analysis, is a means of detecting illegal sub-program use and control-flow standards violations such as detecting unreachable code, infinite loops, knots, and recursive procedure calls. It uses source code as input together with definitions of the standards to be observed. It produces bug reports and a program call graph. See Chapter 7 for a discussion of structure analysis tools.

## 13.4   Function Value Analysis

All paths through functions must either return a value or be explained by a comment.

# 13.5   Symbolic Execution

Symbolic execution represents a mid-point between running individual test sets through a program, and carrying out a proof of its correctness using a rigorous correctness argument.

It involves executing (interpreting) a program symbolically. During the execution, the values of variables are held in algebraic form and the outcome of the program is represented as one or more expressions. Decisions are handled by following both outcomes while remembering the condition value corresponding to each of the paths now being followed separately.

At the end of the evaluation, there will be two facts about each path through the program: a list of the decision outcomes made along the path and the final expression of all the variables expressed algebraically. Together these define the function of the program and can be compared with the required function — this is the test.

For example, given the code fragment shown in Figure 13.4,

```
Input x, input y
z: = x + y
x: = x**2 + y**2
y: = z + x
```

**FIGURE 13.4**  Code fragment

we can rewrite it in terms of the final values of x, y, and z (Figure 13.5).

```
Input a, input b
x: = a**2 + b**2
y: = a + b + a**2 + b**2
z: = a + b
```

**FIGURE 13.5**  Code fragment rewritten

These definitions can then be used as bases for condition coverage tests and path analyses.

Loops require external assistance to determine the number of iterations, unit calls can be handled either by solving for the unit separately and then supplying equations for the call parameters or by including the entire unit in the code to be solved. Conditional jumps require that each possible path be separately solved.

Note that this example excludes such constructs as arrays or parallelism. Symbolic evaluation is very useful for code fragments such as an $LCSAJ_1$ but less valuable for longer and more complex code.

For further details see [Linger] and the *CUTE* tool in section D.10 in Appendix D.

# 13.6   Mutation Testing

One major problem when all tests cases have been designed and executed for all tests is to be reasonably confident that the cases will find all bugs. Mutation analysis helps by identifying omissions.

Mutation analysis validates tests and their data by running them against many copies of the program each containing a different, single, deliberately-inserted change. If the tests discover the change then they are assumed to be *good*. Typical mutations are exchanging all + and . There are two theories underlying the approach:

1. That a large number of bugs are caused by elementary programmer bugs such as using AND instead of OR, + instead of , and SQRT(X) instead of X**2 or vice versa. For some reason this is called the *competent programmer* theory.
2. The second theory is called the *coupling effect* theory, which implies that if a test case can find a simple bug it can find a more complex one also.

Mutation testing creates one or more copies of some original piece of code and changes it such that one or more instructions are different. Code may be added to expose the difference. Thus code as shown in Figure 13.6

```
x = a + b
y = c + d
```

**FIGURE 13.6** Code before mutation

could be mutated and the mutation checked for, as shown in Figure 13.7.

```
x = a + b
if (a + b) <> (a - b) then mutant 1 detected
if (a + b) <> (a * b) then mutant 2 detected
if (a + b) <> (b - a) then mutant 3 detected
if (a + b) <> (a + b) then mutant 4 detected
y = c + d
```

**FIGURE 13.7** Code with a mutation check

The test case which exposes the mutant is said to have "killed" it.

## 13.7   Mutation Testing Problems

Several problems have been identified with mutation testing:

- The sorts of changes made may not reflect the bugs really in the program (for example, multiple or timing bugs), which the tests may be poor at finding. Also a large number of target mutants may be required. These however may be simply produced using a series of operating system commands and a random number generator. Generating all the mutants possible is very costly even with the aid of a tool such as Mothra. ([Howden 3] proposes weak mutation testing wherein only the state immediately after the mutation is compared with the unmutated state.) In practice, of the 22 operators used in Mothra [DeMillo 2] only 5 are shown to be essential:
  - ABS, which forces each arithmetic expression to take on the value 0, a positive value, and a negative value
  - AOR, which replaces each arithmetic operator with every syntactically legal operator
  - LCR, which replaces each logical connector (AND and OR) with several kinds of logical connectors
  - ROR, which replaces relational operators with other relational operators
  - UOI, which inserts unary operators in front of expressions
- In practice, if the software contains a fault, there will usually be a set of mutants that can only be killed by a test case that also detects that fault [Geist].
- Mutated code may also correct a bug in the original code and thus hide it.
- If the code is simply wrong in that its logic is deficient, no amount of mutation testing will reveal this.
- Instrumenting mutated code to expose the errors they are presumed to exhibit generates large amounts of code and a mutant placed early in the code may itself block the execution of a later one.
- The system under test may use a different language from those covered by market-available tools. One solution is to look at the changes in the code using the difference files in the code management system and identify those most common. This will probably require some script to identify the differences but once written will give you a profile to work with.

Should the tests fail to discover the changes made, the tests may be judged *bad* and improved. Mutation tests are valuable in discovering the minor, but important coding lapses even experienced programmers make. See section 18.10 and [Mills 72], [DeMillo 1], [Heidler], [Voas], and [Offutt] for more details.

## 13.8   Fault Injection

The purpose of fault injection is to answer the question: *How well will this software behave in the future?* It does this by simulating both programmer faults and faults induced by connected systems such as failing sensors, and introducing source code changes in an effort to render the software more "*brittle*" in that some bug is more likely to appear. Having exposed the bug by causing it to "*propagate*" the "*brittleness*" of the software is also exposed by the amount of change required to expose the bug. The process is:

- An input (either from a "normal" source such as keyboard or file or one artificially injected which deliberately corrupts some data during program execution) provokes a fault.
- The fault *infects* a data state after execution. (If it doesn't then it will not be visible — this is particularly a problem with fault-tolerant code.)
- The infected data state *propagates* to some output (Figure 13.8).

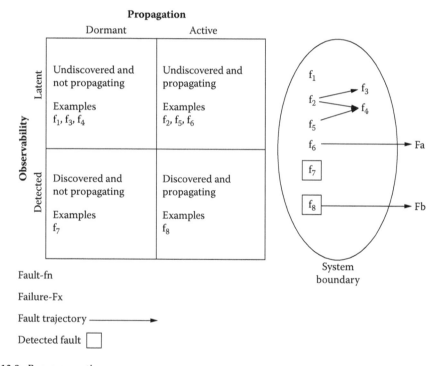

**FIGURE 13.8**  Bug propagation

Bugs can be said to *propagate* in that their effects are visible in program states beyond the state in which the bug existed. Thus if the bug is an inability to handle some input, inputting some illegal input may expose it. If the bug is an inability to pass or receive some system input or output, then artificially inducing a fault may cause that system input or output to exhibit it. Propagated bugs are observable as faults at the system, application, and output levels.

The degree to which some fault is evident is the answer to the question. If no bug creates any error, then the system is immune to data or programmer faults. Note that you need really big perturbations to find the really tough bugs.

Fault injection is applied to inputs, code, and internal data states.

- **Inputs** (particularly rare-event inputs) can be determined from operational profiles (see Chapter 7). Note those inputs which are excluded (particularly the rare event ones) since these may expose unexpected bugs. Rare-event inputs can be determined from the legal inputs and be used to determine some sense of legal system behavior. This can then be compared with illegal inputs to determine how well the system copes. Input types include sensor data, operator input, and even the results of system calls. Inputs will usually be created with a random number generator which avoids creating replacement values identical to the original values. The inputs used need to be captured for the test to be repeatable.

- **Outputs** can be data or events such as removing a file. They allow us to determine whether a bug has been exposed so we must define the set of legal outputs as a baseline. We can determine if an output has exposed a bug by comparing the output of two runs, one with illegal inputs and the other without. Outputs can be big and determining the existence of bugs can require some automation. Outputs may be rare if (for example) we are testing the ability of a rare particle sensor buried in a mountain waiting for a quark to appear or an emergency shut-down of a nuclear plant.
- **Interfaces.** If an anomaly is injected into the interface outputting information from X and none was injected into X itself, this has the effect of simulating a fault on X without having to modify X. In this way X can be treated as a black-box (legacy or COTS software). Such tests assume that a grammar of the inputs and outputs is available. Such a definition needs to exist if a wrapper is to be defined.
- **Code** is the key area where fault injection is deployed. It is essential that some mutated code propagate the bug to an output. This means that the problem, having been created by the mutated code becomes evident at some later state of the system. Highly-defensive code may not do this in which case the observability of any bug in it may be nil and fault-injection won't work. Code can have assertions added. The assertion can be used to provoke some output in the code which will indicate the presence of a fault (Figure 13.9).

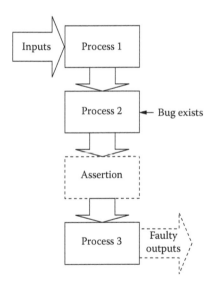

**FIGURE 13.9** Assertion demonstrating a bug

## 13.8.1 Analysis

Having injected faults, much data will be generated. A first step (assuming any event of interest has been observed) is to determine how probable it is based on a level of confidence (Figure 13.10). Thus, where the p(robability) of the event having occurred / n(umber of opportunities for it to occur = tests) is useful, the Confidence Level% is shown in Table 13.1, where p = probability of events, n = sample, zc = (see Table 13.1).

```
confidence level  = p ± z_c (SQRT (p(1-p)/n))
```

**FIGURE 13.10** Confidence-level equation

**TABLE 13.1**  Confidence levels

| Confidence level% | 99.73 | 99 | 98 | 96 | 95.45 | 95 | 90 | 80 | 68.27 | 50 |
|---|---|---|---|---|---|---|---|---|---|---|
| zc | 3 | 2.58 | 2.33 | 2.05 | 2 | 1.96 | 1.645 | 1.28 | 1 | 0.6745 |

### 13.8.1.1  Example

Assume that we have run a trial of 60,000 tests of which 150 found errors. Therefore there is a %probability of finding 150/60000 errors (0.25%). We need to know how confident we can be of the probability of the bug rate being %0.25. Using the equation above we can calculate that there is a 95% confidence that the probability lies between $(0.25 + 0.003464823)\%$ and $(0.25 - 0.003464823)\%$, that is between 0.253464823% and 0.246535177%. Here's how:

| | |
|---|---|
| Tests run (n) | 60000 |
| Errors found | 150 |
| % Probability of an error | 0.25 |
| (1p) | 0.75 |
| p*(1p) | 0.1875 |
| p*(1p)/n | 0.000003125 |
| SQRT(p*(1p)/n) | 0.001767767 |
| zc = 1.96* SQRT(p*(1p)/n) | 0.003464823 |
| Confident to 95% that the probability of finding the errors lies between | 0.253464823 |
| and | 0.246535177 |

Alternatively we could calculate the confidence level that the bugs found were 99.73% probable:

| | |
|---|---|
| Tests run (n) | 60000 |
| Errors found | 150 |
| % Probability of an error | 0.25 |
| (1p) | 0.75 |
| p*(1p) | 0.1875 |
| p*(1p)/n | 0.000003125 |
| SQRT(p*(1p)/n) | 0.001767767 |
| $z_c = 3$ | 0.005303301 |
| Confident to 99.75% that the probability of finding the errors lies between | 0.255303301 |
| and | 0.244696699 |

The fault-injection analysis process is shown in Figure 13.11. This is now supported by a number of tools. See section D.10 in Appendix D.

## 13.8.2  Testability

Fault injection can be used to demonstrate the testability (or otherwise) of code using sensitivity analysis. Code which exhibits few failures (such as highly fault-tolerant code) may still have bugs, but these are not being exhibited by the test data set used. An answer is to use fault injection to create bugs artificially to determine how effective the software is at containing the failure.

[Friedman] proposes a set of algorithms for determining testability. See also [Voas]. These are outlined in section 18.2.

- The *propagation estimate* of each code location $l(score_l)$. This defines the degree to which variables can be used to propagate errors.
- The *infection estimate* of each code location $l$ in each mutant ($score_{IM}$). This defines the degree to which a mutated program exhibits a change as a result of being a mutant (as compared with an unmutated program).
- The *execution estimate* of each code location $l(score_l)$. This defines the degree to which some test set executes some code.

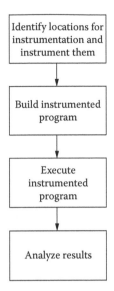

**FIGURE 13.11**   Fault-injection process

## 13.8.3  Conclusions

These scores will indicate:

- The areas of code which most need testing (execution estimates)
- The best *test cases* to be used (propagation and infection estimates) by scoring each test case against:
  - Number of locations exercised
  - Number of data state infections created
  - The number of visibly-propagated mutants

*Test cases* thus scored can be assembled in suites and the suites themselves scored.

## 13.8.4  Exhibiting Bugs

Q1: *What kinds of faults cannot be injected?*
  Distributed faults involving many variables simultaneously, can be as difficult to inject as they would be to test for conventionally. The number variables to be tested for can be reduced by "program slicing" to see which variables interact. Implication: almost any fault can be injected — the problem is balancing the risk of the fault against the cost of fault injection. Fortunately there are tools available to minimize this cost.

Q2: *What kind of software is unamenable to fault injection?*
  - Code which never produces an output or which can never be expected to terminate (such as an operating system) may also be difficult to inject.
  - Code which has timing vulnerabilities may exhibit anomalies precisely because it has been instrumented. It is usually possible (for example, by using a code profiler to detect where delays are non-critical) to instrument code such that it isn't slowed enough to make a difference.
  - Compiled code whose execution thread is indeterminable such as the PowerPC. The PowerPC processor allows dynamic instruction reordering and out-of-order instruction execution though this effect is allegedly masked by a completion buffer.
  - Code whose inputs or outputs cannot be defined. This is particularly the case with COTS software.

Q3: *Can simulating unfeasible anomalies produce useful information?*
  Yes. You can't know they're **always** infeasible and they will show you how vulnerable the system is to that anomaly (when you realize it isn't unfeasible) and possibly others.

Q4: *Just because one simulated anomaly exposes a bug does it mean that any one will?*
There is evidence (See [Voas]) that 84% of variables corrupted, exhibited the same bug. This is still a research area.

Q5: *Where do we inject faults?*
- Decide on the event of interest: (a train going through signals at red, an altimeter failing, a bank statement that is wrong). In safety analysis terms this would be a "top event."
- Identify the software states which might create this.
- Identify the code and variables required to create each state.
- Prune the set of code and variables by slicing.

Q6: *When can we apply fault injection?*
When the code compiles, it can be shown to return the same output for a given input and can be shown to end.

Q7: *The code being executed is compiled code; how does injecting faults in compiled code to provoke a bug tell me what's wrong with the original source?*
It doesn't until you have (1) found a bug and (2) decompiled the compiled code. Identify the question you are trying to answer about the code and instrument as little as possible, and only use a code/chip combination for which a decompiler is available. There remains the possibility that even decompiled code will not reveal a programmer fault. Generally faults should be injected into source code.

Q8: *If using (say) a PowerPC how do I know how the fault-injected code was executed?*
You don't. This is one of the limitations of fault-injection on some processors.

Q9: *Having got the data, what do we look for?*
See section 13.8.3.

Q10: *How do we identify timing sensitivities?*
Use the algorithms shown in section 18.2 to perturb the perturbable timing-related variables (as opposed to those which are system- or processor-determined). This can be used to simply cause synchronizations to be grossly delayed (thus simulating deadlock) or programs can be mutated to provoke control-flow errors. Thus code could be mutated to provoke race conditions. Such attempts amount to deliberate sabotage rather than random mutation and their ability to expose fault is thus reduced.

### 13.8.5   Case Study

A (fictitious) aircraft has a control program for the actuators of its ailerons. Buried deep in the code is an algorithm using a calculation of the sine of an angle. Fault injection changed this to a tangent of an angle. (The example is shown as an Excel function.)

TAN(x * PI()/100)

where 90 > x < 270. Using random data it was discovered that the data of 90° and 270° would cause the ailerons to invert at those settings (and at no other: TAN(90°) and TAN(270°) are undefined) (Figure 13.12).

## 13.9   Test Data Generators

Test data generators can be considered as being of two types. The first are those which allow the user to set up values as he chooses throughout a test run, as with good harnesses or debuggers. The second class (called input generators) are those which actually derive a set of test data needed to comprehensively exercise the code under test. Such generators are particularly useful for testing compilers in that a compiler must be able to handle every legally-possible input string and generating them all by hand is time-consuming. Useful literature on test data generators includes [Bazzichi], [Duncan], [Intermetrics], and [Homer]. They are invaluable for random testing.

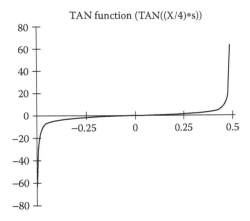

**FIGURE 13.12** A TAN function

## 13.10 Failure Mode Effects and Criticality Analysis

This is a technique for identifying system problems as early as possible, even before having written the requirements specification. It uses a form similar to the one shown in Figure 13.13 to contain the data.

It is time-consuming to prepare and in the case of software requires considerable imagination. It makes no allowance for multiple failures. It can be very cheaply implemented on a spreadsheet. A failure mode entry is the equivalent of a *top event*.

It can be used to include human error, procedural problems, and business process problems.

| Failure Mode Effects and Criticality Analysis | | | | | | |
| --- | --- | --- | --- | --- | --- | --- |
| System: | | Prepared by: | | Date: | | |
| Item/ feature | Failure modes | Cause of failure | Possible effects | Probability | Criticality | Possible action to reduce failure rate, or effects |
| Story Editor | "eats" characters | Interference with toolbar and inability to return control on time | Loss of stories | 0.2 | 1 | Use a less complex plug-in |

**FIGURE 13.13** Failure mode effects and criticality analysis form

# 14

# Unit Test Process

## Story: The Rampant Raj

Once upon a time there was a set of developers, some of whom were proud of never having unit-tested their code. But others had to write clever things which used the operating system a lot. They got fed up of being complained about and started unit testing some of their code. Then they recruited another developer whom we'll call Raj — because that was his name. He was a very conscientious developer who was always stressed and unit-tested everything he did.

So the day came when Raj was given one of the nastiest bits of code to write. It had lots of timing implications and had to cope with some pretty bizarre issues. Other nasty bits of code were farmed around the other developers including those who said they had never unit tested in their lives before and weren't about to start now.

And their code was quite terrible and the release was a disaster. All except for the bits which Raj built. So when they were sacked, he was kept.

## 14.1 Managing Unit Testing

This is akin to cat-herding or managing developers. Unless (unwisely: see section 14.6) your organization has split unit testing from development, you will not manage the writing of unit tests. Most of the contents of this section are therefore for background information. You will however need to know if a release heading your way has been sufficiently unit-tested. Here are some questions to be asked:

- How much of the code has been exercised by the unit tests?
- Were the unit tests run just before the build or some time before?
- Has the rigor of unit testing been related to the risk the unit represents?

You may be asked to initiate unit testing in an effort to show developers how many bugs they could have found before system testing begins.

## 14.2 Purpose of Unit Testing

The purpose of unit testing (sometimes referred to as module testing) is to:

- Limit the scope of testing such that it is possible to find bugs in a humanly-manageable way.
- Remove as many bugs as possible before integration testing begins.

- Provide programmers with some objective evidence of the worth of the units they have produced by measuring it against either the specification from which it was coded or the harness and inputs which they have used.

There is some argument about what is a unit. Here are a few guidelines:

- The print-out of a unit should reside on a single sheet of paper.
- If there are more than four levels of nesting in the unit, then perhaps it should be split in two.
- If the cyclomatic complexity (see section 18.8.4) of a unit is greater than 10 then it is getting too complex.
- If it is content-coupled with another unit then it isn't a good unit.

See [BS 7925-2] and [IEEE 1008] for more on this. Developers of an eXtreme or agile persuasion sometimes propose writing unit tests before they write code. This is excellent for many reasons principally because it increases the probability of a bug being found in the stage it's been created.

The unit test process is:

- Plan the unit tests.
- Design the tests, the test environment, and operator instructions.
- Identify and acquire the test data.
- Code and execute the tests.
- Analyze the results.

The coding process is ignored here since it can occur at any point. While these activities are listed consecutively they may require some iteration. Thus when designing tests you may realize that they haven't been specified sufficiently and you will have to modify the specifications as a result. Similarly the test execution may show that the test data is insufficient or unrealistic.

Unit tests are the lowest-level tests possible. They may employ several of the techniques mentioned in section 12.9. Since the code behavior is evident to the programmer, the tests chosen will usually be white-box types. Once they are confident that the code matches the unit specification they can begin black-box testing.

## 14.3   Identify the Test Baseline

The test baselines will consist of the test plan, the high-level design specifications, the unit specifications, the code, and possibly the requirements specifications (typically where high-level units are being exercised by simulating user inputs).

Clearly in a well-managed project, all the specifications will be both available and consistent. If not, these baselines may be considered to be of descending order of importance:

- If the requirements specifications aren't being met, then the project is doomed. However the requirements specifications will rarely say anything code-specific. Requirements specifications are always the most important specification of any project.
- The high-level design specifications should logically supersede the unit specifications. In practice they will either be so high-level that it is difficult to trace the unit design to them or very unspecific and inconsistent. They are of course a Good Thing To Do because they are the only thing standing between the project and architectural entropy. This is why a good project will be thrice designed: the first two attempts were just sketches to clear the mind.
- Logically the unit specifications should supersede the code — in practice they often ceased to relate to the code, three releases back.
- The code itself may be all you have (in the event that the project is very old and very mismanaged). You may be told "*It's worked for 20 years — now fix it.*" In this unhappy event you can either try and guess from the code what it is supposed to do, undertake an extensive re-engineering job rewriting a set of unit specifications perhaps and then the unit test or resign.

- The test plan may contain good stuff about the level of testing required, the resources available, and the testing criteria to be adopted. It will mostly depend on the other baselines however.

You will need to know things about any unit: how bug-prone it is, what risk it represents, how often it will be used, how complex it is. You or the programmers will use many of the techniques from Chapter 11 through Chapter 13.

## 14.4  Identify Unit Characteristics

A number of approaches to identifying object-oriented unit characteristics have been developed. These can help in determining the approach to be taken:

- *Depth of Inheritance Tree* (DIT). [Chidamber 1], [Chidamber 2] and [Basili 96] have attempted to identify the most predictive of the object-oriented metrics so far proposed and found that DIT was the best predictor of fault proneness. [Glasberg] predicted and confirmed that classes at the root of a hierarchy or that are deepest in a hierarchy will have a lower fault-proneness compared to those in the middle of the hierarchy.

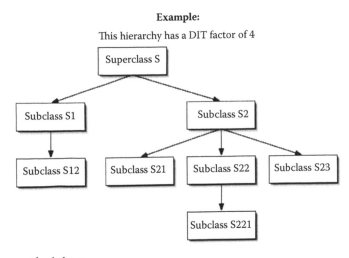

**Example:**

This hierarchy has a DIT factor of 4

**FIGURE 14.1**  Classes and subclasses

- *Number Of Children* (NOC). The number of immediate subclasses. Thus in Figure 14.1, the NOC of S2 is 3. Note that the negative co-efficiency of NOC shown in Table 14.1 is highly counter-intuitive because few classes have more than one child and reuse reduces the probability of bug-proneness.
- *Average Method Complexity* (AMC) of a unit is simply the sum of the complexities (see section 18.8.4 in Chapter 18) of all the methods in that unit divided by the number of methods.

$$average\ method\ complexity = \frac{\sum_{all\ methods} cyclomatic\ complexity}{\sum all\ methods}$$

- *Weighted Methods per Class* (WMC). WMC measures the complexity of an individual class by summing the complexities of all methods of a class.
- *Response For a Class* (RFC). The number of methods in the set of all methods of a class that can be invoked in response to a message sent to an object of that class.
- *Coupling Between Object classes* (CBO). Two classes are coupled when methods declared in one class use methods or instance variables of the other class [Chidamber 2].

Note that there is a large number of object-oriented metrics in the literature many of which are proposed as determiners of test rigor.

## 14.4.1  Coefficients of Object-Oriented Metrics

The coefficients of the metrics are shown in Table 14.1 (taken from [Basili 96]):

**TABLE 14.1**  Average coefficients of object-oriented metrics

| Metrics | Coefficient | Odds ratio | Priority | Comment |
|---|---|---|---|---|
| WMC | 0.22 | 2% | 3 | More methods per object class increase object size and complexity, and probably hinder testing. |
| RFC | 0.09 | 9% | 4 | The probability of a bug increases as the RFC, particularly for new or heavily modified classes. It also hinders testing. |
| NOC | 3.38 | 96% | 2 | The probability of a bug decreases as the NOC. Larger NOCs need more testing. Most classes have NOC = 0. > 1 NOC is bad. |
| DIT | 0.48 | 62% | 1 | The deeper the inheritance tree (probably) the more it hinders testing. Most classes have DIT =0 and rarely DIT >10. |
| CBO | 0.14 | 15% | — | The more-highly-coupled the object (probably) the more it hinders testing and induces bugs. Most classes have CBO = 0. |
| AMC | — | — | — | Complex methods (probably) hinder testing and induce bugs. |

- *Coefficient* is the estimated regression coefficient. The larger the coefficient, the stronger the impact (positive or negative), according to its sign of the explanatory variable on the probability of a fault being detected in a class.
- *Odds ratio* represents the ratio between the probability of having a fault and the probability of not having a fault. Thus DIT correlates at 0.53 and its odds are 74% more probable that it contains a fault than that it doesn't. The odds are metric-specific: don't use them to compare the metrics since the metrics have different ordinal scales.

See section D.6 in Appendix D for details of tools which will automatically extract these metrics.

- Complexity metrics: section 18.8.4
- Fortest: www.fortest.org.uk, Formal Methods in testing
- [Sherriff] for details of the *Programatica* project
- NASA (satc.gsfc.nasa.gov/support/STC_APR98/apply_oo/apply_oo.html)
- [ckjm] and [Hackystat] for details of a process monitoring tool in section D.6 in Appendix D

## 14.4.2  Select Unit *Test Cases*

Several techniques are available to help select unit *test cases*. The value of these techniques is that, for a given amount of testing effort, they increase the probability of discovering bugs, and thus increase testing effectiveness. They are described in section 2.8.1 and section 2.2.

Some advice is given by [Hamlet] which is partly counter-intuitive:

- It is a mistake to refine a partition just to make its tests more alike. The finer partitions will be more homogeneous but will probably have uniform failure rates.
- Combining testing methods to create partition intersections, for example by refining a structural partition with a feature- or specification-based partition, will not be an improvement over either method used alone. (There is no reason to believe that the finer partitions include any with high failure rates and a high-failure partition may be diluted.)
- Dataflow testing methods, particularly those that involve more of the program context, should be superior to full path testing. (The dataflow partitions are failure-prone because they concentrate on difficult programming situations: full path testing refines the dataflow partitions without any evident increase in the expected failure rate.)

# 14.5 Unit Test Development

## 14.5.1 Identify Unit Test Objectives and Pass-Fail Criteria

Test objectives depend on unit criticality, baselines, test techniques, and tools available.

Of these, unit criticality should be defined first. It is pointless to devote a lot of time to defining a lot of test objectives for lightly-used units only to insufficiently-test more-critical units later. The criticality of units should be defined in the test plan. The criticality is determined to some extent by the integration strategy (*which units do we need for build* n?), partly by expected frequency of use (typically I/O-related units) and partly by their function, in that they support some critical feature.

The pass/fail criteria should be unambiguous. For example:

> The unit has passed the test if the output string contains no commas or full stops.

or

> The unit has failed the test if any message other than Next Entry is displayed.

When using a test harness such as xUnit, you may find it simpler to simply:

- List the methods.
- Create stubs for all the missing classes and methods referenced by the test.
- Compile and run the test and watch it fail.
- Implement enough functionality to get the test to succeed.
- Simplify the code as much as possible.

Do not think that simply because your developers use xUnit that they have unit-tested thoroughly. Even unit tests bear some level of design.

## 14.5.2 Design the Tests, the Test Environment, and Operator Instructions

Unit test specification may begin with the unit specification itself. This may consist of some graphic and/ or textual description of the unit, structured into inputs, outputs, processing, the algorithm employed, and constraints. These can all be considered as a series of targets that have to be hit such that the unit tests should attempt to prove that the unit doesn't do what the specification or some other baseline says (this assumes that the unit specification is correct). In many cases tools are available which will analyze the code and create a unit test on-the-fly.

Alternatively unit creation begins with unit test creation. Developers will identify methods and data a unit must be able to handle and create an increasingly-complex unit test *before* writing the code.

Some developers simply hack code and rely on a (very expensive) unit test tool to interpret and evaluate their output by creating an automated unit test on-the-fly.

Unit tests however created, will use a number of approaches drawn from section 12.9; also see Chapter 13. These can be used as the basis of three kinds of specifications:

1. Unit test specifications.
2. Test tool specifications. These will define the various harnesses to be used for testing as well as any more-specialized tools such as analyzers, generators, comparators, and commercially-available tools.
3. Test data specifications. These will define the test data to be acquired either based on the requirements of the individual tests or on data to be acquired from the real world.

Test tools and test techniques are highly inter-related. While all the techniques shown here can be used with pencil and paper, such an approach will exhaust both the testers and the budget. The budget-conscious manager will therefore match the risk to the project against the cost of buying in a particular tool and using a particular technique. A possible approach is:

- Identify all the techniques required.
- Identify all the tools required to support those techniques.
- Identify all those tools which are free off the web.
- Identify all those tools which must be bought-in.
- Identify the cost of bought-in tools in terms of the number of tester-days cost to buy versus tester days saved.
- Identify the cost of free tools in terms of the number of tester-days cost to learn the use of, versus tester-days saved.
- Identify the cost of build-in-house tools in terms of the number of tester-days cost to buy versus tester-days saved.
- Quantify the risk to the project if the testing fails to discover the bugs those tools are expected to find.
- Cut out the tools you can't justify.
- Identify the cost of all the program design and coding tools used. Your test tool costs should be about a third and if your total project budget doesn't allow at least a third to be spent on test and review activities then you are already in trouble.
- Argue the choice with your best friend taking the place of a most unfriendly accountant.
- Add one costly tool to the list so it can be knocked out.

Beware of the argument "*Why don't you use the X tool? After all we've got it already.*" This is the equivalent of the small boy with a hammer to whom everything appears to be a nail. You are in fact a man with a nail. Make sure that what you choose really is a hammer. Be very clear about why X is more trouble than it's worth.

### 14.5.3   Identify and Acquire the Unit Test Data

Once the unit test data has been specified, identify its sources and copy it. While this may seem a trivial exercise, in real-time applications it requires great accuracy. Consider for example the difference between radar data acquired at 2 a.m. and that acquired at 9 a.m. when the skies are presumably fuller. In these last two cases the kind of data can be defined to a limited extent in that the frequency and kinds of signals can be statistically analyzed, and predictions can be made but a new system operating in a relatively-unknown environment may require data whose complexity is both unknowable and unquantifiable.

### 14.5.4   Notes

Always leave room for notes on the test specification or as unit test code header comments, and add them as they come. It is usually the case that the test designer will get to know the unit very well and can leave useful reminders for the test operators or later programmers.

### 14.5.5   Identify How Long Each Unit Test Needs to Run

To show that an implementation is correct requires either analysis or dynamic testing. For non-trivial applications, dynamic testing cannot give the level of confidence needed for critical systems. [Littlewood 98] has shown that to demonstrate that complex software, has a failure rate better than $10^n$ failures/hour needs $10^n$ hours of dynamic testing. Where $n$ is c. 9 (in high-integrity applications), dynamic testing is an impractical means of showing compliance, as any realistic testing will only sample a tiny fraction of the input space. See section 18.6.

### 14.5.6   Unit Test Coverage Strategies

Here is one approach:

- Call 90% of the classes. Hitting 100% is feasible but lengthy. Leave this until later.
- Get 100% decision/condition coverage in each class.
- Provoke 90% of the error codes.

See section 2.8.1. Note that most unit test tools (such as the *Visual Studio* add-ins) consider that exercising the code to be "coverage." Thus they mostly provide only statement coverage.

### 14.5.7   Code and Execute the Tests

The tests are coded and run. It is advisable that all unit tests have a dry-run before use in case they themselves are buggy. This is where section 13.6 is invaluable. While there are advantages in having the same programmer write the unit tests, it is essential that all unit tests be reviewed by another programmer.

### 14.5.8   Analyze the Results

In addition to the simple pass-fail output of a typical unit test run, there may be other valuable information which can be gained from analysis of the results:

- What sorts of bugs have been found? Could they be the same as in other units coded by the same programmer?
- Where have they been found? Is there a particular construct which is causing problems for that programmer? Is a part of the unit specification ambiguous?
- Was the test run efficient? Did it find many bugs? Did it require much operator intervention? How quickly can it be run again?

If a test finds a bug, it can be kept for regression testing but should otherwise be scrapped, otherwise there is a danger that it may simply train the software to pass that test. Scrapping a test may simply consist in changing the test data.

## 14.6   Why the System Test Group Should (Not) Unit Test

There are occasional suggestions made that a special group of testers should unit test the code. Table 14.2 is a list of some of the arguments and rebuttals.

**TABLE 14.2**  Unit-testing arguments

| Argument | Rebuttal |
|---|---|
| It provides a quality gate. | True — but at a disproportionately high cost of having testers learn the code. |
| It provides management with evidence of code quality. | So will tests written by developers. |
| It eliminates obvious problems. | |
| The developers aren't. | They can be persuaded — particularly if those who stringently unit-test get the pay rises. |
| A lot of the problems system (and later test phases) finds could be found by unit tests. | Correct — but they are still best written by the developers. |
| It's less-expensive to find a bug in the same phase as it's been created than to find it later. | |
| It gets feedback to programmers ASAP. | |
| It identifies and enforces a common set of programming practices. | This is better done by code editing tools. |
| The (critical) developers have left and no one understands the code they wrote. Possibly by unit-testing it some light might be shed. | Correct. Whoever writes unit tests is then in a good position to document the code as well. Someone must maintain the code and they are the people best suited to unit-testing it. |

## 14.7   What We Have to Do to Unit Test

There are 5 phases:

### 14.7.1   Set-Up Phase

1. Plan the project.
2. Identify the 3 most bug-scarred units.
3. Identify 3 potential unit-testing tools.
4. Unit-test the units against the tools and identify:
   - Which tool found the most problems
   - Which tool fared best against bebugged code
   - Which problems were found by all the tools
   - Which tool was the easiest to learn
   - Which tool was the easiest to use
   - Which tool was the fastest
   - Which tool provided the best value
   - What problems each tool exhibited
5. Report on the success/otherwise of the project so far, and identify the tool to be used.
6. Decide how Unit test bugs are to be reported (probably as a separate category).

### 14.7.2   Integration Phase (to Show the Effects of Consistent Use to Developers)

1. Plan the phase.
2. Analyze the codebase to identify the top 10% of the most bug-exhibiting units (measured by the number of bug-related changes).
3. Identify which build attempts had been made, and how many failed.
4. Identify the modules which provoked the fails.
5. Discuss the units with the developers to identify the remaining life of each unit, potential for short-term enhancement of the unit, and the amount of time spent fixing it over the last 12 months (to see if it's worth using).
6. Unit-test those units and have the bugs found, fixed.
7. Estimate the number of bugs to be found in that release, make and system-test the release, and (when the release is made) compare this number with the number of bugs found by the system test team (see section 18.10.3.2). This will give us an immediate estimate of the payback. (Unfortunately the estimates may have an error rate which may hide the effects of any improvements.) Measure also the time it takes to execute a complete cycle of system tests and compare the number of test steps per person/day executed. (Possibly a better estimate.)
8. Repeat the unit tests for each new build.
9. Report findings.

### 14.7.3   Assessment Phase

This identifies how much unit testing by developers has occurred and how unit testing could be incorporated as a quality gate. Example: *no code to be accepted into configuration management without the corresponding unit tests and results.*

1. Audit all development units to identify which have unit tests already written.
2. Identify the configuration management processes and build a CM process model.
3. Agree the process with the developers and the project and configuration managers.
4. Agree with project management that (from some date) all code will be unit tested.

5. Revise the process model to show a quality gate preventing code from being checked-in without unit tests and results.
6. Take control of the configuration management tool or audit the codebase before the next release to identify which units have no unit tests. Refuse to accept any release without unit tests and results of all the build items.
7. Report on:
   • The results of the audit
   • The number of units found to have no unit tests or whose tests could not or had not been run
   • Process change, showing the process model and the changes to it
   • The bugs found and fixed before release and the bugs found and fixed after release
   • The change in the number of bugs found after the release and the relative speed of testing

### 14.7.4 Handover Phase

The entire process and toolset is handed over to developers to run. The system test manager reviews the execution of unit tests and writes a report.

### 14.7.5 Unit Regression Testing Procedures

Inevitably, system testing will uncover bugs which will necessitate changes to units. Developers' temptation to make a quick fix and continue with system testing should be resisted: units which have been changed should be re-tested. Ensure they repeat the unit tests, if necessary in the context of an integrated SW/HW skeleton (which, if it contains such tools as an In-Circuit Emulator (ICE) may provide superior facilities for testing to a simple test harness) or using a tool such as *xUnit*. Whichever approach is adopted, remember that this is now a unit-testing activity rather than a system test. The unit testing may be restricted to only a subset of the original tests, and the change may require additional tests to be devised.

Changes should be made to a copy of the unit source taken from the configuration-controlled source, and this copy should be put back under configuration control after satisfactory completion of unit tests.

## 14.8 Unit Test Evaluation

How d'you know if a build has been unit-tested well? You look at the unit tests, and the results or you rely on the smoke and confidence tests (as always).

Unit testing is a critical starting point for the agile development movement, and is commonly practiced by all competent system houses as a matter of course. Its value is so self-evident that few stop to convince those who don't unit test, relying on peer pressure much of the time. If your company hasn't quite got around to mandating that all code be unit tested before it's put under configuration management, here are a few arguments to get them started. They assume you already have a test team which system tests, and that the developers are split into units.

### 14.8.1 How We'll Know if We've Unit-Tested Successfully

1. The first full-scale execution of unit tests delays the project considerably.
2. Unit-testing will initially exhibit a large number of bugs. These will then reduce dramatically.
3. The number of system test bugs will be lower than expected.
4. The time taken to execute a test cycle will be shorter (as measured by the number of tests steps executed).
5. Developers have greater confidence in their code.
6. Builds break for other reasons.
7. Regression or smoke tests rarely fail.
8. The number of unexpected system interactions is much reduced.

### 14.8.2  What It'll Cost Us to Unit Test

The cost of the phases:

- Introductory (2 man-months spent assessing the tools available)
- Integration (2 man-days per unit — assuming an automated tool is used, otherwise two man-days overall). The fix time is not counted
- Assessment (2.5 man-months overall)
- Handover (1 man-month)

The cost of the tool eventually chosen (15 man-months or possibly nil).

### 14.8.3  Why We Shouldn't Unit Test (Some Frequent if Daft Arguments)

1. It will delay releasing. (*Not true — it will speed it up.*)
2. It will cost tester time. (*True — it will also distract testers from preparing system tests — we must plan this in.*)
3. Developers know the code far better than the testers. (*Exactly. They can write better tests faster than testers.*)
4. Unit test bugs wouldn't be seen at system test level (*This is mostly drivel because if they are visible at unit test level they will — given a number of coexisting bugs — eventually be visible at system test level*).
5. System test bugs aren't visible at unit test level. (*Sometimes true — but unit testing will leave fewer to be found.*)
6. Developers can spend their time better than in writing unit tests. (*Also drivel since a well-chosen tool will minimize such time — any time so spent would be more than recouped by the time not spent finding and fixing bugs at system test time.*)
7. Developers and testers will have to learn how to use the tool. (*True.*)

### 14.8.4  Unit-Test Deliverables

You will worry about these only on an high-ceremony project. The project manager or design authority will worry only about these if they are deliverables to a client or if there is an history of failed or very buggy builds. These deliverables are however looked for by auditors and safety advisors:

- Unit-testing plan
- Unit-test-tool assessment report
- Integration-phase report
- Unit-testing tool
- Unit tests
- Unit-test audit report
- Configuration-management process models
- Handover-phase audit report

## 14.9  Unit-Test Tool Criteria

- Must work in a .NET (or whatever) environment.
- Must use MS (or whatever) compilers, etc.
- Must provide code-profiling facilities so we can identify which units are the most used.
- Must provide both an automated (*"paste the code in here and look for the results here"*) and manual facilities.
- Must enable either all code line execution or identify unreachable/unexecutable lines.
- Must exhibit clear pass/fail criteria.

- Must support test data detection/analysis. (It should be capable of defining acceptable test data for a unit, allowing us to redefine that data, parsing it and identifying if it is unacceptable and why.)
- Must help us get test execution statistics easily. (Lines of code executed / total lines of code, decision points traversed / total number of decision points, unit complexity.)
- Must exercise all the unit interfaces.
- Must exercise all the unit defaults.
- Must exercise all the unit error messages.
- Must exercise all the boundaries, and limits for each input class.
- Should create its own framework.

# 15

# System and Acceptance Testing

System testing is a way of attempting to prove that the system doesn't meet its requirements specifications and cannot be used. It can consume as much as half the testing resources.

It answers two big questions:

1. Have we got sufficient coverage of the system? (See section 2.8 and section 15.4 for ways of answering this.)
2. Is the build fit to be released? See section 4.6.5 for ways of answering this.

This chapter describes the system test process and issues you need to be aware of when system testing.

## 15.1 System Test Process (Figure 15.1)

The system test process has many activities. Here is an idealized one:

1. Prepare
   a. (Assuming you're just starting) Get your terms of reference written and signed. Make sure it covers what you're supposed to test, dates, resources, and your reporting structure. See Appendix B.
   b. Assess the current status of the project. Identify the stakeholders, particularly third parties. Read the *contract*, the *project plan*, and any other *overview* documents you can find. Check if there's a *quality plan* you must conform to. Find out the project's history. Look at the risks (see Chapter 3) the project faces and identify the project processes in particular the development process and see how testing relates to it. See section B.7 in Appendix B.
   c. Test planning checklist in Appendix B to give you an idea of what to look for.
   d. If you haven't already written a strategy document write it. See section 8.3. Use this as a basis for getting agreement from the major stakeholders about the big problems you face.
2. Plan the system tests. See section 8.5. Read section B.1 and B. 7 both in Appendix B. Ensure you have *Usability testing*, *Performance testing*, and *Metrics* planned. Build a test *process model*. Start a *risk log* if it doesn't yet exist (see Chapter 3). Check if there's some form of operations acceptance document (see section B.18 in Appendix B) for which you must prepare. Estimate the bugs to be found (see section 18.10) and how long testing will take. List the risks faced by your company, your product, and you. Assign some probabilities of these risks occurring, the costs if they do, and the cost of prevention. Draw a *process model* of how you are going to write the tests. Show the baselines and all the deliverables on it. Then:
   a. Identify the *baselines*. There may be many ranging from the official (requirements specification), the contract, contract clarifications, emails, old systems, manuals, (*UML* and other) models, and documentation, marketing documents, and gossip. Some of these elements may

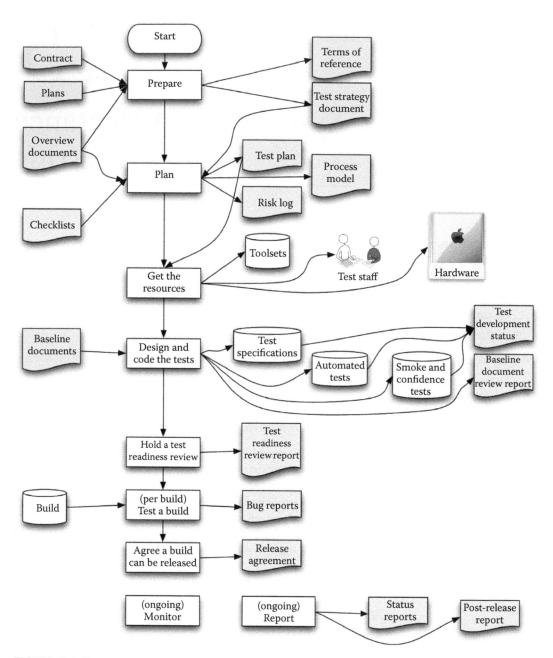

**FIGURE 15.1** System test process

not be available until well after the project has started. If you don't have any baselines, use the manuals but remember that the manuals may only describe 50% of the product (but they may anyway describe functionality you would otherwise be unaware of). If you don't even have the manuals and you don't have any functional specifications then write them. This is again a matter of the risk you run if you don't have a sufficient baseline. Review the baselines. The baselines may not be consistent or sufficient, but you need a coherent story to write tests against. Reviewing (and even modeling) the baseline elements you have will help ensure that you as the testers have as clear idea as possible of what the system is supposed to do.

    b. Identify the test environment in terms of:
       i. Physical relations to the developers (are you in the same room different floor, building or continent?)
       ii. Hardware: networks, PCs, screens cabling, routers, in-circuit emulators, uninterruptible power supplies
       iii. Software: test tools (such as capture-replay tool), test utilities (code analyzers, performance tools) Ensure you have (access to) the test writing, test running, and bug management tools you need. Write this up in the plan. You can then circulate the plan to whoever needs to know about these things. See section 15.3.1 for more on this.
    c. Identify the deliverables.
3. Get the resources: tools, hardware.
    a. Check your access to the configuration management database.
    b. Recruit the staff, bearing in mind that:
       i. You have a deadline to meet.
       ii. You have risks to mitigate.
       iii. No team leader should have to manage more than 5 staff.
       iv. Match staff abilities to the work to be undertaken and the deliverables.
       v. Staff want career progression.
       vi. You'll have to do some teaching and mentoring.
       vii. Testing takes at least half as much effort as Development. So if you have 12 developers you will need at least 6 testers. If you have less, you will not find the bugs fast enough. Here is a way of estimating staff. There are two states you want to avoid:
         • Testers (with no tests left to write or automate or documents to review) are waiting for developers to finish a build (too many testers).
         • Developers (with no systems left to design, code, unit-test, debug or optimize) are waiting for testers to finish testing (not enough testers).
In practice there is always something, not on the critical path, which developers and testers can be doing while they are waiting for a build to be made or tests to be finished. This is why keeping a log of project events (in this case delays) is very useful.
    c. Agree the process model with the staff.
    d. Have a *what we want to do better this time* meeting to tease out any ideas, hopes, and gripes.
    e. Ensure you have maintenance contracts in place for any tools. Should you find bugs in them this will delay testing.
    f. Ensure you have enough hardware: you may need to run system tests on more than one release at a time if developers come up with a fix which they need to have tested urgently "to see if it works."
4. Design and code the tests:
    a. Get the test objectives. These are simple one-line definitions of the test. See section 15.3.1.
    b. Specify the tests: (have the staff you've recruited) write the test objectives based on the baselines. Remember that test objectives are not a substitute for the requirements specification, but if push comes to shove, and you are the first person to remark on the lack of a requirements specification, your test objectives may become a *de facto* set of requirements. In that case write them for the testers' benefit first, and the developers, technical writers, trainers and users second. Review these objectives; this will show you how many of the staff think properly and how much training they need. See section 15.3.3.
    c. Write the tests: concentrate on the best-documented, soonest-to-be-delivered, and smallest feature. Get that written up asap and try it out.
       i. (Ongoing) Identify test automation candidates and automate them.
       ii. (Ongoing) Write as much of the rest of the tests as you can from the documentation you have and as the features become available. Specify any missing requirements, have them agreed with the management, developers, and possibly clients, and write tests to cover them.

  iii. (Ongoing) Review the tests and the process of building them.

  iv. (Ongoing) Identify the smoke and confidence tests, and automate them.

5. Hold a test readiness review. See section 6.6. This may reveal that you are not ready to run the tests because:

  a. They're not all written because your planning was amiss: admit failure to your manager, work out what can be run, and put in place a plan to write the rest. Maybe the features wouldn't have been ready in time anyway.

  b. They can't be run on the environment as it is: identify what needs to be changed, and issue a memo to identify what needs changing or adding, and the control you need over the environment.

  c. The requirements have changed or continue to change. As a. above.

  d. (Some) Tests cannot be run because the code isn't ready: identify which and issue a memorandum to the parties concerned.

6. (Per build) Test a build. Report the bugs found.

  a. Accept a release. Run the smoke and confidence tests.

  b. (Ongoing) Write the bug reports.

7. (Ongoing) Report:

  a. To the project manager and other stakeholders.

  b. Write the post-release report.

  c. Run the smoke and confidence tests on each build.

  d. Run the tests on each build.

  e. Write the weekly reports.

8. (Ongoing) Monitor the test process.

  a. Identify your priority actions and the dates by which they must be achieved; this is where the test strategy document discussed in section 8.3 is useful.

  b. Update the metrics.

  c. Replan your tests: by now your ideas should be firming up (and your suspicions hardening).

9. Agree that the build can be released.

## 15.2 Plan the System Tests

Start during the requirements analysis phase by preparing a skeleton system test plan and draft system testing specification. Update these iteratively thereafter.

 Remember:

1. Formality is essential in system testing and no software should be system tested that is not properly configuration-managed or lacks release details.

2. If any of the code hasn't been unit tested you're almost certainly heading for mega-trouble.

3. Begin system testing with a set of smoke, confidence, bug fix, and regression tests, that test to see if the release is usable, worth testing, and whether the bugs which have allegedly been fixed since the last release, really have been. This is because the system test cycle can be long, sometimes over two months, and it would be pointless to undertake (say) three-quarters of it, only to find that some key feature was missing or some bug had only been half fixed. A regression test set can also be useful to allow briefly-tested (and therefore unofficial) releases to be made to satisfy some other project group or the customer.

4. Since validation and verification are concerned ultimately to reduce risk, balance the amount of effort to be devoted to the system tests with respect to:

  a. The strong correlation between code complexity (see section 18.8.4) as measured by [McCabe] and others and the bug-proneness of software

  b. The more risk-laden parts of the software, so they get more-rigorous testing

  c. The number of times that some software is executed to ensure that the riskier units are the more heavily exercised.

Estimate all these factors when planning system and other tests. To simplify this, build a chart, relating system tests both to the features and the units used as discussed below.

5. Identify the criteria for
   a. Halting system testing
   b. Restarting system testing
   c. Deciding on a release to the field

   And get them accepted by all groups and the customer. See section 2.4 for a discussion on how to estimate when to stop testing and section 8.5.9 for a discussion of how to specify test suspension criteria.

6. Not all the bugs will be:
   a. Discovered by the system tests, because we live in an imperfect world
   b. Fixed in time for the next release, because if some bug is discovered right at the end of some system testing cycle it may be faster and more economic to recommence the next cycle of system tests with the bug unfixed, rather than keep highly-trained staff doing nothing for several weeks

   Therefore to speed system testing identify and have assigned sufficient developers to handle bug-fixing during the system test cycle, and test staff to provide system test support when the system is in the field.

7. Ensure testers can "play" with pre-release fragments so they can learn the system better. You don't want them still to be learning how the system works and designing tests at the moment the first release is made.

8. If you have to demonstrate a system to customers, execute several dry-runs first.

9. Where safety is important, have any system tests which find a bug rewritten. Otherwise the tests will tend to *train* the software to adapt to the tests. The original tests may always be re-applied if necessary.

10. Include any acceptance or certification tests in the system test set. Rigorous customers may have an extensive test set of their own. Compare the coverage of this set with that of your own and identify any shortcomings on either side. See section 15.11 and section 15.13.2 for discussions of these issues.

11. Get system test data from the customer and make sure it's realistic: the customer may be loth to release actual data, either for reasons of confidentiality or simple embarrassment, and may adjust the data actually offered to minimize his short-term problems.

12. Allow 10% for contingency.

## 15.2.1 Test Time Proportions

There is a rule of thumb that testing and reviewing require 50% of all the effort expended in the rest of the project (whether you planned it or not). So if you measure testing and reviewing time as a proportion of all other time spent on the project and discover that it is much less than 50% of that time, be sure that either the project will be abandoned or that time will grow because of the number of bugs discovered in the field which need to be corrected.

Because no one will believe you, except people who test software, here are some figures drawn from [Belford]. They are drawn from large software projects of the 1950s and 1960s. All the figures are expressed as percentages.

TABLE 15.1   Analysis of effort on six major projects

|  | Analysis and design | Coding and reviewing | Checkout and test |
|---|---|---|---|
| SAGE | 30 | 14 | 56 |
| NTDS | 30 | 20 | 50 |
| GEMINI | 33 | 17 | 50 |
| SATURN V | 32 | 24 | 44 |
| OS 360 | 33 | 17 | 50 |
| CFC/BUILD 2 | 55 | 15 | 30 |
| Average | 35.5 | 17.89 | 46.67 |

Note that effort spent on testing and checkout was at least equal to effort spent on the rest of the project in four out of the six cases. The CFC project whose build 2's effort proportions are cited above had the following effort expenditure expressed in man-days.

**TABLE 15.2**    Effort expended on the CFC project

| Build | Subsystem 1 | Subsystem 2 | Subsystem 3 | Total |
|-------|-------------|-------------|-------------|-------|
| 1     | 1480        | 898         | 2843        | 5221  |
| 2     | 4093        | 2030        | 1809        | 7932  |
| 3     | 5171        | 2881        | 2730        | 10782 |
| Total | 10744       | 5809        | 7382        | 23935 |

## 15.2.2   Bug Experience

In addition to the bug models given in the section 18.10 some industry experience can be a useful guide.

[Endres] discusses bugs found in DOS/VS. This was written in IBM DOS macro-assembler language. The system was modular with 81% of units having an average of 425 instructions. Some of the statistics are pertinent The figures for the number of bugs per unit is given.

**TABLE 15.3**    Bugs per unit reported by Endres

|       | Number of units | Number of bugs per unit | Total |
|-------|-----------------|-------------------------|-------|
|       | 112             | 1                       | 112   |
|       | 36              | 2                       | 72    |
|       | 15              | 3                       | 45    |
|       | 11              | 4                       | 44    |
|       | 8               | 5                       | 40    |
|       | 2               | 6                       | 12    |
|       | 4               | 7                       | 28    |
|       | 5               | 8                       | 40    |
|       | 3               | 9                       | 27    |
|       | 2               | 10                      | 20    |
|       | 1               | 14                      | 14    |
|       | 1               | 15                      | 15    |
|       | 1               | 19                      | 19    |
|       | 1               | 28                      | 28    |
|       | 220             | 0                       | 0     |
| Total | 422             |                         | 516   |

The figures are interesting in that 78% of the bugs are caused by 21% of the units, and 7% of the units account for 32% of the bugs. So simply fixing those 7% would make a 32% difference to the bug rate. The three most erroneous units were also the largest in the system, with more than 3000 instructions. The relationship between size and bug-susceptibility wasn't substantiated by other studies, possibly the use of macro-assembler was an important factor.

- [Radatz] noted that bugs in 5 major defense-related systems could be classified thus:
  - 30% faulty algorithms and mathematics
  - 24% faulty data handling
  - 11% interface and I/O handling bugs
  - 11% deviations from specifications
  - 6% wrong execution order (mostly in assembler)
  - 5% timing bugs

These figures are untypical in the high level of algorithm faults shown. This was probably due to the highly technical nature of the software. The bugs were discovered as follows:
- 45% in debugging
- 35% in testing
- 10% in the design phase
- 5% in the requirements specification

The bug profile suggests major coding bugs. Reviews or walk-throughs seem not to have been used.
- [Belford] gives a rate of bugs discovered during system testing at one bug in every 268 lines of code compared with one bug in every twenty-eight lines of code during unit testing. The system had 5372 lines of code and used 511 *test cases*.

The bug detection can be shown as in the following.

**TABLE 15.4** Bug detection rates on the CFC project

| Build | Design walk-through | Unit level testing | System level testing |
|---|---|---|---|
| 1 | n/a | n/a | 0 |
| 2 | 44 | 290 | 18 |
| 3 | 63 | 223 | 20 |
| Totals | 107 | 513 | 38 |

[RADC] gives a rate of bugs discovered during system testing of two JOVIAL projects at one bug in every thirty-five lines of code.

[Basili 87] and [Selby] conducted an experiment with thirty-two professional programmers (from NASA Goddard and CSC) and forty-two advanced students (from the University of Maryland) using code reading, functional testing using equivalence partitioning, boundary-value analysis, and structural testing using 100% statement coverage on four unit-sized programs. They discovered that:

- With professional programmers code reading detected more faults and faster than functional or structural testing
- Fault numbers detected, speed of fault detection, and effort required, varied as the type of software
- Code reading detected more interface faults than did the other methods
- Functional testing detected more control bugs than did the other methods
- Code readers gave better estimates of percentage of faults detected than testers.

[Lipow] gives the following AT&T data in Table 15.5.

**TABLE 15.5** Faults discovered in each phase reported by Lipow

| Phase | Percentage of all faults generated in phase |
|---|---|
| System requirements | 4 |
| Software requirements | 6 |
| High-level design | 24 |
| Detailed design | 28 |
| Code and unit test | 33 |
| Integration test | 5 |
| System test | 0 |
| Total | 100 |

This table is interesting in that it contradicts later experience in which the requirements analysis phase is the richest source of faults. Lipow's experience suggests that coding was the major source of bugs. This may have been due to inexperience with the language. It is surprising that no bugs were generated when fixing bugs at the system testing stage — as might reasonably have been expected.

Lipow also shows the costs of fault fixing in Table 15.6.

**TABLE 15.6**   Relative cost of fixing faults having found them in later phases of software development[a]

| Occurred in phases | Found in phases | | | | | | |
|---|---|---|---|---|---|---|---|
|  | 1 | 2 | 3 | 4 | 5 | 6 | 7 |
| 1. System requirements | 1.0 | 1.3 | 2.4 | 3.3 | 6.8 | 26 | 96 |
| 2. Software requirements |  | 1.0 | 1.8 | 2.4 | 5.1 | 19 | 72 |
| 3. Preliminary design |  |  | 1.0 | 1.3 | 2.8 | 11 | 39 |
| 4. Detailed design |  |  |  | 1.0 | 2.1 | 8.0 | 30 |
| 5. Code and unit test |  |  |  |  | 1.0 | 3.8 | 14 |
| 6. Integration and (system) test |  |  |  |  |  | 1.0 | 3.7 |
| 7. Operation |  |  |  |  |  |  | 1.0 |

[a] Calculated with reference to [Boehm 89].

# 15.3   Design and Code the Tests

This section identifies a minimal number of things which must be there in the system test specifications for you as system test manager to be sure that a good job is being done. Many requirements specifications are still prose-based and it is essential that you are confident that:

- They are consistent.
- The system tests cover them completely.

What follows is a procedure for transforming a prose-based requirements specification into a system test. Those projects fortunate enough to have the requirements specification written in a semi-formal method such as Yourdon, Jackson, SSADM, CORE, or a formal method such as Z, will find the transformation much simpler.

The procedure for writing system tests consists of the following steps:

- Identify the test baseline
- Identify the test objectives
- Write the test specifications
- Define the test environment
- Define the test data
- Define the operator actions
- Define the pass/fail criteria
- Add any notes

These are discussed in the following sections. Note that the order in which these processes are defined is not fixed, and they may be iterated several times. Following this procedure will result in tests that are explicit, consistent and repeatable. They may not however, find all the bugs. System tests must:

- Relate to the requirements specification such that it should be possible to trace each requirement to one or more *test cases* and results which demonstrate successful compliance with requirements.
- Have *test cases* for each requirement assertion. In some cases (such as fault handling or failure mode operation) you may need to use special means to force execution of exception handling code, but this can usually be achieved with a debugging tool.

## 15.3.1   Identify the Test Baseline

Put simply, any document defining *what* the system does (rather than *how*) can be a system test baseline. This set of documents can include:

- **Business requirements:** written such that only senior managers would ever read them.
- **Functional requirements:** written in immense detail and liable to change without notice.

- **Use cases:** written to be invaluable to a programmer or analyst but not a user.
- **Business rules:** written for accountants by accountants.

The test baseline includes everything you need to show that some bug has occurred. This will usually be the specification: unit, interface, high-level design or requirements. But, particularly in the case of system and acceptance testing, you may need other means because of the kinds of bugs discussed in section 4.1. To find them requires a great exercise of the imagination and to prove that some system is acting in an anomalous way with respect to the real world may require access to such documents as operational concepts documents, weather maps, legal papers, and other means of describing the system's environment.

## 15.3.2  Identify the Test Objectives

System test objectives should be:

- Requirements oriented: they should require no knowledge of system internals and should be prepared from the requirements specification.
- Comprehensive enough to provide a systematic check of all of the functions of the system: all classes of valid input should be accepted, all classes of invalid input should be rejected, and all functions should be exercised.

Many of the methods discussed earlier apply; the only difference is that we are now planning the testing of a system comprising a large number of units rather than for a single unit.

**Problem:** big, badly-managed projects may actually have several requirements specifications. This is because the requirements' change cycle has become so unwieldy, and the documentation management so weak, that enterprising engineers, faced with planning a major new subsystem, baulk at having to update and greatly extend the existing requirements specification, and instead issue their own. This may reflect both reality and the contents of several related requirements specifications at several points. Do not be deceived. Somewhere in there, there are some horrible discrepancies.

**Problem:** small, badly-managed projects consisting of a few enthusiastic coders, a care-free manager, and uncritical users, may end up with a mass of frequently-working code and documents which are essentially *aspirational*.[1] Somewhere in there are the occasional consistencies.

The solution is:

- Identify all the documents and their review reports, which could conceivably be held to be requirements specifications.
- Review two until you have identified a worthwhile discrepancy.
- Get hold of your friendly QA auditor and have him audit your project quickly. Ensure he flags up the problem clearly.
- Flag the problem yourself to senior management in writing, requesting extra resources to cope with the extra amount of reviewing you will have to do.
- Review all the requirements specifications (modeling them if necessary) down to enough detail to identify those areas which are either contradictory, better covered in some other document or not a requirement.
- Advise senior management that you will not be testing those parts without a request in writing and extra resources.
- Ensure that the contradictory requirements are removed or resolved.

Naturally you will notice that telling senior management of these problems will not endear you to them, both because you want more resources, and because it was their dimness in allowing control of the requirements specification (and much else) to get out of hand that has precipitated the crisis. If they

---

[1] An *aspirational* document expresses a desire on someone's part. See back copies of the *Journal of Porcine Aviation* for more on this.

aren't told however, you will be forced into the impossible position of having to test the untestable, in that while your test finds a bug (because it is consistent with specification A) some manager claims that no bug in fact exists because the system is consistent with specification D. Meanwhile the customer is firmly focussed on specification C and will hit the roof when the bug is found to have persisted.

- **Moral 1: never reinforce failure.** If some manager wants to play silly-buggers with the requirements specification, don't reinforce him in his stupidity.
- **Moral 2: scream last and nobody cares.** If you wait until the system testing has started before observing the bug no one will want to know. (*Why did you wait? Were you hoping the bug would go away?*) Scream first and (of course) you're just complaining. Scream last and you're too late.
- **Moral 3: don't wait to be shot at.** The QA department[2] has given you enough grief in the past; now's their chance to be loved. Quality is being compromised. QA should support you: it's difficult for management to shoot *two* messengers.

Having (somehow) established the baselines, each assertion in each baseline becomes the basis for a potential test objective. Thus let us imagine a requirements specification for a drinks machine which contains the assertion shown.

```
When a coin is inserted, and one of the choice buttons is pressed, then a cup will descend into
the output station, and the chosen drink will be poured into the cup.
```

**FIGURE 15.2**  A raw assertion in a requirements specification

This assertion can now be analysed as shown.

```
When (a coin is inserted) and (one of the choice buttons is pressed) then (a cup will descend
into the output station) and (the chosen drink will be poured into the cup).
```

**FIGURE 15.3**  An analysed assertion

Notice that the assertion is rendered into a logical proposition. It can be simplified even further:

IF [replacing when] (A and B) then (C and D)

To test this proposition we should derive all the possible inverse permutations of it. That is we should generate a set of counter propositions or hypotheses which contradict the original one:

If (A and B) then (C and not D)
If (A and B) then (not C and not D)
If (A and B) then (not C and D)
If (A and not B) then (not C and not D)
. . .
If (not A and B) then (not C and not D)
If (not A and B) then (not C and D)
. . .

This is a large number of hypotheses to test. We can prune them by deciding which are not useful by substituting the original parts for A, B, C, and D. This shows that (If (not A and B) then (not C and not D)) is not useful since it reads as shown in Figure 15.4.

---

[2] The people who audit you. Sometimes confused with the people who test the code. Two quite different jobs. See Chapter 1.

```
If (not (a coin is inserted into the machine) and (one of the choice buttons is pressed)  then
(not (a cup will descend into the output station) and not (the chosen drink will be poured into
the cup))
```

**FIGURE 15.4**  A not-very-useful test objective

This may be terrible English but it asserts that if you don't put a coin in the machine you don't get anything out. Similarly (If (A and not B) then (not C and not D)) shows that if you put a coin in the machine but you don't press a choice button, nothing will happen. Both these tests are important since they demonstrate that the machine works as intended, but they are not very useful as test objectives since they are unlikely to find bugs. Compare these objectives with:

**If** (not A and B) **then** (not C and D)

which proposes that if no money is inserted and the choice button is pressed then some drink will squirt from the machine without being held in a cup. Could this happen? This is what you should test for, and the first step is to write the test specification.

## 15.3.3  Specify the Tests

Here is how the test specification for the objective shown in the last section could be written.

```
Test No:          System test specification

ST/2300.124       Test author: G. Rosso     Date: February 9, 2008
Test objective:
Attempt to prove that if no money is inserted into the machine and a choice button is
pressed then some drink will be ejected without a cup descending
```

**FIGURE 15.5**  A system test objective

Now we have a problem. We have an excellent test objective to try and hit, but no idea of how to force the machine to commit the bug we are searching for. This is the moment when we realize that testing is indeed creative. There is the obvious approach to take; tell the operator to press all the choice buttons one after the other but unless the machine is very buggy this will produce nothing. We need to look at the test environment.

## 15.3.4  Define the Test Environment

The test environment consists of all the test tools, hardware, and software needed for the test, it also includes the state of the system under test. To run the test whose objective we have defined we will need a drinks machine suitably loaded with drinks and cups, and switched on. We will also need some coins to insert into the machine. The coins, cups, and drinks are of course test input data.

To define the states of the machine it would be useful to draw a Finite State Machine diagram. For the moment we can make a list:

- Machine completely loaded/unloaded
- Machine partly loaded
- Machine switched on/off
- Machine with/without a coin in but no button pressed
- Machine with two coins in but no button pressed
- Machine being cleaned

Here are 6 possible states (there may be more) that the machine may be in. We need to try and reduce the number of states by eliminating those which clearly can't produce the bug (such as the machine in the completely unloaded state, and the machine with one or more coins inserted), and then try them all. We could take the cases of:

- The machine containing no cups
- The machine being cleaned while it is switched on
- The machine with a pen-knife inserted in the coin slot

and see if they will produce the bug. Using the case of the machine containing no cups, the test case specification can now be added to.

```
Test environment:
Drinks machine, drinks
System status before the test:
Drinks machine switched on, no cups in the machine.
System status after the test:
Drinks machine switched on, no cups in the machine.
```

FIGURE 15.6   System test definition details

Another advantage of defining the system status both before and after the test is that when a lot of tests need to be run, we can relate one test to another such that the system status *after* the first test is the same as the system status *before* the next test. In this way a whole test series can be run without having to check or change the status during the run.

### 15.3.5   Define the Test Data

In the example we are using coins, cups, and drinks. For many other tests some definition of test files, the kinds of data in those files, and the sources of those data would be included here. Try and get some test data from the customer.

### 15.3.6   Define the Operator Actions

In the example we are using the operator actions can be written thus:

```
Operator actions:
Press each choice button in turn
```

FIGURE 15.7   System test operator actions

### 15.3.7   Define the Pass/Fail Criteria

```
Pass/fail criteria:
If any liquid leaves the machine without entering the cup then a bug has occurred.
```

FIGURE 15.8   System test pass-fail criteria

### 15.3.8   Notes

When writing the test it may be possible to add notes to the test specification which may help the operator or the programmer who should find the bug.

## 15.4   System Test Coverage

To assess system test coverage consider:

- You need to have a requirements specification (so you can estimate which features have been covered).

- The requirements specification will change (*check how you'll hear of these*).
- The system may have been defined using a number of use cases which you may use as the basis of scenarios.
- Each system feature in the requirements specification will probably be exercised using a number of screens and pull-downs.
- The same screen may be accessed by more than one pull-down.
- The same screen or pull-down may be used by more than one feature.
- Each screen will have some combination of check boxes and fields (see section 8.2.1).
- Any attempt to exercise a GUI by simply exercising every element will fail to provoke any important errors since they are highly-unlikely to fail. The only test is to use the GUI objects to achieve some objective. It is the combination of GUI objects used which determines the useful, bug-exhibiting test.

The combinatorial explosion of all these possible elements makes any attempt at a comprehensive approach to test coverage estimation near-impossible.

Here is an approach:

1. List all the scenarios (extracted from the use cases if possible).
2. List all the screens, pull-downs, fields, and other GUI objects used by the application.
3. Create a diagram showing the relationships between the GUI components and the GUI objects, and the possible transitions between them.
4. Create a spreadsheet mapping the GUI objects used by each scenario to the scenario.
5. Map the tests to the scenarios (probably on another worksheet).
6. Map the tests to the GUI objects.
7. Identify which scenarios can be linked.

You are now in a position to define for each test:

- The (sub-)feature(s) tested (a test might cover more or less than a single feature)
- The proportion of GUI objects exercised by a test
- The proportion of scenarios tested

You will also be able to determine:

- Which scenarios exercise the largest number of features
- The scenarios which exercise the most GUI objects
- The least-exercised GUI objects
- The size and contents of all fields

Assure and demonstrate the system test coverage both of the features and the attributes (reliability, speed, number of users supported, security etc.) of the system. Do this with the aid of two charts, one of which plots the system attributes against the various system tests which most exercise that attribute, and the other which plots the system features against the various system tests.

**TABLE 15.7**  Example chart plotting the system attributes against the various system tests which most exercise that attribute

| System test name/attribute | 023-56 | 023-57 | 023-58 | 023-59 | 023-60 | 023-61 | 023-62 | 023-63 |
|---|---|---|---|---|---|---|---|---|
| Reliability | x | | | | | | x | x |
| Usability | | | x | | | x | x | x |
| Response time adequacy | | | | | x | | x | |
| Execution speed | | x | x | | x | | | |
| Overload tolerance | x | | | | x | | x | x |

**TABLE 15.8**   Example chart plotting the system features against the various system tests

| System test name/ feature name | 023-56 | 023-57 | 023-58 | 023-59 | 023-60 | 023-61 | 023-62 | 023-66 |
|---|---|---|---|---|---|---|---|---|
| file: print.d | | | | | | | | |
| collect | | | x | | | | | |
| yrstrncmp | x | | | x | | | x | |
| print BA table | | | | | x | | x | |
| print literals | x | | | | x | | x | x |
| print msg | | x | | | x | | | |
| print prompt | | | | | | | x | |
| print range status | | | x | | | | | x |
| print test pages | | | | | | | | |
| user range | | x | x | x | | | | |
| valid response | | x | | x | | x | x | |

Consider system tests against the following categories:

- **Configuration testing:** can the system be used on different hardware and operating system configurations? See section 15.10.1.
- **Conversion and cutover testing:** how well will the new system match the behavior of the old? How well is the data migrated? See in section 15.10.3.
- **Documentation and training testing:** do the user guides and other such documents do their job? Are users sufficiently-trained? See section 15.10.7.
- **Installation testing**: which tests the installation procedures. See section 15.10.2.
- **Performance testing:** does the system fulfil requirements for response times and throughput? See Chapter 16 and sections A.7 and A.8 in Appendix A.
- **Stress testing:** at what point will the system break, what warning will it give, and how will it manage the break? See Chapter 16.
- **Procedure testing:** do the procedures work, do they relate to the system? See section 15.10.7.
- **Reliability (resilience) testing:** does the system have a sufficiently long MTBF? See section 16.8, the discussion in section 18.4, and the Resilience Checklist in Appendix B.
- **Resource use testing:** how well does the system use its memory, CPU, network, and disks? See section 15.10.5.
- **Security testing:** can the system security be compromised? See section 15.10.4.
- **Usability testing:** is the user interface usable? See Chapter 17.

If system tests are classified in this way we can run a set of tests to ensure that some attribute has been maintained in a new release. This may become important once the complete set of features is present and tested, and confidence in the attribute needs to be quickly established.

The system *test cases* should systematically cover the features of the system. Where workflow diagrams exist, devise *test cases* to cause execution of all paths in this diagram. Alternatively instrument the code to ensure that all units are exercised by one or more *test cases*.

Define the selection and extent of tests by engineering judgment based on the requirements.

## 15.5   Is It Worth All This Work?

This depends on the risk level. But given the following states:

1. If the possibility that some combination of features could hide a major bug
2. If the system has many features, screens, and screen objects
3. If the risk of a system failure is in some way catastrophic

then YES. Additionally a spreadsheet like the one shown above will show you clearly which:

- Objects are under- or over-tested
- Tests cover which objects
- Scenarios have no, too few or too many tests against them
- Scenarios have a higher priority (and which tests mapped against them should be in the regression test set)
- Scenarios cover the same objects too often and could be split
- States cannot (or should not be able to) be reached
- Scenarios provoke the most bugs (if you map the bugs found, against first the tests and then the scenarios)

Other questions remain:

1. *How can I show that I have exercised all the code using this level of coverage?* Get the source code instrumented to show which statements have been executed, hope that the system's timing is sufficiently robust to cope with the delays this instrumentation will impose, run all your tests, and then look at the results. You will be lucky to hit more than 90% since some code can only be exercised by errors.

2. *What sort of metrics will this let me use?* You will be able to show each day:

$$\% \ GUI \ objects \ exercised = \frac{\sum GUI \ objects \ exercised \ by \ tests \times 100}{\sum GUI \ objects \ in \ each \ test}$$

(note that this will be greater than the total number of objects in the system since some will be exercised more than once)

$$\% \ scenarios \ exercised = \frac{\sum scenarios \ exercised \ by \ tests \times 100}{\sum scenarios}$$

$$\% \ features \ exercised = \frac{\sum features \ exercised \ by \ tests \times 100}{\sum features}$$

3. *How do I define a feature?* You don't. Management defines features by writing a specification for it, identifying which GUI objects it employs. If management has failed to have a definition of each feature specified then either rewrite the user manual to suit your purposes or do as suggested in section 8.2.1 in Chapter 8.

4. *How can I define a way of testing every feature/feature combination?* If by feature you mean some capability such as "edit a document," then you can:
   a. List all the screens and GUI objects involved in defining that feature (see Figure 15.9).
   b. Group them by objects on a (very large) spreadsheet as shown in Figure 15.10.
   c. Identify test-by-test what GUI objects are used and what values are assigned. This can result in a seriously large number of tests: the example above employs some 279,552 different combinations plus whatever arguments are used to search with.
   d. Create a spreadsheet. In this example the user has used the sequence **Word** > **File** > **Open** > **button (New Folder)**, which has opened a screen (new folder) as shown in Figure 15.11.
   e. The only features available to the user at present are to input a folder name in place of "untitled folder."
      i.   Hit button (Create) (default)
      ii.  Hit button (Cancel)

FIGURE 15.9    "Open" screen

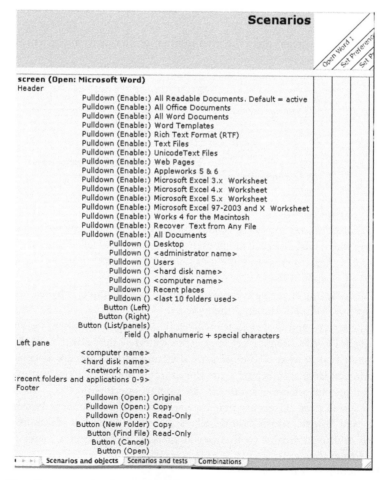

FIGURE 15.10    "Open" screen rendered on a spreadsheet

**FIGURE 15.11** Feature/feature interaction example

      iii.  Choose menu item (Hide Word)
      iv.  Choose menu item (Hide Word (shortcut))
      v.  Choose menu item (Hide Others)
      vi.  Choose menu item (Hide Others (shortcut))

5. Represent this interaction like this:

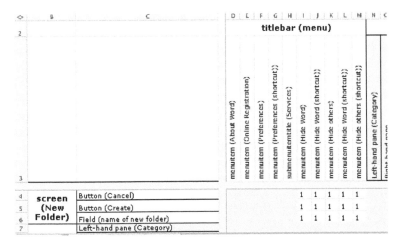

**FIGURE 15.12** Feature/feature interaction matrix example

6. *This could be an enormous number and quite unfeasible for testing with.*
   – Some feature/feature interactions aren't supposed to happen.
   – Unforeseen feature/feature interaction is a product killer and won't go away.
   – You will need to take some engineering decisions, and prune the choices accordingly.

7. *How else can I test feature/feature interaction?* Test automation and rigorous unit testing will help. If you don't test each feature (however defined) with every other one you'll never be sure.

See [Beizer 1] for more on black-box testing.

## 15.6   Test Support Software and Tools

System testing often needs software or hardware to support the testing activity.

Identify any software or hardware to support integration and/or system testing including the version/ serial numbers and place them under configuration control to ensure that tests can be repeated as and when necessary.

## 15.7   Regression Testing

There are two parts of a system regression test:

- Establish that the features tested in the *last* release are still present. So run the tests of the least release first.
- Establish that no memory leaks occur. Memory leaks are a major cause of delay since they are hard to find. It is useful therefore to run system regression tests in parallel with normal system tests (possibly over seventy-two hours using a regression test suite on a dedicated machine) to establish this.

The system regression test suite will normally change as the extra features are added for each build. It is the one part of system testing whose automation can usually be justified for any non-trivial system.

System testing should produce a key deliverable called the *system regression test set*, which is the set of test case data designed to exercise a system over most or all of its features. Its purpose is to support retesting when system changes are made (this is *also* known as regression testing). All that is required is to save the cases that we have constructed; very little effort is involved if this is done as a by-product of systems testing; however preparing these *test cases* at any other time may be expensive.

Start identifying the criteria for regression testing during requirements specification time. These will include:

- What features will be available from release 1?
- What will be the principal requirements incorporated into each release?
- What will be the most common way in which the system will be used?
- What are the most important requirements? (why? Is their importance self-evident or has it more to do with customer politics?)
- What requirements are time-critical?
- Which requirements are usability-critical?
- Which tests are the easiest to run, and the most indicative?
- Which features are the most customer-revenue-critical?

Such criteria give you a filter which you can distribute to all testers so they can flag down possible requirements and therefore tests of interest. You can then prioritize them. As testing progresses you can add the following criteria:

- Which features have contained the greatest number of bugs?
- Which tests have found the largest number of bugs?
- Which operator actions have found the largest number of bugs?

At some point you should be in a position to automate these tests.

## 15.7.1 Regression Test Identification and Prioritization

Regression tests need to answer the question *"has anything broken since the last release"* fast. This requires that the regression tests are prioritized such that those which have historically found the most bugs get run first. There are two solutions to this:

- Ensure that every bug that a test exposes is listed against that test such that only those tests which have already found bugs are run.
- Ensure that the titles of all bugs are constructed such that you can use them to determine which operator (or other) actions are most likely to exhibit bugs.

Thus most bugs will be reported against a feature such as (say) an Alerts Editor. The operator action might be written thus *"When I close the Alerts Editor it causes an unhandled exception error."*

This can be used as the title *"Closing the Alerts Editor causes an unhandled exception, when memory is low."* Such titles can then be extracted from the bug-management tool and parsed into <subject>, <verb>, <object>, and <condition> strings:

- Subject: "closing the Alerts Editor"
- Verb: "causes"
- Object: "unhandled exception"
- Condition: "when memory is low"

These can be kept in a spreadsheet and sorted on <feature>, <subject>, <object>, <condition>, and <priority> (Table 15.9). This will allow you to determine just how often some action is likely to be error-provoking and thus become a candidate for inclusion in a regression test.

**TABLE 15.9**  Regression test candidate examples

| Feature | Subject phrase | Verb phrase | Object phrase | Condition phrase | Priority |
|---|---|---|---|---|---|
| AE | Closing AE | causes | message (error unhandled) exception | when memory is low | 1 |
| AE | Closing AE | generates | message (error) | | 1 |
| AE | Closing alert | displays | no prompt | | 3 |

Other approaches to prioritization include:

- Key features: testing key features first (which is the most common approach to regression-testing since if a key feature is missing the release will be rejected)
- Change: testing changed functions first
- Time since last run: assuming that system test runs do not run every test prepared
- Risk: allocated to the feature in a risk assessment session

# 15.8 Localization Testing

Localization testing can be approached by language set. Assuming you have developed in English then:

- Prioritize your language sets.
- Within each set prioritize the languages.
- Test the top priority language within each set to iron out the primary difficulties. Then test the others.
- Use the localization checklist in Appendix B to identify the issues to be checked for.
- Consider using a specialist agency for testing more than 3 languages unless you have a very polyglot test team.
- Have one person act as review team leader of all manuals and help files, and have all bugs (and any change needed is a bug) routed through that person. This will limit duplication. He should liaise with the technical editor or author(s).

See [Tuthill] and [Lunde].

# 15.9  System Integration and Operations Testing

The purposes of these tests are to check that:

- The system coexists with others on the network (there are no .dll conflicts for example)
- System shut-down and start-up occur without incident
- System upgrades (particularly service packs) have no untoward effect
- Backups can be taken
- Unused parts of databases can be archived-off, and their space reclaimed
- Desktops can be updated remotely
- No security breaches occur
- Systems can be restored after failure

The process requires:

- A dedicated environment
- The time for some reliability testing
- Written procedures (which must be followed slavishly for any procedural errors to be found)
- A means for monitoring the effects on virtual users

# 15.10  Non-Functional Testing

## 15.10.1  Configuration Testing

This is where you test that the system works on every possible configuration. The (few) configurations you will have in your test laboratory are most unlikely to approximate to the configurations found in the field.

Configuration testing implies that you must take a number of tough decisions on the permutations of boxes and software you will choose, and the number of tests you will run on them. This is also true of web testing. Figure 15.13 shows a typical web architecture.

To test this you have a number of tasks:

- **Task 1:** identify the architecture. Draw yourself a picture like the one above. Identify the possible combinations of boxes (for example each application might reside on a separate box). Identify all the places where the OS, Middleware-software-to-be-tested, and co-resident applications may reside.
- **Task 2:** identify the possible combinations of Browser/Client OS, Back Office/ERP, Applications, Middleware, eCommerce server, Web Server, and database. Note that the application you are testing may also have several elements such as an engine, web components, and stored procedures which may be distributed all over the architecture or confined to a box. Therefore you must also check which combinations of your software to be tested are legal and with which other applications might they be contractually-expected to coexist. Do this using a spreadsheet looking like Table 15.10.

  The spreadsheet can get big: hopefully you will find there are some excluded combinations. Thus the browser/client OS combinations are independent of the others. Remember to include:
  - All supported versions of support packs
  - All supported versions of security patches
  - Differing versions of each piece of software
  - All supported foreign language versions of both OS and application.

  This spreadsheet is part of your test plan and is a major tool in negotiating resources. You should consider testing one combination extensively, 3 fairly intensely, and install and run a regression test, on every one of the others. Justify your decisions to minimally-test some particular combinations. Ensure your plan is agreed so that when some particularly-obscure combination causes everyone major grief you will have at least "shared the responsibility." See Appendix B for checklists including web-related issues.

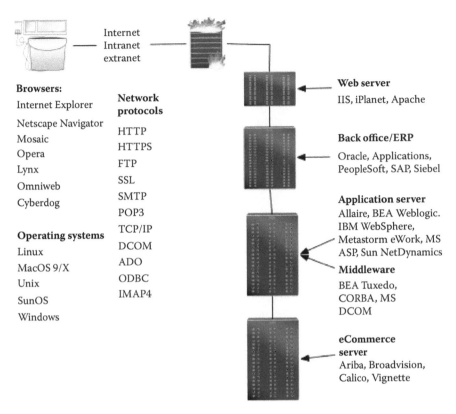

**FIGURE 15.13** eCommerce architecture example

- **Task 3:** identify the priorities of these combinations. Typically this will require a visit or two to the marketing department and Support desk to discover what your customers use most (and what gives them the most grief). From this you can identify a list of the top 3 combinations which you should use as a base list and test first. Only when these are shown to work well should you begin testing variants of these.
- **Task 4:** identify the interfaces available to all these components and the operating systems on which they run. You need to be able to access the logs and run-time details of all operating systems, and applications running on servers. In particular special-purpose engines may be completely transparent to the user (and thus the system interface tester) but may throw-up run-time bugs which need to be captured for investigation.
- **Task 5:** identify the testing tasks to be executed to provide sufficient control of the application to be tested and write them into the plan. Most of the application can be tested through the browser but where some user interface exists at the server end it may be valuable to hand- or script-test that too.

Do not attempt to do configuration testing without having automated the testing of all your primary features. You will have neither the time nor the coverage to draw any useful conclusions.

Configuration testing is not well supported by the industry because of the combinatorial explosion problem wherein not simply the mass of middleware variations, but (even worse) individual settings in each piece of middleware has inhibited tool use. At some point a tool will doubtless be developed which will automatically identify all possible interfaces and settings of each piece of middleware you specify, and will then build a database of these to generate a set of tests on the fly which you can run overnight, and which will reveal illicit combinations of settings, and middleware components. Until then, see the Cosmic project in section D.16 in Appendix D.

**TABLE 15.10**   Web testing combinations spreadsheet

| Software | Combination | | | | | | | | | | |
|---|---|---|---|---|---|---|---|---|---|---|---|
| | 1 | 2 | 3 | 4 | 5 | 6 | 7 | 8 | 9 | 10 | 11 |
| **Browsers** | | | | | | | | | | | |
| Internet Explorer | * | * | * | * | * | * | * | * | | | |
| Netscape Navigator | | | | | | | | | * | * | * |
| Mosaic | | | | | | | | | | | |
| Opera | | | | | | | | | | | |
| Firefox | | | | | | | | | | | |
| **Client operating systems** | | | | | | | | | | | |
| Linux | * | | | | | | | | * | | |
| MacOS 9/X | | * | | | | | | | | * | |
| UNIX | | | * | | | | | | | | * |
| SunOS | | | | * | | | | | | | |
| Windows NT | | | | | * | | | | | | |
| Windows 2000 | | | | | | * | | | | | |
| Windows XP | | | | | | | * | | | | |
| Windows ME | | | | | | | | * | | | |
| **Back Office/ERP** | | | | | | | | | | | |
| Oracle applications | * | | | | | | | | | | |
| … | | | | | | | | | | | |
| Siebel | | | | | | | | | | | |
| Application server | | | | | | | | | | | |
| Allaire | | | | | | | | | | | |
| … | | | | | | | | | | | |
| Metastorm eWork | | | | | | | | | | | |
| Middleware | | | | | | | | | | | |
| BEA Tuxedo | | | | | | | | | | | |
| … | | | | | | | | | | | |
| **Server operating systems** | | | | | | | | | | | |
| Linux | * | * | | | | | | | | | |
| … | | | | | | | | | | | |
| Windows ME | | | | | | | | | | | |
| Palm OS | | | | | | | | | | | |

## 15.10.2   Installation Testing

This is so obvious we all forget it. Find the least-experienced person in the building, and put them in a room with access to help, a manual, (a) computer(s), access to the bug management database, and the release medium. Have them install it. Marvel at the number of things which went wrong. Congratulate them on every goof they make: they're saving someone else a lot of trouble. Write a checklist of things to look for next time and then review the bugs the person raised.

Do not use an experienced tester for this purpose: they know too much.

## 15.10.3   Conversion or Cutover Testing

Three elements must be managed when performing cutover and cutover testing:

1. **Operator training and documentation.** Worst case: the operators must be trained in a completely new system, and then revert to using the old system until cutover, during which time they will forget how to use the new system.
2. **Data restructuring.** Worst case: the data for the new system must be restructured for the new system such that it be completely incompatible with the old.

3. **System substitution.** Worst case: the whole system must be changed during a high-traffic period (because there's never a low-traffic one), and no fall-back is possible.

Possible solutions:

1. Create a copy of the old system in a model office and rehearse the cutover on it:
   a. **Copy the data** available on the old system (*oldSystemData1*) at that point and then capture a copy of all changes made for some manageable and useful period thereafter (*laterInputs*). Copy the system state at the end of that period (*oldSystemData2*).
   b. **Build a simulator** to input transactions captured in *laterInputs* as if they were live transactions using the new system.
   c. **Test the simulator** by identifying a set of transactions from the *laterInputs* and run them using real operators. Then reload the test system with the *oldSystemData1* and run the same transaction set using the simulator. Compare the results to be sure that both the transactions had the same outcomes and were committed at the same times.
   d. **Run the simulator** using the *laterInputs* and look for cases of row locking and consequent freezes. Compare the current state of the system(s) with *oldSystemData2*. In particular look for anomalies in related systems.
2. Alternatively, investigate the possibility of a simulator to translate
   a. Staff input directly from the old system into a rehearsal copy of the new such that the staff are oblivious of the presence of the rehearsal system but the input they create maintains the rehearsal system as if they were using it live, and exhibits errors.
   b. Newly-input data from the old to the new structures on the fly such that the old and new systems can be run in parallel.
3. Give operators a refresher course just before cutover. Have staff retrieve all out-of-date documentation at the moment of cutover and remove all cribs from staff desks related to the old system.

See the definition of *cutover* for other, less fraught strategies.

Note that it will probably be unfeasible to use automated tools to check the behavior of a live system but it might be feasible to check sample transactions against an oracle.

## 15.10.4 Security Testing

A test manager is involved like any other manager in the security process. This (very roughly) consists of seven phases each motivated by critical questions:

1. *What have we got, what are the threats, what are the warning systems, and how do we protect ourselves now?* Identify assets and their values, the threats to those assets, indicators of risk, and the current protection strategy employed by the enterprise. Use the checklists in section B.11 in Appendix B.
2. *What do we have to do to protect them against the threats?* Identify security requirements based on a view of the assets, threats, protection strategies, and risk indicators.
3. *What is our information infrastructure, where are the assets on it, and how are they threatened?* Map the assets, threats, and warning mechanisms against the infrastructure. Look at data flows, the possible movement of assets (logical or physical), how they can be accessed, and the way in which threats can occur.
4. *How are our assets vulnerable?* Analyse each asset's vulnerabilities to each threat, identify intrusion scenarios, and protection requirements, identify existing and missing security policies.
5. *What are the risks?* Define them (see Chapter 3) in a prioritized list risk.
6. *How do we secure ourselves?* Identify approaches and map them against the risks and threats. Choose the best.
7. *Do our defenses work?* Test the system against the security policies and use penetration tests to identify other weaknesses.

The process may be conducted according to a standard such as [TCSEC], [OCTAVE^SM] or [ISO/IEC 17799]. Note that in the latter case there are a number of test-related requirements listed in Table B.1 in Appendix B. Security concerns have generated a rich crop of security standards around the world many of which are simple copies of the others.

Security policies may be written against Common Criteria defined in [ISO 15408] and will in effect create a mass of new requirements against which tests must be created. One of the primary tests of the defenses is penetration testing. This will normally be carried out by specialist testers. See [ISECOM] for more on this. Common Criteria defines 8 levels of assurance:

- **CC EAL0: inadequate assurance.**
- **CC EAL1: functionally tested.** Provides analysis of the security functions, using a functional and interface specification of the TOE, to understand the security behavior. The analysis is supported by independent testing of the security functions.
- **CC EAL2: structurally tested.** Provides analysis of the security functions using functional and interface specifications, and the high level design of the subsystems of the TOE. Uses independent testing of the security functions, evidence of developer "black-box" testing and evidence of a development search for obvious vulnerabilities.
- **CC EAL3: methodically tested and checked.** The analysis is supported by "grey box" testing, selective independent confirmation of the developer test results and evidence of a developer search for obvious vulnerabilities. Requires development environment controls and TOE configuration management.
- **CC EAL4: methodically designed, tested, and reviewed.** Analysis is supported by the low-level design of the modules of the TOE and a subset of the implementation. Testing is supported by an independent search for obvious vulnerabilities. Development controls are supported by a life-cycle model, identification of tools, and automated configuration management.
- **CC EAL5: semiformally designed and tested.** Analysis includes all the implementation. Assurance is supplemented by a formal model, a semiformal presentation of the functional specification, high level design, and a semiformal demonstration of correspondence. The search for vulnerabilities ensures relative resistance to penetration attack. Requires covert channel analysis and modular design.
- **CC EAL6: semiformally verified, designed, and tested.** Analysis is supported by a modular, and layered approach to design, and a structured presentation of the implementation. The independent search for vulnerabilities must ensure high resistance to penetration attack. The search for covert channels must be systematic. Development environment and configuration management controls are further strengthened.
- **CC EAL7: formally verified, designed, and tested.** The formal model is supplemented by a formal presentation of the functional specification and high level design showing correspondence. Evidence of developer "white-box" testing and complete independent confirmation of developer test results are required. Complexity of the design must be minimized.

Security testing will normally be driven by the security manager who will hopefully cover many more areas than software. The test management concerns lie in accommodating the needs of the specialist penetration testers and analysing, extending, and executing the test database to cover the large number of tests required by the security policy.

The OSTMM [OSTMM] defines six test types which define the depth of the penetration test performed:

- **Blind/black-box:** the auditor knows nothing of the target but the target is aware of what, how, and when the penetration tester will be testing.
- **Double-blind/black-box:** the penetration tester is unaware of the target and the target is unaware of what, how or when the penetration tester will be testing.

- **Gray box:** the penetration tester is aware of the operational security measures of the target, and the target is aware of what and when the penetration tester will be testing.
- **Double-gray box:** the penetration tester is aware of the operational security measures of the target, and the target is aware of what and when the penetration tester will be testing.
- **Tandem/white-box:** the penetration tester has detailed knowledge of the target, its processes, and operational security, and the target is aware of what, how, and when the penetration tester will be testing.
- **Reversal:** the penetration tester has detailed knowledge of the target, its processes, and operational security, but the target knows nothing of what, how or when the penetration tester will be testing.

The ISECOM approach leads to the definition of a single-value Risk Assessment Value metric for a site based on a method shown in the manual. See section D.15 in Appendix D.

## 15.10.5  Resource Use Testing

A resource in this context is a processor/memory pair or a peripheral such as a disk, an undercarriage assembly, an on-board railway management system or a radar system. Resource use becomes an issue particularly in embedded systems such as aircraft, cars, and other safety-critical systems where it is essential to know:

- How much memory a resource consumes
- How much processor time a resource consumes
- When a process will stop using that resource
- Whether and how probably that resource will become locked by being contended for by more than one process
- The resources to which a unit or process is allocated, and which it uses

Sometimes the figures can be given precisely because the process (such as system startup) can be precisely measured. Sometimes it can only be given as part of an equation (such as the length of time a sort routine takes to run). Resource use testing is concerned to show that:

- Absolute figures hold under all circumstances
- In the given operating profile the constant representing the resource use is valid

See [Sahner] for details of a tool with which to undertake performance analysis and [Burns] for ways of estimating resource timing. Timing testing is particularly susceptible to Heisenberg effects and so test the testing environment first, and ensure it is neutral. The baseline for this test will be the predictions made against the system design. The method will involve in-circuit analyzers and a test rig. The measurements will be in nanoseconds.

## 15.10.6  Help Testing

No one reads help files until they're desperate. Consequently they need a quite different structure (if similar content) to user documents. User documents are for reference and thus contain more structure. Help documents are best written against a task analysis identifying the primary tasks, and the most-probable keywords which users will look for when trying to undertake those tasks. If you can persuade UTCs to talk out loud while executing the tests you will have some idea of these keywords.

Help should have:

- Titles that flag attention
- Definitions that fix ideas
- Worked examples
- Cross-references to related sections

There is no obvious baseline for help testing. A task analysis (see section 17.6.3) will give you some structure and an idea of what users are *believed* to be wanting to do. An approach to help testing would be to:

- Review the system *as is*
- Have an expert "use" the help to do the primary tasks
- Observe UTC's reactions when they turn to the help during usability testing

See section 18.5.10 and section 18.5.11.

### 15.10.7 Documentation and Training Testing

## Paper Killer

The biggest railway crash in Britain would have occurred in Woking. It would have been caused by a failure to check a document. The document was a work instruction to an operator to undo some bolts on a non-operational structure beside the railway track preparatory to removing it.

Unfortunately whoever prepared the note failed to indicate the correct bolts.

Fortunately the operator on having removed two bolts felt a certain movement through his boots. It was it seems only at this moment that he realized that the bolts held a very large signal gantry in place. This signal gantry was operative and spanned the main London-to-Portsmouth railway line. A lot of trains use that line every minute.

The operator checked his document, replaced and tightened the bolts, and went to see his supervisor.

There are two kinds of documentation to be tested: help files and user documentation. There are four kinds of training materials to be tested: lectures, demonstration playback, training documentation, and courseware. There are three simple if obvious approaches:

1. **Read it:** three kinds of person should read it: a subject matter expert (to ensure it says the right things), a literate person (to ensure it is both well-structured and logical), a user (to show that it can be used) or not.

2. **Review it:** when you have completed the last two activities there are few more-effective ways of teasing out hard-to-find bugs than sitting down a few knowledgeable people and briefly examining each page of a manual to see if each is happy with it. There are good books and courses on reviewing. The reviewer might pretend to be a particular kind of user but being (presumably) knowledgeable will be unlikely to approach the document with the same uncertainty as a generally naïve user. See section B.7.5 in Appendix B.

3. **Check all the illustrations and all the URLs contained in the documents and help files:** if any URL is not under your company's control consider investing in a link-rot service or software to ensure as far as possible that it is kept up-to-date.

4. **Use it:** even reference documents can be user-tested. To take an extreme case: assuming that a manual contains function definitions written by one programmer for an SDK to be used by another, you can test it by taking it to some reasonably-competent programmer, ask him to write something using those functions, and see how easy (or possible) this is.

Very few people read for pleasure and or have a reading age greater than sixteen. Thus it is unlikely that an average user will access any document more than is absolutely necessary. It is even less likely that any UTC will comment on the usefulness of the documents. Documents must therefore be seen as:

- Essential pre-requisites to starting up the system (a get-you-started guide)
- An adjunct to the help system during the usability tests

The best that can be hoped for from a document test is either that users will comment that they are trying to find out how to do X (and can't) or that the information is there, but in the "wrong" place.

There is a number of other ways of assessing a document including a readability index (see section 17.5). None has been found more than indicatively useful in practice.

To determine which physical pages have been accessed try using a light glue on the outer edge of the pages such that each is lightly attached to the next. After the session the unaccessed pages can be determined.

See section 18.5.12.

## 15.10.8 Procedure and Business Process Model Testing

A procedure can be defined by:

- The process model
- The requirements (or other) specification of the system
- The definition of the forms[3] referred to in the process model
- The dataflow definitions in the process mode
- The screen displays
- The command sequences needed to obtain system services
- The rationale[4] of the business process (sometimes known, rarely defined)
- The working knowledge of the existing process held by existing users
- The throughput requirements (define them yourself and let the users disagree)
- The task definitions (not written)[5]

The procedure may be defined in a manual but this will depend on the availability of the information shown above.

Testing the procedure is required as a defense against the following risks:

- That the procedure doesn't work:
  - Some dataflow of the model doesn't connect with the rest of the outside world
  - Activity A depends on or impedes activity B which depends on or impedes activity A (deadlock)
  - Activity A provokes activity B which provokes activity A (race)
  - The throughput is too high for a user to support, (or the system to support that number of calls made on a server)
- The system (as a whole) is too tightly-coupled (any delay in any activity delays the rest of the system)
- The system (as a whole) is too loosely-coupled (any input requires too much time to provoke an output)
- Some form (paper or electronic) doesn't contain:
  - The data required for some input
  - The space for some data to be entered

---

[3] These may not exist at the moment when you try to define the tests, and you will depend on the dataflow definitions and the thoughtfulness of the developers and analysts in maintaining the interface design documentation.

[4] We need to know why a process is there to be able to test how well the system satisfies that rationale and how the system (and process) may evolve. This may be shown in the functional inventory.

[5] The task definitions are essential for a user-centered view of the system.

- That the data is faulty in that it is:
  - Missing at some critical point
  - Wrong (gigo)
  - Late
- That the system doesn't support the procedure properly:
  - The data, while present, cannot be accessed (screen A is needed to answer one part of a query and screen B another, they are mutually exclusive, and the response time is slow)
  - The data isn't available on the screen or form at the time it is needed
  - The interface is awkward (too many keystrokes, keystroke-combination/meanings change between modes, slow reaction, display is confusing or unclear)
  - The error messages are unclear
  - The system fails to handle a user's faulty behavior sufficiently
- The training doesn't support the procedure properly:
  - The course doesn't provide feedback to the pupils and teachers, on how well they're doing
  - The course doesn't cover all the processes
  - The course fails to concentrate on the critical processes
  - Some key feature isn't covered in the course
- Operators can't understand the rationale behind the processes
- Operators are overloaded cognitively
- The documentation doesn't support the procedure:
  - The manuals aren't user-oriented (they're system-oriented, rather than task-oriented)
  - Not all the commands are described
  - Not all the screens are described
  - Not all the features described are available
  - Some process in the model isn't in the documentation
  - Some process in the documentation isn't in the model
- The throughput has been wrongly assessed

## 15.10.9   Procedure Test Method

The procedure test method covers:

- **Bounding the procedure** to be tested: either by participants (*swim-lanes*), threads (sign-on for a supply, read a meter, get a bill, pay it) or functions (customer-handling, back to <company_name>, complaints)
- **Identifying:**
  - The process models of the procedure.
  - The specifications defining the support available for the procedure.
  - All the forms, display types and data streams involved.
  - All the user classes involved.
  - All the transactions involved (in this context a transaction may start with some request and end with its satisfaction or some error message).
  - All the task objectives of each user class (probably means writing a task/objective matrix). (See section 15.10.10.) These may be the same as the transactions.
  - All the training and other documentation for all the users.
- The **procedure location** (in terms of some model office)
- A set of **target objectives and metrics** for each procedure which it is reasonable to expect the procedure to achieve when it is running properly
- All the **constraints** (temporal, physical, logistic) affecting the procedure
- **Desk-checking:**
  - That the training and other documentation covers the activities needed for each user class and each task
  - That every dataflow on the process diagram is tested

- – That every user task objective can be met in terms of some key-stroke commands, data entry, form-filling or other activity (like physically reading a meter)
- **Modeling the dataflows** of that procedure in an executable model
- **Executing the model** to see if it works (does it have any sources which are always empty or sinks which always overflow, do all the flows match). Building the model such that it can be executed will in itself be a major validation task
- **Identifying the dominant dataflows** (those which cause the greatest effect on the others)
- Identifying the dataflow profiles over a twenty-four-hour period, and possibly annually
- **Training** the (subset of user) staff
- **Formally testing** the (subset of user) staff to establish:
  - – How well each member had learned the procedure
  - – How well the procedure had been formally taught
- **Creating the test environment** by physically creating the model office environment, installing the systems and documentation
- **Specifying the tests** by:
  - – Defining the procedure boundaries in terms of other procedures, user interfaces, IT-system interfaces, organizational responsibilities, and marking these limits on the process model
  - – Identifying all data-flows across the process boundaries, and for every dataflow its volume and frequency, the processes which act on it, and whether they cause the dataflow to become transformed, sunk into or sourced from that procedure
  - – Matching every dataflow to a paper form or screen (or part thereof), and matching every form or screen to some part of some user documentation
  - – Matching every process to some description in the user documentation (note: engineering and psychological judgment must be used here — the amount of explanation required for a procedure varies as the target audience. The only rule possible is that some description must exist)
  - – Identifying the rationale of the procedure and the major flows through it
  - – Identifying possible bug conditions in terms of:
    - Faulty or missing data input or output at each human interface (note that faulty system processing is assumed to have been tested elsewhere)
    - Faulty human behavior
    - Constraints, temporal and otherwise
  - – Preparing a set of test objectives for every transaction written bearing in mind presumed training and available documentation
  - – Preparing tests scripts from the test objectives, to show exit and entry conditions
  - – Preparing test scenarios based on:
    - Major flows through the procedure
    - Principal bug conditions
    - Matched exit/entry conditions
  - – Preparing expected results and data with which to "drive" the procedure, based on the executed model
- **Executing the tests**
- **Executing the procedure** with the trained staff and monitoring both their behavior and the output
- Assessing the results in terms of the expected results, the execution time, the data throughput, and operator errors observed
- **Feeding the results** back into:
  - – The model and recalibrating it
  - – The user training program and modifying it
  - – The system and changing it
  
  Until the metrics identified above have been satisfied

See also section A.3.4 in Appendix A.

### 15.10.10 Task/Objective Matrix Example

An employment agency (*EmpAgy*) has a number of standardized workflows or objectives for their staff. (*Create candidate, Create temporary vacancy etc.*) Each of these is formed from a number of a number of tasks some of which are widely used and are shown as << includes >> in the spreadsheet shown in Figure 15.14. The order in which the tasks are executed is shown by figures in the cells. The advantage of such a matrix is that it is simple to detect:

- Which objective uses the most tasks
- Which task is the most used

| # | A | B Create candidate | C Create temporary vacancy (withheld) | D Create temporary vacancy (not withheld) | E Create permanent vacancy (withheld) | F Temp applies for job | G Perm applies for job | H Temp... |
|---|---|---|---|---|---|---|---|---|
| 1 | | | | | | | | |
| 2 | << Include SC001a Create candidate >> | | | | | 1 | 1 | |
| 3 | << Include SC001c Create temporary vacancy (not withheld)>> | | | | | 2 | 2 | |
| 4 | << Include SSC001f Shortlist | | | | | 7 | 7 | |
| 5 | << Include SSC001g Automatic Unassign >> | | | | | 13 | | |
| 6 | << Include SSC001i Find candidate >> | | | | | 9 | 9 | |
| 7 | << Include SSC001j Assign Candidate >> | | | | | 10 | 10 | |
| 8 | << Include SSC002c Candidate searches for vacancy >> | | | | | 3 | 4 | |
| 9 | << Include SSC002e Payroll>> | | | | | 12 | | |
| 10 | << Include SSC002f Export candidate>> | | | | | 8 | 8 | |
| 11 | << Include SSC102 Logon (Internet)>> | 1 | | | | | | |
| 12 | Candidate appears in vacancy | | | | | 6 | | |
| 13 | Candidate applies for vacancy | | | | | 5 | 5 | |
| 14 | Click on option Country Field System | 3 | | | | | | |
| 15 | Create Vacancy | | 1 | 1 | 1 | | | |
| 16 | Fill in mandatory fields and Click "Search" | 5 | | | | | | |
| 17 | Select "Candidates" and "New" | 4 | | | | | | |
| 18 | Select Cost Centre | 2 | | | | | | |
| 19 | Send Vacancy to EmpAgyWeb automatically (not withheld) | | | 2 | | 4 | 3 | |
| 20 | Send Vacancy to EmpAgyWeb automatically (withheld) | | 2 | | 2 | | | |
| | System displays candidates page with unique ID number at | | | | | | | |

FIGURE 15.14  Task/objective matrix example

## 15.11  Conduct a Test Readiness Review

See section 6.6 for more on this. Issue a test readiness review report. If you have serious doubts about the release or its testing this is your last opportunity to voice them, and have something done. If you fail to take this opportunity and later have problems you should have foreseen…

## 15.12  Beta Testing Process

See section 6.8 for more on this. The beta test process consists of the following stages:

1. **Plan beta testing.** This will show:
   a. Who is running the beta tests
   b. What the expected dates are
   c. What will be provided to beta testers
   d. How you will interface with beta testers (specially-trained or existing Support staff)
   e. How you will handle the bug reports
      i.  Interface to test team ("why didn't we find this one?", "can we reproduce this?"
      ii. Interface to the developers: "this is a stinker — beware!"
   f. How you will report progress to management
   g. What rewards management is prepared to make to diligent beta testers (a T-shirt for everyone who submits a bug, a bottle of champagne for every 10 priority-1 bugs found by a single beta tester)
   h. Identify beta test minimum feature set (time may be short and it may be preferable to have early user views on a partial but useable release with time to do something rather than late user views on a full release with "no" time to fix them)
2. **Identify beta test candidates.**
3. **Find out from marketing which customers are:**
   a. Most typical of their market sector
   b. Least likely to complain publicly if the software fails
   c. Most accustomed to/likely to benefit from beta tests
   d. Most likely therefore to undertake beta tests
   e. Least likely to object to close cross-questioning by development staff (you never know — it might be essential)
   f. Most likely to submit useable bug reports
   And will therefore make the best beta test candidates.
4. **Get feedback from the candidates:**
   a. Call the candidate on the phone
   b. Identify who the primary contact is, what they do, and how much time they expect to be able to devote
   c. Get telephone extension numbers, email, and location addresses
   d. Confirm how, if at all, the beta test will be of value to the person's organization
   e. Identify if the person can be trusted to do any testing at all and how his boss views beta testing
   f. Identify which features they will most probably use
   g. Obtain any user documentation showing how they use the product
   h. Ensure that the beta test candidate cannot damage his company by using the system and will preferably be able to play with it in a completely isolated environment (this may not be obvious to the beta test candidate)
   i. Encourage the beta tester to regard usability bugs as being of the greatest importance; stress the value they bring by being awkward and highlighting usability issues (" We believe it works — only you can tell us if it works well")
5. **Finalize the beta test candidate list.** Make sure you have enough candidates if some drop out. Ensure market sector and feature coverages are sufficient. Call the beta test candidates and tell them they've been chosen.
6. **Prepare beta test assets.** Don't expect beta users to be skilled in test preparation. This will be the first time they have used the new version of the software in their firm. Help them with check lists,

suggested use patterns (install, use uninstall, install, use features A–M, close down, startup, use features N–Z, close down, install, use features A, C, E, G, B, D, F, AB, CD, ... close down, uninstall, uninstall — can you?), recommended test environments and test procedures. In particular a one-page sheet on how to fill in bug reports so that testers can repeat the bug. If these are based on their existing in-house documents so much the better. Consider having special builds for really big customers. Warn them how limited the timescales are. Stress the value of usability bugs.

7. **Provide beta test candidates with testing assets.** Call them two days later to ensure they've arrived. Make a fuss of them, but keep it brief. This way they know you care, you're in contact, and you won't waste their time.

8. **Provide beta test candidate with beta test software.** Warn them two days in advance that a release is coming. Check they have the test environment available, get them excited. Courier the release and latest documentation, this makes it seem special even if it could equally well be downloaded. Call the users the next day to check it has arrived and have they had any problems installing it. Find out the configuration they installed it on. Warn them how limited the timescales are.

9. **Get bug reports from beta test candidates.** Thank them personally and briefly by telephone. Compare the bugs with those already found:
   a. Is some feature buggier than was thought?
   b. Was some features coverage incomplete?

10. **Report to management.** To what extent has the beta test program shown up the alpha test program? Are there hardware-specific problems? Are there performance problems? What are the implications for the alpha test suites and the final release date? Are the number and severity of the bugs worse than expected?

11. **Send feedback to beta test candidates.** Do not tell them who else is participating, but report daily on progress. If a new release is required warn them asap so they don't waste their time testing the old one. Try and discover how many of the features they are covering.

12. **Send feedback to the test team.** Which test suites need revising, which test environments need changing, what performance regimes need changing.

13. **Identify how much code was changed** as a result of beta testing. Compare this with the amount of code changed as a result of alpha testing and use this as a way of justifying the cost of beta testing.

# 15.13   Acceptance Testing

## 15.13.1   As a Subset of System Testing

Acceptance testing as a subset of system testing is designed to demonstrate to the customer that the system generally meets requirements. It occurs when all the bugs found in the system testing have been cleared or a concession to ignore them has been obtained from the customer. It ends when the acceptance test certificate is formally signed off by the customer.

To achieve a level of confidence in the delivered system, the customer will want to be confident of the process of its development. This does not mean that the customer will want to carry out comprehensive validation and verification of the design and implementation: these are clearly your responsibility.

Since acceptance testing can be thought of as a subset of system testing all the issues mentioned in the previous section apply. In very large systems however, each sub-system may be so large as to require a separate system test.

Incorporate any acceptance tests proposed by the customer in the system tests. Identify very-important system tests for inclusion as candidate acceptance tests. You can then propose these tests to the customer as the basis of the acceptance test schedule.

Get acceptance test data from the following sources:

- Parallel running, in which the outputs of new and old systems are compared
- File conversion, in which existing input data for an old system is converted, and the results compared with that of the old system (this is essentially a batch version of parallel running)

Can the customer's staff run the system? If they're critical to a successful transition-to-use, then their ability must be tested too.

### 15.13.2 Challenge Testing

There is an argument that says that the customer should write the acceptance tests, keep them secret from the developers and then acceptance-test the product away from the developer. This practice would, if followed, lead to much greater rigor on the part of developers. It is rare that customers are capable of writing tests of any rigor, and it would be essential, for contractual reasons, for the baselines for such tests to be known to the developers.

Note that it is perfectly possible for:

- a set of acceptance tests to be written which are quite orthogonal to the system tests
- customers both to prepare and execute their "own" acceptance tests, which will cause considerable delay in fielding the system
- any customer proposing to write their "own" acceptance tests to first review all the existing system tests to avoid duplication (for the sake of economy as well as common sense); you should be able to determine the objectives of the customer's tests from the questions the customers later ask

## 15.14  Test a Build

The objective in testing a build is to answer the following questions:

- Can the release be installed?
- Do the major features work?
- Has any feature which used to work, stopped working?
- Do the new features work?

When testing a build beware:

- The build doesn't install on the test environment.
- The build doesn't work even minimally.
- You don't know what's in the build.
- Some previously-working features now fail.
- The new features (which is what the build has been created for) are either missing or don't work at all.

Testing a build involves the following steps, designed to handle such threats:

1. **Check the release note.** Every build will have a release note as described in section 8.10. You will be told that *"it's just coming"* and *"it's being written now."* Observe gently that you had made it clear from the outset that the tests would begin *after* the release note had been reviewed and not before. Why be so difficult? This is a critical moment when you show your teeth for the first time. Fail to get your way on this and you will lay down a marker for the rest of the test cycle that you are a person who can be leaned upon. When the project manager finally hands you the note, and smiles with gritted teeth, hand it back to him, and ask him please to sign it.
2. **Install the system.** This may be the subject of a major test. If so don't run that test yet. Assume it can be installed with some agreed set of settings and install it with those.
3. **Run smoke tests.** The name derives from the old engineering principle that in the event some equipment is switched on and smoke seen to billow from it, there is probably something wrong. Smoke tests are designed to answer the question *"Do we have any grounds for rejecting this release straight away?"* and should be runnable within sixty minutes elapsed time. For the smoke test set choose tests which exercise each major feature but no more. Smoke tests are invaluable as a way of avoiding testers wasting their time by trying to test unusable builds. They should be run by

one person. Should any fail, the entire build should be rejected. Choose them from the set of system tests to show every primary feature of the release. If any test finds a bug, then reject the release. Don't accept the excuse that you can "test: *those bits which do work*," because the bits which don't almost certainly hide major bugs, and the working bits will very probably fail the next time round. Knowing that a release has failed its smoke test is news developers need fast.

4. **Run confidence tests.** A confidence test answers the question "*Can we be confident that having started to test this build we will be able to finish testing without finding that some feature really doesn't work?*" They cover all the major features in more depth than the smoke tests, and if only a few fail it is worth continuing testing the release. You will run confidence tests as soon as smoke tests have been completed. Confidence tests should exercise all features to some depth, and should rarely require more than 4 hours to run.

5. **Run regression tests.** The purpose of a regression test is to establish that none of the functionality a system possessed before the last changes has deteriorated. A system regression test will be run as soon as a new build of a release is received. See *Regression testing* below for more on this.

6. **Run the system tests.** These are drawn from the set of tests covering the features of this release as defined in the release note.

## 15.14.1  System-Testing Issues

1. Software releases for system testing should have been constructed from software and hardware which has previously undergone unit testing, and is therefore under configuration control.
2. Ask the developers where they think the most serious bugs lie.
3. Never let the developers think the testers are criticising them. If they were not human the developers wouldn't make mistakes, and there would be no work for testers. If the system tests are well-written they will find extraordinary bugs.
4. Morale is everything: give your staff recognition when they find a bug, particularly a serious bug.
5. The first time the system tests are completely run, the ratio of tests run per day will be very low because even experienced staff need time to get to know the tests and procedures.
6. Some bugs will be found in an unstructured manner:
   a. The fact that some bugs are found as a result of inspired guesswork by staff does not mean that the time spent preparing tests was wasted, rather that having the security of a known testing procedure gave staff the time and motivation and a framework to try out new ideas.
   b. Document any inspired guess-work so that all staff can exploit the experience.
7. Bug reporting:
   a. Report all bugs found to the developers within twenty-four hours. Otherwise they may waste time looking for the same bug. This can usefully take place at 5 p.m. with a weekly review meeting on Monday mornings.
   b. In general, don't report a bug to the developers until it can be repeated. Exceptions: those obscure, rare, hard to replicate, but dangerous system bugs which absolutely *must* be found.
8. Tell test staff when they should abandon attempts to find a difficult bug. Usually thirty minutes is enough; any bug which cannot be repeated in this time should be noted and searched for at the end of a system test run. It may have been found by then anyway.
9. Charts:
   a. If the charts of bugs found and fixed show that something is going wrong then take immediate action. If the charts show the effect you want, then the action was worthwhile. If it doesn't, investigate whether the action was undertaken properly or whether the chart was wrong in the first place.
   b. Charts will at best be 95% correct; only those discrepancies over 5% are worth worrying about.

    c. Circulate a selection of charts as shown in the bug tracking graphs in Chapter 7 regularly. These are useful not only for your management purposes but for explaining progress at your regular bug reporting meetings with the developers. Hold these on Monday mornings such that if testing has occurred throughout the weekend,[6] all staff can be kept up-to-date.

10. Once system testing is satisfactorily completed, the system-tested code should be held separately from the rest of the project code under configuration control. As this is a major baseline, take and archive a master copy. Access to, and control of, the system-tested code is with the project librarian.

11. Tools are also available to show the status of *code* at a glance. Table 15.11 shows the output of one.

**TABLE 15.11**  A project status table[a]

| Unit | Function | SW eng. | Status | Est. NCSS | Actual NCSS | Complexity | Faults | Statement coverage (%) |
|---|---|---|---|---|---|---|---|---|
| Display | | F. B. | System test | 390 | 442 | | 8 | 55 |
| | Match | | | | 73 | 8 | 6 | 96 |
| | Get user string | | | | 100 | **42** | | 100 |
| | Get add edit | | | | 64 | **25** | 2 | 32 |
| | Get main input | | | | 56 | 5 | | 45 |
| | Get delete input | | | | 53 | 7 | | 60 |
| | Get one line | | | | 36 | 11 | | 100 |
| | Get plot menu | | | | 60 | 8 | | 25 |
| ARC | | F. G | Insp. | 60 | 0 | **72** | 4 | 0 |
| SUM | | G. C. | Coding | 100 | 209 | | | |
| CRL | | A. L. | Insp. | 215 | 480 | **236** | 1 | 0 |
| SUB | | B. G. | Design | 250 | 1279 | | 4 | 85 |

[a] The bold figures represent problem areas.

    Use information like this, together with a table relating code to features, to identify the more-problematic features.

12. You may need to know the status of features rather than code. In this case look at:
    – Figure 8.16 to identify test preparation and coverage levels
    – Figure 8.20 to show the status of testing of each feature
    – Figure 8.21 to show how fast you are finding the bugs and the developers are fixing them

# 15.15  Monitor the Test Process

If you have set things up well for yourself you will have several channels by which to monitor the test process:

- The numbers of tests run (as a proportion of those planned) which you can get from the test management tool
- The number of bugs found
- The amount of code turmoil (see section 18.9.8)
- The feedback from the testers at the morning meetings
- Running a few tests yourself
- Use the measures and charts in section 18.10 to monitor release readiness

Beware of the following:
- **Developers creating as many or more bugs than are being fixed.** This will become evident from the bug charts (which never level off) and the level of code turmoil (which never dips). See also section 18.10.2.2.

---

[6] Is weekend testing ever a Good Idea? No. Does it happen? Well …

- **Mid-release requirement changes.** This sounds daft but it happens. As a test manager you must manage it. Ensure that not only the tests directly affected are changed, but that those tests which are only slightly related to the requirement (which you will have identified from the test/feature matrix such as the one in Table 15.8) are also reviewed.
- **Unannounced environment changes.** These cause major upsets. Make sure they cannot happen. If developers need to change the test environment, ensure they must ask you first. Otherwise many of the bugs you find may be false, testers time will have been wasted and friction occur.
- **Unauthorized installation of a new release.** This will occur on the grounds that the developers need to know whether some proposed fix works. Only accept if the current release is so bad that it is pointless to continue testing it. Otherwise:
  - Identify the tester in charge of the feature needing to be tested.
  - Get him to estimate the duration of that retesting.
  - Warn the project that there could be a delay in completing the present release.
  - Try and get some more resources (say from *Support*) to help.
  - Have the tester run tests on the allegedly-fixed release on a separate machine or system.
  - Continue the other tests as before.

  Arbitrarily installing a new release before you have finished testing an old one is a trick played by irresponsible project managers who are terrified you will find too many bugs, and who therefore attempt to limit coverage by ensuring you only ever have time to test a few features superficially. That this will become very evident to any customer who uses the software is not their problem. You, the test manager, failed to provide adequate coverage, and It's All Your Fault. Moral: you alone decide when a new release is loaded.
- **Bugs not being found as fast as you expect:**
  - Is it because many features don't work properly and thus prevent testers from fully exploring them? As the bugs get fixed, testers will find the others – but only as fast as they get fixes.
  - Is this because the testers have little experience of the system? As they gain experience they will find bugs faster.
  - Is this because the bugs take longer to document or require many attempts to demonstrate their presence? Plan better next time.
  - Did you estimate wrongly?
  - Is the system very different from what you had been led to expect?
    - If the requirements were surreptitiously changed, then make this clear to management immediately: someone might be trying to make a fool of you and your staff.
    - If the appearance differs but the functions are as expected then make a note to check the UI better next time.

  If code turmoil is low, the features are stable, the coverage is demonstrably thorough, the tests well-written, but the cumulative bug graph, while flattening, is lower than you estimated, perhaps you are confronted with a really solid system.
- **Testers finding far more bugs than you estimated.** Estimate better next time. If code turmoil is high warn management. Congratulate the testers.
- **Developers deciding to fix only the top severity bugs.** A lot of low-priority bugs mask high-priority bugs. They also make for a quite terrible user experience. Get some agreement with management that for any feature more than x *not-serious-enough-to-fix bugs* (perhaps per feature) = 1 *serious-enough-to-fix* bug, and get them fixed. See section 17.2 in Chapter 17 for a little story.
- **No severity-1 bugs being found.** If this is an high-risk system then this may be good news, particularly if the developers have an history of making very solid releases. Otherwise, particularly if there is an history of severity-1 bugs being reported from the field, check:
  - If the highest-severity bugs are correctly-classified
  - If all end-to end scenarios have been completed
  - If many variations of each scenario have been tested

- If the bugs which have been found are found as often as you expect, but are more serious than they appear (see section 15.15.1 for an example)
- If critical bits of the requirements specification have been correctly mapped to one or more tests
- If the system as a whole is approaching the stability profile you expect
- If *fault injection* in Chapter 13 has been used to test the tests' ability to find high-severity bugs

If the preceding seven statements are true it is probable that no severity-1 bug has been found because it wasn't there. See section 18.2 in Chapter 18 for further tests to run to establish how close the system is to exhibiting a bug. See Table 2.3 for a way of determining this.

- **Having to abandon test runs** because they are untestable: testers are finding so many top-severity bugs that they are losing faith in the possibility of a release succeeding. This is not your problem directly, but it could help if you identify the parts of the system which *can* be tested such that you can propose to management which bits might be worth keeping while the rest be completely rewritten.
- **Previously-stable code is exhibiting bugs** (*"which the testers ought to have found"*). Maybe you should. Maybe they are newly-injected. Load a previously-tested release on a spare machine (or system) and re-run the tests. Do this for a number of bugs. If they are indeed newly-injected, create a table like the one shown in Figure 8.25.
- **Evidence of poor performance.** You'll get this by having created some performance tests to be run in tandem with the system tests, by modeling or (most improbably but seriously) by complaints from testers. Advise management but beware of any attempts to divert you from system testing: get a stable release before you ask for a fast one.
- **Bugs not being fixed in time.** This is not your responsibility but ensure that this failure to fix is clear to your management, in your daily report. It could simply be that the developers are being assiduous in unit-testing.
- **Fixed bugs not being cleared in time**. Retesting bug fixes must be the first thing to be done on a release after smoke and confidence tests. Developers need to know that the fixes work. Testers hate retesting because it's boring. Some find it a challenge to squeeze one last bug from an otherwise impeccable feature. Show how seriously you take this work by clearing some bugs yourself.
- **Users disliking the system.** The system is presumably fairly stable and usability tests are being conducted (see Chapter 17). Such a dislike could presage some major contractual and requirements changes or may simply indicate that users are at last devoting enough attention to the system. Management will need reassurance and evidence that the dislike is unreasonable which you can maybe provide from the usability test results.

## 15.15.1 Proportions of Bugs Ranged by Seriousness

Every project has a bug proportion profile which shows the percentages of bugs ordered by severity. They tend to be quite stable within development and testing teams. Here are three expressed in percentages (Figure 15.15). Projects 1 and 2 had largely the same development and testing teams.

The figure shows the bugs found in three projects. Projects 1 and 2 seem anomalous in that very few *Low* bugs are reported (the testers tended to ignore them because of the large number of *Critical* and *High* bugs).

Such a table is useful in that once you have reasonably-stable proportions for one team, and an estimate of total bugs for a release, you can give some estimate of the highest-severity bugs.

| Project | Critical | High | Medium | Low |
|---------|----------|------|--------|-----|
| 1 | 22 | 43 | 27 | 8 |
| 2 | 25 | 42 | 24 | 9 |
| 3 | 20 | 36 | 17 | 27 |

**FIGURE 15.15** Bugs found in three projects expressed as percentages

## 15.16  Report

Prepare a daily report. It may be unwelcome, but surprises are even less welcome. Use the format in section 8.18. At the end of testing a build, write an end-of-system-test report using the format shown in the example in section A.9 in Appendix A. The purposes of the reports are:

- To discipline yourself to keep your eye on the bugs, give you the space to stand back from the issues and keep things in perspective
- To demonstrate that you are on top of the problem (project managers may not be accustomed to this in test managers)
- To prepare people for that unhappy moment (which may never come) when you have to tell them that this build is no good

Be tactful but truthful in the wording. One manager became very upset because I had referred to (untested) bug fixes as "allegedly-fixed" bugs. I should have said "untested fixes," and left unimplied the possibility that any of the Very Wonderful fixes the release contained might, er, fail. Several didn't.

## 15.17  Agree That the Release Is Ready

Agreeing to a release is the biggest decision you can make as measured by the repercussions on the users and the company. If you have put in place the metrics and reporting systems detailed elsewhere in the book you will have sufficient information on which to take the decision. Here is a last-minute list of things to do:

1. Talk to the testers. Do they have any misgivings, were there any serious but irreproducible problems they recently encountered?
2. See section 2.4 and section 4.6.5.
3. Look again at the project risks and decide if they have been sufficiently addressed.
4. (Refuse to) sign the release note.

# 16

# Performance and Stress Testing

## 16.1 General

Well-specified systems will include performance objectives in terms of speed, bug tolerance, throughput, user response, etc. In general, performance testing should:

- Test the system to its performance specifications to ensure that it can meet requirements
- Then test the system beyond its performance specification until it breaks down (that is, until some aspect of the system behavior becomes unusable at that load) and then analyze how and why it has failed: is it what you would expect? If not, have you uncovered a bug or deficiency? (This is strictly-speaking load testing.)

You need to test the system early: to discover that the system won't support more than 10% of the contracted number of users some 2 weeks before release is, er, a tad late. You will also need to refine your performance test harness as the system itself is developed. It can take 10 man-weeks to set up a running performance test so this is best assigned to someone early on to prepare for and be ready to run as soon as a testable build is to hand.

## 16.2 Service Level Agreements

Service level agreements (SLAs) are generally concerned with little more than the provision of working boxes and a help desk. Some organizations may need 24/7 service with persistent monitoring in real-time of the state of several networks in which case you may be involved on either side of the fence. The issues are:

1. **Service reliability:** some organizations deploy a set of persistent 24/7 services for their users. These include grid tools such as the Globus Toolkit and GRAM gatekeeper [Foster] or an SRB server [Rajasekar] as well as SSH servers and such monitoring frameworks as the Network Weather Service [Wolski]. These services may be susceptible to temporal bugs and external factors (e.g., misconfiguration). Therefore periodically run test suites in order to discover problems before the users detect any interruption.

   Several Grids create a suite of tests for verifying local service availability when setting it up:
   a. NCSA TestGrid Project [NCSA]
   b. The UK Grid Integration Test Scripts [GITS]
   c. The Inca test harness and reporting framework [Smallen]
   These use scripts that run a set of tests and display the results on a web page.

2. **Service monitoring.** In addition to basic service reliability, most organizations deploy a wide range of monitoring software. Cluster monitoring tools include Ganglia [Massie], CluMon [Clumon], and

BigBrother [BigBrother]. Each collects data about cluster resources. Inca's data collection framework can complement such monitoring tools and act as a uniform interface to multiple data sources. Grid monitoring tools used by many organizations include the Globus Toolkit's Monitoring and Directory Service [Zhang], Condor's Hawkeye [Hawkeye], the European Data Grid's RGMA [RGMA] (based on the Global Grid Forum's Grid Monitoring Architecture [Tierney]), GridLab's Testbed Status Monitoring Tool [Holub], SCALEA-G [Truong], and MonALISA [MonALISA]. See [Gerndt] for a survey of other monitoring tools.

3. **Benchmarking.** Benchmarks show how applications should perform on grids and are used to detect performance problems. Thus the TeraGrid deploys high-performance networking, data storage facilities, and clusters using data to verify that the hardware and software functions at the expected capacity. Several projects including the GRASP project [Chun] and GridBench [GridBench] examine the need for common Grid benchmarks.

4. **Site interoperability certification.** As a project grows, it is likely to collaborate with similar projects. When two projects collaborate, they need to verify the compatibility of their project environments; while they may define a higher-level service agreement of common functionality they may have no way to verify it.

5. **Software stack validation.** Any SLA must accommodate updates. These may be deployed by local system administrators according to local constraints, update, and installation procedures. Organizations need to verify that such updates do not interfere with the existing environment. Automated test suites need to be run directly after changes and before the system is deployed to ensure a stable environment.

6. **Metrics.** Service level agreements require that participating sites must deploy a common user environment, such as the TeraGrid Hosting Environment, that includes a software stack and default user environment. Tools such as the TeraGrid Hosting Environment require users to develop applications for a common environment rather than independently. Site autonomy makes such agreements difficult to implement since sites may interpret service agreements differently. So continuously validate and verify SLAs by measuring compliance using metrics. SLAs often center on timing and resource issues:

   a. Client tests of connections to ISPs
   b. Ping tests
   c. Transaction response times
   d. CPU use as a percent of total use
   e. I/O speeds
   f. Memory use
   g. Network throughput
   h. Bandwidth use

Look at section 18.7 for ways of defining issues to be incorporated in an SLA.

# 16.3 Performance Testing: Tool Use

Performance testing involves using a tool to create a series of virtual users who will access a user interface, typically a website, *en masse*. The tool will then report on the number of user transactions and the speed with which they are attempted and completed, and identify how many failures occur. You can then draw conclusions about the overall throughput of the website or application and set about determining where the bottlenecks occur.

The performance test harness will look something like Figure 16.1.

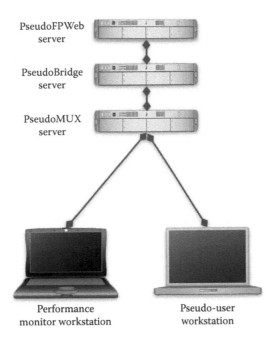

PseudoFPWeb
server

PseudoBridge
server

PseudoMUX
server

Performance
monitor workstation

Pseudo-user
workstation

**FIGURE 16.1**  Performance testing environment

There is a large number of performance tools, both commercial and open source. See section D.7 in Appendix D.

# 16.4  Performance Testing: Requirements

Performance specifications must show:

- Maximum, average, and 95% transaction response times; see [Nielsen 1] for a discussion on maximum response timing
- Load profiles: the users and their transactions over 24- 7-, or 12-hour periods and per week or month (for example people buy more cold things in the summer)
- Database volumes (number of records in production databases)
- The questions the performance tests are expected to answer

See [Gerrard 2] and section B.14 in Appendix B for more on this.

# 16.5  What Is the Baseline for Performance Tests?

Performance tests have baselines too. They're just subtler and rarely well-specified. Tests answer questions. Performance tests are generally intended to answer the question "where's the bottleneck?" See section B.14 in Appendix B. The baseline for finding the bottleneck is the components which make up the system and their configuration. This configuration might change as the bottlenecks are teased out. Note that performance tests are rarely concerned with speed alone: speed of execution is dependent on processor speed and memory, and these can usually be simply changed (wait long enough, and Moore's law will give you all the speed you want). When systems are nominally optimized for speed, you start "real" performance testing which looks at the system-as-a-whole and each component. The baseline for this test is the system as configured for the test, the set of inputs to be used and the definitions in the requirements specification. If they're not there then use the checklist to write them, circulate them, and get agreement.

## 16.6   Performance Testing: Process

To performance test:

1. **Identify performance elements** (see section B.14 in Appendix B).
2. **Define questions** the performance tests must answer.

---

# How Not to Do It

---

The CEO and company founder wanted the system performance tested.
    CEO: "I want to know what its performance is."
    Test Manager (warily): "The system can come in many configurations. D'you have any one in mind?"
CEO: "Just string some boxes together and see how fast it is."
TM: "OK, I can put together what appears to be a typical box configuration. How complex must the application be?" (and the application could be terribly simple, or verging on rocket science).
CEO: "I just want to know how fast it is."
TM: "Has a customer been complaining?"
CEO: "You betcha."
TM: "So how complex is their application? Can we have a copy of it to test here?"
The test manager never got to see the errant application. Eventually he persuaded the CEO that stringing some boxes together wasn't the answer, and that one had to look for answers to questions that salesmen, developers, and indeed any other stakeholder could *use*.

---

See section A.8.7 in Appendix A for examples.

3. **Establish a common measure.** This is critical. There must be a measure of system performance which all stakeholders can agree on and use. (See section D.7 in Appendix D for details of some measures and the organizations defining them.) Thus one page may load fast because it has little on it. Another may have to be built with a lot of fields and .jpgs. A transaction involving the first and not the second will run far faster. Simply to say that one configuration is faster than another is meaningless unless the transactions run on both are somehow comparable and compared using that measure.
4. **Prioritize the questions** with the stakeholders. Plan and specify the tests. Agree on a reporting protocol.
5. **Identify the test environment**(s) **and resources** required. Ensure it is loaded like the "real thing" with similar levels of background tasks.
6. **Code and prepare the tests.** Run several trials to check that the results are repeatable and conclusive.
7. **Define the loads** and validate them.
8. **Run the tests** and analyze the results. Look for counterintuitive results. Thus it was only when several tests were run that we discovered that a 100 MB Ethernet network was running slower than a 10 MB Ethernet network. (100 MB switches can perform better than 100 MB hubs.)
9. **Report the results** such that the stakeholders can take action.

# Case Study: The Awkward Measure

W hen defining measures there may be a conflict between what is useful and what is true. Here's an example (see section A.8 in Appendix A for background).

The BizRools system is a workflow application generator. It can create very simple or insanely complex applications. Its speed is partly dependent on its engine. The engine accepts engine transactions and does something with them depending on the BizRools coded in them. It is very simple to measure how many BizRools the engine processes in a second.

Unfortunately neither users nor salesmen nor analysts ever *see* an engine transaction. They see screen forms. Some of these screen forms have lots of pull-down fields. These are very slow to draw and require many engine transactions. A screen with a single button on it takes only one. **Problem:** get all stakeholders to agree on a common measure in an uncommon world.

**Solution:**

- Get a selection of 60 screen forms from a number of applications which all stakeholders agree are typical.
- Get the stakeholders to sort them into big, small, and medium sets.
- Eliminate from each set any which have not been chosen by all stakeholders.
- Create a profile of all screen elements giving the average and standard deviations of all the screen elements of each set.
- Create applications involving screens conforming to the profile and run them. Measure the engine transactions of each screen.
- Use the method shown above to identify the critical factors involved and the weight to be accorded each.
- Execute the screens in a representative manner.

10. **Tune the system** (and repeat from step 7 if necessary).
11. Decide on a new set of questions.

See Figure 16.2.

## 16.7 Stress Testing

The purposes of stress testing are to discover:

- At what load point the system fails
- How much warning the system gives before failing
- What happens when it does fail (what was the cause? memory leak? resource loss?)
- How long it takes to get it working again
- Whether it can restart by itself[1]

Stress testing requires that you:

- Create a set of known loads
- Subject the system to them
- Monitor the results

See Figure A.43 in Appendix A for an example of a system which was severely stressed and shed load.

---

[1] Not strictly-speaking a performance-testing issue but it's during performance testing that you will find out if there's a problem.

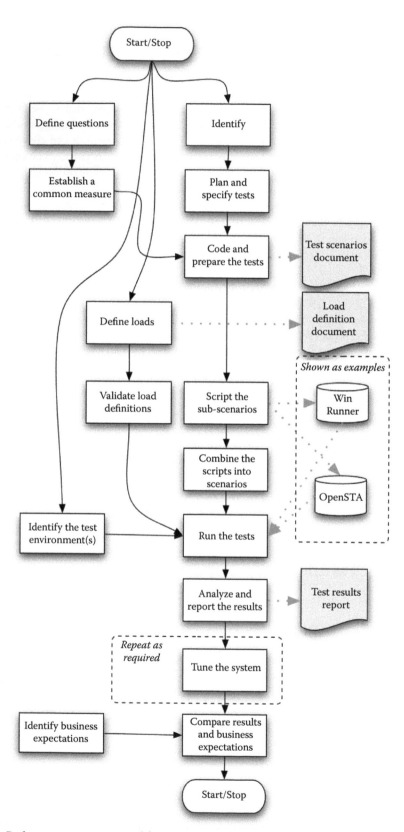

**FIGURE 16.2**  Performance test process model

# 16.8   Reliability Testing

The purpose of reliability testing is to see:

- How reliable the system is when stressed (how long is the MTBF?)
- What hidden problems does a period of extended load throw up

Accordingly you need first to discover at what stress point the system begins to fail. This will be evident either because the system collapses completely, begins to shed load (for example: many transactions are simply dropped from the queue), or the response time begins to rise exponentially. That point, for that system configuration, is the maximum stress point.

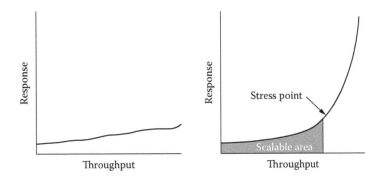

**FIGURE 16.3**   Relationship between response time and throughput

Reliability testing:

- Is similar to load testing except that reliability testing tests systems at the limit whereas load testing simply subjects them to a statistically-representative load to see if the system can cope with it
- Requires
  - Some estimation involving a clock to determine:
    - How many errors have occurred in some interval
    - What is the average interval between the errors
  - A test harness capable of executing a very large number of tests in a short space of time to give the output any statistical relevance

See [Lyu] for more on software reliability. See section D.16 in Appendix D for details of tools. See [Wagner] for a discussion on the use of SMERFS. See also section 18.6.

# 17

# Usability Test Process

If you want some good books on usability read [Norman], [Nielsen 1], [Nielsen 2], [Dix], or [Stanton]. If you want a specialized book on usability testing read [Dumas]. If you want to manage usability testing read on.

## 17.1   Why We Should Usability Test

Everybody now realizes the value of usability testing. Yeah yeah. But when they do, here's why. We usability test to:

- Act as a meeting point between the users, the developers, and the usability (HF/HCI) staff
- Clarify notions of usability with respect to this product (to feedback to developers early)
- Discover what use is being made of the system now
- Reduce the cost of support (one useful driver is the cost of each problem per user/month)
- Find out what objectives the users currently have (and how the availability of the system may change them)
- Minimize the possibility that users will simply refuse to use the system (Aka *acquiring competitive edge*)
- Prioritize system testing better
- See what performance means to users
- Provide training feedback
- Create a database of usability attributes against which you can judge future releases

## 17.2   When Should We Usability Test?

Early usability testing requires some form of representation of the final product (usually in the form of a model or prototype) and relies on modeling or rapid prototyping techniques/tools. This could indicate usability problems associated with a particular set of requirements.

Late usability testing requires the completed product.

# Story

There was once a meeting in a Very Big Organization where the Users had Clout. One of the users had filed a lot of bug reports about how the (in-house-developed) system was unusable. There were more than 30 such bug reports, and they were all true. And one by one the project management (who oddly did not have the same level of clout as the user) decided that these bugs were too low a level even to be considered for fixing.

"Gentlemen," said the user, "you have just effectively rejected 30 bugs. Doesn't it occur to you that, put together, they constitute one very large bug with the headline *This System Is Unusable?*" And the test manager (who should have seen this) hung his head in shame that he had said it not. And lo, the system was never fielded (but for other reasons, having to do with it not working), and the test manager kept this story close to his heart. Until today.

## 17.3   What Is the Baseline for UI Tests?

The UI question *"Can someone use this?"* requires that you decompose the question into subquestions. The subquestions are:

"What is this?" (user guide, introductory course, and version xyz of the system)
"Who is someone?" (naïve user, trained user, experienced user, administrator)
"What do we mean by use?" (install the system, start the system up, process some inputs, close the system down, uninstall the system)

By decomposing the usability questions you can thus arrive at such test objectives as:

Given a user guide and the introductory course, can a(n) { naïve user | trained user | experienced user | administrator | ... } { install | uninstall } the system using UI version xyz, and complete task X in 10 minutes making only *n* mistakes?

This test can then be further decomposed into test objectives covering system installation and uninstallation and the various tasks and varieties of valid and invalid inputs. Hopefully, there is a UI specification or guideline against which you can work. If not look at section B.12.2 in Appendix B.

## 17.4   How to Usability Test

Usability testing can range from simple heuristic evaluation to a full usability test in a lab. Both are discussed below. In addition it is usual for HCI specialists to conduct informal sessions showing card-based mock-ups to potential users.

### 17.4.1   Inputs

The inputs to usability testing should consist of:

- The requirements specification (this should specify the usability goals [see section B.12.2 in Appendix B])
- A task analysis of each role in the system (see section 17.6)
- Case studies and customer visit reports
- User diaries
- Use-case scenarios
- Prototype interfaces (can be card models)

### 17.4.2   Heuristic Evaluation

Heuristic evaluation is very similar to a peer review:

- Select some evaluators. These are clever folks, often with a degree in psychology, who ask odd questions and then make surprisingly acute observations about systems.
- Have the evaluators compare the user interface to current good practice.[1]

---
[1] No, there are no absolutes. Current "good practice" is still a good way of identifying what's not working well.

- Ask one or more evaluators (who can be real users, HF experts, or a focus group) to follow scripted scenarios or use checklists. See [Veenendaal] for an example.
- Raise bug reports of poor usability, frustrations, etc.
- Convene a meeting to review the issues raised and discuss possible improvements.
- Have users attempt to use a documentation-free product, and try to identify where some document would have been useful such that the documents to be written are minimal and essential. Use a Subject Matter Expert (SME) sparingly to provide essential input.

You may find that developers and HCI specialists will run such reviews very early on. Variations of this approach are called *participatory design, focus group research, pencil-and-paper evaluations, design walk-throughs, structured walkthroughs, expert evaluations*, and *usability audits*.

Tests may also involve favored customers having two users attempt a task on a single computer, talking as they do so, or having trusted users complete user diaries or a field questionnaire.

## 17.4.3   Exploration Phase (Figure 17.1)

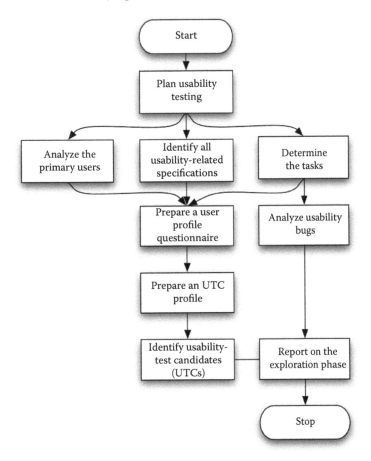

**FIGURE 17.1**   Exploration phase process

- **Plan usability testing.** What are the big questions to be answered? Prioritize them. Review the scenarios against the questions.
- **Analyze the primary users** of the system by number and frequency of use, and build a set of user profiles.
- **Identify** all usability-related **specifications.**

- **Determine the tasks** to be tested. These should be *most-frequently-used, critical* or *high risk,* and *complex.*
- Using this overall assessment prepare and **distribute a user profile** questionnaire to existing users to determine:
  - What their overall working objectives are with respect to the proposed system
  - What their use scenarios are, and how these scenarios relate to the objectives and are patterned over time
  - What time or performance constraints they work under
  - What their major triggers and interrupts are
  - What systems they currently have available
  - What features of these systems they use the most
  - What they think of each proposed feature (use Lickert scales: 0 < 4, terrible < marvelous)
- **Prepare a Usability Test Candidate** (UTC) **profile** and identify the number of UTCs.
- **Identify UTCs** among the staff or general public. Ensure that you include some particularly unable people. If necessary pre-test them with an IQ test. Note that there is some dispute about the minimal number required. For non-web usability testing 5 candidates were long believed to be sufficient ([Nielsen 3], [Virzi], and [Lewis]), however [Barnum] cited research that more than 10 users are preferable.
- **Analyze** any current outstanding usability **bugs:**
  - As far as possible identify duplicate bugs
  - Build a bug profile in descending order of duplication
  - Map the most duplicated (= most-frequently-occurring) bug against the scenarios
  - Identify the most-problematic scenarios
  - Validate the allegedly most-problematic scenarios with the usability-test-candidate staff
  - Identify possible usability metrics
- **Report** on the Exploration phase.

## 17.4.4   Inception Phase (Figure 17.2)

- **Update** the usability test plan.
- **Recruit the UTCs** (you may need more than you thought — they may not all be available. You may need a week just to find 10.) This will involve:
  - Defining a user profile
  - Ensuring its statistical relevance
  - Determining if any reward or honorarium is required
  - Preparing an UTC screening questionnaire
  - Preparing an UTC product assessment questionnaire (see [Veenendaal] for an example)
  - Advertising for UTCs
  - Interviewing them, screening them, grading them, and dealing with the excluded
  - Training them in the product as users would be
  - Scheduling their presence in the testing environment
- **Define a usability test environment** (PC in a room with an observer, PC with a two-way mirror, CCTV, webex, user manuals, user instructions, playback software, screen capture software). Make sure you have serious hard disk space available since the captured data will possibly take up terabytes).
- From the use profile questionnaires and interviews with users, **identify** a number of **scenarios** incorporating the major features of the system, the key features of the new release, and validate them with the UTCs.
- **Build a matrix of user/work scenarios** covering the tasks. Break the tasks into logical steps and define each in terms of what to do (create a new item with the name "New item"), avoiding system-specific terms. Include in each task a definition of what a functional failure would be, such that an observer can identify it unambiguously.

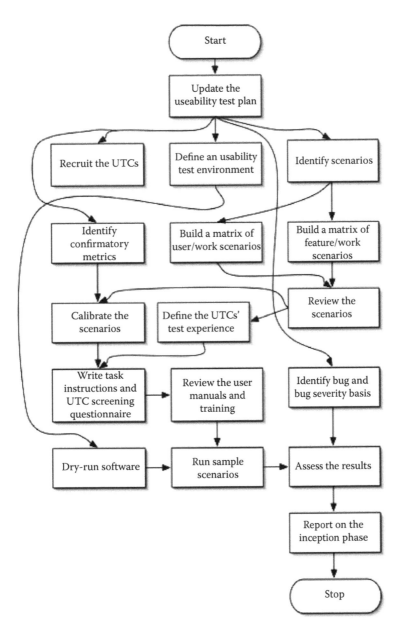

**FIGURE 17.2** Inception phase process

- **Build a matrix of feature/work scenarios** (essentially the same as the *Task/objective matrix example* in section 15.10.10 by mapping the current features of the system against the scenarios.
- **Review the scenarios** for clarity and relevance (use the *Usability checklist* in section B.12 in Appendix B).
- **Identify some source of confirmatory metrics** (perhaps system use logs) to compare and report on alleged and actual use over some period. See section 18.5.
- **Calibrate the scenarios** using expert users (possibly drawn from the training and testing staff to find the best possible execution time. A novice will need between four and six times the length of time of an expert. When you have calibrated your tests check that the probable elapsed time of the real tests with novices is in that proportion. This will give you your expert task time metric to determine the product ease-of-use metric (see Chapter 18).

- **Define the UTCs' test experience** as a process. This may be a simple memo or a more complex model. You need to know what the UTCs will experience from the moment they walk into the building to the moment they leave. Otherwise UTCs may be:
  - Insufficiently prepared
  - Unamenable to return for follow-up (is it too long?)
  - The experience may be too unrealistic to be useful)
- **Write** UTC and observer **task instructions,** and validate them with the users, training staff, and the usability guru. If necessary write a UTC screening questionnaire to exclude participants who are too knowledgeable, clever, or the reverse.
- **Review the user manuals and training** expected to be ready for the start of the tests.
- **Identify the basis on which a fault can be defined**:
  - *"X takes 'too' long."*
  - *"I can't find the X."*
  - *"I don't know what I'm supposed to do now."*
  - *"Why doesn't it do X?"*
  - *"I can't do X."*
  - *"What does that mean?"* (often of some ill-composed message).
  
  See section C.5 in Appendix C.
- **Identify the basis for determining the severity of a usability bug.** This is quite critical: while bugs are normally defined in terms of *"it doesn't work,"* usability bugs need to be defined in terms of *"it doesn't work for me."* Management may then say that the HCI people are *"crying wolf."*
- **Dry-run the test capture-playback** and any other software with some pseudo-UTCs.
- **Run a sample set of scenarios** with the pseudo-UTCs.
- **Assess the results:**
  - Which user goals were not met?
  - Which tests can we eliminate?
  - Were the users representative?
  - Which provoked cognitive overload?
  - What questions do we need to ask before and after the tests?
  - Has the user profile changed?
  - Does any part of the test environment impede testing?
  
  And modify the scenarios and materials as required.
- **Report** on the Inception phase.

## 17.4.5  Execution Phase (Figure 17.3)

- **Identify and prepare the environment:**
  - Room: needs to be either pleasantly neutral — flowers, nice pictures on the wall, or as similar as possible to the work environment. It needs to be booked to allow for overruns.
  - Equipment: ensure that each UTC has as much space as required to read and work with, and that the PC (or whatever) is of an identical specification to that used in the field.
  - Staff: ensure that the observers and test administrator are trained, and that UTCs are subject to as little stress as possible (unless having stressed UTCs is essential for the test). Ensure there is access to developers should some issue require extra help.
  - UTCs: confirm their status (selected, rejected, retain for later consideration). Get the signed non-disclosure agreements. Send those selected a confirmatory pack.
- **Run the tests:**
  - Decide the priorities: frequency of task execution, criticality of the task (to the user), feature instability,[2] feature readiness (when things are getting very rough).

---

[2] A lousy reason for inflicting a fragile user interface on the poor UTCs but sometimes developers need to know.

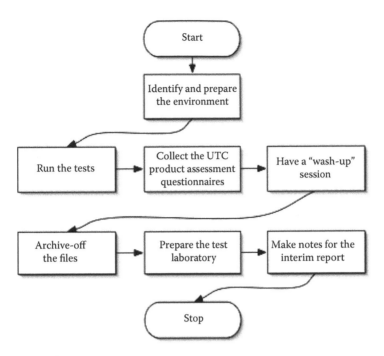

**FIGURE 17.3**  Execution phase process

- Greet the UTCs.[3]
- Train the UTCs both in the product and in thinking aloud. (*Demonstrate this to the UTCs.*) Clarify what testing is for, what a bug is, and how bugs are identified and assessed. Ensure that the UTCs realize they are valued participants and that their value lies in the fact that *they don't know.*
- Answer their questions. Ensure that they realize it is the product which is being tested, not them, and that the more problems they bring up, the more you will learn (and be grateful). Ensure that they feel useful and wanted. Ensure that they know they can leave at any time — at the cost of only receiving a partial fee.
- Synchronize the videotapes and any capture-replay software.
- Distribute the task instructions. Ensure they are all different such that no UTC can judge their speed relative to the others.
- Run the scenarios.
- Record the bugs.
- Collect the UTC product assessment questionnaires.
- Have a "wash-up" session to collect UTC's views. Get key quotations for the final report. Thank the UTCs.
- **Archive-off** the video and any keyboard and screen copying files.
- **Prepare the test laboratory for the next session.**
- **Make notes** for the interim report.

## 17.4.6   Evaluation Phase (Figure 17.4)

- **Triage the problems** encountered to remove duplicates (and count the number of duplicates).

---

[3] More than one UTC at a time? With directional microphones and enough observers this is feasible and you'll get results faster. The background hubbub may soothe the users slightly and need not intrude. Minimize distraction by having each user seated facing a different wall.

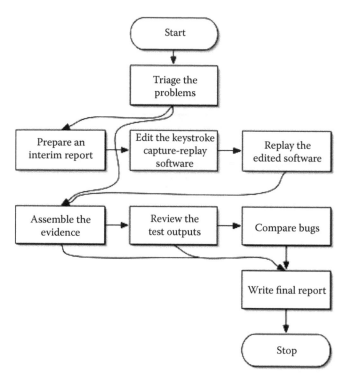

**FIGURE 17.4**  Evaluation phase process

- **Prepare an interim report** for immediate feedback to developers and management.
- **Edit** the keystroke capture-replay software, screen capture software, and videotapes to show only those **scenarios** in which users experienced difficulties (get this from the session protocol). Listen for more key quotations.
- **Replay the edited software** (possibly with the original users present so the human factors' experts can question them).
- **Assemble the evidence of the problems** from the sessions and combine them with the UTC product assessment questionnaires and the triaged bugs. Use section 18.15 in Chapter 18 to correlate the scores so that you can relate overall (dis)satisfaction to its primary causes.
- Have the HCI staff **review the test outputs** and identify any further bugs. Enter them on the main bug management database.
- **Compare** any newly-found **bugs** against those found by testers. Is there a trend? Which features are the most difficult?
- **Write a final report** giving full details. Possibly include a highlight videotape. This should cover test design, execution, and results. The usability plan can be included as an appendix.

## 17.5  Readability Indices

There are lots of readability indices.

### 17.5.1  Gunning Fog Index

The Gunning Fog index is designed to show the number of years of education required to read some text:

> Gunning Fog index = (average # of words/sentence + percentage of words of three
> or more syllables) * 0.4

This formula implies that short sentences written in plain English achieve a better score than longer and more-complex sentences.

Thus, *The New York Times* has an average Fog index of 11–12, *Time* magazine is about 11. Technical documentation typically is between 10 and 15, and professional prose rarely exceeds 18. The BBC News website is around 9.

## 17.5.2   Flesch–Kincaid Index

$$\text{Flesch–Kincaid index} = 0.39 * \text{average \# of words per sentence} + 11.8 * \text{average \# of syllables per word} - 15.59$$

The BBC News website is about 6.

## 17.5.3   Flesch Reading Ease Index

$$\text{Flesch Reading Ease index} = 206.835 - 1.015 * \text{average \# words per sentence} (84.6 * \text{\# of syllables per word})$$

High scores are good. Anything below 50 implies limited readability. The BBC News website is about 57.

## 17.5.4   Lexical Density Test

$$\text{Lexical Density index} = 100 * (\text{\# of different words / total \# of words})$$

The lexical density of a text tries to measure the proportion of the content (lexical) words over the total words. Texts with a lower density are more easily understood.

As a guide, lexically dense text has a lexical density of around 60–70% and those which are not dense have a lower lexical density measure of around 40–50%.

## 17.5.5   Passive Index

$$\text{Passive index} = 100 * (\text{\# of sentences containing passive verbs / \# of sentences})$$

See juicystudio.com/services/readability.php#readresults for a quick calculator.

# 17.6   Task Analysis

## 17.6.1   Summary

Task analysis identifies what a user must do to achieve a task in terms of actions and/or cognitive processes. It is conducted to understand an existing pattern of work and the information flows within it. These information flows are important to defining the requirements of any new system by mapping (parts of) a task to one or more features.

## 17.6.2   Method

Task analysis requires that the analysts meet the users (much as in systems analysis) and ask them for details of their work. They then decompose the task definitions into their constituent subtasks. This will show an overall structure of the main user tasks.

To decompose a task, ask "*how is this task done?*" If a subtask is identified at a lower level, we can build up the structure by asking "*why is this done?*" The task decomposition can be carried out using the following stages:

- Identify the task to be analyzed.
- Break this down into between 4 and 8 subtasks, specified in terms of objectives.
- Draw the subtasks as a layered diagram.
- Decide upon the level of detail into which to decompose in terms of decision processes, rationale, screen layouts, metrics, and constraints. Add a narrative to the document.
- Have someone uninvolved in the analysis review it for consistency and sufficiency.

See [Hackos], [Kirwan], and [Preece] for more on this.

### 17.6.3   Hierarchical Task Analysis

Some human factors analysts find it useful to classify tasks (as decomposed) according to psychological theories. One which is particularly cited is that of [Gagné]. In this the decomposition levels may be related to the following:

- **Motor skills** are bodily movements involving muscular activity such as starting a car, shooting a target, swinging a golf club, or hitting a key.
- **Attitude** affects an individual's choice of action toward some object, person, or event such as visiting a museum or writing a letter.
- **Verbal information:**
  - Labels and facts define names or are used in a response to some input. The response may be naming or citing a (set of) fact(s). Examples: identifying objects, people, or events, or recalling a person's birthday or hobbies.
  - Bodies of knowledge refers a body of related facts such as the meaning of a text or a rule or regulation.
- **Cognitive strategy** (metathinking) is an internal process by which the learner controls his ways of thinking and learning, such as engaging in self-testing to decide how much study is needed; knowing what sorts of questions to ask to best define a domain of knowledge and the ability to form a mental model of the problem.
- **Intellectual skills** include:
  - Discrimination: to make different responses to the different members of a particular class. This is critical to (for example) reading a gauge correctly.
  - Abstraction: the ability to classify all members of a particular class according to some common denominator. Thus *canoe, bus, train,* and *car* are all examples of the abstract concept *transport.*
  - Rule using: applying a rule to a given situation or condition by responding to a class of inputs with a class of actions.
  - Problem solving: combining rules to solve problems in a new situation.

By so relating tasks it is easier for a psychologist to determine the level of difficulty a task may pose the user and the level of help or prompts a user might need.

## 17.7   Who Is Involved in Usability Testing?

### 17.7.1   Test Users (Aka UTCs)

The test users sit at the computer and perform the scenarios. They should ideally be the target end users or people with similar backgrounds. If you have enough test users you might pair them to encourage them to speak aloud during the tests. In this case, choose pairs with similar levels of experience. Ensure that they realize that the more problems they encounter and talk about, the better. Successfully completing a scenario doesn't help you much.

### 17.7.2  Administrator

The administrator runs the usability test users. The administrator should appear neutral. The administrator greets the UTCs, lists the "rules" of the testing process, gives the scenarios to the test users, and encourages them to "*think aloud*," preferably by demonstrating how to "think aloud" himself.

The administrator never helps or guides test users except when they reach an impasse. In this case, once the associated usability problem has been observed, the administrator can explain how the software failed, how to complete the task, possibly reset the machine, and then instruct the test users to move on to the next task.

On rare occasions the administrator will call for technical help. The administrator should monitor the UTCs and observers for signs of UTCs in difficulty, and may ask questions to keep them "*thinking out loud*" such as "*Is this what you were expecting? What are you looking for?*" or "*What do you think the application is telling you?*"

### 17.7.3  Observers

The observers watch the test users as they perform the scenarios and note where the test users experience difficulty. Ensure the observers remain silent and expressionless, if sympathetic and interested, throughout the test. They should never even hint that the UTC's ability is being judged. Observers should indicate to the administrator when intervention is needed. Observers are particularly concerned to note:

- Where the test user got misled
- Where the test user need to know something that he couldn't possibly have known
- Where the test user succeeded
- Where the test user noticed when he made a mistake, whether he recovered, and if the mistake could have been prevented

Observers should note these moments possibly using a simple code in their notes (they use the pre-printed assessment notes). They are probably HF experts.

### 17.7.4  Recorder

The recorder observes the test user and records the metrics. Thus if one of the metrics is user task time (see section 18.5), the recorder would have a stopwatch. Like the observer, the recorder should remain silent and expressionless throughout the test. The recorder can be supplanted by capture-replay software and a camcorder.

## 17.8  How Will We Know if We've Usability-Tested Successfully?

1. When you have accounted for two issues:
   a. Speed of execution
   b. User mistakes
   Any human factors expert will point to a host of other metrics involved in human factors' analysis. They are right, but if you haven't assessed the speed at which users can work and the number of mistakes they make, all else is pointless.

   Having said that, focusing solely on speed and mistakes in assessing usability would be like focusing on the speed of the fastest car and the number of crashes as the only factors to be considered in assessing a formula-1 car's design.

   The centrality of these two issues can be judged from the fact that excluding them would clearly render the entire usability assessment pointless. Given enough PhDs and enough time, even the daftest user interface can be negotiated.
2. When you have accounted for all the questions you needed to ask.
3. When an HF bug is treated as something to be fixed and when developers are sensitive to the threat implied by a lot of small bugs.
4. When your customers:
   a. Stay on your website beyond the home page

b. Register
c. Repeatedly return to your website
d. Reduce calls to your helpline and Support desk
5. When your training time reduces.
6. When your website page views increase.

## 17.9   What It'll Cost Us to Usability Test

Table 17.1 is an example drawn from experience with a 110,000-line system.

**TABLE 17.1**   Cost of usability testing example

| | |
|---|---|
| **Heuristic evaluation** | |
| Heuristic evaluation (two HF experts * five days @ $500 per person per day) | 5000 |
| Heuristic evaluation (five users * one day @ $320 per person per day) | 1600 |
| **Exploration phase** | |
| Plan usability testing | 500 |
| Analyze the primary users | 1000 |
| Identify all usability-related specifications | 100 |
| Determine the tasks | 3000 |
| Prepare and distribute a user profile questionnaire to existing users | 1500 |
| Prepare a UTC profile and identify the number of UTCs | 500 |
| Identify usability-test candidates | 100 |
| Analyze any current outstanding usability bugs | 400 |
| Report on the Exploration phase | 500 |
| **Inception phase** | |
| Update the usability test plan | 250 |
| Recruit the UTCs | 1500 |
| Define a usability test environment | 750 |
| Identify a number of scenarios and validate them with the UTCs | 2500 |
| Build a matrix of user/work scenarios | 250 |
| Build a matrix of feature/work scenarios | 250 |
| Review the scenarios | 1920 |
| Identify some source of confirmatory metrics | 500 |
| Calibrate the scenarios | 2640 |
| Define the UTCs' test experience | 125 |
| Write UTC and observer task instructions, and validate them with the users, training staff, and the usability guru. If necessary write UTC screening questionnaire | 1920 |
| Review the user manuals and training | 1000 |
| Identify the basis on which a fault can be defined | 200 |
| Identify the basis for determining the severity of a usability bug | 200 |
| Dry-run the test capture-playback and any other software with some pseudo-UTCs | 330 |
| Run a sample set of scenarios with the pseudo-UTCs | 1320 |
| Assess the results | 200 |
| **Execution phase** | |
| Identify and prepare the environment | 1000 |
| Run the tests | 12700 |
| **Evaluation phase** | |
| Triage the problems | 533 |
| Prepare an interim report | 500 |
| Edit the software | 1000 |
| Replay the edited software | 2540 |
| Assemble the evidence of the problems | 500 |
| Have the HCI staff review the test outputs and identify all bugs | 1000 |
| Compare the newly-found bugs against those found by testers | 250 |
| Write a final report giving full details | 1000 |
| Total | 51078 |

# 17.10   Why We Shouldn't Usability Test

- When the user interface is too small to pose a risk.
- When the RoI of a usability test is too small.

Table 17.2 is an example of an RoI calculation of a usability test. Thus the RoI = (412,500 − 62190) / 62190 = 563%.

**TABLE 17.2**  RoI on usability calculation

| Action | Gain | Loss |
|---|---|---|
| We do the test and discover five problems. Each would cost a user one minute per day. | | |
| We fix the five problems during the prototype stage and we will save the users an average of one minute per day per problem. The cost of fixing is $500 per problem. | | $2500 |
| (500 users use this software * five minutes * 220 days a year) / 60. | 9,167 hours per annum | |
| Each user costs $15 per hour. | $137,500 | |
| Assume a product life of three years. | $412,500 | |
| Deduct the cost of the usability tests. | | $51,078 |
| Deduct the cost of the usability test environment. | | $3,000 |
| Deduct the simple interest on usability testing (5% per year for three years). | | $8,112 |
| Totals | $412,500 | $62,190 |

[Weinschenk] proposes a useful table to clarify management thinking. Table 17.3 is an example. See also [Schaffer].

**TABLE 17.3**  Usability RoI calculation

| Product | Problem | Result | Cost of not fixing | Usability fix to apply | RoI |
|---|---|---|---|---|---|
| Website | High click-out (90% of users never progress beyond the page they access first) | Low sales | $2.7m p.a. | Redesign the site and test for navigability, $120,000 | 96% |

# 17.11   Usability-Testing Deliverables

You need to know what you're getting for your money and what can be reused. These deliverables can be picked over by a lot of people:

- Usability test plan covering the phases: *Exploration, Inception, Execution,* and *Evaluation.* This should follow the format of the test plan as shown in section 8.5 in Chapter 8.
- Scenario test materials:
  - A script for the administrator. This supports a consistent presentation from one participant to the next, and limits fatigue. This is based on the UTC experience process model.
  - Logistics notes for the administrator help keep track of details about the environment or the order of activities to ensure consistency:
    - Sufficient videotapes and audiotapes
    - Checklists of how to reset the equipment and environment between participants
    - Copies of all reference documentation
    - One set of test materials (per participant, for the administrator and for each observer)
    - Copies of background questionnaires, non-disclosure forms, and videotape release forms
  - Pre-printed assessment notes (such as questions with check-boxes or lists of key issues to observe) simplify recording test results data and ensure that key issues are noted consistently.

- Product assessment questionnaires to give to the participant to elicit participant opinions.
- A handout or videotape instructing participants on how to *"think aloud."* It is useful for later analysis for users to announce out loud that they are about to *"create a file"* or *"run scenario 23.2"* such that this can be picked up on tape. When users say out loud that they are having difficulties and announce that they have failed to achieve something, it makes videotape editing much easier. Alternatively the administrator can intervene and ensure that the problems are recorded.
- Task instructions, pictures of objects to be identified, and lists of items to rank or rate. These are derived from the usability test specification.
- UTC screening questionnaire which asks for the same information collected during oral screening, to verify participant characteristics.
- Non-disclosure form and videotape release forms (check with your legal department if you videotape participants' faces)
- Confirmation pack for UTCs (thank-you letter, manuals, handouts, joining instructions, schedule)
- Exploration phase plan
- User profiles
- Completed UTC screening questionnaires
- Bug analysis
- Work scenarios (with mapped bugs)
- Matrix of user/work scenarios
- Matrix of feature/work scenarios
- UTC/staff list
- Exploration phase report
- Usability test specification
- Edited videotape, playback software, and screen record output
- Final report

## 17.12 Usability Test Specification

This is derived from:

- Work scenarios (with mapped bugs)
- Matrix of user/work scenario
- Matrix of feature/work scenario
- Product specifications
- User profile questionnaires

and should specify:

- Goals
- Context (who, doing what, under what circumstances)
- Work rate criteria (worst case, planned level, best case, now level), sometimes expressed as a percentage of existing or competitive products
- Measurement method (metric, data collection technique setting)
- Result (file created, patient heart rate being monitored, train route set)
- Ease of learning (see section 18.5.16 in Chapter 18):
  - Within a given exposure time
  - After a given level of training
  - On reusing the system after a given lapse of time
- Ease of use:
  - The time to complete the task
  - The number of times a user refers to "help" or a manual
  - A number of "misunderstandings"

**TABLE 17.4** Usability specification

| | Context | | | Performance criteria | | | | | Measurement method | | |
|---|---|---|---|---|---|---|---|---|---|---|---|
| Result | Who | Doing what | Under what circumstances | Worst case | Planned level | Best case | New level variables | Metric | Data collection technique | What and where |
| Improved installation time | Service engineer | Installing system | At customer site | 1 day without media | 1 hour without media | 10 minutes without media | Many can't install | Time to correctly install | Observation (checklist, timing device) | Laboratory and field |
| Newsbreak creation and sending | Journalist | Using news system | At newsdesk with feeds | 3 minutes | 45 seconds | 30 seconds | Level of interruptions | Time to create and send newsbreak | Keyboard buffer monitor | Test system with live feeds |
| Patient heart monitor set up | Nursing technician | Using ECG machine | Accident and emergency area | 5 minutes | 60 seconds | 120 seconds | Training of technician, noise, and confusion | Time from moment the ECG unit is beside the bed to the moment the trace is visible and valid | CCTV | Simulated A&E environment |

- Usefulness
- The number of commands the user should use
- The *productivity* or *work rate* (see section 18.5.5)
- The level of reliability
- Attractiveness metric (see section 18.5.17)

On the previous page is a sample row from a usability specification table (Table 17.4).

## 17.13   Usability Test Warnings

- If you haven't analyzed the tasks (see section 17.6) you are immediately running into trouble. The only basis for scenario development will then be use-case scenarios and these will lack critical metric and other data.
- Establish the seriousness of HCI bugs early on or you'll have arguments and later attempts to foist a poor or unusable interface onto reluctant users.
- Getting UTCs is non-trivial. Allow lots of time and keep in contact with them regularly before the test (or they may not turn up).
- Don't try to run tests for more than 6 hours a day. No individual session should last more than 2 hours with a 15-minute break thereafter. The administrators will be exhausted even if the UTCs aren't. Ensure all participants know where the lavatory is, and keep them well supplied with drinks and biscuits.
- Don't let developers or management ruin the relevance of the tests by adding newly-developed features to the release at the last moment.
- Don't give staff or UTCs access to the main bug management database but if necessary create a second one to simplify triage.
- 1 in 6 UTCs may not come.
- Know how to reset the system if it crashes.
- Ensure that users know that the more difficulties they have, the more they are helping you. Make every effort to alleviate any sense of guilt that they are failing to achieve some outcome. Treat every problem they have as an interesting event.

See also [Kantner] and section D.14 in Appendix D.

# 18

# Metrics

*The quality of a swordsmith is measured by the longevity of his customers.*

**—Fred Brooks, *The Computer Scientist as Toolsmith***

Metrics are ways of answering questions. Without knowing the question they are there to answer, they are a waste of time. To determine the metrics you need for any project, work top-down:

- Define the goals (business and technical). What are we trying to do? (Example: build a better mousetrap.)
- Define the questions (which in turn clarify the goals). What do we mean by "*better mousetrap*"? (Example answer: requiring, designing, constructing, testing, and deploying a mousetrap.)
- Define the metrics which allow us to determine the answers to the questions. (Example "How do we build a better mousetrap?" can be extended to "*How long does it take us to build a mousetrap? How much material does it cost to build a mousetrap? Does anyone build a mousetrap faster? Given n mice in a house, how many can the mousetrap be expected to catch in a 24-hour period?*")

See [Basili 84] and [Offutt] for more on this.

As a test manager you typically need to be able to predict:

- How many bugs exist in a release (see section 18.10).
- How much it costs on average to fix a bug. (You need to have all programmers filling in time sheets with separate codes for hours spent bug-fixing, designing, etc.)
- What proportion of bugs will be Priority 1, 2, 3, etc.
- How many bugs it is reasonable to leave in a release. (None? When you find life on Jupiter boring, try planet Earth for a while There have always been bugs found in the field. Look at the figures for the last three releases you made. None were found in the field? D'you believe that?)
- When you are likely to have finished testing. (Once you have established how many bugs you expect to find, then you can estimate how many you will find each day. You can get rough estimates of that from the last time(s) you ran a system test.)
- How much of the code have you exercised? There are tools you can use to instrument your code-instrumentation tool; see Appendix D.

You will also need to get answers to a lot of other questions which could involve many of the metrics in this chapter.

## 18.1  Functionality Metrics

### 18.1.1  Interoperability Metrics

Interoperability has come into its own as a result of:

- The military realizing that their systems didn't interoperate in the field as they had back at base.

- An embarrassing series of hiccups as various business mergers, toasted at many dinners with much fine wine, fell apart as the terrible truth dawned that the systems used by the merging companies couldn't be merged.
- The realization on the part of accountants, investment analysts, and other good folks charged with due diligence that they could no longer declare a total ignorance of software and expect to get away with it.

All these folks need a process for determining interoperability. Here are the latest:

- [LISI] (Levels of Information Systems Interoperability) is a set of models and associated processes developed by the U.S. DoD C4ISR Working Group in 1998 for assessing information systems' capabilities and implementation in context with the degree of interoperability required. It is supported by the Carnegie-Mellon Software Engineering Institute.
- [NC3TA] (NATO C3 Technical Architecture) is a similar structure to LISI, but developed by NATO.

See [Tolk] for ways of comparing these systems and a number of test issues.

## 18.1.2   Problems of Interoperability: Semantics

The advent of XML has exposed a number of problems in how we think of interoperability. Simply defining an XML model is, unhappily, insufficient: we also need to define the context in which it is used.

---

**Example of How Context Changes Meaning**

Data: the statement, "I'm going to kill you."
  **Context 1:** said by small, unarmed boy whom you recently prevented from assaulting his brother.
  **Context 2:** said by psychotic, martial arts expert, and amateur militiaman armed with a loaded AK-47.

---

In essence what matters is not simply *how* data is used in a system, but what it was intended to mean and the context it was intended to be used in when it was created (which we commonly call *semantics*). For a simple (but very expensive) example of data abuse (or *failure to preserve semantics*), see the story under *Terms Used* in the Glossary. Failure to preserve semantics lead to the re-emergence of some very old bug types:

- **Semantic conflicts:** the concepts of different local schemata do not match exactly, but must be aggregated or disaggregated. They may overlap or be subsets of each other, etc.
- **Descriptive conflicts:** there are homonyms, synonyms, different names for the same concept, different attributes, or slot values for the same concept, etc.
- **Heterogeneous conflicts:** the notations used to describe the concepts differ, thus one concept might be described in *UML* and the other in the SADT™.
- **Structural conflicts:** different structures are used to describe the same concept, thus in one local schema an attribute is used while in the other schema a reference to another concept is used to describe the same part of a view of "reality."

**Testing** is of limited value until such conflicts are resolved. Identifying that such conflicts exist may be a major problem, however. One approach is:

- Use a data dictionary to define data structure, meaning, and contexts of definition and use.
- Trace data from creation through use to destruction, look at how it is used, and what possible meaning is being derived from it.
- Compare the data's use to the dictionary definition.

This second approach follows the adage, *"Don't ask me what it means. Tell me how it's used, and I'll tell you what it means."*

## 18.1.3 Problems of Interoperability: Control and Ownership

In any relationship between at least two systems one must be able (at the very least) to sever relations with the other. One may thus be said to dominate or have control over another. This relationship can be expressed using deontic logic (see section A.3 in Appendix A). With very large systems composed of other systems these relations can become very complex. The circumstances under which system A may control system B may also vary. Thus a system for managing police radio communications may normally be under the control of the police. In the event of a terrorist attack, control may be ceded to some other organization consisting of government, military, and emergency services. Conditions for such a cession may involve a complex protocol which must be followed to ensure that the cession of control is complete and does not create more problems than it solves. Thus in the event of a terrorist attack ambulances carrying road accident victims should not be diverted from their current task until the victims have reached an accident and emergency center. However, should the attack involve poison gas, you don't want ambulances driving through gas clouds.

The control of some system may also be locality-related. A terrorist attack in Memphis should not necessarily affect the emergency services operation in Seattle.

Should a dominating system become incapacitated, it might be essential that controlled systems detach themselves from it and reconfigure themselves on the fly. Having such facilities presents great security issues since *rogue* systems might then be able to *go local*, control some area, and create chaos.

The effective cooperation of systems, like humans, requires a degree of altruism. One objective to be pursued when testing such systems is whether any part of the system, by being selfish, can disrupt the workings of the whole and whether completely selfless systems can ever cooperate (*"after you," "no, no, my dear chap, after you," "no, no, I insist"*).

If your system has its loci of control, and rules of control cession and acquisition defined using deontic logic, then you will be in a position to:

- Identify if any of rule is inconsistent with any another in any circumstance.
- Use the rules as test objectives to see if the system violates them at any moment.

Since the rules may exhibit combinatorial complexity, try using a logic-based tool such as Prover, Java rules, or Manageability as discussed in section D.4 in Appendix D.

## 18.1.4 Problems of Interoperability: Evolution

Regression testing of interoperable systems needs to account for:

- **Stability:** the more changed a system is, the less interoperable it is likely to be since its relation with other components or systems is more likely to be impaired.
- **Ownership:** the fewer the owners, the greater the probability of interoperability being maintained through evolution.
- **Relationships between systems:** the greater the interoperation relationships, the greater the coordination needed to maintain interoperability while evolving the system.

The LISI method as currently described remains unsatisfactory since there is no conclusive way to relate interoperability levels either over time or between systems. Each statement of interoperability of some set of systems still needs a standard defining and will need to be recalibrated as systems evolve. The approach remains useful as a way of structuring one's view of the problem. Interoperability continues to pose major problems for procurers and developers of systems alike. It remains a research area.

## 18.1.5   Accuracy Metrics

# Story

There was a government auditor in Africa who had to audit a government farm the size of a county. There were many cows on this farm. He told the manager he was going to count them. All of them. After a tactful silence, the manager said he would arrange to have all the herds (there were several) brought in one by one over the next week slowly so the cattle didn't lose too much weight. The auditor would be given a table, a sunshade, a supply of water, and a chair.

The next morning the auditor went forth. At the foot of a small hill he found the table, sunshade, water, chair, and a herdsman. He signaled that he was ready and the cattle were driven past, one at a time.

By lunchtime on the third day the auditor had counted over 250,000 head of cattle. This surprised him since the previous auditor had only tallied 110,000 some three years earlier, whereafter there had been a drought, several cattle sales, and the occasional rustling. Fecundity was one thing, but these cows were porn stars.

He decided to take a walk around the hill. Was it possible that the herdsmen were simply driving a small herd round and round it?

Accuracy implies that some figure is true + some percentage. In other words, the true figure exists within some limits. See section 18.10.4 for 2 measures of accuracy: *magnitude of relative error* (MRE) and *balanced relative error* (BRE). Note that *precision* is merely the means by which some measure is expressed. Thus 1/3 is more precise than 33.33333%.

## 18.1.6   Security Metrics

Security metrics focus on assets, threats, vulnerabilities, and defenses. There is currently no accepted set of metrics to use for any of these. What metrics there are, tend to fall into one of three groups:

1. **Interview-based metrics,** in which the Great and Good are asked about the assets they have to protect, the levels of threats, and the defenses they have in place.
2. **Process-related metrics,** in which responses to questionnaires are correlated and results derived.
3. **Artefact-related metrics,** which define attributes of assets, threats, and defenses, often in relation to some theory.

A number of metrics in use have been grouped under these headings. More can be derived from section B.11 in Appendix B.

See [Herzog] for details of the Risk Assessment Values approach. Security metrics remain a research area.

## 18.1.7   Accountability Metrics

"Accountability" is a vague term which is entirely task-dependent on its meaning. In essence it means that we are responsible (or "accountable") for our actions. Insofar as a system commits an action without direct human intervention, it is useful to be able to record this for later analysis. To this extent, accountability relates to the degree to which a relation can be traced between a person's (or a system's) action and its result.

**Example**

A train has crashed. Four sets of computers are involved:

- The train's computer
- The trackside computer
- The signaling computer
- The overall system monitoring computer

The accountability of each of these systems can be measured as:

1. The amount of **data** relating to the history of the decisions each took which is available (measure in MB or whatever)
2. **Time** taken to determine which actions it took (if this is a matter of reading and tracing through a lot of log files, then identify this as the time)
3. The **degree of control** it exercised (measure this as the total number of functions controlled/total number of system functions)
4. The **ease** with which each computer's contributions to the disaster can be determined (**data/time**)
5. The **potential for preventing** the disaster which the computer had (create a fault-tree diagram to show the controls and count the number of controls the system could have independently exerted on the event; repeat for the number of joint controls)

## 18.2 Testability

Testability can be considered the inverse of fault tolerance. Code which tolerates faults will not, by definition, exhibit them. Code may also be perfectly correct, yet rather difficult to test. Examples:

- COTS software (or any other) executables
- Assembler code
- Those parts of "C" which manipulate bits directly
- Code of so monolithic a nature that it is impossible to assure any useful degree of coverage

Software can be temporarily rendered more testable by including assertions in it.

See [Friedman], [Voas], and section 13.8 in Chapter 13 for discussions of how to (partly) solve this. [Friedman] suggests an approach to determining testability involving fault injection in three stages: *propagation, infection,* and *execution* (PIE). They depend on repeated executions of the software.

### 18.2.1 (Revised) Propagation Analysis Algorithm

This algorithm is to determine the propagation estimate of a variable in some code location. It is very expensive to create for large programs, but is a very powerful way of determining the testability of a program since the more variables which propagate errors, the more testable a program is.

1. Identify a testing distribution D
2. Let L = { all locations to be analyzed in the program }
3. For each $l$ in L set counter$_l$ = 0
4. Set the following constants: x1: = 10, x2: = 90, x3: = 900, t1: = 5, t2: = 10
5. Find x1 *test cases* according to D which exercise $l$
6. For each of the x1 *test cases*:
   a. Completely execute the program without any change and check the result
   b. Perturb the data state of a variable $a$ located after $l$, continue execution of the program, and check the result
   c. Increment counter$_l$ whenever the results from a and b differ

7. If $counter_l$ > t1, then
   a. L: = L – $l$
   b. $score_l$: = $counter_l$/x1
8. Repeat steps 5–7 for each $l$ in L
9. Find x2 cases according to D which exercise $l$ in L
10. For each of the x2 cases:
    a. Completely execute the program without any change and check the result
    b. Perturb the data state of a variable $a$ located after $l$, continue execution of the program, and check the result
    c. Increment $counter_l$ whenever the results from a and b differ
11. If $counter_l$ > t2, then
    a. L: = L – $l$
    b. $score_l$: = $counter_l$/(x1 + x2)
12. Repeat steps 9–11 for each $l$ in L
13. Find x3 cases according to D which exercise $l$ in L
14. For each of the x3 cases:
    a. Completely execute the program without any change and check the result
    b. Perturb the data state of a variable $a$ located after $l$, continue execution of the program, and check the result
    c. Increment $counter_l$ whenever the results from a and b differ
15. $score_l$: = $counter_l$/(x1 + x2 + x3)
16. Repeat steps 13–15 for each $l$ in L

The *propagation estimate* of $l$ is $score_l$.

## 18.2.2 Data Corruption

Data corruption requires that data be changed from the original. Data can be changed as follows:

- "Bit flipping," in which the binary representation of data is perturbed, possibly to produce all 0s and all 1s.
- Modifying existing data such that it is a function of the existing data (and thereby possibly conforms to the same grammar and is therefore a more-credible simulacrum of a programmer's error).
- Simply substituting a random string.
- Analyzing the variables being perturbed to see if they are "live." Primary candidates are those involved in LCSAJ decisions (see section 12.8). Note that in the event that the original data was "wrong" in the first place, the corrupted data might be correct.

## 18.2.3 (Revised) Infection Analysis Algorithm

This algorithm is to determine the degree to which a mutant program exhibits a change in the state of the software. This is the *infection estimate*.

1. Identify a testing distribution D
2. Let L: = set of all mutants of the program
3. For each mutant M with location $l$, set $counter_{IM}$: = 0
4. Set the following constants: x1: = 10, x2: = 90, x3: = 900, t1: = 5, t2: = 10
5. Find x1 *test cases* according to D which exercise $l$
6. Execute location $l$ in mutant M for each case in x1
   a. Compare the resulting data states
   b. If any differ from the unmutated program increment $counter_{IM}$ for a maximum score of x1

7. For each mutant $M$
   If counter$_{IM}$ > t1
   a. L: = L − M
   b. score$_{IM}$: = counter$_{IM}$/x1
8. Find x2 *test cases* according to D which exercise $l$
9. Execute location $l$ in mutant M for each case in x2
   a. Compare the resulting data states
   b. If any differ from the unmutated program increment counter$_{IM}$ for a maximum score of x1 + x2
10. For each mutant M
    If counter$_{IM}$ > t2
    a. L: = L − M
    b. score$_{IM}$: = counter$_{IM}$/(x1 + x2)
11. Find x3 *test cases* according to D which exercise $l$
12. Execute location $l$ in mutant M for each case in x2
    a. Compare the resulting data states
    b. If any differ from the unmutated program increment counter$_{IM}$ for a maximum score of x1 + x2 + x3
13. For each mutant M
    score$_{IM}$: = counter$_{IM}$/(x1 + x2 + x3)

The infection estimate of each $l$ in M is score$_{IM}$

## 18.2.4 Mutation Strategies

- Look at the mutation operators of Ada83 and relate them to the language of the program being mutated.
- Exploit LCSAJs (see section 12.8).
- Create "off-by-one," operator change, and offset (add $n$ to some constants) errors.
- Analyze the changes in existing code using the configuration management database and identify the top 10. Note this can give rise to some very large, and thus unwise, changes.
- In principle, mutate as little as possible; programmers make mistakes, but only little ones. Big mistakes will create obvious errors.

Note also that the original code might have been wrong in the first place and that the mutated code is correct (and therefore won't exhibit an error).

## 18.2.5 Revised Execution Analysis Algorithm

This algorithm is to estimate the degree to which a test set executes some code.

1. Identify a testing distribution D
2. Let L: = set of all locations of the program to be analyzed
3. For each location $l$ in L, set counter$_l$: = 0
4. Set the following constants: x1: = 10, x2: = 90, x3: = 900, t1: = 5, t2 = 10
5. Execute the program with x1 *test cases* according to D
   for each $l$ in L do
   a. increment counter$_l$ whenever $l$ is executed
   b. for each $l$ in L do
   c. if counter$_l$ > t1, then
   d. L = L − 1
   e. score$_l$: = counter$_l$/x1

6. Execute the program with x2 *test cases* according to D
   for each *l* in L do
   a. increment counter$_l$ whenever *l* is executed
   b. for each *l* in L do
   c. if counter$_l$ > t2, then
   d. L = L − 1
   e. score$_l$: = counter$_l$/(x1 + x2)
7. Execute the program with x3 *test cases* according to D
   for each *l* in L do
   a. increment counter$_l$ whenever *l* is executed
   b. for each *l* in L do
   c. if counter$_l$ > t3, then
   d. L = L − 1
   e. score$_l$: = counter$_l$/(x1 + x2 + x3)

The *execution estimate* of each *l* is score$_l$.

   Note that instrumenting every location in some code in an effort to see if it might be executed may not only be computationally-expensive, but have the effect of skewing any timing expectations. It could also require several compilations of the code.

## 18.3   Performance Metrics

Chapter 16 discusses the need to define a set of questions before looking at the metrics for performance testing. This is why this section is sometimes titled with questions.

### 18.3.1   How to Calculate Influences on Performance

The figures obtained in section A.8.1 in Appendix A are examples of the need to be able to identify a set of influences based on a series of tests.

   The process was as follows:

1. A set of 32 tests were run using 5 binary variables ($2^5 = 32$):

| | |
|---|---|
| QA (100T Ethernet connection) | Support (10T Ethernet connection) |
| Complex form | Simple form |
| SQL server | Oracle |
| Separate database | All applications and database on the same machine |
| Separate networks | Same network |

2. The time taken by each test was obtained by running the tests using a WinRunner script 100 times and dividing the resulting overall times by 100. This gave the table shown in Figure 18.1 (only the first 4 rows are shown).
3. The load time in seconds corresponding to each filled cell of each column of the table was then multiplied by its lower neighbor to get the **variable outcome.** Thus in the example shown in Figure 18.2, because cells AF2 and AF3 (and several others in the AF column) are *filled*, the corresponding "*Load time in seconds*" readings in column AN are multiplied.
4. Divide all the possible outputs involving this variable (**variable outcomes**) by the combinations of all possible variables to give the **normalized variable outcome** (Figure 18.3).

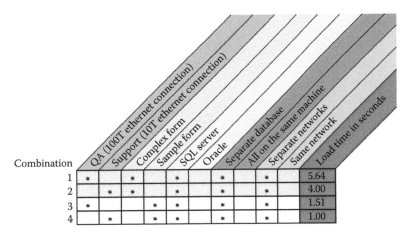

**FIGURE 18.1** Performance influence table: data entry

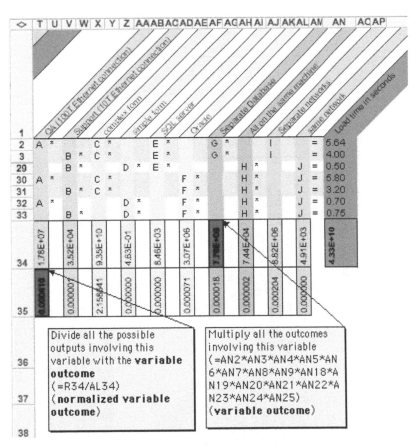

**FIGURE 18.2** Performance influence table: determining the variable outcomes

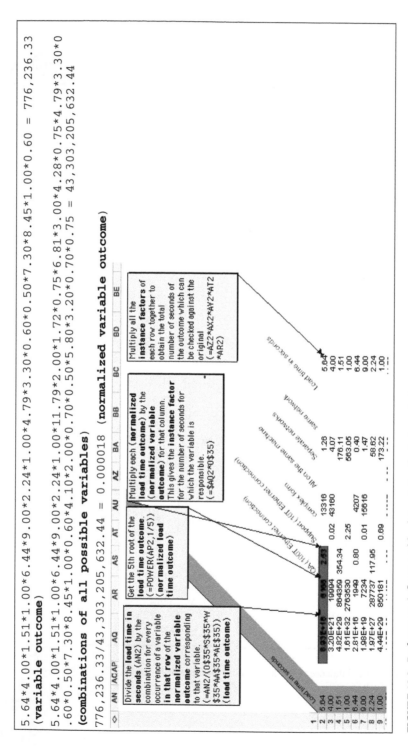

**FIGURE 18.3**　Performance influence table: determining the instance factors

5. Divide the load time in seconds (AN2) by the combination (for every occurrence of a variable in that row) of the normalized variable outcome corresponding to that variable. (=AN2/(O$35* S$35*W$35*AA$35*AE$35)) to give the **load time outcome.**

> 5.64/(0.000409940264*2.158641085808*0.000000195404*0.000017925609*0.000203741407)
> = 8,930,821,698,201,400,000 (**load time outcome**)

6. Get the 5th root of the load time outcome (=POWER(AP2, 1/5)) to give the **normalized load time outcome** (6168.481744).
7. Multiply each **normalized load time outcome** by the **normalized variable outcome** for that cell. This gives the instance factor for the number of seconds for which the variable is responsible (=$AQ2*O$35).

> 6168.481744*0.00040994 = 2.528709037

8. Multiply all the instance factors of each row together to obtain the total number of seconds of the outcome which can be checked against the original load time in seconds (=AZ2*AX2*AV2 *AT2*AR2).

> 2.5287091*13315.53868*0.001205*0.110573*1.25677 = 5.6399999

9. Multiply all the 16 instance factors for each column and take the 16th root to give the normalized instance factors (Figure 18.4).

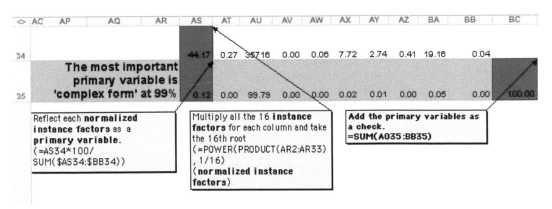

**FIGURE 18.4** Performance influence table: determining the primary variables

10. Reflect each normalized instance factors as a primary variable.
11. Add the primary variables as a check (Figure 18.5).

## 18.3.2 Efficiency Metrics

In software, efficiency is the ability of the system to use resources such as CPU cycles, memory, caches, buffers, disk space, database, and network access to obtain the maximum throughput at the minimum cost to other processes or user response. This efficiency is usually denominated by a *cost*, often expressed in CPU cycles. The operation whose efficiency is to be measured can be denominated in terms of operations achieved or inputs consumed. Thus an operation to read several records from a database might be expressed in terms of bytes read per CPU cycle. In this way a comparison can be drawn between the value of (say)

| | | QA (10UT Ethernet connection) | Support (10T Ethernet connection) | complex form | simple form | SQL server | Crack |
|---|---|---|---|---|---|---|---|
| 8.93E+18 | 6168 | 2.53 | | 13316 | | 0.00 | |
| 3.20E+21 | 19994 | | 0.02 | 43160 | | 0.00 | |
| 4.82E+29 | 864359 | 354.34 | | | 0.00 | 0.17 | |
| 1.61E+32 | 2763530 | | 2.25 | | 0.00 | 0.54 | |
| 2.81E+16 | 1949 | 0.80 | | 4207 | | | 0.14 |
| 1.98E+19 | 7234 | | 0.01 | 15616 | | | 0.51 |
| 1.97E+27 | 287737 | 117.95 | | | 0.00 | | 20.40 |
| 4.44E+29 | 850181 | | 0.69 | | 0.00 | | 60.28 |
| 1.95E+20 | 11427 | 4.68 | | 24667 | | 0.00 | |
| 1.67E+22 | 27823 | | 0.02 | 60059 | | 0.01 | |
| 5.74E+30 | 1418111 | 581.34 | | | 0.00 | 0.28 | |
| 1.26E+33 | 4170443 | | 3.39 | | 0.00 | 0.81 | |
| 3.10E+17 | 3150 | 1.29 | | 6800 | | | 0.22 |
| 6.89E+19 | 9283 | | 0.01 | 20038 | | | 0.66 |
| 3.93E+28 | 523529 | 214.62 | | | 0.00 | | 37.12 |
| 3.48E+30 | 1283008 | | 1.04 | | 0.00 | | 90.98 |
| 1.36E+22 | 26725 | 10.96 | | 57691 | | 0.01 | |
| 4.74E+24 | 86124 | | 0.07 | 185912 | | 0.02 | |
| 3.45E+32 | 3217101 | 1318.82 | | | 0.00 | 0.63 | |
| 1.45E+35 | 10769458 | | 8.75 | | 0.00 | 2.10 | |
| 5.73E+19 | 8945 | 3.67 | | 19309 | | | 0.63 |
| 3.34E+22 | 31977 | | 0.03 | 69028 | | | 2.27 |
| 1.58E+30 | 1096179 | 449.37 | | | 0.00 | | 77.73 |
| 4.79E+32 | 3436190 | | 2.79 | | 0.00 | | 243.65 |
| 1.22E+23 | 41411 | 16.98 | | 89393 | | 0.01 | |
| 3.00E+25 | 124548 | | 0.10 | 268854 | | 0.02 | |
| 4.20E+33 | 5303467 | 2174.10 | | | 0.00 | 1.04 | |
| 1.51E+36 | 17214709 | | 13.99 | | 0.00 | 3.36 | |
| 4.75E+20 | 13655 | 5.60 | | 29477 | | | 0.97 |
| 1.32E+23 | 42093 | | 0.03 | 90863 | | | 2.98 |
| 1.16E+31 | 1631575 | 668.85 | | | 0.00 | | 115.69 |
| 6.25E+33 | 5743347 | | 4.67 | | 0.00 | | 407.25 |
| | | 44.17 | 0.27 | 35716 | 0.00 | 0.06 | 7.72 |

**The most important primary variable is 'complex form' at 99%**    0.12   0.00   99.79   0.00   0.00   0.02

**FIGURE 18.5** Performance influence table: identifying the most important primary variable

locking a large number of records against expected adjacent reads from a database versus the cost involved in *un*locking such records to allow another process to read them too and thus resolve a contention.

## 18.4   Resilience (Robustness) Metrics

Resilience is often measured as the Mean Time Between Failures (MTBF). This ignores the effect of system degradation: a system which is partly degraded may have a much shorter MTBF than one which is not. Testing must account for this possibility. A baseline for such a set of tests is a fault model which can account for the threats to the system's optimal behavior. Such models should be executable since it is the failing system's dynamic behavior which is of interest. The system resilience checklist is shown in section B.14.4 in Appendix B.

## 18.4.1   Process

Identify:

- The system's maximum MTBF (system working but lightly-loaded)
- The system's MTBF and load, when loaded such that some bottleneck will become evident if loaded any further (system stressed to the maximum acceptable limit)
- The fully loaded system's MTBF when subjected to threats { A | B | ... }
- The interactions between the system layers as the system's MTBF falls
- The behavior of the system when subjected to multiple simultaneous threats
- The status of critical features as the system degrades

From the results of this analysis you should be able to identify:

- The most critical threat and threat combination
- The most vulnerable part of the system
- The most-critical system interactions

See section 18.6 for a discussion of MTBF, and section 18.4.3 for details of a useful resilience modeling approach.

## 18.4.2   Mean Time to Failure

This is measured usually against a clock (alternatively, use CPU cycles) and assumes:

- **Constant execution load.** Simply having the software loaded and running is mostly meaningless if it is given nothing to do.
- Measurement against some **error threshold.** Trivial errors may neither stop the process nor be useful to record. You need a minimum error severity below which no event is of interest nor is recorded.

### Example

A system was tested using three severity levels $P_{1-3}$ (see Table 18.1). Bugs occurred according to the elapsed times in the *Time* column (1) and with the severities shown in the *Bug Severity* column (2). The elapsed times were listed according to bug severity in columns (3), (5), and (7). The interval times were then identified and the mean interval of each severity shown in the bottom row.

**TABLE 18.1**   MTTF Example

| Bug Severity | Time | P3 Elapsed | P3 Interval | P2 Elapsed | P2 Interval | P1 Elapsed | P1 Interval |
|---|---|---|---|---|---|---|---|
| P3 | 180 | 180 | 180 | | | | |
| P2 | 477 | | | 477 | 477 | | |
| P3 | 855 | 855 | 675 | | | | |
| P1 | 894 | | | | | 894 | 894 |
| P3 | 1170 | 1170 | 315 | | | | |
| P3 | 1382 | 1382 | 212 | | | | |
| P2 | 1525 | | | 1525 | 1048 | | |
| P3 | 1660 | 1660 | 278 | | | | |
| P3 | 2163 | 2163 | 503 | | | | |
| P2 | 2210 | | | 2210 | 685 | | |
| P1 | 2316 | | | | | 2316 | 1422 |
| P3 | 2594 | 2594 | 431 | | | | |
| P2 | 2606 | | | 2606 | 396 | | |
| **MTTF** | | | **370.57** | | **651.50** | | **1158.00** |

### 18.4.3 Markov Chain

One way of determining a system's resilience (or availability) is to model it as a Markov chain. The two circles in Figure 18.6 represent two states of the system: working (1) and failed (0). Assuming that the system is in state 1, there are two possible outcomes: it can stay in state 1 or move to state 2. The parameters are as follows:

- *a* is the probability of failure that the system moves to state 0, given that it is in state 1.
- *b* is the probability that it will move from a failed state to a working state, given that it is in a failed state.
- *1-a* is the probability that it will continue to work, given that it is working.
- *1-b* is the probability that it will continue to fail, given that it is failing.

In this case we want to find the probability that the state will be in each state.

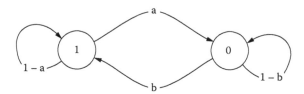

**FIGURE 18.6**  A system modeled as a Markov chain

### Example

Let us assume that the probability of the system working after some time period (*1-a*) = 0.85 and the probability of it being repaired given that it has failed (*1-b*) = 0.65. From this we see that *a* = 0.15 and *b* = 0.35 (Figure 18.7).

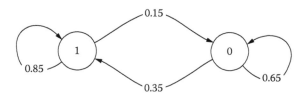

**FIGURE 18.7**  A system modeled as a Markov chain with probabilities

We need to know what the probabilities are after a number of iterations (say 4). Here are the iterations modeled as a tree (Figure 18.8).

Adding the probabilities of being in the 1 and 0 states after four iterations gives us p(1) = 0.71875 and p(0) = 0.28125. Note the table of iterations below. Expressed as a graph (Figure 18.9), this suggests that the iterations will converge. Here are the equations:

$$p(1) = \frac{b}{a+b}$$

and

$$p(0) = \frac{a}{a+b}$$

**TABLE 18.2** The iterations converge the values

| Iteration | 1 | 2 | 3 | 4 |
|---|---|---|---|---|
| p(1) | 0.85 | 0.775 | 0.7375 | 0.71875 |
| p(0) | 0.15 | 0.225 | 0.2625 | 0.28125 |

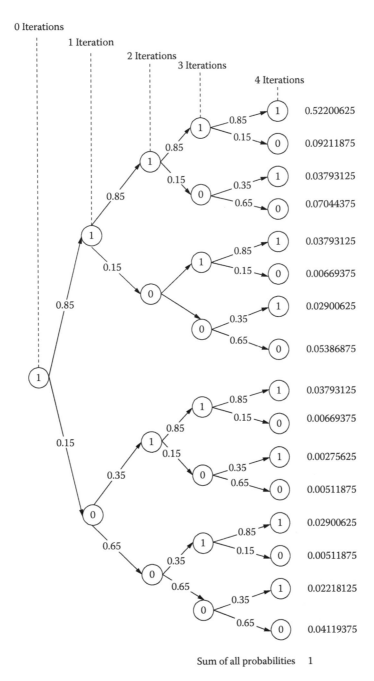

Sum of all probabilities   1

**FIGURE 18.8** A system modeled as a Markov chain with probabilities after 4 iterations

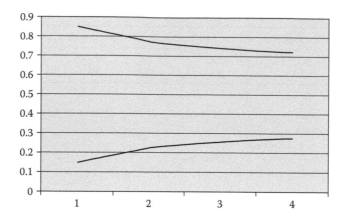

**FIGURE 18.9** The iterations converge the values

Resolving for a and b gives us p(1) = 0.7 and p(0) = 0.3. Note:

- Markov chains are history-free in that changes are entirely dependent on the current state.
- Multiple-state Markov chains are essential for modeling different levels of failure. The two-state chain in Figure 18.6 is very simple and purely for illustration.
- The probabilities can be estimated from a number of runs of a fault model.
- The Markov chains can be decomposed to become as complex as the system being modeled.
- The probabilities can be estimated by counting the number of times the system was in that state divided by the total number of times the system was in any state.
- States are usually measured using a number of runs of an executable model aggregated over some time periods.
- High resilience is simply b/a where the smaller the figure, the higher the resilience.

The data collected from runs is of two kinds: time series and summary. The summary data is derived from the time-series data. They answer two questions:

1. What is the average ability of the system to recover from a failure? (Useful when comparing the resiliencies of systems.)
2. What is the probability of the system recovering from a fault at this moment? (Useful when trying to determine the system's most vulnerable moment.)

# 18.5   Usability Metrics

There are many usability metrics about, some under false names. Here is an attempt to be rational. Some usability metrics are shown as exclusive, multiple choices. They aren't either. See also [Sauro] who has attempted to combine 4 of them.

## 18.5.1   How to Identify a Set of Usability Metrics

When talking to users and HF experts during the heuristic evaluation and the user profiles prepared during the Inception phase (see section 17.4.4), try and identify the issues or goals which the product's usability must address (see section B.12 in Appendix B).

Get the answers to these questions in both textual and metricated form.

## 18.5.2 Usability Problem Density

$$problem\ density = \frac{number\ of\ problems\ a\ user\ encounters}{time(test)}$$

Note that such problems may not be bugs in the system or, if they are, may be duplicates of an existing bug. See the discussion in Appendix C.

## 18.5.3 Ease-of-Use Metric

$$ease\ of\ use = \frac{expert\ task\ time}{user\ task\ time}$$

Measure the expert after giving him every chance to "warm up." Allow time between tests to refresh.

## 18.5.4 Work Rate Metric

$$work\ rate = \frac{\%\ of\ task\ completed}{time(task)}$$

Requires that the tasks are well-defined and finite and that the software be robust. Assumes several tasks. If there be but one, then assess what proportion of that was completed. Note that if the tasks are of very varying lengths, then some other measure must be made. One possible (sub)task measure is hitting "*Return*" or "*OK*."

## 18.5.5 Productivity Metric

$$productivity = \frac{number\ of\ tasks\ completed}{time(test)}$$

As *Work rate* in section 18.5.4. Assumes that the tasks are of similar length or difficulty.

## 18.5.6 Task Fit Metric

$$task\ fit\ score = \frac{number\ of\ features\ used}{number\ of\ features\ available}$$

This is of greater use in an early evaluation. Should some feature remain unused after every possible task has been executed, then its value can be questioned. However, that some task uses few features is unimportant compared with whether it be achieved.

## 18.5.7 Activity Error Rate

$$activity\ error\ rate = \frac{number\ of\ errors}{productivity}$$

One of the key metrics. If it rises faster than the productivity rate, then it implies that some usability limit is being reached. Compare with % of users successful in the next section.

## 18.5.8   % of Users Successful

$$\% \ of \ UTCs \ successful = \frac{number \ of \ UTCs \ completing*100}{number \ of \ UTCs}$$

An early indicator of problems. A variation of this distinguishes those not needing administration help (as opposed to documentation or "help" menu help) from those who do. If more than 10% of UTCs cannot complete without administration help, then either the UTC selection or the interface needs revision (or both).

## 18.5.9   % of Users Successful within Time Metric

$$\% \ of \ UTCs \ successful \ within \ time = \frac{number \ of \ UTCs \ completing \ within \ time*100}{number \ of \ UTCs}$$

Should not be less than 70%.

## 18.5.10   Help (Reading) Rate

$$help(reading) \ rate = \frac{time \ spent \ reading \ documents}{time(test)}$$

Low scores are good.

## 18.5.11   Help (Menu) Rate

$$help(menu) \ rate = \frac{time \ spent \ reading \ help \ menu}{time(test)}$$

Low scores are good.

## 18.5.12   Document Success Rate

$$document \ success = \frac{times \ documents \ consulted \cup task \ completion}{number \ of \ times \ documents \ consulted}$$

Measure the number of times that document consultation is followed by successful completion of a task compared with all the times attention shifts to the document (high scores are good). Implicitly a good document will provide the answer immediately and thus require a single access, including table of contents and index. Multiple accesses without success imply that the user has difficulty in navigating the document.

## 18.5.13   Document Navigation Success Rate

$$navigation \ success = \frac{times \ table \ of \ contents \ or \ index \ consulted}{number \ of \ times \ documents \ consulted}$$

Measure the amount of time spent consulting the index and table of contents compared with the reading the rest of the document (low scores are good). Note that this ignores any help given by cross-references.

## 18.5.14   Mean Time to Complete Task

$$mean\ time\ to\ complete\ task = \frac{\sum task\ completion\ times}{number\ of\ UTCs}$$

Limiting the number of UTCs or failing to control for user types will have a negative effect on the credibility of this metric.

## 18.5.15   Understandability (Communicativeness) Metrics

Collect the following data for each UTC:

- % of time spent using the "help" system
- % of time spent consulting a manual
- % of time spent asking for help from the administrator
- % score from an UTC product assessment questionnaire

Measure each as a proportion of the total time spent using the product. Identify and eliminate outliers. Get the mean for the product and compare it with other products or releases. This will answer two questions:

1. How easy is the product to understand? (Any score of above 30% is "not very.")
2. Has understandability improved since the last release? (Compare the two scores.)

Beware of using too few UTCs. This could skew your results.

## 18.5.16   Learnability Metrics

Collect the following data for each UTC:

- Initial training time (ITT)
- Subsequent training time (relearnability) for some gap in use (STT)
- Score for UTC's ability (pre- and post-training) (UTCS)

You need to control for many factors:

- A UTC (and everyone else) forgets, so test their ability to remember.
- Some people have longer gaps between system use than others, so allow for this. There are statistics showing the ability to forget over time, from psychology books.
- A well-designed system will have visual clues which aid retention. Designers need to know if they work.
- Some systems are easier to learn than others, usually those involving a large degree of transfer of knowledge from a comparable system.
- Some *parts* of a system are easier to learn than others. Designers need to know which.

Eliminate any outliers. Use multiple regression analysis (see section 18.10.3.2) to relate the ITT, STT, and UTCS for the candidates, and then compare the resulting equation with other releases or products.

## 18.5.17   Attractiveness Metric

Any one of the following:

- The number of favorable/unfavorable comments
- The level of fatigue (measure using a short test of a trivial word-processing task [Bangor], or the UTC's response times before and after the usability test session)
- The result of a set of scored UTC product assessment questionnaires

### 18.5.18  Human Interface Design

[Michael] has proposed a crude but interesting metric for comparing user interfaces by identifying the factors that impede users such as much keyboard input and big input fields. It uses a function which might be construed either as a GUI object (more precise) or as a system feature.

$$HID = KMS + IFPF + ALIF + (100 - BR)$$

where

      KMS = average number of keyboard to mouse switches per function
      IFPF = average number of input fields per function
      ALIF = average string length of input fields
        BR = percentage of buttons whose functions were identified via inspection by first time users (*10)

A large HID indicates a hard-to-learn system and the likelihood of errors in using it.

HID might be usefully employed as a means of comparing the (un)usability of GUI objects by using calculating an absolute HID for each GUI component.

## 18.6  Reliability

Reliability can be defined as the mean time between failures of some software. There is a simple measure of reliability:

$$MTBF = MTTF + MTTR$$

where

      MTBF is mean time between failures
      MTTF is mean time to fail
      MTTR is mean time to repair

In the software context, MTTR is usually measured as the length of time a system takes, given some failure, to trap its settings, halt its processes, restart, and achieve the same state as when it failed.

### 18.6.1  General

Some of the problems of reliability assessment and testing can be determined from the unit shown in section 18.12.2. For a reliability estimate of $10^9$ hours of operation of that unit alone, more than $10^9$ hours of operation must have occurred with all possible data inputs. This is a mere 114,468.9 years. Alternatively, with 228,938 processors the job might be done in 6 months. This is possible, if improbable. The set of all possible data for some non-trivial program is likewise enormous. The value of reliability as a measure is consequently limited.

Reliability estimates require some failure and vast quantities of time to be accurate. Only after this extraordinarily long time should a failure occur. If it doesn't, can one be certain that the test was valid? One answer to this would be to look at section 18.2.

### 18.6.2  Reliability Profile

Reliability profiles derive from two kinds of reliability model:

1. The **reliability growth model** assumes that the reliability of some software increases monotonically as bugs are fixed. This implies that the failure rate is decreasing. The failure times are the only inputs to such models; they require no details of the software structure to operate. A number of reliability growth models have been defined; see [Goel-Okhumoto], [Jelinsky], [Littlewood 81], [Verrall], [Musa 3], and [Musa 4]. Some of these are embodied in SMERFS (see section D.16 in Appendix D).

2. The (reliability) **structural model** predicts the reliability of systems from the intrinsic reliability of their components. This is useful as components are integrated. It relies much on the history of hardware development. A model of this type can be found in [Littlewood 81]. These often use bug seeding as a means of estimating reliability. See section 18.10.6.

Both models can be used to build up a reliability profile of a system. Such a profile needs to be matched by reliability targets in the test planning phase such that for each component

- the reliability measure (possibly the number of class-, or severity-1 failures per day of testing)
- test coverage and type
- maximum effort expended

can be defined beforehand such that the degree to which the product meets or exceeds its expected profile can be decided. Use the *Weibull approach to release readiness estimation* in section 18.10.11 to create a profile from several previous releases and see how well the new release matches it. If the bug detection profile of the new release matches or exceeds the older ones one, then you have a better basis for deciding that the release is ready.

### 18.6.3 Musa Model of Software Reliability

The following MTBF model has been developed by [Musa 1]. It consists of a series of equations:

The number of bugs which some set of tests will find

$$n = N_o * (1 - EXP((-C*t)/N_o*T_o)) \qquad \text{(Equation 18.1)}$$

The probability of the system not failing after some time spent testing

$$R(t) = EXP(-t/T) \qquad \text{(Equation 18.2)}$$

The number of bugs found given some change in MTBF

$$\Delta n = N_o * T_o * ((1/T_1) - (1/T_2)) \qquad \text{(Equation 18.3)}$$

The number of bugs found given some change in MTBF

$$\Delta t = ((N_o * T_o)/C) * \ln(T_2/T_1) \qquad \text{(Equation 18.4)}$$

where

$\Delta n$ = number of bugs to be found by some set of tests during some time t
$\Delta t$ = time spent testing
$N_o$ = the total number of bugs in the system
$T_o$ = the MTTF at the start of testing
$T_1$ = the MTTF at the start of some testing
$T_2$ = the MTTF at the end of some testing
$C$ = the testing *compression* factor

### Example

Given a large program:

- Which is believed to contain about 300 bugs
- Whose MTBF at the start of testing is 1.5 hours

and a set of tests whose compression factor is assumed to be 4 (i.e., we're using the program 4 times more intensely than a user normally would), we can find:

- The amount of testing required to reduce the remaining bugs to 10
- The reliability of that program after that testing, over a 50-hour period

like this:

- We want to know the amount of testing required to reduce the remaining bugs to 10. We know that $N_0 = 300$ and $T_0 = 1.5$. We assume that $T_1 = T_0$ because no testing has (presumably) begun yet. From Equation 18.4 we can show that:

$$\Delta t = ((300*1.5)/4*\ln(\mathbf{T_2}/1.5)$$

- But we still don't know $\mathbf{T_2}$. To find this we should use Equation 18.3. We know $\Delta n$ because we want the number of bugs found to be $(300 \quad 10) = 290$. Therefore we have:

$$290 = 300*1.5((1/1.5)(1/T_2)), T2 = 45$$

- Substituting for $T_2$ in the previous equation gives:

$$\Delta t = 300*1.5((1/1.5)(1/45) = 382.6 \text{ hours}$$

- We need to find the reliability of that program after that testing, over a 50-hour period. We know that at $T_2$ (that is the period at the end of testing) the MTTF = 45, and we can use Equation 18.2 thus:

$$R(t) = R_{50} = EXP(50/45) = 33$$

- which implies that the program has a 67% probability of finding some bug during the next fifty hours of running.

## 18.6.4   Reliability of Two Elements in a Series

The reliability of two elements connected in series can be expressed graphically as:

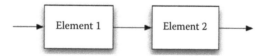

and mathematically as:

$$\text{reliability of element 1*reliability of element 2}$$

## 18.6.5   Reliability of Two Elements in Parallel

The reliability of two elements connected in parallel can be expressed graphically as:

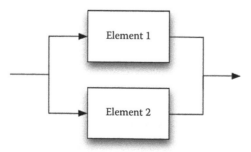

and mathematically as:

[1((1reliability of element 1)*(1reliability of element 2))]

## 18.6.6 Reliability of *m* Out of *n* Elements

The reliability of *2* out of *3* elements can be expressed graphically as:

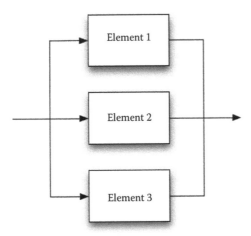

and mathematically as:

$$R^3 + 3R^2(1-R)$$

**Example**

Assume the reliability of each element to be 0.89 and that 2 out of 3 elements must work:

$$0.89^3 + 3*0.89^2*0.1 = 0.942599$$

The formula for *m* out of *n* elements generally is expressed as:

$$\sum_{k=m}^{n} \frac{n!}{(n-k)!k!} R^k (1-R)^{n-k}$$

# 18.7  Availability

## 18.7.1  Coexistence

At one level coexistence is the inverse of *interference.* Processes coexist on a processor or in a network to the extent that they don't interfere with each other. The response time of a process can thus be expressed as:

Response time = Computation time + Interference time

for some period of time. Interference in this case would be a function of the time to execute all the processes of higher priority. The worst case would be the maximum. See [Burns] for more on this.

When considering the degree of interference between applications on a network, use Table 18.3 to construct a model of the system's behavior.

**TABLE 18.3**  Coexistence metrics

| Domain and metric | Actions | | |
| | Concurrency | Scaling[a] | Coordination |
| --- | --- | --- | --- |
| **Time** | | | |
| Average time to process a transaction | Average time to process a transaction per network node | % change in time to process a transaction per node with addition/deletion/update | Average time to process transaction coordinations |
| **Rate** | | | |
| Average number of transactions processed per unit of time | Average number of transactions processed per unit of time per network node | % change in transactions per node with addition/deletion/update | Average number of transaction coordination tasks per unit time |
| **Resource use** | | | |
| Number of transactions processed | Average number of transactions per node | % change in transactions per node | Total transaction interactions |
| **Reliability** | | | |
| % total transactions missing a deadline | Average number of transactions missing a deadline | % change in the number of transactions missing a deadline | Average number of transactions using out-of-date data |
| **Availability** | | | |
| Average time a transaction spends in a queue | Maximum number of transactions handled simultaneously | % change in transaction queue length | % of time spent coordinating tasks |

[a]  This doesn't account for load shedding. If a system begins to shed load it may not be due to applications interfering with each other, but simply due to overloading. This table will be useful only if the system does *not* shed load.

- Find a common currency such as a "typical" transaction for each application whose resource use you can compare. Bear in mind that "typical" transaction behavior can vary as the transaction content. Thus a user may download a small video clip or Ben Hur.
- If some transactions are very large with respect to others, they will interfere by reason of processing use alone. Control for this by identifying transactions from all applications and identifying those which use the same number of CPU cycles to process. Check this use against increasing levels of system stress to see if any divergence in the number of cycles used occurs.
- Test at least against:
  - An unstressed system
  - A stressed system
  - An overstressed system

  This will give you the percentage changes.
- Test with every combination of application and all primary transaction types of each application. This is why coexistence metrics are rarely sought.
- Create a set of matrices relating the applications and use the scaling percentages and the coordination data to show for each pair of applications the degree of upset each causes or suffers (Table 18.4).

**TABLE 18.4**  Example of a coexistence metric: some interference between applications B and D is evident

| Application | % change in time to process a transaction per node with addition/deletion/update | | | | |
| | A | B | C | D | E |
| --- | --- | --- | --- | --- | --- |
| A | | | | | |
| B | 1.08 | | | | |
| C | 1.8 | 0.7 | | | |
| D | 0.89 | **25.8** | 0.03 | | |
| E | 2.6 | 1.8 | 6.9 | 0.9 | |

### 18.7.2 Availability Metric

Availability is the probability that the system will still be operating to requirements at a given time. This is defined as

$$availability = \frac{MTTF}{MTTF + MTTR} \times 100$$

MTTR is an indirect measure of maintainability. Availability is more sensitive to MTTR than to MTTF.

## 18.8  Maintainability Metrics

Maintainability is a function of several attributes:

- Analyzability (as discussed in section 18.8.1)
- Complexity (as discussed in section 18.8.2)
- Coupling
- Dependency of one piece of code on another

[Hordijk] also claims that it is a function of the quality of the maintenance team. Maintainability is not amenable to testing. It is an attribute both of the architecture and the legibility of the code. Consequently the only input a test group can offer is to use maintainability assessment tools such as those in [LaQuSo], or Jdepend (see section D.6 in Appendix D). As code becomes less maintainable (= more entropic) any bugs found in that code will become increasingly hard to fix. This will lead to the injection of more bugs and increasing code turmoil.

Maintainability is ill-defined. Various authors have approached the subject, but no consensus has arisen. Various tools have been created:

- [Berns] described a *Maintainability Analysis Tool* for use with FORTRAN on a VAX. It's old, but it gives a good idea of what can be achieved and what to look for in a maintainability analysis regime.
- [Muskens] described a *Software Architecture Analysis Tool.*
- SQAE (see section D.6 in Appendix D).

See Figure 18.10 for an example of a maintainability comparison of three applications; also see [Belady] for a discussion of a maintainability model, and the Glossary at the end of this book for a maintainability index.

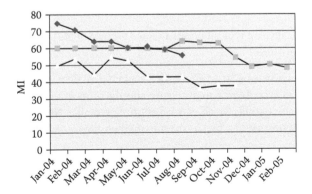

**FIGURE 18.10**  Example of a maintainability comparison of three applications; none of them is improving, although efforts are sporadically made

## Conclusion

As a test manager you have a responsibility to advise the project manager about the release date. You may also have a responsibility to advise the PM about code quality. Increasing difficulty in maintaining code is an early warning that the bug count will rise and the release will be late. Therefore:

- Ensure you get read-only access to the code libraries.
- Identify a maintainability toolset and regime from which you can draw conclusions (the *maintainability index* is one approach). Ensure it is accepted, tool-supported, and easy-to-use.
- Propose it to the project manager and design authority.
- Establish what you believe to be limits beyond which the code may be considered dangerously unmaintainable.
- If possible, set up an alerting system for you and the project manager and design authority.
- Monitor the state of the code base weekly.
- Attempt to relate the maintainability of the code to the number of unit tests, the code turmoil, and the number of bugs predicted and found. You will need to have data from at least 3 releases to have a minimally-accurate prediction.

## Hypothesis

There is some level of maintainability below which code turmoil will increase such that early attempts at predicting bug levels will consistently underestimate the final number. Thus if you have attempted to predict bug levels using (say) one of the methods shown in section 18.10, you will find that beyond that point the bug-fixing abilities of the maintenance team have been overwhelmed by the unmaintainability of the code and the number of bugs increases at a rate which equals and eventually exceeds that of bug detection.

## 18.8.1   Analyzability Metrics

This is the degree to which some person can read the code and understand it. See [Berns] for a useful discussion.

## 18.8.2   Complexity Metrics: McCabe's Measure

From the directed graph, McCabe's cyclomatic complexity measure is computed using the following formula:

$V(g)$ = number of control paths between decisions − number of decisions
        + number of unconnected control paths between decisions

Alternatively:

$V(g)$ = number of binary decisions + ((n − 1)*(n − times multiway decisions)

> (Multiway decisions are typically implemented using SELECT statements. Each is counted as n − 1 binary decisions.)

$V(g)$ reflects the decision-making structure of the program. [McCabe] recommends that for any given unit the value V should not exceed ten. This also represents the number of *test cases* required for that code. Use this value as an indicator of units which may benefit from redesign. Note that this formula differs from McCabe's original. This is because of a bug in the use of graph theory. See [Henderson] for full details.

## Code Complexity

Analyzers report on the underlying structure of the code, procedure by procedure. You can select which ones are to be analyzed.

**Code Structure**

To analyze fully the subject code structure many testing tools first reduce it to a series of connecting basic blocks. These basic blocks are discrete processing elements of the program. See Figure 13.1.

Thus, a statement will only reside in one basic block, and also, if one statement in a basic block be executed, every statement within that basic block will also be executed. This allows optimization of code contained within a basic block; any expression used within a basic block may be computed once at the head of the block and used repeatedly within the block with absolute confidence.

Interconnections between basic blocks are given by many test tools and from that information a directed graph representation of the program may be obtained. The basic blocks will form the nodes of the directed graph and the branches are the arcs.

**Knots**

Complexity analysis will report control-flow knots. A control-flow knot is defined as occurring when two control-flow jumps cross.

**Intervals**

Interval reduction is a way of showing the structuredness of a program. The better the structure the easier the program is to think about and the less likely is it to have bugs.

The advantages of McCabe is that:

- It enables developers to concentrate unit testing and inspection time on the more complex code.
- It gives system testers early warning of those parts of the system most likely still to contain bugs.

# 18.9   Process Metrics

## 18.9.1   Fix Backlog Metric

This is a metric whose usefulness depends much on the definition of *fixed*. Consider the bug life cycle:

1. A bug is embodied in code (it may derive of course from a faulty requirement or design).
2. The code is unit tested without the bug being found.
3. The code containing the bug is incorporated into a build.
4. The build is released to the testers, who system-test it and find the bug. The bug is then *open*.
5. Project management agrees that the bug must be fixed and it is scheduled for fixing.
6. A developer changes and unit-tests the code, believing it to be *fixed*.
7. As 3 above. At this point many development managers claim the bug is *fixed*. It isn't really *fixed* until it's *closed*. It may still fail.
8. The build is released to the testers, who system-test it and declare the bug dead. Only at this point the bug can be considered *closed*.

All this time the testers are discovering other bugs. You need to know to what extent the developers are coping with the bugs testers find.

$$fix\ backlog = \frac{number\ of\ bugs\ closed\ during\ the\ month}{number\ of\ bugs\ found\ during\ the\ month} * 100$$

This is of course the metric equivalent of Figure 18.11. More than 100% implies that the developers are coping. Monitor this using limits of 95% (any less means you need more developers) and 105% (any more and you need fewer developers).

Keep a separate *Fix backlog metric* for each bug severity level, otherwise developers may be tempted to inflate their scores by fixing the simpler and low-severity bugs first.

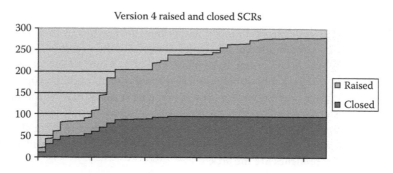

**FIGURE 18.11** Bugs found and fixed overall

## 18.9.2 Mean 30-Day Fix Response Time

The mean 30-day fix response time is the mean time taken to close a bug measured from the moment it is raised to the moment it is closed (usually by the tester who raised it). Relate this to the priority level of the bug. The formula is:

$$\text{mean 30-day fix response time} = \frac{\displaystyle\sum_{\text{all fixes in last 30 days}} \text{fix closed time} - \text{bug open time}}{\text{number of fixes in the last 30 days}}$$

Graph the output daily and use it to monitor the developers' bug fixing speed. Note that if the testers fail to close (or reopen) bugs speedily, it will reflect unfairly and badly on the developers.

## 18.9.3 Mean Age of Bugs

In principle every bug should be detected in the same phase in which it is created. The quality of the development process can be measured by the speed with which a bug is detected. The speed can be calculated from:

- **The date a bug is fixed.** When a bug is fixed some change is made to the source code or documentation. The fix is then reviewed and tested, and the change put under configuration management. Thus the moment of change can be dated.
- **The date a bug is created.** Similarly the moment the bug was created can be determined. A bug exists from the moment a null file was first populated with code and saved. If this cannot be determined, assume the middle of the phase in which it was first possible to create the bug.

$$\text{Mean age of bugs} = \frac{\displaystyle\sum_{\text{number of bugs}} \text{date a bug is fixed} - \text{date a bug is created}}{\text{number of bugs}}$$

### Example (Figure 18.12)

The development process is bad. The lowest mean was in May 2004. Unless development phases are very long it seems certain that bugs are being found in the next phase. Better reviewing is needed.

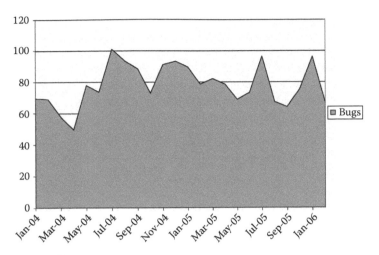

**FIGURE 18.12**  Mean age of bugs

### 18.9.4   Mean Age of Open Bugs

The mean age of open bugs is usually calculated at the end of each month for each severity since the most severe tend to be fixed fastest. The formula is

$$mean\ age\ of\ open\ bugs = \frac{\displaystyle\sum_{all\ open\ bugs} present\ time - bug\ open\ time}{number\ of\ open\ bugs}$$

The calculation can be plotted monthly and used to allocate developer time for fixing.

### 18.9.5   Example of Mean Age of Open Bugs (Figure 18.13)

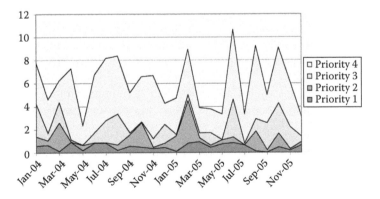

**FIGURE 18.13**  Mean age of open bugs example chart

The chart shows that heroic efforts are occasionally made to limit bug ages, and the average age is never more than 11 (weeks). Most priority-1 bugs are fixed within 3 days. Whether developer effort was well spent on fixing all those priority-3 bugs in May 2004 is questionable. Perhaps management wanted a high bug-fix figure and developers complied.

## 18.9.6   % Delinquent Fixes

Some fixes fail when they are delivered to a customer or a system test team. Some fixes are made late and some fixes are not yet made, but should have been. All are delinquent. They can be compared on a rolling 30-day period with the total number of fixes made in that period. Any rise of 1% above 0 is an exception. If the rise continues, it means that bug fixing is insufficiently-resourced because the pressure to fix one bug is distracting developers from fixing others. The metric is:

$$\% \; delinquent \; fixes = \frac{\sum\limits_{over \; 30 \; days} delinquent \; fixes}{\sum\limits_{over \; 30 \; days} total \; fixes} \times 100$$

Calculate this for every severity level of interest.

## 18.9.7   Requirements Turmoil

A critical element in the assessment of project stability is the degree to which requirements change. This can be assessed either by having the requirements held in a tool with versions configuration-managed or by simply keeping individual versions in text form.

Text versions can be compared and differences identified automatically. From these the following can be derived:

- The number of inserts, deletes, and changes
- The sections changed
- The dates on which these changes occurred

Put these into a spreadsheet and then combine it with another spreadsheet devoted to *Code turmoil* as shown below.

## 18.9.8   Code Turmoil

This is a measure of the amount of change code has suffered over some period compared with some other period expressed as the percentage of changes (inserts, deletes, or updates).

Tools exist to analyze this but the base data can be obtained by extracting an history file from the configuration management database giving for each unit for each day a list of the inserts, deletes, or updates which have occurred.

This list can be big: 40 MB for a 100 KLOC system over 24 months and thus unamenable to simple manipulation on a spreadsheet. However it is not difficult to write some simple program to:

- Read the history file
- Output a file containing the following: <date> <unit name> <No. of inserts> <No. of deletes> <No. of updates> <bug number$_1$> ... <bug number$_n$>

This list can then be read into a spreadsheet and manipulated to show:

- Turmoil by unit over time
- Total turmoil of the system over time
- Which is the most changed unit
- Which units attracted the most bugs

The data can then be augmented by output from code analysis and fault-injection tools to show:

- Code complexity (see section 18.8.4) of each unit
- Degree of coupling of each unit

- Knots
- Dataflow bugs
- Percentage of paths exercised by unit testing
- Testability of each unit

It is then possible to cross-refer these analyses such that the code turmoil can be related to each of these characteristics such as to be able to answer the following questions by using multiple regression analysis (see section 18.10.3.2):

- *To what extent does the code complexity, degree of coupling, knots, or dataflow bugs of units affect the probability that the unit harbors bugs?* (One suspects, positively.)
- *To what extent does the percentage of paths exercised by unit testing and the testability of each unit affect the probability that the unit harbors bugs?* (One hopes, negatively.)

In addition there is a number of other questions which can be answered with code turmoil data:

- *How much turmoil does a critical bug cause on average?* (Assuming you have related those bug numbers to the criticality of the bug which provoked them) you can identify which units have been changed as a result.
- *Which bugs have created the most turmoil?*
- *Which requirements changes have caused the greatest turmoil?*
- *Which units have reached such a state of turmoil that they should be rewritten?* (Which units have constant or increasing turmoil levels throughout the period of the project, order by turmoil level, and pick off the worst 10%.)
- *How long does it take to resolve a bug* (timed from the moment the bug is authorized for resolution to the moment the changes are entered in the configuration management database)?
- *What is the turmoil level of each build and what is the relationship between turmoil level and bugs raised in each build?*
- *Is the turmoil trend rising or dropping?*
- *How many changes were needed to fix a bug?*
- *What evidence is there that large numbers of code changes to fix a bug imply that that bug was not properly fixed?* (Check which bugs have reappeared by looking at the bug management output, and then list all the bugs in order of the number of changes they have provoked and see how many are common. This could be a sign of lack of unit tests, developers under pressure, or entropic code structure.)

## 18.9.9  Case Study of Code Turmoil

Here is a snapshot of the code turmoil of a project taken from its configuration management database. The columns are calculated as shown in Table 18.5 and Table 18.6.

**TABLE 18.5**  Code turmoil data key

| Column title | Meaning and calculation |
| --- | --- |
| Non-commented source statements (NCCS) | Taken from the configuration management database at 1700 hours each Friday |
| Difference | The absolute difference between one week's code size and the next (ABS(A-B)) |
| Inserts | Number of insertions of new code |
| Deletes | Number of lines of code deleted |
| Updates | Number of lines of code updated |
| Total turmoil | Sum of *inserts, deletes,* and *updates* for some period |
| % turmoil | 100*total turmoil of that period/(total turmoil) |

**TABLE 18.6**  Code turmoil data

| Week | NCCS | Difference | Inserts | Deletes | Updates | Total turmoil | % turmoil |
|---|---|---|---|---|---|---|---|
| 01.Aug.04 | 128000 |  | 470 | 946 | 877 | 2293 | 1 |
| 07.Aug.04 | 130000 | 2000 | 941 | 806 | 218 | 3965 | 3 |
| 13.Aug.04 | 131400 | 1400 | 714 | 860 | 993 | 3967 | 3 |
| 19.Aug.04 | 129000 | 2400 | 132 | 551 | 450 | 3533 | 2 |
| 25.Aug.04 | 152234 | 23234 | 215 | 15 | 760 | 24224 | 15 |
| 31.Aug.04 | 148999 | 3235 | 522 | 209 | 499 | 4465 | 2 |
| 06.Sep.04 | 123899 | 25100 | 392 | 399 | 216 | 26107 | 21 |
| 12.Sep.04 | 123414 | 485 | 111 | 720 | 164 | 1480 | 1 |
| 18.Sep.04 | 144565 | 21151 | 383 | 872 | 955 | 23361 | 16 |
| 24.Sep.04 | 134343 | 10222 | 560 | 725 | 882 | 12389 | 9 |
| 30.Sep.04 | 130000 | 4343 | 927 | 242 | 663 | 6175 | 4 |
| 06.Oct.04 | 120000 | 10000 | 360 | 417 | 389 | 11166 | 9 |
| 12.Oct.04 | 117868 | 2132 | 625 | 673 | 576 | 4006 | 3 |
| 18.Oct.04 | 119990 | 2122 | 34 | 505 | 312 | 2973 | 2 |
| 24.Oct.04 | 120000 | 10 | 59 | 933 | 115 | 1117 | 0 |
| 30.Oct.04 | 119980 | 20 | 870 | 378 | 474 | 1742 | 1 |
| 05.Nov.04 | 118980 | 1000 | 932 | 255 | 566 | 2753 | 2 |
| 11.Nov.04 | 117890 | 1090 | 157 | 254 | 452 | 1953 | 1 |
| 17.Nov.04 | 117355 | 535 | 259 | 124 | 279 | 1197 | 1 |
| 23.Nov.04 | 117450 | 95 | 8 | 457 | 116 | 676 | 0 |
| 29.Nov.04 | 117460 | 10 | 478 | 533 | 359 | 1380 | 1 |

The chart shows a project in which the August period had few changes (due to holidays?) and which then was greatly disrupted (Figure 18.14). Turmoil being low, a release was made at the end of October in which few bugs were found and changes ceased at the end of November. See [Suardi] for more on code turmoil.

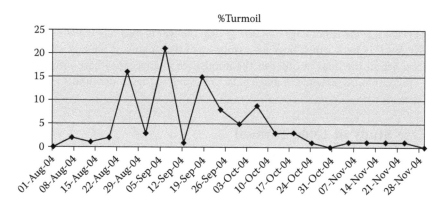

**FIGURE 18.14**  Code turmoil from August to November

## 18.9.10  Process Efficiency

By tracking the phase in which a bug was created as well as those in which it was found, you can assess the efficiency of the bug minimization ability of the system as a whole. First you create a table with rows and columns representing the project processes: requirement, design, coding, system testing, etc. Add on the various reviews and inspections and enter the bug totals (Figure 18.15). Then calculate the phase (process) defect removal effectiveness rates as shown in Figure 18.16 … and include a nice picture.

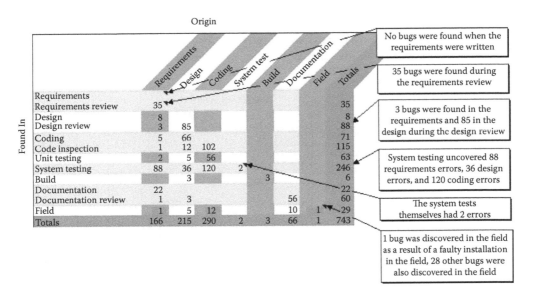

**FIGURE 18.15** Bug data showing the phase in which each is created and found

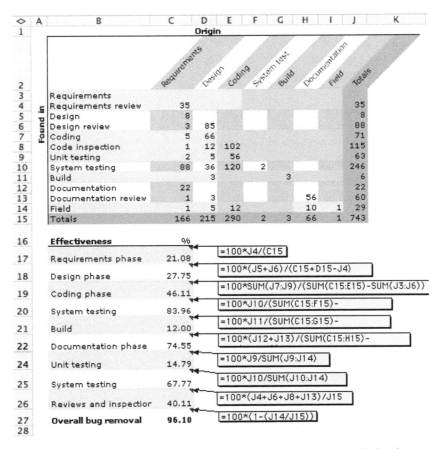

**FIGURE 18.16** Bug data showing how the bug removal effectiveness of each phase is calculated

Note that:

- The field phase doesn't create bugs and has therefore been excluded.
- The bug detection rate assumes that all the bugs are removed and that the changes/fixes are not themselves buggy (Figure 18.17).

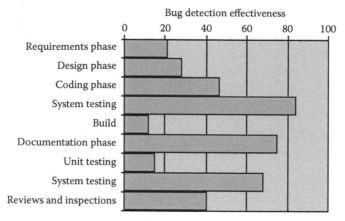

FIGURE 18.17  Bug detection effectiveness chart

Having established the table you are now in a position to:

- Persuade management to add resources for reviewing, inspections, and/or testing.
- Set phase-based bug detection and removal targets.
- Measure the result of such improvements.

# 18.10  Estimates of Bugs in the System

There are three questions which plague test managers:

- How effective are the tests at finding bugs?
- How many bugs are there in the software?
- When will the system be ready to release?

Here are some equations which can help.

## 18.10.1  Bug (Defect) Density Model

Each system has two characteristics (of many): the number of bugs and the number of non-commented lines of source code (KLOC):

$$bug\ density = \frac{bugs}{KLOC}$$

This can be calculated for each release such that given the size of any release the number of bugs can be calculated.

## 18.10.2  Bug (Defect) Density Model Caveats

There is a number of problems with this approach:

- The number of bugs must include both those found in the field and those found while testing. You cannot know the total number of bugs found in the field until the product is withdrawn from use. Thus the estimate is at its most accurate at the moment it is least useful.

- Bug densities vary: they are essentially a measure of the ability of the developers and analysts to err. Some err more than others, and may or may not improve over time.
- Some bugs may be hidden for a long time until exposed by some major change to the system.
- The measure is dependent on the language being used. There is likely to be a higher defect density in a very terse language like C++ than in a very prolix language like Cobol. Don't rely on comparisons of systems using different languages.
- There is as great a range of bugs as your classification system allows. So to know for example (see below) that your system is expected to have 1320 bugs found in it before the release doesn't tell you how many of those will be priority-1 bugs causing blue screens of death and customer database deletions. Practice shows that there is usually a stable proportion between the priorities when measured over a large number of releases. Exceptions to this rule occur when:
  - Management discourages anyone from reporting anything but the most serious bugs.
  - Attempts are made to reduce the priority levels of the most-critical bugs.
- Reusing well-tested code can have a big effect.

**TABLE 18.7** Bug density of four releases

| Release number | 4 | 4.1 | 5 | 5.1 |
|---|---|---|---|---|
| Code size totals by release | 75896 | 163289 | 200053 | 205121 |
| Problem numbers by release | 511 | 1580 | 3515 | 466 |
| Lines per bug | 148.52 | 103.35 | 56.91 | 440.17 |

The figures shown have been entirely skewed by the substitution of 3rd-party custom controls in Release 5.1 for (much buggier) homecrafted controls. The bug density of one per 440 lines was quite unpredictable from any preceding case.

An alternative to using KLOCs as a denominator is the *Function point* metric described later.

### 18.10.2.1 Case Study of Bug Density Used to Predict Release Readiness

Assume that:

- The first version of system X has 10 KLOC (KLOC = 1000 lines of executable code).
- 550 bugs were detected before release and 50 were detected in the field.
- Assume that sales of the system were sufficient to warrant building a further release (the 50 bugs found in the field had not precipitated lawsuits or bankruptcy).

Then

- The system has a total of 600 bugs.
- The system has a bug density of 600/10,000 = 0.06.
- The test efficiency (ability to find bugs before release) is 550/600 = 0.917.

Now assume that version 2 of System X has a bug density of 0.1 and has had to be withdrawn to avoid litigation. Clearly the bug count of version 3 had better be closer to 0.06 than 0.1. Assuming that:

- The target bug density > 0.06.
- The KLOC = 22.
- The test efficiency remains the same (0.917).

Then

- The total number of bugs expected to be found is 1320 (22000*0.06).
- The number of bugs expected to be found before release to the field is 1210 (22000*0.06*0.917).

This is a primitive example. A less-primitive one would show a range of test efficiencies and bug densities with standard deviations within which releases could be made.

### 18.10.2.2 Case Study of What Happens When Bug Density Is (Fairly) Static, But the Code Grows Uncontrollably

A project has several releases. Each release has:

- a number of lines of code (LOC) shown as thousands of LOC (KLOC), This increases from 106 to 440 KLOC
- a number of bugs per 10 KLOC overall which varies between 1 and 40
- a number of bugs per 10 KLOC per release which varies between 2 and 185.

Unfortunately (as in the last example) the size of the software as measured by KLOCs is increasing fast. The number of bugs is therefore also increasing.

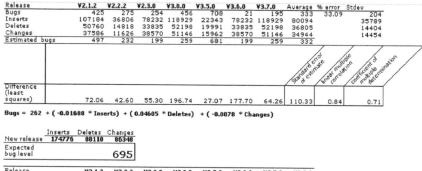

| Release | V2.1.2 | V2.2.2 | V2.3.0 | V3.0.0 | V3.5.0 | V3.6.0 | V3.7.0 | Average | % error | Stdev |
|---|---|---|---|---|---|---|---|---|---|---|
| Bugs | 425 | 275 | 254 | 456 | 708 | 21 | 195 | 333 | 33.09 | 204 |
| Inserts | 107184 | 36806 | 78232 | 118929 | 22343 | 78232 | 118929 | 80094 | | 35789 |
| Deletes | 50760 | 14818 | 33835 | 52198 | 19991 | 33835 | 52198 | 36805 | | 14404 |
| Changes | 37586 | 11626 | 38570 | 51146 | 15962 | 38570 | 51146 | 34944 | | 14454 |
| Estimated bugs | 497 | 232 | 199 | 259 | 681 | 199 | 259 | 332 | | |

| | | | | | | | | Standard error of estimate | Linear multiple correlation | coefficient of multiple determination |
|---|---|---|---|---|---|---|---|---|---|---|
| Difference (least squares) | | 72.06 | 42.60 | 55.30 | 196.74 | 27.07 | 177.70 | 64.26 | 110.33 | 0.84 | 0.71 |

Bugs = 262 + ( -0.01688 * Inserts) + ( 0.04605 * Deletes) + ( -0.0078 * Changes)

| | Inserts | Deletes | Changes |
|---|---|---|---|
| New release | 174776 | 88110 | 86348 |
| Expected bug level | | | 695 |

| Release | V2.1.2 | V2.2.2 | V2.3.0 | V3.0.0 | V3.5.0 | V3.6.0 | V3.7.0 | V3.8.0 |
|---|---|---|---|---|---|---|---|---|
| KLOC (overall) | 106 | 128 | 173 | 240 | 242 | 286 | 353 | 440 |
| 10*Bugs/KLOC overall | 40 | 21 | 15 | 19 | 29 | 1 | 6 | 16 |
| 10*Bugs/KLOC per release | 29 | 57 | 22 | 27 | 185 | 2 | 11 | 27 |

**FIGURE 18.18** What happens to an out-of-control project 1

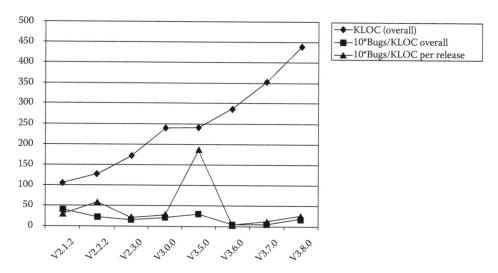

**FIGURE 18.19** What happens to an out-of-control project 2

In addition note that the quality of the 10*bugs/KLOC/release is also very variable. Release 3.5 was a major problem. Two solutions to the project's dilemma were:

- Greatly reduce the bug rate, probably by unit testing (which had been negligible).
- Reduce the code size by having a tool check for dead code and rewriting the larger units in a more-elegant way.

Well-managed projects have:

- A decreasing bugs/KLOC/release level
- A flat bugs/KLOC/overall level
- Regular code culling to reduce its growth

## 18.10.3  Bug Prediction KLOC Estimate [Takahashi]

The following model has been proposed by [Takahashi] and can be applied only when coding is finished. This uses the following equation to predict the number of bugs per 1000 lines of code:

The number of bugs per KLOC =

$$67.98 + 0.46*f_1 - 9.62*f_2 - 0.08*f_3$$

where

$f_1$ = the number of bug reports required to change the design and code during the coding phase per KLOC

$f_2$ = the average number of years experience of programming of all programmers involved

$f_3$ = the number of pages of new and modified high- and low-level design documents used per KLOC

### A Worked Example

$$f_1 = 10, \ f_2 = 5.3, \ f_3 = 8$$

The number of bugs per KLOC = 20.954

## 18.10.4  A Worked Example of Bug Prediction Using Multiple-Regression

This is a simple method of predicting bugs. It requires that:

- You have made several releases already and are able to identify the total number of bugs found in each release.
- You can identify the number of lines of code inserted, changed, and deleted, and the number of bugs fixed for each release:

The project had already made 5 releases and wanted to know what the bug level was likely to be for the next. Using a spreadsheet derived from the equations in section 18.15, an initial estimate of 797 bugs overall was given. The mean BRE (see below) of this figure is 16% so you should allow for between 670 and 925 bugs to be found (797 bugs ± 16%).

Various caveats are in order:

- The equation depends entirely on the number of *inserts, updates,* and *deletes.* These will increase as builds are made and tested accurately. To predict the number of bugs to be found before the release is made requires that you estimate the total number of *inserts, updates,* and *deletes* to be made by the moment of release. You can estimate these by taking weekly history files from the configuration management database, plotting them on a chart, and observing the trends.
- As the number of bugs found in old releases rises (since not everyone updates to new ones) you will need to recalibrate the model.
- Multiple regression analysis is very sensitive to extremes in the input data.
- The number of bugs shown is the total. In practice you have only to get the overall proportion of critical, high, medium, and low bugs from the project to get a good estimate of how to split the total predicted. This release might be a little different though.
- You need to allow for error by calibrating against the original data. In this case two estimating error approaches have been used:

–   Magnitude of Relative Error (MRE) is calculated as

$$\frac{|actual - estimate|}{actual}$$

This can lead to an exaggeration since under-estimates are insufficiently weighted. Note the mean relative error bias, which is an underestimate of 0.03 or 3%.

–   Balanced Relative Error (BRE) is calculated as

$$\frac{actual - estimate}{\min(actual, estimate)}$$

This balances over- and under-estimation evenly. Note the *Mean Balanced Relative Error* bias below of 0.01 or 1%.

See [Miyazaki] for more on MRE and BRE; also see Figure 18.20 for a bug prediction spreadsheet, and section 18.15 for more on this.

| Release | V2.1.2 | V2.2.2 | V2.3.0 | V3.0.0 | V3.5.0 | V3.6.0 | V3.7.0 | Average | Stdev |
|---|---|---|---|---|---|---|---|---|---|
| Bugs | 425 | 275 | 254 | 456 | 708 | 240 | 295 | 379 | 155 |
| Inserts | 107184 | 36806 | 78232 | 118929 | 22343 | 78232 | 118929 | 80094 | 35789 |
| Deletes | 50760 | 14818 | 33835 | 52198 | 19991 | 33835 | 52198 | 36805 | 14404 |
| Changes | 37586 | 11626 | 38570 | 51146 | 15962 | 38570 | 51146 | 34944 | 14454 |
| Estimated bugs | 477 | 246 | 291 | 330 | 689 | 291 | 330 | 379 | |

| | Inserts | Deletes | Changes |
|---|---|---|---|
| New release | 174776 | 88110 | 86348 |

Bugs = 281 + ( -0.01671 * Inserts) + ( 0.03953 * Deletes)  + ( -0.00053 * Changes)

| Expected bug level | 797 |
|---|---|

| | |
|---|---|
| Mean Magnitude of Relative Error | 0.14 |
| **Mean Balanced Relative Error** | **0.16** |
| Mean Relative Error Bias | -0.03 |
| **Mean Balanced Magnitude of Relative Error Bias** | **-0.01** |

FIGURE 18.20   Bug prediction spreadsheet

Who cares about this figure of between 669 and 925 bugs? If no one else, you do. With this figure in mind you are in a position to refute any suggestions that there are only 254 bugs to be found (as in version 2.3.0). These bugs will take longer to find than in version 2.3.0, and since you can estimate the average time it takes you to find a 100 bugs (based on the length of time you took to find all the others), you'll be in a better position to estimate when the release is ready. You will not be loved for telling management that system testing will possibly take longer even than version 3.5.0, but then you're not paid to be loved.

## 18.10.5   Twin Test Team Model (Remus and Zilles)

It is sometimes the case that more than one team is involved in testing a system. Team 1 may consist of (say) testers, whereas team 2 consists of (say) users. The rationale is that the testers release nothing to the users until it is of a useable quality. An advantage of this approach is that eventually both teams are testing the same system and sometimes finding the same bugs.

The bugs found (and in particular the duplicated bugs) are invaluable. Record them all and mark the duplicates. Our objective is to estimate the total number of bugs in the system. We know:

•   The bugs found by team 1 and team 2
•   The duplicates

We need to find the test effectiveness of each team. This can be expressed as:

$$effectiveness\ of\ team\ 1 = \frac{number\ of\ bugs\ found\ by\ team\ 1}{total\ number\ of\ bugs}$$

$$effectiveness\ of\ team\ 2 = \frac{number\ of\ bugs\ found\ by\ team\ 2}{total\ number\ of\ bugs}$$

Here's the clever bit: the test effectiveness of team 1 can be measured as being some proportion of the faults found by team 2. Team 1 found

$$\frac{duplicates}{number\ of\ bugs\ found\ by\ team\ 2}$$

of all the bugs found by team 2. Similarly team 2 found

$$\frac{duplicates}{number\ of\ bugs\ found\ by\ team\ 1}$$

of all the tests found by team 1. Put into equations this is:

$$effectiveness\ of\ team\ 1 = \frac{duplicates}{number\ of\ bugs\ found\ by\ team\ 2}$$

and

$$effectiveness\ of\ team\ 2 = \frac{duplicates}{number\ of\ bugs\ found\ by\ team\ 1}$$

The test effectiveness of the two teams is

$$effectiveness\ of\ both\ teams = effectiveness\ of\ team\ 1 \times effectiveness\ of\ team\ 2$$

Thus we have a way of calculating total number of bugs in the system:

$$total\ number\ of\ bugs = \frac{duplicates}{effectiveness\ of\ both\ teams}$$

## Twin Test Team Model Example

Given the expanded equation:

$$total\ number\ of\ bugs = \frac{duplicates}{\frac{duplicates}{bugs\ found\ by\ team\ 2} \times \frac{duplicates}{bugs\ found\ by\ team\ 1}}$$

and some data:

- Bugs found by team 1 = 50
- Bugs found by team 2 = 60
- Duplicates = 30

we can see the total number of bugs (= 100). Thus we can also calculate the number of bugs left to be found (= 20).

> *bugs left to be found = total number of bugs − bugs found by team 1 − bugs found by team 2 + duplicates*

### Twin Test Team Model Caveat

The value of this estimate is limited since it will probably change over time. This is because:

- The estimate is most useful at the end of system testing (since all the figures will grow until then).
- Not all features are in place (and some will be buggier than others).
- Critical bugs are discovered that inhibit the testing of major features until they're fixed.
- The cost of the method is the number of duplicates found.

Nevertheless it is useful as a means of getting a working hypothesis and comparing it with others.

## 18.10.6  Bug Seeding Model

Another technique for answering such questions as "how many bugs has the system got in it?" is called bug seeding or bebugging. This technique requires that bugs be randomly inserted into a program. This can be done by using a standard set of random numbers to define the non-comment source code lines to be seeded and then seeding them, and assumes you have seeded a system homogeneously with a representative set of faults.

A set of tests may then be run. The effectiveness of the tests may be assessed from the number of seeded bugs found, to give two equations:

$$test\ effectiveness = \frac{number\ of\ seeded\ bugs\ found}{number\ of\ seeded\ bugs} \tag{1}$$

$$estimated\ number\ of\ bugs = \frac{number\ of\ unseeded\ (indigenous)\ bugs\ found}{test\ effectiveness} \tag{2a}$$

or put more simply

$$estimated\ number\ of\ bugs = \frac{number\ of\ unseeded\ bugs\ found \times number\ of\ bug\ seeded}{number\ of\ seeded\ bugs\ found} \tag{2b}$$

These are however very crude functions and make no allowance for the possibility that the seeded and indigenous bugs found might be unrepresentative.

A seeded bug is often of the following type:

- Assignment operator used rather than a comparison operator ("= =" rather than "=") or the reverse
- A "Greater Than" operator used rather than a "Less Than" operator (">" rather than "<"), or the reverse
- *Off-by-one* bug (particularly in DO loops) "FOR I = 1 to n" rather than "FOR I = 1 to n+1" or "FOR I = 1 to n − 1"

If you need to know what sort of bugs your developers make, look at the code history files (showing which lines were added/deleted/modified) and of course the bug reports.

Bug seeding models require that you use a distribution model such as the binomial or Poisson distributions (see [Shooman], [Mills 72], and below for further details).

## 18.10.7   Bug Types through the Life-Cycle

Some interesting data has come out of IBM and ICL (now Fujitsu).[1] It suggests that most bugs in high-level documents are due to things being "missing," whereas in low-level documents rather more are "wrong" (see Table 18.8 and Table 18.9).

**TABLE 18.8**   IBM data on bug types

| IBM data | Missing | Wrong | Extra |
|---|---|---|---|
| | | % | |
| Design | 61 | 34 | 5 |
| Code | 26 | 62 | 12 |

**TABLE 18.9**   ICL data on bug types

| ICL data (Omega Project) | Total defects | Missing | Wrong | Extra |
|---|---|---|---|---|
| | | | % | |
| (High-Level) Requirements | 203 | 63 | 34 | 3 |
| Development plans | 451 | 61 | 33 | 6 |
| Product specifications[a] | 1627 | 56 | 40 | 4 |
| Design specifications | 503 | 53 | 39 | 8 |
| Alpha test specs | 472 | 71 | 26 | 3 |
| Beta test specs | 290 | 51 | 39 | 10 |
| Code listings | 228 | 26 | 45 | 29 |
| Total and averages | 3774 | 54 | 37 | 9 |

[a]   Lower-level requirements.

## 18.10.7   Binomial Distribution

You need to know how much you can rely on your estimate. The probability of $k$ seeded bugs being detected in some software with $r$ bugs already detected (Pr(n, k, N, r)) is given by the equation:

$$\Pr(n,k,r) = \dfrac{\left(\dfrac{n!}{(n-k)! \times k!}\right) \times \left(\dfrac{\left(\dfrac{r \times n}{k}\right)!}{\left(\left(\dfrac{r*n}{k}\right)-r\right)! \times r!}\right)}{\dfrac{\left(\dfrac{r \times n}{k}+n\right)!}{\left(\left(\dfrac{r*n}{k}+n\right)-(r+k)\right)! \times (r+k)!}}$$

---

[1]   ivs.cs.uni-magdeburg.de/sw-eng/us/experiments/gilb/

In Excel notation:

$$= \text{FACT}(n)/(\text{FACT}(n-k)*\text{FACT}(k))*(\text{FACT}((r*n)/k))/ (\text{FACT}(((r*n)/k)-r)* \text{FACT}(r)) /$$
$$(\text{FACT}(((r*n)/k)+n)/ (\text{FACT}((((r*n)/k)+n)-(r+k))*\text{FACT}(r+k))) \qquad (18.7)$$

where

    n = number of seeded bugs
    k = number of detected seeded bugs, which can be found from Equation (18.2) (see section 18.10.2)
    r = detected indigenous bugs

**Note 1:** it is as well to seed the bugs sparingly such that the seeded bugs are likely to be less than the indigenous ones. Otherwise you will be attempting to find factorial $n < 0$ and the attempt will fail.
**Note 2:** the value of the test depends on:

- The probability that the proportion of seeded bugs found to those inserted is the same as the proportion of indigenous bugs found of the total of indigenous bugs.
- The seeded bugs being of the same type and severity as the indigenous ones, thus the choice of seeded bugs is critical. Use bug reports to determine the mix.

**TABLE 18.10**    Binomial distribution example

| | | |
|---|---|---|
| Number of seeded bugs | n | 10 |
| Number of detected, seeded bugs | k | 9 |
| Number of detected indigenous bugs | r | 20 |
| Total indigenous bugs | N | 22 |
| Probability of finding k and r | Pr | 0.4657258 |
| Test efficiency | | 0.9 |

**Example**

A unit was selected and 6 bugs were introduced into it. Of these, 5 were detected by the unit tests, which also detected 20 unseeded or indigenous bugs (see Table 18.10). From this it was concluded that:

- The unit probably contains 22 indigenous bugs.
- The probability of the bugs being found was 0.4657258.
- The efficiency of the tests was 90%.

## 18.10.9  Poisson Distribution

When performance testing you may find it more useful to estimate the probability of bugs being found over a period of time. Here, a version of the Poisson distribution provides a solution. The equation is:

$$\frac{e^{-\lambda t} \bullet \lambda t^r}{r!}$$

| | =(EXP(-B1*B2)*POWER((B1*B2),B3))/FACT(B3) |
|---|---|

| | A | B |
|---|---|---|
| 1 | lambda ($\lambda$) | 0.05 |
| 2 | t | 50 |
| 3 | r | 1 |
| 8 | | 0.205212497 |

where

    $\lambda$ = a constant representing the frequency with which a bug is found
    t = time the software is tested
    r = number of bugs found

**Example**

Assuming that:

- Bugs occur at the rate of 0.05 of a bug each day
- The software is tested for 50 days

then the probability of finding a single bug ($r$) is 0.21.

## 18.10.10  Zero-Failure Approach to Release Readiness Estimation

Assuming all the major bugs (are believed to) have been teased out of the system we need to know how much time must be spent testing before a product may be released. This method is described by [Brettschneider]. It is based on some period being defined during which no further failures must be found if some level of reliability (measured as $n$ bugs or less being found by the customer) is to be achieved. It assumes that:

- The product is being constantly tested at the same intensity.
- The probability of a bug remaining in the product is proportional to the time spent testing the product without finding one.
- 0.5 of a bug = 0.0 of a bug (this simply adds statistical conservatism).

The method uses the equation

$$p(t) = a \times e^{-f(t)}$$

This is calculated thus:

$$a \times \frac{\ln(\frac{f}{0.5+f})}{\ln(\frac{0.5+f}{s+f})}$$

where

$a$ = no. of test hours since the last problem was observed
$f$ = expected number of field failures
$s$ = number of test failures discovered to far

Thus, assuming:

- A total of 500 hours of testing of which the last 50 hours have exhibited no errors ($a = 500 50 = 450$)
- A target of no more than 1 field failure ($f = 1$)
- A total of 15 errors discovered so far during the first 450 hours of testing ($s = 15$)

we can calculate (using the following Excel formula):

$$= a^*(LN(f/(0.5+f))/LN((0.5+f)/(s+f)))$$

giving 77.08.

Thus if no error is observed in the following 22.52 (77.08 – 50) hours of testing the product can be released. If one is, then the clock must be restarted and 76 hours of fault-free testing on a new release must occur before release readiness is demonstrable.

## 18.10.11   Weibull Approach to Release Readiness Estimation

At the start of testing you will have done your estimates and established a total for the number of bugs you expect to find. You then need to establish:

- How long it will take to find them
- When you can release

Here is a method of doing both. Start by downloading the bugs found so far from the database of the bug-tracking tool (Figure 18.21). Then echo that raw data through to another page (because you will want to update it) such that you have:

**FIGURE 18.21**   Adding the raw bug data

- The date of the bugs (column F)
- Each bug's severity (critical, high, medium, and low in this case) echoed as a 1 in the related severity column (Figure 18.22)

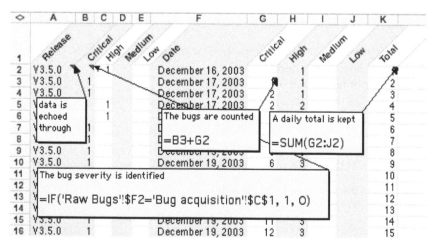

**FIGURE 18.22**   Echoing and preparing the raw bug data

- The running total of that bug severity
- A total column for checking

Then on another sheet prepare the predicted and actual data:

- The total number of bugs predicted (you can vary this)
- The start date

- The expected duration (of the system, or other tests)
- Two Weibull parameters: $c$ (scale parameter) and $m$ (shape parameter)
- A column of 100 moments (each of 0.01), which will be used in the calculation; the purpose of the 100 moments is to limit the number of dates from which we sample the bug levels

Weibull curves have been shown (see the discussion in [Kan] and [Weibull]) to be manipulable to approximate to bug detection curves. Using the 100 moments we can create a list of the predicted bugs and manipulate the rate (the curves) at which they are predicted to be found, to match the rate at which they are actually found. To do this we need to tweak the $c$ and $m$ variables such that the curves match as much as possible (Figure 18.23).

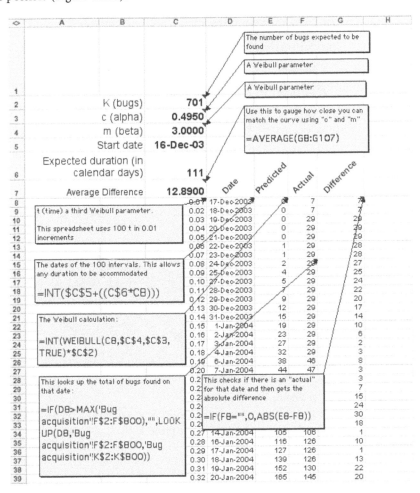

**FIGURE 18.23** Preparing the predicted and actual data

From the 3 columns **Date, Predicted,** and **Actual,** create a graph like the one shown in Figure 18.24.

Use the *Average Difference* figure to match the curve best (start with the $c$ and when that has minimized the *Average Difference* as much as possible use $m$).

If the difference becomes irreconcilable (for example, the actual appears to be about to grow higher than the predicted) then raise $K$ (*bugs*) and lengthen the *Expected Duration*.

The value of this approach is that you can begin matching the actual versus predicted very early.

Use the **G, H, I,** and **J** columns of Figure 18.22 to create another table showing the bug severity distribution (Figure 18.25).

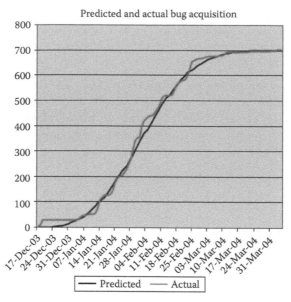

FIGURE 18.24   The Weibull curve (also known as the probability density function)

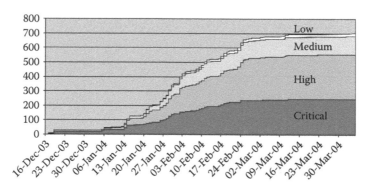

FIGURE 18.25   Bug severity distribution

Use the source data as shown in Figure 18.26 (in Excel).

**Note:** holding *m* = 2 makes the Weibull curve the *Rayleigh* curve, which can be used to model the bug detection curves (among many other things) of the entire project.

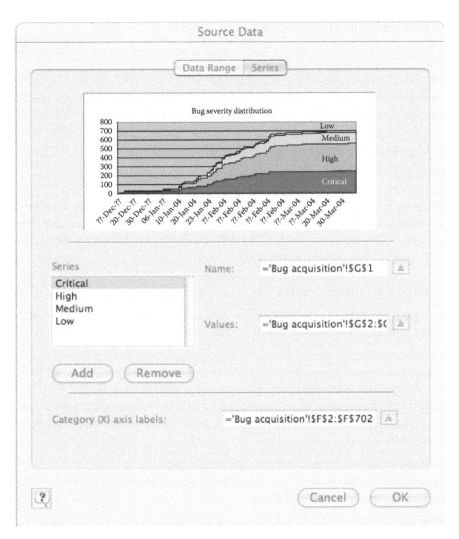

**FIGURE 18.26**  Bug severity distribution source data

## 18.11   Function Point Metric

Given the variability of the KLOC metric between project groups and even within a project over time as an estimate of project size some alternative means called the *function point* (FP) has been researched [Albrecht]. Function point analysis can be used to:

- Estimate system component size
- Estimate effort at an early stage
- Validate effort estimates derived in some other way
- Rank system functions into complexity order
- Ensure that either the system is very well understood or at least identify those parts which are not clearly defined
- Estimate bug quantity (as at 2002, the U.S. military estimated there would be 5 bugs per function point)

Applying the method requires some analysis of the system. Once that exists, the calculation takes a few man-hours for most systems.

### 18.11.1  Overview of the Function Point Method

Albrecht's method counts certain features and employs simple arithmetic to derive a number which represents the system's size and complexity.

The method lets us size a system by assessing the size of the system's information model, its external interfaces to other systems, and the number and complexity of transactions. It can be used at any stage of the lifecycle, from requirements specification onwards.

### 18.11.2  Use of the Function Point Results

Albrecht derived several formulae, based on an analysis of 41 IBM projects, relating FPs to effort-months and lines of COBOL and PL/l.

Function points are however reasonable indicators of the delivered program size, usually measured as the number of high-level language statements. But FPs alone are not a good predictor of effort, since the Albrecht method leaves out many of the COCOMO cost drivers which allow for the risk to the project of, for example, using less experienced staff or fewer tools.

### 18.11.3  Function Point Inputs

You can only apply function point analysis or any systematic method of estimation when you have at least a minimal functional specification with the following details:

- An information model, identifying all objects in the real world about which the system will have to keep information. These might be shown as an entity-relationship diagram, the set of datastore items in a detailed dataflow diagram, or in an *UML* activity diagram.
- A list of functions provided by the system or a list of events to which the system must respond.
- A list of constraints, specifying the performance, availability, reliability, and other non-functional requirements.

The final stage is performing the function point calculation itself.

### 18.11.4  Function Type Definitions

There are five sources of functionality to be identified and recorded:

1. **Logical internal files** containing data which the users wish to maintain within their system. They correspond to "entities" in the system data model. These are not necessarily the same as the files defined during system design.
2. **External interface files** that enter or leave the bounds of the system and are used or maintained in other systems.
3. **External inputs.** Typically user data entry, but these may represent batch processes.
4. **External outputs.** Typically user data entry, but may represent batch processes. Information which the user gets from the system, typically reports and displays.
5. **External inquiries.** A combined input/output operation. The user enters a request for information and receives an immediate reply. The format and processing would be less complex than for a report.

Each source of functionality is classified as simple, average, or complex. While functions are incompletely defined in many requirements documents, identifying their existence early on is more important than classifying it. By default, assume average complexity.

With care, the counting may be based on dataflow and structure diagrams resulting from the application of the Yourdon or *UML* techniques, but check the level of detail implied by any diagrams to see if functions can be identified from it.

For reference, the Albrecht complexity weightings are summarized here.

**TABLE 18.11**    Albrecht weightings

| | Complexity weight | | |
| --- | --- | --- | --- |
| Function type | Simple | Average | Complex |
| Logical internal file | 7 | 10 | 15 |
| External interface file | 5 | 7 | 10 |
| External input | 3 | 4 | 6 |
| External output | 4 | 5 | 7 |
| External enquiry | 3 | 4 | 6 |

The complexity classification is based on standards.

## 18.11.5   Function Point Assessment Process

The calculation is performed in three stages:

1. Classification and counting of five user function types: external user inputs, outputs, enquiries, "internal" files, and "external" files. Each is classified as simple, average, or complex and the results are weighted and summed to produce a function count (FC).

$$\textit{function count} = \sum_{i=1}^{5}\sum_{j=1}^{3} w_{ij} \times x_{ij}$$

where $w_{ij}$ = the weighting factors of the 5 components by the three complexity levels, and $x_{ij}$ = the numbers of each component in the system.

2. A value adjustment factor (VAF) is then calculated by considering 12 systemwide cost drivers:
   a. Data communications
   b. Distributed functions
   c. Performance
   d. Heavily-used configuration
   e. Online data entry
   f. End-user efficiency
   g. Online update
   h. Complex processing
   i. Reusability
   j. Installation ease
   k. Operational ease
   l. Facilitation of change
   and the impact of performance requirements.

$$VAF = 0.65 + 0.01 \sum_{i=1}^{14} c_i$$

where $c_i$ = the score of system characteristic $i$.

3. Deriving the function point value (FPV), which is simply the product FC × VAF.

See www.ifpug.org/ for further details.

## 18.12   Test Case Estimation

A critical part of the planning and management of testing is to balance the risk of a bug remaining in the code against the effort required. This involves asking a number of pertinent questions as the tests are being planned:

1. How many bugs does the software contain?
2. How many bugs will we find?
3. How many bugs can we risk allowing to remain in the system once the testing is finished?
4. How many tests should be written?
5. How long should the tests be run for?
6. Which parts of the system should we test most thoroughly?
7. What are the best sorts of test to use? (See section 2.2 in Chapter 2.)
8. When will the release be in a fit state? (When the number of bugs found (2) = number of bugs the software is believed to contain (1) overall, less the number we can afford to leave in (3).)
9. How many bugs are likely to be introduced per fix? (How many bugs are found in a release containing fixes which weren't there when the tests were run on the immediately-preceding release? How many fixes were made in that release? *Caveat*: this estimate is only feasible if the release is entirely testable; that is, there is no bug which inhibits access to any feature.)
10. Is the structure of the code so entropic that it is better to throw it away and start again? (Are the numbers of bugs introduced per fix rising? Then identify the features with the largest numbers of bugs and rewrite the top 20%. Repeat until the rate of bug introduction starts to drop.)
11. Which features have the most/least bugs? (Ensure the bug-management tool lists the feature names.)
12. Which tests have found the most/least bugs? (Ensure the bug-management tool lists the test names.)
13. How many lines of code per bug per release?
14. How many (critical) bugs are found per build? (Are we getting better?)

Answers to these can be found using statistical estimations based on many years of experience of software development.

This chapter discusses these questions beginning with the question of the complexity of code and the limits to which it can be tested.

Note that there is no foolproof method of test-case estimating yet discovered. All one can currently attempt is to use several approaches and see how well, if at all, they converge.

### 18.12.1   The Difficulty of Estimating System Test Cases

The table in Figure 18.27 shows various counts of words, tests, and test steps. It was derived from a big project whose requirements specifications were prose-based and feature-specific in that each specification corresponded to a feature. The tests were written using TestDirector™ and each test consisted of at least one test step.

| Feature | No of words in spec | No of words in test | No of tests | No of test steps | words (spec/test) | words/tests | words/test steps |
|---|---|---|---|---|---|---|---|
| 1 | 2963 | 2646 | 23 | 55 | 1.12 | 128 | 53 |
| 2 | 4277 | 1201 | 16 | 41 | 3.56 | 267 | 104 |
| 3 | 6425 | 13248 | 66 | 254 | 0.48 | 97 | 25 |
| 4 | 26112 | 29718 | 62 | 368 | 0.88 | 421 | 70 |
| 5 | 5693 | 2655 | 15 | 58 | 2.14 | 379 | 98 |
| 6 | 3439 | 2513 | 50 | 60 | 1.37 | 68 | 57 |

FIGURE 18.27   Features and tests

The number of words of each feature requirements specification and test were counted. The specifications and scripts were all written by the same groups of analysts and testers.

**Conclusions**

1. None of the figures are anything more than indicative. Other business analysts and testers may be more or less terse.
2. There is no necessary relationship between specification size and test size. Feature 3 for example generated 1 test word for every 0.48 specification words, whereas feature 2 generated 3.56.
3. Persuade the project manager to have the system modeled using *UML* down to Activity diagram level. Then use section A.2 in Appendix A to derive the test objectives.

## 18.12.2 The Limits of Testing

Figure 18.28 shows a typical unit. It has a McCabe complexity value (see section 18.8.4) of 9, derived from the 8 decision points plus 1. See also D6 and the Terms Used section for further details of the [McCabe] complexity measure. It has 2 loops totaling 24 possible iterations and therefore the number of paths it could execute are

```
(6¹²+6¹¹...6¹) * (8²+8¹)  = 1.88074E+11
```

**FIGURE 18.28** A typical unit

Assuming a test could be written, executed, and analyzed every 5 minutes it would require 9 million years to completely test the unit. The solution to this problem is to divide the unit into the 13 *basic* blocks shown and then test each basic block.

While this limitation is particularly true of units it is also true of systems as a whole. To minimize this problem we need to be able to divide it into bits. In this case a useful way is to divide the unit into *basic* blocks, each of which is then tested. There are 13 basic blocks and the objective is to show that for every possible input to every block there is a correct output. In this way only 13 sets of tests need be defined.

However we still need to know how many cases each set of tests should contain. This is where the methods shown in Figure 18.29 come in handy.

## 18.12.3 Test Case Estimation (Like Last Time)

Assuming that several releases have already been made, one very crude approach is to identify the number of:

- Features in the last $n$ releases
- *Test cases* created for the last $n$ releases
- Bugs found in the field and in-house for the last $n$ releases
- Projected new features[2]

Use section 18.15 to estimate the number of *test cases*.

**Example**

Assume we have the following input:

| Release | V2.1.2 | V2.2.2 | V2.3.0 | V3.0.0 | V3.5.0 | V3.6.0 | V3.7.0 |
|---|---|---|---|---|---|---|---|
| Test cases | 390 | 260 | 267 | 430 | 680 | 205 | 281 |
| Features | 9 | 6 | 6 | 12 | 15 | 5 | 6 |
| Bugs (found in house) | 425 | 275 | 254 | 456 | 708 | 240 | 295 |
| Bugs (found in field) | 25 | 6 | 8 | 30 | 49 | 8 | 12 |
| Estimated test cases | 396 | 271 | 240 | 435 | 675 | 218 | 273 |

---

[2] How big is a feature? If your company specifies things well, this will be obvious from the requirements specification. Each feature will perhaps occupy an individual section. If some features are far bigger than others, try counting the words used to describe it, use the average as a common denominator, and mark each feature as being 0.9 or 1.1 of that common feature.

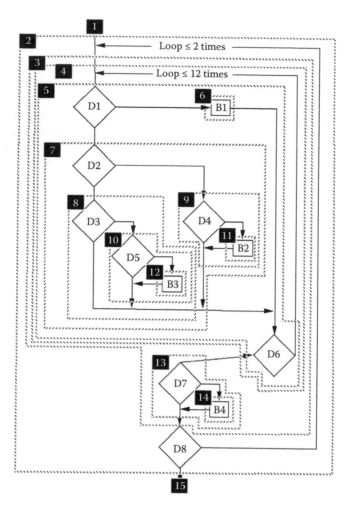

**FIGURE 18.29**  Number of executable paths

and that we calculate that there will be 450 bugs (see section 18.10), of which 400 will be found in-house and 50 in the field. We will need to write a total of 316 (±13, the Mean Balanced Relative Error):

| | Features | Bugs (found in house) | Bugs (found in field) |
|---|---|---|---|
| New release | 14 | 400 | 50 |

Test cases = -61 + ( 7.10095 * Features) + ( 1.12826 * Bugs (found in house)) + ( -3.46093 * Bugs (found in field))

| Minimum No. of test cases | 303 | | Expected number of test cases | 316 | | Maximum No. of test cases | 329 |
|---|---|---|---|---|---|---|---|

| | |
|---|---|
| Mean Magnitude of Relative Error | 0.04 |
| **Mean Balanced Relative Error** | **0.04** |
| Mean Relative Error Bias | 0.00 |
| **Mean Balanced Magnitude of Relative Error Bias** | **0.00** |

Possibly this may impose an unacceptable load on *Support*, and management wants no more than 25 bugs to be found in the field. This shows we will need 431 (±17) *test cases*. Does management want to spend 19% more on testing just to drop the Support costs by 50%?

| | Features | Bugs (found in house) | Bugs (found in field) |
|---|---|---|---|
| New release | 14 | 400 | 50 |

Test cases = -61 + ( 7.10095 * Features) + ( 1.12826 * Bugs (found in house)) + ( -3.46093 * Bugs (found in field))

| Minimum No. of test cases | 303 | Expected number of test cases | 316 | Maximum No. of test cases | 329 |
|---|---|---|---|---|---|

| | |
|---|---|
| Mean Magnitude of Relative Error | 0.04 |
| **Mean Balanced Relative Error** | **0.04** |
| Mean Relative Error Bias | 0.00 |
| **Mean Balanced Magnitude of Relative Error Bias** | **0.00** |

Notice how small is the Mean Balanced Relative Error. Unless the new release is very unusual, the estimates (in this case) will be correct to 4%. Had the input figures fluctuated greatly the MBRE would have been bigger and the estimate subject to a bigger variation.

Note that attempting to use the number of screens as an estimate is unwise. Developers are rather good at coding up screens. It's the stuff behind them which causes the problems.

## A Variation

If the developers are brave enough to predict the code size, you can substitute the code size for the features:

- Get the average code size of the last $n$ releases at the start of system testing ($KLOC_{S1} \ldots KLOC_{Sn}$).
- Get the average code size of the last $n$ releases at the end of system testing ($KLOC_{E1} \ldots KLOC_{En}$).
- Identify the average growth rate of the code:

$$\% average\ code\ growth = \frac{\sum_{n} \dfrac{KLOC_{En} - KLOC_{Sn}}{KLOC_{En}}}{n} \bullet 100$$

- Get the code size estimate at the start of the new project ($KLOC_{Ns}$).
- Multiply it by (($100 + \%$ *average code growth*)$/100$) to give the estimated $KLOC_{Ne}$ at the end of the project.
- Use the code sizes in the equation.

## Another Example

| Release | V2.1.2 | V2.2.2 | V2.3.0 | V3.0.0 | V3.5.0 | V3.6.0 | V3.7.0 | Average | Stdev |
|---|---|---|---|---|---|---|---|---|---|
| Test cases | 390 | 260 | 267 | 430 | 680 | 205 | 281 | 359 | 150 |
| Code size | 195530 | 63250 | 150637 | 222273 | 58296 | 150637 | 222273 | 151842 | 63732 |
| Bugs (found in house) | 425 | 275 | 254 | 456 | 708 | 240 | 295 | 379 | 155 |
| Bugs (found in field) | 25 | 6 | 8 | 30 | 49 | 8 | 12 | 20 | 15 |
| Estimated test cases | 402 | 267 | 238 | 427 | 677 | 221 | 281 | 359 | |

| | Code size | Bugs (found in house) | Bugs (found in field) |
|---|---|---|---|
| New release | 794776 | 425 | 25 |

Test cases = -65 + ( 0.00005 * Code size) + ( 1.26496 * Bugs (found in house)) + ( -3.2009 * Bugs (found in field))

| Minimum number of test cases | 416 | Expected number of test cases | 432 | Maximum number of test cases | 448 |
|---|---|---|---|---|---|

| | |
|---|---|
| Mean Magnitude of Relative Error | 0.04 |
| **Mean Balanced Relative Error** | **0.04** |
| Mean Relative Error Bias | 0.00 |
| **Mean Balanced Magnitude of Relative Error Bias** | **0.00** |

### 18.12.4 Test Case Estimation [Capers Jones]

Capers Jones [Jones 1] and [Jones 2] suggest two equations exploiting Function Points (see below):

$$\text{system test cases} \approx FP^{1.2}$$

$$\text{acceptance test cases} \approx FP \times 1.2$$

Capers Jones also suggests that

> Civilian projects tend to average about 2 *test cases* per function point, while military software projects tend to average about 3 *test cases* per function point.[3]

### 18.12.5 Why Use Function Points for Test Estimation?

Function points have many advantages over simple lines of code:

- They are language-independent. If you are testing a system being translated from one language to another any estimates based on the original language may be quite useless.
- They are programmer-independent. The difference in productivity between best and worst programmers may be as high as 5:1. This may also be reflected in the code size and the bug levels, too.
- They can be defined before a line of code has been written.
- They can be used in place of deletions, inserts, and changes in an effort to predict bug levels. At a very crude level 3, old versions of a system could be analyzed to identify their function points and total bugs. They can then be analyzed to show:

$$\text{total new bugs in a new version} = \frac{\text{new FPs} \times \text{average old bugs}}{\text{average old FPs}}$$

- More subtly, the weighted function points for the { Logical Internal File | External Interface File | External Input | External Output | External Enquiry } of a new version can be related to the bug level for that version using multiple regression analysis.

## 18.13 Cost of Finding and Fixing a Coding Bug

### 18.13.1 The Equation

Here is a simple equation to calculate the cost of someone writing a test and the cost of someone finding and fixing the bug which the test exhibits.

$$\text{cost of a bug (found in-house)} = (\text{test preparation time} + \text{test execution time} + \frac{(\text{finding and fixing time})}{\text{No of bugs}}$$

Thus a test which required 50 tester-hours to write and 2 tester-hours to run finds 24 bugs. Each bug takes an average of 2.7 hours to locate and fix:

= 50+2+(24*2.7)

= 116.8, or 4.87 hours per bug

Assuming that testers cost \$45 per hour and developers \$50, this gives a cost per bug of \$232.50.

---

[3] www.qucis.queensu.ca/FAQs/SE/archive/funcpoints

This equation can be extended to cope with requirements-level bugs by including all the personnel involved in the phases needed to echo through a changed requirement back into code. It is also one of the main bases on which you can justify test automation. As the cost of test development decline relative to test execution, automated testing becomes increasingly cost-effective.

## 18.13.2  How to Calculate the Cost of Finding and Fixing Bugs

Let us begin with some assumptions.

- We need to know the cost of:
  - Coding
  - Bug finding and fixing
- We know:
  - The amount of time each developer spends on developing overall (from the time sheets)
  - The developer responsible for finding and fixing each bug (from the unit headers where the reason for the unit's modification is listed)
  - The amount of time each developer spends on average per week in company meetings, emailing, telephoning, getting in pizzas at night, chatting over coffee (guess)
  - The date each:
    - Buggy unit was retrieved from the bug management database
    - Fixed unit was returned to the configuration management database
  - That developers:
    - Either design systems, write code, debug code, unit test, lead other developers, or advise other staff
    - May be temporarily assigned to fix bugs on other projects
    - Spend time (maybe 20%) in company meetings, emailing, telephoning, getting in pizzas at night, and chatting over coffee
    - Have to fix bugs on releases other than the one they are (mostly) working on

We can of course always ask developers to account for every half-hour of their time. This suggestion will be met with little cries of delight from the developers. Possibly. Alternatively we can use the data mentioned above to calculate from the configuration management database:

- The time spent bug fixing identified from the time when every unit modified by that developer for Project X and any other was retrieved from to when it was resubmitted to the configuration management database for bug fixing ($D_{iBfxX}$ and $D_{iBfxY}$)
- This will show a number of slots occupied by bug fixing:

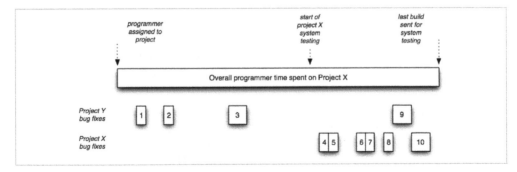

- From the time sheets identify how many hours developer ($D_i$) has worked since the start of project X ($D_{it}$)
- From experience identify how much of a developer's time is spent *not* developing ($D_{iNt}$)

From this we can calculate how much time the developer has spent coding on Project X

$$coding\ time = D_{it} - (D_{iNt} + D_{iBfxX} + D_{iBfxY})$$

and bug fixing on Project X: ($D_{iBfxX}$)

**Note 1.** Supervisory staff such as team leads may spend only 40% of their time developing as opposed to team leading. The chief developer or design authority may only ever design. Thus their costs might be better assigned proportionately to all developers.

**Note 2.** You may consider non-development time ($D_{iNt}$) as part of the cost of development.

## 18.14   Some Metrics from the "Real" World

[McCormack] cites the following statistics culled from a number of HP and Agilent projects:

1. The median project involved 9 people developing 70,000 LOC for a product totaling 170,000 LOC over 14 months at a mean rate of 26.4 LOC/day. The mean bug rate was 18.8 bugs reported by customers per month per million LOC.
2. The biggest negative effect on productivity was an incomplete requirements specification (0.473 correlation at the $p < 5\%$ level).
3. The biggest reducing effects on the bug rate they discovered were:
   a. An early prototype
   b. Design reviews (requirements reviews never seem to have occurred)
   c. Integration or regression testing when checking in code (presumably to the configuration management system)

Since the study took no account of the system test defect rate (the ability of the system test staff to find bugs before release), its value to the software engineering community is limited. Conclusion: the result of any study depends primarily on the questions asked and the data gathered.

[Weinschenk] cites the following:

1. Every $1 invested in user-centered design returns between $2 and $100 [Pressman].
2. Nearly 80% of software life cycle costs occur during the maintenance phase [Pressman].
3. According to The Standish Group, 60% of that maintenance phase is due to re-work because the user requirements were not clear in the beginning.
4. Approximately 63% of software projects exceeded their estimates with the top four reasons all related to product usability:
   a. Frequent requests for changes by users
   b. Overlooked tasks
   c. Users' lack of understanding of their own requirements
   d. Insufficient user-to-analyst communication and understanding [Lederer].
5. An average of 48% of application code is devoted to the user interface, and 50% of the development time required for the entire application is devoted to the user interface portion [Myers B].

Mistrust any bug estimate outside the range of 10 to 40 per KLOC.

[McCormack] cites the following interesting figures. They come from a study of 29 projects whose median KLOC size was 70 new for a total of 170 KLOC and whose median staffing level was 9 people over a median 14 months (Table 18.12). They concluded that 74% of the defect rate is accounted for by:

- The existence of an early prototype
- Testing code before check-in
- The use of design reviews

**TABLE 18.12** McCormack's project statistics

| Variable | Description | Mean | Median | Std dev | Minimum | Maximum |
|---|---|---|---|---|---|---|
| Field bug rate | Average number of customer-reported bugs per month per million lines of new code in the first 12 months after release | 18.8 | 7.1 | 23.1 | 0.0 | 80 |
| Productivity | New LOC written per person-day | 26.4 | 17.6 | 24 | 0.7 | 85 |
| Functional (requirements) specification complete | Percentage of functional specification complete before coding | 55 | 55 | 32 | 0 | 100 |
| Design specification complete | Percentage of design specification complete before coding | 20 | 10 | 26 | 0 | 80 |
| Design review | If designs reviewed then 1, else 0 | 0.79 | 1 | 0.51 | 0 | 1 |
| Code review | If code reviewed then 1, else 0 | 0.52 | 1 | 0.41 | 0 | 1 |
| Daily build | If design changes incorporated into code base and compiled daily then 1, else 0 | 0 | 1 | 0.48 | 0 | 1 |
| Daily regression test | If regression test run when code is checked into code base then 1, else 0 | 1 | 0.51 | 0.48 | 0 | 1 |

They also noted that:

- None of the three factors mentioned above could be considered in isolation.
- There was a strong correlation between having a largely-complete requirements specification before coding and productivity.
- Design reviews decrease defect rates.
- Testing code before check-in decreases defect rates.
- The success of daily builds greatly affects project success.

Note however that this study (like many others) failed to:

- Relate the bugs found before release to those found in the field (which would have indicated the test efficiency)
- Identify the level of feature coverage achieved (which could then have been related to test efficiency)

No Nobel Prize winner has ever exceeded 2.1 meters in height.

# 18.15 Multiple Regression Analysis

Here is a simple example of multiple regression analysis. We have 12 (wholly fictitious) units together with their bugs, coupling levels, and complexity levels (see section 18.8.4). We want an equation whereby we can find the expected number of bugs given the *coupling* and *complexity*. We also want to know if the coupling and complexity affect the levels of bugs positively or negatively. We enter the data as shown in Figure 18.30

| | Unit 1 | Unit 2 | Unit 3 | Unit 4 | Unit 5 | Unit 6 | Unit 7 | Unit 8 | Unit 9 | Unit 10 | Unit 11 | Unit 12 |
|---|---|---|---|---|---|---|---|---|---|---|---|---|
| Bugs | 64 | 71 | 53 | 67 | 55 | 58 | 77 | 57 | 56 | 51 | 76 | 68 |
| Coupling | 57 | 59 | 49 | 62 | 51 | 50 | 55 | 48 | 52 | 42 | 61 | 57 |
| Complexity | 8 | 10 | 6 | 11 | 8 | 7 | 10 | 9 | 10 | 6 | 12 | 9 |

**FIGURE 18.30** Multiple regression: data input

and perform some calculations as shown in Figure 18.31.

| | | Unit 1 | Unit 2 | Unit 3 | Unit 4 | Unit 5 | Unit 6 | Unit 7 | Unit 8 | Unit 9 | Unit 10 | Unit 11 | Unit 12 | Totals |
|---|---|---|---|---|---|---|---|---|---|---|---|---|---|---|
| X1 | Bugs | 64 | 71 | 53 | 67 | 55 | 58 | 77 | 57 | 56 | 51 | 76 | 68 | **753** |
| X2 | Coupling | 57 | 59 | 49 | 62 | 51 | 50 | 55 | 48 | 52 | 42 | 61 | 57 | **643** |
| X3 | Complexity | 8 | 10 | 6 | 11 | 8 | 7 | 10 | 9 | 10 | 6 | 12 | 9 | **106** |
| | | | | | | | | | | | | | | |
| X2*X2 | | 3249 | 3481 | 2401 | 3844 | 2601 | 2500 | 3025 | 2304 | 2704 | 1764 | 3721 | 3249 | **34843** |
| X3*X3 | | 64 | 100 | 36 | 121 | 64 | 49 | 100 | 81 | 100 | 36 | 144 | 81 | **976** |
| | | | | | | | | | | | | | | |
| X1*X2 | | 3648 | 4189 | 2597 | 4154 | 2805 | 2900 | 4235 | 2736 | 2912 | 2142 | 4636 | 3876 | **40830** |
| X1*X3 | | 512 | 710 | 314 | 737 | 440 | 406 | 770 | 513 | 560 | 306 | 912 | 612 | **6796** |
| X2*X3 | | 456 | 590 | 294 | 682 | 408 | 350 | 550 | 432 | 520 | 252 | 732 | 513 | **5779** |

**FIGURE 18.31** Multiple regression: calculations

Then we create an equation by identifying three variables: A, B, and C. Note that the number of units (12) is the first value of A in the top row. Numbers have been rounded for clarity (Figure 18.32).

| | | | | | | | |
|---|---|---|---|---|---|---|---|
| (A) | (The number of units) | 12 | A + | 643 | B + | 106 | C = | 753 |
| (B) | | 643 | A + | 34843 | B + | 5779 | C = | 40830 |
| (C) | | 106 | A + | 5779 | B + | 976 | C = | 6796 |
| (D) | Multiply (A) by 106/12 | 106 | A + | 5679.8 | B + | 936.3 | C = | 6652 |
| (E) | Subtract (D) From © | | A + | 99.167 | B + | 39.67 | C = | 145 |
| (F) | Multiply (A) by 643/12 | 643 | A + | 34454 | B + | 5680 | C = | 40348 |
| (G) | Subtract (F) from (B) | | | 388.92 | B + | 99.17 | C = | 482 |
| | | | | | B + | | C = | |
| (H) | Multiply (E) by 388/99 | | | 388.92 | B + | 155.6 | C = | 567 |
| (I) | Subtract (H) from (B) | | | | | −56.4 | C = | −85 |
| | | | | | | | C = | **1.51** |
| (J) | Substituting in (H) | | | 388.92 | B + | 234.3 | = | 566.71 |
| | | | | 388.92 | B + | | = | 332.37 |
| | | | | | | | B = | **0.85** |
| (K) | Substituting in (A) | 12 | A + | 549.51 | + | 159.7 | = | 753.00 |
| | | | | | | | A = | **3.65** |
| (L) | **Bugs =** | **3.7** | + | **0.8546** | *Coupling + | **1.506** | *Complexity | |

**FIGURE 18.32** Multiple regression: equations

Note that in Equation (L) (Figure 18.32) all the values are positive. This means that (as expected) there is (in this case) a positive correlation between *coupling, complexity,* and levels of bugs. Note that this is purely to demonstrate how multiple regression can be used to derive an equation. It uses fictional data and thus proves nothing real about the relationship between *coupling, complexity,* and levels of bugs in reality. The Equation (L) can then be used to derive the set of estimated bugs in the original table (Figure 18.33). The average error is thus shown to be +3.4762. The worst-seen error was 11.

| | Unit 1 | Unit 2 | Unit 3 | Unit 4 | Unit 5 | Unit 6 | Unit 7 | Unit 8 | Unit 9 | Unit 10 | Unit 11 | Unit 12 | |
|---|---|---|---|---|---|---|---|---|---|---|---|---|---|
| Bugs | 64 | 71 | 53 | 67 | 55 | 58 | 77 | 57 | 56 | 51 | 76 | 68 | |
| Coupling | 57 | 59 | 49 | 62 | 51 | 50 | 55 | 48 | 52 | 42 | 61 | 57 | |
| Complexity | 8 | 10 | 6 | 11 | 8 | 7 | 10 | 9 | 10 | 6 | 12 | 9 | |
| | | | | | | | | | | | | | |
| Estimated bugs | 64 | 69 | 55 | 73 | 59 | 57 | 66 | 58 | 63 | 49 | 74 | 66 | |
| | | | | | | | | | | | | | Average |
| Difference (least squares) | 0 | 2 | 2 | 6 | 4 | 1 | 11 | 1 | 7 | 2 | 2 | 2 | **3.4762** |

**FIGURE 18.33** Multiple regression: substitution

But we need to know to what extent the number of bugs in each unit can be attributed to the combined effect of coupling and complexity. To do this we need to find first the *linear correlation coefficient* (Figure 18.34) of X1 and X2, X1 and X3, and X2 and X3, from which we can obtain the results shown in Figure 18.35. From this we can see that 0.71 (71%) of the variation in the number of the bugs between units is explained by the coupling and complexity.

Conclusion: (in this case) the coupling and complexity are good predictors. Try to reduce them.

| | |
|---|---|
| Linear correlation coefficient of X1 and X2 = | 0.819645083 |
| Linear correlation coefficient of X1 and X3 = | 0.769816802 |
| Linear correlation coefficient of X2 and X3 = | 0.798407457 |

**FIGURE 18.34** Linear multiple correlation coefficients

| | |
|---|---|
| Coefficient of multiple correlation = | 0.841756673 |
| **Coefficient of multiple determination =** | **0.708554296** |

**FIGURE 18.35** Multiple determination coefficient of bugs

This example was adapted from [Spiegel], which should be consulted if you want to use more variables and a larger number of examples. Note that some of Microsoft's best researchers [Nagappan] have concluded that:

- For each project they could find a set of complexity metrics that correlated with post-release defects, but there was no single set of metrics that predicts post-release defects in all projects.
- Predictors are accurate only when obtained from the same or similar projects.

## 18.15.1 Multiple Regression Equations

The following equations are for multiple regressions on four variables, where $X_1$, $X_2$, $X_3$, and $X_4$ are the variables you want to use as input and estimate the value of and N is the number of the data used.

$$\sum X_1 = aN + b\sum X_2 + c\sum X_3 + d\sum X_4 \qquad (18.8)$$

$$\sum X_1 X_2 = a\sum X_2 + b\sum X_2^2 + c\sum X_2 X_3 + d\sum X_2 X_4 \qquad (18.9)$$

$$\sum X_1 X_3 = a\sum X_3 + b\sum X_2 X_3 + c\sum X_3^2 + d\sum X_3 X_4 \qquad (18.10)$$

$$\sum X_1 X_4 = a\sum X_4 + b\sum X_2 X_4 + c\sum X_3 X_4 + d\sum X_4^2 \qquad (18.11)$$

Solve these using simultaneous equations for a, b, c, and d. Then (assuming that is the variable you want to estimate) use Equation (18.12) with these variables:

$$X_1 = a + bX_2 + cX_3 + dX_4 \qquad (18.12)$$

## 18.15.2  Standard Deviation

To get the standard deviation for $X_1$, $X_2$, $X_3$, and $X_4$, use:

$$stdevX_n = \sqrt{\frac{\sum X_n^2}{N} - \left(\frac{\sum X_n}{N}\right)}$$

where $n = 1, 2, 3, 4$.

## 18.15.3  Standard Error of Estimate

To get the standard error of estimate for $X_1$, $X_2$, $X_3$, and $X_4$, use:

$$stderr_{est} = \sqrt{\frac{\sum (X_n - X_{n,est})^2}{N}}$$

where $n = 1, 2, 3, 4$.

## 18.15.4  Linear Multiple Correlation

To get the linear multiple correlation, use:

$$\sqrt{1 - \frac{(standard\ error\ of\ estimate)^2}{(standard\ deviation)^2}}$$

## 18.15.5  Coefficient of Multiple Determination

To get the coefficient of multiple determination, use:

$$(linear\ multiple\ correlation)^2$$

# Appendix A

## Examples

## A.1 Case Study: Getting Test Objectives Out of a Use Case

Use cases:

1. Are a collection of related scenarios that describe actors and operations in a system, can be organized hierarchically but not decomposed.
2. Can be formalized (such as preconditions, operations, and post-conditions) and used for testing.
3. Can be collected together to form a Use-Case model.
4. Are used to get an overall view of a set of features. Not for drilling down to the details. Unfortunately details are essential to get system test objectives written.

## A.2 Case Study: Withdraw Cash Use Case

This example is extremely limited and is only concerned with showing how the process of test development from a set of *UML* diagrams can work.

### A.2.1 Description

This case describes how a bank customer uses an ATM to withdraw money from a bank account.

### A.2.2 Use-Case Diagram (Figure A.1)

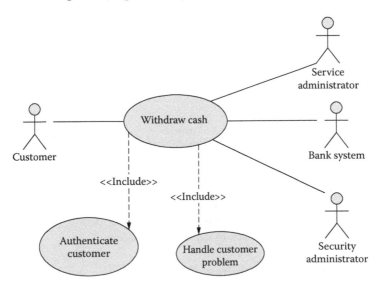

**FIGURE A.1** Use-case diagram for the Withdraw Cash use case

## A.2.3  Preconditions

1. The bank customer must possess a bank card.
2. The network connection to the bank system must be active.
3. The system must have sufficient cash to be dispensed.
4. The cash withdrawal service option must be available.
5. The receipt printer has enough paper and ink.

## A.2.4  Activity Diagram (Withdraw Cash)

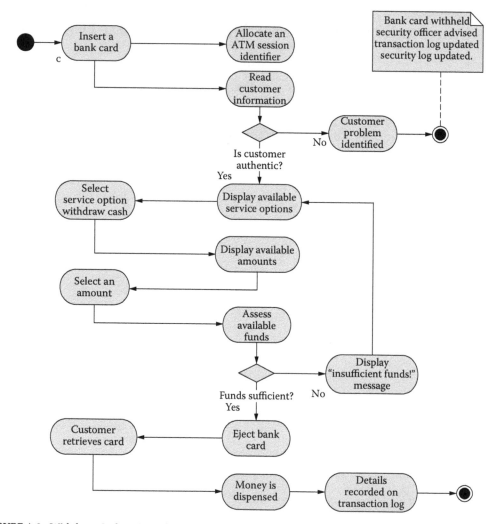

**FIGURE A.2**  Withdraw Cash activity diagram

The problem with Figure A.2 is that it has too much detail. You can't easily identify those actions which, if tested, would indicate if the system was not working. Nor can you identify which parts of the diagram refer to or represent the <<include>> parts of the Use case diagram.

## A.2.5  Sequence Diagram (Withdraw Cash)

The sequence diagram in Figure A.3 includes messages from the two <<includes>> use cases: *Authenticate Customer* and *Handle Customer problem.* By using the sequence diagram it is much more evident that the system test baselines are to be derived from actions concerning the bank card, ATM, and Transaction log objects.

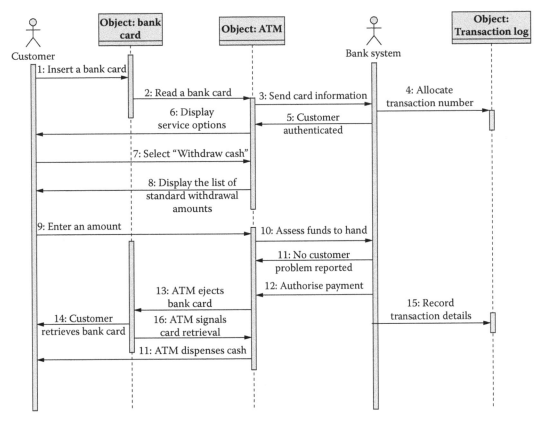

**FIGURE A.3** *UML* Sequence diagram example "Withdraw Cash"

## A.2.6 Informal Specification (Withdraw Cash)

{ Insert Card }

 The Use case begins when the actor Customer inserts a bank card into the card reader on the ATM.

{ Read card }

 The card reader reads the bank card information from the card.

 The ATM transmits the card information to the bank system.

 The bank system allocates an ATM session identifier to enable bugs to be tracked and synchronized between the ATM and the bank system.

{ Authenticate Customer }

 Include use case "Authenticate Customer" to authenticate the use of the bank card by the individual using the machine.

{ Select Withdrawal }

 The bank system displays the service options currently available on the machine.

 The Customer selects "Withdraw cash."

{ Select Amount }

 The bank system prompts for the amount to be withdrawn by displaying the list of standard withdrawal amounts.

 The Customer enters an amount to be withdrawn.

{ Confirm Withdrawal }

 The bank system assesses funds to hand.

{ Validate the Withdrawal }
Include use case "Handle the Bank Refusing the Withdrawal" if there are insufficient funds in the Customer's account to be dispensed.
The bank system authorizes payment.
{ Eject Card }
The ATM ejects the bank card.
The Customer takes the bank card from the machine.
{ Dispense Cash }
The ATM signals the card has been retrieved.
The ATM dispenses the requested amount to the customer.
The bank system records the transaction details in the Transaction log.
{ Use Case Ends }
Use case ends.

## A.2.7 Sequence Diagram (Handle Authentication Failures)

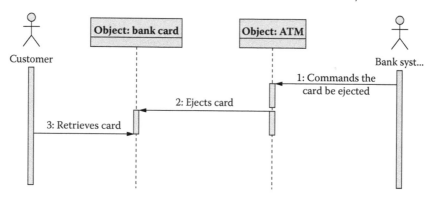

**FIGURE A.4** *UML* Sequence diagram example "Handle Authentication Failures"

## A.2.8 Informal Specification (Handle Authentication Failures)

At { Authenticate Customer }, if the bank card is not authenticated but not retained, then:

1. { Eject Card }
2. The system ejects the Customer's bank card.
3. The Customer takes the bank card from the machine.
4. The use case resumes the basic flow at { Use Case Ends }.

## A.2.9 Sequence Diagram (Handle the Bank Refusing the Withdrawal)

See Figure A.5.

## A.2.10 Informal Specification

At { Validate the Withdrawal }, if the bank system rejects the transaction, then:
If the bank system rejected the withdrawal because there are insufficient funds in the account the bank system, the ATM:

1. Informs the Customer that the withdrawal has been rejected because the account does not have sufficient funds.
2. The bank system records a transaction log entry for the transaction including the reason given for the transaction's rejection.

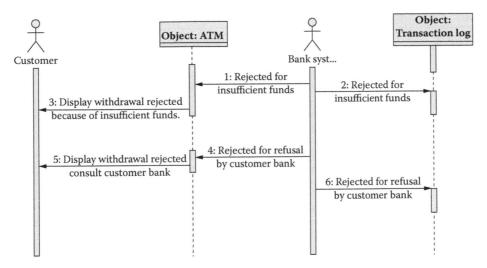

**FIGURE A.5**  *UML* Sequence diagram example "Handle the Bank Refusing the Withdrawal"

If the bank system rejects the withdrawal for any other reason, the ATM:
1.  Informs the Customer that the withdrawal has been rejected by the Customer's Bank and that the Customer should contact the Bank for further details.
2.  The bank system records a transaction log entry for the transaction including the reason given for the transaction's rejection.
3.  The ATM ejects the bank card.

Resume the use case from { Use Case Ends }.

## A.2.11  Test Steps

The test steps listed in Table A.1 are derived from the Use case shown above. They are trivial and exclude many features of ATMs. Many more *test cases* could be derived showing variations: this simple case is presented purely for illustrative purposes. It is a trivial matter to enter such steps into a test management tool.

**TABLE A.1**  Withdraw cash test

| Step | Description | Expected | Derived from |
| --- | --- | --- | --- |
| 1 | Customer inserts bank card | ATM displays service options. | 1, 6 |
| 2 | Customer selects "Withdraw cash" | ATM displays list of standard withdrawal amounts | 7, 8 |
| 3 | Customer enters an amount < Customer balance | ATM ejects bank card | 9, 13 |
| 4 | Customer retrieves bank card | ATM dispenses cash | 14, 17 |
| 5 | (Read Transaction log) | (Transaction log shows Transaction number, time, and cash dispensed details.) | 4, 15 |

## A.2.12  Use Case Glossary

The glossary in Table A.2 contains terms that are used in this use case.

**TABLE A.2**  Use case glossary

| Term | Definition |
|---|---|
| ATM | Automatic Teller Machine. |
| ATM ID | An alphanumeric identifying an ATM. |
| ATM session identifier | Unique alphanumeric identifier includes the ATM ID. |
| ATM withdrawal limit | The maximum a customer may withdraw in any 24-hour period from an account. |
| bank card | Bank debit card, contains the card issuer ID, Customer ID, PIN, and bank card number. |
| bank card information | Information recorded on the bank card. |
| bank card number | 20 character alphanumeric code. |
| bank system | Networked system connecting the bank and the ATM. |
| card issuer | The organization administering the card. May not be the organization managing the ATM. |
| communication retry number | The number of attempts to be made to re-establish communication between an ATM and a bank. |
| confiscated cards | Set of cards held internally in the ATM for later retrieval by bank staff. |
| customer | Anyone trying to use one or more of the available service options and with an account held with a card issuer. |
| customer's bank | The bank in which the cardholder keeps the account against which the card is to be debited. |
| event log | Log of all system events maintained both locally at the ATM and centrally. The event log entry includes the video image and any bank card information (excluding the PIN) that it managed to read. |
| list of standard withdrawal amounts | Collection of service options. |
| other amount | A service option. Lets you select some amount not necessarily included in the list of standard withdrawal amounts. |
| overdraft limit | The maximum amount a customer may owe a bank on an account. |
| PIN | Personal Identification Number. |
| service option | A user-visible option displayed on the ATM screen. |
| transaction details | Contains { ATM ID, Date, Time, Customer ID, bank card information, service option, ATM session identifier, and PIN number }. |
| transaction log | Log of all transaction details maintained both locally at the ATM, and centrally. Contains a reference to the video image. The local image does not contain the PIN number used. |
| Withdraw cash | A service option. Enables a customer to withdraw money from the machine up to either his overdraft limit or the ATM withdrawal limit. |
| Withdraw Cash withdrawal receipt | Service option implying the ATM's ability to produce cash in an authorized transaction. |

# A.3  Case Study: Getting Test Objectives Out of Business Rules

## A.3.1  Introduction

A business rule typically defines some aspect of a business such as determining what is an acceptable salary level for an employee:

> BR1: An employee's salary cannot exceed the limit set for the position he/she holds.

A business rule may be buried in a legacy system and not immediately obvious to current users since it constrains operations within the organization rather than it defines operations. Defined operations are normally embodied in applications, typically employee payment systems, customer relations systems or manufacturing systems which will tend to have specifications (however outdated) retained somewhere. Defined operations are typically defined in Requirements specifications. Business rules affect workflow processes and persistent data.

Constrained operations follow what is called "deontic" logic whereby "can," or "must" relations are defined, thus:

- Any employee can be promoted.
- All employees must have an employee number.

and their negatives

- No employee can be paid less than the minimum wage.
- Employees must not work more than 80 hours per week.

(See [Chellas] for an introduction, also onegoodmove.org/fallacy/branches.htm.). These constraints are sometimes buried in code or stored procedures unannounced by any comments. Exceptionally they are coded in XML. Over the years a number of business rule extraction tools have evolved to identify and extract them: these include integrity constraints in database systems [Ullman], triggers in active database systems [Paton], constraints in object-oriented systems (e.g., coordination contracts [Andrade 1], [Andrade 2] and IBM's Accessible Business Rules (ABR) [IBM 1]), expert systems (e.g., OPS5 [Brownstone] and CLIPS [Riley]), and knowledge-based inference engines (e.g., ILog JRules [ILog], Common-Rules [IBM 2] and Versata Logic Server [Versata]). Alternatively they may be used to structure a BizTalk-based application (see [Herring]).

## A.3.2 Hierarchy

Business rules can thus be seen to exist in a hierarchy.

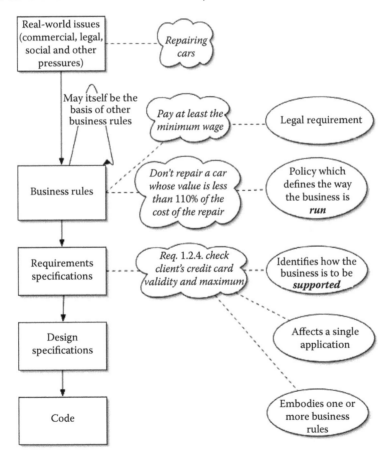

**FIGURE A.6** A business rule in a hierarchy

Business rules differ from requirements in that business rules:

1. Identify constraints on how a business is run rather than how the business is supported by its IT systems.
2. Can apply to more than one system, whereas a requirement applies to one system only. If a requirement applies to more than one system there is the:
   - Danger that, should it become obsolete, it will not be removed from the requirements set of every system to which it applies
   - Possibility that it will be expensively duplicated
3. Are the basis against which requirements are defined or by which they are constrained.
4. Define the environment within which a bug exists, rather than the bug itself.
5. Are ideally implemented as something separate from code such that they can be easily changed.
6. May be the basis against which two systems in a Trading Partner Agreement are being compared.

## A.3.3  Business Rule Types

There are three business rule types:

1. Conditional (IF x THEN y). Examples:
   - IF <<prospective customer has no valid driving license>> THEN <<do not rent him a vehicle>>.
   - IF <<water temperature > 100°C>> THEN <<switch off the kettle>>
2. Invariant (x is always true). Examples:
   - Absolute zero is always 273°C.
   - No more than 10% of all business class seats should be upgrades from Economy in any quarter.
3. Deontic (x may/must (not) do y). Examples:
   - Only project managers may sign time sheets.
   - Train doors must be shut and locked before departure.

Note that while the opposite of "MUST" is "MUST NOT," the opposite of MAY is (of course) MAY NOT which can also be interpreted as "SHOULD NOT."

## A.3.4  Business Rule Testing Process

Before any attempt is made to test business rules they must be defined. A number of notations exist for defining them. See [Business Rules Group], [OCL], [CBL], [BRML], [Ross 2], [SRML] and [Warmer].

Once defined, their propagation must be reviewed such that every system, which needs to embody them, has its requirements reviewed to ensure they embody the business rules fully, consistently, and without contradiction.

In principle insofar as every business rule is traced to one or more requirements there is no need for extra testing. In practice there is. There are several problems inherent in business rules:

- They may not be universally applied, by oversight.
- They may not be universally applicable. Thus even in a single company each division may have business rules specific to that division but common to several applications. They may only apply under some conditions or in some contexts.
- They may not be applied at all. Very Wonderful Policy Statements may be made which are never realized, perhaps because for fear of bankrupting the company.
- They may be misapplied.
- They may (have) become obsolete.
- They may change dramatically for example when tax changes are announced.
- They may conflict.

thus:

```
BR1: When a rental car has covered over 16,000 kilometers since its last
     service it must be withdrawn from rental availability and sent for a
     service.
BR101: If the only rental car available has been withdrawn for servicing but
       is not expected to exceed 110% of the allowable inter-service distance
       by the time the next rental ends then retrieve the car from the
       service queue and rent it.
```

In this case the second rule can be held to be superior to and therefore overriding the first. Rules may override on the grounds of recency, authority (for example *Corporate rules* override *Divisional rules*) or ascribed precedence (*Rule 21 is held to override rule 10*).

- They may remain undetected until the system embodying them is shut down.
- Applying them may cause performance bugs, particularly if every firing of an expert system rule or stored procedure trigger, necessitates a call to a business rule manager.

A process for testing them is:

1. Confirm with the business representatives that all business rules have been extracted. If they can't then you need to undertake a business rule discovery exercise.
2. Review all the requirements.[1] See if any requirements are equivalent. If they are then:
   - List each as a business rule.
   - Discover why it wasn't already listed.
   - Discover why it was created (this could give you pointers to other hidden rules).
   - See what other systems or processes they might apply to.
3. Review all the process models. What rules do they embody? Does any rule apply to any system?
4. Review each rule against the Business rules testing review checklist in Appendix B.
5. Map the rules against process models and requirements specifications. Identify which rules are:
   - Not embodied in any system
   - Only embodied in a manual process ("check that the driver's license is current")
6. Review all manual processes to see if under some circumstance the rule could be misapplied.
7. Review all system tests to identify which ones test business-rule-related requirements.
8. Identify all rules which either are insufficiently-tested or not tested at all, and write tests for them.

Note that this does not allow for performance effects of rules which must be accounted for as part of performance testing. Since the "strength" of rules may influence the order in which they are fired, rule developers may do much tweaking and this will have a performance effect.

# A.4 Case Study: Test Coverage

This example uses Microsoft Word as the system under test.

## A.4.1 List All the Scenarios

The primary use cases for MS Word (Figure A.7) are:

---

[1] If at all possible every textual requirement should be identifiable as a single paragraph often of only one sentence. It should mostly take the form of an assertion "X is true IF/WHEN Y."

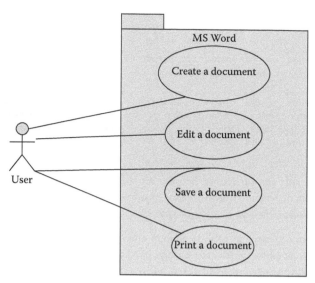

**FIGURE A.7** A simple set of use cases for Word

1. Create a document.
2. Edit a document.
3. Save a document.
4. Print a document.

## A.4.2 List All the GUI Objects

The Word "File" Pulldown (Figure A.8) is transformed into Figure A.9, and the resulting screen shown in Figure A.10 is also specified (Figure A.11). Specifying such a set of GUI objects is non-trivial and Word (for example) might require 5 man-days simply to decompose in this manner. Once done however the rest of the work becomes simpler.

**FIGURE A.8** Example: Word "File" Pulldown...is transformed into:

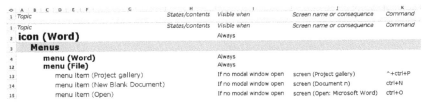

| Topic | States/contents | Visible when | Screen name or consequence | Command |
|---|---|---|---|---|
| Topic | States/contents | Visible when | Screen name or consequence | Command |
| **icon (Word)** | | Always | | |
| **Menus** | | | | |
| **menu (Word)** | | Always | | |
| **menu (File)** | | Always | | |
| menu Item (Project gallery) | | If no modal window open | screen (Project gallery) | ^+ctrl+P |
| menu Item (New Blank Document) | | If no modal window open | screen (Document n) | ctrl+N |
| menu Item (Open) | | If no modal window open | screen (Open: Microsoft Word) | ctrl+O |

**FIGURE A.9** Example: Word "File" Pulldown, specified…and the resulting screen:

**FIGURE A.10** Example: Word "Project Gallery" screen…is also specified:

| Topic | States/contents | Visible when |
|---|---|---|
| **screen (Project gallery)** | | If called by pull-down |
| **Left-hand pane (Category)** | | If screen (Project gallery) = open |
| Blank documents | | If screen (Project gallery) = open |
| My Templates | | If screen (Project gallery) = open |
| Based on Recent | | If screen (Project gallery) = open |
| Business forms | | If screen (Project gallery) = open |
| Brochures | | If screen (Project gallery) = open / templates/Brochures" exists |
| Agendas | | If screen (Project gallery) = open / Office/Templates/Business Forms/ |
| ... | | |
| **Right-hand pane** | | If screen (Project gallery) = open |
| Examples | Shows examples of Left-hand pane" chosen | If screen (Project gallery) = open |
| **Lower pane** | | If screen (Project gallery) = open |
| Pull-down (View) | Catalog/List | If screen (Project gallery) = open |
| Pull-down (Show) | All Office Documents/Word Documents/Excel Documents/Powerpoint Documents/Entourage Documents | If screen (Project gallery) = open |
| Pull-down (Create) | Document/Template | If screen (Project gallery) = open |
| **Button (Open)** | Default = active | If screen (Project gallery) = open |
| **Button (Cancel)** | Default = active | If screen (Project gallery) = open |
| **Button (OK)** | Default = chosen | If screen (Project gallery) = open |
| **Tick box (Show Project gallery at startup)** | on/off | If screen (Project gallery) = open |
| **screen (Open: Microsoft Word)** | | If called by pull-down |
| Header | | If screen (Open: Microsoft Word) |

**FIGURE A.11** Example: Word "Project Gallery" screen, specified

Specifying such a set of GUI objects is non-trivial and Word (for example) might require 5 man-days simply to decompose in this manner. Once done, however, the rest of the work becomes simpler.

### A.4.3 Create a Diagram Showing the Relationships between the GUI Components, the GUI Objects, and the Possible Transitions between Them

This can also get large. Figure A.12 is a top-level view of Word. For each of the menu items shown above there is either a lower-level set of menu items or a screen. The user activity on the screens' objects can be shown using a simple state transition diagram or flow chart (Figure A.13).

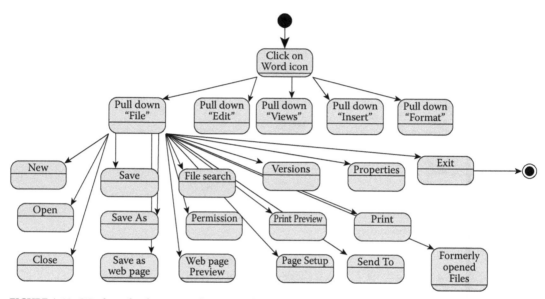

**FIGURE A.12**   Word top-level menus and contents shown as an *UML* activity diagram

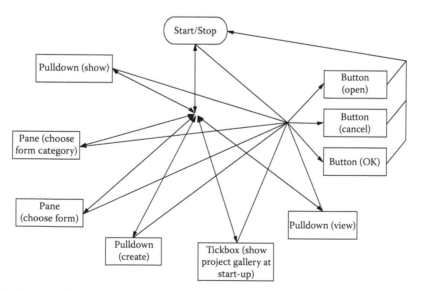

**FIGURE A.13**   State transition diagram showing user-initiated events within the Project Gallery screen

Note that the arrows on the chart (Figure A.13) imply that the mouse can move from any GUI object to any other GUI object save the three buttons. Once one of these is pressed, control passes from the Project Gallery screen.

### A.4.4 Map the GUI Objects Used by Each Scenario to the Scenario

The objects used in the scenarios are echoed to another worksheet and are shown on the left (Figure A.14) with the lowest-level objects ranged right. The order in which each is used is shown by the numbers in each column. For the sake of simplicity all scenarios assume that Word be opened afresh each time. In practice this would be restructured so that each scenario could interface with another.

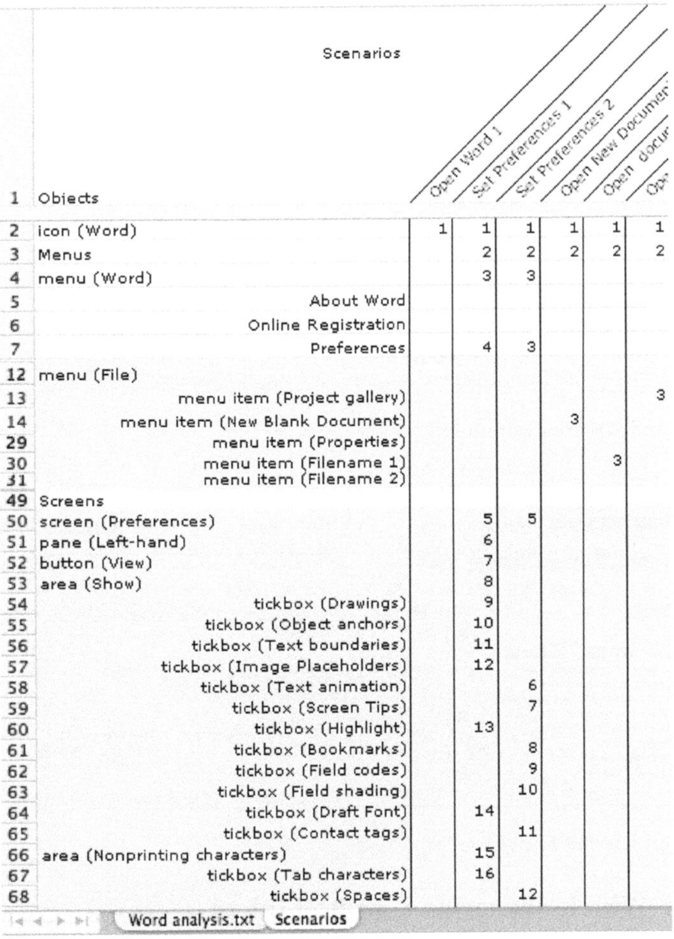

| # | Objects | Open Word 1 | Set Preferences 1 | Set Preferences 2 | Open New Document | Open document | Op... |
|---|---------|:-----------:|:-----------------:|:-----------------:|:-----------------:|:-------------:|:-----:|
| 2 | icon (Word) | 1 | 1 | 1 | 1 | 1 | 1 |
| 3 | Menus | | 2 | 2 | 2 | 2 | 2 |
| 4 | menu (Word) | | 3 | 3 | | | |
| 5 | About Word | | | | | | |
| 6 | Online Registration | | | | | | |
| 7 | Preferences | | 4 | 3 | | | |
| 12 | menu (File) | | | | | | |
| 13 | menu item (Project gallery) | | | | | | 3 |
| 14 | menu item (New Blank Document) | | | | 3 | | |
| 29 | menu item (Properties) | | | | | | |
| 30 | menu item (Filename 1) | | | | | 3 | |
| 31 | menu item (Filename 2) | | | | | | |
| 49 | Screens | | | | | | |
| 50 | screen (Preferences) | | 5 | 5 | | | |
| 51 | pane (Left-hand) | | 6 | | | | |
| 52 | button (View) | | 7 | | | | |
| 53 | area (Show) | | 8 | | | | |
| 54 | tickbox (Drawings) | | 9 | | | | |
| 55 | tickbox (Object anchors) | | 10 | | | | |
| 56 | tickbox (Text boundaries) | | 11 | | | | |
| 57 | tickbox (Image Placeholders) | | 12 | | | | |
| 58 | tickbox (Text animation) | | | 6 | | | |
| 59 | tickbox (Screen Tips) | | | 7 | | | |
| 60 | tickbox (Highlight) | | 13 | | | | |
| 61 | tickbox (Bookmarks) | | | 8 | | | |
| 62 | tickbox (Field codes) | | | 9 | | | |
| 63 | tickbox (Field shading) | | | 10 | | | |
| 64 | tickbox (Draft Font) | | 14 | | | | |
| 65 | tickbox (Contact tags) | | | 11 | | | |
| 66 | area (Nonprinting characters) | | 15 | | | | |
| 67 | tickbox (Tab characters) | | 16 | | | | |
| 68 | tickbox (Spaces) | | | 12 | | | |

Word analysis.txt  Scenarios

**FIGURE A.14**  Example of a scenario/object cross-reference

### A.4.5 Map the Tests to the Scenarios

Given a set of tests (in, say, TestDirector) looking like Figure A.15, you can map each of these tests against a scenario like the one shown in Figure A.16.

### A.4.6 Map the Tests to the GUI Objects

You can examine each of the steps using the Test steps pane (Figure A.17). Pick out from the Description column the objects which are being used and check that each corresponds to those in the Word analysis worksheet.

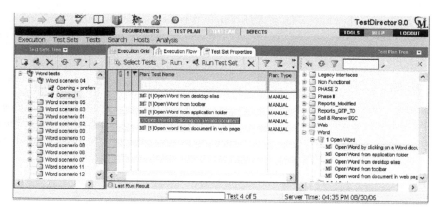

**FIGURE A.15**  TestDirector™ Test Schedule pane

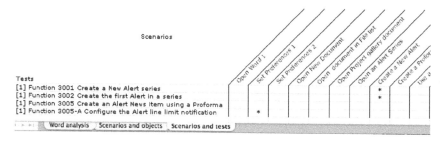

**FIGURE A.16**  Tests and Scenarios worksheet

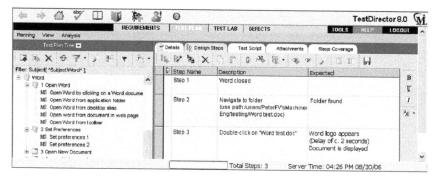

**FIGURE A.17**  TestDirector Test Steps pane

## A.4.7  Identify Which Scenarios Can Be Linked

This is critical. An executed scenario will leave the software in a state which the next scenario can exploit. Failing to exploit it can hide a bug.[1] Each scenario will leave the software in some state (Figure A.18).

The states can then be matched to create large scenarios. A scenario can have an end state in which various things are true such as a Word document being Open and a particular set of Preferences being true.

---

[1] For example, just creating a cross-reference in Word will rarely provoke a bug. Creating several in a large (50 MB) document without frequent saves will usually crash Word. In versions of Word around 1998 creating a table and then changing the width of some cells would crash it if the table were in a footer.

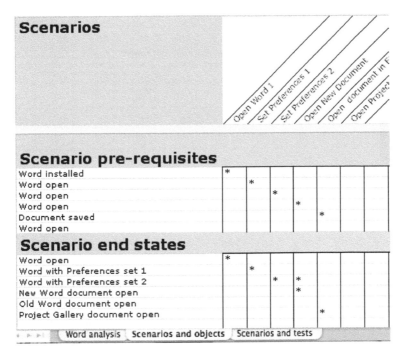

**FIGURE A.18** Scenario prerequisites and end states

## A.5 Example: Requirements Traceability Using TestDirector™

TestDirector™ is a widely-used tool sold by Mercury. It is web-based and has limited editing and data manipulation facilities. It is thus best used with the aid of a spreadsheet. It has built-in links to a number of requirements management tools but these are of little use when using it to manage tests. A number of test specification tools can also be linked to it.

All the requirements are listed directly in TestDirector as the basis of tests, as shown in Figure A.19.

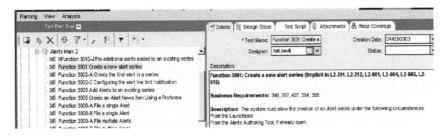

**FIGURE A.19** TestDirector™ Test Details pane

Each is then translated into test steps (Figure A.20) which are then batched into runs (Figure A.21). Each test may have attachments. As tests are run, the results are added to the run schedule (Figure A.22). These are then added to a spreadsheet which is updated daily to show the current position.

## A.6 Example: How to Get a Report Out of TestDirector

The TestDirector reporting mechanism wins few awards for intuitiveness. Getting a report out requires you to:

1. Set a filter (otherwise you will endanger several forests when you try and print it).

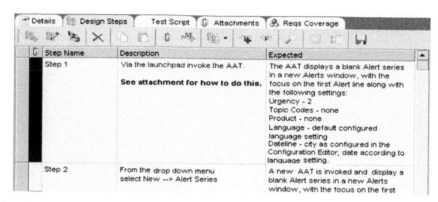

**FIGURE A.20** TestDirector™ Design Steps pane

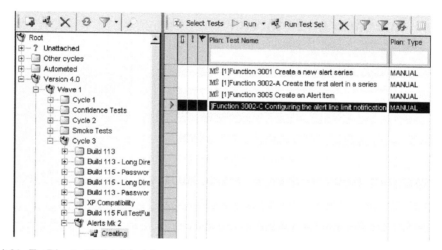

**FIGURE A.21** TestDirector™ Test Schedule pane

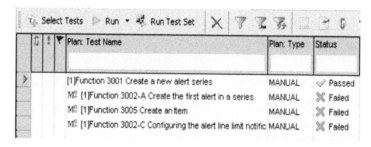

**FIGURE A.22** TestDirector™ Test Runs pane

2. Choose a report.
3. Define the fields to be shown.
4. Save it to disk.
5. Print it (you can print before saving it to disk but I wouldn't).

The reports may be essential for saving tests to disk or printing them off for review.

## A.6.1 Set a Filter

1. Log into TD > Go to the Test Plan tab (Figure A.23).
2. Click on the filter icon, the Filter Window opens (Figure A.24).

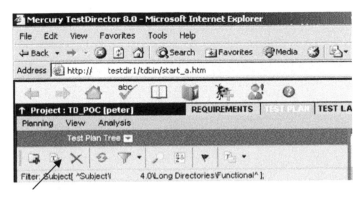

**FIGURE A.23** TestDirector™ (Test Plan tab)

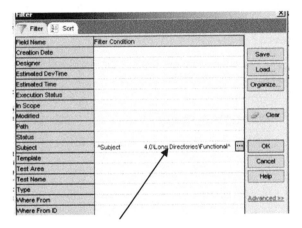

**FIGURE A.24** TestDirector™ (Filter window)

3. Assuming that you just want to print off the tests you've written, click on the Subject bar. A three-dot browse button appears, hit it, and the test folders are displayed. Click on the one you want and drill down until you get to the level you need (Figure A.25).

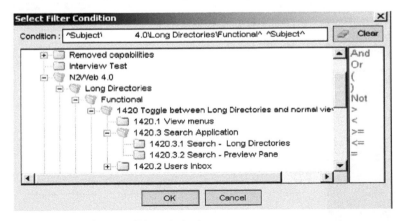

**FIGURE A.25** TestDirector™ (Filter Condition window)

4. Notice that the filter pathname is entered at the top. Add more sets of tests using the And/Or etc. constructs on the right-hand pane followed by a repetition from Filter window. Click OK.
5. Hit the Save button and the Save Filter window is displayed (Figure A.26).

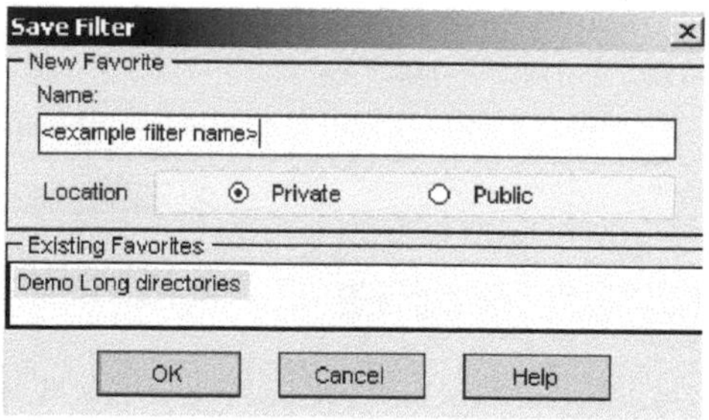

**FIGURE A.26**  TestDirector™ (Save Filter window)

6. Enter a name and hit OK. The window vanishes and the Completed filter window is displayed as in Figure A.24.
7. Hit OK and the Test: plan tab is displayed. Go to subtab Reports and pull down a report type.

## A.6.2 Choose a Report

8. Choose a report type. The report window displays the types and you can choose the report you want filtered by the filter currently set (Figure A.27).

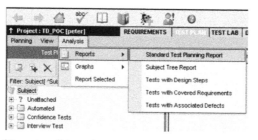

**FIGURE A.27**  TestDirector™ (Reports pulldowns)

9. Report Window (planning report) lists the title of each test with a load of administrivia detail (Figure A.28).

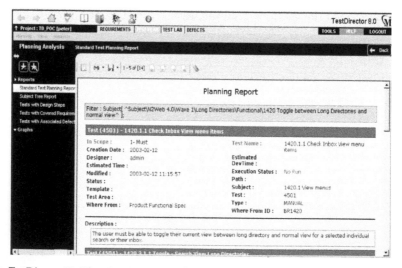

**FIGURE A.28**  TestDirector™ (Planning Reports window)

10. Report Window (Subject Tree Report) which lists the tests in their hierarchy (Figure A.29).
11. The Report Window (Tests with design steps) shows each test with its details and steps (Figure A.30).

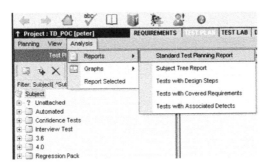

**FIGURE A.29** TestDirector™ (Subject Tree Report window)

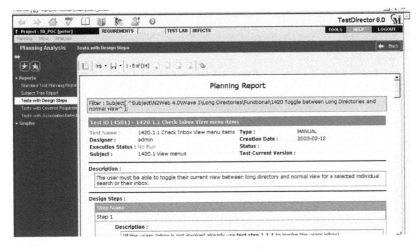

**FIGURE A.30** TestDirector™ (Tests with Design Steps Report window)

12. Report Window (Tests with covered requirements) shows each test with its details and related requirement(s) (Figure A.31).

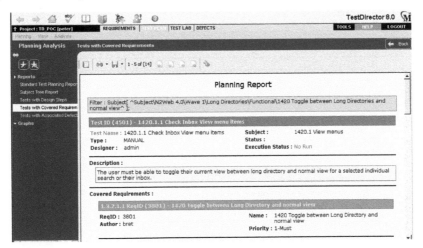

**FIGURE A.31** TestDirector™ (Tests with Covered Requirements window)

13. Report Window (Tests with associated defects) shows each test with its details and any defect(s) (Figure A.32).
14. Configure the report by pressing the button (Figure A.33).

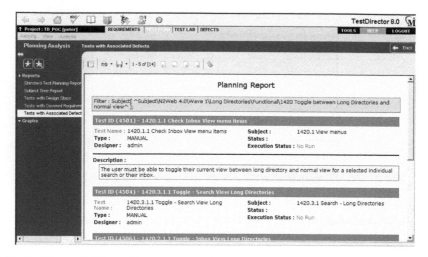

**FIGURE A.32**   TestDirector™ (Tests with Associated Defects window)

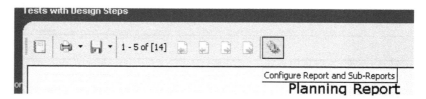

**FIGURE A.33**   TestDirector™ (Report Configuration button)

15. The report configuration window is displayed. If you want to limit the fields to be displayed hit the Custom fields button (Figure A.34).

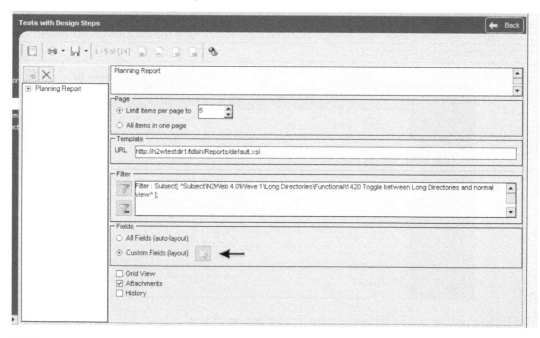

**FIGURE A.34**   TestDirector™ (Custom Fields button)

16. This will display the custom fields window allowing you to choose the fields available to be displayed, the fields to be displayed and the order in which this happens (Figure A.35).

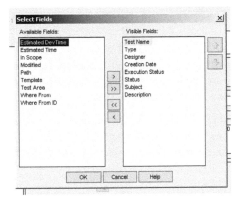

**FIGURE A.35** TestDirector™ (Custom Fields window)

17. Generate a report by pressing the button (Figure A.36) …

**FIGURE A.36** TestDirector™ (Generate a Report button)

18. Save the report to disk by hitting Save (Figure A.37)

**FIGURE A.37** TestDirector™ (Save All Pages of a Report pull-down)

19. …and at length a Save window opens (Figure A.38).

Note that the report can only be saved in .html. This file can however be then opened and edited in Word.

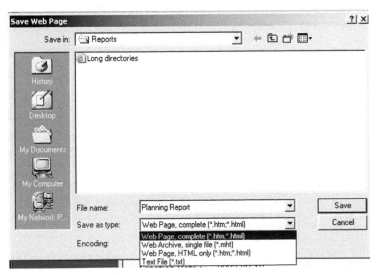

**FIGURE A.38** TestDirector™ (Save window)

# A.7  Case Study: Performance Testing (Throughput)

The Flying Pun Agency is a major player in the employment of secretaries and ancillary workers. It has offices throughout the world and a development center in a major African capital. It also has server farms in the Middle East.

It is attempting to move from a client–server-based system to a web-based system (FPWeb). For historic reasons it has decided to have the two systems coexist. During this period all branch offices will have PCs capable of running both an application client and a browser-client. They want to know if the proposed system will support the number of clients expected to use it.

1. **Plan the tests.** A test plan was written. It covered three pages and was largely what is shown in this section. The questions to be answered were:
   a. Can the system sustain the maximum transaction rate with sufficient headroom for a 10% per annum expansion?
      i.   What are the transactions?
      ii.  How many are there per second?
      iii. What are the maxima?
   b. If not
      i.  what is the maximum sustainable transaction rate?
      ii. where and what are the bottlenecks?
2. **Get the figures.**
   a. Environment:
      i.    8 hours per day worked
      ii.   1200 users
      iii.  180,000 assignments per annum
      iv.   0.95% assignments made on Mondays
      v.    10 candidates found for every one finally assigned
      vi.   39 candidate-related scenarios
   b. Key dates:
      i.   Friday afternoon, Monday, and Tuesday. Monday is the day of the heaviest traffic.
      ii.  Month's end
      iii. 1 day payroll
   c. 30,000 temporary workers rely on the weekly payroll
3. **Identify the critical profiles.** The scenarios (for example, "Create vacancy") were matched against transaction types (for example, "Create temporary vacancy," "Create permanent vacancy"). Numbers were either "guesstimated" from sample branches or obtained from system logs (Figure A.39).

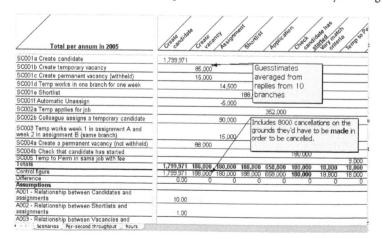

**FIGURE A.39**  Scenario lists

The figures were extracted from the scenarios and recast as weekly averages (Figure A.40).

| Annual total | Weekly average | Hourly average | Per second | % | user mode (80%) | Admin mode (20%) |
|---|---|---|---|---|---|---|
| 1,799,971 | 34615 | 865 | 0.24 | 10.82 | 8.66 | 2.16 |
| 188,000 | 3615 | 90 | 0.03 | 1.13 | 0.90 | 0.23 |
| 171,000 | 3288 | 82 | 0.02 | 1.03 | 0.82 | 0.21 |
| 188,000 | 3615 | 90 | 0.03 | 1.13 | 0.90 | 0.23 |
| 658,000 | 12654 | 316 | 0.09 | 3.96 | 3.16 | 0.79 |
| 180,000 | 3462 | 87 | 0.02 | 1.08 | 0.87 | 0.22 |
| 18,800 | 362 | 9 | 0.00 | 0.11 | 0.09 | 0.02 |
| 18,000 | 346 | 9 | 0.00 | 0.11 | 0.09 | 0.02 |
| 630,000 | 12115 | 303 | 0.08 | 3.79 | 3.03 | 0.76 |
| 6,301,899 | 121190 | 3030 | 0.84 | 37.88 | 30.31 | 7.58 |
| 6,301,899 | 121190 | 3030 | 0.84 | 37.88 | 30.31 | 7.58 |
| 180,000 | 3462 | 87 | 0.02 | 1.08 | 0.87 | 0.22 |
|  |  |  |  | 100 | 80 | 20 |
| 16,635,570 | 319915 | 7998 | 2 |  |  |  |

**FIGURE A.40** Weekly averages

The weekly average number of transactions were then modeled to show the daily maxima (Figure A.41). From this it could be seen that a worst-case daily maximum was 4.2222 transactions a second.

| | 0900 | 1000 | 1100 | 1200 | 1300 | 1400 | 1500 | 1600 | |
|---|---|---|---|---|---|---|---|---|---|
| Transactions | | | 800 | | | | | | |
| | | | 800 | | | | | | |
| | | | 800 | | | | | | |
| | | | 800 | | | | | | |
| | | | 800 | | | | | | |
| | | | 800 | | | 800 | | | |
| | | 800 | 800 | | | 800 | | | |
| | | 800 | 800 | | | 800 | | | |
| | | 800 | 800 | | | 800 | 800 | | |
| | | 800 | 800 | | | 800 | 800 | | |
| | | 800 | 800 | | | 800 | 800 | | |
| | | 800 | 800 | 800 | 800 | 800 | 800 | | |
| | | 800 | 800 | 800 | 800 | 800 | 800 | | |
| | | 800 | 800 | 800 | 800 | 800 | 800 | | |
| | | 800 | 800 | 800 | 800 | 800 | 800 | | |
| | 800 | 800 | 800 | 800 | 800 | 800 | 800 | 800 | |
| | 800 | 800 | 800 | 800 | 800 | 800 | 800 | 800 | |
| | 800 | 800 | 800 | 800 | 800 | 800 | 800 | 800 | |
| per hour | 2400 | 10400 | 15200 | 6400 | 6400 | 11200 | 8800 | 2400 | 7900 |
| per second | 0.6667 | 2.8889 | 4.2222 | 1.7778 | 1.7778 | 3.1111 | 2.4444 | 0.6667 | |

**FIGURE A.41** Daily transaction profile

4. **Create the test environment.** The test environment mimicked the real one. Non-test-system-derived loads were simulated and the load level checked using Performance Monitor (Figure A.42).

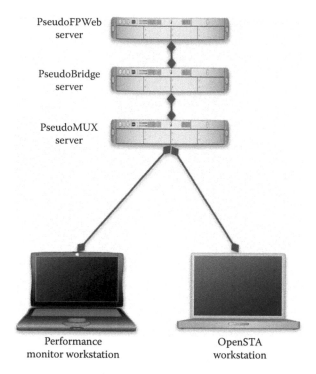

PseudoFPWeb
server

PseudoBridge
server

PseudoMUX
server

Performance
monitor workstation

OpenSTA
workstation

**FIGURE A.42** Performance test environment

5. **Get the performance testing tool.** The OpenSTA tool was used and scripts were written to mimic the candidate registration process being executed by 15,200 virtual users an hour.

6. **Write and run the scripts and report.** The scripts were run and the results shown in the report extract (shown in Figure A.43 and Figure A.44). The tests were run with the same number of users (100), but a decreasing ramp-up time such that the number of virtual users (VUs) connecting to the site increased with each test. All VUs were in a single batch. Thus 100/$n$ VUs per second would hit the site where $n$ is the ramp-up time in seconds. The test established that the system was quite incapable of supporting the load levels required. The system could not manage 1 user transaction a second without load shedding, and 4 user transactions per second was out of the question. Subsequently the network was changed to speed-up processing. This too proved inadequate, and a further analysis was conducted (similar to the one shown in section A.8) to determine

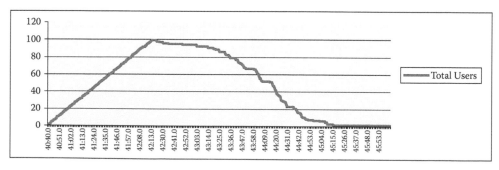

**FIGURE A.43** Performance test report.
When the ramp-up time = 100 seconds (1 user every second), all 100 users attempted to visit the site and 16 users were refused.

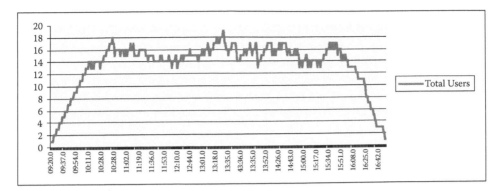

**FIGURE A.44** Performance test report.
When the ramp-up time = 400 seconds (1 VU every 4 seconds), a maximum of 19 VUs accessed the site simultaneously and no VU was refused access to the site.

where the bottleneck was in the processing. This identified that the bottleneck was (a) the "Create candidate" scenario and (b) the interface between the web and the legacy system retained especially and solely for the "Create candidate" scenario, which required that the legacy system be abandoned, and its data migrated. Much later it was discovered that the legacy system had been decreasingly adequate for the preceding 14 months as the load had grown.

## A.7.1 Conclusions

1. The network cannot support the throughput.
2. The bottleneck lies in the interface between the legacy and web systems.

# A.8 Case Study: Performance Testing (Bottlenecks and Critical Variables)

This section is an edited plan/report of a series of performance tests. This identifies the issues dealt with, the processes, and tools used.

The groups involved were *Testing* and *Support* (which provided much valuable advice and a lot of machines). Where parts have been excluded a "…" is left in their place.

## A.8.1 Executive Summary

The BizRool system is an advanced workflow generator. This section of the plan/report:

- Describes how Testing prepares and execute performance tests of the BizRool system.
- Reports previously-executed performance and stress tests.

The following questions have been answered:

1. *Does switching off the screen/form loading progress bars speed loading the screen/form?* Answer: **yes, it can reduce it by more than half.**
2. *Is Outlook or Internet Explorer faster at opening screen/forms with many BizRools?* Interim answer: **yes, Outlook is on average twice as fast as Internet Explorer.**
3. *Do many fields and BizRools on a screen/form slow the loading of a screen/form and the engine?* Interim answer: **in BREng5.[1] it can slow it by a factor of 10.**

---

[1] A particular version of the BizRool Engine.

4. *Are screen/forms executed all-on-the-same-machine faster with the database on a separate machine?*
    a. **Answer 1:** complex (500 BizRool) screen/forms account for 99.79% of the delay. The difference in Ethernet speed accounts for 0.12% and the separate networks account for 0.05%. Conclusion: reduce or speed up the engine transaction rate for complex forms.
    b. **Answer 2:** removing the form complexity as an issue leaves the difference in Ethernet speeds accounting for 59.9% of the delay, the separate networks accounting for 25.7% and the relatively slow Oracle server accounting for 10%. Conclusion: ensure customers use a 100 MB Ethernet network.
5. Is there any advantage in putting the Engine on a quad-processor machine? Answer: **no. There is virtually no processing advantage.**

## A.8.2  Background

Performance is critical to BizRool's success. Salesmen and customers need some statement of performance. Developers need to know how much they must adjust the code.

## A.8.3  Objectives

Define a plan and reporting method for performance and load testing. Load testing will provide answers to the questions detailed in section A.8.7.

Long term, the aims of performance testing are as follows:

1. Provide customers with benchmarks defined in terms of transactions, user BizRools, and transactions per hour
2. Provide *Development* and *Support* staff with figures to allow diagnosis, prediction, and improvement of BizRool performance.

This document is intended to be used as a record of questions answered, work in progress, and questions yet to be answered.

## A.8.4  Strategy

The overall strategy for fulfilling those aims consists of 2 phases:

1. **Load testing** in which a number of statistically-relevant loads are applied across three kinds of systems, and the effects are observed
2. **Stress testing** in which the loads used in the previous phase are increased so that:
    a. The system collapses.
    b. The effects of the stress on the various components can be observed.
    c. Alternative configurations can be attempted in an attempt to stave off the collapse.

The strategy will be articulated to find the answers to a number of questions shown in section A.8.7.

## A.8.5  Method

See Chapter 16.

## A.8.6  Architecture

The BizRool architecture is shown in Figure A.45.

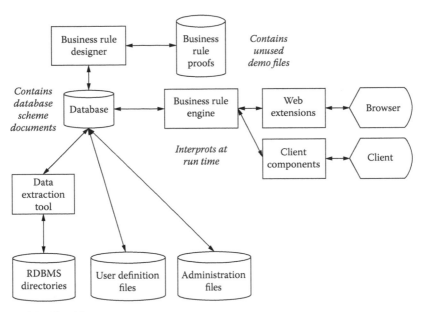

**FIGURE A.45**  BizRool architecture

The critical interfaces are:

1. Between the database and the engine
2. Between the engine and the clients

*DET* and *BizRool Designer* do not present performance problems.

## A.8.7  Questions to Be Answered

The tests will be executed to answer the questions in the following order of priority:

1. What are the typical loads imposed by current users?
2. To what extent does the structure and content of an application affect the transaction rate?
3. To what extent are screen/form design and process design, factors affecting response time and throughput?
4. What is the effect of moving the database and engine onto the same machine?
5. What is the effect of adding a second BizRool engine to a separate server?
6. At what point does the addition of an extra engine have *no* appreciable effect on the Performance of the system?
7. What is the effect of adding a BizRool webserver on a separate box?
8. What is the effect on response time and throughput does the increase in the memory of { web server | database server | engine } for a given number of BizRools per hour and users?
9. What is the effect on response time and throughput does the increase in the number of processors of { web server | database server | engine } for a given number of BizRools per hour and users?

## A.8.8  Results Analysis

Two primary results will be looked for: response time and throughput:

1. Response time and *throughputs* (per request, especially screen/forms, lists, attachments, and *submits*)
2. Throughput = # of Transactions per unit time

These will be graphed for each test, and the "elbow" of the response/throughput curve will be identified such that the limits of scalability can be determined.

## A.8.9   Phase: Load Testing

This phase is designed to:

1. Determine typical BizRool configurations in terms of hardware, applications and throughput.
2. Identify the relative 'weight' of different BizRools.
3. Determine the importance of screen/form type and size.

During this phase, a mix of transactions and user BizRools will be used.
Load can be increased by either:

- Having virtual users perform transactions more quickly

or

- Increasing the number of virtual users

The load testing phase will attempt to answer the following questions:

...

- **What is the effect of adding a BizRool webserver on a separate box?**
  - Method: Using the configuration described in *Test environments* below, add a separate web server, and run the three applications against it. Measure the average times required to display all screen/forms and execute all useful paths. Add a second engine on a separate server. Repeat the process.
  - Results: % change in the response time and throughput as a result of adding a BizRool webserver on a separate box to a two-server configuration.

...

- **Does switching off the screen/form loading progress bars speed loading the screen/form?**
  - Method: Use PBFIELDTHRESHOLD= 0 to switch off the screen/form loading progress bar
  - Results: It can reduce it by more than half.

| Case | Load time in seconds |
|---|---|
| Oracle ODBC driver & default BizRool install settings (PBFIELDTHRESHOLD=100) | 14 |
| Oracle ODBC driver & PBFIELDTHRESHOLD=200 | 8 |
| Oracle ODBC driver & PBFIELDTHRESHOLD=0 | 6 |

...

- **Is Outlook or Internet Explorer faster at opening screen/forms with many BizRools?**
  **Method 1** — BREng5:
  The screen/form contains 500 fields each with a BizRool. The engine was BREng5.
  Results 1: Yes: with 500 BizRools, the results on each are:

| Form load | Outlook | IE |
|---|---|---|
| Screen/form with 500 custom variables loads in: | 1 min | 3m 54s |

  **Method 2** — BREng5 Submit with screen/form reload: The screen/form contains only 1 field, even though there are 500 BizRools. The engine was BREng5.
  - We added "Re-open folder" checked to reload screen/form.
  - We removed all the fields on the screen/form.
  **Result 2** BREng5 — Submit with screen/form reload:

| Screen/form load/submit | Outlook | IE |
|---|---|---|
| Screen/form load time [with 500 custom variables and no field on screen/form]: | 1.0 sec | 2 sec |
| Screen/form submit time (with screen/form reload): | 4.5 sec | 7 sec |

**Method 3** BREng5 — 800+ BizRools

| Screen/form load/submit | Outlook | IE |
|---|---|---|
| Screen/form load time [with 800+ custom variables and no field on screen/form]: | 1.5 sec | 2.5 sec |
| Screen/form submit time (with screen/form reload): | 8.5 sec | 13.0 sec |

The readings on a 800 MHZ (W2K) and 1 GHz (NT) boxes are similar.

| Screen/form load/submit | Outlook | IE |
|---|---|---|
| Screen/form load time [with 500 custom variables but only one field]: | 1.0 sec | 2 sec |
| Screen/form submit time: | 2.5 sec | 3 sec |

Also assigning all these custom variable values either on "When BizRool started" or on "When user loads screen/form" seems to make little or no difference.

- **Do many fields and BizRools on a screen/form slow the loading of a screen/form and the engine?**
  1. **Discussion:** Variables can be accessed either in the database or the screen/form. Using BREng5 and maintaining more than 500 variables in one application can have disastrous consequences for system performance. A screen/form with one Custom Variable on it but with an application with 500 variables referenced in the database, can take on average (1 GHz p2) 10 seconds to load or submit. Without the variables in the database, either of these operations takes 1 second. This will be repeated using an BREng6 engine and clients.
  2. **Method 1 — BREng5 and increase the number of variables** Test Environment: BizRool 5.3 engine and web server on a machine running Windows 2000 Professional, 1.7 GHz CPU, 512 MB RAM, virus scanner stopped. SQL Server 7 SP5 is on a 2nd machine running Windows 2000 Server, 350 MHz CPU, 320 MB RAM.

     Scenario: This scenario includes the processing of a blank screen/form (no fields) for load and submit (with the screen/form reload option checked since this reflected the Customer requirement). In this particular scenario, we did not reference a custom variable, just had 100s of them in the database associated with the application.
  3. **Result 1 — BREng5 and increase the number of variables**

| BizRools | blank screen/form load (secs.) | from submit to screen/form reloaded (secs.) |
|---|---|---|
| 0 | < 1 | < 1 (Base case) |
| 289 | 2 | 6 |
| 339 | 2 | 8 |
| 389 | 2 | 10 |
| 439 | 2 | 11 |
| 489 | 2 | 12 |
| 589 | 3 | 14 |
| 689 | 4 | 18 |
| > 800 | > 6 | > 23 |

  4. **Comment** (see Figure A.46): The obvious issue here was the slow database server. This led us to advise the Customer to get a faster database server. However, we were surprised at the trend that was exposed — that so much processing was taking place even though we were not referencing the variables.

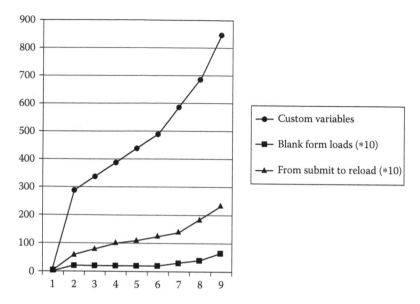

**FIGURE A.46**  BREng5 increase the number of variables

- **Are screen/forms executed all-on-the-same-machine faster with the database on a separate machine?**

    **Method 1**: *Testing* and *Support* will each dedicate 2 machines. *Support's* will have a 10T Ethernet connection; *Testing's* will have a 100T Ethernet connection. Each will test using a complex and a simple screen/form on a single application, using SQL server and Oracle. The two sets of machines will have different processor speeds. This will hopefully be identifiable (and therefore eliminable as a factor) when running the screen/forms by expressing the speeds of the execution of a complex screen/form on a single machine with a SQL server, as percentage differences, i.e. *Support's* machines are (say) 10% faster than *Testing's*. Once this is established as a baseline, it should be possible to identify the difference which small screen/forms, SQL versus Oracle etc. and the network make.

    This will be repeated using an BREng6 engine and clients.

    **Environment**:
    - The "same machines" environment uses SQL server.
    - The "separate machines" environment has several clients, each running scripts, pointing at a webserver running the BREng6 web components pointing at an BREng6 engine, pointing at an (Oracle) database.

    **Results** (Figure A.47):
    - Answer 1: complex (500 BizRool) screen/forms account for 99.79% of the delay. The difference in Ethernet speed accounts for 0.12% and the separate networks account for 0.05%. Simple screen/forms load on average more than 4 times faster than complex screen/forms. (19: 88).
    - Answer 2: removing the form complexity as an issue leaves the difference in Ethernet speeds accounting for 59.9% of the delay, the separate networks accounting for 25.7% and the relatively slow Oracle server accounting for 10%.

    For details about how the *%influence on delay* is calculated see section 18.3.

- **Is there any advantage on putting the Engine on a quad-processor machine?**

    Traditionally one anticipates that the major issue on a multi-CPU system will be contention.

    Since TITAN was already set up for extended tests using the Test Harness, *Testing* used that machine on its own.

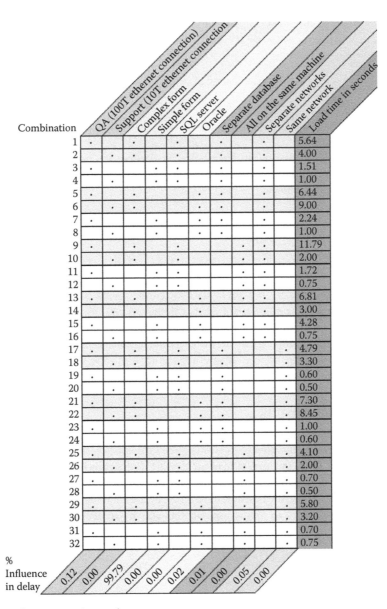

**FIGURE A.47**  Performance testing results

Two test runs were done, each for two hours. The first was of the engine running on all 4 CPUs, the second with the engine set to use only 1 CPU (via the Engine's registry setting). The idea was to see how many BizRools could be performed over a fixed period of time (measured by counting number of events in BizRools table for the test application).

**Setup:**
- TITAN 4 x Pentium V
- 1 GB RAM
- Windows 2000 Server SP2
- SQL Server 7.00.0961

Subs1 and TH3 Test Harness scripts were run against BizRool application 3.

Test Harness Logs and BizRool application were cleared down and the system rebooted between each run.

**Results:**

| Configuration | No. of events generated over 2 hours |
|---|---|
| 1 CPU | 14,268 |
| 4 CPUs | 14,464 |

In separate shorter runs, Testing also measured 2 Performance counters which can be used to give an indication of contention: Context switches per second and System calls per second. Typical measurements were as follows:

| Configuration | Context switches/second | System calls/second |
|---|---|---|
| 1 CPU | 45,656 | 113,086 |
| 4 CPUs | 48,312 | 117,892 |

**Conclusions:** These tests are not particularly scientific, being based on a very small sample. Nonetheless, given that the only variables between the test runs was the number of CPUs used by the engine, we can conclude that the Engine's Performance on a multi-CPU configuration appears to be no better than on a single CPU. The Performance counter data indicate that more contention is occurring but not by the orders of magnitude feared. It may be, that the bottleneck here is SQL Server running on the same machine.

## A.8.10 Phase: Stress Testing

This phase of testing is not designed to determine optimal BizRool configurations (but see the end of this section), rather this phase will attempt to evaluate the load which different BizRools apply. Thus we can rank the following BizRools in terms of load on the various parts of the system. This is necessary to provide a baseline understanding of BizRool under load.

This will be performed against the baseline system (see above) and load added until the system is no longer scalable. It is not intended to mimic user BizRool (say by simulating think time and/or mix of BizRool type).

## A.8.11 Definitions

| Term | Meaning |
|---|---|
| BizRool complexity | (of a BizRool application) The number of (published) BizRools. |
| main path | (in workflow creation) That path connecting the creation of a folder with its archiving via the BizRools of the highest priority. |
| MTS | Microsoft transaction server |
| path | (in workflow creation) the process by which a folder can be created and used through to being archived. There may be several of these depending on the complexity of the map |

**FIGURE A.48** BizRool performance glossary

## A.8.12 Test Environments (see Figure A.49 through Figure A.51)

| No web (a) | SQL Server 2000 + Win 2000 | Engine + Win 2000 | | Outlook 2000 sp2+ Test harness |
|---|---|---|---|---|
| Web (b) | Oracle 8/9i | Engine + Win 2000 | Web Server + extensions + IIS + MTS + Win 2000 | Outlook 2000 sp2 + Test harness |
| Hardware | P5 quad processor 1 GHz processor and 512 Mbytes RAM | P5 server with 1 GHz processor and 512 Mbytes RAM | P5 server with 1 GHz processor and 512 Mbytes RAM | P5 machines with 1 GHz processor and 512 Mbytes RAM |

**FIGURE A.49**  Test environment 1

| No web (a) | SQL Server 2000 + Engine + Win 2000 | Outlook 2000 sp2 + Test harness |
|---|---|---|
| Web (b) | SQL Server 2000 + Engine + Win 2000 | Browsers (IE5.5) + Test harness |
| Hardware | P5 quad processor 1 GHz processor and 512 Mbytes RAM | P5 with 1 GHz processor and 512 Mbytes RAM |

**FIGURE A.50**  Test environment 2

| Web(b) | Oracle 8/9i + Win 2000 | *m* Engines | n web servers + IIS 5 | Proxy server + Oracle 8i/9i |
|---|---|---|---|---|
| Clients (IE5.5)+ Test harness | | | | |
| Hardware | P5 quad processor 1 GHz processor and 512 Mbytes RAM | P5 with 1 GHz processor and 512 Mbytes RAM | P5 with 1 GHz processor and 512 Mbytes RAM | P5 with 1 GHz processor and 512 Mbytes RAM |
| P5 with 1 GHz processor and 512 Mbytes RAM | | | | |

**FIGURE A.51**  Test environment 3

1. *Test harnesses.* The previously-developed test harness will be used. In addition a number of test scripts will be developed using the WinRunner tool.
2. *BizRool application 1.* A very simple application involving a single screen/form and few BizRools.
3. *BizRool application 2.* A simple application involving three screen/forms and few BizRools.
4. *BizRool application 3.* A complex application involving many screen/forms, and several BizRools.
5. *Hardware sources*
   a. Testing has access to 20 machines which are Pentium V 1 GHz with 512 MB of RAM. All of them have been ghosted such that it is a simple matter to load any OS and DB combination.
   b. *Support* can supply access to 3 Dell 1 GHz servers.
   c. Development can supply access to 4 machines including the Quad processor.
6. *Test input parameters.* Testing will use an input parameters file. This will contain and define:
   a. Transaction mix (see Table A.3)

**TABLE A.3**   Transaction mix

| Transaction | Subtransaction | % | Notes |
|---|---|---|---|
| Login |  | 10 | NB 9 am login flood |
| Filter |  | 10 | NB web only |
| DisplayList |  | 10 | NB In-Tray/Watch size |
| Screen/form: | Blank | 13 |  |
| Screen/form: | Folder [page] | 18 |  |
| Screen/form: | Action | 13 |  |
| Refill |  | 0 |  |
| Attachment |  | 0 |  |
| Close: | Submit | 24 |  |
| Close: | Cancel | 2 |  |
| Raise flag |  | 0 | NB non-user BizRools?? |
| Total |  | 100 |  |

b.  Test application characteristics. The test applications will be graded as shown in Table A.4.

**TABLE A.4**   Test application characteristics

| Characteristic | Small | Medium | Large |
|---|---|---|---|
| # BizRools | 10 | 100 | 500 |
| Screen/form size (as measured by # of screen/form elements, grids etc.) | 1 screen/form = { 5 buttons + 2 entry fields + TH1 } | Screen/form 1 = { 5 buttons + 2 entry fields }<br>Screen/form 2 = { 10 buttons 5 entry fields + 1 gif + 2*2 grid } |  |
| Server scripts (measured by # lines) | None | 2 * 10 lines | 5 * 10 lines |

7.  *Data Sources.* The BREng5.3 and BREng6 Engines will provide counters of each transaction type in its performance counters. These can be saved to file via standard Microsoft Management Console mechanisms, so we can get our percentages for each type, with minimal fiddling about. The following data is required:

a.  Number of users/license (Table A.5). Average is 242. the maximum is 3623.

**TABLE A.5**   Number of users/license

| # of users/ license | <100 | 101–200 | 201–300 | 301–400 | 401–500 | 501–600 | 601–700 | 701–800 | 801–900 | 901–1000 | 1001–1100 |
|---|---|---|---|---|---|---|---|---|---|---|---|
| % of total | 54 | 15 | 11 | 7 | 1 | 3 | 2 | 3 | 1 | 1 | 1 |
| Number of licenses | 86 | 24 | 17 | 11 | 2 | 4 | 3 | 4 | 2 | 1 | 1 |

b.  Size of applications used (measured as shown in Table A.3 and Table A.4).

c.  Hardware environments.

8.  *Database Environments.*

a.  For database, engine, and web server on a single box, use SQL Server 2000.

b.  For separate database box 1, also use SQL Server 2000.

c.  For separate database box 2, use Oracle 8i or 9i running on a big UNIX box.

d.  In BREng6.1 we can compare Oracle, SQL, and DB2.

9.  *BizRool Clients.* For Phases 1 & 2, separate figures will be produced for web client and for the universal clients: Outlook & GroupWise. The Universal clients are believed to load the server to the same extent. A check will be made on this.

a.  For Phase 3, figures will be obtained for the clients in use *in situ*.

b.  No attempt will be made to assess the performance of any clients until the server is well-proven.

# A.9 Example: End-of-System-Test Report

This is included as an example of an end-of-system-test report. It describes the status of a system as it leaves the system-test phase and enters an integration phase in which its ability to coexist with other systems is tested.

The report's underlying message was that the release was unfit for any further testing due to the large number of unfixed problems. The consequence was that several more "releases" were made before Integration testing occurred.

## A.9.1 Management Summary

### Purpose of This Report

This report defines the quality of the Wave 1 software at the moment of its handover by System test to other testing teams.

### Apologies

This report presupposes some knowledge of the product as well as software testing. It is intentionally brief.

### Structure of the Report

The report identifies an idealized method of defining a system's quality and then discusses what has been done to define the quality of this system. It then draws a number of conclusions.

### Conclusions

1. The system needs all *Critical* and most *High* problems fixing before it is ready for Integration testing with companion systems.
2. System test has raised more errors in this release than in any other so far.
3. System testing of Wave 1 raised slightly fewer bugs than expected. This was partly due to a lack of fixes (see #9 below).
4. Several subfeatures were not available in the release and tests could not be run because of this.
5. The feature exhibiting the largest number of bugs is Alerts.
6. Few specifications showed user scenarios; these are critical to exercising the system in a convincing manner and exposing bugs.
7. The value of the system test to the product can be measured by the number of bugs it finds as a proportion of all bugs in the release.
8. 143 *Critical* and *High* bugs have been raised in V4.0 so far. 42 are fixed. To go into what is effectively the next release with only 29% of *Critical* and *High* bugs fixed is to court major problems and consequent delays.
9. The need to continue System test testing beyond the 3-release limit currently imposed will be seen from the number of bugs raised in the Integration environment. If they are over 336 then it was preferable to let System test continue testing for at least another cycle.

## A.9.2 The Quality of a System

The quality of a system can be defined in two senses: the quality of the process and the quality of the product.

1. The quality of the development process within the product is undefined apart from the testing, configuration management, and release processes. No audits of the development process have yet occurred.
2. The quality of the product can be defined in functional and non-functional terms. At a non-functional level the customer has identified a number of Business Process Measures but these are unrelated to management-level questions such as "what would be the effect on the system of adding an extra server/memory/processor?" and are mostly concerned with throughput. System test testing is not required to test these.

At a functional level all the customer requirements are defined in the System Requirements specifications. All the features of the release are defined in one or more system functional specification (See section A.9.8 for a list).

The quality of testing can be determined by looking at the number of problems reported from the field as a proportion of the number of problems found while testing. Ideally this is nil.

The number of bugs raised is at best a relative guide to test or product quality. A large number of bugs might simply mean an excellent test set, a small number might mean excellent software.

### A.9.3  What We Did

1. Review functional specifications. Each functional area was assigned to a tester who was responsible for reviewing the functional and other specifications, liaising with the developers, and creating the tests.
2. Create tests. We created tests based primarily on the functional specifications using the TestDirector tool. As the features stabilized, these tests were then extended. Special-to type tests of a highly complex and repetitive nature, to do with internal product coding were scripted using WinRunner. These tests were found to be both a major identifier of bugs and a very fast way of getting excellent coverage.
3. Test coverage. Test coverage is measured as a percentage of the requirements and is displayed in charts as shown in section A.9.9 in Appendix A.

### A.9.4  What Testing Has Shown

Since the primary objective of testing is to find bugs the charts in Figure A.52 through Figure A.54 illustrate our achievement.

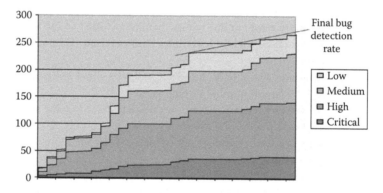

**FIGURE A.52**  Bugs raised by severity

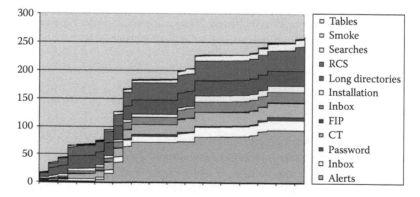

**FIGURE A.53**  Bugs raised by features

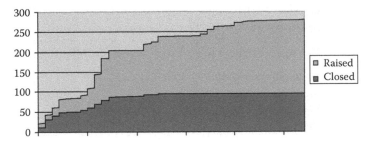

**FIGURE A.54** Bugs raised and closed overall

143 *Critical* and *High* bugs have been raised in V4.0 so far. 42 are fixed. To go into what is effectively the next release with only 29% of *Critical* and *High* bugs fixed is to court major problems and consequent delays (Table A.6).

**TABLE A.6** Current bug status

| | |
|---|---|
| Critical | 40 |
| High | 103 |
| Medium | 91 |
| Low | 35 |
| Total | 269 |

Note the expected number of bugs raised by System test shown in Table A.7. The discrepancy between predicted and found is probably due to the lack of fixes.

**TABLE A.7** Overall bugs predicted and found

| Total bugs found before Wave 1 | Environment | % | Predicted for V4 Wave 1 | Actually found in Wave 1 | % difference |
|---|---|---|---|---|---|
| 310 | DEV | 6 | 51 | 16 | 68 |
| 1985 | System test | 40 | 329 | 269 | 18 |
| 649 | Production | 13 | 108 | | |
| 2029 | Integration testing | 41 | 336 | | |
| 1 | Training | 0 | 0 | | |
| 6 | DPS | 0 | 1 | | |
| 4980 | Total | 100 | 825 | | |

Note the levels of bugs for some previous releases in Table A.8.

**TABLE A.8** Bug levels in some previous releases

| Release | Total | Critical |
|---|---|---|
| 2.1 | 426 | 64 |
| 2.2 | 275 | 94 |
| 2.3 | 254 | 46 |
| 3 | 452 | 94 |
| 3.5 | 713 | 246 |

### A.9.5 Why Estimate the Number of Bugs to Be Found and What Makes Us Think the Estimate Is Correct?

We estimate the number of bugs to be found so we have a way of identifying:

- How good or otherwise our testing is.
- How many developers will be required to fix bugs.
- How many bugs remain in a release after testing has finished.
- When testing should stop.

There is a number of ways of estimating bug counts:

- **Bugs per line of code**: this is primitive and of limited value as a predictor since the variation is too high and sensitive to both team and language changes.
- **Bugs by number of Requirements satisfied**: this too is likely to be a poor predictor.
- **Bugs per function point**. No function point analysis has been undertaken.
- **Bugs in relation to inserts, deletes, and updates per release**: this is the approach taken using multiple regression analysis (see section 18.10.5 in Chapter 18). It generates an equation requiring regular recalibration. The recalibration is needed because as fixes are made the code changes, and because bugs in past releases are being constantly recorded.

Try to average out a number of these approaches. In particular, recalibrate the last approach for *Critical, High, Medium,* and *Low* bugs for each release.

The accuracy of the last approach can be shown in relation to the preceding releases. The equation used works for them all. With increasing numbers of releases this equation will improve in predictive power. Once data from 10 releases has been obtained, a simple data mining tool can also be employed.

### A.9.6 What the Graphs Don't Show

We still have persistent problems with:

1. Installing on a completely clean machine. Without installing a 3.5 release, and thus "dirtying" the machine, Version 4 installations fail. The definitions of the "clean install environment" are not available.
2. Obtaining a satisfactory virtual environment with which to test XP installations. It is difficult to test all the features on an XP environment due to the large number of XP regression tests required. Automating the regression tests set would be a preferred solution.
3. Obtaining specifications in a timely manner. Alerts features were still changing until 12 working days before the release. The latest X specification was delivered on Monday 2nd of May, 13 days before the expected end of X testing.
4. The features withdrawn from the release and moved to later releases: had this been decided earlier it would have simplified planning.
5. Stopping testing too early. Were a proper test-and-fix cycle adopted, at least two further cycles would have been needed. As it was the bug detection rate was artificially low. Figure A.51 shows the angle at which bugs are being acquired in the last few days. It would have been far sharper at this point were bugs being fixed as they are found. This line should be nearly flat for System test testing to be ended.
6. TestDirector and its inability to generate graphs and Excel outputs simply, accept input and save it in a stable manner.
7. The fact that several subfeatures were not available in the release and tests could not be run because of this.
8. That System test suffered a week's test delay due to the poor initial quality of Wave 1, release 4. Two patches were necessary.

## A.9.7  What We Would Do Differently Next Time

1. Issue daily reports and keep a daily log based on them. While reports were issued on most days this was not consistently done.
2. Insist on getting scope documents earlier.
3. Get virtual machine environments established before testing started.
4. Insist on having scenarios for all users defined in the PFS.[1] On the rare occasions they are provided they have proved to be an important way of exposing bugs.
5. Always install onto at least one clean machine.
6. Always raise a bug even if the problem is likely to be test-environment-related.

## A.9.8  Appendix: Functional Specifications for Wave 1

Table A.9 shows the status of a number of specifications at the start of a new "wave" of releases. One "Backwards compatibility" is simply missing. (Most of) the others have PRS (Product Requirements Specifications) or PFS (Product Functional Specifications) or UI (User Interface Specifications). All the specifications were in fact to hand but several were not signed off (and thus had "0.n" numbers) and tended to be changed with minimal warning.

**TABLE A.9**  Functional Specifications for Wave 1

| Description/functionality | Spec. | Team leader | System tester | PRS | PFS | UIS |
|---|---|---|---|---|---|---|
| Backwards compatibility | Not Found in DOCLIB: Backwards compatibility PFS | Laxman | Lucy | — | — | — |
| Long directories | Long Directories Requirements Catalogue | Laxman | Shakir | — | 1.1 | 1.4 |
| Password security | Password Security PFS | Ken | Shakir | 0.1 | 1.1 | 0.4 |
| Alerts | Alerts Business Workflow Scenarios (Alert Authoring) | Paul | Mat/Mark | 1.0 | 2.0 | 0.3 |
| Windows XP compatibility | Windows XP Compatibility PRS | Ken | Lucy | 0.1 | | |
| Codes | Codes | Vaso | Lucy | 1.0 | | 1.0 |
| | Guide to Requirements Documentation | | | | 0.3 | |

This suboptimal state caused some problems since some tests had to be redesigned "on the fly" and then later reviewed.

Based on this table management were advised that testing would be problematic, slow, and likely to overrun.

## A.9.9  Appendix: Test Coverage

The scale shows the state of tests during a system test. Tests marked as N/A were not runnable since they referred to features missing from that Wave. Some tests could not be run due to the late arrival of specifications. Some Alerts tests could not be run due to the bugs already raised (Figure A.55).

---

[1] *Product Functional Specification.* A lower-level form of requirements specification used by developers and coders rather than PRS (*Product Requirements Specification*) used by management and sales.

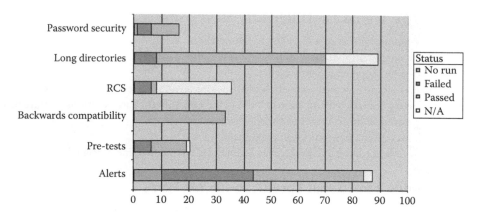

**FIGURE A.55**  Feature quality

## A.10  Example: Test Function Report

This is an example of a report written on taking over a test function. It concentrated entirely on the bug status since there were neither staff nor tools to be reported on (Figure A.56).

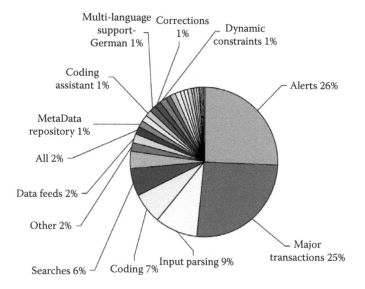

**FIGURE A.56**  Sources of bugs

1. 26% of bugs are unrelated to any unit; you can't be sure that any of the other figures aren't hopelessly-skewed.
2. The Major Transactions are the biggest single source of bugs. Alerts remain a big problem.
3. Only 3% of bugs are found in the field; either users have given up reporting them or 97% of the bugs are found in testing. But see Figure A.57. Some releases are buggier than others. Figure A.57 shows that:
   a. 2.0.51, 2.0.57, and, 2.0.58 were buggy (or well-tested), and that recent releases are also exhibiting many bugs.
   b. There was a large number of releases made.
   c. Little testing appears to have occurred on the earlier releases.

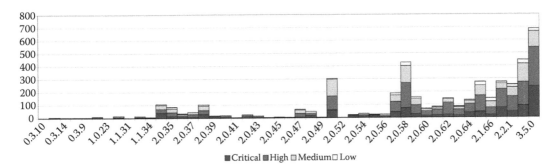

FIGURE A.57  Release history

As the interval between releases grows, the number of bugs tends to grow also. Figure A.58 shows that the release decision-making process was out of control. Taken with the chart in the preceding figure it shows that virtually no time at all was being allowed for the testing of releases 2.0.40–2.0.46 and the accumulated bugs only became evident in release 2.0.51 when a better attempt was made at testing them.

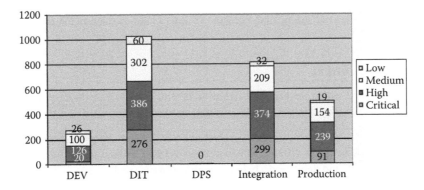

FIGURE A.58  Release interval analysis

Some test environments find more bugs. Who uses the DPS environment? The reduction in bugs from system test to production is good but should the number of production-environment bugs not be added to the total found in the field (136)? This would mean that 15% are found in the field, which is high (shouldn't be over 10%) (Figure A.59).

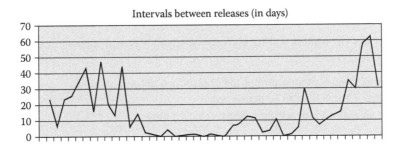

FIGURE A.59  Bug-finding ability of test environments

An increasing number of bugs are being designated "unfixable" whereas before they were simply designated "by design." If a large number of bugs are in fact features then either the testers need more training or the specifications need more care. Allegedly "unfixable" bugs merit close management attention. *Why are they being raised? What cannot be fixed?* (See Figure A.60.)

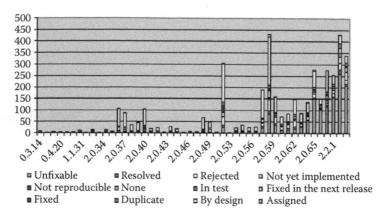

FIGURE A.60   Bug resolution

## A.11   Case Study: Testing a Formal Requirements Specification (TransitCard Ticketing System)

This section provides the context and background details of a system fragment called the TransitCard Ticketing System. It:

- Identifies the document structure of the TransitCard development
- The context of the system to be developed
- Illustrates an approach to testing a safety-critical system
- ...

> The ticketing system is not only mission- but also safety-critical. Accounting for everyone in the system at any time is essential in case of an emergency. So this specification is detailed. The documentation structure below shows the specifications which were created.

### A.11.1   Documentation Structure

This section identifies the relationships between the various kinds of documents used in this example (Figure A.61).

### A.11.2   System Context

This system is concerned with a ticketing subsystem to be employed on an underground system. It has four parts: the ticket, the ticket charger, the ticket reader and access controller, and the station computer.

- **Ticket.** The ticket is a SmartCard called a TransitCard. It can accept a charge of up to $100.
- **Ticket charger.** The ticket charger can issue new TransitCards, display the balance of existing cards, accept credit and debit cards, banknotes and coins as small as 10p, and issue paper receipts (Figure A.62).
- **Ticket reader and access controller unit:** The ticket reader and access controller accepts and returns tickets, returns invalid tickets and issues an alert to the user, admits passengers or inhibits their access, displays the balance of the ticket, displays whether the access point may be used for entry or egress (Figure A.63 and Figure A.64).
- **Station computer:** The Station computer manages one or more Ticket reader and access controller units.

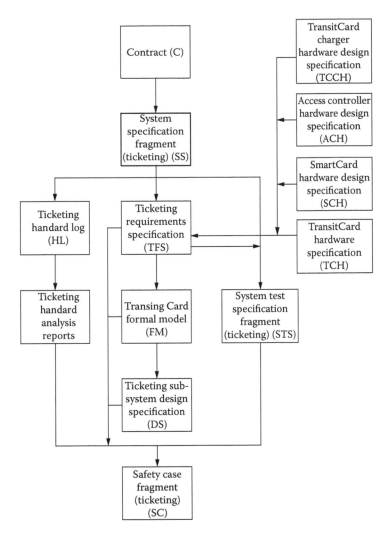

**FIGURE A.61** Ticketing subsystem documentation structure

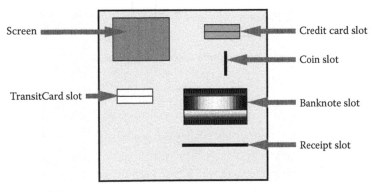

**FIGURE A.62** TransitCard Charger

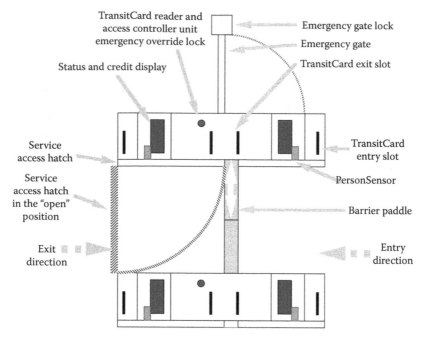

**FIGURE A.63** 2 Access controller and card reader unit system diagram

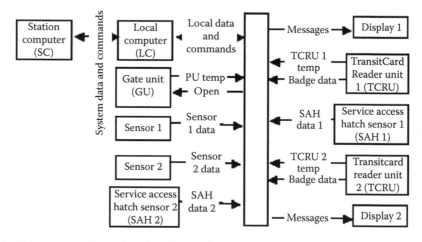

**FIGURE A.64** 2 Access controller and card reader unit functional diagram

## A.11.3 Specification

This is the primary natural-language specification which is used as the basis for writing system tests.

**Interfaces.** Table A.10 shows the interfaces which have been defined.
**Constraints:** The features listed in Table A.11 are safety-related.

**TABLE A.10** Interfaces of the ticketing system

| Interface name | Explanation | From | To |
|---|---|---|---|
| PU temp | Paddle unit temperature | Paddle Unit (PU) | Local Computer (LC) |
| ... | | | |
| Sensor 2 data | Person has passed sensor 2 | Sensor 2 | |

**TABLE A.11** Constraints

| Ref. | Feature | Safety-relationship |
|---|---|---|
| 21.8.4–13.5 | The TransitCard reader and Access Controller ... indicates whether the access point may be used for entry or exit. | In an emergency it must be clear to passengers by which gates they can leave. |
| 2.5.1–1.1 (not shown) | The Station computer manages one or more TransitCard reader and Access Controller units. It can be used to: ... reconfigure individual TransitCard reader and Access Controller units to accommodate changes in passenger flows. | In the event of an emergency it is essential that intending passengers be prevented from entering the station and current passengers be allowed to leave. |
| ... | | |
| 2.5.1–2 (not shown) | Emergency overrides can also be commanded remotely from a Master computer. | It must be possible for a central controller to take over control in the event of the absence or incapacitation of staff. |

Assumptions

1. Accounting will use cents at $1 = 100$. The administration charge is reflected neither on the card nor in the specification.
2. The Barrier position is not part of the TransitCard's data but is shown since it is central to the card's function.
3. The TransitCardID is not modeled since it is only ever recorded on the card. It is shown for *completeness'* sake alone.
4. The formula for calculating the station-to station cost is also not shown since in practice it could be implemented as a table maintained in ...
5. Several messages have been excluded but the model could be extended to include them.

## A.11.4 System Use

This section is a series of assertions which can be used as baselines for system tests. They are reflected in the schemas of the Z specification and must be consistent with it.

The system is used as follows:

**Passenger**

20.11.4–1 Passengers buy a TransitCard using the TransitCard charger. This will cost at least $11 and allow them to travel anywhere on the system.

20.11.4–2 Passengers insert their TransitCards into the TransitCard reader and Access Controller unit. This displays the balance left on the card.

20.11.4–2.1 If the balance is insufficient to allow passengers to go anywhere on the system (that is to the farthest possible station) the TransitCard is refused, a message is displayed, and a buzzer sounds.

20.11.4–3 Passengers insert their TransitCards into the TransitCard reader and Access Controller unit in order to leave the station.

20.11.4–3.1 Unless the station is the same as the one they left, they are charged according to the shortest distance between the two stations.

20.11.4–4 Passengers can refill their TransitCards using the TransitCard charger to a maximum of $100.

...

**TransitCard**

20.11.4–5 The ticket is a smartcard called a TransitCard incorporating a microprocessor.

20.11.4–6 It can accept a charge of up to $100.

20.11.4–7 Passengers may purchase TransitCards for $11 (this includes a £1 administration fee, the remaining $10 is a credit).

20.11.4–8 Recharging the card will incur a charge equal to the journey time bought.

20.11.4–9 Each TransitCard is uniquely numbered for security purposes. The number is not humanly-visible.

20.11.4–10 Cards are not transferable within the Railway system, for MMI and financial reasons.

20.11.4–11 The TransitCard is sufficiently robust to withstand $10^6$ traverses of a TransitCard reader.

20.11.4–12 The microprocessor contains sufficient memory to record permanently:

20.11.4–12.1 A 16-digit identity code.

20.11.4–12.2 A 5-digit value code. The two last digits are after the decimal point. The card may thus contain up to $999.99 in value though the system will impose a $100 limit.

20.11.4–12.3 The name of the station where the journey began.

20.11.4–12.4 The card status.

...

**TransitCard reader and Access Controller unit**

20.11.4–13 The TransitCard reader and Access Controller unit

20.11.4–13.1 Accepts and returns TransitCards

20.11.4–13.2 Returns invalid TransitCards and issues an alert to the user

20.11.4–13.3 Admits passengers or inhibits their access

20.11.4–13.4 Displays the balance of the TransitCard

20.11.4–13.5 Indicates whether the access point may be used for entry or exit

20.11.4–14 No other tickets can be used on the system

...

20.11.4–15 To journey from station A to station B the passenger inserts the TransitCard in the TransitCard entry slot.

20.11.4–15.1 If there is insufficient credit in the TransitCard to make the longest journey

20.11.4–15.1.1 The TransitCard is returned

20.11.4–15.1.2 A buzzer sounds, and

20.11.4–15.1.3 The display screen advises the passenger that the TransitCard has been refused.

20.11.4–15.2 If there is sufficient credit in the TransitCard, and the passenger has passed the first sensor:

20.11.4–15.2.1 The screen displays the remaining credit

20.11.4–15.2.2 The TransitCard moves to an intermediate position.

20.11.4–15.3 As soon as the passenger has retrieved the card from the TransitCard retrieval slot, the barrier paddle moves out of the passenger's way.

...

20.11.4–17 Any attempt to duplicate the card identity number with the result that more than one card with the same number be used on the system at the same time will trigger an alarm when either card is used to obtain egress. It is up to station staff to determine which is the duplicate card.

...

## A.11.5  Specification of the TransitCard System

This is a semi-formal definition of the possible states of the Transit card and is included so you can compare it with the natural-language descriptions and with the Z schemata.

The TransitCard system is here modeled as a state machine from the viewpoint of the card. The possible transitions are illustrated below.

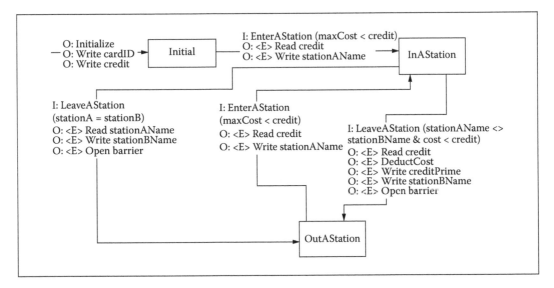

**FIGURE A.65**  State machine view of the TransitCard

### Statuses of the Card

The card may be in one of the following states:

- Blank and uninitialized as it is received from the factory.
- Initialized with a credit of $10.
- InAStation after a user has put the card through a reader and it has been accepted as having enough credit to permit the shortest journey.
- OutAStation after a user has put the card through a reader and it has been debited with the cost of the journey.

### Operations

The card may move between states as follows:

- **Initialization** when the *TransitCardCharger* initializes a card before issuing it.
- **EnterAStation** when a user puts the card in a machine to enter to a station.
- **LeaveAStation** when a user inputs the card in a machine to leave a station.

The following non-state-changing operations may also occur:

- **CreditMyCard** when a user wants to increase the credit on a card.
- **RejectMyCard** when a card is found to be short of funds.

## Data Structure

The card has the following data on it:

1. **status:** the card's status as shown above.
2. **stationAName:** the name of the station at which the card was last used to enter the system.
3. **cardBalance:** the current value of the card.
4. **TransitCardID:** the unique card identifier.

The system is aware of two other data:

1. **minCost:** the minimum cost of traveling between any two stations.
2. **journeyCost:** a given function which returns the cost of travel between any two stations.
3. **additionalCredit:** the amount of credit entered by a user which is added to the card's cardBalance.

## Errors

The following errors have been defined:

1. *Rejected* after a user has put the card through a reader and it has been found to have insufficient credit to cover the cost of the journey.
2. *Too much credit* after a user has attempted to credit the card with more credit than is allowed.

## Data Invariants

1. Credit and cost are always positive.
2. JourneyCost < minCost < 10000.

# A.11.7  The Z Model

This is the formal specification of the TransitCard. It is modeled as a state machine with 3 states and 3 transitions.

## A.11.7.1  Data Definitions

The card will have some data on it:

```
[BARRIER_POSITION,MESSAGES,STATION_NAME]

CREDIT == ℕ₁

COSTVAR == ℕ₁

STATION_NAME ::= Blank | Station_1 | Station_2 | ...
               | Station_N

COST == ℕ₁
```

and some messages

```
STATE ::= Initialised | InAStation | OutAStation

MESSAGES ::= Card_Rejected | Too_Much_Credit | OK

BARRIER_POSITION ::= Barrier_Up | Barrier_Down
```

### TransitCard Schema

The TransitCard contains the entry station name and the card balance. The journeyCost is calculated from the entry to the exit station and is always less than or equal to **minCost** — the minimum cost of using the system.

```
┌─TransitCard──────────────────────────────────────────────
│ entryStationName,exitStationName : STATION_NAME
│ state : STATE
│ minCost : COSTVAR
│ cardBalance : CREDIT
│ journeyCost : STATION_NAME × STATION_NAME ⟶ COST
├──────────────────────────────────
│ ∀ minCost : COSTVAR;
│    journeyCost : STATION_NAME × STATION_NAME
│                   ⟶ COST •
│   journeyCost (entryStationName,exitStationName)
│    ≤ minCost ≤ 1000
└──────────────────────────────────────────────────────────

ΔTransitCard ≙ TransitCard ∧ TransitCard′

ΞTransitCard ≙ [ ΔTransitCard |
                  θ TransitCard = θ TransitCard′ ]
```

The Transit card can be modified and therefore exists in two states: *after* and *before*. It can also simply be read without being modified. The values of the *after* and *before* states are bound to the TransitCard by use of Ξ.

### Initialization Schema

The card is initialized by having a credit $10, the card's initial status (blank) and **entryStationName** (blank) recorded on it.

```
∃ TransitCard′• Initialise
⇔ TransitCard′ •
[TransitCard′|state′ = Initialised
    ∧ stationAName′ = Blank ∧
cardBalance′ = 1000
```

### EnterAStation Schema

The card is inserted into the card reader to gain access to a station. The old entryStationName is overwritten. If:

1. There is sufficient credit (minCost < cardBalance)
2. The TransitCard is in the "**InAStation**" state (which would mean that someone had jumped a barrier)
3. Entry is permitted and a message "OK" is displayed, the card status is changed, and the barrier is lifted.

```
This is the part of the specification which proves the system's integrity.
Each part of the proof is composed of a header and a body.
The header will contain the schema name such as "EnterAStation0" and the
input/output parts of the schema such as:

entryStationName?: STATION_NAME          (Get the station name)
message!:          MESSAGES              (Display any messages)
Barrier_Position!: BARRIER_POSITION      (Get the barrier position)

state, state?:     STATE                 (The card's state)
```

The body contains the various conditions and actions, and should be read to mean:

"IF
state ≠ InAStation                    (Since the transition is
                                       "EnterAStation0" you cannot be both
                                       about to enter it and already be
                                       in it.)
cardBalance ≥ minCost                 (There's enough money on the card
                                       to cover the minimum travel on the
                                       system)
THEN
StationAName = entryStationName?      (Write the name of the station where
                                       the card entered the system to
                                       the variable StationAName)
Message! = OK                         (Possibly make a happy sound to
                                       indicate all is well or just display
                                       a message saying "OK")
Barrier_Position!: Barrier_Up
State = InAStation                    (the card is now in the station)"

```
┌─EnterAStation0────────────────────────────────────────────┐
│ ΔTransitCard                                               │
│ entryStationName? : STATION_NAME                           │
│ message! : MESSAGES                                        │
│ Barrier_Position! : BARRIER_POSITION                      │
│ state,state? : STATE                                       │
│ ──────────────────────────────────────────────            │
│ state ≠ InAStation                                         │
│ cardBalance ≥ minCost                                      │
│ stationAName = entryStationName?                           │
│ message! = OK                                              │
│ Barrier_Position! = Barrier_Up                            │
│ state = InAStation                                         │
└───────────────────────────────────────────────────────────┘
```

The EnterAStation definition is completed in the *RejectMyCard schema* section.

## LeaveAStation Schema

The card is inserted into the card reader to leave a station. If:

- The exit station name exitStationName is the same as the entry station name entryStationName, or
- There is sufficient credit to pay for the travel between the two stations (cardBalance > journeyCost)
- Exit is permitted, the card status is changed to "InAStation" and the barrier is lifted. Otherwise a message "There is insufficient credit on your card" is displayed.

Note that the use of minCost should always guarantee that cardBalance > journeyCost. This is an added precaution.

```
┌─LeaveAStation0──────────────────────────────────────┐
│ ΔTransitCard                                         │
│ entryStationName,exitStationName? : STATION_NAME     │
│ message!  : MESSAGES                                 │
│ Barrier_Position!  : BARRIER_POSITION                │
├──────────────────────────────────────────────────── │
│ (cardBalance                                         │
│   ≥ journeyCost (entryStationName,exitStationName?)  │
│  ∧ cardBalance'                                      │
│     = cardBalance                                    │
│       - journeyCost (entryStationName,              │
│                          exitStationName?))          │
│ ∨ (entryStationName = exitStationName?)              │
│ message! = OK                                        │
│ Barrier_Position! = Barrier_Up                       │
│ state = OutAStation                                  │
└──────────────────────────────────────────────────── ┘
```

PreLeaveAStation0 ≙ pre LeaveAStation0

```
┌─PreLeaveAStation0───────────────────────────────────┐
│ TransitCard                                          │
│ entryStationName,exitStationName? : STATION_NAME     │
├──────────────────────────────────────────────────── │
│ state = InAStation                                   │
│ ∨ (cardBalance                                       │
│     ≥ journeyCost (entryStationName,exitStationName?)│
│   ∨ entryStationName = exitStationName?)             │
└──────────────────────────────────────────────────── ┘
```

The LeaveAStation definition is completed below in the *RejectMyCard schema*
...

## RejectMyCard Schema

If:

- cardBalance < minCost or
- cardBalance < journeyCost

the card is rejected by the card reader, a message "Card_Rejected" is displayed, and the barrier stays down.

```
┌─RejectMyCard────────────────────────────────────────┐
│ ΔTransitCard                                         │
│ entryStationName,exitStationName? : STATION_NAME     │
│ message!  : MESSAGES                                 │
│ barrier!  : BARRIER_POSITION                         │
├──────────────────────────────────────────────────── │
│ ((cardBalance < minCost                              │
│   ∨ cardBalance                                      │
│     < journeyCost (entryStationName,                 │
│                       exitStationName?))             │
│  ∧ (message! = Card_Rejected                         │
│    ∧ barrier! = Barrier_Down))                       │
└──────────────────────────────────────────────────── ┘
```

EnterAStation ≙ EnterAStation0 ∨ RejectMyCard

LeaveAStation ≙ LeaveAStation0 ∨ RejectMyCard

...

## A.11.8  System Test of "Enter A Station"

### Test Environment

The test will require an operational barrier, a separate card reader, and a TransitCard.

### Test Objectives

**TABLE A.12**  System test of "Enter A Station"

| Precondition | Expected result | Failure |
|---|---|---|
| Card inserted with the card having cardBalance ≥ minCost | • Barrier opens.<br>• Card is returned. | Any combination of:<br>• the barrier will not open<br>• the card is rejected<br>• the card is retained<br>• a warning message displayed<br>• a warning sound generated |
| Card inserted with the card having cardBalance < minCost | • Barrier remains shut.<br>• A warning message displayed. | Barrier opens. |
| Card inserted with the card having state = InAStation | • Barrier remains shut.<br>• A warning message displayed.<br>• Card is retained. | Barrier opens.<br>OR<br>Card is returned. |
| Card inserted and ejected with the card having cardBalance ≥ minCost<br>AND<br>Barrier open | • (Check by using a hand-held reader). The card balance should only change on leaving the station.<br>• Station B name should be blank until the card leaves the station.<br>• The TransitCardID must never change | state ≠ InAStation<br>OR<br>cardBalance has changed<br>OR<br>StationBName ≠""<br>OR<br>TransitCardID has changed |

# Appendix B
## Checklists

The purpose of these checklists is to give you some points to think about, not boxes to tick.

## B.1  Test Manager's Terms of Reference

Use this as a way of giving yourself some power as well as responsibility. It will also enable you to see (as people suck their teeth meditatively) where some of the more sensitive or absent parts of the project lurk.

1. **Quality:**
   a. You are expected to ensure that the requirements of the company software quality system are fulfilled.
   b. All work must comply with the company software quality system as defined in the company quality manual.
   c. You must exercise quality control of all test deliverables either personally or by delegation. If quality control authority is delegated to one of your project staff, such delegation does not absolve you from responsibility for its execution.
   d. You are required to use the standards agreed as part of the quality plan for the project (see section 8.21 in Chapter 8).
   e. You must ensure that all test staff are familiar with and have access to all the standards necessary for them to undertake the tasks assigned to them.
   f. You must ensure that you monitor the use of these standards.

2. **Project administration:**
   You are expected to ensure that all required administrative actions are taken for the purposes of testing of the project's deliverables.

3. **Project reporting:**
   a. You are expected to report effectively to the project manager on the test progress and performance against the test plan. In particular you are expected to give early warning of potential and actual problems.
   b. You are expected to progress all bugs reported to the bug reporting meetings up to the point where responsibility for the bug is accepted by the project manager or development team.
   c. You are to advise the project manager of the status of all bugs found in a timely manner.

4. **Constraints:**
   You are expected to take account of the following constraints in the planning and management of the project:
   a. <<list anything here which will affect product quality or delivery>>
   b. ...

5. **Absence from work:**
   You must ensure that arrangements are made for another member of the project team to deputize for you in the event of your absence and to ensure that the relevant staff member is advised.

6. **Acceptance certificates:**

You are responsible for obtaining the client's signature on acceptance certificates. You are also responsible for filing the signed acceptance certificates with the project office.

7. **Archiving:**

You are responsible for ensuring that all test records are properly archived in accordance with company policies.

8. **Progress meetings:**

You are responsible for:

   a. organizing regular weekly progress meetings with your manager at which your test status report will be discussed
   b. chairing the weekly Test Forum
   c. chairing the defect review meetings

You will be expected always to give a factual and honest account of test project progress.

9. **Client and subcontractor meetings:**

You are required to attend client meetings if requested by the client. You may request subcontractor meetings with the agreement of the project manager. You will be expected to keep a record of these meetings and file them with the project office.

10. **Test subcontractor obligations:**

   a. You must ensure that any test subcontractor is notified in advance of his/her obligations to the company under the contract as incorporated in the project plan.
   b. You will be expected to monitor any test subcontractor's performance against the project plan and to document any instances of late performance on their part in your progress reports to the project manager.

11. **Expertise:**

You are expected to provide test expertise to the project team test methods and principles, test tools, etc.

12. **Test and commissioning areas:**

You are responsible for:

   a. test scripts and test cases to ensure their maintenance and to account for changes introduced
   b. test tools and hardware
   c. the proper use of any test and commissioning areas and of hardware, including rigs — unless a specific waiver has been obtained — whether owned by the company or not

13. **Confidentiality:**

You are responsible for ensuring that the confidentiality of any client information released to you or the test team is maintained and for taking all necessary steps in this respect.

14. **Correspondence:**

You are responsible for ensuring that your manager receives copies of the following promptly:

   a. any contractual correspondence — that is, any document which may affect the company's contractual applications
   b. a weekly test status report, including minutes of progress meetings
   c. all project correspondence of contractual importance bearing the company letterhead is to be signed by your manager

15. **Overruns:**

You must notify your manager at the earliest moment should your forecasting reveal an actual or potential resource or time overrun.

16. **Overtime:**

All staff overtime must be authorized in advance by you and the project manager and you must also check all such claims.

17. **Planning:**
    a. You must prepare a test plan in accordance with company standards in a timely manner.
    b. You must ensure that all members of the test team are familiar with the test plan.
18. **Progress monitoring:**
    You are required to monitor the actual progress and resource use against the test plan. You must take all necessary steps to adhere to the time and resource use targets as far as possible.
19. **Purchasing (materials and expenses):**
    a. You are responsible for raising all purchase requests for material and expense items. These must be in accordance with the test plan. You must obtain proper authorization for these from the project manager
    b. All purchasing activities must follow company procedures
20. **Securing staff:**
    a. While it is the line manager's responsibility to secure staff for the project, you should ensure that written agreements exist for all imported project staff and consultants and that the agreements are signed by the respective line managers.
    b. You should also ensure that the relevant line managers of all imported project staff and consultants are aware of the respective start and end dates of their staff's involvement.
21. **Test staff:**
    You are expected to:
    a. contribute to the appraisal of your test staff
    b. contribute to the development of the company staff assigned to you while the project is in progress
    c. endeavor to develop staff abilities through exposure to new responsibilities, methods, and tools and arranging for training
    You are responsible for:
    a. assigning work to your test staff and for monitoring their performance
    b. maintaining test staff morale; this entails ensuring that each team member not only understands, but identifies with the company's goals. You should ensure that your team is kept properly informed of relevant matters by means of face-to-face meetings at intervals
    c. ongoing management of the test staff, who may report in to the various business managers, but have been assigned to the project
    d. negotiating the availability of resources from the business and planning their availability and utilization with the business managers
    e. monitoring of any client staff assigned to your test team
    You may not commit staff to another manager's direction without further reference to the project manager.
22. **Test subcontracts:**
    You are responsible for the management of any test subcontracts, except as authorized in the approved test plan, you may not subcontract any part of the work outside the company without the prior approval of the project manager.
23. **Time sheets:**
    You are responsible for collecting and approving the time sheets for all assigned test team members at the end of each month.
24. **Deliverables:**
    You will deliver:
    a. a comprehensive test strategy and test plan that is feasible, achievable, thorough, and accepted by the project manager (this will include the resource matrix and schedule for the test program)
    b. a defined test process that details roles, responsibilities, triage framework, communication channels, escalation points, etc.
    c. a test pack that includes all the necessary test cases and scripts for executing the test program

# B.2    What Test Managers Do Checklist

There are quite essential things test managers do. If you aren't doing them, then ask yourself why. This first checklist is intended for the test manager's use and to raise management issues. The others are phase-specific and can be used by anyone involved in that phase to raise technical issues.

## B.2.1    Generally

1. Check if you have your terms of reference. Are they sufficient? (See section B.1.)
2. Recruit staff.
3. Obtain SW and HW test resources.
4. Authorize releases.
5. Assess testing providers.

## B.2.2    Assess

1. The **contract** or **bid**: Look for contractual stipulations concerning testing.
2. The **safety** status: Are there any safety-related issues? Review safety issues according to the section B.10.
3. The **security** status: Are there any security-related issues? Review security issues according to section B.11.
4. The **product quality** status (see section B.7):
   a. bugs:
      i.   number of bugs released to the field (Check with Support)
      ii.  number of bugs found internally
      iii. the cost of finding and fixing a bug
      iv.  the number of bugs found in the same phase as they were created
      v.   the number (age and levels) of unfixed bugs (Is there a mass of low-level unfixed bugs which together render the system unusable?)
      vi.  evidence of bug fixing introducing more bugs (see section 2.7.5 in Chapter 2, section 18.9.8 in Chapter 18, and Figure 8.25)
   b. stakeholders:
      i.    project management's view (Do they see testing as a defense against trouble or as a largely-avoidable expense?)
      ii.   developer's view of product quality (They probably know what's wrong; are they doing a lot of overtime?)
      iii.  marketing's view of product quality (They know what's right, but watch the way the topic changes when you mention the embarrassing bits.)
      iv.   customer's view of product quality (If you are ever allowed anywhere near a customer other than for showing-the-quality-flag purposes, be pleasantly surprised.)
      v.    safety manager's view (How well is testing contributing to the safety case?)
      vi.   quality assurance manager's view (Is there a testing process defined? Does it work? Is it followed? Is there enough evidence to show that it's followed?)
      vii.  Support's view of the product (Which release provoked the largest number of calls? What was the test coverage of that release?)
      viii. tester's view of product quality
      ix.   third-party supplier's view of product quality
      x.    the channels of communication existing between stakeholders (Do they work? Are they all informal? Is there a danger of missing essential information?)
   c. releases:
      i.   the number of patches released in the last 24 months and what they covered
      ii.  the number of test runs abandoned

       iii.  the state of the configuration management

       iv.  the number of stable components

   d.  release timing:

       i.    length of time since last release

       ii.   median inter-release periods over the last year

       iii.  number of failed builds

       iv.  amount of slip from planned to actual dates in the last 5 releases

       v.    next deadline

   e.  documentation:

       i.    business process models

       ii.   requirements specifications

       iii.  design specifications

       iv.  safety analyses

   f.  performance:

       i.    any evidence of non-functional feature failures (speed, bottlenecks, and/or usability)?

       ii.   is there a performance specification or plan? (see section A.8 in Appendix A)

5. The **history**:

   a.  how long has the product existed?

   b.  why did your predecessor leave?

   c.  how many releases have been made?

   d.  what is the staff turnover level?

   e.  how long have key staff (project manager, team leaders) been in post?

   f.  is there any evidence of premature releasing?

   g.  are there any requirements documents?

   h.  are there any test standards?

   i.  are there any tests?

   j.  is there a plan?

6. The **test environment**:

   a.  test tools

   b.  test specifications

   c.  tests (Are they well-written? Were they themselves tested? Were they ever reviewed? How much of the functionality was covered? Have you watched the automated test suites being run? Are any never run? Why?)

   d.  bug management:

       i.    bug classification scheme

       ii.   bug management software (Is there a bug recording system?)

       iii.  bug detection charts

7. The **state of the test team**:

   a.  ratio of testers to developers

   b.  morale of testers (tester turnover as a proportion of all staff)

   c.  experience and qualifications of testers

   d.  aspirations of testers

   e.  division of testers between releases

8. The **state of the documentation**. Is it usable or shelfware?

   a.  training (Are the training courses sufficient to get new testers up to speed on the product as it is?)

   b.  support (How much time does Support spend resolving issues training should have fixed? How often does Support identify an unfixed bug in the field, how long does it take them to recognize this, how fast does such a bug get fixed, and how much does it all cost?)

   c.  safety management (Can every hazard be traced to some set of tests? How are the results of tests fed back to safety management?)

   d.  human factors management (Is there a set of tests covering every task identified in the task analysis?)

9. The **state of plans and budgets**: Is there a plan and a requirements specification? Is there a Risk log? Does it reflect the problems the project has really suffered?

10. The **state of reporting**: Are there weekly reports provided by all stakeholders to the project manager?

## B.2.3  Plan

1. **Identify** (see section B.7):
   a.  common terms (Are we all singing from the same hymn sheet?)
   b.  current status of project
   c.  test scope (Do you only system test or do you unit and integration-test too?)
   d.  interacting groups/stakeholders
   e.  expectations/commitments of each stakeholder group (documents, test results)
   f.  key dates which must be met
   g.  baseline documents
   h.  performance issues
   i.  risks:
      i.    key metrics which will signal that major risks will occur
      ii.   *Risk log*
      iii.  fault analyses
   j.  test plan review points
   k.  test data providers
2. **Prepare:**
   a.  strategy documents
   b.  test process model
   c.  test preparation monitoring document(s)
   d.  test execution monitoring document(s)
3. **Define:**
   a.  contractual, environmental, and legal constraints
   b.  testing environment, (tools, hardware, networks, disks, physical space, licenses)
   c.  staff acquisition and release
   d.  tool evaluation and acquisition
   e.  third-party services and software
   f.  baselines:
      i.   baseline document list
      ii.  baseline document review
   g.  relations with stakeholders
   h.  test team:
      i.   responsibilities (the terms of reference of all testers and test groups)
      ii.  training requirements
   i.  test development
   j.  build acceptance (entry criteria)
   k.  test execution
   l.  test conclusion (exit criteria) and release authorization
   m.  metrics identification, acquisition, and use
   n.  key dependencies, deliverables, and responsibilities
   o.  schedule
   p.  how you will monitor test development, execution progress, and feature coverage
   q.  bug management
   r.  configuration management
   s.  non-functional issues to be tested for

    t.  test data acquisition and quality control processes
    u.  regression, smoke, and confidence test identification process and criteria
    v.  risks and contingencies

## B.2.4  Estimate

1. Number of bugs to be found
2. Release date
3. Cost of testing. Ensure developers log the amount of time they spend fixing bugs as opposed to developing new features.
4. Baseline availability. What have you not got, when will it be available, how can this delay you and by how much?
5. Basic events (from Fault Tree Analysis) which will require testing

## B.2.5  Monitor

1. **Build and release management.** How many incoming builds were unusable? How many releases you made to other groups contained bugs you should have found?
2. **System test preparation.** Identify:
   a.  features
   b.  the risk level of each feature
   c.  coverage levels
   d.  the baseline document status (non-existent, draft, reviewed, released)
   e.  the tasks each tester has
3. **Assess risk and test status for each feature.**
4. **System test execution:**
   a.  bug levels, causes, and resolution
   b.  unit test execution and the amount of code being covered by unit tests
   c.  the quality of each release relative to others
   d.  current issues

## B.2.6  Report

1. **Daily** on the status of:
   a.  baseline review
   b.  test creation and execution
   c.  feature coverage and status
   d.  contribution to the safety case
   e.  security issues
   f.  likely problems
   g.  test environment
   h.  crashes
   i.  risks
   j.  bug status and estimates
   k.  schedule slippage
   l.  current issues
2. **Per release** on the:
   a.  quality of that release
   b.  problems encountered and their root causes in the:
       i.   system being tested
       ii.  test environment
   c.  safety and security statuses

    d.  non-functional characteristics, coverage, and status

    e.  risks

    f.  release metrics

### B.2.7  Manage Relations With

1. Assessment and certification bodies
2. Business analysts and technical writers
3. Developers
4. Human resources
5. Project manager
6. Quality assurance staff
7. Safety staff
8. Testers

## B.3  Communication, Team Compatibility, and Motivation Checklist

1. Does the team communicate well both with you and each other?
2. Does the project manager understand the risks and see you as part of the way with which they will be managed?
3. Is your team familiar to you; have you worked together on a team project before?
4. Are tasks delegated in a fair manner amongst your team?
5. Is your team motivated to create a good product?
6. Does your team have enough product knowledge to test well?

## B.4  Bid Review Checklist

1. Do we have the requirements?
2. Do we have any experience of this market?
3. Do we know what our prospect's experience of the system is?
4. Is the proposed work central to the company's future?
5. Is the proposed work a new direction for the company?
6. Is the proposed work pure research or integration of an existing solution or both?
7. How long will it be before the proposed research can be translated into a product?
8. What unusual constraints does the RFP impose?

## B.5  Requirements Analysis Checklist

### B.5.1  Requirements Analysis General Checklist

1. Do the documents conform to standards?
2. Has an initial concepts document or some such been prepared? Have the requirement mapping against initial concepts documents been mapped against this?
3. Is each requirement separately identifiable?
4. What checks for completeness and consistency have been made on the requirements?
5. Which requirements are the most likely to change? Why?
6. How and where are the boundaries of the system defined? Are they clear? Do they include the user classes?
7. From what H/W, communications, or application bugs must the system always recover?

8. Within the requirements specification, is there a clear and concise statement of:
   a. each safety- or mission-related function to be implemented?
   b. the information to be given to the operator information at any time?
   c. the required action on each operator command action command action command including illegal or unexpected commands?
   d. the communications requirements between the system and other equipment?
   e. the initial states for all internal variables and external interfaces?
   f. the required action on power-down and recovery?
   g. the different requirements for each phase of system operation? (e.g., start-up, normal operation, shutdown)
   h. the anticipated ranges of input variables and the required action on out of-range variables?
   i. the required performance in terms of speed, accuracy, and precision?
   j. the constraints put on the software by the hardware (e.g., speed, memory size, word length)?
   k. internal self-checks to be carried out and the action on detection of a failure?
   l. any components to be replaced while the system is running? Is any downtime foreseen?
9. Can each requirement be reinterpreted in terms of IF ... THEN ... ELSE?[1]

## B.5.2 Traceability Checklist

1. Is the specification traceable to any initial concepts, ITT, or other document that may have preceded the requirement?
2. From which higher-level document has this specification been developed?
3. Is the higher-level document under configuration management?
4. Is the higher-level document list listed in the document reference list?
5. Is the rationale of any derived requirement adequate?

## B.5.3 Attributes Checklist

1. What assumptions have been made? Where are they listed?
2. What requirements do they affect most?
3. Are expected requirements such as testability, reliability, reusability, modifiability, accuracy, performance, and usability all specified?
4. Is any requirement inconsistent with any other?
5. Are the requirements easy to understand and unambiguous?
6. Which requirements pose big technical challenges?
7. Which requirements are critical to the success of the project?
8. Are there any requirements for concurrency or data synchronization?
9. Have adequate provisions been made for all foreseeable future extensions to the system?
10. Is there evidence that the requirement is feasible?
11. Are any requirements insufficient?
12. Has a risk assessment been performed? Are the results to hand?
13. Can you map every requirement to a system test?
14. Must any legacy system or data be incorporated?

## B.5.4 Business Rules Testing Review Checklist

1. What purpose does the rule serve? (*Does it make sense? If it doesn't, either you don't understand it or the person who defined it doesn't.*)

---

[1] If it can't, then it's probably too vague to be testable. Simply saying "x is true/available" can be tested for, but having proved that it is true (or not) you have nothing left to relate it to the rest of the system.

2. What influenced the creation or modification of a rule? (*If this is an utterly sound business reason then the rule is pretty solid. Otherwise...*)
3. To which areas of the business does it apply?
4. Where is a rule implemented (*in which applications and/or processes*)?
5. In which jurisdictions is a rule enforced?
6. How each rule will be enforced?
7. Where will each rule be enforced; for example, within which implementation component, object or work task?
8. Who/what is responsible for enforcing each rule?
9. Which events should cause each rule to be enforced?
10. From which basis was it derived? (*Was it some legal requirement or was it "the way we've always done things"? Has the basis changed or is the basis liable to change?*)
11. When was the rule created?
12. When did the rule become effective?
13. Is the rule still in effect, and, if not, when was it discontinued?
14. Are there previous versions of a rule?
15. Was the rule retired or replaced and, if so, why?
16. Who can answer particular kinds of questions about a rule?
17. Who has been involved with a rule over time and in what way?
18. Where can more information about a rule be found?
19. Have all the possible conditions been identified?
20. Do any conditions conflict? Real example: "IF the train is in the goods yard and the train is not in the automatic train protection area THEN display xxxxxxx" (*the goods yard was in the automatic train protection area*).
21. Is any condition logically infeasible? Real example: "IF the system detects the last cheque being processed THEN send 'last cheque' signal" (how is the system to know this if you don't tell it?).
22. Does no invariant ever vary? Example: "Settlement day is always Thursday" (*except when Thursday is a bank holiday*).
23. Are the permissions and restrictions sensible? Example: "It must be impossible for a system administrator to have user access."

## B.6  Risk Management Checklist

1. Is there a *Risk log*?
2. Can it have entries deleted?
3. Can you delete entries from it?
4. If so, how many have been deleted, and can you get a copy that's six months old and see what's been deleted?
5. If so, can you get an old copy and see what has been deleted?
6. Does it list the critical product features and the cost if any one fails?
7. Is there any evidence of defeaturing?
8. If there is, then what was defeatured and what risk did it represent?
9. Does the *Risk log* list the core features of the system and what it would cost if any one failed?
10. To what extent has the project been defeatured?
    a. Why?
    b. When?
11. How many of the risks actually happened?

# B.7 Test Planning Checklists

## B.7.1 Test Planning General Checklist

1. With what customer-specific or other international standards must the project comply? Where are these defined?
2. What test plans exist? How will the test activities test be echoed in the project plan?
3. What extra hardware and software is required for testing?
4. What assessment procedures are used for customer-supplied hardware or software or subcontractor-supplied hardware or software?
5. What are the customer assessment criteria? How was this defined?
6. Do the various documents conform to company standards?
7. Are all the necessary output documents mentioned in the plan(s) in sufficient detail?
8. Are the methods to be used sufficient and sufficiently specified?
9. Does every test make sufficient allowance for range?
10. Are details of the types and quantities of bugs already found in the specifications to hand?
11. Is there evidence of a direct relationship between the criticality of some software and the plans and tests for that software?
12. Is there evidence that successful tests (those that find bugs) are withdrawn and rewritten? If not what steps are taken to prevent the tests from training the software to pass?
13. Are there any difficulties in tracing the tests to their baseline tests?
14. Is there any evidence of compromise in the evaluation of test results?
15. Are test plans and specifications produced in concert with the system analysis and design?

## B.7.2 Test Environment Checklist

1. Are the various test environments (unit, integration, and system) sufficient and sufficiently specified?
2. Do the test environment specification environment specifications include the details of the test data suites?
   a. How do you know these test suites are valid?
   b. Are any special tools required?
3. Is the software tested in the final use environment (i.e., the target processor and the actual peripherals, memory, etc.) rather than in an emulator?
4. What evidence is there that the quality of the code has deteriorated? Complexity of units > 10? Illicit unit binding? Greater unit binding?
5. Will there be sufficient hardware to do adequate integration and testing?
6. Is there any problem with developing realistic scenarios and test data to demonstrate any requirements?
7. Have acceptance criteria been agreed for all requirements?
8. Has sufficient time been allowed for product integration?
9. Is the product design and documentation adequate to maintain the code?
10. Are the test specifications adequate to fully test the system? Consider the risk of poorly written requirements or specifications.
11. Have you calibrated the (load-generation and any white-box) tools?
12. How do you know the tools are not imposing a Heisenberg effect?

## B.7.3  Configuration Management Checklist

1. How is the software configuration managed?
2. Who is the configuration manager?
3. Is there a software-based system to help with the configuration management?
4. Is there a change control board? Who is on it? How often does it sit?
5. What is the procedure for controlling changes?
6. How can staff suggest changes?
7. What relationships exist with hardware configuration control? Do hardware developers just dump kit for the testers to test against or are you warned in advance of critical changes?
8. What baselines have been defined? How have they been defined?
9. What means are available for customers to introduce changes into the requirements?
10. Has a baseline release been defined for the next release?
11. What baselines are under configuration management?

## B.7.4  Test Readiness Review Checklist

1. Does the review package include all baseline documents and unit test results?
2. Has the requirements specification been:
    a. updated, reviewed, and approved?
    b. checked to ensure that each requirement is traceable to one or more tests?
    c. analyzed to expose all safety- or mission-critical requirements?
3. Has all the code been peer-reviewed and approved?
4. Is the testing environment:
    a. adequately documented?
    b. adequately configuration-managed?
    c. operational?
5. Does the test plan identify:
    a. the testers?
    b. all possible test scenarios?
    c. the tests by priority?
    d. all risks, mitigation plans, and issues?
    e. test suspension and restart criteria?
    f. all user goals and scenarios concerning the documents?
6. Does the test plan address user guide, operations, maintenance, and business process validation?
7. Have all unresolved bug reports been analyzed to ensure they will not impede the testing effort?
8. Have all workarounds and non-functioning software components been identified in the test specification?
9. Have operational profiles of all major user groups been defined?
10. Has the acceptance and/or failure criteria been identified for every test?
11. Have all scenarios been identified and documented?
12. Has a feature/test matrix been developed?
13. Are all requirements traceable to one or more tests?
14. Are all tests traceable to one or more requirements?
15. Have any usability issues been identified concerning the testing activities?
16. Have any safety issues been identified concerning the testing activities?
17. Have any security issues been identified concerning the testing activities?
18. Is the new release under configuration management?
19. Are technical risks, mitigation plans, and issues documented with plans for tracking and closure?
20. Are there any risks, issues, or requests for action that require follow-up?
21. Is the architecture susceptible to common-mode failure?

22. In the event of failure of a load-balanced server, how long does it take the remaining servers to rebalance?
23. In the event of failure of any part of a fault-tolerant system, how long does it take for the system to recover?
24. How long does it take for (part of) a restarted system to recover?
25. Is there any evidence of high and persistent code turmoil? If there is it may imply that the release will be unstable. Comment on this in the report as a warning to management.

### B.7.5  User Documentation and Business Process Testing Checklist

1. Is there a documentation plan? Does it address:
   a. the documents' structure, objectives, and readership?
   b. the relationships between the documents?
   c. the role of each document?
2. Does each document have a table of contents, index, and glossary?
3. Has each document been spell-checked?
4. Does any document say anything the inverse of which would be ridiculous?
5. Is the objective of each document clear?
6. Can each document be related to one or more user tasks?
7. Can any feature of the system not be found (by reference to the documentation) to be fully explained?
8. Does each document relate to a version of the system and is this relationship explicit?

## B.8  Quality Review Checklist

1. What comparable projects have ended in disaster, and why?
2. How many bugs are reported from the field?
3. Is there any evidence that users are failing to report bugs or that they have given up reporting bugs?
4. How many users use the software and for what proportion per day?
5. What errors have been found in the field which should have been found in unit/system test/UAT, etc. testing?
6. Which parts of the system exhibit the most bugs?
7. Which parts of the system give users the most problems?
8. At what point does the return on testing become negative? When should we stop?
9. Is the test function failing? Evidence?
   a. dissatisfied customers?
   b. too many bugs found by customers?
   c. bugs being found too late to be fixed?
   d. only trivial bugs being found by testers?
10. What are the root causes?
    a. Is the test environment being constantly changed by the developers?
    b. Are releases being made irrespective of the bug status?
    c. Are the testers finding bugs too slowly?
    d. Are the testers failing to find bugs which only surface when the users find them?
    e. Have the testers the wrong tools?

## B.9  Localization Checklist

### B.9.1  General

1. Character sets
2. Keyboards

3. Text filters
4. Loading, saving, importing, and exporting high- and low-end ASCII
5. Hot keys
6. Error message identifiers
7. Hyphenation rules
8. Spelling rules
9. Sorting rules
10. Grammar
11. Underscoring rules
12. Capitalization and lower-case conversion rules
13. Paper sizes
14. Data formats
15. Address formats
16. Postcodes
17. Tax regimes
18. Decimal separators
19. Date and time rules
20. Rulers and measurements
21. Acculturated graphics
22. Acculturated output
23. Punctuation
24. Diacritical marks

### B.9.2  Manuals

1. Documentation testing
2. Help file testing

### B.9.3  Language Groups

1. European alphabetic
2. Middle Eastern
3. South Asian
4. Southeast Asian
5. East Asian
6. Additional modern
7. Archaic
8. Symbols
9. Special areas and format characters

## B.10  Safety Testing Checklist

### B.10.1  General

1. What levels of safety does the project deal with?
2. Is it clear which parts of the system are safety-critical?
3. How are safety-related issues managed in the project? Is there a means whereby a safety-related issue can be raised with any manager and quickly-resolved? Is there a means by which safety-related changes can be quickly identified and resolved?
4. Have all hazard-related failures revealed by the tests been advised to the safety manager?
5. Have all safety requirements and constraints been reflected in tests?
6. Have tests of unintended behavior been specified?

7. Have tests been specified to cope with or reveal hardware failures?
8. Do tests include critical operator behavior?

## B.10.2  Hazard Analysis Checklist

1. Has a hazard analysis been included in the project plan?
2. Do safety requirements originate from a systematic hazard analysis of the system and if not, on what basis was the safety requirements specification formulated?
3. Is there a formal procedure to check the safety requirements specification against the known hazards?
4. Has the system's ability to cope with every hazard identified in the hazard analysis been tested? Have hazard-related failures been induced, perhaps by fault injection?
5. If using fault tree analysis:
   a. have all top events been identified?
   b. have all basic events been identified?
   c. has every basic event been matched to some (set of) test(s)?
   d. have the probabilities of the basic events been established?
   e. have all minimal cut sets been identified?
6. If using event tree analysis:
   a. has every protection branch stage been related to some test?
   b. have the probabilities of each failure been estimated?
7. If using cause-consequence analysis, has every cause been tested?
8. If using failure modes, effects, and criticality analysis, has every component been tested to demonstrate that its MTBF can be met?

## B.10.3  Safety-Related Functions Checklist

1. Is there a clear and concise description of each safety-related function to be implemented by the system, e.g., interlocks, alarms, trips, input data, validity checks, reversionary modes?
2. Are the system inputs relating to each safety-related function defined with regard to range, accuracy, noise limits, bandwidth, etc.?
3. Are the system outputs relating to each safety-related function defined with regard to range, accuracy, update frequency, etc.?
4. Has the system sampling rate and accuracy been defined?
5. Is it consistent with the defined inputs and outputs?
6. Mode changes:
   a. Are the safety-related functions defined for every operating state of the system, e.g., start-up, normal operation, shutdown, maintenance, auto, manual, training? For example, different interlocks may apply in different modes, certain trips or alarms may be inhibited or may operate at different alarm levels during start-up.
   b. Are the necessary conditions for a safety transition between the operating states adequately defined and are unsafe transitions inhibited?
   c. What evidence is there that the effects of any power system changeover have been analyzed?
   d. Does the specification avoid the need for the safety functions to be inhibited under certain conditions? If not have adequate grounds for inhibiting safety functions been established?
   e. Have facilities been specified to apply inhibitions to states in a controlled way, to ensure that the inhibited state is clearly indicated and to ensure the removal of inhibitions after maintenance?
   f. Have procedures for the safe use of inhibitions been developed covering the actions to be taken before, during, and after their application?
7. Safety performance requirements:
   a. Have safety performance requirements (speed, accuracy, etc.) been specified where necessary?
   b. Have they been adequately researched?

    c.  Has a safety target been specified in respect of the system as a whole or in respect of the safety-related systems?

8.  Recovery from failure:

    a.  Has sufficient attention been given to survivability? (e.g., reversionary mode requirements and redundancy)?

    b.  Have safe system and state definitions been identified so that a safe state can be achieved in the event of failures?

    c.  Have provisions been specified to enable all operational settings to be readily inspected to ensure that they are correct at all times?

    d.  Has a means been specified of limiting the ranges of main control inputs (such as trip settings) to safe values, either in hardware or software?

    e.  Are there any requirements for disconnected systems to be reconnected after recovery?

    f.  Are there any requirements for data integrity or maintenance following power failure?

    g.  What evidence is there that the effects of any utility failure have been analyzed?

    h.  What evidence is there that common mode failure has been sufficiently considered?

    i.  Does the system have built-in self-testing facilities?

    j.  Is its failure reporting facility itself failure-independent?

    k.  Are failures automatically recorded?

9.  Human interfaces:

    a.  Has the role of the operator in maintaining safety been defined? For example, manual control may sometimes be necessary.

    b.  Is the user–system interaction defined for every operating state? For example, the control options given to the operator and the system response to both correct and incorrect selection of options may need to be defined.

    c.  In the event of the failure of automatic control, is sufficient information given to the operator to allow him to assume safe manual control?

    d.  Have the provisions been specified for ensuring safety during maintenance and modification of the system?

    e.  Have all error messages been specified?

    f.  Does the system generate any warnings? Are these consistent with human factors definitions and task analysis?

    g.  Does the system generate any status or maintenance data? Are these consistent with human factors definitions and task analysis?

10.  Testing:

    a.  Have provisions been specified for the testing of safety functions with a minimum of physical operations? For example, have provisions been specified to avoid the need for disconnections at terminals or other undesirable means for:

        i.  the injection of test signals?

        ii.  the monitoring of the results?

    b.  For configurations including those having diverse features:

        i.  Are the safety specifications developed by different people?

        ii.  Is the safety requirements specification checked against the known hazards by different people?

        iii.  Is the safety requirements specification written in more than one format?

    c.  Are there test requirements for different prototype builds?

    d.  Is there a requirement to range-test all mission-critical parameters?

## B.10.4  Fault Tree Analysis Notation

In fault tree analysis we begin with a (hazard) list of top events which Must Not Happen. Each is then decomposed to identify what could cause it to happen, using logic gates in a notation like the one shown in Figure B.1.

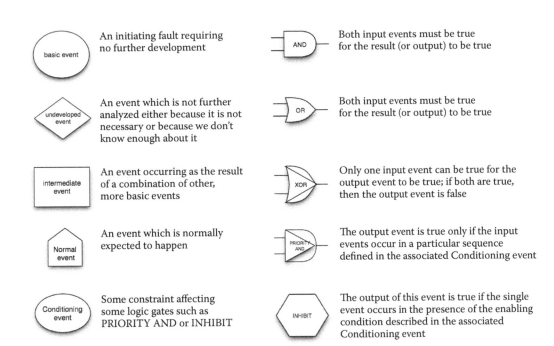

**FIGURE B.1** FTA symbols

# B.11 Security Testing Checklist

## B.11.1 General

1. What levels of security does the project deal with?
2. What steps have been taken to ensure the security of project hardware, software, and documentation?
3. What steps have been taken to ensure the security of customer hardware, software, or documentation?
4. With what security standards must the project comply?
5. Does the company have a security policy or other standard?
6. Has this standard been identified as defining this document?
7. Does this document:
   a. conform?
   b. have a clearly defined purpose and scope?
   c. contain references to policies, directives, procedures, standards, and terminology?
   d. specify the project risk objectives and policy toward risk?
   e. identify project assumptions and constraints as they relate to the risk management process?
   f. provide an overview of the risk management process?
   g. define risk parameters for analyzing and categorizing risks?

## B.11.2 User Registration and Management Checklist

1. Will the system use an existing registration, user management, and permissioning system or
   a. Will the system use an existing feature for user registration, management, and permissioning?
   b. If this system is used for trading will it be protected by two-factor authentication?
   c. Will there be a formal process in place for registering and removing users from the system?
   d. When passwords are given to users, will there be a process in place to ensure that they are kept confidential?

e. Will there be a secure process in place to reset forgotten passwords?

f. For any sensitive manual processes involved in this system, will a separation of roles be enforced to ensure that no single person is solely responsible for the entire process?

2. Will all the default and test user IDs be disabled?
3. Will there be a process in place to review user access rights regularly?
4. Have all accounts with administrator level or elevated privilege been reviewed to ensure that the access is actually required?
5. Are all user IDs associated with a named individual?
6. Will the system store or process any personal information that relates to identifiable individuals?
7. Will security awareness training be put in place for end users of the system?
8. Password management:
   a. Will the system verify that all passwords follow the company standard for password complexity?
   b. Will passwords be stored in encrypted form within the system?
   c. Will passwords be encrypted when they are transmitted across networks?
   d. Will the system enforce temporary user lockout if there have been five failed attempts to enter the correct password?
   e. Will there be a regime of elapsed-time-dependent enforced password changes?
9. Session management:
   a. Will the system use cookies or a similar token for session management?
   b. Will user sessions timeout after 15 minutes of inactivity?
   c. Will sessions be limited to eight hours before re-authentication is required?
   d. Will a banner be displayed during the log-in process to indicate that unauthorized access to the system is not permitted?
   e. Will the system display the date and time of when the user last accessed the system each time they log in?
10. System authentication
    a. Will all access between the servers within the system on the same network be authenticated?
    b. Will all access between remote servers be authenticated?
    c. Will it be possible for a single User ID to be used more than once at the same time?

## B.11.3  System Defenses Checklist

1. Against virus and worm infection:
   a. Is the company standard build to be used for all operating systems within the system?
   b. Have all the operating systems had the relevant security lockdown scripts applied?
   c. Is the use of system utilities restricted to those provided with the standard build?
   d. Will anti-virus software be activated on all servers within the system with a process in place to ensure virus update signatures are regularly applied?
   e. Will all the servers and applications within the system be registered and covered by the patch management program?
2. Against denial of service attacks
3. Against Trojan horses

## B.11.4  System and Data Classification and Validation Checklist

1. Has a business effect assessment been completed, reviewed, and signed off by the customer?
2. Have all the different types of data held within the system been documented and classified as public, confidential, or secret?
3. Has a permissions matrix been documented that defines all the user types, the data, and what sort of access users have to the data within the system?

4. What data security and integrity methods are used?
5. What safeguards do they offer against corrupt data?
6. How does the system cope with insufficient or missing data?
7. Will the information that is input into the system, be validated at the server to ensure that it contains the expected type and amount of data?
8. Network design:
    a. Has a network design been documented that covers the physical design, logical architecture, dataflows, and all the protocols used?
    b. Has the network design been reviewed to ensure that it follows best practice?
    c. If the system is connected to the Internet will it be connected through a firewall?
    d. If the system is accessible from a network other than the Internet, will it be protected by a firewall?
    e. Are sufficient access controls enforced for all firewall tunnels?
9. Encryption: Will all confidential or secret data be encrypted when it passes over untrusted networks such as the Internet?
10. Remote management: Will remote management of this system be necessary by any group?
11. Event logging:
    a. Will the system create and maintain a log of the following activities:
        i.    failed log-in attempts?
        ii.   successful logins?
        iii.  log off events?
        iv.   passwords changes?
        v.    creation, deletion, and modification of accounts and permissions?
        vi.   changes to confidential data?
        vii.  use of privileged functions?
        viii. administration activities?
        ix.   accesses to the audit log?
        x.    changes to the audit log?
    b. Will system logs be retained for six months?
    c. Is access to the audit logs restricted and monitored?

## B.11.5  Dealing with a Third-Party Company Checklist

1. Will a third party be involved in the hosting, maintenance, or provision of the system?
2. Has a non-disclosure agreement been signed by the third party?
3. Has an outsourcing due diligence investigation been completed and a report provided?
4. Has a security schedule been included in the contract with the third party?
5. If information is shared with a third party, have you consulted the legal department to ensure that the contracts and data processing warranties are in place?
6. Is data to be transmitted to a third party to be encrypted?

## B.11.6  Other Security Issues Checklist

1. If the system is regulated, for example by the FSA, SEC, or another authority, has the company security office been consulted?
2. Will the system involve any new cryptographic components?
3. Has the company security office been involved in developing security content for product launch or sales materials?

## B.11.7 Security Testing Checklist

1. Are all the Internet-facing servers within the system registered with the corporate web office?
2. Do the test plans for the system include tests to verify that security functionality has been properly implemented?
3. If the system is rated high on the business effect assessment or if it is Internet facing, has the company security office been consulted to determine whether or not additional security testing is required?
4. Has the security test covered the following?
    a. application testing
    b. back doors in code
    c. denial of service testing
    d. directory permissions
    e. document grinding (electronic waste research)
    f. exploit research
    g. firewall and application control list
    h. intrusion detection systems
    i. manual vulnerability testing and verification
    j. network surveying
    k. password cracking
    l. PBX testing
    m. port scanning
    n. privacy review
    o. redundant automated vulnerability scanning
    p. review of IDS and server logs
    q. security policy review
    r. services probing
    s. social engineering
    t. system fingerprinting
    u. trusted systems testing
    v. user accounts
    w. wireless leak tests

## B.11.8 Procedures for Testing Setup Checklist

1. Is traffic from the production system isolated from development and test environments?
2. Are the accounts used for testing different to real ones used on the production system?
3. Has consent from the Global Privacy Officer been granted for the use of any personal or confidential production data in a test or development system?
4. Have you consulted the legal department to establish how long data needs to be retained within the system?

## B.11.9 BS ISO/IEC 17799: 2000 Information Technology Code of Practice for Information Security Management Test Checklist

See Table B.1.

**TABLE B.1**  BS ISO/IEC 17799: 2000 Information Technology Code of Practice for Information Security Management Test checklist

| Standard reference | Heading | Questions |
|---|---|---|
| 2.3.1 | Security requirements in outsourcing contracts | … The contract should address … how the security of the organization's assets are maintained and tested, the right to audit, physical security issues, and how the availability of the services is to be maintained in the event of disaster. |
| 8.2.2 | System acceptance | Are system acceptance criteria established for new information systems, upgrades, and new versions? Are suitable tests carried out before acceptance? |
| 8.4.1 | Information backup | … Are the backup media regularly tested to ensure that they can be restored within the period allotted in the operational procedure for recovery? |
| 8.1.5 | Separation of development and operational facilities | Are the development and testing facilities isolated from operational facilities? For example must development software be run on a different computer to that of the computer with production software? |
| 8.4.3 | Fault logging | Are faults reported and well managed? Does this include corrective action being taken and checked and a review of the fault logs? |
| 10.1.1 | Security requirements analysis and specification | Are security requirements incorporated as part of the requirements specifications of new or existing systems? Do the security requirements and controls identified, reflect the business value of information assets involved and the consequences of a failure of security? |
| 10.2.1 | Input data validation | Is data input validated? Are there controls for: different type of inputs to provoke error messages and procedures for responding to such messages…? |
| 10.2.2 | Control of internal processing | Are risks identified in the processing cycle and validation checks included? Are controls identified to mitigate risks during processing? |
| 10.2.4 | Output data validation | Is the output data validated? |
| 10.4.2 | Protection of system test data | Are system test data protected and controlled? Is use of operational data containing personal information avoided for test purposes? |
| 10.5.2 | Technical review of operating system changes | Are there are processes or procedures in place to ensure the application system is tested after a change to the operating system and before being put back into production? |
| 10.5.5 | Outsourced software development | Are there controls over outsourcing software? Do these cover licensing arrangements, escrow arrangements, contractual requirement for reviews and testing before installation to detect malicious code etc? |
| 11.1.3 | Writing and implementing continuity plan | Are plans developed to restore business operations within the required period following an interruption or failure to business process? Are such plans regularly tested and updated? |
| 11.1.5 | Testing, maintaining and re-assessing business continuity plan | Are business continuity plans tested regularly to ensure that they are up-to-date and effective? |

# B.12  Usability Checklist

## B.12.1  Introduction

1. Has a task analysis been performed for every role within the requirements?
2. Can each human-factors requirement be traced to a task analysis?
3. Is the adequacy of the requirement for human factors and the human–system interface sufficiently assured?

4. Are there any requirements to provide help and diagnostics to operators?
5. What evidence is there that the system's various operations will be comprehensible to the users?
6. To what extent is the system pushing the cognitive abilities of its users to the limit?

## B.12.2   Usability Goals Checklist

1. Can 90% of users install the product in less than 15 minutes?
2. Can 75% of users use the key features after 1 day's instruction and 1 day's practice?
3. Can 75% of users use the key features after using the tutorial for 2 hours?
4. Which feature is the hardest to use?
5. How often do users use your product?
6. Do infrequent users have to relearn how to use your product each time they use it?
7. Do users need to learn new tasks easily or perform complex tasks?
8. Is an average user able to use the product in less than 3 times the time of an expert?
9. Is the work rate for an experienced user greater than 50% per hour?
10. Is the productivity for an experienced user greater than 30 tasks per hour?
11. Which scenario is the least well-supported by the system? What is the lowest task fit of all the scenarios?
12. Is the activity error rate rising?
13. How many naïve users succeed given time in accomplishing their tasks compared with those who give up?
14. Are more than 70% of naïve users successful within time?
15. Is the documentation useable?
16. Is the documentation easy to access?
17. What is the mean task completion time for novice, average, and expert users?

## B.12.3   Users and Tasks Checklist

1. Do you have a clear definition of who will use the system?
2. Can you identify >10 aspects in which the end user differs from you in knowledge, skills, computing experience, outlook, etc.?
3. What assumptions are being made about the users?
4. Have these assumptions been validated?
5. Can you classify the people who will use the system into groups who share similar attributes and will therefore require similar user interfaces?
6. Can you state the goals and operations which the user will want to perform with the system?

## B.12.4   User interface consistency checklist

1. Are the styles of interaction used consistently, e.g., not switching from function keys in one part of the system to a command line in another?
2. Is the screen layout consistent with similar items, e.g., menus or error messages using the same part of the screen on all screens?
3. Is the terminology used consistently, e.g., is the same part of the interface always referred to by the same word?
4. Are the keys on the keyboard used consistently? Are the abbreviations consistent and is there a simple rule used to form abbreviations?

## B.12.5   User Control Checklist

1. Can users stop any process taking longer than 3 seconds and return the system to a known state?
2. Can the user undo the previous action?

3. Is the user warned if the action can't be undone?
4. Are there any unexplained delays in the operation of the system?
5. Can the user change system, client, or server defaults?
6. Are any functions allocated to the system which users prefer to perform themselves?
7. Is the user capable of performing the functions that have been allocated to him/her or are they just the functions that can't be automated?

## B.12.6  User Performance Checklist

1. Can the user perform frequent operations rapidly?
2. Are shortcuts provided for skilled users?
3. Are defaults used sensibly?
4. Are the shortcuts displayed in an accessible form so the user is supported in becoming skilled in using the parts of the system they are interested in?
5. Is any human operation, expected by the system, difficult or impossible to achieve?

## B.12.7  User Interface Assessment Checklist

1. Is the interface efficient?
   a. Can tasks be performed with keyboard strokes?
   b. Does the site relate to how users work?
   c. Are response times fast enough?
   d. Do the windows fit on the screen?
   e. When opening a window does it appear above previously-opened windows?
   f. Do the words fit the window?
   g. Do the window titles match the window's function?
   h. Can the windows be resized?
   i. Do all buttons function as expected?
   j. Is there a screen refresh after a window is minimized or closed?
   k. How much can be entered into a field before it reacts?
   l. Does the screen match the screen shots in the manual?
   m. Does the "X" (close) button in the upper right corner work?
   n. Does the "–" (minimize) button work?
   o. Does the GUI freeze when a window is adjusted?
   p. Do the windows display correctly in either large or small font mode?
   q. Do all menu commands work?
   r. Are all non-functional buttons grayed out?
   s. Do all keyboard shortcuts work?
   t. Are all read-only data fields locked?
   u. Do windows or dialogs completely fit on the screen at low display resolutions?
   v. Does the tab key access the input fields and/or buttons in a logical order?
2. Is it intuitive?
   a. Does it exploit users' mental models?
   b. Does it behave consistently?
   c. Is it visually consistent?
3. Is it supportive?
   a. Does it allow mistakes to be shown and easily undone?
   b. Does it provide advice? tools? reference materials?
4. Is it engaging?
   a. Do users feel in control?
   b. Do users enjoy their experience?

## B.12.8  Usability Test Checklist

1. Tests:
   a. Is every scenario covered? Does every scenario need to be covered?
   b. Does every test have defined beginning and end states (so you can relink them)?
   c. Do the tests exercise all the user interface features?
   d. Are the tests prioritized?
   e. Are all the major errors exercised?
2. Test environment:
   a. Can you monitor the test environment remotely?
   b. Are users aware when you are monitoring the test environment?
   c. Is it easy to reset the test environment before a new set of users arrives?
   d. Have you tested the test environment to be sure that it records what users do correctly?
   e. Are you aware of how dissimilar the hardware is to that used in the "real world"? Does this matter?
   f. Do the users have all the support material to hand?
   g. Do you have all the questionnaires, logistic notes, etc. needed?
   h. Do you have a process model of the user experience?
   i. Are all the cameras working and with fresh videotapes?
   j. Is the sound quality adequate?
   k. Is the bug management system coping with the load?
3. UTCs' test experience definition:
   a. Do you have a definition of the users?
   b. Does this definition distinguish between groups of users in > 10 ways?
   c. What assumptions do you make about the users? How d'you know these are valid?
   d. Do you have (a) task definition(s) for each user class?
4. User instructions:
   a. Have you used them (possibly with an inexperienced member of staff as the "user" and also an experienced user, to compare timings)?
   b. Have you recorded the behavior of your prototype users to be sure the output of the recording system is usable?

# B.13  Web Issues Checklist

## B.13.1  General

1. Is everything on the screen visible at all supported monitor bit depths?
2. Will the client side run on the browsers specified?
3. Does the client side need any special plug-ins?
4. Are the client machine and browser settings, including security and multimedia correct?
5. Are the Java versions compatible?
6. How critical is the website or service you are testing (on a scale of 1–5) (see Table 5.1).
7. With what web standards must you comply? (See www.w3.org/TR/ for lists.)
8. Does the client side (need to) interface with any commonly-available applications such as the Microsoft Office suite?
9. Can the server-side structure handle the expected load? Where are the bottlenecks? What are the limits and will the system fail gracefully if overloaded?
10. Are you considering the interaction between browser controls (particularly forward/back/reload buttons) and the application? Check the following:
    a. Input data is available if the user hits the "back" button.
    b. A page on which a user has input data cannot be left without the user being asked to submit the data and warned that it will be lost if he doesn't.

   c. When using a web-mail system, and a user selects a message in the incoming list and the text of that message is displayed, and if the user returns to the incoming list page using the back button, the previously displayed message is not checked as "read."

   d. When a user reaches a page with an access counter and then uses only the back and forward buttons to re-display the page, the value of the counter is not incremented.

   e. When a user authenticates himself by submitting a username and a password, and during the navigation returns to the log-in page, and then goes forward simply using the browser buttons, the session expires.

   f. Only the first browser page in any sequence has both the forward and back buttons simultaneously disabled.

   g. The first browser page in any sequence never has the back button enabled.

   h. The first browser page in any sequence can never have the forward button enabled.

There are several useful checklists in [Nguyen], [Gerrard 1], and [Splaine]. These books are worth reading for their insights into Web testing as well.

## B.13.2 Web Configurations Checklist

1. Which client hardware are you targeting? { PC | PDA | cell phone | other }
2. Which browser set are you targeting? { Internet Explorer 6 | Internet Explorer 5 | FireFox | Mozilla | Netscape 7 | Netscape 4 | Opera 8 | Opera 7 | AOL }?
3. What server structure is required? { all on one box | two-box | three-box | other }
4. Which operating systems will the client use? { Linux | PalmOS | Windows CE | Windows XP | Windows 2000 | Windows 98 | Windows NT | Windows 2003 | Windows 95 | Mac }?
5. Which server operating systems are you targeting? { Windows XP | Windows 2000 | Windows NT | Windows 2003 | Linux | MacOS | UNIX | Solaris }
6. Which plug-ins must your clients use? How widely-used are they?
7. What bits of the web are you testing? { browser | Web application | legacy application | business rules | database }
8. Which languages will the site be offered in? Have you allowed for all kinds of address formats and scripts?
9. Where is the business logic? Is it hard-coded into the application or in a separate "rules" section?
10. Have you checked all the links at the application level?
11. Are any links dynamic? How could they change? How can you be sure you have tested the possible changes?
12. Can it be installed on the hardware specified?
13. Can it be uninstalled from the hardware specified?
14. Can it co-exist with other commonly-found applications?
15. Are there any server-side limitations? (one-box only? dedicated server?)

## B.13.3 Web Usability Checklist

1. Does every page load within eight seconds? *Don't keep them waiting, particularly for home pages.*
2. Does the page tell the user they've arrived? *If your home page doesn't stand out because it informs and attracts, redesign it.*
3. Do they know where they are? *If they've googled you, they might not hit the home page first. No one asks for help in cyber space. They just click out.*
4. What could the user want to do now?
5. How much does the user have to learn and remember? D'you need a PhD to navigate this site? Yeah, well, er. Is it clear, quick, and literate?
6. Can they talk back? *Contact phone, e-mail, fax, and snail mail?*

7. Do the interaction styles the users must adopt vary through tasks, moving for example from mouse to keyboard without the opportunity for command keystrokes to be used?
8. Are command keystrokes consistent?
9. Are screen layouts consistent through tasks?
10. Are the terms used consistently through tasks?
11. Can a user stop a process at any time and return to known state? If not, in what period of time can this be done?
12. Can a user undo any previous action other than those for which he is given due warning of their irreversibility?
13. Is the user given clear and sufficient warning before taking any irrevocable step?
14. Are delays explained to users?
15. Can the user change the defaults?
16. Does the user have a help file available at every step of a task?
17. Can the user perform frequent operations rapidly?
18. Are there shortcuts? How difficult are these to learn for the novice?

# B.14  Performance Checklists

## B.14.1  Performance Requirements Checklist

1. Has the system performance been defined in the requirements specification?
2. Have the performance requirements been specified in terms of:
   a. goals, questions, and metrics:
      i. Are the questions sufficient to answer the needs of the stakeholders?
      ii. Can any question be removed without jeopardizing the effectiveness of the plan?
      iii. Does the plan show exactly how each question will be answered?
      iv. trigger event, periodicity, rate, response event, response time, and response type?
   b. throughput (traffic volumes):
      i. percent throughput growth over a year?
      ii. ability of the system to scale?
   c. stable workload (possibly as n users + m applications):
      i. operations as seen by the client under various transaction rates and workload mixes?
      ii. conditions under which the server degrades suddenly?
   d. use patterns/load profile (during the day, week, month season, year)?
   e. load spike characteristics { time-of-day | height | frequency | other }?
   f. users:
      i. number of users?
      ii. growth in the number of users over { a year | ramped-up in the { morning | afternoon }}?
      iii. behavior patterns { repetitive over a long period | time-coherent | user-class-coherent | other }?
      iv. types { accounting | sales | customer | administrators | other }
      v. work { database access | other }?
      vi. characteristics { typing speed | number of pauses | mean pause length | mean consecutive simultaneous transaction quantity | think times | other }?
   g. response:
      i. latency (response times end-to-end) { average case | best case | 95% | worst case }?
      ii. response time variance as the configuration changes?
   h. web server hit rate when backing a website?
   i. database:
      i. volume expected at the start of use?
      ii. percent database growth per annum?

      iii.  access patterns (moments when table or row locking causes bugs, multiple-concurrent updates, other contention bugs)?

3. What is the definition of the minimum:
   a. server CPU speed, memory size, disk speed, and throughput?
   b. client CPU speed, memory size, disk speed, and throughput?
4. What is the system architecture?

## B.14.2 Performance Management Checklist

1. Have any studies been made to see if the performance targets are reachable?
2. Has any part of the system been simulated to determine its performance?
3. Has the performance of the system been identified in terms of the component behavior?
4. Who are the stakeholders involved in performance?
5. Have the individual components been performance-tested?
6. Have any performance bottlenecks been identified?
7. Do you have to meet a Service Level Agreement?
8. What is the:
   a. test database size?
   b. data distribution across the network (to simulate bottleneck[2])
   c. concurrent applications (which 20% of concurrent applications are present during / contribute to 80% of the bugs?)
   d. bug rate and bug breakdown?
   e. levels of output and bug detection?
   f. query type which provokes the most performance bugs?
9. pass/fail conditions:
   a. one user fails (is this a fail?)
   b. critical task fails (is this a fail?)
   c. "with n users 90% of all transactions have response times of < 5 seconds" (is this a pass?)
   d. "with n users do any transactions have response times of > 45 seconds" (is this a pass?)

## B.14.3 Performance General Checklist

1. To what extent is browser activity affected by { cookies | database state | session variables | client-side scripts | browser visualization controls }?
2. To what extent are screen/form design and process design, factors affecting response time and throughput?
3. What is the slowest browser page to load?
4. To what extent does the structure and content of an application affect the transaction rate?
5. What is the effect of:
   a. moving the database and applications onto the same machine?
   b. adding a second web server?
   c. mounting the web server on a separate box?
6. What is the effect on:
   a. response time and throughput given an increase in the memory of { web server | database server | application server } for a given number of transactions per hour and users?
   b. response time and throughput given an increase in the number of processors of { web server | database server | application } for a given number of transactions per hour and users?
   c. a client's response time as the # of users accessing the server increases?

---

[2] Ask: are we concerned to test for bottlenecks?

7. At what point does the addition of an extra application and web server have no appreciable effect on the performance of the system? (At what point can it be shown that the database is the bottleneck?)
8. How much:
    a. warning do we get if the system is about to collapse?
    b. headroom do we have if (say) our site hit rate rises by 1000%? (You should have at least 300% of current average load available on principle.)
    c. does anti-virus software on the { client | server } affect throughput?
    d. does load-balancing facilitate or impede throughput or response time?
    e. does the system leak memory? How d'you monitor this?
9. What is the maximum:
    a. load the system can sustain while keeping an acceptable transaction response?
    b. # of users which the fastest server can handle?
    c. # of users which the system can handle before the response time exceeds 10 seconds?
    d. and minimum transaction times?
    e. Acceptable abandonment rate (of users due to slow response)?
10. Are the bottlenecks the same, irrespective of the configuration?
11. Which loads applied to which part of the system will most quickly cause system failure?
12. Which affects submission speed more?
    a. screen/form complexity (defined as the number of fields)
    b. data size (measured by the total amount of new data in a submitted screen/form)
13. At what point does screen/form complexity or data size affect throughput or response time?
14. To what extent does the structure and content of an application affect the transaction rate?
15. How fast can the system recover from a load spike? (Run two heavy spikes close together and see how far apart they have to be for the resources to be recovered.)
16. To what extent is browser-response time location-dependent?
    a. Which is the slowest location? { Americas | EMEA | Middle East | Asia }
    b. Which are the fastest mirror sites?
    c. Is mirror-site speed time-of-day-dependent?
    d. Is browser-response time, time-of-day-, and location-dependent?

## B.14.4  Resilience Checklist

1. Have resilience requirements covered the following threats:
    a. hardware failures?
    b. software failures?
    c. network failures?
    d. mis-operation?
    e. server capacity exhaustion (I/O, CPU, memory, disk)?
    f. higher than expected traffic volumes?
    g. bad input data?
    h. fail-safe behavior?
    i. system degradation?
2. Is there a resilience specification? Does it cover:
    a. the logical deployment of the system?
    b. the partitioning of the servers into a number of layers each focusing on a different aspect of the functionality described? (Is each layer of the architecture described and the interfaces and dependencies between each layer defined?)
    c. a high-level overview of the physical deployment of the architecture?
    d. the main business use cases supported by the system and the corresponding dataflows between the layers?
    e. The start and end of each flow?

    f.  port numbers, protocols, and traffic volumes?

    g.  the resilience and scalability characteristics of the system with reference to the layers and public interfaces described earlier?

    h.  the effects of single, partial, and multiple failures?

    i.  any platform deficiencies identified in the previous sections?

    j.  availability of the system?

    k.  need for rollback of transactions?

    l.  a summary of the responses to non-platform issues (i.e., those typically of an operational or process nature) identified earlier (or are these in the Risk log)?

    m.  a control policy or escalation strategy to coordinate restoration in a network that spans multiple layers and region expressed as a set of rules?

    n.  the requirements of a Service Level Agreement?

3. Is there a document relating the resilience specification to existing or new tests?
4. What features must the system have at all times?
5. What is the essential data for those features?
6. Is there a reversionary mode?
7. What is the most vulnerable part of the system?
8. Is there a fault model?

    a.  Has the fault model been simulated to show the effects of more than one failure?

    b.  Does the model show the probabilities of moving to a failure state?

9. To what extent can transactions be "wound back" in the event of a system failure:

    a.  automatically?

    b.  manually by reference to the transaction log?

## B.14.5 Availability Checklist

1. **General:**

    a.  Analyze business impact to identify:

        i.  all critical applications

          •  which functionality is critical commercially?

          •  which functionality is critical operationally?

        ii.  the availability requirements for each application (hours of operation)

        iii.  the application's recovery requirements (maximum recovery time)

        iv.  the costs of an application outage (loss of revenue, customers, business)

        v.  any application dependencies (resources, other applications, and so on)

        vi.  requirements to extend service hours

        vii.  time zone considerations

          •  24-hour services

          •  others

    b.  Define service level objectives for applications:

        i.  hours of service

        ii.  maximum number of outages that can be tolerated

        iii.  application recovery times

        iv.  minimum/maximum application response times

        v.  capacity requirements

          •  the levels of (degraded) service

          •  the reliability/availability of each service level

    c.  Identify and evaluate all the critical components involved in supporting a given application and the effect of their failure (FMECA):

        i.  the failures which are evident to users

        ii.  which mission-critical functions can be executed manually in an emergency

    d. Identify the time lost through planned and unplanned outages (time for backups, database restructuring, and reinstallation). Identify root causes of unplanned outages.

    e. Identify maintenance requirements:

       i. minimum and maximum service times for hardware/software

       ii. concurrent maintenance or downtime requirements

2. **Performance.** Identify:

    a. the user-evident bottlenecks and their causes

    b. mission-critical components

    c. components associated with the largest server loads

    d. time taken to activate a back-up-system as an operational system

    e. time taken to restart after a system crash

    f. the minimum demand of each mission-critical component on the infrastructure

    g. which components and functionality can be dynamically scaled

    h. types of faults needing to be tolerated: timing (e.g., timing overruns), semantic, (wrong output values) and system (memory overruns due to bad pointers)

3. **Failure scenarios.** What is the availability needed in the event of:

    a. planned maintenance and shutdown

    b. system crash

    c. communication failure

    d. system hang

# B.15  Coding and Unit Testing Review Checklist

1. Is there sufficient data to establish the integrity of the design available? Typically this data will include logic diagrams, algorithms, and design storage allocation charts.
2. Do formal proofs of these algorithms exist and have they been checked?
3. Is any part of the design document insufficient for a programmer to write unit tests based on it?
4. Does the design include sufficient details of function flow, timing, sizing, storage requirements, memory maps, database size, and other performance factors?
5. What is the criticality of the unit?
6. Is every unit matched by some unit test?
7. Is a sufficient set of unit metrics available?
8. Is the intensity of testing of the unit related to the risk of it failing?
9. Will sufficient paths and variations executed by the tests be exercised to have confidence in the unit? Do you know how the unit will be used in practice? How do the rigor of your tests relate to the unit's criticality?
10. Is the test feasible? Will it not take too long? What confidence have you that the test will find bugs? Are the following exercised:

    a. unit interface interfaces?

    b. defaults?

    c. error messages?

    d. input class boundary and limits, for each input class?

    e. every primitive statement at least once?

    f. every conditional statement for all of its outcomes?

    g. loops, at the extremes of their application?

    h. every state of each variable on the input data interface?

    i. all other requirements of the unit specification (e.g., reusability, speed, size)? Is the test input data fully detailed?

    j. the unit with invalid data states?

    k.  arithmetic functions, with the sets of input values which give the maximum and minimum computed results to ensure that no overflow conditions are reached?

    l.  do distinct elements of input vectors and matrices have distinct values for the purpose of catching indexing errors?

    m.  were all operations that might cause erroneous execution (i.e., divide by zero, taking square root of negative number, etc.) proved impossible?

11. Are all expected outputs fully detailed?

12. Has a regression test set for that unit been identified?

13. Is sufficient information available to enable test repeatability?

14. Is the test method designed to simulate exceptional conditions as well as normal conditions, thereby finding faults as well as proving correct operation?

15. Does any unit have any simulator or hardware dependencies? Are they addressed in the test plan? Is the test harness support adequate?

16. Are there any requirements or design changes outstanding which could invalidate the test?

17. Is all necessary test software described and provided?

18. Are the unit test specifications consistent with the unit design?

19. Are there standards for software testing:

    a.  for the control of changes to the software tests?

    b.  for generating and maintaining adequate records of the tests carried out and their results?

    c.  for correcting any deficiencies in the specification, design, or code revealed during test?

    d.  which ensure that any necessary modifications are subject to the original standards and procedures at each phase?

    e.  which ensure that test results are analyzed to reveal any areas of the software which show an unexpectedly high rate of failures in test?

    f.  which ensure that the reasons for a high rate of failure are established?

20. Is each software unit tested individually before software–software integration?

# B.16  Software–Software Integration Test Review Checklist

1. Is the software–software integration strategy clear? Is the rationale for the software–software integration strategy clear? Is there an integration test for every build step?

2. Are the assumptions behind the integration strategy assumptions explicit? Are they likely to change?

3. Have all automated checks been run and have they failed to find any errors?

4. Are there any errors such as overflow/underflow or divide by zero that must be identified, repaired, or require special recovery?

5. Does the bug handling contain adequate error-detection facilities allied to bug containment, recovery, or safe shutdown procedures?

6. Are software packages reused? If so:

    a.  have they been developed and tested to the same integrity level?

    b.  have any modifications to them been carried out to the original standards and procedures?

    c.  is there a procedure change control for the control of changes to library programs?

7. Have all mission-critical elements been distributed over redundant elements?

8. Has compatibility between the interfaces been defined?

9. Has every requirement been mapped to some system feature?

10. Does every mapping represent a sufficient transformation of some requirement with respect to the configuration management plan?

11. If graphic and prose definition are used, is there evidence that consistency checks on both have been carried out?

12. Does each integration test cover the relevant interfaces sufficiently?
13. Does each integration test cover the relevant features which that build level represents, to give you confidence that the build is worth continuing?
14. Do you have a sufficient regression test for each integration step?

# B.17  System Test Review Checklist

1. Is the system test preparation and execution planned to allow sufficiently for overruns?
   a. Is there a sufficient number of system test cycles built in?
   b. Has sufficient time been allowed for bug fixing in between?
2. Has the system test documentation been checked to ensure that all the requirements of the requirements specification have been tested and are met?
3. Is every requirement matched by one or more system tests?
4. Is every system test traceable to some requirement?
5. Have all the test objectives been reviewed?
6. If part of a multiply-redundant system fails under test?
   a. is the root cause of failure established?
   b. are similar items inspected for a similar potential cause of failure?
7. Is there sufficient independence in the testing of diverse equipment and functions?
8. Is there a software system test on host specification? Does it ensure that there are criteria for the test coverage (for example, is each control flow path through the program tested to ensure that each statement is executed at least once)?
9. If not, that the coverage of the tests is known?
10. Is graceful degradation test of the system in all modes tested for?
11. Is fault tolerance test of the system in all modes tested for?
12. Do you have tests of inter-system data transfer?
13. If you have to integrate with existing systems, do you have:
    a. definitions of the interfaces with the other systems?
    b. the requirements specifications of the other systems?
    c. definitions of the dataflowing across these interfaces?
    d. stubs, drivers or other harnesses to simulate the interfaces with these other systems?
14. Do you have definitions of all business processes which your system supports? Can you identify which processes trigger which system features?
15. Do you have copies of sufficient test data? Have you validated it?
16. Are any data structure changes proposed before go-live?
17. Do you have a simple database test which writes a record, reads it back and compares it, updates it and compares it, and finally deletes it and checks that it no longer exists?
18. Has training been given, appropriate to the risks to be carried out and the staff involved?
19. Are testing and commissioning procedure sufficiently explicit in their detail so that they do not leave interpretations or important decisions to be made by testing and commissioning staff?

# B.18  Operations Acceptance Checklist

Table B.2 is included for completeness because it marks the limit of the responsibility of the test manager. Unless testing has an exceptionally-wide remit, the test process is over once section 2.7 is complete. It identifies a number of quality gates. You might want to add more.

**TABLE B.2**  Operations acceptance checklist

| Project Name: | | | | | | |
|---|---|---|---|---|---|---|
| **1. System documentation** | | | | | | |
| No. | Support | Requirement | Comments | Owner | Date | Pass[a] |
| 1.1 | | Physical deployment design signed-off | | | | |
| 1.2 | | Project installation specification signed-off | | | | |
| 1.3 | | Site guide signed-off | | | | |
| 1.4 | | Run book/Operations guide signed-off | | | | |
| 1.5 | | Training documentation complete | | | | |
| 1.6 | | Work instructions complete | | | | |
| 1.7 | | Other documents complete | | | | |
| **2. System summary** | | | | | | |
| No. | Support | Requirement | Comments | Owner | Date | Pass |
| 2.1 | | Requirements specifications signed-off | | | | |
| 2.2 | | Network diagram (all components and connectivity) signed-off | | | | |
| 2.3 | | System overview (Management summary), trouble shooting, Support & Escalation guide, alerting and Management systems guide signed-off | | | | |
| 2.4 | | Hardware list (including server names, IP addresses, DNS names, network components, disk details, licenses) signed-off | | | | |
| 2.5 | | Software list (including O/S, databases, versions, licenses), assets register updated signed-off | | | | |
| 2.6 | | Customer base profile (total users, concurrent users, geography, key times, key contacts) signed-off | | | | |
| 2.7 | | All testing undertaken and signed-off | | | | |
| 2.7.1 | | Unit testing complete | | | | |
| 2.7.2 | | System testing complete | | | | |
| 2.7.3 | | Reliability testing complete | | | | |
| 2.7.4 | | Performance testing complete | | | | |
| 2.7.5 | | User acceptance testing complete | | | | |
| 2.7.6 | | Load testing complete | | | | |
| 2.7.7 | | Security testing complete | | | | |
| 2.7.8 | | Operations testing complete | | | | |
| 2.7.9 | | Business continuity/disaster recovery testing complete | | | | |
| 2.8 | | Ownership (service, product/ business owners & other key individuals) identified and agreed | | | | |
| 2.9 | | Is a business continuity plan/ disaster recovery plan delivered with this project, or "back out" specified if not? | | | | |

**TABLE B.2** Operations acceptance checklist (continued)

| No. | Support | Requirement | Comments | Owner | Date | Pass |
|---|---|---|---|---|---|---|
| 2.10 | | FFT (fitness for launch) date defined and agreed with Operations | | | | |
| 2.11 | | Systems cabinets labeled on the server floor; floor plan updated | | | | |
| 2.12 | | System test packs complete | | | | |
| 2.13 | | Operations notified of the change/go-live | | | | |
| **3. Installation** | | | | | | |
| No. | Support | Requirement | Comments | Owner | Date | Pass |
| 3.1 | | Installation guide complete and signed-off | | | | |
| 3.2 | | Security & compliance review complete | | | | |
| **4. Routine operation** | | | | | | |
| No. | Support | Requirement | Comments | Owner | Date | Pass |
| 4.1 | | Operations support requirements defined (including third party); support rosters available | | | | |
| 4.2 | | Timetable and explanation of business-critical scheduled jobs/tasks (including housekeeping) | | | | |
| 4.3 | | Database recovery procedures specified (including times and data timeliness considerations) | | | | |
| 4.4 | | Security administration (types of user, access levels, authorizations, meets Operations standards) | | | | |
| 4.5 | | User administration specified and agreed with Operations | | | | |
| 4.6 | | Data retention guidelines specified and agreed with Operations | | | | |
| 4.7 | | Training provided for all relevant groups | | | | |
| 4.8 | | Maintenance window defined and agreed with Operations | | | | |
| 4.9 | | System remote access method agreed with Operations | | | | |
| 4.10 | | Routine (weekly/monthly/yearly) procedures defined and Operations schedules amended | | | | |
| 4.11 | | Customer alerting processes defined and agreed with Operations | | | | |
| 4.12 | | Media/tape requirements created and labeled, back up procedures & on-/off-site media storage procedures defined | | | | |
| 4.14 | | Service monitoring/reporting (who, when, for whom) agreed with Operations | | | | |
| **5. Exception conditions** | | | | | | |
| No. | Support | Requirement | Comments | Owner | Date | Pass |
| 5.1 | | All critical processes and dataflows identified | | | | |
| 5.2 | | All critical processes and dataflows alerted | | | | |
| 5.3 | | All *Critical* alerts have actions to be taken | | | | |

| 6. Capacity planning | | | | | | |
|---|---|---|---|---|---|---|
| No. | Support | Requirement | Comments | Owner | Date | Pass |
| 6.1 | | Capacity group engaged and system/platform placed "under watch" | | | | |
| 6.2 | | System scaling and limits defined | | | | |
| Signatories | | Name | Signature | | | Date |
| Project manager | | | | | | |
| Test manager | | | | | | |
| Operations manager | | | | | | |
| Other | | | | | | |

ᵃ Y(es), N(o), DMP (Defect Management Plan).

# B.19  Metrics Checklist

1. Have you asked the big metrics questions:
   a. How is the quality of the product to be measured?
   b. How is the test performance to be measured?
   c. How is the development process to be measured?
   d. How is customer satisfaction to be measured?
   e. How will release readiness be determined?
2. Do you have a set of questions agreed with project management which can be answered by metrication?
3. Do you have a metrics plan to answer these questions?

# B.20  Very Wonderful New Approaches Checklist

You will occasionally be asked to adopt some Very Wonderful New Approach. Here are some awkward questions to pose first:

1. Has someone bothered defining a process model of this approach complete with inputs and outputs?
2. What will it cost me to get the inputs?
3. What will the outputs buy me? How many man-days will this save?
4. Who else needs these outputs?
5. How is this better than what I am doing at present?
6. Does this approach have tool support? All of it? How much?
7. Has anyone written a paper on this? Is there a manual?
8. Has anyone ever used this in industry? Are they still in business?

Here are some totally irrelevant answers:

1. X promotes this.
2. I want you to try this.
3. We need to sharpen up our approach.
4. We need more rigor.
5. The CEO/Board wants …
6. It's a new approach.
7. Haven't you read … ?

# Appendix C

## Category and Priority Classifications for Bug Reporting

## C.1 Purpose

This appendix contains requirements for a category and priority classification scheme which can be applied to all bugs detected in the deliverable software or its documents that have been placed under configuration management. It has been proposed with the expectation that:

1. It will not always be possible to attach a hazard- or mission-criticality level to some software fault found (say) during an inspection or unit test, nor would it be useful to do so since such a fault would (hopefully) be fixed before the work-product in which it was found was released for system test.
2. It will be used mostly within the software development groups.
3. It will be a simple matter to add fields in order to extend the scheme to include any hazard, risk assessment, or mission-criticality scheme envisaged.
4. The software bug reporting system will be used throughout the life of the system such that accurate bug reporting is possible.
5. Human factor (usability) bugs may not reflect any logical failing of the system. They may better be recorded as a special category of problem due to poor interface design. Their existence cannot be determined by simple repeatability but rather by the probability of occurrence. Thus if 10 users out of 15 report difficulty in locating some feature, the fact that 5 users have reported no difficulty does not deny the existence of a problem. The bug can be said to have a probability of 10/15 of being evident.
6. Some means is devised to prevent usability bugs from being ignored. One simple approach is to agglomerate them:
   a. Ten priority-4 usability bugs on the same feature is the equivalent of a priority-3 bug on that feature.
   b. Ten priority-3 usability bugs on the same feature is the equivalent of a priority-2 bug on that feature.
   c. Ten priority-2 usability bugs on the same feature is the equivalent of a priority-1 bug on that feature.
   
   To clear such an agglomeration, all the bugs constituting it must be cleared. Play around with the figures as you think fit: you must get your senior management and the project manager to agree to them.

It is useful to relate bugs to the criticality of the feature or function in which they are found.

## C.2  Classification by Category

Bugs detected during software operation can be categorized as follows:

1. **Performance** bug (PF): There is a plausible argument that the item will not meet the performance objectives stated in the requirements. This is classified by *DoD-STD-2167*, Appendix A, as either a software bug or a design problem, depending on whether it is found in the software or in some design document.
2. **Data** bug (DA): Some data item or type is either missing or extra.
3. **Interface** bug (IF): Some call is missing, incorrect, or extra. Note that this does not apply to HCI bugs which are classified as (HF) below.
4. **Feature** (CA): Some key feature is missing, incorrect, or extra.
5. **Documentation** bug (DC): Some document is incomplete, ambiguous, or inconsistent either with itself or some other document. (The documentation of some code in the form of comments or any other means is included in this definition. It is classified by *DoD-STD-2167*, Appendix A, as a documentation problem.) As a rule of thumb every paragraph to be changed in a document can count as a single bug.
6. **Standards** bug (ST): Some quality system standard has been violated or is insufficient.
7. **Human-Factor** bug (HF): Some human factor bug has been observed or there is a plausible argument that it exists. (This is classified by *DoD-STD-2167*, Appendix A, as a design problem.)
8. **Logic** bug (LO): Some logic is found to be inconsistent either internally or with some specification. (This is classified by *DoD-STD-2167*, Appendix A, as either a software bug or a design problem, depending on whether it is found in the software or in some design document.)
9. **Test environment** bug (TE): Some test environment is found to be insufficient to support some test type or inconsistent with its specification.
10. **Test coverage** bug (TC): Some test is found to be insufficient to exercise some software.
11. **Other** bug (OT): Some other bug has been observed.

## C.3  Classification by Severity Approach 1

Bugs detected in the software or its documents can be classified by severity as follows:

1. Severity 1. A system component bug that does one of the following:
   a. Prevents the accomplishment of an operational or mission-essential feature specified by base-lined requirements.
   b. Prevents an operator from accomplishing some operational or mission-essential feature.
   c. Jeopardizes personnel safety.
2. Severity 2. A bug that does one of the following:
   a. Adversely affects the accomplishment of an operational or mission-essential feature specified by baselined requirements so as to degrade performance such that no workaround solution is known.
   b. Prevents an operator from accomplishing some operational or mission-essential feature specified by baselined requirements so as to degrade performance such that no workaround solution is known.

3. Severity 3. A bug that does one of the following:
   a. Adversely affects the accomplishment of an operational or mission-essential feature specified by baselined requirements so as to degrade performance and for which a workaround solution is known.
   b. Prevents an operator from accomplishing some operational or mission-essential feature specified by baselined requirements so as to degrade performance and for which a workaround solution is known.
4. Severity 4. A bug that causes operator annoyance or inconvenience, but which does not affect a required operational or mission-essential feature.
5. Severity 5. All other bugs.

# C.4 Classification by Severity Approach 2

Here is an alternative set of definitions of problem severities:

1. *Critical*: Bug prevents a user from fulfilling an essential task. Such a failure materially affects the users' ability to function.
2. *High*: As *Critical* but a workaround exists.
3. *Medium*: Bug interferes with but does not completely inhibit some required function.
4. *Low*: Bug causes irritation to staff or customers.

Note that these definitions do not determine fix priorities. Perhaps, for example, a *High* severity bug might need to be fixed before a *Critical* severity one.

# C.5 Beizer's Taxonomy

[Beizer 3] has proposed an excellent bug taxonomy. I won't reproduce it (although he offers it free if you make the appropriate citations) because his book is worth buying for its insights into testing.

## C.6  Bug Severity Calculation Matrix

The table in Figure C.1 shows another means of determining the severity of a bug. For any line of the table, if all the conditions listed in the vertical columns are true, then a bug of that severity has been found

| Characteristic | Supporting system(s) produce(s) materially | Supporting system(s) fail catastrophically | Supporting system(s) is/are rendered unusable | Fails to produce a result in a timely manner | One or more key features of the product cannot be | Problem causes unacceptable interruption to work | Incorrect/inaccurate data is transmitted to | One or more parts of the system cannot be | Crashes, or freezes occur which can be | Destroys, changes, or conceals data | Problem limits but does not prevent system use | Performance acceptably degraded | < 10 Non-key features inhibited | > 10 Non-key features inhibited | Annoys the user | Fails regularly | No workaround exists | Workaround exists |
|---|---|---|---|---|---|---|---|---|---|---|---|---|---|---|---|---|---|---|
| Critical | X | | | | | | | | | | | | | | | X | X | |
| | | X | | | | | | | | | | | | | | X | X | |
| | | | X | | | | | | | | | | | | | X | X | |
| | | | | X | | | | | | | | | | | | X | X | |
| | | | | | X | | | | | | | | | | | X | X | |
| | | | | | | X | | | | | | | | | | X | X | |
| | | | | | | | X | | | | | | | | | X | X | |
| | | | | | | | | X | | | | | | | | X | X | |
| | | | | | | | | | X | | | | | | | X | X | |
| | | | | | | | | | | X | | | | | | X | | |
| High | X | | | | | | | | | | | | | | | X | | X |
| | | X | | | | | | | | | | | | | | X | | X |
| | | | X | | | | | | | | | | | | | X | | X |
| | | | | X | | | | | | | | | | | | X | | X |
| | | | | | X | | | | | | | | | | | X | | X |
| | | | | | | X | | | | | | | | | | X | | X |
| | | | | | | | X | | | | | | | | | X | | X |
| | | | | | | | | X | | | | | | | | X | | X |
| | | | | | | | | | X | | | | | | | X | | X |
| | | | | | | | | | | | | | X | | | X | | |
| Medium | | | | | | | | | | | X | | | | | X | | |
| | | | | | | | | | | | | X | | | | X | | |
| | | | | | | | | | | | | | X | | | X | | |
| Low | | | | | | | | | | | | | | | X | X | | |

**FIGURE C.1**  Bug severity calculation matrix

# Appendix D

## Tools

## D.1 Automated Testing Tools

| Name | Details |
|------|---------|
| Automated Test Designer | www.atyoursideconsulting.com<br>Commercial requirements-based test case generating tool. Translates from natural language requirements specifications to a formal language using a Cause–Effect Definitions tree and then uses a neural network algorithm to produce the minimum number of *test cases* to cover the requirements. It can be integrated with Mercury TestDirector™. |
| Automated Test Tools (Java) | www.manageability.org/blog/stuff/opensource-automated-test-tools-written-in-java/view |
| Push-To-Test | www.pushtotest.com<br>A free, web-oriented framework and utility to build intelligent test agents to drive services, as real users are expected to. An optional package can be used to turn test activity into a summarized set of reports to identify scalability and performance problems. |

## D.2 Dynamic Analysis Tools

| Name | Details |
|------|---------|
| CASE Supplier List | www.dcc.ufrj.br/~schneide/es/2001/1/g07/vendor.html<br>Includes dynamic analysis tools |
| Coverity | www.coverity.com<br>Automates the detection of software defects and security vulnerabilities for complex software as developers write code. |
| EDEM (Expectation-Driven Event Monitoring) | www.ics.uci.edu/~dhilbert/edem/<br>Tool which can be used to illuminate how applications are used, to uncover mismatches in actual versus expected use and to increase user involvement in the evolution of interactive systems. |
| LDRA | www.LDRA.co.uk<br>A commercial suite of tools for code and dynamic analysis. |
| MaC | www.cis.upenn.edu/~rtg/mac/download.php3<br>Run-time Monitoring and Checking tool from Penn State. Monitors and checks running systems against a formal requirements specification |
| RECON3 | www.cs.uwf.edu/~recon/recon3/index.html<br>A free toolset to help understand and debugs. *Support*s C/C++ and FORTRAN 77 and may also be used with other programming languages. |
| SUIF | suif.stanford.edu/research/analysis.html<br>(Stanford University Intermediate Format group)<br>Two dynamic analysis tools. |
| Valgrind | valgrind.org<br>A suite of tools for debugging and profiling Linux programs which detect memory management and threading bugs, perform detailed profiling, speed up, and reduce memory use. It runs on x86/Linux, AMD64/Linux, PPC32/Linux |

*(continued)*

| Name | Details |
|------|---------|
| VeriSoft | cm.bell-labs.com/who/god/verisoft/<br>A tool which automatically searches for coordination problems (deadlocks, etc.) and assertion violations in a software system. It integrates automatic test generation, execution, and evaluation in a single framework. |

## D.3  Executable *UML* Tools

| Name | Details |
|------|---------|
| Kabira | www.kabira.com<br>ObjectSwitch |
| Kennedy-Carter | www.kc.com<br>*UML*/x*UML* |
| Project Technologies | www.projtech.com<br>BridgePoint |

## D.4  Formal Methods' Tools

| Name | Details |
|------|---------|
| ARS | The Database of Automated Reasoning Systems: ftp://sail.stanford.edu/pub/clt/ARS/README |
| Formal Methods | www.chopwell.ncl.ac.uk/pub/fm_tools/fm_tools_db<br>Tool database.<br>www.comlab.ox.ac.uk/archive/formal-methods.html |
| Fortest | www.fortest.org.uk<br>Formal Methods in testing. |
| Java rules | www.javarules.org/<br>Hosts information related to building business rule applications or rule-based systems using the Java programming language. |
| Manageability | www.manageability.org/blog/stuff/rule_engines/view<br>Open source rule engines written in Java. |
| Prover | www.prover.com/<br>A tool and plug-in set in wide use in the railway industry allowing a wide variety of systems to be modeled and conclusions drawn. |

## D.5  Localization Links

| Name | Details |
|------|---------|
| Unicode | www.unicode.org/versions/Unicode4.1.0/ |
| TCM Globalization Testing | 8001/tcm2/opensource/tcm_index.cgi?action=list_projects<br>(username: guest, password: 123) |
| Solaris | opensolaris.org/os/community/int_localization/relatedlinks/ |

# D.6  Metrics Tools

| Name | Details |
|------|---------|
| ckjm | Chidamber and Kemerer Java Metrics. The program calculates Chidamber and Kemerer object-oriented metrics by processing the bytecode of compiled Java files. The program calculates the following metrics for each class and displays them on its standard output, following the class's name:<br>• WMC: Weighted methods per class<br>• DIT: Depth of Inheritance Tree<br>• NOC: Number of Children<br>• CBO: Coupling between object classes<br>• RFC: Response for a Class<br>• LCOM: Lack of cohesion in methods<br>• Ca: Afferent coupling (not a C&K metric)<br>• NPM: Number of Public Methods for a class (not a C&K metric)<br>www.spinellis.gr/sw/ckjm/doc/indexw.html |
| ergoBrowser | www.ergosoft.com<br>Allows better capture of metric data |
| JDepend | www.clarkware.com/software/Jdepend.html\<br>Java metrics extraction tool. |
| Krakatau metrics | www.powersoftware.com |
| McCabe | www.mccabe.com |
| Mitre (SQAE) | www.mitre.org/work/tech_transfer/sqae.html<br>Maintenance method, framework, and toolset. Handles 64 languages including Ada, Assembler, C, C++, COBOL and Copy libraries, FORTRAN, Java, LISP, Pascal, and PL/1. |
| RSM metrics | www.msquaredtechnologies.com |
| SD metrics | www.sdmetrics.com |

# D.7  Performance-Testing Tools

| Name | Details |
|------|---------|
| Grinder | A Java-based framework for running test scripts across a number of machines. These tests can be merely functional tests or can be load, stress or performance tests. It is freely available under a BSD-style Opensource license.<br>grinder.sourceforge.net |
| Henning | www.cs.columbia.edu/~hgs/internet/traffic-generator.html<br>Henning Schultzrinne's load generator page. |
| ICIR | www.icir.org/models/trafficgenerators.html<br>ICIR's traffic modeling page |
| Load Testing Tool | www.loadtestingtool.com<br>Web server performance testing tool. |
| Loadrunner | www.mercury.com |
| OpenSTA | www.opensta.org |
| OpenSTA add-ons | www.trickytools.com/php/opensta.php |
| Performance Measurement Tools Taxonomy | www.caida.org/tools/taxonomy/performance.xml<br>List of tools for measuring Internet performance. |
| Rational Performance Tester | www-306.ibm.com/software/awdtools/tester/performance/index.html |
| SPEC (Standard Performance Evaluation Corporation) | www.spec.org<br>• **SPECweb2005 v1.02** emulates users sending browser requests over broadband Internet connections to a web server. It provides three new workloads: a banking site (HTTPS), an eCommerce site (HTTP/HTTPS mix) and a support site (HTTP). Dynamic content is implemented in PHP and JSP.<br>• **SFS97_R1 (3.0).** A benchmark designed to evaluate the speed and request-handling features of NFS (network file server) computers using versions 2 and 3 of the NFS protocol. |

*(continued)*

| Name | Details |
|------|---------|
| SPEC (Standard Performance Evaluation Corporation) (continued) | • **SPECimap.** Currently under development by SPEC to be an industry-standard benchmark to measure the performance of corporate email servers. This will test a server's ability to process email requests, based on the Internet standard protocols SMTP and IMAP4. |
| | • **MAIL2001.** Measures a system's ability to act as a mail server servicing email requests, based on the Internet standard protocols SMTP and POP3. Characterizes throughput and response time of a mail server system under test with realistic network connections, disk storage, and client workloads. |
| | • **SPECjvm98** allows users to evaluate performance for the combined hardware and software aspects of the JVM client platform. On the software side, it measures the efficiency of JVM, the just-in-time (JIT) compiler and operating system implementations. On the hardware side, it includes CPU (integer and floating-point), cache, memory, and other platform-specific performance. |
| | • **JBB2005.** A benchmark for evaluating the performance of servers running typical Java business applications, JBB2005 represents an order processing application for a wholesale supplier and can be used to evaluate performance of hardware and software aspects of Java Virtual Machine (JVM) servers. |
| | • **SPECjAppServer2004.** Measures the performance of J2EE 1.3 application servers. Includes an enhanced workload by adding a Web tier, JMS, and other changes to SPECjAppServer2002. |
| | • **OMP2001.** Measures performance using applications based on the OpenMP standard for shared-memory parallel processing. Consists of OMPM2001 and OMPL2001, which contains larger working sets and longer run times than OMPM2001. |
| | • **HPC2002.** Measures the performance of high-end computing systems running industrial-style applications and is especially suited for evaluating the performance of parallel and distributed computer architectures. |
| TPC (Transaction Processing Performance Council) | www.tpc.org |
| | A non-profit corporation founded to define transaction processing and database benchmarks, and disseminate performance data to the industry. Creates and maintains audited benchmarks. Regards a transaction as it is commonly understood in the business world: a commercial exchange of goods, services or money. A typical transaction, as defined by the TPC, would include the updating to a database system for such things as inventory control (goods), airline reservations (services) or banking (money). Publishes the following benchmarks: |
| | • **TPC-App.** Application Server and web services. Simulates the activities of a business-to-business transactional application server operating in a 24/7 environment. The workload exercises commercially-available application server products, messaging products, and databases associated with such an environment. |
| | • **TPC-C.** Online transaction processing. Simulates a complete computing environment in which a user population executes transactions against a database. The benchmark is centered on the principal activities (transactions) of an order-entry environment. These activities include entering and delivering orders, recording payments, checking the orders' status, and monitoring the stock levels at the warehouses. While the benchmark portrays the activity of a wholesale supplier, |
| | • **TPC-H.** Represents decision support environments where users don't know which queries will be executed against a database system; and are therefore ad hoc. Pre-knowledge of the queries may not be used to optimize the DBMS system. |
| W3Org | www.w3.org/qa/tools/ |
| | World Wide Web consortium's test toolbox. |

# D.8  Risk Tools

| Name | Details |
|------|---------|
| Mitre risk tool | www.mitre.org/work/sepo/toolkits/risk/ToolsTechniques/RiskMatrix.html |
| | An application to identify, prioritize, and manage key risks. Created some years ago to support a risk assessment process. |

## D.9  Security Tools

| Name | Details |
|------|---------|
| CRAMM | A British-government-approved approach to security assessment, commercialized by Siemens Insight Consulting. Provides a staged approach to hardware, software, physical, and human aspects of security. It is divided into three stages:<br>1. Asset identification and valuation<br>2. Threat and vulnerability assessment<br>3. Countermeasure selection and recommendation<br>www.cramm.com |
| Splint | www.splint.org<br>Tool for checking "C" source for security vulnerabilities. |

## D.10  Source Code Comprehension and Analysis Tools

| Name | Details |
|------|---------|
| Clover | Commercial Java code coverage analysis tool.<br>www.cenqua.com/ |
| CUTE (a Concolic Unit Testing Engine for C and Java) | A tool to test sequential C programs (including pointers) and concurrent Java programs systematically and automatically. Combines concrete and symbolic execution in a way that avoids redundant *test cases* as well as false warnings. The tool also introduces a novel race-flipping technique to efficiently test and model-check concurrent programs with data inputs.<br>osl.cs.uiuc.edu/~ksen/cute/ |
| Emma | Opensource toolkit for measuring and reporting Java code coverage.<br>emma.sourceforge.net |
| Fault Injection Test Harness | fault-injection.sourceforge.net/ |
| GROK | grok2.tripod.com/code_comprehension.html<br>Source code comprehension tool site |
| Jester | Java mutation testing tool.<br>jester.sourceforge.net/<br>www-128.ibm.com/developerworks/library/j-jester/ |
| Propane | www.deeds.informatik.tu-darmstadt.de/hiller/<br>Fault-injection tool being developed by Martin Hiller. |
| SPIN | spinroot.com/spin/whatispin.html<br>For details of the SPIN model checker |
| static source code analysis tools | www.spinroot.com/static/<br>Static source code analysis tools for C<br>www.splint.org/links.html<br>Static checking tool site |
| Understand | www.scitools.com |

## D.11  Static Analysis Tools

| Name | Details |
|------|---------|
| CMU | www.cs.cmu.edu/~aldrich/courses/654/tools/<br>List of tools that have been evaluated by students at Carnegie-Mellon University and their reports |
| Queen's | www.qucis.queensu.ca/Software-Engineering/archive/static.html<br>List maintained by Queen's University, Kingston, Ontario, Canada |
| SPIN | www.spinroot.com/static/<br>List maintained by the ACM for SPIN, a "C" tool. |
| Testing FAQs | www.testingfaqs.org/t-static.html<br>List maintained by testingfaqs.org. |

## D.12  Unit Testing

| Name | Details |
| --- | --- |
| Apollo | ajax.sourceforge.net/apollo/api/overview-summary.html<br>Test skeleton toolkit. |
| AUT | Advanced Unit Testing is a unit test engine that provides features that go beyond other unit test engines such as NUnit and CSUnit. Conversely, certain features, most notably a command line driven interface, do not exist in AUT.<br>www.marcclifton.com/Projects/AdvancedUnitTesting/tabid/102/Default.aspx |
| Hackystat | The Hackystat Project is an open source community of researchers and practitioners who are developing and evaluating new techniques for automated collection and analysis of software engineering process and product data.<br>www.hackystat.org/hackyDevSite/home.do |
| Harness it | Commercial unit test harness.<br>www.unittesting.com/ |
| JUnit | www.JUnit.org<br>Java unit test tool. |
| MbUnit | MbUnit is an extensible .Net test framework. As in NUnit, tests are created at runtime using Reflection and custom attributes. MbUnit differs from NUnit in its extensibility and contains a number of tests that go beyond the simple unit testing, such as combinatorial testing, data oriented testing, etc.<br>www.mertner.com/confluence/display/MbUnit/Home |
| NCover | Unit code coverage tool which tells you which lines in your unit have actually been exercised.<br>www.ncover.org |
| NUnit | www.nunit.org/ |
| Parasoft | www.parasoft.com/jsp/products/home.jsp |
| Programatica | Programatica project (object-oriented unit test) www.cse.ogi.edu/~hallgren/Programatica/tools/<br>www.cse.ogi.edu/PacSoft/projects/programatica/default.htm |
| Unit testing FAQ | www.testingfaqs.org/t-unit.html |

## D.13  Web Tools

| Name | Details |
| --- | --- |
| Apache Foundation | jakarta.apache.org/<br>www.apache.org/foundation/<br>Provides organizational, legal, and financial support for a broad range of open source software projects. Apache projects deliver enterprise-grade, freely available software products that attract large communities of users. |
| Lisa | www.itko.com/<br>"Wizard"-based test script generator |
| Netmechanic | www.netmechanic.com<br>Site devoted to a range of commercial tools for net testing and maintenance. |
| Testweb | www.origsoft.com/Products/testweb.htm<br>Browser script record and playback toolset. |
| WAI | www.w3.org/WAI/ER/existingtools.html<br>List of evaluation, repair, and transformation tools for web content accessibility maintained by the Web Accessibility Initiative. |
| Worksoft | www.worksoft.com<br>Specify-Test data generator. |
| codehouse | www.codehouse.com/browser_watch/ |
| opendemand | www.opendemand.com/openload/<br>Web Application Load Testing Software / Load Testing Tool<br>IBM and Open Demand: simple, stress, and load testing software for performance tuning of websites. |
| Doit | doit.sourceforge.net/<br>Doit: Simple Web Application Testing. |

# D.14  Web Usability Test Tools and Facilities

| Name | Details |
| --- | --- |
| Alucid | www.alucid.com<br>Offers a usability suite. |
| Max | zing.ncsl.nist.gov/hfweb/proceedings/lynch/<br>Tool for assessing site accessibility. |
| NIST | zing.ncsl.nist.gov/WebTools/<br>Offers a free Web Metrics Testbed. |
| otal | www.otal.umd.edu/guse/testing.html<br>Contains a number of free usability testing methods and tools. |
| U.S. government | www.usability.gov/guides/index.html<br>Includes a number of U.S. government usability resources. |
| Usable | usablenet.com<br>Offers a "Web: Usability Index" based on its assessment of a site against its in-house and customer-provided usability rules. |
| W3C | www.w3.org/TR/WCAG10/<br>Web Content Accessibility Guidelines 1.0<br>www.w3.org/WAI/eval/<br>Evaluating Web Sites for Accessibility, a multi-page resource suite outlining approaches to evaluating websites for accessibility. Provides general procedures and tips for evaluation during website development and monitoring of existing sites.<br>www.w3.org/QA/<br>Testing blog for the W3C. |

# D.15  Web Security

| Name | Details |
| --- | --- |
| OWASP (Open Web Application Security project) | www.owasp.org<br>Opensource non-subscription, collaborative community. Its projects and local chapters produces free, unbiased, Opensource documentation, tools, standards, and facilitates conferences, local chapters, articles, papers, and message forums. The OWASP Foundation is a not-for-profit charitable organization. Participation in OWASP is free and open to all. |
| ISECOM (Institute For Security and Open Methodologies) | www.isecom.org<br>An Opensource, subscription-based, collaborative community with non-profit status in the USA and Spain. It provides practical security awareness, research, certification, training support, and project-support services.<br>Has the Open Source Security Testing Methodology Manual (OSSTMM) and a lot of useful standards, tools, guides, and checklists. |

# D.16  Other Tools

| Name | Details |
| --- | --- |
| City University of New York | unlser1.unl.csi.cuny.edu/faqs/software-engineering/tools.html<br>Tool list |
| CommonTest | commontest.sourceforge.net/ |
| COSMIC | (Component Synthesis using Model Integrated Computing). Comprises a collection of DSMLs and model interpreters that apply MDD technologies to QoS-enabled component middleware technologies along seven points of integration. Includes Opensource toolkit.<br>www.dre.vanderbilt.edu/cosmic/ |
| Dr Dobb's Journal | Good site for techie test articles.<br>www.ddj.com |
| E-tester | www.rswsoftware.com/products/etester_index.shtml |

*(continued)*

| Name | Details |
|---|---|
| Grove Consultants | www.grove.co.uk/pdf_Files/Tool_List.pdf<br>A list of commercially-available tools |
| JDepend | www.clarkware.com/software/Jdepend.html |
| JGrasp | Lightweight development environment generating software visualizations.<br>www.jgrasp.org |
| Jstyle | www.codework.com |
| LaQuSo | www.laquso.com/<br>Research collaboration of Technische Universiteit Eindhoven and Radboud Universiteit Nijmegen. Has a number of interesting services and tools. |
| Mitre Corporation | www.mitre.org/work/tech_transfer/downloadable_software.html |
| NASA | sw-assurance.gsfc.nasa.gov |
| Open source | csharpsource.net/<br>developers.sun.com/<br>dmoz.org/Computers/Programming/Software_Testing/<br>forum.textpattern.com/viewtopic.php?id=9329<br>freshmeat.net/<br>javasource.net/opensource/testing-tools<br>opensourcetesting.org/index.php<br>testing.tigris.org/<br>testingfaqs.org/<br>www.freefire.org/<br>www.opengroup.org/testing/downloads.html<br>www.osdl.org/<br>www.pushtotest.com/Docs/javatestanddesign.html<br>www.voip-info.org/wiki-Open+Source+VOIP+Software<br>www-128.ibm.com/developerworks/java/library/j-cobertura/ |
| Open Source Initiative (OSI) | www.opensource.org/ |
| Opensource Testing | www.opensourcetesting.org |
| Ovum | www.ovum.com<br>Ovum maintains a list of commercially-available tools |
| Project analyzer | www.aivosto.com |
| QA Forum | www.qaforums.com |
| Rational | www.rational.com/products/robot/index.jsp |
| Reviews | tejasconsulting.com/open-testware/ |
| Silk test | www.segue.com/html/s_solutions/silk/s_family.htm |
| sitepoint | www.sitepoint.com/forums/showthread.php?t=100332 |
| SMERFSV | Statistical Modeling and Estimation of Reliability Functions For Software<br>An interactive program for software reliability modeling that supports eleven different models; six using as input data the time between error occurrences, and five using the number of detected errors per testing period. The former include Littlewood and Verrall's *Bayesian Model*, Moranda's *Geometric Model*, John Musa's *Basic Execution Time Model*, and his *Logarithmic Poisson Model*, the *Jelinski-Moranda Model*, and an adaptation of Goel's *Non-Homogeneous Poisson Process* (NHPP) *Model* to time between error data. The latter models include the *Generalized Poisson Model*, Goel's NHPP Model, *Brooks, and Motley's* Model, Yamada's *S-shaped Growth Model*, and *Norman Schneidewind's Model*.<br>The program lets you perform a complete software reliability analysis by:<br>• entering either of the two types of model data,<br>• modify that data if necessary including transforming it,<br>• doing a preliminary model analysis to help select candidate models that are most appropriate for the entered data set,<br>• fitting the appropriate models,<br>• determining the adequacy of the fits.<br>The new version lets you analyze risks with some of these measures to help determine the optimum release time and/or time for reengineering of the software.<br>See also W. Farr and O. Smith, *Statistical modelling and estimating of reliability functions for software user guide.* Technical report NAVSWC TR-84373, Naval Surface Weapons Centre, 1993.<br>www.slingcode.com/smerfs/downloads/ |

| Name | Details |
|------|---------|
| Software QA Test | www.softwareqatest.com |
| Software reliability prediction tools | See Vs. Casre & SMERFS<br>Compares CASRE SMERFS and PRISM (from RIAC)<br>www.softrel.com/frstalt.com |
| Software Testing and Online Resources | www.mtsu.edu/~storm/ |
| software.testing | groups.google.com/group/comp.software.testing |
| Sourceforge | sourceforge.net/projects/autoalert/ |
| SQA test | www.sqa-test.com/webtest.html<br>A lot of test resources |
| SQAzone | www.sqazone.com/Home.html |
| SSADM | www.webopedia.com/TERM/S/SSADM.html |
| StickyMinds | www.stickyminds.com<br>(includes *Better Software* magazine) |
| Système Evolutif | www.evolutif.co.uk |
| Test standards | www.testingstandards.co.uk/<br>www.ieee.org |
| Testing Craft | www.testingcraft.com/ |
| Testing Foundations | www.testing.com/ |
| Testing stuff | www.testingstuff.com/references.html |
| Testingfaqs | www.testingfaqs.org/ |
| TET | www.tetworks.opengroup.org |
| University of Magdeburg | www.smlab.de/toolvendors.html<br>Tool list |
| Web test | www.softwareqatest.com/qatweb1.html |
| Wilson Mar | www.wilsonmar.com/ |
| XP Wiki | www.xpdeveloper.com |

# References

## Books and Papers

[Abe]  Abe Joichi, Ken Sakamura, and Hideo Aiso. *An analysis of software project failure.* In Proceedings of the 4th International Conference on Software Engineering, September 1979.

[Albrecht]  A. J. Albrecht. *Measuring application development productivity.* In Proceedings of the Joint IBM/SHARE/GUIDE Applications Development Symposium, October 1979.

[Andrade 1]  L. Andrade, J. L. Fiadeiro, and M. Wermelinger. *Enforcing business policies through automated reconfiguration.* In Proceedings of Automated Software Engineering (ASE 2001), M. Feather and M. Goedicke (Eds.), San Diego, pp. 426–429, November 2001.

[Andrade 2]  L. F. Andrade and J. L. Fiadeiro. *Coordination: The evolutionary dimension.* In Proceedings of Technology of Object-Oriented Languages and Systems, TOOLS Europe 2001, W. Pree (Ed.), Zurich, Switzerland, pp. 136–147, March 2001.

[Andrews]  Mike Andrews and James A. Whittaker. *How to break Web software.* Reading, Massachusetts: Addison-Wesley, 2006.

[Argyris]  C. Argyris. Skilled incompetence. *Harvard Business Review,* September-October 1986, p. 74.

[Atkinson]  Colin Atkinson and Thomas Kühn. Model-drivel development: A metamodelling foundation. *IEEE Software,* September/October 2003.

[Aubert]  Benoit A. Aubert, Sylvie Dussault, Michel Patry, and Suzanne Rivard. *Managing the risk of IT outsourcing.* Cirano Montréal, 1998.

[Bangor]  Aaron W. Bangor. *Ambient display technology and ambient illumination influences on visual illumination influences on visual fatigue at VDT workstations.* Ph.D. thesis, Virginia Polytechnic Institute and State University.

[Barnum]  Carol Barnum, Nigel Bevan, Gilbert Cockton, Jakob Nielsen, Jared Spool, and Dennis Wixon. Panel paper: *The "magic number: 5": Is it enough for Web testing?* CHI 2003, April 5–10, 2003, Ft. Lauderdale, Florida.

[Basili 84]  V. R. Basili and D. M. Weiss. A methodology for collecting valid software engineering data. *IEEE Transactions on Software Engineering,* SE-10, no. 3, November 1984, pp. 728–738.

[Basili 87]  V. R. Basili and R. W. Selby. Comparing the effectiveness of software testing strategies. *IEEE Transactions on Software Engineering,* SE-13, no. 12, December 1987.

[Basili 96]  Victor R. Basili, Lionel C. Briand, and Walcelio L. Melo. *A* validation of object-oriented design metrics as quality indicators. *IEEE Transactions on Software Engineering,* vol. 22, no. 10, October 1996.

[Bazzichi]  F. Bazzichi and I. Spadafora. An automatic generator for compiler testing. *IEEE Transactions on Software Engineering,* FE-8 (4), 1982.

[Beizer 1]  Boris Beizer. *Black box testing.* New York: John Wiley & Sons, 1995.

[Beizer 2]        Boris Beizer. *Software system testing and quality assurance.* New York: Van Nostrand Reinhold, 1984.

[Beizer 3]        Boris Beizer. *Software testing techniques, second edition.* New York: Van Nostrand Reinhold, 1990.

[Belady]          M. M. Belady and M. M. Lehman. *The evolution dynamics of large programs.* IBM research report RC5615, 1975.

[Belford]         P. C. Belford(CSC) and C. Broglio(FAA). *A quantitative evaluation of the effectiveness of quality assurance on a large-scale software development effort.* IFIP, 1981.

[Berns]           Gerald M. Berns. Assessing software maintainability. *CACM*, vol. 27, no. 1, January 1984.

[Bieman]          J. M. Bieman and J. L. Schultz. Estimating the number of test cases required to satisfy the all-DU-paths testing criterion. In Richard Kemmerer, Software Engineering Notes, *ACM*, pp. 179–186, vol. 14, no. 8, December 1989.

[BigBrother]      www.bb4.com.

[Birman]          Ken Birman. The Untrustworthy web services revolution. *IEEE Computer,* February 2006.

[Boehm 75]        B. Boehm, R. MacLean, and D. Urfrig. Some experience with automated aides to the design of large-scale reliable software. *IEEE Transactions on Software Engineering,* SE-1, 1975, pp. 125–133.

[Boehm 88]        B. Boehm and F. Belz. Applying process programming to the spiral model. Proceedings of the 4th International Software Process Workshop, 1988.

[Boehm 89]        B. Boehm. *Software engineering economics, second edition.* Prentice-Hall, 1989.

[Boehm 91]        B. Boehm. Software risk management. *IEEE Software,* 8, 1, 1991.

[Brettschneider]  Ralph Brettschneider(Motorola). Is your software ready for release? *IEEE Software,* July 1989.

[BRG]             Business Rules Group. Final Report 1.3, July 2000.

[BRML]            *Business Rule Mark-up Language.* www.oasis-open.org/cover/brml.html.

[Brooks]          Fred Brooks. The computer scientist as toolsmith-II. *CACM,* March 1996.

[Brownstone]      I. Brownstone, R. Farrell, E. Kant, and N. Martin. *Programming expert systems in OPS5: An introduction to rule-based programming.* Reading, Massachusetts: Addison-Wesley, 1985.

[Burns]           Alan Burns and Andy Wellings. *Real-time systems and programming languages, second edition.* Reading, Massachusetts: Addison-Wesley, 1997.

[Carr M]          Marvin J. Carr et al. *Taxonomy-based risk identification.* Software Engineering Institute at Carnegie Mellon University, Pittsburgh, Pennsylvania, 1993.

[Carr N]          Nicholas G. Carr. IT doesn't matter. *Harvard Business Review,* 2005, reprint.

[CBL]             Common Business Language. www.xcbl.org

[Chellas]         Brian F. Chellas. *Modal logic: An introduction.* Cambridge University Press, 1980.

[Chidamber 1]     S. R. Chidamber and C. F. Kemerer. *Towards a metrics suite for object-oriented design.* Proceedings of the ACM Conference on Object-Oriented Programming, Systems, Languages, and Applications (Oopsla 91), ACM Press, 1991.

[Chidamber 2]     S. Chidamber and C. Kemerer. A metrics suite for object-oriented design. *IEEE Transactions on Software Engineering,* vol. 20, no. 6, pp. 476–493, 1994.

[Chun]            G. Chun, H. Dail, H. Casanova, and A. Snavely. *Benchmark probes for grid assessment.* Technical report CS2003-0760, University of California, San Diego, July 2003.

[Clumon]          *Clumon cluster monitoring Webpage.* www.clumon.ncsa.uiuc.edu.

[Cohen]           Cynthia F. Cohen, Stanley J. Birkin, Monica J. Garfield, and Harold W. Webb. Managing conflict in software testing. *CACM,* vol. 47, no. 1, pp. 76–81, 2004.

[Cooper]          R. G. Cooper. *Winning at new products, third edition.* Cambridge, Massachusetts: Perseus Publishing, 2001.

[Cusumano 1]      M. A. Cusumano and R. Selby. How Microsoft builds software. *CACM,* June 1997.

| | |
|---|---|
| [Cusumano 2] | M. A. Cusumano. *The business of software.* Free Press, 2004. |
| [DeMillo 1] | R. A. DeMillo, R. J. Lipton, and F. G. Sayward. Hints on test data selection: Help for the practicing programmer. *IEEE Computer,* vol. 11, pp. 34–41, April 1978. |
| [DeMillo 2] | R. A. DeMillo and A. J. Offutt. Constraint-based automatic test data generation. *IEEE Transactions on Software Engineering,* vol. 17, pp. 900–910, September 1991. |
| [Dix] | Alan Dix, Janet Finlay, Gregory Abowd, and Russell Beale. *Human–Computer Interaction.* Prentice Hall, 1998 (www.hcibook.com/). |
| [Dixon 1] | Norman E. Dixon. *On the psychology of military incompetence.* Futura, 1988. |
| [Dixon 2] | Norman E. Dixon. *Our own worst enemy.* Futura, 1987. |
| [Dumas] | Joseph S. Dumas and Janice C. Redish. *A practical guide to usability testing.* Intellect, 1999. |
| [Duncan] | A. G. Duncan and J. S Hutchinson. *Using attribute grammars to test designs and implementations.* 5th International Conference on Software Engineering, San Diego, March 1981. |
| [Dyer] | M. Dyer. *Software designs of certified reliability.* in Reliability 85. |
| [Endres] | A. Endres. An analysis of errors and their causes in system programs. *IEEE Transactions on Software Engineering,* June 1975, pp. 140–149. |
| [Fairfield] | P. Fairfield, D. Hedley, and M. A. Hennell. *Test coverage analysers.* Alvey deliverable A35. Alvey Directorate. Project SE/031. |
| [Farrell-Vinay] | *A grammar of incompetence.* IASTED 2001. |
| [Foster] | I. Foster and C. Kesselman. Globus: A metacomputing infrastructure toolkit. *International Journal of Supercomputer Applications,* 11, 2, 115–128, 1997. |
| [Freedman] | D. P. Freedman and G. M. Weinberg. *Handbook of walkthroughs, inspections and technical reviews.* New York: Dorset House Publishing, 1990. |
| [Friedman] | Michael Friedman and Jeffrey M. Voas. *Software assessment: Reliability, safety, testability.* New York: Wiley Press, 1995. |
| [Gagné] | R. M. Gagné and L. J. Briggs. *Principles of instructional design.* Holt, Rinehart and Winston, 1974. |
| [Geist] | R. Geist, A. J. Offutt, and F. Harris. Estimation and enhancement of real-time software reliability through mutation analysis. *IEEE Transactions on Computers,* vol. 41, pp. 550–558, May 1992, special issue on Fault-Tolerant Computing. |
| [Gerndt] | M. Gerndt, R. Wismuller, Z. Balaton, G. Gombs, P. Kacsuk, Z. Neth, N. Podhorszki, H.-L. Truong, T. Fahringer, M. Bubak, E. Laure, and T. Margalef. *Performance tools for the grid: State of the art and future.* Technical report cited in Smallen et al., *The Inca test harness and reporting framework.* IEEE, 2004. |
| [Gerrard 1] | Paul Gerrard and Neil Thompson. *Risk-based E-business testing.* Artechnical, 2002. |
| [Gerrard 2] | Paul Gerrard. *Client-server performance testing.* www.evolutif.co.uk, 2002. |
| [Gervasi] | Vincenzo Gervasi and Bashar Nuseibeh. *Lightweight validation of natural language requirements: A case study.* Proceedings of the 4th IEEE International Conference on Requirements Engineering (ICRE2000), IEEE Computer Society Press, June 2000. |
| [Gilb] | Tom Gilb and Dorothy Graham. *Software inspection.* Reading, Massachusetts: Addison-Wesley, 1993. |
| [GITS] | *The UK Grid Integration Test Script-GITS,* www.soton.ac.uk/_djb1/gits. html. |
| [Glasberg] | Daniela Glasberg, Khaled El Emam, Walcelio Melo, and Nazim Madhavji. *Validating object-oriented design metrics on a commercial Java application.* NRC-ERB 1080, National Research Council of Canada, September 2000. |
| [Goel-Okhumoto] | A. L. Goel and K. Okhumoto. Time-dependent error-detection-rate model for software reliability and other performance measures. *IEEE Transactions on Reliability,* 1979, R-28. |
| [GridBench] | G. Tsouloupas and M. Dikaiakos. *GridBench: A tool for benchmarking grids.* In Proceedings of the 4th International Workshop on Grid Computing, 2003, pp. 60–67. |
| [Hackos] | J. Hackos and J. Redish. *User and task analysis for interface design.* Wiley, 1998. |
| [Halstead] | M. H. Halstead. *Elements of software science.* New York: Elsevier North Holland, 1977. |

[Hamlet]            R. Hamlet. Theoretical comparison of testing methods. *Software Engineering Notes, ACM,* vol. 14, no. 8, December 1989, pp. 28–37.

[Hawkeye]           Hawkeye. www.cs.wisc.edu/condor/hawkeye.

[Heidler]           W. Heidler et al. *Software testing measures.* U.S. Air Force Rome Air Project Center, Technical report 82-135, May 1982.

[Henderson]         B. Henderson Sellers. Modularisation and cyclomatic complexity. *CACM,* vol. 35, no. 12, December 1992, pp. 17–19.

[Herring]           Charles Herring and Zoran Milosevic. *Implementing B2B contracts using BizTalk.* Proceedings of the 34th Hawaii International Conference on System Sciences, IEEE, 2001.

[Herzog]            *Security metrics — RAVs (Risk Assessment Values).* www.isecom.org/securitymetrics.shtml

[Hetzel]            Bill Hetzel. *The complete guide to software testing, second edition.* Wellesley, Massachusetts: QED Information Sciences, 1988.

[Hollocker]         Charles P. Hollocker. *Software reviews and audits handbook.* Wiley-Interscience, 1990.

[Holub]             P. Holub, M. Kuba, L. Matyska, and M. Ruda. *Grid infrastructure monitoring as reliable information service.* In 2nd European Across Grids Conference, 2004.

[Homer]             W. Homer and R. Schooler. Independent testing of compiler phases using a test case generator. *Software: Practice and Experience,* January 1989.

[Hooks]             Ivy F. Hooks. www.complianceautomation.com/papers/ ManagingRequirements.pdf

[Hordijk]           Wiebe Hordijk and Roel Wieringa. *Surveying the Factors that Influence Maintainability.* ESEC-FSE'05, ACM, September 5–9, 2005.

[Howden 1]          W. E. Howden. Methodology for the generation of program test data. *IEEE Transactions on Computers,* TC-24, May 1975.

[Howden 2]          William E. Howden. Weak mutation testing and completeness of test sets. *IEEE Transactions on Software Engineering,* 8, 4, 371–379, July 1982.

[IBM 1]             IBM. *Accessible Business Rules.* www.research.ibm.com/AEM/abr.html.

[IBM 2]             IBM. *Overview of IBM CommonRules.* www.research.ibm.com/rules/commonrules-overview.html.

[Intermetrics]      *Text generator tutorial.* Technical report IR-MA-557-2. Intermetrics Incorporated, Cambridge, Massachusetts, March 1986.

[Jelinsky]          Z. Jelinsky and B. Moranda. Software reliability research, in W. B. Freiberger (Ed.), *Statistical computer performance evaluation.* Academic Press, 1972.

[Jensen]            Randall W. Jensen and Charles C. Tonies. *Software engineering.* Prentice-Hall, 1979.

[Johnson]           Philip Johnson, Carleton Moore, Joseph Dane, and Robert Brewer. Empirically-guided software effort guesstimation. *IEEE Software,* November/December 2000.

[Jones 1]           Capers Jones. *Software cost estimation in 2002(c)* (in Crosstalk). www.stsc.hill.af.mil/crosstalk/2002/06/ jones.html

[Jones 2]           Capers Jones. *Applied software measurement, second edition.* New York: McGraw-Hill, 1996.

[Kan]               Stephen H. Kan. *Metrics and models in software quality engineering.* Reading, Massachusetts: Addison-Wesley, 1995.

[Kantner]           Laurie Kantner. Techniques for managing a usability test. *IEEE Transactions on Professional Communication,* September 1994.

[Kelly 1]           Tim Kelly. *A systematic approach to safety case management.* University of York, UK. www-users.cs.york.ac.uk/~tpk/04AE-149.pdf.

[Kelly 2]           Tim Kelly. *Concepts and principles of compositional safety case construction,* May 2001, COMSA/2001/1/1.

[Kirwan]            B. Kirwan and L. K. Ainsworth (Eds.), *A Guide to Task Analysis.* London: Taylor & Francis, 1992.

[Kwan]              Irwin Kwan and Daniel M. Berry. *Specify first or build first? Empirical studies of requirements engineering activities: A survey.* School of Computer Science University of Waterloo, Ontario, Canada.

[LaQuSo]            www.laquso.com

| | |
|---|---|
| [Lederer] | A. L. Lederer and J. Prassad. Nine management guidelines for better cost estimating. *CACM*, 35, 2, 51–59, 1992. |
| [Lehman] | Manny Lehman. Private communication. |
| [Levinson] | Stanley H. Levinson and H. Tazewell Daughtrey. *Risk analysis of software-dependent systems.* Presented at Probabilistic Safety Assessment International Topical Meeting, Clearwater Beach, Florida, January 1993. |
| [Lewis] | J. R. Lewis. Sample sizes for usability studies: Additional considerations. *Human Factors*, 36, 368–378, 1994. |
| [Linger] | R. C. Linger, H. D. Mills, and B. I. Witt. *Structured programming:Theory and practice.* Reading, Massachusetts: Addison-Wesley, 1979. |
| [Lipow] | M. Lipow. Quantitative demonstration and cost considerations of a software fault removal methodology. *Quality and Reliability Engineering International*, vol. 1, pp. 27–35, 1985. |
| [Littlewood 81] | B. Littlewood. Stochastic reliability growth: A model for fault removal in computer programs and hardware design. *IEEE Transactions on Reliability*, R-30, 1981. |
| [Littlewood 98] | B. Littlewood, P. Popov, L. Strigini, and N. Shryane. *Modelling the effects of combining diverse software fault removal techniques.* Esprit long term research project 20072, DeVa (Design for Validation), December 1998. |
| [Liuying] | Li Liuying and Qi Zhichang. *Test selection from UML statecharts.* Technology of Object-Oriented Languages and Systems, 1999. TOOLS 31 Proceedings, pp. 273–279. |
| [Lunde] | Ken Lunde. *CJKV information processing.* O'Reilly, 1999. |
| [Lutz] | Robyn R. Lutz and Inds Carmen Mikulski. Requirements discovery during the testing of safety-critical software. *IEEE Software*, 21, 2, March/April 2004. |
| [Lyu] | Michael R Lyu (Ed.). *Handbook of software reliability engineering.* New York: McGraw Hill, 1996. |
| [MacCormack] | Alan MacCormack, Chris Kemmerer, Michael Cusumano, and Bill Crandall. Tradeoffs between productivity and quality in selecting software development practices. *IEEE Software*, September/October 2003. |
| [Mangione] | Carmine Mangione. *Software project failure: The reasons, the costs*, www.cioupdate.com/ reports/article.php/1563701. |
| [Massie] | M. Massie, B. Chun, and D. Culler. *The ganglia distributed monitoring system: Design, implementation, and experience.* Parallel Computing, April 2004. |
| [McCabe] | T. J. McCabe. A complexity measure. *IEEE Transactions on Software Engineering*, December 1976. |
| [McCartney] | *Successful IT: Modernising Government in Action.* www.ogc.gov.uk/index.asp?id=377. |
| [McCormack] | Alan McCormack et al. Trade-offs between productivity and quality in selecting software development best practices. *IEEE Software*, September/October 2003. |
| [Memon] | Atif M. Memon, Mary Lou Soffa, and Martha E. Pollack. *Coverage criteria for GUI testing.* ACM SIGSOFT Software Engineering Notes, Proceedings of the 8th European Software Engineering Conference held jointly with 9th ACM SIGSOFT international symposium on Foundations of Software Engineering, ESEC/FSE-9, vol. 26, issue 5, September 2001. |
| [Michael] | James B. Michael, Bernard J. Bossuyt, and Byron B. Snyder. *Metrics for measuring the effectiveness of software-testing tools.* Proceedings of the 13th International Symposium on Software Reliability Engineering (ISSRE'02). |
| [Mills 72] | H. D. Mills. *On the statistical validation of computer programs.* Technical report FSC-726015, IBM Federal Systems Division, 1972. |
| [Mills 87] | H. D. Mills and M. Dyer. A formal approach to software error removal. *Journal of Systems and Software*, 1987. |
| [Minto] | Barbara Minto. The pyramid principle. *Financial Times*, Prentice Hall, 2001. |

[Miyazaki]      Y. Miyazaki et al. Method to estimate parameter values in software prediction models. *Information and Software Technology,* vol. 33, no. 3, 1991.

[MonALISA]      H. B. Newman, I. C. Legrand, P. Galvez, R. Voicu, and C. Cirstoiu. *MonALISA: A distributed monitoring service architecture.* Proceedings of the Conference on Computing and High Energy Physics (CHEP), 2003.

[Munoz]         C. U. Munoz. An approach to software product testing. *IEEE Transactions on Software Engineering,* November 1988.

[Musa 1]        John D. Musa. *Software reliability engineering.* New York: McGraw-Hill, 1998.

[Musa 2]        John Musa. A theory of software reliability and its application. *IEEE Transactions on Software Engineering.* SE-1, no. 3, pp. 312–327, 1975.

[Musa 3]        John Musa. Operational profiles in software reliability engineering. *IEEE Software,* March 93. Special issue devoted to operational profiles.

[Musa 4]        John D. Musa and K. Okhumoto. *A logarithmic Poisson execution-time model for software reliability assessment.* Proceedings of the 7th International Conference on Software Engineering, Silver Spring, Maryland, 1984.

[Muskens]       Johan Muskens, Michel Chaudron, and Rob Westgeest. *Software architecture analysis tool.* Proceedings of the 3rd Progress Workshop on Embedded Systems, 2002.

[Myers B]       Brad A. Myers. User interface software tools. *ACM Transactions on Computer–Human Interaction 2,* pp. 64–108, March 1995.

[Myers G]       Glenford J. Myers. *The art of software testing.* Wiley, 1979.

[Nagappan]      Nachiapan Nagappan, Thomas Ball, and Andreas Zeller. *Mining metrics to predict component failures.* ACM Proceedings of the 28th International Conference on Software Engineering, Shanghai, 2006.

[NCSA]          NCSA TestGrid Project, grid.ncsa.uiuc.edu/test.

[Nguyen]        Hung Q. Nguyen. *Testing applications on the Web.* Wiley, 2001.

[Nielsen 1]     Jakob Neilsen. *Designing Web usability: The practice of simplicity.* New Riders, 2000.

[Nielsen 2]     Jakob Neilsen. *Usability engineering.* Boston: Academic Press, 1993.

[Nielsen 3]     Jakob Neilsen. *Why you only need to test with 5 users.* Alertbox, 2000, www.useit.com/alertbox/2000319.html.

[Norman]        Donald A. Norman. *Emotional design: Why we love (or hate) everyday things.* Basic Books, 2002.

[OMG]           Object Management Group, www.omg.org.

[OCL]           The Object Constraint Language, www.agilemodeling.com/artifacts/constraint.htm#OCL.

[Offutt]        A. J. Offutt. The coupling effect: Fact or fiction. *Software Engineering Notes,* December 1989, pp. 131–140.

[OSTMM]         Herzog et al. *The open source security testing methodology manual.* Available from www.isecom.org/osstmm/.

[Parnas]        David L. Parnas, A. J. van Schouwens, and P. Kwan. Evaluation of safety-critical software. *CACM,* June 1990, pp. 636–648.

[Paton]         N. W. Paton and O. Diaz. Introduction in N. W. Paton (Ed.), *Active rules in database systems,* Springer, 1999, pp. 1–28.

[Preece]        J. Preece, Y. Rogers, H. Sharp, D. Benyon, S. Holland, and T. Carey. *Human–computer interaction.* Reading, Massachusetts: Addison-Wesley, 1994.

[Pressman]      R. S. Pressman. *Software engineering: A practitioner's approach.* New York: McGraw Hill, 1992.

[Presson]       E. Presson. *Software test handbook.* U.S. Air Force Rome Air Project Center Technical report 84-53, March 1984.

[Prince II]     Project management for business. *CCTA,* 1997.

[Radatz]        Jane W. Radatz. *Analysis of IV and V data.* Report RiSED-81319. Logicon Inc., San Pedro, California, 1981.

[RADC]          Software reliability study [RADC-TR-74-250], October 1974.

[Raistrick]    Chris Raistrick, Paul Francis, John Wright, Colin Carter, and Ian Wilkie. *Model-driven architecture with executable UML.* Cambridge, 2004.

[Rajasekar]    A. Rajasekar, M. Wan, R. Moore, W. Schroeder, G. Kremenek, A. Jagatheesan, C. Cowart, B. Zhu, S.-Y. Chen, and R. Olschanowsky. Storage resource broker managing distributed data in a grid. *Computer Society of India Journal,* special issue on SAN, 33, 4, 42–54, October 2003.

[Rapps]    S. Rapps and E. J. Weyuker. Selecting software test data using dataflow information. *IEEE Transactions on Software Engineering,* SE-11(4), pp. 367–375, April 1985.

[Reason]    James Reason. *Human error.* Cambridge, 1997.

[Remus]    H. Remus and S. Zilles. *Prediction and Management of Program Quality.* Proceedings of the Fourth International Conference on Software Engineering, Munich, 1979, IEEE Computer Society, pp. 57–64.

[Reifer]    Donald Reifer. Web development: Estimating quick-to-market software. *IEEE Software,* November/December 2000.

[Rich 81]    D. J. Richardson and L. A. Clarke. *A partition analysis method to increase program reliability.* Proceedings of the 5th International Conference on Software Engineering, 1981, pp. 244–253.

[Rich 89]    D. J. Richardson, O. O'Malley, and C. Tittle. Approaches to specification-based testing. In Kemmerer, *Software Engineering Notes,* vol. 14, no. 8, pp. 86–96. ACM, December 1989.

[Riley]    G. Riley. *CLIPS: A tool for building expert systems.* www.ghg.NET/clips/CLIPS.html, 2001.

[Rosenblum]    D. S. Rosenblum and D. C. Luckham. *Testing the correctness of tasking supervisors with TSL specifications.* In Kemmerer, *Software Engineering Notes,* vol. 14, no. 8, pp. 187–196. ACM, December 1989.

[Ross]    R. G. Ross, *Principles of the business rule approach.* Reading, Massachusetts: Addison-Wesley, 2003.

[Royce]    W. W. Royce. *Managing the development of large software systems.* IEEEWescon, 1970.

[Sachs]    M. Sachs, A. Dan, T. Nguyen, R. Kearney, H. Shaikh, and D. Dias. *Executable trading agreements in electronic commerce,* IBM T. J. Watson Research Center, 2000.

[Sahner]    Robin Sahner, Kishnor Trivedi, and Antonio Pulliafito. *Performance and reliability analysis of computer systems.* Kluwer, 1996.

[Sauro]    Jeff Sauro and Erika Kindlund. *A method to standardize usability metrics into a single score.* Paper presented at CHI 2005, Portland, Oregon (www.measuringusability.com/SUM/).

[Schaffer]    Eric Schaffer. *Institutionalisation of usability.* Reading, Massachusetts: Addison-Wesley, 2004.

[Sherer]    Susan A. Sherer. *Software failure risk.* Plenum Press, 1992.

[Sherriff]    Mark Sherriff and Laurie Williams. *Tool support for estimating software reliability in Haskell programs,* www4.ncsu.edu/~mssherri/papers/SW04.pdf.

[Shooman]    M. L. Shooman. *Software engineering.* McGraw-Hill, 1983.

[Smallen]    Shava Smallen, Catherine Olschanowsky, Kate Ericson, Pete Beckman, and Jennifer M. Schopf. San Diego Supercomputer Center, *The Inca test harness and reporting framework,* IEEE, 2004.

[Spiegel]    Murray R. Spiegel and Larry J. Stephens. *Statistics, third edition.* McGraw, 1998.

[Splaine]    Steven Splaine and Stefan Jaskiel. *The Web testing handbook.* STQE Publishing, 2001.

[SRML]    *Simple Rule Markup Language,* www.oasis-open.org/cover/srml.html.

[SSADM]    SELECT Software Tools plc, Gloucestershire, England.

[Stanton]    *Handbook of human factors and ergonomic methods.* Boca Raton, Florida: CRC Press, 2004.

[Suardi]    Luigi Suardi. How to manage your software product life cycle with MAUI. *CACM,* vol. 47, no. 3, March 2004.

| [Takahashi] | M. Takahashi and Y. Kamayachi. An empirical study of a model for program error prediction. *IEEE Transactions on Software Engineering*, January 1989. |
| [Tierney] | B. Tierney, R. Aydt, D. Gunter, W. Smith, M. Swany, V. Taylor, and R. Wolski. *A grid monitoring architecture.* www.ggf.org/documents/final.htm. |
| [Tolk] | Andreas Tolk and James A. Muguira. *The levels of conceptual interoperability model.* 2003 Fall Simulation Interoperability Workshop. |
| [Truong] | H. Truong and T. Fahringer. *SCALEA-G: A unified monitoring and performance analysis system for the grid.* In 2nd European Across Grids Conference, 2004. |
| [Tuthill] | Bill Tuthill and David Smallberg. *Creating worldwide software: Solaris International developer's guide, second edition.* Prentice Hall PTR, 1997. |
| [Ullman] | J. D. Ullman and J. Widom. *A first course in database systems.* Prentice-Hall, 1997. |
| [Veenendaal] | Erik van Veenendaal. Questionnaire based usability testing. In *Project Control for Software Quality*, Rob Kusters, Adrian Cowderoy, Fred Heemstra, and Erik van Veenendaal (Eds.), Shaker Publishing, 1999 (www.ucc.ie/hfrg/questionnaires/sumi/). |
| [Verrall] | B. Littlewood and J. L. Verrall. A Bayesian reliability growth: A model for computer software. *IEEE Transactions on Reliability, Applied Statistics*, 1973. |
| [Versata] | *Versata Logic Suite.* www.versata.com. |
| [Virzi] | R. Virzi. Refining the test phase of usability evaluation: How many subjects is enough? *Human Factors*, 34, 457–468, 1992. |
| [Voas] | Jeffrey M. Voas and Gary McGraw. *Software fault injection: Inoculating programs against errors.* New York: Wiley Computer, 1997. |
| [Wagner] | Stefan Wagner and Tilman Seifert. *Software quality economics for* (sic) *defect detection techniques using failure prediction.* In 3-Wo SQ '05, May 2005. ACM 1-59593-122-8/05/0005. |
| [Wallace] | Linda Wallace and Mark Keil. Software project risks and their effect on outcomes. *CACM*, April 2004. |
| [Warmer] | Warmer and Kleppe. *The Object Constraint Language.* Reading, Massachusetts: Addison-Wesley, 1998. |
| [Weibull] | W. Weibull. A statistical distribution function of wide application. *Journal of Applied Mechanics*, vol. 18, 1951. |
| [Weinschenk] | Dr. Susan Weinschenk. *Usability: A business case.* Human factors International Inc., Fairfield, Iowa. |
| [Wei-Tek] | Wei-TekTsai, Lian Yiu, and Ray Paul. Rapid embedded system testing using verification patterns. *IEEE Software*, July/August 2005. |
| [Wiegers] | Karl Wiegers. *Peer reviews in software: A practical guide.* Reading, Massachusetts: Addison-Wesley, 2001. |
| [Wolski] | R. Wolski, N. Spring, and J. Hayes. The Network Weather Service: A distributed resource performance forecasting service for metacomputing. *Journal of Future Generation Computing Systems*, 15(5-6), 757–768, October 1999. |
| [Yourdon] | Ed Yourdon. *Structured walkthroughs.* Prentice-Hall, 1989. |
| [Zhang] | X. Zhang, J. Freschl, and J. Schopf. *A performance study of monitoring and information services for distributed systems.* In Proceedings of HPDC-12, 2003. |

# Related Standards

This book is consistent with, and related to, the following standards and publications:

| [AICPA TSC] | (US) *AICPA — Trust Services Criteria; including SysTrust/WebTrust.* www.aicpa.org/trustservices |

| | |
|---|---|
| [AICPA SGP] | Standard of Good Practice for Information Security (Information Security Forum) www.isfsecuritystandard.com/index_ie.htm The American Institute of Certified Public Accountants, www.aicpa.org |
| [ANSI] | American National Standards Institute, www.ansi.org |
| [ASBDC-US] | (US) The Association of Small Business Development Centers, www.asbdc-us.org |
| [BIS Basel II] | *Basel II – The New BASEL Capital Accord.* Bank for International Settlements. www.bis.org/publ/bcbsca.htm |
| [BIS SP] | *Sound Practices for Mgmt & Supervision of Operational Risk.* www.bis.org/publ/bcbs96.pdf |
| [BITS ] | *BITS Framework: Managing Technology Risk for Information Technology Service Provider Relationships.* Financial Services Roundtable. www.bitsinfo.org. www.bitsinfo.org/bits2003framework.pdf The Technology Group for The Financial Services Roundtable, www.bitsinfo.org |
| [BR] | Building *Security in the Digital Economy: an Executive Resource*; www.businessroundtable.org/pdf/814.pdf Business Roundtable, www.businessroundtable.org |
| [BS 7799] | BS 7799 – Parts 1 & 2, Code of Practice for Information Security Management |
| [BS 4778] | BS 4778 – *Quality vocabulary Part 1 1987 International terms.* Equivalent of ISO 8402: 1986. |
| [BS 5750 1] | BS 5750 – British standard for quality systems. |
| [BS 5750 13] | Part 13 *Guide to the application of BS 5750: Part 1 to the development, supply, and maintenance of software.* Equivalent to ISO 9000-3. Quality management and quality assurance standards - Part 3: Guidelines for the application of ISO 9001 to the development, supply, and maintenance of software. |
| [BS 7925-2] | BS 7925-2: 1998 *Standard for software component testing.* BSI. London. 1998 |
| [BSI] | British Standards Institute. www.bsi.org.uk |
| [BSA ISG] | *Information Security Governance: Toward a Framework for Action* www.bsa.org/resources/loader.cfm?url=/commonspot/security/getfile.cfm&PageID=5841 |
| [BSA SC] | *Security Checklists for Mid, Large, and Small Businesses, Government Agencies, and Consumers.* global.bsa.org/usa/policy/security/checklists.phtml |
| [BSA PCS] | *Partnering for Cyber Security: A CEO's Blueprint for a More Secure America*; www.bsa.org/security |
| [BSA CGF] | *Corporate Governance Framework.* A recent publication that outlines the rôles, and responsibilities of everyone in the corporation in terms of information security. TechNet's evaluation tests for the corporate governance principles developed by BSA. www.bsa.org/policy/security-index.cfm |
| [BSA] | Business Software Alliance. www.bsa.org |
| [BSI-de] | Bundesamt für Sicherheit in der Informationstechnik. www.bsi.bund.de/cc/ |
| [C4ISR 98] | *C4ISR Interoperability Working Group*, Department of Defense. Levels of Information Systems Interoperability (LISI). Washington, DC: 1998. |
| [CERT] | Computer Emergency Response Team. Carnegie Mellon CERT Coordination Center. A centre of Internet security expertise, located at the Software Engineering Institute, a federally funded research and development centre operated by Carnegie Mellon University. www.cert.org |
| [CESG] | The Information Assurance arm of GCHQ (UK Government Communications HQ). www.cesg.gov.uk/ |
| [CIAO] | Critical Infrastructure Assurance Office (formerly U.S. Dept. of Commerce, now IAIP of DHS) |
| [CICA ITCG] | *Information Technology: Control Guidelines* 1998. Chartered Accountants of Canada. www.cica.ca |

| | |
|---|---|
| [CIS] | *Consensus Benchmarks and Consensus Benchmark Scoring Tools* The Center for Internet Security. www.cisecurity.org |
| [*CompSecGloss*] | *Computer Security Glossary*. www.radium.ncsc.mil/tpep/library/rainbow/NCSC-TG-004.pdf |
| [COSO] | Committee of Sponsoring Organizations for the Commission on Fraudulent Financial Reporting, www.coso.org |
| [CSE] | Communications Security Establishment. Canada's national cryptologic agency. It provides the Government of Canada with foreign signals intelligence in support of defence and foreign policy, and the protection of electronic information and communication. www.cse-cst.gc.ca/index-e.html |
| [DEF STAN 05-95/1] | 05-95/1 *Quality system requirements for the development, supply, and maintenance of software*. Replaced AQAP-13. It embodies requirements found in ISO 9001 and text from ISO 9000-3. Much of its text renders the provisions of ISO 9000-3 more strict by replacing should by shall. Also contains a number of supplements which extend the standard. |
| [DHS] | Department of Homeland Security, www.dhs.gov |
| [DISA ] | *Security Technical Implementation Guides*. csrc.nist.gov/pcig/cig.html Defense Information Systems Agency. www.disa.mil |
| [DTI] | *Code of Practice for Information Security Management*: Department of Trade and Industry, and British Standard Institute. London. 1993. 1995. (Became BS 17799). www.dti.gov.uk/industries/information_security/ |
| [ETSI 873-1] | ETSI ES 201 873-1: The Testing and Test Control Notation version 3; Part 1: TTCN-3 Core Language. V2.2.1 (2002- 10), 2002; also an ITU-T standard Z.140. |
| [ETSI 873-3] | *ETSI ES 201 873-3: The Testing and Test Control Notation version 3; Part 3: TTCN-3 Graphical Presentation Format.* |
| [EU] | *EU Data Protection Directive*. (aspe.os.dhhs.gov/datacncl/eudirect.htm).europa.eu.int/comm/internal_market/privacy/docs/95-46-ce/dir1995-46_part1_en.pdf, europa.eu.int/comm/internal_market/privacy/docs/95-46-ce/dir1995-46_part2_en.pdf |
| [FedCIRC] | Department of Homeland Security Federal Computer Incident Response Center. The US federal government's trusted focal point for computer security incident reporting, providing assistance with incident prevention and response. www.fedcirc.gov |
| [FFIEC] | *Audit IT Examination Handbook* and *Audit Examination Procedures*. www.ffiec.gov. www.ffiec.gov/ffiecinfobase/index.html Federal Financial Institutions Examination Council, www.ffiec.gov |
| [FISMA] | *Federal Information Security Management Act of 2002* – U.S. Congress, 2002 www.fedcirc.gov/library/legislation/FISMA.html |
| [FSR] | Financial Services Roundtable, www.fsround.org |
| [FTC] | *Federal Trade Commission enforcement guidelines/actions*. www.ftc.gov/ogc/brfovrvw. htm.www.ftc.gov/opa/2003/11/cyber security.htm Federal Trade Commission, www.ftc.gov |
| [GAISP] | *Generally Accepted Information Security Principles* (Generally Accepted Systems Security Principles) (GASSP), June. 1999. web.mit.edu/security/www/gassp1.html (Detailed Principles are under development (ISSA) www.issa.org/gaisp.html) |
| [GAISP C] | Generally Accepted Information Security Principles Committee. www.issa.org/gaisp.html |
| [GASSP] | *Generally Accepted System Security Principles*. International Information Security Foundation. www.polivec.com/knowledgebase/gassp/GASSP.doc |
| [GLBA] | (US) Gramm, Leach, Bliley Act — *The Financial Modernization Act of 1999*. www.ftc.gov/privacy/glbact/ |
| [HIPAA] | *Health Information Portability and Accountability Act*. www.hhs.gov/ocr/hipaa/ |

[IAIP]          Information Assurance and Infrastructure Protection Directorate of the DHS. www.dhs.gov

[ICAEW]         *Turnbull Report — Internal Control — Guidance for Directors on the Combined Code.* Institute of Chartered Accountants in England & Wales (ICAEW). www.icaew.co.uk/ index.cfm?AUB=TB2I_6242, MNXI_47896
                Institute of Chartered Accountants in England & Wales, www.icaew.co.uk

[ICC]           *Information Security for Executives.* Business and Industry Advisory Committee to the OECD and International Chamber of Commerce, Paris, November 2003. www.iccwbo. org/uploadedFiles/ICC/policy/e-business/pages/InfoSecurityAssurance.pdf
                International Chamber of Commerce, www.iccwbo.org

[IDEF]          IEEE standard 1320.1.1 Mar-96. Language Formalization for IDEF0 Function

[IEEE 1008]     ANSI/IEEE Std 1008-1987 *Software Unit Testing.* Defines an integrated approach to systematic and documented unit testing.

[IEEE 1012]     ANSI/IEEE Std 1012-1986 *Software Verification and Validation Plans.* Provides uniform and minimum requirements for the format and content of Software Verification and Validation Plans for both critical and non-critical software.

[IEEE 1540-2001] ANSI/IEEE 1540-2001 *IEEE Standard for Software Life Cycle Processes — Risk Management.*

[IEEE 729]      ANSI/IEEE Std 729-1983 *Glossary of Software Engineering Terminology.* Establishes definitions for most of the software engineering terms in general use.

[IEEE 829]      ANSI/IEEE Std 829-1983 *Software Test Documentation.* Defines the content and format of documents that cover the testing process.

[IEEE 90]       IEEE. *IEEE Standard Computer Dictionary: A Compilation of IEEE Standard Computer Glossaries.* New York, NY: 1990.

[IEEE 982]      ANSI/IEEE Std 982. 1-1988 *Standard Dictionary of Measures to Produce Reliable Software.* Defines measures currently used as indicators of reliability. This standard presents a selection of applicable measures, the proper conditions for using each measure, the methods of computation and a framework for a common language among users.

[IEEE 982G]     IEEE Std 982. 2-1988. *Guide to the Use of IEEE Standard Dictionary of Measures to Produce Reliable Software.* Provides the conceptual insights, implementation considerations and assessment suggestions for the application of IEEE Std 982. 1.

[IEEE 983]      ANSI/IEEE Std 983-1986 *Guide to Software Quality Assurance Planning.*

[IFAC]          *International Guidelines on Information Technology Management—Managing Information Technology Planning for Business Impact.* International Federation of Accountants, New York. 1999. www.ifac.org
                International Federation of Accountants, www.ifac.org

[IIA]           The Institute of Internal Auditors, Inc. (and IIA Research Foundation), www.TheIIA.org

[ISA]           *Common Sense Guide for Senior Managers: Top Ten Recommended Security Practices.* www.isalliance.org/news/requestform.cfm
                Internet Security Alliance, www.isalliance.org

[ISACA COBIT]   *COBIT – Control Objectives for Information and Related Technologies.*

[ISACA ITGIG]   *IT Governance Implementation Guide.* www.isaca.org/Template.cfm?Section=Browse_ By_Topic&Template=/Ecommerce/ProductDisplay.cfm&ProductID=503

[ISACA]         The Information Systems Audit and Control Association, www.isaca.org

[ISECOM]        An open, collaborative, security research community www.isecom.org

[ISF]           Information Security Forum, www.securityforum.org

[ISO 15408]     ISO 15408 — *Common Criteria.* csrc.nist.gov/cc/ccv20/ccv2list.htm 618

[ISO 21827]     ISO 21827 — *System Security Engineering Capability Maturity Model.* www.iso.ch/iso/ en/CatalogueDetailPage.CatalogueDetail?CSNUMBER=34731&ICS1=35&ICS2= 40&ICS3

[ISO TR 13335]    ISO TR 13335 *Guidelines for the Management of Information Security, Parts 1-5.* www.iso.org/iso/en/StandardsQueryFormHandler.StandardsQueryFormHandler

[ISO TR 13569]    ISO TR 13569 *Banking and Related Financial Services – Information Security Guidelines.* 9/9/2003. www.iso.org/iso/en/stdsdevelopment/techprog/workprog/TechnicalProgramme ProjectDetailPage.TechnicalProgrammeProjectDetail?csnumber=37245

[ISO 13 407]      *Human-Centred Design Processes for Interactive Systems.* ISO Genève. www.iso.ch

[ISO/IEC 17799]   BS ISO/IEC 17799: 2000 (BS 7799-1: 2000): *Information Technology - Code of Practice for Information Security Management.* ISO Genève. 2000.

[ISO 7498-2]      Open Systems interconnection security architecture.

[ISO 10181-1 ... 7] *Information technology — Open Systems Interconnection — Security frameworks for open systems: Overview, Authentication framework, Access control framework, Non-repudiation framework, Confidentiality framework, Integrity framework, Security audit, and alarms framework.* Note that ISO 10181-8 remains unissued.

[ISO/IEC 9126-1]  ISO/IEC standard 9126 *Software engineering product quality — Part 1: quality model.* ISO Genève. 2001. www.iso.org/iso/en/CatalogueDetailPage.CatalogueDetail?CSNUMBER= 33441&ICS1=35&ICS2=40&ICS3.www.iso.ch/iso/en/prods-services/popstds/infor-mationsecurity.html

[ISO]             International Organization for Standardization, www.iso.org

[ISSA]            *Generally Accepted Information Security Principles.* www.issa.org/gaisp.html
                  Information Systems Security Association, www.issa.org

[ITGI BBITG]      *Board Briefing on IT Governance.* www.itgi.org. www.itgi.org/Template_ITGI.cfm?Section =ITGI&CONTENTID=6658&TEMPLATE=/ContentManagement/ContentDisplay.cfm

[ITGI COBIT]      *Governance, Control, and Audit for Information, and Related Technology.* Information Technology Governance Institute. www.isaca.org/cobit.htm

[ITGI GBDEN]      *Guidance for Boards of Directors, and Executive Management.* 2001. www.itgi.org. www.itgi.org/template_ITGI.cfm?Section=Recent_Publications&Template=/ TaggedPage/TaggedPageDisplay.cfm&TPLID=43&ContentID=657

[LISI]            Levels of Information Systems Interoperability, C4ISR Architectures Working Group, 30 March 1998, available at: US DoD, OSD (C3I), CIO, Director for Architecture and Interoperability Website: www.c3i.osd.mil/org/cio/i3/

[NACD]            *Information Security Oversight: Essential Board Practices.* www.nacdonline.org/pub-lications/pubDetails.asp?pubID=138&user=1B8BBA1982AA45348559A2C66 A2BA20A
                  National Association of Corporate Directors, www.nacdonline.org

[NC3TA]           NATO Allied Data Publication 34 (ADatP-34): "NATO C3 Technical Architecture (NC3TA), Version 4.0", March 2003; obtainable via the NATO standard website: www.nato.int/docu/standard.htm

[NCSA]            National Cyber Security Alliance, www.staysafeonline.info

[NERC]            *Interim Security Guidelines: Standard 1200 — Cyber Security.* ftp://ftp.nerc.com/pub/ sys/all_updl/standards/Urgent-Req-CyberStnd-3- 3121.pdf
                  North American Electric Reliability Council www.nerc.com

[NIST GAPP]       *Generally Accepted Principles and Practices.* csrc.nist.gov/publications/nistpubs/index. html

[NIST 800-12]     *The Computer Security Handbook.* 1995. csrc.nist.gov/publications/nistpubs/index.html

[NIST 800-14]     *Generally Accepted Principles and Practices for Securing IT Systems.* 1996. csrc.nist.gov/ publications/nistpubs/index.html

[NIST 800-18]     *Guide for Developing Security Plans for Information Technology Systems.* December 1998. csrc.nist.gov/publications/nistpubs/index.html

[NIST 800-27]     *Engineering Principles for IT Security.* csrc.nist.gov/publications/nistpubs/index.html

[NIST 800-30]     *Risk Management Guide for Information Technology Systems.* csrc.nist.gov/publica-tions/nistpubs/index.html

| | |
|---|---|
| [NIST 800-37] | *Guide for The Security Certification and Accreditation of Federal Information Systems.* csrc.nist.gov/publications/nistpubs/index.html |
| [NIST 800-50] | *Building an Information Technology Security Awareness and Training Program.* csrc.nist. gov/publications/nistpubs/index.html |
| [NIST 800-53] | *Recommended Security Controls for Federal Info Systems* (draft). csrc.nist.gov/publications/nistpubs/index.html |
| [NIST 800-55] | *Security Metrics Guide for Information Technology Systems.* csrc.nist.gov/publications/nistpubs/index.html |
| [NIST 800-60] | *Guide for Mapping Types of Information and Information Systems to Security Categories, Volumes 1 & 2.* csrc.nist.gov/publications/nistpubs/index.html |
| [NIST AISPA] | *Automated Information Security Program Review Areas;* csrc.nist.gov/cseat/index.html |
| [NIST CG] | *NIST Configuration Guides.* csrc.nist.gov/pcig/cig.html |
| [NIST] | National Institute for Standards and Technology, www.nist.gov |
| [NSA CG] | *NSA Configuration Guides.* www.nsa.gov/snac |
| [NSA SNAC] | *The 60 Minute Network Security Guide.* www.nsa.gov/snac/support/download.htm National Security Agency, www.nsa.gov |
| [OCTAVE^SM^] | *Operationally Critical Threat, Asset and Vulnerability Evaluation^SM^.* A framework for identifying and managing information security risks which defines a method to enable an organization to identify the information assets that are important to the mission of the organization, the threats to those assets, and the vulnerabilities that may expose those assets to the threats. By putting together the information assets, threats, and vulnerabilities, the organization can begin to understand what information is at risk. With this understanding, the organization can design and implement a protection strategy to reduce the overall risk exposure of its information assets. www.sei.cmu.edu/publications/documents/99.reports/99tr017/99tr017abstract.html |
| [OECD] | *Guidelines for the Security of Information Systems and Networks.* www.oecd.org/document/42/0, 2340, en_2649_33703_15582250_1_1_1_1,00.html Organization for Economic Cooperation and Development, www.occd.org |
| [PCAOB] | Public Company Accounting Oversight Board. www.pcaobus.org |
| [PIPEDA] | *Personal Information Protection and Electronic Documents Act.* Canada. www.pipeda.org |
| [SANS] | *SANS Step-by Step Guides* store.sans.org Systems Administration, Audit, and Network Security Institute, A leader in information security research, certification and education.www.sans.org |
| [SEI] | Carnegie Mellon University Software Engineering Institute, www.sei.cmu.edu |
| [SNAC] | Systems and Network Attack Center, www.nsa.gov/snac |
| [SOX] | *Sarbanes-Oxley Act.* frwebgate.access.gpo.gov/cgi-bin/getdoc.cgi?dbname=107_cong_public_laws&docid=f: publ204.107.pdf |
| [SSE-CCM] | *SSE-CCM: Model Description Document,* V 2.0 April 1. 1999. www.sse-cmm.org/ |
| [TCSEC] | DoD 5200.28-STD. *Department of Defense Trusted Computer System Evaluation Criteria.* www.radium.ncsc.mil/tpep/library/rainbow/5200.28-STD.html csrc.nist.gov/publications/history/dod85.pdf |
| [TechNet] | *Corporate Information Security Evaluation for CEOs.* TechNet www.technet.org/cybersecurity |
| [TheIIA] | *Information Security Management and Assurance.* Three report series from IIA, NACD, CIAO, et al. www.theiia.org/esac/index.cfm?fuseaction=or&page=rciap |
| [*UML* TP] | *UML Testing Profile. Version 1.0 formal/ptc/03-08-03.* OMG. 2005. Defines a test modelling language for designing, visualizing, specifying, analyzing, constructing, and documenting the artefacts of test systems. |
| [US-CERT] | U.S. Computer Emergency Readiness Team, www.us-cert.gov |
| [US-CIB] | *Information Security Assurance for Executives.* The Business and Industry Advisory Council to the OECD. www.uscib.org/docs/information_security_biac_icc.pdf |

[US-FDA]        USFDA — U.S. Food & Drug Administration; *Title 21 Code of Federal Regulations Electronic Records; Electronic Signatures Pt1: 9 Pt 2: 11 20. FDA 21 CFR Part 11* www.fda.gov/ora/compliance_ref/part11

[VISA]          *VISA Cardholder Information Security Program.* Digital Dozen usa.visa.com/business/merchants/cisp_index.html?ep=v_sym_cisp

[WB]            *Risk Mitigation in Financial IT Transactions.* June 2002. wbln0018.worldbank.org/html/FinancialSectorWeb.nsf/(attachmentweb)/E-security-RiskMitigationInFinancial Transactionsv4/$FILE/E-security-Risk+Mitigation+In+Financial+Transactions+v+4.0.pdf

                World Bank, www.worldbank.org

[WH]            *The National Strategy to Secure Cyberspace.* www.whitehouse.gov/pcipb

[You've Been    CA SB 1386 (the *You've Been Hacked* Act). info.sen.ca.gov/pub/01-02/bill/sen/sb_1351-
Hacked]         1400/sb_1386_bill_20020926_chaptered.html

# Glossary

## Abbreviations Used

**ACM** — Association for Computing Machinery

**ACS** — Access Control Server

**AICPA** — American Institute of Certified Public Accountants

**AICPA SGP** — AICPA Standard of Good Practice

**AICPA TSC** — AICPA Trust Services Criteria

**AMC** — Average Method Complexity

**ANSI** — American National Standards Institute

**API** — Application Programming Interface

**AQAP** — Allied Quality Assurance Publication

**ARS** — Automated Reasoning Systems

**asap** — As Soon As Possible

**ASBDC-US** — Association of Small Business Development Centers

**ASL** — Action Specification Language

**ASP** — Active Server Pages

**ATP** — Acceptance Test Procedure

**BIS** — Bank for International Settlements

**BITS** — BITS Framework: Managing Technology Risk for Information Technology Service Provider Relationships

**BNF** — Backus–Naur Form

**BOGSAT** — Bunch of Guys Sitting Around a Table

**BPM** — Business Performance Measure

**BS** — British Standard

**BSA** — (1) British Standards Institute; (2) Business Software Alliance

**CACM** — Communications of the Association for Computing Machinery

**CASE** — Computer-Aided Software Engineering

**CBO** — Coupling Between Object Classes

**CCM** — CORBA Component Model

**CERT** — Computer Emergency Response Team

**CFC** — Central Flow Control[1]

**CGF** — Corporate Governance Framework

**CGI** — Common Gateway Interface

**CIAO** — Critical Infrastructure Assurance Office

**CIS** — Center for Internet Security

**COBIT** — Control Objectives for Information and Related Technologies

**COCOMO** — Constructive Cost Model

**CORBA** — Common Object Request Broker Architecture

**COSO** — Committee on Sponsoring Organizations

**COTS** — Commercial Off-The-Shelf

**CSE** — Communications Security Establishment

---

[1] A U.S. air traffic control program.

**CWM** — Common Warehouse Metamodel
**DACC** — Design Assertion Consistency Checker
**DCL** — DEC Control Language
**DEF STAN** — Defense Standard
**DFD** — Dataflow Diagram
**DHS** — (U.S.) Department of Homeland Security
**DIT** — Depth of Inheritance Tree
**DMP** — Deficiency Management Plan
**DMZ** — Demilitarized Zone
**DOD** — (U.S.) Department of Defense
**DOM** — Document Object Model
**DSDM** — Dynamic Systems Development Method
**DSI** — Delivered Source Instruction
**DSML** — Domain-Specific Modeling Language
**DTI** — (UK) Department of Trade and Industry
**EDEM** — Expectation-Driven Event Monitoring
**EJB** — Enterprise Java Beans
**ETA** — Event Tree Analysis
**ETSI** — European Telecom Standards Institute
**EU** — European Union
**FC** — Function Count
**FDA** — (U.S.) Food and Drug Administration
**FISMA** — (U.S.) Federal Information Security Management Act
**FMECA** — Failure Mode Effects and Criticality Analysis
**FP** — Function Point
**FSM** — Finite State Machine
**FSR** — Financial Services Roundtable
**FTA** — Fault Tree Analysis
**FTC** — (U.S.) Federal Trade Commission
**GAISPC** — Generally Accepted Information Security Principles Committee
**GAPP** — Generally Accepted Principles and Practices
**GASSP** — Generally Accepted System Security Principles
**GIGO** — Garbage In, Garbage Out
**GUI** — Graphical User Interface
**HIPAA** — Health Information Portability and Accountability Act
**HTML** — Hypertext Markup Language
**HTTP** — Hypertext Transfer Protocol
**IAIP** — Information Assurance and Infrastructure Protection (Directorate of the DHS)
**ICAEW** — Institute of Chartered Accountants in England & Wales
**ICE** — In-Circuit Emulator
**IDEF** — Military equivalent of SADT
**IDL** — Interface Description Language
**IEEE** — Institute of Electrical and Electronics Engineers
**IIA** — The Institute of Internal Auditors
**IIOP** — Internet Inter ORB Protocol
**IP** — (1) Intellectual Property; (2) Internet Protocol
**ISACA** — The Information Systems Audit and Control Association
**ISAPI** — Internet Server Application Programming Interface
**ISF** — Information Security Forum
**ISG** — Information Security Governance
**ISO** — International Organization for Standards

**ISSA** — Information Systems Security Association
**ITCG** — Information Technology: Control Guidelines 1998
**ITGIG** — IT Governance Implementation Guide
**ITT** — Initial Training Time
**ITT** — Invitation To Tender
**J2EE** — Java 2 Platform, Enterprise Edition
**KDSI** — 1000 DSIs
**KLOC** — 1000 lines of (executable) code
**KPQM** — Key Performance Quality Measure (aka BPM)
**LCSAJ** — Linear Code Sequence and Jump
**LDRA** — Liverpool Data Research Associates
**LISI** — Levels of Information Systems Interoperability
**MDA** — Model-Driven Architecture
**MDD** — Model-Driven Development
**MOD** — (UK) Ministry of Defence
**MOF** — (In *UML*) Meta-Object Facility
**MPI** — Merchant server Plug-In
**MTBF** — Mean Time Between Failure
**MTTF** — Mean Time To Fail
**MTTR** — Mean Time To Repair
**NCSA** — National Cyber Security Alliance
**NCSS** — Non-Commented Source Statements
**NIST** — National Institute for Standards and Technology
**NOC** — Number of Children
**NSAPI** — Netscape Server Application Programming Interface
**OCT** — Operationally Critical Threat
**OMG** — Object Management Group
**OMT** — Object Modeling Technique
**PCA** — Performance and Coverage Analyzer
**PCAOB** — Public Company Accounting Oversight Board
**PCS** — Partnering for Cyber Security
**PIM** — Platform-Independent Model
**PIPEDA** — Personal Information Protection and Electronic Documents Act
**POF** — Probability of Failure
**PSI** — Platform-Specific Implementation
**QMS** — Quality Management System
**QoS** — Quality of Service
**RAD** — Rapid Application Development
**RFC** — Request for Change
**RFC** — Response for a Class
**RFP** — Request for Proposal
**RMI** — Remote Method Invocation
**ROI** — Return on Investment
**RSS** — Rich Site Summary
**SADT** — Systems Analysis and Design Technique
**SC** — Security Checklist
**SCA** — Source Code Analyzer
**SCR** — Software Change Request
**SDK** — Software Development Kit
**SEI** — (Carnegie Mellon University) Software Engineering Institute
**SME** — Subject Matter Expert

**SNAC** — Systems and Network Attack Center
**SOAP** — Simple Object Access Protocol
**SOX** — Sarbanes–Oxley Act
**SPEC** — Standard Performance Evaluation Corporation
**STT** — Subsequent Training Time
**SUT** — System Under Test
**TCB** — Trusted Computing Base
**TOE** — Target of Evaluation
**TTCN** — Testing and Test Control Notation
**TTCN-3** — Testing and Test Control Notation (3rd edition)
**UDDI** — Universal Description, Discovery and Integration
*UML* **TP** — *UML* Testing Profile
*UML* — Universal Modeling Language
**URI** — Uniform Resource Identifier
**URL** — Uniform Resource Locator
**UTC** — Usability-Test Candidate
**UTCS** — UTC Score
**VAF** — Value Adjustment Factor
**VEE** — Virtual Execution Environment
**WMC** — Weighted Methods per Class
**WSDL** — Web Services Description Language
**XMI** — XML Metadata Interchange
**XML** — eXtensible Markup Language
**XP** — eXtreme Programming

## Terms Used

# Story

G etting the names right matters. There was once a launch of two satellites held one above the other on the launch vehicle. One was called the "top" satellite and one the "bottom." Unfortunately one was also called the "first" satellite (because it was the first to be loaded on the rocket) and the other was called the "second."

The in-orbit launch failed. Guess why.

| Term | Explanation (italicized text refers to terms explained in this section) |
| --- | --- |
| 3rd-line support call | A call made by a support group within an organization as a result of a *customer problem*, to the test group in an effort to determine if the *customer's problem* is known, or represents a new *bug*. The call may also be made direct to a development group, and the test group only advised once a fix for the *problem* is determined upon and needs *testing*. |
| acceptance criteria | The criteria a software product must meet successfully to complete a *test phase* or meet *delivery requirements*. (ANSI/IEEE-729) |
| acceptance test | A test conducted to determine whether or not a system satisfies its *acceptance criteria* and thus to enable the *customer* to determine whether or not to accept the system. (ANSI/IEEE-729) |

| Term | Explanation (italicized text refers to terms explained in this section) |
|---|---|
| acceptance test procedure | The procedure to be adopted for the running of an *acceptance test*. Normally documented in an *acceptance test plan*. |
| acceptance test process | *Formal testing* conducted to determine whether a system satisfies its *acceptance criteria* and to enable the *customer* to determine whether or not to accept the system. See also *qualification testing, system testing*. (ANSI/IEEE-729) Sometimes misused by agile programming adherents to mean *system testing*. |
| access control server | (In *credit-card authentication*) A component in the *issuer domain*, which verifies whether authentication is available for a card number and authenticates *transactions*. |
| accuracy | A *quality* of that which is free of *error*. (ISO) A qualitative assessment of freedom from *error*, a high assessment corresponding to a small *error*. (*ISO*) A quantitative measure of the magnitude of *error*, preferably expressed as a function of the relative *error*, a high value of this measure corresponding to a small *error*. (ISO) A quantitative assessment of freedom from *error*. Contrast with *precision*. (ANSI/IEEE-729) |
| acquirer | The business wanting to let its *customers* use their credit cards to buy the *acquirer's* goods or services. |
| acquirer domain | (In *credit-card authentication*) Contains the systems and functions of the *acquirer* and its *customers*, such as *merchants*. |
| Action Specification Language | (In *UML*). An implementation-independent language for specifying the processing of the methods and state actions of object models. |
| active server pages | Allows dynamic creation of HTML pages by a Web server for return to a browser. Originally a Microsoft-only product, but now supported on other, non-Windows platforms. Compare with *common gateway interface* and *Java server pages*. |
| actor | (In use cases). Any user or other autonomous object which interacts with the system being modeled; can thus be another system. |
| ad click | See *click through*. |
| algorithm | • A finite set of well-defined rules for the solution of a *problem* in a finite number of steps; for example, a complete specification of a sequence of arithmetic operations for evaluating the sine of $x$ to a given *precision*. (ISO) <br> • A finite set of well-defined rules that give a sequence of operations for performing a task. (ANSI/IEEE-729) |
| algorithm analysis | The examination of an *algorithm* to determine its *correctness* with respect to its intended use, to determine its operational characteristics or to understand it more fully in order to modify, simplify or improve it. (ANSI/IEEE-729) |
| alpha release | Any version of the software which has not passed *system testing*. This may include partial *releases*. |
| anomaly | Some corruption of a program's internal state through data or code changes. Such changes may be accidental (*faults*) or deliberate *fault injection*. [Voas] |
| Apache Server Application Programming Interface | *Application Programming Interface* or *Protocol*, allowing Apache servers to *interface* with Web-based applications. |
| aperiodic bug | A *transient bug* that becomes active periodically (sometimes referred to as an intermittent *bug*). Because of their short duration, transient *faults* are often detected through the *anomalies* that result from their propagation. |
| Application Programming Interface | • A set of routines, *protocols* and tools for building software applications. An API provides some or all of the building blocks with which to develop a program. A programmer assembles the blocks. <br> • Most operating environments, such as MS-Windows, provide an API for programmers to write applications consistent with them. APIs are supposed to guarantee that all programs using a common API will have similar *interfaces*. When true, this makes it easier for users to learn new programs. |

| Term | Explanation (italicized text refers to terms explained in this section) |
|---|---|
| arbiter | • (In *UML*). A property of a *test case* or a *test suite* used to evaluate test results and to assign the overall *verdict* of a *test case* or *test suite* respectively. There is a *default* arbitration *algorithm* based on functional, *conformance testing*, which generates Pass, Fail, Inconclusive, or Error as a *verdict*. The arbitration *algorithm* can be user-defined. See also *test expected result*. A better word would be "criterion."<br>• One who is chosen by the parties in a dispute to decide the difference between them. (OED) |
| assertion | A logical expression. In software, the specifying of a *program state* that must exist or a set of conditions that program variables must satisfy at a particular point during program execution; for example, *A is positive and A is greater than B*. See also *input assertion, output assertion*. (ANSI/IEEE-729) |
| asset specificity | The state of a productive asset of being limited to a single use. If this asset (such as a client-specific software system) is costly, much effort will be made to reuse it. |
| assure (quality) | To provide confidence that specified *requirements* will be or have been, met. *Note:* In AQAPs and STANAGs, the term *assure* is used specifically for purchaser's activities. (AQAP-15) |
| asymmetric information | A contractual state in which access to information by one party (or parties) to a *transaction* is better than access by another party. This can be used as a source of power in determining the outcome of the *transaction*. A common example is where the seller of a good knows much more about the characteristics of that good than the buyer. |
| attractiveness | (In *human factors*). An attribute of *usability* which defines how pleasant (or otherwise) the system is to use. |
| automated test generator | A *software tool* that accepts as input a computer program and test criteria, generates test input data that meet these criteria, and sometimes determines the expected results. (ANSI/IEEE-729) |
| automated verification system | A *software tool* that accepts as input a computer program and a representation of its specification and produces, possibly with human help, a *correctness proof* or disproof of the program. See also *automated verification tools*. (ANSI/IEEE-729) |
| automated verification tools | A class of *software tools* used to evaluate products of the software development process. These tools aid in the *verification* of such characteristics as *correctness, completeness, consistency, traceability, testability* and adherence to standards. Examples include *design analyzers*, *automated verification systems*, *static analyzers*, dynamic analyzers and standards enforcers. (ANSI/IEEE-729) |
| availability | • The probability that software will be able to perform its designated system function when required for use. (ANSI/IEEE-729)<br>• The ratio of system up-time to total operating time. (ANSI/IEEE-729)<br>• The *availability* of an item to perform its designated function when required for use. (ANSI/ASQC A3-1978)<br>• May be expressed in terms of a probability *A (t)* of the system being available at time *t*. Compare with *reliability*.<br>• *Availability* is usually measured in terms of the long-run fraction of time that a system is working. |
| availability model | A model used for predicting, estimating, or assessing *availability*. (ANSI/IEEE-729) |
| average method complexity | Object-oriented *metric*: greater method *complexity* is likely to:<br>1. Be more difficult to maintain<br>2. Reduce application comprehensibility<br>3. Reduce application *reliability*<br>4. Be more difficult to test |
| backsourcing | The process whereby a client reasserts control of an outsourced project. Aka *on-shoring*. |
| Backus–Naur form | A meta-language used formally to describe the syntax of a language devised by John Backus and Peter Naur. |

| Term | Explanation (italicized text refers to terms explained in this section) |
|---|---|
| baseline | • A specification or product that has been formally *reviewed* and agreed upon, which thereafter serves as the basis for further development and can be changed only through formal change control procedures. (ANSI/IEEE-729)<br>• A configuration identification document or a set of such documents formally designated and fixed at a time during a configuration item's life cycle. *Baselines*, plus approved changes from those *baselines*, constitute the current configuration identification. For configuration management there are three *baselines*, as follows:<br>  1. Functional *baseline*. The initial approved functional configuration. (ANSI/IEEE-729)<br>  2. Allocated *baseline*. The initial approved allocated configuration (ANSI/IEEE-729)<br>  3. *Product baseline*. The initial approved or conditionally approved product configuration identification. (DoD-STD 480A) |
| baselined requirement | A *requirement* expressed in a document under configuration management. Others may exist in *customers'* heads, the backs of envelopes and similarly unstable places. |
| basic block | A maximal *sequence* of one or more consecutive, executable statements in a source code program such that the *sequence* has only one entry point (the first statement executed), one exit point (the last statement executed) and no internal branches. |
| basic event | (In *fault tree analysis*). One of a set of *events* which, if it occurs, will provoke a *top event*. The set may have one or more members. |
| bebugging | See *bug seeding* or *fault injection*. |
| Bell–La Padula model | A formal state transition model (aka a *state diagram*) of computer *security policy* that describes a set of access control rules. In this formal model, the entities in a computer system are divided into abstract sets of subjects and objects. The notion of a secure state is defined and it is proven that each state transition preserves *security* by moving from secure state to secure state, thereby inductively proving that the system is secure.<br>A system state is defined to be "secure" if the only permitted access modes of subjects to objects are in accordance with a *security policy*. In order to determine whether an access mode is allowed, the clearance of a subject is compared to the classification of the object and a determination is made as to whether the subject is authorized for the access mode. [*CompSecGloss*] |
| beta release | The first version of the software that has passed *system testing* in a special-purpose test environment. The software may not be suitable for general use until it has undergone a *beta test*. |
| beta test | A set of tests executed by persons within organizations which either use earlier versions of the software or who are typical of those who will. The tests may be provided by the organization creating the software, the user, the user's organization, or any permutation of the three.<br>The purpose of a *beta test* is to test the software in circumstances as close to *live* operational use as possible. |
| black-box testing | Black-box or *functional testing* means *testing* software without using any knowledge of its design or construction. The software functions are tested against its specification. (*Testing* done using knowledge of the construction is known as white-box or *structural testing*.) |
| boundary-value analysis | A technique for the selection of *test cases* and *test data* whereby the specification is analyzed to determine the boundaries of the domain of input variables across which the software's behavior should change. (MoD 00-55) |
| branch metric | The number of *units* in the system in which all the branches have been executed at least once, divided by the number of *units* in the system. (Adapted from IEEE *Computer*, page 88. July 1989) |
| breadcrumb navigation | A quick way for a user to know how the current Web page relates to the home page by showing the hierarchy of links back to the home page. |
| bridge | (In x*UML*). A class containing the bridge operations required for a single required *interface*. |
| bridgehead team | (In *outsourcing*) The people whom the supplier sends to work with *customer staff* and vice versa. |
| browsing session | A period during which *Web objects* are transferred with intervening idle periods. |

| Term | Explanation (italicized text refers to terms explained in this section) |
|---|---|
| buffer time | A period of time artificially inserted in a plan in the form of a pseudo-activity to allow for slippage. |
| bug | • A *defect* in a program. Compare with *anomaly* and *failure*. [Voas]<br>• An accidental condition that causes a functional *unit* to fail to perform its required function. (ISO)<br>• A manifestation of an *error* in software. A *bug*, if encountered, may cause a *failure*. (ANSI/IEEE-729)<br>• A software bug that can lead to *failure*. It is the result of an *error* in development. (MoD 00-55) |
| bug analysis | • The process of investigating an observed *bug* with the purpose of tracing the *fault* to its source. (ANSI/IEEE-729)<br>• The process of investigating an observed software *fault* to identify such information as the cause of the *fault*, the phase of the development process during which the *fault* was introduced, methods by which the *fault* could have been prevented or detected earlier and the method by which the *fault* was detected. (ANSI/IEEE-729)<br>• The process of investigating software *errors*, *failures* and *faults* to determine quantitative rates and trends. (From ANSI/IEEE-729) |
| bug category | One of a set of classes into which a *bug*, *fault* or *failure* might fall. Categories may be defined for the cause, *criticality*, effect, life cycle phase when introduced or detected, or other characteristics of the *bug*, *fault*, or *failure*. (ANSI/IEEE-729) |
| bug data | A term commonly (if imprecisely) used to denote information describing software *bugs*, *faults*, *failures* and changes, their characteristics and the conditions under which they are encountered or corrected. (ANSI/IEEE-729) |
| bug density | A measure of the number of *bugs* or *defects* per 1000 lines of executable code. |
| bug detection | The discovery of a *bug*. Aka *defect* detection or *defect* arrival. |
| bug model | A mathematical model used to predict or estimate the number of remaining *faults*, *reliability*, required test time, or similar characteristics of a software system. See also *bug prediction*. (ANSI/IEEE-729) |
| bug prediction | A quantitative statement about the expected number or nature of software *bugs*, *faults* or *failures* in a software system. See also *bug model*. (ANSI/IEEE-729) |
| bug recovery | See *failure recovery*. |
| bug report metric | The number of unresolved but found *bugs* in a system. (Adapted from IEEE *Computer*, page, p. 88. July 1989) |
| bug resolution | Some decision taken consequent on the discovery of a *bug*. This decision can be one of the following types:<br>• Fixing the *bug*<br>• Deferring fixing, for example until after some *release*<br>• Reclassification of the *bug* as already known<br>• Reclassification of the *bug* as several *bugs* which merely appear to be one<br>• Reclassification of the *bug* as non-existent and having been wrongly identified as a *bug* |
| bug seeding | See *fault seeding*, *fault injection* and *bebugging*. |
| build | An operational version of a software product incorporating a specified subset of the *features* that the final product will include. (ANSI/IEEE-729)<br>Some set of linked software resulting from a *build step*. |
| build definition item | (In configuration management). Defines the process by which derived items are constructed. |
| build level | Some clearly identifiable level of *feature* achieved by a *build* step. |
| build step | Some clearly identifiable moment during software *integration* when some software has been integrated and *integration* tested; aka *integration step*. |

| Term | Explanation (italicized text refers to terms explained in this section) |
|---|---|
| built-in test | Some facility for *testing* incorporated into the hardware to be tested. May be interruptible (*IBIT*) or continuous (*CBIT*). |
| built-in test equipment | The hardware containing the *BIT*. |
| bunch of guys sitting around a table technique | Approach to solving any *problem* relying more on group solidarity than ability. |
| business effect assessment | An assessment of the business impact of some change. |
| business performance measure | A measure of a system's operational *feature* as it affects the business in which the system is used. |
| business requirement | Some high-level definition of a *requirement* in language which the funding agency (aka *business*) understands, as opposed to the more-complex and detailed *functional requirement* which it will usually give rise to. |
| business rule | A *business rule* is a statement that defines or constrains some aspects of a business. |
| callgraph | Graphic representation of a number of procedures whose *nodes* represent procedures and its edges represent which procedures can call which others. |
| cannot-happen effect | (In executable *UML*). Some system (mis)behavior for which no recovery action has been designed. Should at least provoke an entry in the system log. |
| capability | A system's human-evident behavior as specified in a *requirements specification*. Aka *feature*. |
| capacity | (Of a system). The *rate* at which data may be passed to or through the system over time. |
| case study | (In usability testing). The results of a *usability* exercise designed to show the feasibility of some approach. May involve a prototype in (literally) cardboard or software form. Alternatively a *case study* may demonstrate the value of a complete redesign of some *interface* based on the cost of support and lost *customers*. Will normally address many of the issues raised in a strategy document. |
| certificate | Piece of paper containing some verifiable *assertion* and a (number of) signature(s) of (a) person(s) supposedly capable of verifying that that *assertion* be true, such that the piece of paper can be accepted in some court of law as evidence either that the *assertion* was true or that it was reasonable for a person to believe it was true. A *certificate* may be issued in the name of some body, in which case the person(s) whose name(s) appear(s) on the *certificate* are assumed to be officers of that body. |
| certification | • A sequential procedure for continuously projecting software MTTF from recorded interfail data. [*Dyer*]<br>• A process, which may be incremental, by which a *contractor* provides *objective evidence* to the contracting agency that an item satisfies its specified *requirements*. (2167A)<br>• A written guarantee that a system or computer program complies with its specified *requirements*. (ANSI/IEEE 729)<br>• A written authorization that states that a computer system is secure and is permitted to operate in a defined environment with or producing sensitive information. (ANSI/IEEE 729)<br>• The formal demonstration of system acceptability to obtain authorization for its operational use. (ANSI/IEEE 729)<br>• The process of confirming that a system, software sub-system, or computer program is capable of satisfying its specified *requirements* in an operational environment. *Certification* usually takes place in the field under actual conditions and is used to evaluate not only the software itself, but also the specifications to which the software was constructed. *Certification* extends the process of *verification* and *validation* to an actual or simulated operation environment. (ANSI/IEEE 729)<br>• The procedure and action by a duly authorized body of determining, verifying and attesting in writing to the *qualification*s of personnel, processes, procedures, or items in accordance with applicable *requirements*. (ANSI/ASQC A3-1978) |
| change control board | Project-level group of stakeholders which authorizes changes to a system. |
| classification society | Body authorized to certify an organization to some standard such as ISO 9000. |

| Term | Explanation (italicized text refers to terms explained in this section) |
|---|---|
| click out | User behavior on a website indicating that they have left the site. Can be the basis of a *bug report*: it can mean either something doesn't work or they're fed up. |
| click past | User behavior on a website indicating they have accepted some page by clicking either "*OK*" or (in the case of a pop-up) "*Cancel*." |
| click rate | A measure of the amount of times a Web icon is clicked versus the amount of times it's viewed. |
| click-through | The process of a visitor clicking on a web icon (possibly an advertisement) and going to the related website.<br>Also called *ad clicks* or requests. |
| client-side script | A *script* which is executed on the browser. Compare with *server-side script*. |
| closed bug | A *bug* which has been fixed. Compare with *open bug*. |
| code audit | An independent *review* of source code by a person, team, or tool to verify *compliance* with software design documentation and programming standards. *Correctness* and efficiency may also be evaluated. See also audit, *static analysis*, *inspection* and *walk-through*. (ANSI/IEEE-729) |
| code turmoil | The percentage of a system's code which has changed over some period of time. |
| coding rule | (In *UML*). The *interfaces* of a SUT use notation, such as XML, which have to be respected by the test systems. Hence, *coding rule*s are part of a *test specification*. (Aka notation) |
| cognitive dissonance | The discomfort felt on discovering a discrepancy between what you already know or believe and new information or interpretation. |
| cohesion | The degree to which the tasks performed by a single program module (*unit*) are functionally related. Contrast with *coupling*. (ANSI/IEEE-729) |
| commercial off-the-shelf | Software which can be obtained in readily usable form from a commercial distributor. Will normally have an API to allow programmers to interface with it. |
| common cause | An *event* that affects more than one *component* or subsystem such that more than one *failure* occurs. |
| common gateway interface | A *protocol*, supported by *scripts* in several languages, which allows a web server to exchange data with another application possibly residing on another server. Compare with *active server pages* and *Java server pages*. |
| common mode failure | Where separate or redundant processes fail because of some *event* which affects them all. (MoD 00-55) |
| common object request broker architecture | An OMG-distributed computing platform specification that is independent of implementation languages. |
| common warehouse metamodel | An OMG specification for data repository *integration*. |
| communications commonality | The extent to which some system uses standard or common communication *protocols* and *interfaces*. |
| communicative-ness | The extent to which a system provides useful outputs and a friendly *interface* with the user. |
| company "jolly" | A trip, meal, or other non-work-related diversion typically outside office hours, wholly or partly paid for by the company. |
| comparator | A *software tool* used to compare two computer programs, files, or sets of data to identify commonalities or differences. Typical objects of comparison are similar versions of source code, object code, database files, or test results. (ANSI/IEEE-729). A typical example is the grep facility in UNIX™. |
| compatibility | The ability of two or more systems to exchange information. Compare with *interoperability*. (ANSI/IEEE-729) |

| Term | Explanation (italicized text refers to terms explained in this section) |
| --- | --- |
| completeness | Attribute frequently claimed of some specification's ability to define a system, which cannot logically be achieved since a "complete" specification would have all the characteristics of the completed system itself. A better term would be "sufficient" (for the use of all the stakeholders using that specification). (PF-V) |
| complexity | The degree of complication of a system or system *component* determined by such factors as the number and intricacy of *interfaces*, the number and intricacy of conditional branches, the degree of nesting, the types of data structures and other system characteristics. (ANSI/IEEE-729) See also *cyclomatic complexity*. |
| compliance | The fulfillment by a *quality system*/procedures of specified *requirements*. (AQAP-15) |
| component | • (In the ADA language system). A *component* is a value that is a part of a larger value or an object that is part of a larger object. (ANSI/MIL-STD-1815A)<br>• A collection of related *units*.<br>• A basic part of a system or program. (ANSI/IEEE-729) |
| component test | A test of a component. This is often to see that the component *interfaces* with the other components and that its *performance* is acceptable. This will usually occur without a user *interface*. |
| compression factor | (In testing). The ratio of equivalent operating time to testing time or the amount to which the test is believed to exercise the software compared with the way the software is believed will be exercised by a real user. |
| computer software component | A functionally or logically distinct part of a CSCI. Computer *components* may be top-level or lower-level. (ANSI/IEEE-729, DOD-STD-2167A) |
| computer-aided software engineering | An environment for software development which should provide tool support for at least two primary software development phases (*requirement*, design, coding *unit*, and *system testing*) and minimize or eliminate data loss between phases. |
| conceptual integrity | A characteristic of a system that is based on an overriding theme. |
| concession | A document which when authorized by a design and development facility, allows a manufacturing facility to deviate from some design. See also *waiver*. |
| confidence interval | A definition of the degree of confidence of some estimate of probability. A 95% confidence estimate implies that if some test were taken 60,000 times with a probability of (say) 0.45 + 0.004, the results would be within that probability range 95% of the time (0.454062019 => results >= 0.449983417). It is thus a measure of the stability of the estimate. |
| confidence test | A test which is the second to be run on a *build* after a *smoke test*, to determine if the *build* has minimally all the *features* expected and that the test team can have enough confidence to test it. |
| configuration audit | The process of verifying that all required configuration items have been produced, that the current version agrees with specified *requirements*, that the technical documentation completely and accurately describes the configuration items and that all change requests have been resolved. (ANSI/IEEE-729) |
| Configuration Manager | Person in charge of managing the configurations and *releases* of all software and hardware. He may be the same as the *project librarian*. |
| conformance | The fulfillment by a product or service of specified *requirements*. (AQAP-15) |
| connection | • A reference in one part of a program to the identifier of another part (that is, something found elsewhere). See also *interface*. (ANSI/IEEE-729)<br>• An association established between functional *units* for conveying information. (ISO) |
| connectivity | (In interoperability). A measure of the number of *messages* sent by all participating *units* in a network and the number of *messages* received by a network or a data link. |
| consequence | (Sometimes known as the hazard *consequence*). The cost of a *failure* (caused by a *bug*). |

| Term | Explanation (italicized text refers to terms explained in this section) |
|------|--------------------------------------------------------------------------|
| consistency | The extent to which:<br>• The output of some process is consistent with its input. Thus the high-level design process uses the *requirements specification* as input and produces the high-level design document as output. The high-level design must be consistent with the *requirements specification*.<br>• Some document is consistent with or does not contradict itself. Thus if some specification contains some *assertion* on page 5, it should not contradict it on page 505.<br>Inconsistency is a very common *fault* of specifications and a rich source of *bugs*. |
| Constructive Cost Model | A method of evaluating and/or estimating the cost of software development. There are three levels:<br>• **Basic**: Estimates software development effort and cost as a function of program size expressed in estimated DSIs. There are three modes within Basic:<br>  – *Organic:* Projects are typically uncomplicated and involve small, experienced teams. The planned software is not considered novel and is expected to be < 50 KDSIs.<br>  – *Semidetached:* Projects are typically more complicated than in *Organic* mode, and involve teams of people with mixed levels of experience. The software < 300 KDSIs. The project has characteristics of both projects in Organic and Embedded modes.<br>  – *Embedded*: Projects (often *safety*-critical and anyway regulation-constrained) must satisfy a well-written set of *requirements* for code to be burned on a ROM or otherwise built for a special-to-type chip.<br>• **Intermediate**: An extension of the Basic model that estimates effort from a set of "cost drivers" that will determine the effort and duration of the project.<br>• **Detailed**: An extension of the Intermediate model that adds effort multipliers to each phase of the project to determine each cost *driver's* effect on each step.<br>See [*Boehm 89*]. |
| continuous built-in test | A BIT that is continuously executed on some *unit* while that *unit* is switched on and which cannot be interrupted without switching the *unit* off. |
| contract | The individual *contract* which a development organization obtains to perform any given piece of work. |
| contract data requirement list | The list of those documents required to ensure payment of a *contract*. |
| contractor | One who enters into a *contract* to supply a product or provide a service. *Note:* This term is preferred to the terms *supplier, vendor* and *manufacturer,* which are sometimes used in this sense. (AQAP-15) |
| conversion | See *cutover*. |
| coordination | (In *UML*). Concurrent (and potentially distributed) *test components* have to be coordinated both functionally and in time in order to *assure* deterministic and repeatable test executions resulting in well-defined test *verdicts*. *Coordination* is done explicitly with normal *message* exchange between *components* or implicitly with general ordering mechanisms. |
| CORBA component model | An OMG specification of an implementation-language-independent distributed-*component* model. |
| corrective action | Action taken to correct any condition and the cause that adversely affects *quality*. (AQAP-15) |
| corrective maintenance | *Maintenance* performed specifically to overcome existing *faults*. (ISO) See also *software maintenance*. (ANSI/IEEE-729) |
| correctness | The extent to which software<br>• Is free from design *bugs* and from coding *bugs*; that is, *fault* free (ANSI/IEEE-729)<br>• Meets its specified requirements (ANSI/IEEE-729)<br>• Meets user expectations (ANSI/IEEE-729) |
| correctness proof | See *proof of correctness*. |

| Term | Explanation (italicized text refers to terms explained in this section) |
|---|---|
| coupling | A measure of the interdependence among modules (*units*) in a computer program. Contrast with *cohesion*. (ANSI/IEEE-729). There are many kinds of coupling:<br>• *Call coupling:* Unit X calls unit Y without passing any parameters, without sharing any common variable references or references to any external media.<br>• *Parameter coupling:* X calls Y passing some data items as parameters.<br>• *Shared data coupling:* X calls Y and both refer to the same data object globally or non-locally.<br>• *External device coupling:* X calls Y and both access the same external medium (e.g., a sensor, a file or an actuator). |
| coupling between object classes | Object-oriented *metric* defined as the count of the classes to which this class is coupled. (Class) *coupling* means two classes are coupled when methods declared in one class use methods or instance variables of the other class. [Chidamber 2]. The greater the *coupling*, (1) the worse the design and possibility of reuse since more dependent; (2) the higher the sensitivity to changes in other parts of the design and therefore the more difficult the *maintenance*; and (3) the more rigorous the *testing* needed. |
| coverage criteria | A series of criteria which define the degree to which *test cases* exercise (or cover) the logic of a program as expressed in the *unit* specification or the source code. The weakest such criterion is that every statement be exercised at least once, while more stringent criteria are concerned with branch coverage, condition coverage, etc. |
| critical design review | Determines whether the detailed software designs as defined by the software design description satisfy the *requirements* in the software *requirements specification*. (ANSI/IEEE-729) |
| critical piece first | Pertaining to an approach to software development that focuses on implementing the most critical aspects of a software system first. The critical piece may be defined in terms of services provided, degree of *risk*, difficulty, or some other criterion. (ANSI/IEEE-729) |
| critical section | A segment of code to be executed mutually exclusively with some other segment of code that is also called a critical section. Segments of code are required to be executed mutually exclusively if they make competing uses of a computer resource or data item. (ANSI/IEEE-729) |
| criticality | A classification of a software *error* or *fault* based upon an *evaluation* of the degree of effect of that *error* or *fault* on the development or operation of a system (often used to determine whether or when a *fault* will be corrected). (ANSI/IEEE-729) |
| cultural discontinuity | That unhappy state wherein two groups of people fail to share norms and values. In the context of *off-shoring*, it usually means that each group has a different set of expectations of roles, processes, common language, relations, hierarchy, and/or ethics. |
| customer | The person or body for whom the software is being developed. Usually the person who pays for the software, but in the event that the software is being developed only for use within the developing organization, a pseudo-*customer* may be appointed to provide a *customer interface* for the *developers*. |
| customer staff | The people who will end up using the system. |
| customer visit report | (In usability testing). A report on the outcomes of visit by *developers* and *usability* staff to the premises of a *customer* for the purpose of assessing the use of some system. |
| cut set | (In *Fault Tree Analysis*). A minimum set of *basic events*, together with the associated Boolean logic (but without any intermediate (or pseudo-) *events*) sufficient to cause a *top event*. |
| cutover | The process by which an old system is turned off and the new one turned on. There are three types:<br>• **Direct cutover:** The new system immediately replaces the old system.<br>• **Parallel cutover:** Both the old and new systems are operated for a few months or until it is clear that there are no bugs in the new system.<br>• **Phased cutover:** The new system is installed in one part of the organization on trial and thereafter installed in other parts. |
| cyclomatic complexity | A measure of the *complexity* of code in some *unit*. |
| dataflow diagram | A notational construct symbolizing a process which consists of inputs, outputs, stores and processes. Each process can be decomposed. |

| Term | Explanation (italicized text refers to terms explained in this section) |
|------|-----------------------------------------------------------------------|
| data latency | The time elapsed between some event (such as transmission of data) and data being received by the user. This time is conventionally divided between<br>• Time of event to time of *observation*<br>• Time of *observation* to time of completion of processing<br>• Time of completion of processing to time of receipt by the user |
| data partition | (In *UML*). A logical value for a parameter used in a *stimulus* or in an *observation*. It typically defines an equivalence class of values (e.g., valid user names.) |
| data pool | (In *UML*). A collection of values used by *test components* as a source of values for the execution of *test cases*. *Data pools* can be represented by *utility parts* or be logically described by constraints. |
| data problem | (DA). *Bug* class indicating that some data item or type is either missing, extra, or not as specified. |
| data space | (In *fault injection*). The set of all possible *data states* of a point in the code. [Voas] |
| data state | (In *fault injection*). See *program state*. |
| debugging | The process of locating, analyzing and correcting suspected *faults*. Compare with *testing*. (ANSI/IEEE-729) |
| debugging model | See *bug model*. |
| decision point metric | The number of modules (*units*) in the system in which all the decision points have been exercised at least once divided by the number of modules (*units*) in the system. (Adapted from *IEEE Computer*, page 88. July 1989) |
| decision table | A table of all contingencies that are to be considered in the description of a *problem* together with the actions to be taken for each set of contingencies. (ISO)<br>A presentation in either matrix or tabular form of a set of conditions and their corresponding actions. (ANSI) |
| default | (In *UML*). A behavior triggered by a test *observation* that is not handled by the behavior of the *test case* per se. *Defaults* are executed by *test components*. |
| default notice | Advice given by a development organization to a *customer* or vice versa that the other is in *default* of some *contract*ual obligation. An action which should be taken as the last step before court proceedings. (P F-V) |
| defeature | To remove a *feature* from the product definition. Sometimes because the *risk* of including the *feature* is too high. |
| defect | See *fault*. |
| defect management plan | Management device for clearing low-level *bugs* post *release*. Any *bug* not considered an impediment to a *release* (generally Medium and Low *bugs*) would be assigned to this plan. Usually consists of a spreadsheet of *bug* IDs, names, the *risk* they pose and the *release* to which they are assigned. |
| delivered source instruction | A line of compilable code. |
| delivery | The point in the software development cycle at which a product is *released* to its intended user for operational use. (ANSI/IEEE-729)<br>The point in the software development cycle at which a product is accepted by its intended user. (ANSI/IEEE-729) |
| demilitarized zone | A computer or small sub-network that sits between a trusted internal network, such as a corporate private LAN and an untrusted external network, such as the public Internet. Typically contains devices accessible to Internet traffic, such as Web (HTTP) servers, FTP servers, SMTP (e-mail) servers and DNS servers. The term comes from military use, meaning a buffer area between two enemies. |
| deontic logic | A logic of permission and obligation whereby "can," "cannot," "must," or "must not" relations are defined. |

| Term | Explanation (italicized text refers to terms explained in this section) |
|------|-----------------------------------------------------------------------|
| depth of inheritance tree | The maximum length from the *node* to the root of the tree.<br>The number of ancestor classes that can affect a class. Thus the deeper a class is in the hierarchy:<br>• The larger the number of methods inherited<br>• The more unpredictable its behavior<br>• The greater the potential reuse of inherited methods |
| design analysis | • The *evaluation* of a design to determine *correctness* with respect to stated *requirements*, *conformance* to design standards, system efficiency and other criteria.<br>• The *evaluation* of alternative design approaches.<br>See also *preliminary design*. (ANSI/IEEE-729) |
| design analyzer | An automated design tool that accepts information about a program's design and produces such outputs as module (*unit*) hierarchy diagrams, graphical representations of control and data structure and lists of accessed data blocks. (ANSI/IEEE-729) |
| design assertion consistency checker | *Software tool* which checks *assertions* inserted in code against the state of the software at the point at which the *assertion* is checked. |
| design authority | Person in charge of the architectural and technical coherence of the system. |
| design inspection | See *inspection*. |
| design review | • A formal meeting at which the preliminary or detailed design of a system is presented to the user, *customer* or other interested parties for comment and approval. (ANSI/IEEE-729)<br>• The formal *review* of an existing or proposed design for the purpose of detection and remedy of design deficiencies that could affect fitness-for-use and environmental aspects of the product, process, or service, or for identification of potential improvements of *performance*, *safety* and economic aspects. (ANSI/ASQC A3-1978)<br>• A formal systematic examination of a proposed design. (AQAP-15) |
| desk checking | The manual *simulation* of program execution to detect *faults* through step-by-step examination of the source code for *bugs* in logic or syntax. See also *static analysis*. (ANSI/IEEE-729) |
| developer | A member of staff who writes real code and sometimes low-level design and *unit* tests. |
| deviation | Written authorization, before manufacture or providing a service, to depart from *requirements* for a specified number of *units* or for the specified service or for a specified time (AQAP-15) |
| diagnostic | A *message* generated by a computer program indicating possible *faults* in another system *component*; for example, a syntax *fault* flagged by a compiler. (ANSI/IEEE-729)<br>Pertaining to the detection and isolation of *faults* or *failures*. (ANSI/IEEE-729) |
| disaster | A condition in which a resource is unavailable as a result of a natural or man-made occurrence that is of sufficient duration to cause significant disruption in the accomplishment of system objectives, as determined by management. Aka catastrophe. |
| document object model | A platform- and language-neutral *interface* allowing programs and *scripts* dynamically to access and update the content, structure and style of documents. The document can be further processed, and the results of that processing incorporated into the presented page. See www.w3.org/DOM/#what for more. |
| documentation problem | *Bug* class indicating that some document is incomplete, ambiguous, or inconsistent either with itself or some other document. (DOD STD 2167A) |
| domain metric | The number of *units* in the system in which at least one legal entry and one illegal entry in every input field has been correctly processed divided by the number of *units* in the system. (Adapted from IEEE *Computer*, page 88. July 1989) |
| drawing change notice | A design *modification* document used as a drawing or parts list which illustrates the changes some revision to the design. |
| driver | A program that exercises some system or system *component* by simulating the activity of a higher-level *component*. See also software *test driver*. (ANSI/IEEE-729) |

| Term | Explanation (italicized text refers to terms explained in this section) |
|------|-------------------------------------------------------------------------|
| drop | A particular *build* of a *release* which is considered suitable for *testing*. In the early stages some attempts at a *build* may fail. It is preferable for management and analysis to record the fact that *build n* failed and to make another. Only a successful *build* becomes a *drop*. Only a successful *drop* becomes a *release*. |
| dry-run | (Usually of a system test) An execution of a critical subset of the system tests or a preliminary version of the software to ensure both that the system tests themselves work and that the software is reasonably stable. (P F-V) |
| dynamic analyzer | A *software tool* that aids in the *evaluation* of a computer program by monitoring execution of the program. Examples include *instrumentation tools*, *software monitors* and tracers. Contrast with *static analyzer*. (ANSI/IEEE-729) |
| dynamic analysis | Execution of a program with *test data* and the analysis of the results. (*MoD 00-55*) The process of evaluating a program based on execution of the program. Contrast with *static analysis*. (ANSI/IEEE-729) |
| dynamic systems development method | A consortium, set up to develop a non-proprietary *rapid application development* method. See www.dsdm.com. |
| ease of use | An attribute of *usability* which defines how quickly users can accomplish a task when they have learned how to use the system. |
| encryption | The process of cryptographically converting plain text electronic data into a form unintelligible to anyone except the intended recipient. |
| Enterprise Java Beans | A *component* standard for the Java platform. |
| entropy | A term derived from nuclear physics (2nd law of thermodynamics.) The name given to one of the quantitative elements which determine the thermodynamic condition of a portion of matter (*OED*). Also used to describe the difference between the energy applied to a process and the output [Jensen]. Entropic software processes generate bad code which in turn leads to *infinite defect loops*. |
| environmental variable | Describes the conditions that affect the way the program runs (the control paths it takes and the data it accesses), but do not relate directly to *features*. |
| equivalence partitioning | A technique for the selection of *test cases* for a piece of software whereby the specification of the software is analyzed to determine partitions of the domain that should be treated equivalently by the software. One *test case* can then be chosen from each equivalence partition. (MoD 00-55) |
| error | • A discrepancy between a computed, observed, or measured value or condition and the true, specified, or theoretically correct value or condition. (ANSI)<br>• Human action that results in software containing a *fault*. Examples include omission or misinterpretation of user *requirements* in a software specification and incorrect translation or omission of a *requirement* in the design specification. This is not a preferred usage. See also *failure*, *fault*. (ANSI/IEEE-729)<br>• A mistake made during specification or development which results in a *fault* in the software. (MoD 00-55) |
| error message metric | The number of *error messages* in the system that have been demonstrated at least once divided by the number of *error messages* in the system. (adapted from IEEE *Computer*. Page 88. July 1989) |
| evaluation | • An assessment of some software or system while in use. One reason why evaluation is important is that all tests before installation are based on an estimate of the manner in which the system will be used. Evaluation enables this estimate to validated and the basis for the tests, including the frequency and severity of the *events* they are supposed to test can be redefined. Compare with *quality control*.<br>• The process of determining whether an item or activity meets specified criteria. (2167A)<br>• (In the Ada language system). The evaluation of an expression is the process by which the value of the expression is computed. This process occurs during program execution. (ANSI/MIL-STD-1815A) |

| Term | Explanation (italicized text refers to terms explained in this section) |
|---|---|
| event | An internal or external occurrence involving equipment, *performance,* human action, and/or software that perturbs some system. (Adapted from IEEE Spectrum page 25. June 1989.) An event may be the occurrence of some *threat.* |
| event tree analysis | (In safety analysis) A decision-tree-based approach which relates the outcomes and probabilities) of some initiating *event* to the various methods used to limit the effects of that initiating *event.* |
| evolution | (of software) Software development and *bug* correction following the first *release.* Sometimes referred to as *maintenance.* |
| exception reporting | A means of reporting *problem*s to a higher level than one's immediate operational manager. Compare with *operational reporting.* |
| executable lines of code | See *lines of code* |
| executable *UML* | A means of developing software using graphic models based on the *UML* notation which eliminates any need for developers to concern themselves with the execution environment. |
| execution estimate | (In *fault injection*). A measure of the degree to which some test set exercises code. |
| execution time | • The amount of actual or central processor time used in executing a program. (ANSI/IEEE-729) <br> • The period of time during which a program is executing. See also run time. (ANSI/IEEE-729) |
| execution time theory | A theory that uses cumulative *execution time* as the basis for estimating *software reliability* (ANSI/IEEE-729) |
| explicit operational profile | An enumerated set of all variables taken together with their associated occurrence probabilities. Its advantage is that you can specify fewer elements — a number equal to the sum of the number of levels of the *key input variable*s. A disadvantage of the explicit approach is that you can miss executing some seldom-used but critical operations while testing, unless you record all combinations of *key input variable*s executed. Compare with *implicit operational profile. [Musa 4]* |
| exposure (to risk) | A vulnerability to loss resulting from accidental or intentional disclosure, *modification,* or destruction of information resources. |
| eXtensible Markup Language | A standard for creating markup languages which describe the structure of data. It is not a fixed set of elements like HTML, but more like SGML (Standard Generalized Markup Language) in that it is a meta-language or a language for describing languages. XML enables authors to define their own tags. XML is a formal specification of the World Wide Web Consortium (www.w3.org). |
| external (environmental) fault | A *fault* arising from outside the system boundary, the environment, or the user. Such *fault*s include phenomena that directly affect the operation of the system, such as temperature, vibration, or nuclear or electromagnetic radiation or any other that affects the input provided to the system. |
| extreme programming | An approach to systems development requiring that programmers write a test for everything they code before coding it. |
| fail operational | A system state that provides a full set of operational *features* in the *event* of any *failure.* |
| fail passive | See *fail safe.* |
| fail recovery | A system state that provides some *feature* in the *event* of some *failure.* |
| fail safe | • A *feature* that attempts to limit the amount of damage caused by some *failure* but which does not provide the *feature* for which the system was originally designed. Aka *fail passive.* <br> • *Safety*-critical software which remains in or moves to a safe state after a *failure.* (MoD 00-55) |
| fail safe state | A state which cannot result in an accident, although function or *performance* may be lost. (MoD 00-55) |
| fail soft | A system that, when a *failure* occurs, provides the *feature* for which the system was originally designed in a degraded form. |
| fails-to-scale | When adding extra resources (engines, clients, web servers etc.) results in no faster *response time* or better *throughput* of a system. |

| Term | Explanation (italicized text refers to terms explained in this section) |
|---|---|
| failure | • The termination of the ability of a functional *unit* to perform its required function. (ISO)<br>• The inability of a system or system *component* to perform a required function within specified limits. A *failure* may be produced when a *fault* (*bug*) is encountered. (ANSI/IEEE-729)<br>• A departure of program operation from program *requirements*. (ANSI/IEEE-729)<br>• The *event* when software does not behave according to its specification — the manifestation of a *fault*. (MoD 00-55) |
| failure modes | The various ways in which systems can fail. These are: *fail safe, fail soft, fail operational, fail recovery.* |
| failure modes effects and criticality analysis | A graphic means of predicting equipment *reliability* by establishing that a product will work without *failure* for some period or will have some minimum inter-fail period. It emphasizes successful functioning rather than hazards or *risk*. It is applied to an already-created design. It is executed by looking at the results of the *failure* of one or more low-level *components* and tracing this to some *safety*-critical *top event* in an effort to show that such a *top event* either cannot occur or has an acceptably-low level of probability. |
| failure rate | • The ratio of the number of *failures* to a given *unit* of measure; for example, *failures* per *unit* of time, *failures* per number of *transactions*, *failures* per number of computer runs. (ANSI/IEEE-729)<br>• In *reliability modeling*, the ratio of the number of *failures* of a given category or severity to a given period of time; for example, *failures* per second of *execution time*, *failures* per month. (ANSI/IEEE-729) |
| failure recovery | The return of a system to a reliable operating state after *failure*. (ANSI/IEEE-729) |
| failure tolerance | The *capacity* of a program to compute an acceptable result even when the program suffers from<br>• one or more *bugs* or<br>• corrupted incoming data. |
| failure-to-scale | The *failure* of a system to permit faster *response time* or better *throughput*, despite the addition of extra resources (engines, clients or web servers etc.). |
| fault | See *bug*. |
| fault compensation | System response to some *fault* intended to mitigate its effect. See also *reversionary mode*. |
| fault containment | • The process that pr*event*s the propagation of *faults* from their origin at one point in a system to a point where it can have an effect on the service to the user.<br>• Where a *failure* in one part of a program is pr*event*ed from causing *failures* in other parts of the system. (MoD 00-55) |
| fault detection | The process of determining that a *fault* has occurred. |
| fault diagnosis | The process of determining what caused the *fault* or exactly which subsystem or *component* is *faulty*. |
| fault injection | The process of injecting *faults* into software to determine how well (or badly) some software behaves. Aka *fault seeding, bug seeding, bebugging*. |
| fault masking | The process of insuring that only correct values get passed to the system boundary in spite of a failed *component*. |
| fault repair | The process by which *faults* are removed from a system. In well-designed fault-tolerant systems, *faults* are contained before they propagate to the extent that the *delivery* of system service is affected. This leaves a portion of the system unusable because of residual *faults*. If subsequent *faults* occur, the system may be unable to cope because of this loss of resources, unless these resources are reclaimed through a recovery process which ensures that no *faults* remain in system resources or in the system state. |
| fault seeding | The process of intentionally adding a known number of *faults* to those already in a computer program for the purpose of estimating the number of *indigenous faults* in the program. Synonymous with *bug seeding*. (ANSI/IEEE-729) |

| Term | Explanation (italicized text refers to terms explained in this section) |
|---|---|
| fault tolerance | • The ability of *safety*-critical software to continue to execute acceptably after a limited number of *failures*. (MoD 00-55)<br>• The built-in *feature* of a system to provide continued correct execution in the presence of a limited number of hardware or software *faults*. (ANSI/IEEE-729)<br>• The number of *faults* a system or *component* can withstand before normal operation is impaired.<br>• The ability of a computer system to continue to operate correctly despite the malfunction of one or more of its *components*. Note: system *performance*, such as speed and *throughput*, may be diminished until the *faults* are corrected. See also *resilience*. |
| fault tree analysis | A graphic representation of all the *failures* from which a system may suffer. The charts used in *fault tree analysis* link the *top events* with *basic events* using *intermediate events* and Boolean operators.<br>*Fault tree analysis* was developed in 1961 by H. A. Watson of Bell Laboratories for the Minuteman program. |
| feature | Some system action(s) or state change which<br>• Cause the system to be bought<br>• Will be useful to some users<br>• Can be defined in some specification possibly in terms of some outcome(s) and/or some GUI objects and their interactions<br>• Are provoked by some input and which generate observable output.<br>Typically, in a Windows-based system, a feature is some user input typically accessing a menu item or keystroke combination which in turn displays a screen which a user can fill in to obtain either an output (e.g., *Ctrl-P > print*) or some state change (e.g., *Page set up*) whose effects can later be observed (e.g., by printing or p*review*ing a document). Aka *capability*. |
| feature problem | *Bug* class indicating that some key *feature* is either missing, incorrect, or extra. (DOD STD 2167A) |
| finite state machine | A computational model consisting of a finite number of states and transitions between these states. (ANSI/IEEE-729) |
| flexibility | An attribute of *usability* which defines how much a system allows adaptation of some percentage variation in task and/or environments beyond those first specified. |
| flow of control | The sequence of operations performed in the execution of an *algorithm*. (ANSI/IEEE-729) |
| flowgraph | Graphic description of a number of *nodes* representing the *program* statements and edges representing the order in which they may be executed. Each *node* is annotated with indications of which program *events* occur as a *consequence* of its execution. |
| formal language | A language whose rules are explicitly established before its use. Synonymous with artificial language. Examples include mathematical or logical languages, such as predicate calculus, Z or VDM. Contrast with natural language. (ANSI/IEEE-729) |
| formal mathematical method | Mathematically-based method for the specification, design and production of software. Also includes a logical inference system for formal *proofs of correctness* and a methodological framework for software development in a formally verifiable way. (MoD 00-55) |
| formal proof of correctness | A way of proving that a computer program follows its specification by a mathematical proof using formal rules. (MoD 00-55) |
| formal qualification testing | A process that allows the contracting agency to determine whether a configuration item complies with the allocated *requirements* for that item. (DOD STD 2167A) |
| formal security policy model | A mathematically-precise statement of a *security policy*. To be adequately precise, such a model must represent the initial state of a system, the way in which the system progresses from one state to another and a definition of a "secure" state of the system. To be acceptable as a basis of a TCB, the model must be supported by, a formal proof that if the initial state of the system satisfies the definition of a "secure" state and if all assumptions required by the model hold, then all future states of the system will be secure. Some formal modeling techniques include: state transition models, denotational semantics models and algebraic specification models. [*CompSecGloss*] |

| Term | Explanation (italicized text refers to terms explained in this section) |
|---|---|
| formal testing | The process of conducting *testing* activities and reporting results in accordance with an approved *test plan*. (ANSI/IEEE-729) and (DoD-STD 2167) |
| formal verification | Showing by formal mathematical proof or arguments that software implements its (formal mathematical) specification correctly. (MoD 00-55) |
| function point | A weighted total of 5 *component*s which abstractly comprise an application. (Number of { external inputs | external outputs | logical internal files | external *interface* files | external inquiries }). *Function point*s were originated by Albrecht and his colleagues in IBM in 1979. |
| functional requirement | A statement of *requirement* written in a language which *developers*, *testers*, technical authors and trainers are likely to find useful. Often derives from a *business requirement*. |
| functional testing | The *testing* of software against a definition of its external behavior, with no knowledge of the internal logic of the software (it is aka *black-box testing* for this reason). There are various techniques for selecting input *test data* to maximize the probability of finding *bugs*. |
| Gantt chart | Aka timeline chart. Shows how long each activity will last. Invented by Henry Laurence Gantt. (1861–1919) during WWI as way of showing ship construction tasks to new workers. |
| garbage-in-garbage-out | What happens to a system incapable of discriminating between good and bad inputs. |
| generic representation | (In *usability*). A description of a system in a form suitable for the design sub-teams who will use it in later stages of the system life cycle. Part of *task analysis*. |
| graceful degradation | Stepwise reduction of function or *performance* as a result of *failure*, while maintaining as many essential parts of the functionality as possible. (MoD 00-55) |
| graph | A model consisting of a finite set of *node*s having *connection*s called edges or arcs. (ANSI/IEEE-729) |
| graphical user interface | A hierarchical, graphical front-end to software that accepts as input user- and system-generated *events* from a fixed set of *events* and produces deterministic graphical output. A GUI contains graphical objects and each object has a set of properties. At any time during the execution of the GUI, these properties have discrete values, the set of which constitutes the state of the GUI. [Memon] These properties may be affected by extraneous *events* such as *link-rot* and timing issues as well as content-related issues such as video streaming. |
| graphical user interface component | Any window and all the objects it contains. GUI *components* can be of two kinds: modeless and modal. A non-modal or modeless *component* can be modified and left without impeding the user from modifying the contents of other windows. A modal *component* must be closed and the changes committed before another *component* can be modified. |
| graphical user interface object | The set of all possible parts of any GUI window. This includes fields, tick-boxes, radio buttons, labeled buttons, panes, pull-downs, icon buttons and palettes. See Table 8.1 for a non-exhaustive list. |
| hazard rate | (Sometimes known as the per *fault hazard rate*). The probability that a *bug* will cause a *failure*. |
| headroom | (In *performance testing*). Colloquial expression of the unused *capacity*. |
| Heisenberg effect | An informal extension of Heisenberg's *Uncertainty Principle* which has a consequence that if an object's position x is defined precisely, then the momentum of the object will be only weakly constrained and vice versa. Thus one cannot simultaneously find both the position and momentum of an object to arbitrary *accuracy*. These *errors* are negligible in general but become critical when studying the very small such as the atom. In the context of system testing this is intended to mean the interference of a test environment on the behavior of a test. |
| heisenbug | A *bug* caused by some attempt to test, itself provoking some *bug*. After *Heisenberg*, a Nazi physicist. |

| Term | Explanation (italicized text refers to terms explained in this section) |
|---|---|
| host machine | • The computer on which a program or file is installed.<br>• A computer used to develop software intended for another computer.<br>• A computer used to emulate another computer.<br>• In a computer network, a computer that provides processing *features* to users of the network. |
| host testing | The process of ascertaining that compiled code executes in accordance with its *baseline* specification when running on a computer other than the one for which the software has been designed. (Compare with *target testing*) |
| human factors | See *usability*. |
| human-factors bug | *Bug* class indicating that some human factor *bug* has been observed or there is a plausible argument that it exists. (DOD STD 2167A) |
| Hypertext Markup Language | The authoring language used to create documents on the World Wide Web. See www.w3.org/MarkUp for more details. |
| Hypertext Transfer Protocol | The *protocol* used over Port 80 responsible for requesting and transmitting data over the Internet. |
| imperfect debugging | In *reliability modeling*, the assumption that attempts to correct or remove a detected *fault* is not always successful. (ANSI/IEEE-729) |
| implicit operational profile | This consists of sets of the *key input variables*' values, with their associated occurrence probabilities. It can be used only when the *key input variables* are independent (at least approximately) of each other with regard to the occurrence probabilities of their values. This is suited to *transaction*-based systems in which processing depends primarily on *transaction* attributes that are generally independent and have known occurrence probabilities. A system to generate personalized direct mail, for example, depends on *customer* attributes (*location*, income, home ownership) that are essentially independent. Compare with *explicit operational profile*. [*Musa 4*] |
| in-circuit emulator | Hardware which simulates the behavior of a processor while allowing engineers to see its internal workings particularly the behavior of its processor(s) and the state of the registers. |
| independent verification and validation | *Verification* and *validation* of a software product by individuals or groups other than those who performed the original design, but who may be from the same organization. The degree of independence must be a function of the importance of the software. (ANSI/IEEE-729) |
| indigenous fault | A *fault* existing in a computer program that has not been inserted as part of a *fault-seeding* process. (ANSI/IEEE-729) |
| inductive assertion method | A *proof of correctness* technique in which *assertions* are written describing program inputs, outputs and intermediate conditions, a set of theorems is developed relating satisfaction of the *input assertions* to satisfaction of the *output assertions* and the information hiding. The technique of encapsulating software design decisions in *units* in such a way that the *unit's* *interfaces* reveal as little as possible about the *unit's* inner workings; thus, each *unit* is a black box to the other *units* in the system. The discipline of information hiding forbids the use of information about a *unit* that is not in the *unit's* *interface* specification. (ANSI/IEEE-729) |
| infection estimate | (in *fault injection*) A measure of the degree to which some program is susceptible to coding *errors*. |
| infinite defect loop | A state reached by code in a project when any attempt to fix *n* bugs results in *m* bugs being introduced and $n \cong m$. |
| informal testing | Any test which does not meet all the *requirement* of a formal test and results of which are not usually deliverable items. (DoD-STD-2167) |
| information flow analysis | Identification of the input variables on which each output variables depend in a computer program. Used to confirm that outputs only depend on the relevant inputs as specified. (MoD 00-55) |

| Term | Explanation (italicized text refers to terms explained in this section) |
|------|-------------------------------------------------------------------------|
| infrastructure failure | • Cascading *failure*: A disruption in one infrastructure causing a disruption in a second infrastructure<br>• Escalating *failure*: A disruption in one infrastructure exacerbating an independent disruption of a second infrastructure (thus the time for recovery or restoration of an infrastructure may increase because another infrastructure is not available)<br>• *Common cause failure*: Disruptions of more than one infrastructure because of a *common cause* (e.g., natural *disaster*, right-of-way corridor, excavation of power cables) |
| initial concepts document | A definition of what the world will be like when the system is running. |
| injection point | (In *fault injection*). Any executable source statement in code which may have a *fault* injected. [Voas] |
| input assertion | A logical expression specifying one or more conditions that program inputs must satisfy in order to be valid. (ANSI/IEEE-729) |
| input space | The program's *input space* consists of all the inputs it can receive. |
| inspection | • A formal *evaluation* technique in which software *requirements*, design or code are examined in detail by a person or group other than the author to detect *faults*, violations of development standards and *other bugs*. Contrast with *walk-through*. See also *code audit*. (ANSI/IEEE-729)<br>• A phase of *quality control* that using examination, *observation* or measurement determines the *conformance* of materials, supplies, *components*, parts, appurtenances, systems, processes or structures to predetermined *quality requirements*. (ANSI N45.2. 10-1973)<br>• The process of measuring, examining, *testing*, gauging, or otherwise comparing the *unit* with the applicable *requirements*. *Inspection* includes deciding whether or not specified *requirements* have been met. (AQAP-15) |
| inspection system | The established management, structure, responsibilities, methods and resources that together provide *inspection* to demonstrate the attainment of *quality*. (AQAP-15) |
| installation and checkout phase | The period of time in the software life cycle during which a software product is integrated into its operational environment and tested in this environment to ensure that it performs as required. (ANSI/IEEE-729) |
| instrumentation | (Of code). The insertion of extra code into a completed *unit* in order to either provoke calls to *scaffolding* or test tools or to display a *message*. Code *instrumentation* is typically used to count the number of times a *unit* is called. The disadvantage of *instrumentation* is that:<br>• It may interfere with the execution of the program in subtle ways particularly if timing is a *problem*.<br>• It may not be removed completely after the tests have been run and may thereafter interfere with the program.<br>See also *program instrumentation*. |
| instrumentation tool | A *software tool* that generates and inserts counters or other probes at strategic points in another program to provide statistics about program execution, such as how thoroughly the program's code is exercised. (ANSI/IEEE-729) |
| integration | The process of combining software elements, hardware elements or both into an overall system. (ANSI/IEEE-729) |
| integration step | An identifiable moment during *integration* when some software *feature* has been achieved. |

| Term | Explanation (italicized text refers to terms explained in this section) |
|---|---|
| integration strategy | The strategy by which the product will be put together. Conventionally there are six strategies:<br>• **Top-down,** in which the user *interface units* are integrated and tested first using *stub*s to simulate the lower-level code. This is then followed by the next level of code until the operating system or *target hardware* is integrated.<br>• **Bottom-up,** in which the *target hardware* or operating system (or whatever is next to the *target hardware*) is integrated with the next-higher code. The code is exercised using *drivers* to simulate the operator and other inputs. This is then followed by the next level of code until the user *interface* is integrated.<br>• **Critical units first,** which requires that these *units* be identified and integrated first. These may be *performance*, function- or operator-critical and thus the *criticality* will impose its own constraints on the *integration*.<br>• **Middle-out,** which is an amalgam of top-down and bottom-up. This is frequently used when no *target hardware* can be used.<br>• **Threaded**, in which all the software required for some *feature* is integrated using some strategy. As soon as that *feature* is demonstrated the next *feature* can be added. In web testing this is sometimes known as *transaction link testing*.<br>• **Big-bang,** in which all the software is integrated at once. Only sensible if the software is known to be very *bug*-free or very small.<br>The strategy chosen constrains the order in which *units* are developed. |
| integration testing | An orderly progression of *tests* in which software elements, hardware elements or both are combined and tested until the entire system has been integrated. See also *system testing*. (ANSI/IEEE-729) |
| intellectual property | The group of legal rights to things people create or invent. Intellectual property rights typically include patent, copyright, trademark and trade secret rights. |
| interface | • A shared boundary. Thus an interface might be a hardware *component* to link two devices or it might be a portion of storage or registers accessed by two or more computer programs (ANSI/IEEE-729)<br>• To interact or communicate with another system *component*. (ANSI/IEEE-729) |
| interface bug | *Bug* class indicating that some call is either missing, incorrect or extra. (DOD STD 2167A) |
| Interface Description Language | A computer language or simple syntax for describing the *interface* of a software *component* and used to write the "manual" on how to use a piece of software from another piece of software, much as a user manual describes how to use a piece of software to the user. |
| interface requirements (specification) | • Specifies the *requirements* for one or more *interfaces* between one or more CSCIs and other configuration items or critical items. (DOD STD 2167A)<br>• A *requirement* that specifies a hardware, software or database element with which a system or system *component* must *interface* or that sets forth constraints on formats, timing or other factors caused by such an *interface*. (ANSI/IEEE-729)<br>• A specification that sets forth the *interface requirements* for a system or system *component*. (ANSI/IEEE-729) |
| interface testing | *Testing* conducted to ensure that program or system *components* pass information or control correctly to one another. (ANSI/IEEE-729) |
| intermediate event | (In *Fault Tree Analysis*). An *event* linking another *intermediate event* with any two of a *top event*, another *intermediate event*, or a *basic event*. |
| Internet Server Application Programming Interface | *Application programming interface* or *protocol* allowing Microsoft Internet Information Servers to *interface* with web-based applications. |

| Term | Explanation (italicized text refers to terms explained in this section) |
|---|---|
| interoperability | The ability of two or more systems to exchange information and to mutually use the information that has been exchanged. Compare with *compatibility*. (ANSI/IEEE-729)<br>• **Operational:** The ability of systems to cooperate and be linked for operational reasons. *Operational interoperability* depends partly on the degree of technical *interoperability* of systems. This approximates to a semantic level of understanding between systems.<br>• **Technical:** The degree to which systems facilitate service or information exchanges between them. This approximates to a syntactic level of understanding between systems.<br>Interoperability can be said to lie along a continuum between complete system integration and simple compatibility. Put crudely: it's the last point along that continuum in which you can expect that some Perl folks can be reasonably expected to lash your systems together and still have someone use them. |
| interval | (In program structuring). An *interval l* with head *node* H is the sub-graph containing H plus any *node*s that can be reached on a path from H and which have all their immediate predecessors in the *interval*. |
| interval reduction | Consider the directed *flowgraph* below: |

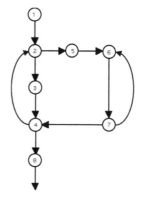

And using a second *interval reduction* reduces to

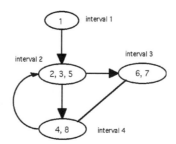

Thus the directed *flowgraph* is reducible in the *interval* sense. However some directed *flowgraphs* are irreducible. An example of an irreducible *flowgraph* is shown below.

Using interval reduction this reduces to:

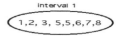

*(continued)*

| Term | Explanation (italicized text refers to terms explained in this section) |
|---|---|
| interval reduction *(continued)* | And this can be further reduced: |
| Invitation To Tender | A document issued by a company to potential suppliers to identify who is prepared to tender for to supply some system or service. |
| issuer | (In *credit-card authentication*). A financial institution that issues credit cards and contracts with each cardholder to provide card services, determines the eligibility of a cardholder to use a credit card in a secure card use system and identifies credit card number ranges eligible to participate in a secure credit card use system. |
| issuer domain | (In *credit-card authentication*). Contains the systems and functions of the *issuer* and its *customers* (cardholders) |
| item review | A *review* by one or more development members other than the author(s) of the item to be placed under configuration management, to ascertain whether the item conforms to the item *acceptance criteria*. If it does the item is accepted. If not the item is rejected and the reason for the rejection is given to the author(s) of the item. |
| Java 2 platform enterprise edition | A platform-independent, Java-centric environment from Sun for developing, building and deploying Web-based enterprise applications online. The J2EE platform consists of a set of services, APIs and *protocols* that provide the functionality for developing multi-tiered, Web-based applications. |
| Java server pages | Java equivalent of *active server pages* but uses a combined markup language (HTML, DHTML, or XML) and Java to generate web pages dynamically. Compare with *common gateway interface* and *active server pages*. |
| key input variable | A variable which differentiates one function or operation from another. |
| key performance quality measure | See *business process measure*. |
| knot | (In control-flow analysis). A place in a control-*flowgraph* in which one control-flow crosses another. There are commonly three kinds of knots: <br> • **Down-down knots** may be regarded as relatively harmless, as they reflect linearization of the directed *graph*. <br> • **Up-down knots** are of more interest, but may legally be constructed from DO or WHILE loop type language constructs. <br> • **Up-up knots** are the most serious: they have no known legal language construct (except FOR loops in the C language) and therefore should not remain in a program. |
| large-scale integration test | Glamorous name for a system test of a very large system. |
| LCSAJ start point | The target line of a control-flow jump or the first line of the program text. An LCSAJ *end* point is any line which can be reached from the start point by an unbroken linear *sequence* of code and from which a jump can be made. The information about the terminating jump is added to the start and end points so that an LCSAJ is characterized by a start line, an end line and the target line for the jump. |
| learnability | An attribute of *usability* which defines how easy is it for users to accomplish basic tasks the first time they encounter a system. |
| line manager | The person with overall financial responsibility for the project. The *project manager* reports to him. |

| Term | Explanation (italicized text refers to terms explained in this section) |
|---|---|
| linear code sequence and jump | A linear *sequence* of executable code that begins at the start of the program or some branch and ends either at the end of the program or some other branch. |
| lines of code | The source code of some system. They are of four kinds:<br>• *Executable lines of code* are the true program and do the work<br>• Data definitions<br>• Pseudo code which contains compiler directives<br>• Comment lines explain what the *executable lines of code* do<br>For the purpose of this book, an LOC is considered to be a non-comment line or *non-commented source statement*. |
| link-rot | The tendency of URLs to fail as the websites to which they refer are modified. |
| liquidated damage clause | A clause in an agreement, which establish the amount of damages to be paid in the event of a breach or cancellation of a contract. |
| live | (Of a line of code). The *quality* of being useable by the program. Code which is not "*live*" is of course "dead." |
| load test | Subjecting a system to a statistically-representative load. |
| load test process | The exercise of a test on the entire system which exercises its essential functions to the limit in an effort to see what the limits are, where the bottlenecks are and what resource use patterns are under load. |
| location | (In *fault injection*). Code statement of one of the following types: assignment, input, output, or condition. |
| lock-in | (In contract negotiation). A situation in which a client is constrained to use a single supplier. |
| log action | (In *UML*). An action to log information in the *test trace*. |
| maintainability | • The ease with which software can be maintained. (ANSI/IEEE-729)<br>• The ease with which *maintenance* of a functional *unit* can be performed in accordance with prescribed *requirements*. (ISO)<br>• Ability of an item under stated conditions of use to be retained in or restored to, within a given period of time, a specified state in which it can perform its required functions when *maintenance* is performed under stated conditions and while using prescribed procedures and resources. (ANSI/ASQC A3-1978)<br>• The *capability* of the software product to be modified. *Modification*s may include corrections, improvements, or adaptations of the software to changes in environment, *requirements* and functional specification. (ISO/IEC 9126-1) |
| maintainability index | A measure of software *maintainability* based on the following equation:<br><br>$171 - 5.2 \ln(\text{ave V}) - 0.23 \text{ aveV}(g') - 16.2 * \ln(\text{aveLOC}) + 50 * \sin(\text{sqrt}(2.4 * \text{perCM}))$<br><br>where aveV = average Halstead Volume V per module (see Halstead *Complexity* Measures);<br>aveV(g') = average extended *cyclomatic complexity* per module;<br>aveLOC = the average count of *lines of code* per module; and, optionally,<br>perCM = average percent of lines of comments per module.<br>Measurement and use of the MI is a process technology, facilitated by simple tools, that in implementation becomes part of the overall development or *maintenance* process. These efforts also indicate that MI measurement applied during software development can help reduce lifecycle costs.<br>See www.sei.cmu.edu/str/descriptions/mitmpm_body.html |
| maintenance | See *software maintenance*, *evolution*. |
| Markov chain | A definition of all possible states of the system together with the probability of the system being in each state. |
| Mean Time To Fail | The average elapsed time between *failures* of a system or component. |
| Mean Time To Repair | The average time it takes to repair a failed component. |

| Term | Explanation (italicized text refers to terms explained in this section) |
|------|-------------------------------------------------------------------------|
| merchant | (In *credit-card authentication*). Entity that contracts with an *acquirer* to accept credit cards or other payment means, manages the online shopping of a cardholder, obtains a card number, then transfers control to the *merchant server plug-in*, which authenticates payment. |
| merchant server plug-in | (In *credit-card authentication*). A component operating in the *acquirer domain* incorporated into the *merchant*'s website to perform secure functions for the *merchant*, such as determining card authentication and validating digital signatures in a secure *message*. |
| message | (In object-oriented programming). A request that an object makes of another object to perform an operation. |
| meta-object facility | An OMG standard, closely related to *UML*, that enables metadata management and modeling language definition. |
| metrics | Quantitative analysis values calculated according to a precise definition and used to establish comparative aspects of development progress, *quality* assessment, or choice of options. |
| minimum cut set | A *cut set* containing no other *cut set*s. If one *event* in the *minimum cut set* does not occur the *top event* will not occur. |
| modal window | Any window which must be closed before any other window can be opened. A non-*modal window* can be opened and left without impeding the user from opening other windows. |
| model-driven architecture | An approach to IT system specification which separates the specification of functionality from the specification of the implementation of that functionality on a particular technology platform. |
| modifiability | • The degree to which a system or component facilitates the incorporation of changes, once the nature of the desired change has been determined [Boehm 78]. <br> • The ease and success with which <br>   – a module in a subsystem can be changed without side effects within that or any other subsystem and <br>   – a system written in one language can be transformed into another usually by designing modules with minimum coupling and maximum *cohesion*. <br> Modifiability allows systems to be metamorphic or polymorphic, through modularization, data encapsulation and abstraction. |
| modification | A change made to software. (ANSI/IEEE-729) <br> The process of changing software. (ANSI/IEEE-729) |
| modularity | The extent to which software is composed of discrete *components* such that a change to one *component* has minimal effect on other *components*. (ANSI/IEEE-729) |
| MQSeries | A middleware product from IBM which runs on many platforms and allows applications to send *messages* to other applications. |
| mutant | A variant of a program in which one or more semantic *errors* have been deliberately made. Used in *fault injection*. |
| mutation | See *program mutation*. |
| Netscape Server Application Programming Interface | *Application programming interface* or *protocol* allowing Netscape servers to interface to web-based applications. |
| network fault tolerance | A measure of the number of *failures* the network can sustain before a disconnection occurs. In a system where the *failure* of $n$ *node*s will provoke a service *failure* its *fault tolerance* can be defined as $n-1$. Compare with *resilience*. |
| node | • An end point of any branch of a network or *graph* or a junction common to two or more branches. (ANSI/IEEE-729) <br> • In a tree structure, a point at which subordinate items of data originate. (ANSI) <br> • In a network, a point where one or more functional *units* interconnect transmission lines. (ISO) <br> • The representation of a state or an *event* using a point on a diagram. (ANSI) |

| Term | Explanation (italicized text refers to terms explained in this section) |
|---|---|
| non-commented source statement | See *lines of code*. |
| non-conforming software | Software which does not conform to some *requirement*. Includes software infected with viruses, logic bombs, and Trojan horses. |
| non-functional requirement | Any *requirement* which is not a *feature*. *Non-functional requirements* are generally expressed in terms of such qualities as *reliability, maintainability* etc. They are thus commonly referred to as the "*ilities*." |
| number of children | Object-oriented *metric* defined as the number of immediate subclasses. The greater the number of children the greater the:<br>• reuse, since inheritance is a form of reuse<br>• likelihood of improper abstraction of the parent class or of misuse of subclassing<br>• potential influence a class has on the design<br>• need to test the methods in that class |
| Object Management Group | An open membership, not-for-profit consortium that produces and maintains computer industry specifications for interoperable enterprise applications. (www.omg.org) |
| Object Modeling Technique | Forerunner of the (Rational) Unified Process |
| objective evidence | (In *testing*) Something which demonstrates the *conformance* of a product or service or the effectiveness of a system or parts of it (AQAP-15) |
| observation | • (In *UML*). *Test data* reflecting the reactions from the SUT and used to assess the SUT reactions which are typically the result of a *stimulus* sent to the SUT. Aka test output.<br>• (In *quality assurance*) A written definition of some non-*compliance* with the *quality system*. |
| off-shoring | As *outsourcing* but the supplier is outside the country of the *customer*. |
| online testing | Where equipment or software is tested while it is operating. (MoD 00-55) |
| on-shoring | See *backsourcing*. |
| open bug | A *bug* which has been raised but not fixed. Compare with *closed bug*. |
| operational reliability | The *reliability* of a system or software subsystem in its actual use environment. *Operational reliability* may differ considerably from *reliability* in the specified or test environment. (ANSI/IEEE-729) |
| operational reporting | The usual relationship with one's immediate manager. Compare with *exception reporting*. |
| operational state | Pertaining to the status given a software product once it has entered the operation and *maintenance* phase. (ANSI/IEEE-729) |
| operational testing | *Testing* performed by the end user on software in its normal operating environment. Part of *system testing*. (DoD) |
| operator fault | Some *fault* created by a person considered to be a part of the system. Note that the roles of user and operator are considered separately; the user is considered to be external to the system while the operator is considered to be a part of the system. Compare with *user fault*. |
| oracle | (In testing). Some means of defining the truth of some statement by matching it against some accepted authority, often a *subject matter expert* or an existing system whose output can be accepted as true. |
| other bug | *Bug* class indicating that some other bug has been observed. (DOD STD 2167A) |
| output assertion | A logical expression specifying one or more conditions that program outputs must satisfy in order for the program to be correct. (ANSI/IEEE-729) |
| outsourcing | The process of having software or other facility created by some supplier for a *customer*. |

| Term | Explanation (italicized text refers to terms explained in this section) |
|---|---|
| overall relationship contract | (In *outsourcing*). A superior contract between *customer* and supplier dominating all subsidiary contracts for the supply of software and/or services. Eliminates repetition of detail in and constrains lower-level contracts. |
| overload | (Of a system). The state in which more data must be exchanged than a system can transmit, measured as the sum of all *messages* remaining in queues after their assigned transmission period for all system *nodes*. |
| partial correctness | (In *proof of correctness*.) A designation indicating that a program's *output assertions* follow logically from its *input assertions* and processing steps. Contrast with *total correctness*. (ANSI/IEEE-729) |
| pass/fail criteria | Decision rules used to determine whether a software item or a software *feature* passes or fails a test. See also *arbiter*. |
| path analysis | Program analysis performed to identify all possible paths through a program, to detect incomplete paths or to discover portions of the program that are not on any path. (ANSI/IEEE-729) |
| path condition | A set of conditions that must be met in order for a particular program path to be executed. (ANSI/IEEE-729) |
| path expression | A logical expression indicating the input conditions that must be met in order for a particular program path to be executed. (ANSI/IEEE-729) |
| peer review | A *review* of some work product by a person of the same level of experience as the author. |
| performance | A measure of the ability of a computer system or subsystem to perform its functions; for example, *response time*, *throughput*, number of *transactions*. (ANSI/IEEE-729). See also *performance requirement*, *trigger event*, *periodicity*, rate, *response event*, *response time* and *response type*. |
| performance bug | *Bug* class indicating that there is a plausible argument that the item will not meet the *performance* objectives stated in the *requirements*. (DOD STD 2167A) |
| performance evaluation | The technical assessment of a system or system *component* to determine how effectively, operating objectives have been achieved. (ANSI/IEEE-729) |
| performance requirement | A *requirement* that specifies a *performance* characteristic that a system or system *component* must possess; for example, speed, *accuracy*, frequency. (ANSI/IEEE-729) |
| performance testing | Testing conducted to evaluate the compliance of a system or component with specified performance requirements. [IEEE] |
| performance and coverage analyzer | A software development tool to analyze the run-time behavior of application programs. |
| periodicity | (In *performance testing*). The nature of a *trigger event*: periodic, (regularly occurring), aperiodic (not recurring at regular *intervals*), or sporadic (occurring at irregular *intervals*, having no pattern or order). |
| permissioning | Means of determining the access rights of a person to a system. |
| persistent bug | A *fault* which is evident for a long period of time. Sometimes termed hard *faults*. Persistent *faults* usually are the easiest to detect and diagnose, but may be difficult to contain and mask unless redundant hardware is available. |
| pert chart | A method of presenting a project's critical path and links, devised by Dupont and Remington Rand in the 1950s. Often used to model "what if" *scenarios* by changing elapsed times to give managers a better understanding of *delivery* obstacles. |
| Petri net | An abstract, formal model of information flow, showing static and dynamic properties of a system. A *Petri net* is usually represented as a *graph* having two types of *nodes* (called places and transitions) connected by arcs and markings (called tokens) indicating dynamic properties. See also *state diagram*. (ANSI/IEEE-729) |

| Term | Explanation (italicized text refers to terms explained in this section) |
|------|------------------------------------------------------------------------|
| ping test | A ping test checks to see if a system on the Internet is working. Pinging a server tests and records the *response time* of the server. Pinging multiple computers can be helpful in finding Internet bottlenecks, so that data transfer paths can be rerouted more efficiently. |
| platform-independent model | (In *UML*). A complete application specification of a subsystem that contains no information specific to the platform or the technology that is used to realize it. Compare with *platform-specific model.* |
| platform-specific model | (In *UML*). A *platform-independent model* which has been post-processed to create source code for execution on a particular platform and which may therefore contain elements specific to that platform. |
| portability | The ease with which software can be transferred from one computer system or environment to another. (ANSI/IEEE-729) |
| precision | • A measure of the ability of some system to distinguish between nearly equal values; for example four place numerals is less precise than six-place numerals. Nevertheless an accurately computed four-place numeral maybe more accurate than an improperly-computed six-place numeral.<br>• The degree of discrimination with which a quantity is stated; for example, a three-digit numeral discriminates among 1000 possibilities. (ISO)<br>Contrast with *accuracy.* |
| probability of failure | The probability that a program in some environment will fail at the next input. Compare with *reliability* unlike which probability of failure is time-independent. |
| problem | See *fault.* |
| problems per user month | Total *problems* that *customers* report per month/number of open licenses that month. |
| product baseline | The initial approved product configuration identification. (DoD-STD-2167) |
| program instrumentation | Probes, such as instructions or *assertions*, inserted into a computer program to facilitate execution monitoring, *proof of correctness*, resource monitoring or other activities. (ANSI/IEEE-729)<br>The process of preparing and inserting probes into a computer program. (ANSI/IEEE-729) |
| program mutation | A program version purposely altered from the intended version to evaluate the ability of program *test cases* to detect the alteration. (ANSI/IEEE-729)<br>The process of creating *program mutation*s in order to evaluate the adequacy of program *test data.* (ANSI/IEEE-729)<br>Aka *mutation testing.* |
| program state | A set of mappings between all declared and dynamically allocated variables at some point in the program's execution. Aka "*data state*" [Voas] |
| program validation | See *validation.* |
| project bankruptcy | Defined in [Abe] as the moment when project actual costs exceed project planned costs by 20%. See also *Project failure.* |
| project failure | [*Mangione*] cites 4 kinds of *project failure*:<br>• **Hitting the wall before release:** An otherwise successful team suffers some fatal hitch such as market change, team member loss, cash flow *problem* or *requirements* change. The product is never released.<br>• **90% done:** The product suffers from extreme *entropy* and the cost of change becomes prohibitive. This may be due to poor architecture or delaying addressing the riskiest *problems* until too late.<br>• **Endless testing:** The *developers* inject as many *bugs* as the test group discovers.<br>• **Version 2.0:** The product achieves *release* 1, but suffers from extreme *entropy* and the cost of change required for *release* 2 becomes prohibitive. |
| project librarian | The person in charge of all the project documentation. |

| Term | Explanation (italicized text refers to terms explained in this section) |
|------|------------------------------------------------------------------------|
| project manager | The person in charge of all aspects of the project except design. He writes the project plan and the *quality* plan. He may be in charge of the *test manager*. He will have limited financial authority and report to the *line manager*. |
| proof obligations | The *requirement* to prove a theorem to demonstrate the *correctness* of a development step. (MoD 00-55) |
| proof of correctness | • A formal technique used to prove mathematically that a program satisfies its specifications. See also *partial correctness, total correctness*. (ANSI/IEEE-729)<br>• A program proof that results from applying this technique. (ANSI/IEEE-729) |
| propagation estimate | The estimate of the susceptibility of variable *a* in *location l* to a *fault*. The possible outcomes vary from nil (either because the program is highly *fault*-tolerant or because the variable is "dead") to high (in which case the variable deserves extensive *testing*). |
| protocol | • A set of conventions or rules that govern the interactions of processes or applications within a computer system or network. (ANSI/IEEE-729)<br>• A set of rules that govern the operation of functional *units* to achieve communication. (ISO) |
| Public Company Accounting Oversight Board | A United States non-profit corporation established under the Sarbanes–Oxley Act of 2002 to oversee the auditors of public companies in order to protect the interests of investors and further the public interest in the preparation of informative, fair and independent audit reports. |
| qualification | See *verification* and *validation* and *formal qualification testing*. |
| qualification testing | *Formal testing*, usually conducted by the *developer* for the *customer*, to demonstrate that the software meets its specified *requirements*. See also *acceptance testing, system testing*. (ANSI/IEEE-729) |
| quality | See *software quality*. (ANSI/IEEE-729) |
| quality assurance | See *software quality assurance*. (ANSI/IEEE-729) |
| quality assurance manager | The person in charge of the *quality system*. He *assures* the process whereby the system is required, designed, built, tested, installed and handed over. He has nothing to do with either *reviewing* or *testing* but acts as the channel whereby any serious *quality* concerns can be revealed to senior management as required by ISO 9000. Not to be confused with *test manager*. |
| quality assurance representative | Person responsible for signing off the *quality* plan (and thus implicitly any separate *test plans*) and auditing the project against the *quality system*. He reports to the *quality assurance* manager. He has no responsibility for *testing* or *reviewing*. He must be satisfied that all the *quality controls* on the project are satisfactory and will thus be particularly concerned with such issues as *reviews, testing* and configuration management. |
| quality control | The operational techniques and activities that ensure the attainment of *quality* to specified *requirements*. (AQAP-15). Aka *validation and verification*. |
| quality control system | The established management structure, responsibilities, methods and resources that together provide *quality control* to demonstrate the attainment of *quality*. (AQAP-15). See also *quality control* and *quality assurance*. |
| quality metric | A quantitative measure of the degree to which software possesses a given attribute that affects its *quality*. (ANSI/IEEE-729) |
| quality milestone | Some identifiable moment in some development having to do with *quality*. Typically such milestones occur at the end of some *quality*-related activity such as the *review* or system test of a major *deliverable*. As such *quality milestones* may be unrelated to the major management milestones of the development plan. |
| quality system | The organizational structure, responsibilities, procedures, processes and resources for managing quality. |

| Term | Explanation (italicized text refers to terms explained in this section) |
|------|---------------------------------------------------------------------------|
| rapid application development | Any software life-cycle intended to give faster development and better results and to exploit recent advances in development software by minimizing process "ceremony," and documentation.<br>It varies in scope from hacking away in a GUI builder with little analysis and design to complete information engineering frameworks. |
| rate | (In *performance testing*). The frequency of a periodic *event*. |
| recursion | See *recursion*. |
| red team | (In *security testing*). The person(s) conducting a black-box penetration test or ethical hacking activity. |
| redundancy | The inclusion of duplicate or alternate system elements to improve *operational reliability* by ensuring continued operation in the *event* that a primary element fails. (ANSI/IEEE-729) |
| regression test | Some test which is used to demonstrate that the *features* a piece of software had in the previous *build* are still present. |
| regression testing | Selective retesting to detect *faults* introduced during *modification* of a system or system *component*, to verify that *modification*s have not caused unintended adverse effects or to verify that a modified system or system *component* still meets its specified *requirements*. (ANSI/IEEE-729) |
| release | The *delivery* from one group to another or to users of some set of executables and documentation as defined in a *release transmittal note* which constitutes some set of *features* as defined by a *baseline*. A *release* may be subdivided by *waves* and *drops*. |
| release transmittal note | See version description document. |
| reliability | The ability of an item to perform a required function under stated conditions for a stated period of time. (ANSI/ASQC A3-1978). See *software reliability*. *Reliability* can be expressed as the probability $R(t)$ that the system has functioned from time 0-$t$. *Reliability* is time-dependent. (Adapted from IEEE Spectrum page 25. June 1989) (Compare with *availability* and *probability of failure*.) |
| reliability assessment | The process of determining the achieved level of *reliability* of an existing system or system *component*. (ANSI/IEEE-729) |
| reliability evaluation | See *reliability assessment*. |
| reliability growth | The improvement in *software reliability* that results from correcting *faults* in the software. (ANSI/IEEE-729) |
| reliability model | A model used for predicting, estimating, or assessing *reliability*. See also *reliability assessment*. (ANSI/IEEE-729) |
| reliability modeling | The process of creating a reliability model. |
| remote method invocation | Used in Java platforms remotely to invoke the methods of a Java Object. |
| repeatability | See *test repeatability*. |
| request for change | A means of formally requesting some change to a *feature*. May result in changes to specifications, code, tests and user documentation. Compare with *software change request*. |
| request for proposal | A document issued by a potential *customer* indicating generally what the system must be able to do. Tenderers will then issue tenders which respond to all or most of the *requirements* listed therein. |
| requirement | • A condition or *feature* needed by a user to solve a *problem* or achieve an objective. (ANSI/IEEE-729)<br>• A condition or *feature* that must be met or possessed by a system or system *component* to satisfy a *contract*, standard, specification or other formally imposed document. The set of all *requirements* forms the basis for subsequent development of the system or system *component*. See also *requirements* analysis, *requirements* phase, *requirements specification*. (ANSI/IEEE-729) |

| Term | Explanation (italicized text refers to terms explained in this section) |
|------|--------------------------------------------------------------------------|
| requirements execution metric | The number of *requirements* that have been demonstrated to be fully satisfied by the system divided by the number of *requirements*. (Adapted from *IEEE Computer*, page 88, July 1989) |
| requirements inspection | See *inspection*. |
| requirements specification | A specification that sets forth the *requirements* for a system or system *component*; for example, a configuration item. Typically included are functional *requirements*, *performance requirements*, *interface requirements*, design *requirements* and development standards. (ANSI/IEEE-729) |
| Requirements Specification Language | A *formal language* with special constructs and *verification protocol*s used to specify, verify and document *requirements*. (ANSI/IEEE-729) |
| requirements verification | See *verification*. |
| resilience | The extent to which software can continue to operate correctly despite the introduction of invalid inputs. (ANSI/IEEE-729) |
| resource use testing | A deliberate stressing of one or more resources by means of virtual users in an effort to provoke contention for those resources by two or more processes. |
| response event | (In *performance testing*). The *event* marking the end of some behavior which defines some *performance*. |
| response for a class | Object-oriented *metric* defined as the number of methods in the set of all methods that can be invoked in response to a *message* sent to an object of a class. The larger the number the<br>• greater the *complexity* of the class,<br>• greater the *complexity* of the *testing* and *debugging* of the class.<br>Use the worst case value for possible responses to allocate *testing* time. |
| response time | (In *performance testing*). The period between the *trigger event* and the *response event*. |
| response type | (In *performance testing*). A constraint on the response: hard implies that every instance of the use case *scenario* must occur within the *response time* or soft implying that some proportion (possibly an average) of the responses must. |
| reusability | The degree to which a software *unit* or other work product can be used in more than one computing program or software system. [*IEEE90*] |
| reversionary mode | A system state which provides minimum essential functionality in the *event* of catastrophic *failure*. |
| review | • A formal meeting at which some document is presented to the user, *customer* or other interested party for comment and approval.<br>• A formal meeting at which some document is presented to some specially-convened group with the intention of detecting *bugs*.<br>• (Of a *quality system*). The *contractor*'s independent systematic examination of the effectiveness of the *contractor*'s system concerned or parts of it. (AQAP-15)<br>Unlike software audit, this is a *quality control* process. See *design review*. |
| rich site summary | A family of document types for listing updates to a site. RSS documents are readable with RSS readers. This facility is found in most browsers. |
| rigorous correctness argument | An outline of a *proof obligation* showing the main steps, but not all the detail. (MoD 00-55) |
| risk | • A measure of the severity and likelihood of an accident. (MoD 00-55)<br>• The combination of the probability of some *threat* and the *consequence*s of that *threat* to a system's operators, users, and environment.<br>• The probability that a loss of information resources or breach of *security* will occur. |
| risk analysis (of information loss) | An *evaluation* of system assets and their vulnerabilities to *threat*s. *Risk analysis* estimates potential losses that may result from *threat*s. |
| risk assessment | The process of identifying, characterizing, quantifying and evaluating *risk*s and their importance. (Adapted from IEEE *Spectrum* page 25. June 1989). |

| Term | Explanation (italicized text refers to terms explained in this section) |
|---|---|
| risk driver | A variable which causes the *risk* to change and can thus affect the cost or the probability of the *risk*. |
| risk exposure | The period when some entity (product, process, project, system or person) is exposed to some *threat*. |
| risk management | • The process of attempting to minimize the probability of some accident or the *consequences* thereof. (Adapted from *IEEE Spectrum*, p. 25, June 1989).<br>• Decisions to accept *exposure* or to reduce vulnerabilities by either mitigating the *risk*s or applying cost effective controls. |
| robustness | See *resilience*. |
| roll-up patch | A collection of patches intended to resolve a number of *bugs* and allowing users and system administrators to make few and controlled changes rather than update their software whenever a new patch is created. |
| safe side | A system state that is reachable from any other state and is always safe. |
| safety | The degree to which something is free from *threat* to life or property. Compare with *security*. (P F-V) |
| safety case | Document required by law in many countries which explains why some system can be used and how it represents no *threat* to the public or its users or operators. It identifies the:<br>• detailed *safety* planning and control measures that will be used<br>• arguments and proof which show the system to be safe<br>• descriptions of the management and technical procedures used for the development of the *safety*-critical software<br>• resources and organizations required by standard<br>• key staff by name<br>A safety case should communicate a clear, comprehensive and defensible argument that a system is acceptably safe to operate in a particular context. [*Kelly 1*] |
| safety log | A document which includes the results of hazard analysis, modeling reports and the results of checking the formal arguments. |
| scaffolding | Software which takes the place of as-yet unavailable software for the purposes of integrating some system. It consists of *stubs and drivers*. (P F-V) |
| scalability | The degree to which a system reacts to a change in demand. A system will be considered *scalable* while for some set of hardware and *transaction*s, there is a linear relationship between load and *response time* and *throughput*, within some limits. For instance:<br><br><br><br>Scalable      Not scalable beyond *stress point*<br><br>Thus a system can remain scalable if you manage to move the *stress point* to the right. |
| scenario | • (In *Use cases*). A *sequence* of actions and interactions between *actor*s and the system.<br>• (In *usability testing*). A scripted *sequence* of actions between users and the system. |
| scheduler | (In *UML*). A property of a *test context* used to control the execution of the different *test components*. The *scheduler* identifies which *test components* exist and when and participate in which *test case*. It collaborates with the *arbiter* to inform it when it is time to issue the final *verdict* and controls the creation and destruction of *test components*. |

| Term | Explanation (italicized text refers to terms explained in this section) |
|---|---|
| script | (In the context of a *web server*). A piece of code written in any of a number of languages (C++, Javascript, Visual Basic script, Perl, Python, or others). The scripts follow one of a number of *protocols*: *CGI, Apache API, ISAPI, NSAPI*. |
| security | The protection of computer hardware and software from accidental or malicious access, use, *modification*, destruction, or disclosure. Security also pertains to personnel, data, communications and the physical protection of computer installations. (ANSI/IEEE-729). Compare with *safety*. |
| security administrator | The person charged with monitoring and implementing *security controls* and procedures for a system. Whereas each entity or organization will have one Information Security Officer, technical management may designate a number of *security administrators*. |
| security control | Hardware, programs, procedures, policies and physical safeguards which are put in place to *assure* the integrity and protection of information and the means of processing it. |
| security incident or breach | An *event* which results in unauthorized access, loss, disclosure, *modification*, or destruction of information resources whether accidental or deliberate. |
| security policy | The set of laws, rules and practices that regulate how an organization manages, protects and distributes sensitive information. [*CompSecGloss*] |
| seeding | See *fault seeding*. |
| sequence | Some path to be executed through some application. |
| server-side script | A *script* which is executed on the server. Compare with *client-side script*. |
| Simple Object Access Protocol | A popular *protocol* used to remotely invoke operations of a *web object* across the web. A SOAP *message* consists of: envelope, header, body and *fault*.<br>• **Envelope** (mandatory): the root element of a SOAP *message* describing its contents, identifying it as a SOAP *message*.<br>• **Header** (optional) contains application-specific information.<br>• **Body** (mandatory) contains the data intended for the recipient of the *message*.<br>• **Fault** element which carries *error messages* from an SOAP *message*. |
| simulation | The representation of selected characteristics of the behavior of one physical or abstract system by another system: In a digital computer system, simulation is done by software; for example:<br>• The representation of physical phenomena using operations performed by a computer system<br>• The representation of operations of a computer system by those of another computer system. (ISO)<br>Contrast with analytical model. (ANSI/IEEE-729) |
| simulator | A device, data processing system, or computer program that represents certain *features* of the behavior of a physical or abstract system. (ANSI) |
| slicing | (In *fault injection*). A technique to minimize the number of variables and *lines of code* in which to inject (a) fault(s). In static slicing a new program is defined by identifying a particular line of interest together with the variables used to arrive at that line (by using *flowgraph*) and then removing all the lines not required to achieve that line. In dynamic *slicing* further reduces static slicing sizes by deciding on some data set, observing the code not exercised by the use of that data set and eliminating it. |
| small-number bargaining | In contract negotiation, the presence of a monopoly or oligopoly on either of the transacting sides. |
| smoke test | A test which is the first to be run on a *build* to determine if it is capable of being tested. *Failure* of a *smoke test* will usually mean that the *build* is refused by the system test team. The name derives from an approach to the *system testing* of electrical systems whereby the first test was to switch it on and see if it smoked. |
| software change | Any change to any software. |
| software change request | *Fault* or *bug report*. Compare with *Request For Change*. |

| Term | Explanation (italicized text refers to terms explained in this section) |
|---|---|
| software development kit | A set of tools, APIs and documentation for developing software. |
| software maintenance | • *Modification* of a software product after *delivery* to correct *faults*.<br>• *Modification* of a software product after *delivery* to correct *faults*, to improve *performance* or other attributes or to adapt the product to a changed environment. (ANSI/IEEE-729) |
| software monitor | A *software tool* that executes concurrently with another computer program and that provides detailed information about the execution of the other program. (ANSI/IEEE-729) |
| software quality | • The totality of *features* and characteristics of a software product that bear on its ability to satisfy given needs; for example, conform to specifications. (ANSI/IEEE-729)<br>• The degree to which software possesses a desired combination of attributes. (ANSI/IEEE-729)<br>• The degree to which a *customer* or user perceives that software meets his or her composite expectations. (ANSI/IEEE-729)<br>• The composite characteristics of software that determine the degree to which the software in use will meet the expectations of the *customer*. (ANSI/IEEE-729) |
| software quality assurance | The monitoring and correction of software development process(es). Compare with *software quality control*. |
| software quality control | A control of the output(s) of a process. Aka *validation and verification*. Compare with *software quality assurance*. |
| software quality milestone | Some important *quality* moment during a development. Typically the end of some *quality* activity such as *review*, test, or audit of the major deliverables. A point at which a *quality control* checkpoint needs to exist. |
| software quality plan | A plan of all *software quality control* activities. (Compare with the IEEE *software quality assurance* plan standard *730-1984*.)<br>A mandatory *requirement* for each *Contract* operating to AQAP-13 is a *Software Quality Control* Plan identifying the Procedures which will be used during all phases of the *Contract* to perform the work. This plan is referred to in the *Quality System* as the *Software Quality plan*. |
| software query note | A document detailing a *bug* which has been detected by development team during the software specification and design phases, *unit* test or software *integration* phase and requires clarification from the system *design authority*. |
| software reliability | • The probability that software will not cause the *failure* of a system for a specified time under specified conditions. The probability is a function of the inputs to and use of the system as well as a function of the existence of *faults* in the software. The inputs to the system determine whether existing *faults*, if any, are encountered. (ANSI/IEEE-729)<br>• The ability of a program to perform a required function under stated conditions for a stated period of time. (ANSI/IEEE-729) |
| software requirements review | This ensures the adequacy of the *requirements* stated in the software *requirements specification*. (ANSI/IEEE-729) |
| software sneak analysis | A technique applied to software to identify latent (sneak) logic control paths or conditions that could inhibit a desired operation or cause an unwanted operation to occur. Of little use without considerable tool support. (ANSI/IEEE-729) |
| software tool | A computer program used to help develop, test, analyze, or maintain another computer program or its documentation; for example an automated design tool, compiler, test tool, *maintenance* tool. (ANSI/IEEE-729)<br>Compare with support software. |
| software verification and validation readiness review | Evaluates the adequacy of the *verification* and *validation* methods defined in the *quality* plan. (Equivalent of a Software *test readiness review* as defined in *MIL-STD-1521B-1985*) |

| Term | Explanation (italicized text refers to terms explained in this section) |
|---|---|
| source code analyzer | A language-specific tool which accepts source code as input and outputs a series of graphic or textual analysis showing possible sources of *problem*s such as syntactic *errors*, global *interface problem*s, data usage, unused local variables, unused function call results and valid but unusual constructs such as passing structures by value, in the form of call trees and symbol table cross references. |
| Standard Performance Evaluation Corporation | A non-profit corporation whose membership is open to any company or organization that is willing to *support* its goals (and pay its dues). Originally just a bunch of people from workstation suppliers devising CPU *metrics*, SPEC has evolved into an umbrella organization encompassing:<br>• **Open Systems Group** (OSG). The OSG is the original SPEC committee. This group focuses on benchmarks for desktop systems, high-end workstations and servers running open systems environments.<br>• **High-Performance Group** (HPG). The HPG is a forum for establishing, maintaining and endorsing a suite of benchmarks that represent high-*performance* computing applications for standardized, cross-platform *performance evaluation*.<br>• **Graphics Performance Characterization Group** *(GPC)*. The SPEC/GPC Group is the umbrella organization for project groups that develop consistent and repeatable graphics benchmarks and *performance*-reporting procedures. SPEC/GPC benchmarks are worldwide standards for evaluating *performance* in a way that reflects user experiences with popular graphics applications. |
| standards bug | (ST). *Bug* class indicating that some project *quality system* standard has been violated or is inadequate. (DOD STD 2167A) |
| state (transition) diagram | A directed *graph* in which *node*s correspond to internal states of a system and edges correspond to transitions; often used for describing a system in terms of state changes. (ANSI/IEEE-729) See also *Petri net*. |
| static analyzer | A *software tool* that aids in the *evaluation* of a computer program without executing the program. Examples include syntax checkers, compilers, cross-reference generators, standards enforcers and flowcharters. (ANSI/IEEE-729) Contrast with *dynamic analyzer*. |
| static analysis | The process of evaluating a program without executing the program. See also *desk checking, code audit, inspection, static analyzer, walk-through*. (ANSI/IEEE-729) Contrast with *dynamic analysis*. |
| static code analysis | Using mathematical techniques to analyze a program and reveal its structure. It does not need execution of the program, but verifies the program against the specification. Techniques include control-flow, data use, information flow and semantic analysis. (MoD 00-55) |
| statistical test model | A model that relates program *faults* to the input data set (or sets) which cause them to be encountered. The model also gives the probability that these *faults* will cause the program to fail. (ANSI/IEEE-729) |
| stimulus | *Test data* sent to the SUT in order to cause some change in its behavior and to make assessments about the SUT when receiving the SUT reactions to these stimuli. Aka test input. |
| stress point | The point at which the *response time* / *throughput* curve begins to behave exponentially. (Aka *stress elbow*). The point at which the *throughput*/response curve becomes sharply "elbowed" indicating that the system has become overstressed. |
| stress testing | The *testing* of a system under a load to the extent that the system fails, in an effort to see: if the system fails gracefully, what warnings the system gives of impending *failure* and where the bottlenecks are. |
| structural testing | *Structural Testing* uses knowledge of the internal logic of the software to construct *test cases* to achieve the desired *coverage criteria*. It is aka white-box *testing*. |
| stub | • A dummy program *unit* used during the development and testing of a higher-level *unit*.<br>• A *program* statement substituting for the body of a program *unit* and indicating that the *unit* is or will be defined elsewhere. (ANSI/IEEE-729) |

| Term | Explanation (italicized text refers to terms explained in this section) |
|------|--------------------------------------------------------------------------|
| subject matter expert | A person expert in the use of the application to be tested. |
| support desk staff | Persons responsible for helping *customers* use the system. There are usually three levels: simple ("Is it plugged in? No?"), intermediate ("Are you running service pack 3? Can you see the database?") and "third level" (*to the developers:* "Excuse me, but I have a customer on the phone who says the latest release just wiped his hard disk. Would you guys know anything about this?") |
| symbolic execution | A *verification* technique in which program execution is simulated using symbols rather than actual values for input data and program outputs are expressed as logical or mathematical expressions involving these symbols. (ANSI/IEEE-729) |
| system layer | (In system architecture). A view of a part of a system which has been designed such that each layer furnishes part of its *capability*. Thus a system may be divided into applications, middleware, network services and operating system.<br>Layering enables the design a system of systems that has technology independence, *scalability*, decentralized operation, architecture and supporting standards, *security* and *flexibility*. Layering can also accommodate heterogeneity, accounting and cost recovery. |
| system reliability | The probability that a system, including all hardware and software subsystems, will perform a required task or mission for a specified time in a specified environment. See also *operational reliability software reliability*. (ANSI/IEEE-729) |
| system safety | The degree to which some system is free from *threat* to life or property. Normally defined in terms of hazards or system states that when combined with certain environmental conditions could lead to a mishap. |
| system testing | The process of *testing* an integrated hardware and software system to verify that the system meets its specified *requirements*. See also *acceptance testing, qualification testing*. (ANSI/IEEE-729) |
| system under test | The system, subsystem or *component* being tested, exercised via its public *interface* operations and signals by the *test components*. |
| Systems Analysis and Design Technique | Modeling notation developed by Douglas Ross, then of SofTech in the 1970s. It has since been extensively propagated by the U.S. DoD under the opensource name IDEF. |
| target hardware | Computer hardware used by the *Safety*-critical software in the de*live*red equipment. (MoD 00-55) |
| target machine | The computer on which a program is intended to operate.<br>The computer being emulated by another computer.<br>Contrast with *host machine*. (ANSI/IEEE-729) |
| target of evaluation | (In *security assessment*). An IT product or system that is the subject of an *evaluation*. |
| target testing | Execution of tests on the *target hardware*. Contrast with *host testing*. |
| task analysis | (In HCI). The process of identifying how users interact with a system. Consists of *task elicitation, task representation* and *generic representation*. |
| task elicitation | (In HCI). The process of deriving details about a system from stakeholders using interviews, *observation* of *performance* with prototypes and any current system and the analysis of *performance* records. The complementary process is *task representation*. Part of *task analysis*. |
| task representation | (In HCI). A representation of the information derived from *task elicitation* in a form such that it can be checked with the users from whom it was collected. *Task representation* generates users' models which describe the "what is to be done" information and goal specification which describes how well is it to be done. Part of *task analysis*. |
| termination proof | (In *proof of correctness*). The demonstration that a program will terminate under all specified input conditions. (ANSI/IEEE-729) |
| test | Some attempt to prove that some specified *feature* of software and/or hardware is absent, such that this can be established by human-perceivable means. |

| Term | Explanation (italicized text refers to terms explained in this section) |
| --- | --- |
| test bed | • A test environment containing the hardware, *instrumentation tools*, *simulators* and other support software necessary for *testing* a system or system *component*. (ANSI/IEEE-729)<br>• The repertoire of *test cases* necessary for *testing* a system or system *component*. (ANSI/IEEE-729) |
| test bug report | A document reporting on any *event* that occurs during the *testing* process which requires investigation. (Aka *bug report* or software *bug report*). |
| test case | • A set of *test data* and associated procedures developed for a particular objective, such as to exercise a particular program path or to verify *compliance* with a *requirement*. (ANSI/IEEE-729)<br>• A set of inputs, execution conditions and expected results. (MoD 00-55)<br>• (In *UML*). A complete technical specification of a *test objective* showing how the SUT should be tested for a given *test objective* and includes what to test, with which input, result and under which conditions. It may include executable and source code. It is defined in terms of *sequences*, alternatives, loops and *defaults* of stimuli to and output from the SUT either humanly observable or mediated by test software. A *test case* may invoke other *test cases*. A *test case* many use an *arbiter* to evaluate the outcome of its test behavior. A *test case* is a *component* of a *test suite*. |
| test case generator | See *automated test generator*. |
| test case specification | A document specifying objectives, inputs, operator actions, the *baseline* specification, predicted results and the execution conditions and environment for a test (Aka software *test* description). (DoD-STD-2167A) |
| test comparator | A test tool which compares the contents of a *test-expected-result file* with that of a *test-actual-result file* to determine if any *errors* have occurred. |
| test component | (In *UML*). A class of a test system. *Test component* objects realize the behavior of a *test case*. A *test component* has a set of *interfaces* via which it may communicate via *connections* with other *test components* or with the SUT. |
| test configuration | The collection of *test component* objects and of *connections* between the *test component* objects and to the SUT.<br>(In *UML*). The *test configuration* defines both (1) *test component* objects and *connections* when a *test case* is started (the initial *test configuration*) and (2) the maximum number of *test component* objects and *connections* during the test execution. |
| test context | (In *UML*). A collection of *test cases* together with a *test configuration* on the basis of which the *test cases* are executed. Aka *test suite*. |
| test control | (In *UML*). A *test control* is a specification for the invocation of *test cases* within a *test suite*. It is a technical specification of how the SUT should be tested with the given *test suite*. It is the equivalent of a *test procedure*. |
| test coverage | • The ability of some test to exercise some code. Can be expressed in terms of the number of statements executed, paths through the software, conditions, condition combinations, branches, DU paths, LCSAJs and degree to which some software attribute such as *performance* or *usability* is demonstrated.<br>• A measure of how far a test covers the specified *requirements* of a system, *unit* or *component*. (MoD 00-55)<br>• The degree to which some test exercises some system *feature*. |
| test coverage bug | (TC). *Bug* class indicating that some test is found to be insufficient to exercise some software. (DOD STD 2167A) |
| test coverage criteria | Rules to determine whether a *test suite* has adequately tested a program and to guide the *testing* process. |
| test coverage monitor | A *software tool* to measure *test coverage*. (MoD 00-55) |
| test data | Data developed to test a system or system *component*. (ANSI/IEEE-729) See also *test case*. |
| test data file | A file containing *test data*. |
| test data generator | Software for creating fake if credible data. |
| test description | See software *test case specification*. |

| Term | Explanation (italicized text refers to terms explained in this section) |
|------|------------------------------------------------------------------------|
| test design specification | A document specifying the details of the test approach for a software *feature* or combination of software *features* and identifying the associated tests. |
| test driver | A *driver* that invokes the item under test and that may provide test inputs and report test results. (ANSI/IEEE-729) |
| test effectiveness ratio | Three measures of the effectiveness of tests: $$TER1 = \frac{number\ of\ statements\ exercised\ at\ least\ once}{total\ number\ of\ executable\ statements}$$ $$TER2 = \frac{number\ of\ branches\ exercised\ at\ least\ once}{total\ number\ of\ branches}$$ $$TER3 = \frac{number\ of\ LCSAJs\ exercised\ at\ least\ once}{total\ number\ of\ LCSAJs}$$ |
| test environment bug | (TE). *Bug* class indicating that some test environment is found to be insufficient to support some test type or inconsistent with its specification. (DOD STD 2167A) |
| test execution step | A single activity within a test such as "*press a button*" or "*display a screen.*" Can be used for manual or automated tests and as a measure of how large a test is. |
| test expected result | A definition of the expected result of a test. This result may be positive or negative. Thus an expected result may say (positively) "if x = 10 then the SUT has passed" or (negatively) "if 10 > x < 100 the SUT has failed." See also *arbiter*. |
| test harness | Software or a *test driver* used to invoke a module (*unit*) and to provide test input and to monitor and report test results. (MoD 00-55) |
| test invocation | (In *UML*). A *test case* can be invoked with parameters and within a context. The *test invocation* leads to the execution of the *test case*. The *test invocation* is denoted in the *test trace*. |
| test item | A software item which is to be tested. |
| test item transmittal report | A document identifying *test items*. It contains current status and *location* information. |
| test log | A chronological record of all relevant details of a *testing* activity. (ANSI/IEEE-729) |
| test manager | Person in charge of writing the test strategy and *test plan* or the test parts of the quality plan. He may report to the *project manager* or to the *line manager*. He is responsible for test planning, execution and reporting as well as running the test team. |
| test objective | (In *UML*). A test objective is a named element describing what should be tested. It is associated with a *test case*. A test objective should be written in terms of the *failure* it is attempting to provoke. |
| test phase | The period of time in the software life cycle during which the *components* of a software product are evaluated and integrated and the software product is evaluated to determine whether or not *requirements* have been satisfied. (ANSI/IEEE-729) |
| test plan | • A document prescribing the approach to be taken for intended *testing* activities. The plan typically identifies the items to be tested, the *testing* to be performed, test schedules, personnel *requirements*, reporting *requirements*, *evaluation* criteria and any *risks* requiring contingency planning. (ANSI/IEEE-729) <br> • A management document which addresses all aspects related to the test. It should include the test schedule and define the necessary support tools. (AQAP-13) Compare with *quality* plan. |
| test procedure | • A *test procedure* is a document that delineates each step necessary to conduct a test. The steps are in sequence with all inputs and outputs defined. (AQAP-13) See also *test procedure*. <br> • Detailed instructions for the setup, operation and *evaluation* of results for a given test. A set of associated procedures is often combined to form a *test procedures* document. (ANSI/IEEE-729) |

| Term | Explanation (italicized text refers to terms explained in this section) |
|------|-------------------------------------------------------------------------|
| test process | The process of exercising or evaluating a system or system *component* by manual or automated means to verify that it satisfies specified *requirements* or to identify differences between expected and actual results. (ANSI/IEEE-729) Compare with *debugging.* |
| test readiness review | Determination that software *test procedures* are complete and the *developer* is prepared for formal software *performance testing;* results of *informal testing* are also reviewed. (US Military standard 1521B-1985) |
| test repeatability | An attribute of a test indicating whether the same results are produced each time the test is conducted. (ANSI/IEEE-729) |
| test report | A document describing the conduct and results of the *testing* carried out for a system or system *component.* (ANSI/IEEE-729) |
| test specification | Describes the test criteria and the methods to be used in a test to *assure* that the *performance* and design specifications have been specified. The *test specification* identifies the *features* or program functions to be tested and identifies the test environment. (AQAP-13) |
| test step | Some moment within a test in which the operator is expected to do something if only read a screen. This is a useful way of denominating manual tests since each action needs to be specified and the more actions, the bigger the test, the longer it takes and the longer it takes the more management will complain that you're taking too long. This way you can compare the time taken to run 100 3-step tests with 30 10-step tests. |
| test suite | A collection of *test cases* together with a *test configuration* on the basis of which the *test cases* are executed. Aka (In *UML test context*). |
| test summary report | A document summarizing a *sequence* of tests. Normally derived from the *test log.* |
| test trace | (In *UML*). An interaction resulting from the execution of a *test case.* It represents the different *messages* exchanged between the *test components* and the SUT and/or the states of the involved *test components.* A trace is associated with a *verdict* representing the adherence of the SUT to the *test objective* of the associated *test case.* |
| test validity | The degree to which a test accomplishes its specified goal. (ANSI/IEEE-729) |
| testability | • The extent to which software facilitates both the establishment of test criteria and the *evaluation* of the software with respect to those criteria. (ANSI/IEEE-729) <br> • The extent to which the definition of *requirements* facilitates analysis of the *requirements* to establish test criteria. (ANSI/IEEE-729) <br> • The extent to which the software exhibits a *bug.* (PF-V) |
| test-actual-result file | A file produced as the result of some test(s) which may be compared using a *test comparator,* with a *test-expected-result* file to determine if any *errors* have occurred. It can be very useful when combined with (a) software *test data file*(s). |
| tester | Person responsible for specifying, writing, executing and analyzing tests. |
| test-expected-result file | A file produced as during the test preparation phase which may be compared using a software *test comparator,* with a software *test-actual-result file* to determine if any *errors* have occurred. It can be very useful when combined with (a) software *test data file*(s). |
| testing distribution | (In *fault injection*). A definition of where and how many *faults* will be injected in code. May employ the LCSAJ approach or may be determined by the particular questions the *tester* is trying to answer. Its intention is to limit the number of *test cases* developed. It may be useful to work backwards from some known or presumed catastrophic state (a "*top event*" in *safety* terms) and determine what *data states* could trigger such an *event.* The set of all such states can become a testing distribution. |
| testing and test control notation | • A *test specification* and implementation language to define *test procedures* for *black-box testing* of distributed systems. <br> • A TTCN-3 *test specification* consists of four main parts: (1) type definitions for *test data* structures, (2) template definitions for concrete *test data,* (3) function and *test case* definitions for test behavior and (4) control definitions for the execution of *test cases.* <br> • A forerunner of [*UML* TP]. |

| Term | Explanation (italicized text refers to terms explained in this section) |
|---|---|
| thin thread | A complete end-to-end trace through some system of data or *message* using a sample of external input data to produce sample of external output data. |
| threat | Some *event* which can cause harm or loss to some entity (product, process, project, system, or person). |
| throughput | • The number of bits, characters, or blocks passing through a data communication system or portion of that system.<br> – Note 1: Throughput may vary greatly from its theoretical maximum.<br> – Note 2: Throughput is expressed in data *units* per period of time.<br>• The maximum *capacity* of a communications channel or system.<br>• A measure of the amount of work performed by a system over a period of time, e.g., the number of jobs per day. |
| time zone | (In *UML*). A grouping mechanism for *test components*. Each *test component* belongs to a certain *time zone*. *Test components* in the same *time zone* have the same time, i.e., *test components* of the same *time zone* are time synchronized. |
| timer | (In *UML*). Mechanisms that may generate a timeout *event* when a specified time value occurs. This may be when a pre-specified time *interval* has expired relative to a given instant (usually the instant when the timer is started). Timers belong to *test components*. They are defined as properties of *test components*. A timer is started with an expiration time being the time when the timeout is to be issued. A timeout indicates the timer expiration. A timer can be stopped. The expiration time of a running timer and its current status (e.g., active/inactive) can be checked. |
| timing analyzer | A *software tool* that estimates or measures the *execution time* of a computer program or portions of a computer program either by summing the *execution time*s of the instructions in each path or by inserting probes at points in the program and measuring the *execution time* between probes. (ANSI/IEEE-729) |
| timing bug | A timing *fault* occurs when a value, process, or service is delivered before or after the specified time. Timing *faults* cannot occur if there is no explicit or implicit specification of a deadline. |
| tolerance | The ability of a system to provide continuity of operation under various abnormal conditions. (ANSI/IEEE-729) |
| top event | (In *Fault Tree Analysis*). A catastrophic *failure*. |
| top-down testing | The process of checking out hierarchically organized programs, progressively, from top to bottom, using *simulation* of lower level *components*. (ANSI/IEEE-729) |
| total correctness | In *proof of correctness*, a designation indicating that a program's *output assertions* follow logically from its *input assertions* and processing steps and that, in addition, the program terminates under all specified input conditions. Contrast with *partial correctness*. (ANSI/IEEE-729) |
| traceability | The ability of some assertion expressed in some artefact (specification, code, manual, or test) to be related both to any artefact from which it was derived and to any artifact deriving from it. (PF-V) |
| trading partner agreement | Contractual agreement between two commercial entities to enable them to (temporarily) have their systems talk directly to each other. Typically this occurs between major manufacturers and trusted suppliers. See [Sachs] for more on this. |
| transaction | (Part of) some path to be executed through some application which will conclude with some observable outcome. |
| transaction link testing | See *integration strategy (threaded)*. |
| transient bug | A *bug* which is evident for a short period of time. |
| trapdoor | A way of secretly accessing a program or online service. *Trapdoor*s are built into the source code to gain special access to otherwise inaccessible functions. |

| Term | Explanation (italicized text refers to terms explained in this section) |
|------|------------------------------------------------------------------------|
| trigger event | (In *performance testing*). The external unprovoked *event* which initiates the execution of a use case (in *UML*) and whose occurrence bounds the behavior which defines some *performance*. |
| trusted computing base | The totality of protection mechanisms within a computer system, including hardware, firmware and software, the combination of which is responsible for enforcing a *security policy*. A TCB consists of one or more *components* that together enforce a unified *security policy* over a product or system. The ability of a TCB to enforce correctly a unified *security policy* depends solely on the mechanisms within the TCB and on the correct input by system administrative personnel of parameters (e.g., a user's clearance level) related to the *security policy*. [*CompSecGloss*] |
| *UML* testing profile | A definition of a language for *testing* which extends and reuses existing *UML* constructs. [*UML TP*] |
| uncertainty | A measure of the limits of knowledge expressed as a distribution of probabilities around a point estimate. The four elements of *uncertainty* are: statistical confidence (a measure of sampling *accuracy*), *tolerance* (a measure of the relevance of available information to the *problem*), incompleteness and *inaccuracy* of input data and ambiguity in the modeling of the *problem*. (Adapted from IEEE Spectrum page 25. June 1989) |
| underuse | (Of a system). The inverse of *overload*. |
| Unified Modeling Language | An OMG standard language for specifying the structure and behavior of systems. The standard defines an abstract syntax and a graphical concrete syntax. |
| uniform resource identifier | See *uniform resource locator* |
| uniform resource locator | The address of a web page on the World Wide web. Sometimes known as *uniform resource identifier*. |
| unit | • A program *unit* that is discrete and identifiable with respect to compiling, combining with other *units* and loading; for example, the input to or output from an assembler, compiler, linkage editor, or executive routine. (ANSI)<br>• A logically separable part of a program. (ANSI/IEEE-729)<br>• A separately identified part of a computer program which performs a specific function. (MoD 00-55)<br>• The smallest logical entity specified in the Detailed Design which completely describes a single function in sufficient detail to allow implementation code to be produced and tested independently from other *Units*. See also module. |
| unit coupling | A measure of the degree to which *units* are not independent of each other. There are seven levels:<br>• **No coupling** exists when the only relation one *unit* has with another is that it has been compiled with or linked to it.<br>• **Data coupling** occurs when the data between two *units* mentioned in their input-output *interface* is the same in that only a subset of an entire data structure is passed.<br>• **Stamp coupling** occurs when a data structure is shared among more than one *unit* not by common *coupling*, but by passing the data structure using *unit* call and return parameters.<br>• **Control coupling** occurs when one *unit* passes switch, flag, or *unit*-name information from one *unit* to another.<br>• **External coupling** occurs when more than one *unit* references the same external data structure. That is they contain references to the same external data structure.<br>• **Common coupling** occurs when more than one *unit* references the same global data structure. That is they contain references to the same global data structure.<br>• **Content coupling** occurs when a branch within one *unit* passes control to the interior of the other (as opposed to calling it). |
| unit test | A test of the smallest separately-compilable piece of code. |
| unit test process | The process of verifying that a *unit's* source code correctly implements the associated detailed design specification. |
| unity | (in the context of an equation) 1. |

| Term | Explanation (italicized text refers to terms explained in this section) |
|---|---|
| universal description discovery and integration | A central directory service where businesses can publish, register and search for *Web service*s. The data stored is in three categories:<br>• white pages containing such information as name, description and contact details of a company offering the service<br>• yellow pages containing classification data of the category of the company or the service offered; and<br>• green pages containing technical data about a *web service* allowing someone to write an application to use it. |
| usability | • The attribute which determines how easy a system is to use which is defined by its *usefulness*, its *ease of use*, its *learnability*, *flexibility* and its *attractiveness*.<br>• The extent to which a product can be used by specified users to achieve goals with effectiveness, efficiency and satisfaction in a specified context of use (ISO 9241-11)<br>• The ease with which a user can learn to operate, prepare inputs and interpret outputs of a system or *component*. [*IEEE 90*] |
| usability test candidate | (In *usability testing*). Some person with the characteristics of some class of user. The name is preferable to the psychology-derived "test subject" since it leaves them feeling less like goldfish in a bowl. Using the UTC acronym also tends to speed open discussion. Note that very clever UTCs won't find many *bugs* since they will somehow make things work. |
| usefulness | (In *human factors*). An attribute of *usability* which defines the extent to which the system helps the user accomplish their goals. |
| user action log | File containing data drawn from web server logs or special-to-type logs showing user behavior when interacting with an application. |
| user diary | (In *usability testing*). A log of *events* occurring to and kept by a user (possibly with a grudge) of some software. An excellent way of both letting off steam and helping *developers*. Helps to counter any attempt by *developers* to claim that "they were only minor *bugs*." |
| user fault | A *fault* is created by the user in employing the system. Note that the roles of user and operator are considered separately; the user is considered to be external to the system while the operator is considered to be a part of the system. Compare with *operator fault*. |
| user screening questionnaire | (In *usability testing*). Means of distinguishing useful UTCs. Will normally cover: age, sex, highest grade studied, subjects studied at university, computer experience, application experience, attitude towards computers. May include intelligence quotient and (increasingly) reading quotient. |
| user story | In agile development a narration both of what (a *feature* of) the system will do for the user and the basis on which *developers* can estimate of the time it will take to *build*. A *build* will consist of 60–100 user stories. They are supposed to approximate to a *requirements specification* and are the basis of an *acceptance test*. |
| utility part | (In *UML*). A part of the test system representing miscellaneous *components* which help *test components* to realize their test behavior. Examples of *utility part*s are *data pool*s. |
| validated compiler | Where a national or international *certificate* shows that a compiler has been tested against its language definition standard. (MoD 00-55) |
| validation | Showing that a system or computer program satisfies its *requirement*. (MoD 00-55)<br>The process of evaluating software to ensure *compliance* with software *requirements* during the first stages of the software life-cycle. (ANSI/IEEE-729) and with system *requirements* during the Hardware-Software *Integration* phase. See also *verification*. |
| validation action | (In *UML*). An action to evaluate the status of the execution of a *test case* by assessing the SUT *observation*s and/or additional characteristics/parameters of the SUT. A *validation action* is performed by a *test component* and sets the local *verdict* of that *test component*. |
| value bug | See *data problem*. |

| Term | Explanation (italicized text refers to terms explained in this section) |
|---|---|
| verdict | (In *UML*). The assessment of the *correctness* of the SUT with respect to a *test case*. Predefined *verdict* values are pass, fail, inconclusive and *error*. **Pass** indicates that the test behavior gives evidence for *correctness* of the SUT for that *test case*. **Fail** describes that the purpose of the *test case* has been violated. Inconclusive is used for cases where neither a Pass nor a Fail can be assigned. An *error verdict* is used to indicate *errors* (exceptions) within the test system itself. *Verdict*s can be user-defined. The *verdict* of a *test case* is calculated by the *arbiter*. Equivalent to result. |
| verification | • The process of determining whether or not the products of a given phase of the software development cycle fulfill the *requirements* established during the previous phase. (ANSI/IEEE-729) See also *validation*.<br>• Formal proof of program *correctness*. (ANSI/IEEE-729) See *proof of correctness*.<br>• The act of *reviewing*, inspecting, *testing*, checking, auditing, or otherwise establishing and documenting whether or not items, processes, services, or documents conform to specified *requirements*. (ANSI/ASQC A3-1978)<br>• Showing that a development stage in a system or computer program is correct. (MoD 00-55) |
| verification system | See *automated verification system*. (ANSI/IEEE-729) |
| virtual execution environment | A virtual software machine providing an environment in a target computer for an application software program having one or more execution dependencies that are incompatible with a software execution environment on the target computer. (From the United States Patent 5067072) |
| waiver | Written authorization to allow acceptance of a product or service found to depart from specified *requirements* during manufacture or provision of the service. (AQAP-15) |
| walk-through | A *review* process in which a designer or programmer leads one or more other members of the development team through a segment of design or code that he or she has written, while the other members ask questions and make comments about technique, style, possible *errors*, violation of development standards and *other bugs*. Contrast with *inspection*. (ANSI/IEEE-729) |
| wave | A division of a *release* whereby only a subset of *features* of a *release* is developed and system-tested at a time. Each *wave* may be divided into *drops*. |
| web object | An HTML file along with all the files that are embedded in it by reference. |
| web service | A programmable application *component* that can be accessed over the Internet and used remotely. Web services are built to standards and *protocols* such as HTTP, SOAP, XML, WSDL and other *protocols* that support *interoperability* thus enabling the creation of open applications, compatible with many programming languages, operating systems, hardware platforms and which are accessible from any geographic *location*.<br>A web service works thus:<br>• a requesting client application sends its request to the service-providing application using SOAP and<br>• the service-providing application receives the request, processes its business logic and sends the response back also using SOAP. |
| Web Services Description Language | An XML-based method used to identify *web service*s and their access at runtime. |
| weighted methods per class | Object-oriented *metric* defined as the sum of the complexities of all methods of a class. Predicts how much time and effort is required to develop and maintain the class.<br>The larger the number of methods in a class,<br>• the greater the potential impact on children, since they will inherit all the methods defined in the class and<br>• the more likely they are to be application-specific, limiting the possibility of reuse. |
| wildcard | (In *UML*). Special symbols to represent values or value ranges and specify whether a value is present or not, and/or whether it represents any value. *Wildcard*s are used instead of symbols within instance specifications. |

| Term | Explanation (italicized text refers to terms explained in this section) |
|---|---|
| work-around solution | Short-term means of allowing some system to function, albeit in a degraded manner, when no immediate solution to the *bug* can be implemented. |
| workpackage | One of the constituent parts of the activities of a project as defined in the work break-down structure. |
| workpackage completion certificates | A management device by which the work package manager (often the development manager) accepts with his or her signature, that some *workpackage* has been satisfactorily completed. |
| work-product | Generic title for the output of some process or *workpackage*. Thus if the process is *Write requirements specification* the work-product is the *requirements specification*. |
| wrapper | Code added to limit the access to other code by hiding its operations, often to make it seem as if it is an object with methods. |
| XML metadata interchange | An OMG standard that facilitates interchange of models via XML documents. |
| XUnit | Generic name for a family of tools based on J*Unit* which simplify *unit testing* in various languages. |
| zero-failure | An approach to calculating the minimum *bug*-free *testing* time which must elapse if a product is to be delivered with less than some minimum number of undiscovered *bugs* therein. |

# Index

# D

DACC, acronym expansion, 468
daily, 32
    build, invaluable means of testing automated
            build scripts, 96
    test report, 160
dangers
    of executable UML process model, 54
    of extreme/agile/rapid process model, 55
    of formal methods process model, 54
    of Prince II process model, 47
    of spiral process model, 46
    of stage-gate process model, 45
    of synch and stabilize process model, 48
    of unified process model, 49
    of waterfall process model, 43
data
    acceptance test, 274
    bug prediction, 345
    combination, tendency to be infinite, 117
    corruption, as a mutation testing technique, 310
    flag, 128
    flow
        diagram, definition of, 479
        test technique, 220
    illegal, detection of, 19
    items used in a program, 119
    latency, definition of, 480
    mining tool, 402
    partition, definition of, 480
    pool, definition of, 480
    problem, definition of, 480
    space, definition of, 480
    state, definition of, 480
database
    as performance bottleneck, 71
    bug management, 103
        in quality plan, 168
        input to quality plan, 108
        used to identify bug costs, 359
        used to monitor supplier, 196
    card issuer, 75
    configuration management, 7, 24
        check access to, 245
        source of code turmoil data, 24
        to analyse code changes, 311
    drivers as source of memory leaks, 82
    in cutover testing, 91
    in test automation, 100
    interface with web server, 74, 78
    population
        test automation can help, 97
DCL, acronym expansion, 468
dealing with a third-party company checklist, 435

debugging
    definition of, 480
    model, definition of, 480
decision, 27
    (branch) coverage, 26
        test technique, 209
        use of, 19
    multiple condition coverage, 214
    outcome, 19
    point metric, 480
    release
        taken without reference to the test team, 58
    table, 78
        definition of, 480
        test specification technique, 217
        use of, 19
DEF STAN
    05-95/1, 522
    acronym expansion, 468
default
    definition of, 480
    notice, definition of, 480
defeature, definition of, 480
defect, definition of, 480
deficiency management plan, definition of, 480
delivered source instruction, definition of, 480
delivery, definition of, 480
demilitarized zone, definition of, 480
DeMillo
    223, 515
deontic logic, definition of, 480
depth of inheritance tree
    definition of, 481
    metric, 233
design
    analysis, definition of, 481
    analyzer, definition of, 481
    assertion consistency checker, definition of, 481
    authority
        definition of, 481
        role of, 12
            approval of changes, 95
    document used in out-sourcing, 199
    inspection, definition of, 481
    review, definition of, 481
    specification
        baselined on a requirement specification, 10
        reference to in test plan, 134
desk checking, definition of, 481
developer, 41
    as determinant of root cause of failure, 24
    creating bugs as fast as they fix them, 63
    definition of, 481
    expertise, 35
    hours versus tester hours, 57

# G

# P

if at first you don't succeed then bungee
jumping's not for you, 93
it isn't lovely but it works, 219
it's always your fault, 20
little boy with a hammer, 15
man with a nail, 15
many a mickle makes a mess, 289
model(ling) testers, 45
pay for good testing and deliver late, or pay for
support and get a bad reputation, 184
rehearse your project on paper, 9
so which satellite was that?, 470
Terminal litigation, 29
test costs, 10
testing as redemption, 178
The gold team, 171
The rampant Raj, 231
the realistic project manager, 39
what the bleep was that?, 21
strategy, test
assumptions, 130
audience, 130
background, 130
introduction, 130
purpose, 130
related documents, 130
scope, 130
stress
point, definition of, 503
test
process, 396
test, process, 285
testing, definition of, 503
structural
coverage of unit tests, 88
testing, definition of, 503
structure
coverage, by test, 26
server-side, 440
structured programming verification, 117
STT
acronym expansion, 470
metric
learnability, 323
related to UTCs, 323
stub
as deliverable
reference to in test plan, 138
definition of, 503
creating, 51
in partial integration, 87
Suardi, 336, 519
subject matter expert, definition of, 504
submission speed affected by
data size, 444
screen/form complexity, 444

SUIF, 457
suppliers, role of, 13
support, 503
cost, 28
desk staff, 13
definition of, 504
SUT
acronym expansion, 470
symbolic
evaluation
technique, 18
use of, 19
execution
definition of, 504
test technique, 221
synch and stabilize, 24
syntactic analysis, 114
system
agreed maximum number of bugs in a released, 59
analysis
using function points, 351
and data classification and validation checklist,
434
availability
modelled using a Markov chain, 318
big, needs a a separate integration test plan, 87
bugs remaining in for more than one phase, 107
configuration, effect on, bottleneck, 444
defences checklist, 434
earlier version used as a baseline, 60
history, 27
infected with a thousand tiny bugs, 4
inputs, 27
integration and operations testing, 262
layer, definition of, 504
mission-critical, analysis, 37
overload, definition of, 495
performance, xxviii
quality, confidence in, 26
reliability, definition of, 504
resilience modelled using a Markov chain, 318
safety, definition of, 504
shown to have a minimum capability by a
regression test, 40
sizing
derived from requirement specification, 4
test, xxviii, 243
answers a question, 10
coverage strategy, 27
example: ÒEnter A StationÓ, 416
execution time, 3
in xUML, 53
objective, 253
phase, 106
planning, 89

Milton Keynes UK
Ingram Content Group UK Ltd.
UKHW052028071024
449327UK00027B/2476